CW01558465

The Story of White Hall Centre

The Story of White Hall Centre

Outdoor Education across the Decades

Pete McDonald

Published in 2018 by Pete McDonald
26 Grandview Crescent, Opoho, Dunedin, 9010, New Zealand
pete.mcdnz@outlook.com

ISBN 9780473425272   Hardback

All author-publisher royalties from
the sale of this book will be donated
to Parkinsonism Society Otago
Incorporated.

'There were some people who equated White Hall courses with Outward Bound experiences and talked of character development but Longland dissociated himself and White Hall from that idea. The writer heard him say on one occasion words to the effect: "We have umpteen schools where people learn to work but now we have one where they can learn to play."'

Author and source: Norman W Dobson, who was involved in outdoor pursuits in the late 1930s and who worked as a voluntary instructor at White Hall Centre during its first two years, 1951 and 1952. 'Influences on the Development of Outdoor Pursuits in French Children's Education' (PhD thesis, University of Leicester, 1999), pp. 1, 236.

'The obvious first principle is that the youngsters and adults who visit the centre should enjoy themselves. The obvious test is whether they want to come again or not. The aim is the stimulation of a permanent interest in any of the activities. We are persuaded that we have been very successful with this approach and this success must largely result from the general absence of pressure. In detail, there is almost always complete freedom of choice as to which of the specialised activities – rock-climbing, canoeing, caving, and so on are taken and if anyone wishes [they] can just go fell-walking instead. We do not assume that everyone must like these pastimes. No-one is pressed to do anything [they find] difficult or alarming.'

Author and source: Harold Drasdo, who instructed at White Hall for two years, in 1956–8. 'The Character Builders', *Anarchy*, no. 11 (Jan 1962), pp. 25–28 (p. 28).

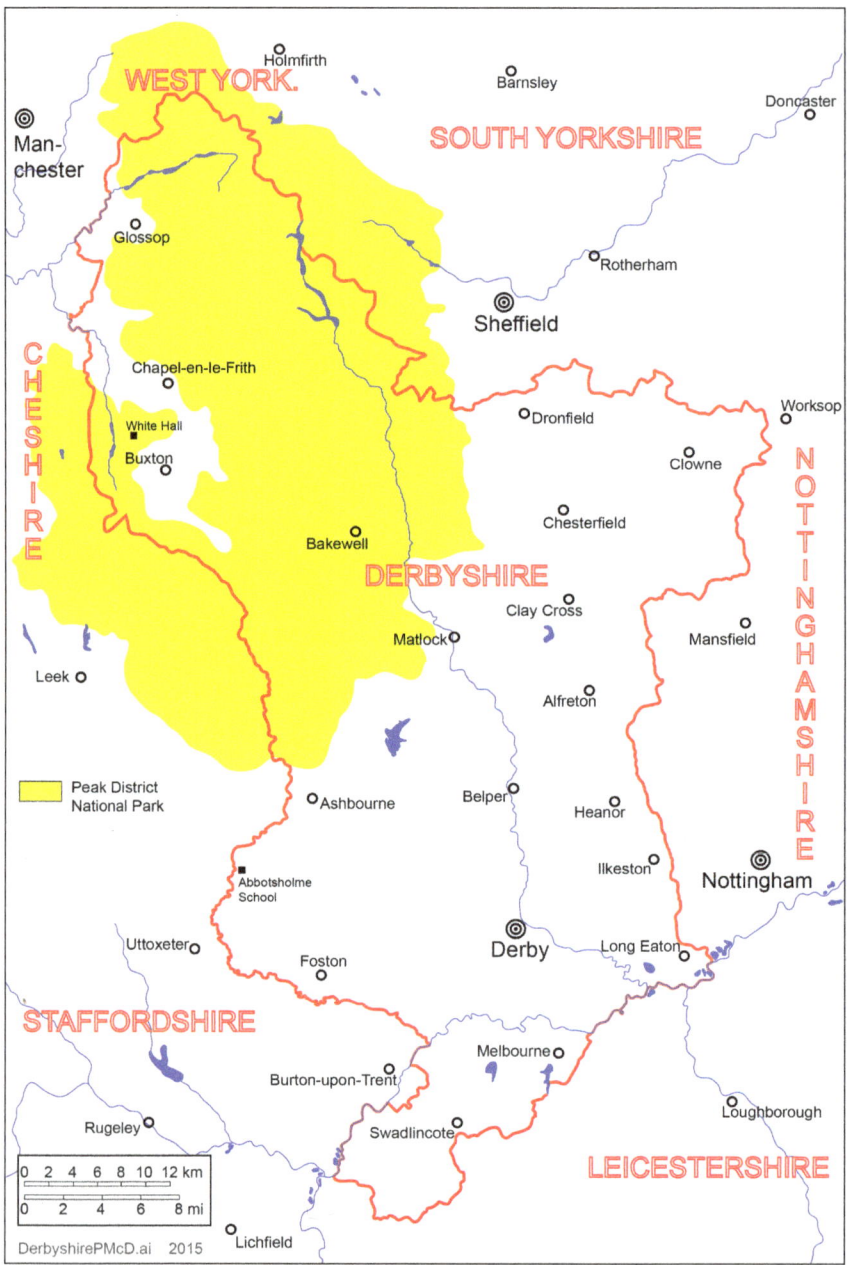

The boundaries of Derbyshire and the Peak District National Park.

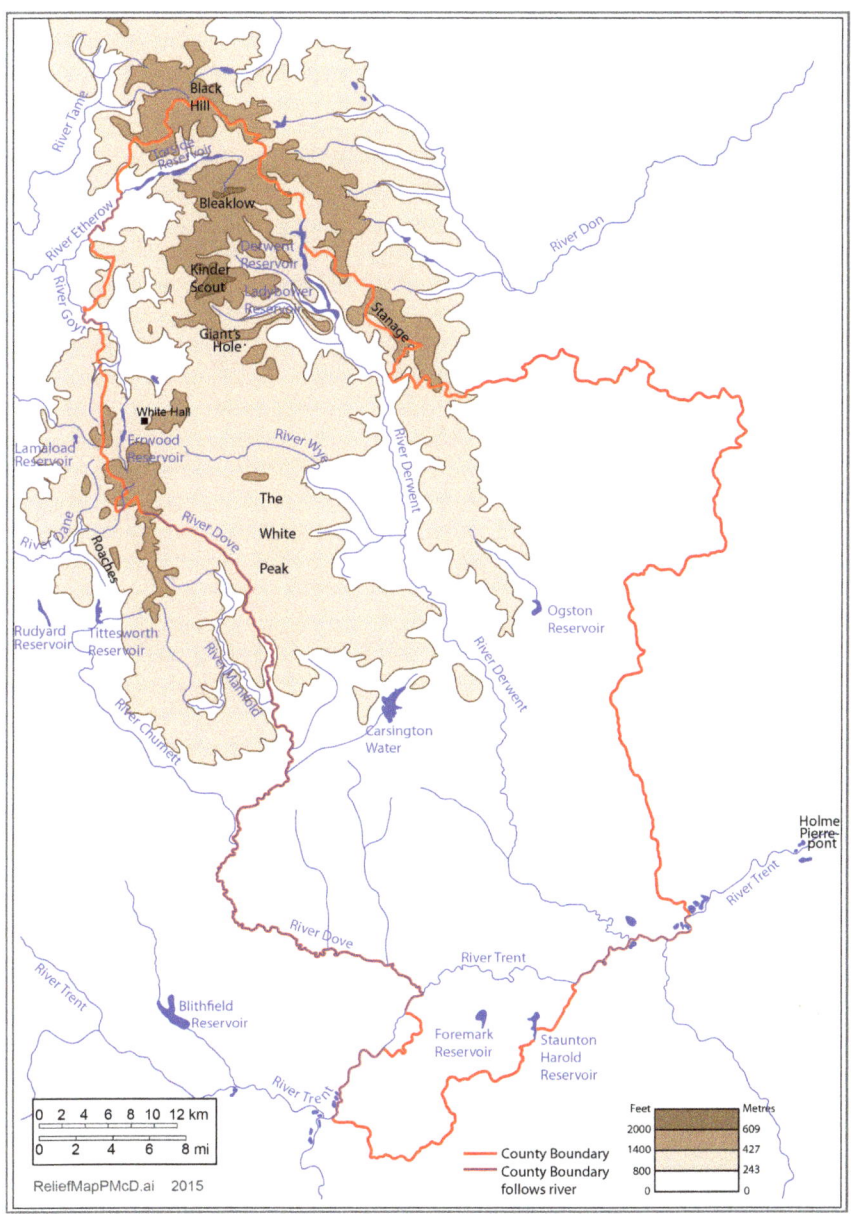

The terrain, rivers and reservoirs of Derbyshire and the Peak District National Park.

Contents

Introduction

White Hall Centre for Open Country Pursuits welcomed its first course members on the evening of Friday 29 December 1950. This was a century and a half after the beginnings of Romanticism and its quest for the picturesque, eighty-five years after the end of the golden age of Alpine mountaineering, and sixty-four years after Walter Haskett Smith made the first ascent of Napes Needle. The general history of mountaineering, including the social, cultural and economic conditions that gave rise to the sport, is well covered by published books. So too are the histories of other adventurous outdoor pursuits such as kayaking, sailing and caving. Similarly, regarding the origins of outdoor education, a number of authors have written about aspects of 17th, 18th and 19th century history that preceded and influenced the growth in the 20th century of a diverse movement that became known as outdoor education or outdoor learning but which can mean different things to different people.[1]

The focus of *The Story of White Hall Centre* is narrower than that of a general history, both in subject and in time-span. The subject is one local education authority (LEA) residential outdoor pursuits centre out of a total number of such places that at its peak may have exceeded one hundred.[2] The establishing of White Hall was largely an initiative of Jack Longland, Derbyshire county council's director of education. During the inaugural weekend in 1950, 'Longland, supported by the Warden of the Centre, Peter Mosedale, stated their aims. These included the provision of basic training in hillcraft in all weathers and in the allied sports of climbing, caving, camping, canoeing, and ski-ing wherever conditions are suitable'.[3]

As for the time-span, Part One covers the first half of the 20th century, with forays into the late 19th, setting the scene for Longland's arrival in Derbyshire. Chapters 1 to 6 each take a theme from this period, before the existence of White Hall Centre. In looking at the growth of outdoor recreation before 1950, I differentiate between what adults were doing (Chapter 2 and 3) and what school pupils were getting up to (Chapter 4).

Part Two is more chronological, covering the first twenty years of the centre, December 1950 – September 1970. A separate chapter is allocated to each wardenship or principalship. A brief summary of national developments concludes each of these chapters; these summaries draw heavily, and with some ruthless condensing, from Ken Ogilvie's voluminous *Roots and Wings*, an all-encompassing history of outdoor education in the UK that taps into the records of a lifetime of committee meetings and conferences.

Part Three covers the period September 1970 – March 1992, including the mountain-training dispute, a national issue that Jack Longland was involved in.

The narrow focus of the title *The Story of White Hall Centre* may tempt some readers to categorise the stories of Jack Longland and of White Hall Centre as merely parts of local history, of little interest outside Derbyshire. This would underrate their importance. Longland had a national presence. In mountaineering he became a ubiquitous and influential patrician figure, president of the Mountain Leadership Training Board (MLTB) and of the British Mountaineering Council (BMC), member of the Central Council of Physical Recreation (CCPR) executive and of the Countryside Commission, and chair of the Sports Council and of numerous symposia and conferences.

The place he set up, White Hall Centre, also gained a national reputation. Writers on outdoor education have frequently described White Hall Centre as Britain's first LEA residential outdoor pursuits centre. A *Buxton Advertiser* article in August 1949 was headed: '"Whitehall" May Be First Country Pursuits Centre: County Plan Submitted to Ministry'.[4] In 1956, Cyril Machin wrote that 'Derbyshire's is the first LEA to establish a centre of this kind'.[5] He may have been wrong. Keswick Youth Centre (later called Denton House), set up by Cumberland education authority, might have been the first LEA outdoor pursuits centre. Not that it matters. What is significant is that a strong consensus seems to exist that identifies White Hall Centre as the mould followed – closely or not so closely – by many of the LEA residential outdoor pursuits centres that sprang up in the 1960s and 70s. So the approaches and ethos that evolved at White Hall in the 1950s hold more than just local relevance.

The centre that grew under the wardenships of Peter Mosedale and Geoffrey Sutton differed in some small and subtle but important respects from the Outward Bound (OB) schools of the 1940s and early 1950s. The reasons for this were partly practical, such as the necessity to find approaches that suited the younger age group and that suited courses of a week instead of a month; and they were partly philosophical, such as reservations about or rejection of the character-training ideas of OB and the Boy Scout movement. To illustrate this difference, I allocate some space and attention to the subject of character training.

For much of his life, Longland was heavily involved in a wide range of national sports and countryside bodies and in a variety of local government and central government groups and commissions. His life and achievements and the centre he set up occupy important places in the history of British outdoor education.

Regarding the different outdoor pursuits discussed in this book, mountaineering and mountaineers have tended to dominate the development of outdoor education in Britain. In *Roots and Wings*, Ken Ogilvie allows the history of mountaineering a generous amount of space. He acknowledges that giving a preponderance of attention to mountaineering, in a book about outdoor education, could attract some criticism. But he also defends the space allocation, arguing that 'many aspects of mountaineering, its aims, motives and effects on people, are intrinsic to Outdoor Learning philosophy'. This does not, he says, belittle the many amazing achievements that have taken place on the oceans and rivers, below ground and in the air.[6]

The history of White Hall Centre provides a local example of this national bias. The Peak District is one of the major climbing areas in Britain. A mountaineer set up White Hall. Two of the folk present at the opening weekend – Longland and Bob Pettigrew – would later serve terms as president of the BMC. Of the many activities provided at White Hall, the primary skill and interest of most of its wardens or principals has been mountaineering and especially rock climbing. Recalling his years at White Hall and at Glenmore Lodge, White Hall's third warden/principal, Eric Langmuir, said: 'I place[d] great store by mountaineering because I considered that the basis for everything else. People could sail or canoe or ski but they had to be mountaineers.'[7] Although the teaching staff have often included one or two expert kayakers, accomplished cavers and well-qualified dinghy sailors, the spread of outdoor skills across the staff has been biased towards climbing.

Despite this slant in staff members' pedigree, climbing has always been just one of the wide assortment of activities offered on White Hall schools' courses. Caving, camping, map-reading or orienteering, moorland walking, and canoeing or kayaking have remained staple activities at White Hall since about 1954. Skiing was an occasional winter extra from the 1950s to the 1990s. Pony trekking appeared on some programmes in the early 1970s. Sailing on Errwood Reservoir was always popular in the 1970s and 80s, until the county's schools' sailing facilities were closed. Mountain-biking arrived at White Hall in 1991.

There is another point about mountaineering that I want to make here, in the Introduction. When I started writing this book, I looked upon mountaineering as being just one aspect, albeit an important one, of the history of the multidimensional movement that became known as outdoor education or outdoor learning. Then, eighteen months into the writing, I realised that a reverse connection also existed; the story of outdoor education in the UK, and in particular the story of White Hall Centre, is an aspect of the history of British mountaineering. But, as I see it, many accounts of the development of British mountaineering, whether short articles or whole books, have understated the role of LEA outdoor pursuits centres during the steady expansion and diversification of the sport in the second half of the 20th century.

If this premise is correct – that historians of UK mountaineering have been slow to scrutinise and reveal the collective national impact of the well-funded residential LEA outdoor centres – why the tardiness? In actuality, there is no mystery behind this reluctance to see the obvious. The long and fierce mountain-training dispute of the mid-1970s was accompanied by the deep antagonism of many grassroots climbers towards outdoor educators in general and towards so-called educational mountaineers in particular. Far from welcoming the potential of outdoor education to promote the attractions of mountaineering, the mountaineering establishment feared the possible negative consequences, and especially the possibility of heightened risk-averseness and of state interference in the conduct of the sport. Vestiges of hostility and distrust may linger in some quarters. Yet this bizarre dispute happened forty years ago. A fresh look at the half-century is overdue.

I did not expect *The Story of White Hall Centre* to contribute that fresh look and hence provide new insights into this period in the history of British mountaineering. However, as an indirect and unexpected result of my research, the book goes some way towards fulfilling exactly this purpose (despite its focusing on only one centre). It tells you, for example, about the magazine article that Jack Longland wrote in 1950, 'Why provide mountain training centres?' Until recently, this clear exposition lay hidden among private papers; it will deserve a mention in any future account of the way that climbing and hillwalking grew in popularity from 1950 onwards. The book also uncovers the considerable public-relations initiatives of Geoff Sutton in the late 1950s, which very deliberately used television, radio, a royal visit and newspapers to improve the public's understanding of and acceptance of rock climbing. For fifty years, the LEA residential outdoor centres boosted the popularity of hillwalking and climbing. Some of you who are reading this will have been introduced to the hills and the crags at an LEA outdoor centre. These residential centres also served, with other outdoor institutions, as hotbeds for the evolution of professional standards in instructing. *The Story of White Hall Centre* may be of interest not just to outdoor educators but also to those members of the mountaineering fraternity who are involved in promoting the sport and in raising awareness of its physical and social benefits.

Immense social and cultural and technological changes have taken place during the lifetime of White Hall Centre. In ordinary conversation in 1950, the word 'environment' was a rarity. Across the Atlantic, a new term, 'risk management', was coming into use in the American insurance industry. The term 'extreme sports' did not exist. In 1950, there were still 300,000 horses working on farms in England. By 1979 the total was 3,575. A study of urban life in the city of Derby, published in 1954, revealed that nine out of ten homes possessed a Bible. Football crowds in 1955 were 'as orderly as church meetings'.[8] Schoolchildren were even more orderly, kept so by the use of a thin flexible cane or a leather tawse. In the UK, life expectancy at birth in 1950 was 71 years for women and 66 years for men.[9] In 2015 the figures were 82.8 for women and 79.1 for men.[10]

In 1950–1, the total number of full-time and part-time students taking courses at universities in the UK was 104,687. By 1980–1, it was 339,925.[11] In 2013–14 the total number of full-time and part-time students at all UK higher education providers was 1,863,860.[12]

The sport of sailing provides a striking example of social change. In January 1950, eleven months before White Hall opened, Combs Sailing Club was founded, based at Combs Reservoir, just two miles north of White Hall. The club's constitution excluded women from membership, implying – intentionally or not – that dinghy sailing was a sport for men only … Fast forward fifty-five years to 7 February 2005: Ellen MacArthur, who had grown up in Whatstandwell near Matlock, crosses the finishing line near the French coast at Ushant to break the world record for the fastest solo nonstop circumnavigation of the globe.

Drawing up an accurate and complete list of past White Hall staff has been a slow and often hesitant process. The exact dates when individuals started and finished have sometimes been difficult to determine. I would welcome news of any errors, so that any future editions can be corrected.

Having worked at White Hall in the 1970s and 80s, I will occasionally add a memory or observation of my own, so here and there you will find me writing in the first person.

Finally, a note on nomenclature. Much of this book discusses residential courses. When stating the length of a course, different sources followed two different conventions. Consider a course that stretched from 2pm on a Monday to 3pm on a Friday. Was this a four-day course or a five-day course? In general use in the world at large, most people would refer to such a course as a five-day course. Course lengths mentioned in the body text of this book follow this convention.

For many years, until recently, White Hall's printed annual programmes followed a different convention. Monday-to-Friday courses appeared as four-day courses (because the fee charged was for four nights of accommodation). Similarly, Monday-to-Sunday courses appeared as six-day courses. The programme extracts reproduced in this book remain in their original state.

White Hall Centre has pioneered excellence in outdoor education for seventy-seven years. This book tries to do justice to that achievement.

Notes

1   In particular, Ken C Ogilvie, *Roots and Wings: A History of Outdoor Education and Outdoor Learning in the UK* (Lyme Regis, UK: Russell House Publishing, 2013), pp. 44–166.

2   Ibid., pp. 383–387.

3   Cyril B Machin, 'The Educational Value of Open Country Pursuits', *Journal of the Midland Association of Mountaineers*, 3, no. 1 (1956), pp. 16–18.

4   '"Whitehall" May Be First Country Pursuits Centre', *Buxton Advertiser*, 27 Aug 1949, p. 3.

5   Cyril B Machin, 'The Educational Value of Open Country Pursuits', *Journal of the Midland Association of Mountaineers*, 3, no. 1 (1956), pp. 16–18 (p. 16).

6   Ken C Ogilvie, *Roots and Wings: A History of Outdoor Education and Outdoor Learning in the UK* (Lyme Regis, UK: Russell House Publishing, 2013), pp. 122–123.

7   Jeff Connor, *Creagh Dhu Climber: The Life and Times of John Cunningham* (no place given: Ernest Press, 1999), p. 173.

8   Asa Briggs, *A Social History of England* (London: Weidenfield and Nicolson, 1983), pp. 290–294, 313.

9   Human Mortality Database, 'United Kingdom: Life Expectancy at Birth', University of California (USA) and Max Planck Institute for Demographic Research (Germany) (5 July 2013) <www.mortality.org> [accessed 8 May 2015].

10   Office for National Statistics, *Statistical Bulletin: National Life Tables, United Kingdom: 2013–2015* (London: Office for National Statistics, Sept 2016), p. 2.

11   B R Mitchell, *British Historical Statistics* (Cambridge: Cambridge University Press, 1988), pp. 811–813.

12   Higher Education Statistics Agency, 'General Student Numbers: Table 1' (2015) <https://www.hesa.ac.uk/stats> [accessed 6 June 2015].

Part One:
Historical Background, 1880–1950

1. Jack Longland's Route to Derbyshire, 1905–49

One day in March 1933 during the long approach to Everest, across the plains of Tibet, the weather is perfect and the going is easy. Jack Longland, aged twenty-seven and a lecturer in English literature at Durham University, happens to spot some solid-looking climbable rock beside the trail. It can be hard for a born rock climber to resist such a temptation; the ability to glide gracefully up steep rock is one of Longland's natural talents, which he had exploited impressively on several Welsh cliffs. When you possess a gift like that, you yearn to use it. Hugh Ruttledge, the expedition leader, knows that Longland is 'one of the best of the modern school of British rock-climbers, whose technique must surely be nearing the limit of which human beings are capable'.[1] Ruttledge takes up the story:

> There can hardly be anything more delightful than marching across the Tibetan levels in such circumstances, before the wind gets up. On the way we found some cliffs which positively invited a halt for a sun-bath on the warm rock. Longland interpreted the invitation differently. To him anything steep is a direct challenge. Selecting a moment when I was at peace with the world, he departed stealthily round a corner, and was well on the way up a vertical pitch before I could develop my parrot-cry of 'Safety first on the way to Mount Everest'. However, Longland shares with lizards the faculty of adhering to perfectly smooth walls.[2]

In later life, Sir John Laurence ('Jack') Longland was well-known as a broadcaster, a mountaineer, and an educational administrator. Of these three identities, the general public knew him best as the question-master of the long-running BBC radio quiz *My Word*, which he chaired for over twenty years. Also, his reputation as a leading rock climber and an Everest mountaineer jumped the gap from climbing literature to national newspapers. Similarly, unlike most educational administrators, who tend to be anonymous figures, he was quite frequently in either the local news or the national news as an educationist, especially while he was director of education for Derbyshire. Less well-known were his winning an athletics blue at Cambridge for pole-vaulting and his participation in November 1927 in the second ascent of the rooftop circuit of Trinity College's Great Court, Trinity being the aristocrat of the Cambridge night-climbing venues.[3]

Michael Westmacott said of him: 'The son of a clergyman, Longland was one of the Establishment, but was often critical of its ways … As a rock-climber, he was brilliant.'[4] Jim Perrin, writing about the climbers of the late 1920s, refers to him as 'the astoundingly gifted young university climber from Cambridge'.[5] This was a man whose legend seems to be based on the truth. Some people are allotted an outrageously diverse range of talents, compared to the rest of us.

The role of most interest to us in this book is that of Longland the educationist. Not that we can ever separate this passionate professional from the athlete with an abiding love of mountaineering or from the panellist with a quick wit and an incisive mind.

Summer Holidays

In 1905 there were just 16,000 private cars on the roads in Britain (compared to a projected 31.4 million for 2015), and most people still considered the car to be a toy.[6] John Laurence Longland was born on 26 June that year, in a Britain whose fields and streets were still full of horses. His father was the curate of St John's, Hagley, Worcestershire. John was the second of five children.

Whereas he was just at the beginning of an eventful life, in the most extraordinary century in human history, three men whose lives would touch his were already partway through theirs. All three harboured ideas on young people and the outdoors. Which of their ideas would come to be espoused by Longland, and which would not, this book will try to determine. The oldest of these three men was Major-General Robert Baden-Powell.

From June to December 1901, Baden-Powell, a popular patriotic figure for his role in the defence of Mafeking, had been on leave in England, recovering from an illness.[7] He had visited the home of Sir George Young, where he had met a man central to this story, Young's third child, Geoffrey. In June 1898 Geoffrey and a friend had invented and staged a very successful manhunt game that took place across the central Lake District fells. Baden-Powell asked him to describe it.[8] This exchange of information led later to the development of the wide games that became popular in Scouting and which would resurge vigorously at White Hall Centre in the 1950s.

In 1905, when Longland was born, Baden-Powell was forty-eight years old and was pondering ways to adapt military training methods for nonmilitary use with groups of boys. His solution, put into writing in the summer of 1907, was a training scheme that sought to develop the whole person, physically, mentally and spiritually, and which emphasised the value of camping and outdoor activities. By 2008, his book of yarns and pictures, *Scouting for Boys*, which had remained in print in various editions and languages for a century, was estimated to have sold more copies worldwide than almost any other text, excluding the Bible.[9]

Aged about twenty-four when Longland was born, Geoffrey Winthrop Young had started a climbing career that would make him one of the best-known British mountaineers of the period before the first world war. In 1903 he had organised the first of what became annual Easter climbing get-togethers at the Gorffwysfa Hotel, at Pen-y-Pass in Snowdonia, occasions that the accounts variously call gatherings or retreats or house parties, typically featuring long days on Lliwedd followed by long nights of intellectual stimulation and inventive relaxation and who knows what other funny business. In time, these highly exclusive Easter meets would become a part of Jack Longland's life. They continued, with breaks during the first and second world wars, until 1947.[10] Echoes of them may have entered the ethos of White Hall Centre, but without the elitist Cambridge-only aspect.

As well as being a climber, Young was a schoolteacher and educationist. From 1905 to 1914 he inspected schools for Her Majesty's Inspectorate.[11] But he believed the English public-schools system to be flawed. Before the first world war, Young and others discussed the possibility of creating the ideal school of the future, whose pupils would spend half the school year in the classroom and half in permanent camp, 'engaged on practical open-air activities and crafts'.[12]

In May 1910 Baden-Powell retired from the army. Being a family friend of the Youngs, he approached Geoffrey Young to ask him about 'the merits of climbing as an exercise and a discipline for boys'. (In the first half of the 20th century, boys dominated all references to aspects of education in the outdoors.[13]) The two men discussed this again after the war.[14] At some point, Baden-Powell commissioned Young to write a 2,000-word paper on climbing as an educative activity for Boy Scouts. Simon Thompson, writing on the history of British climbing, has suggested that this commission was probably the first attempt in Britain to codify the benefits of outdoor education.[15] If so, it was a flop, because the scoutmasters turned down the chance to go climbing, 'at that date still the esoteric enthusiasm of the few'. Young explained: '[climbing] was rejected by all the more earnest leaders, as an expedient unacceptable, on grounds of danger, to the serene Victorian Age and to contemporary parentage'.[16]

Part of the reason for Baden-Powell's initiative was that the scout movement was seeking activities that would attract adolescents. Rock climbing, in the 1910s, still had a long way to go before the public would approve it as a sport for young people.

The third man whose thoughts and activities would influence Longland, to some extent, was Kurt Hahn, the son of a businessman in the German steel industry. Nineteen years old when Longland was born, Hahn was already ruminating on the essential ingredients of education and on what makes a good school. In July and August 1903, aged seventeen, he had taken part in a walking tour of the Dolomites in the company of his uncle and three pupils from Abbotsholme, Cecil Reddie's progressive school on the banks of the River Dove in south Derbyshire.[17] His meeting these three boys had sparked an interest in Reddie's unconventional ideas and methods. It is possible that some ideas originating at Abbotsholme in Derbyshire may have stayed in Hahn's head and travelled firstly to Salem school in Germany (a place I will mention later), and then onwards to Gordonstoun school in Scotland, before branching out to Aberdovey Outward Bound Sea School (OBSS) and to Hertfordshire schools, and then arriving back in Derbyshire at White Hall Centre. (This cross fertilisation of ideas appears to have started in the 1880s and 1890s, through a connection between Reddie and the German educationist Hermann Lietz.[18])

In 1905 Hahn still had nine years of university studies ahead of him, at Oxford and in Germany, until the first world war intervened and opened up for him some important connections that would have significant consequences for the development and dissemination of his ideas on education.

Before I return to the story of the young Longland, I will dwell on Hahn and World War I for a moment longer. Exempted from military service on health ground, and also an ardent and articulate pacifist, Hahn worked for the German foreign office. He became involved in groups that advocated a peaceful end to hostilities, which led to his working closely with Prince Max of Baden, an outspoken Christian.[19]

Young and Hahn will appear frequently in this account of Longland's route to Derbyshire and of the first twenty years of the outdoor centre he set up.

To understand Longland, the man whose career took him to Derbyshire in 1948, we need to go back to the schoolboy at King's School, Worcester, soon after the end of the first world war. What we find is a refined variation on a familiar theme. What should a chap do in the long summer holiday, now that the war is over? Obvious! The classics master will be residing in a gîte above the Rhône valley, encircled by the peaks of the Diablerets; there will be room for you and your younger brother to spend the summer there and study Greek.[20]

He holidayed there two years running. A knowledge of Greek was still one of the hallmarks of a first-class education, as it had been in the medieval grammar schools, and Longland was probably a competent Greek scholar, but his attention was drawn to his surroundings. 'His interest was thus fired, and he searched out thenceforwards every bit of rock available to him on family holidays or within reach of his native Droitwich, to practise his new-found passion.'[21]

Longland's father had become vicar of St Peter's, a Norman church in Droitwich, in 1916. The main outcrop locally was a quarried lump of diorite in the hills on the south side of Worcester. Here, the teenager

Ive Scar Rock, near Great Malvern, Worcestershire, where the boy Jack Longland first tied onto a rope.

first tied onto a climbing rope: 'I remember making my Papa sit on the rope while I was trying to climb the villainous bit of crag called the Ivy Scar Rock on the Malvern Hills, which I think was the most dunderhead thing that I've done in my life.'[22]

A little searching online confirmed that this crag should be left for the birds: 'Truly rubbish. Probably the worst bit of rock I have ever climbed on. Unprotectable, sloping, awkward, loose, lichenous.'

At about the same time as the teenage Longland was surviving this horrible introduction to rock climbing, in 1920 an industrious Kurt Hahn, with the guidance and encouragement of Prince Max, was setting up a progressive co-educational boarding-school at Salem in south Germany near Lake Constance. It was housed in a wing of the prince's castle, a former Cistercian monastery in rolling country with hills and woods all around. 'The aim of the school was to inculcate in the post-war generation self-discipline, enterprise, physical fitness, skills, craftsmanship, and compassion.'[23] Hahn placed greater emphasis on noncompetitive physical activities than on high levels of performance in competitive games.[24] In some ways, Salem was the antithesis of the traditional German schools, which followed narrower curriculums and were rigid and authoritarian, part of a system often stigmatised as a teaching machine. On the other hand, several progressive educational movements in Germany had preceded Salem and had already influenced some parts of the German educational system, taking school work far beyond the three Rs. Expeditions and *schullandheim* (school outdoor centres) were important elements of German educational practice before Hahn started Salem; I do not know whether they influenced his thinking.[25]

From King's School in October 1923[26] Longland went up to Jesus College, Cambridge, where he was Rustat Exhibitioner and Scholar. Here he latched onto a talented coterie of climbers that included Gino Watkins, Ivan Waller and the geologist Lawrence Wager, watched over by the father figure Geoffrey Young, who moved from north Lancashire to Cambridge at the end of 1924.[27] Longland later remembered being a first-year undergraduate: 'When I went to Cambridge I was buttoned-up and callow and shy and as soon as I met him I came very much under the influence of Geoffrey Young.'[28] So much so, according to Jim Perrin, that 'as an eighteen-year-old freshman … Jack Longland was sexually involved with both G. W. Y. and "Len" Young [Geoffrey Young's wife Eleanor]'.[29] Geoffrey Young was homosexual but this did not destroy the Youngs' marriage. 'They found an acceptable *modus vivendi.*[30] (There is a slight chronological hiccup in this paragraph, not yet explained, as the Youngs did not move to Cambridge until Longland's second year.)

The first time Longland climbed properly with a rope was in Wasdale in 1925, where he fell out of Kern Knotts Crack and frightened himself on Keswick Brothers Climb.[31] He first visited north Wales in October 1925: 'Ivan Waller and I arrived in an ancient air-cooled Rover on the first of many week-ends snatched from Cambridge term. We knew nothing of tradition, nothing of the Climbers' Club or of the aura round Pen-y-pass, in fact we chose the Royal Hotel as the obvious centre for a climbing party! We drove through the night, as became usual, and went straight to Idwal to fight our way up the ordinary route on the Slabs.'[32]

By the start of 1926 Geoffrey and Len Young and their two children had moved from a small rented house to a grander house at 5 Benet Place, where there was room for hospitality. They began to hold regular Sunday evening at-homes for their friends. Their house became 'the centre for all the most active ambitious, and no doubt insufferable among young Cambridge climbers'.[33] In the wider student community, the 1920s brought 'a great release of upper-class gaiety amongst the so-called "bright young things" of Oxford and Cambridge'.[34]

Geoffrey Young's Easter parties at Pen-y-Pass were rendezvous for an exclusive climbing fraternity. 'Jack was a dashing figure on these occasions, active on the hills, a witty and stimulating companion, excelling also with his compact muscular figure at such gymnastic contests as arm wrestling and climbing round an upright chair without touching the floor.'[35] The competition was intense, leading on one occasion to Ivan Waller performing a handstand on top of one of Tryfan's summit blocks.[36]

In Cambridge, Longland joined in the local nocturnal sport of roof-climbing but deplored the publicity that this activity later received. 'The whole point about roof climbing,' he said, 'was its quietness and anonymity and the University authorities would not take strong action, such as sending you down, if you kept quiet.' This versatility, Peter Lloyd says, was a foretaste of what was to come in his professional life.[37]

In 1926, while the youthful Longland, average in height, supreme in agility, was learning the games that climbers play, the far older Young was settling into a new job, as a consultant to the Laura Spelman Rockefeller Memorial, a foundation set up by John D Rockefeller to support research in social studies. The work entailed spending long periods in Geneva, Paris and Berlin.[38] Young had heard about Kurt Hahn's residential school at Salem, where Hahn was putting into practice his concept of training to produce a whole, well-balanced adult. Young visited this innovative endeavour and was impressed. He was pleased to discover Hahn's strong conviction that sport should be wider than just team games and athletics, embracing climbing, hillwalking, canoeing and small-boat sailing.[39] In 1926 Hahn was still formulating his Seven Laws of Salem. 'The two men, each a charismatic and mildly eccentric individual, quickly found common ground, their ideas about education being similar.'[40] They will have both approved of the real law passed by the German government in the late 1920s that required every school class to spend one day a month, to be known as *Wandertag* (wandering day), outside the school grounds.[41]

These ideas were to quickly reach Longland, directly from Young and some years before Longland's stint in the Durham coalfields and his subsequent move into educational administration. A question remains, however, about the extent to which Hahn's smooth rhetoric and Young's unrestrained enthusiasm for character training influenced Longland and Peter Mosedale and the formative first few years of White Hall Centre. Chapters 7, 8 and 9 will try to throw some light on this matter.

Longland gained a first class in the Historical tripos in 1926, and a first class with special distinction in the English tripos in 1927. After graduating he stayed on for two years as a bye-fellow of Magdalene College, responsible for the Pepysian Library.[42]

At Whitsuntide in 1928, the West Buttress of Clogwyn du'r Arddu, a six-hundred-foot cliff on Snowdon, remained unclimbed. The author of a 1926 guidebook had written: 'No breach seems either possible or desirable along the whole extent of the West Buttress, though there is the faintest of faint hopes for a human fly rather towards its left side.'[43]

On Whit Sunday, 27 May, two parties of climbers met at the base of the buttress, both intent on exploring this faintest hope. One party was from the Cambridge University Mountaineering Club, the other from the Rucksack Club. Gentlemen all, they jettisoned north-south rivalry for the greater good, which resulted in a combined team of five. Several of them had half-climbed the new route, up a long narrow slab, over the previous few days. Longland – the young and confidant rock gymnast – now completed the job, leading his four companions up the West Buttress by what became known as Longland's Climb. It was no harder than some of the routes on more frequented crags, but it was a psychological breakthrough, a way up an entirely unknown buttress of a formidable precipice. A comment from *The Black Cliff* (1971) is still worth saying today: 'The young climber who today finds this passage scarcely severe might remember that it was led without runners, into the unknown, with little hope of retreat after the crux and no possibility of a rope from above.'[44] Longland, aged twenty-two, had arrived. He would contribute to a surge in climbing standards in the UK.

In 1929 Longland went to East Prussia for a postgraduate year as an exchange fellow at Königsberg University. This coincided exactly with the time when Kurt Hahn in Salem was finalising the educational principles his teachers were to follow, which appeared in writing in 1930 (and which still underpin life and work at Schule Schloss Salem today). Hahn's motivation stemmed from his great concern for young people, but his gift lay in applying the ideas of other educational reformers; his Seven Laws of Salem were not original ideas, yet his adoption of them for the particular purposes of his own enterprising school was determined and successful. The following English version of the 'laws' is from the website of the Schule Schloss Salem:

> Provide young people the chance to discover themselves and face challenges.
> Provide young people with the experience of both victory and defeat.
> Teach them to put pursuit of the common good before personal ambition.
> Make time for silence – make space for contemplation.
> Train imagination and the ability to look ahead and plan.
> Take sports and games seriously, but do not let them dominate.
> Liberate the children of the rich and the powerful from the paralyzing awareness of their privilege.[45]

Looking forwards a couple of years, in March 1931 Geoffrey Young's son Jocelin, eleven years old, would join Salem junior school, an indication of Young's admiration for Hahn's educational methods.[46] Regarding the sons of the rich, Hahn's link with Prince Max was to have one particularly notable consequence: the twelve-year-old Prince Philip of Greece (later the Duke of Edinburgh) would join Salem in September 1933. The effects of this connection still reverberate through some sectors of outdoor education today, particularly in the Outward Bound movement and in the Duke of Edinburgh's award scheme.

Some observers have described the Salem programmes as militaristic asceticism. The school has been called an effort 'to breed modern "princes" of Machiavelli's kind ... leaders in politics and diplomacy, or in industry and commerce'.[47] Jonathan Petropoulos, writing in *Royals and the Reich*, says that these descriptions are rather ungenerous. 'The school featured a significant number of scholarship students from modest background, and many of its graduates emerged with liberal and progressive views.'[48]

Longland was back in north Wales at Easter 1930, where with two novices literally in tow he made the first ascent of the Javelin Blade climb in Cwm Idwal, described by Jim Perrin thus: 'Perhaps the most difficult lead achieved on a mountain crag until the immediate post-war period, and one of the few British climbs of its time which could bear comparison with technical developments on the Continent.'[49] On the crux of Javelin Blade, Longland was forty feet above his belayer. He faced an eighty-foot lob onto a hemp rope tied around his waist. A hemp rope would sustain a man's weight falling about ten feet, but no more than that.[50] Ivan Waller has summarised these sorts of situations: 'At this time nobody wore helmets, runners had not been thought of and pitons were taboo. A fall by the leader was usually fatal especially as the climbs were in general not as steep as the modern ones, so that there was more likelihood of hitting a ledge or projecting rock instead of falling clear, and furthermore there were no harnesses to check your fall in comfort.'[51]

Durham and Everest

In 1929 the US stock market crashed. World trade slumped, prices fell, and credit dried up. The value of British exports halved, plunging its industrial areas – already suffering for other reasons – into poverty. In the coalfields of County Durham the number of miners fell from 172,026 in 1924 to 107,938 in 1931.[52] This was the part of England where Longland came to live when in 1930 he returned from his scholarship in Germany.

Longland's first full-time job was as a lecturer in English literature and language at Durham University. A newspaper notice on 1 July 1930 included him in a list of appointments. He wasn't yet 'Longland of Everest', he was just the more prosaic and unremarkable 'President of the Cambridge Alpine Club'.[53] His stint as a university lecturer would last from 1930 to 1936, a period interspersed by two expeditions.

After he arrived in Durham and before the Everest expedition, Longland began to lecture on climbing and mountaineering, sometimes to the public and sometimes to members of local organisations, such as the Sunderland and District Branch of the Geographical Association.[54] One imagines that he enjoyed this voluntary lecturing, which became a feature of his life in Durham. It was a way for him to meet and talk to ordinary folk and to promote a better public understanding of a sport that he loved. He was a confident speaker, at ease in front of a crowd, whether he was talking to the Workers' Educational Association about rock climbing or to the English Association about the literature of mountaineering.[55]

Still a young man in 1930 and a natural athlete, he became a playing member of Durham City Rugby Club.[56] He also coached athletics with unemployed coal-miners, resulting in one of his protégés winning the pole vault at an international event.[57] Of most interest to us, though, is a reference to perhaps his earliest organisational involvement with novice climbers: a 1933 edition of the student magazine *New Durham* records that Durham Colleges' Mountaineering Club was founded in Michaelmas 1931 under the auspices of Jack Longland.[58]

He had other strings to his bow, too. One of the earliest mentions of him in a Durham newspaper informed the readers in November 1932 that Mr J L Longland was busy rehearsing his part in 'Five Little Plays of St. Francis', which were to be staged in St. Margaret's Hall in aid of the work of the Durham Deaconesses.[59]

*

Longland was no mere crag-rat. He had directed his main attention towards the Alps, climbing there every year between 1925 and 1932. Climbing guidelessly, he had achieved some impressive ridge climbs.[60] His all-round mountaineering ability and his gilt-edged Cambridge credentials made him a natural choice for Hugh Ruttledge's Everest expedition of 1933. The places on the large and expensive expeditions to Everest went to gentlemen from 'the well-to-do middle-classes, with a background of Oxbridge and a decent sprinkling of Army officers and Government officials'.[61]

There are over two hundred books recording the mountaineering history of Mount Everest (Chomolungma).[62] One of the best of them is an anthology edited by Peter Gillman, *Everest: The Best Writing and Pictures from Seventy Years of Human Endeavour*. Only the finest of Everest writing makes it into this book. Ruttledge's *Everest, 1933* is a workmanlike account of the 1933 expedition and it went into at least five editions. It forms a reliable record of the summit attempts by Wager, Wyn-Harris and Smythe, key episodes of the mountain's history. But the writing chosen for the Gillman book is Longland's story of his retreat from a height of 27,500 feet (8,380 metres) in a sudden storm on the afternoon of 29 May 1933.

Unforeseen dramatic happenings in mountaineering can be long-drawn-out battles over several days or short sharp tragedies or near misses. The Longland retreat was none of these extremes; it involved two hours of acute anxiety while he led eight cold and exhausted Sherpa porters down a little known and ill-defined route, easy to lose and close to perilous ground. Readers who have been lost in a vicious snowstorm on steep ground on a British or Alpine mountain will understand how alarming the situation can be; then imagine the same thing happening on the upper reaches of the world's highest mountain.

The furthest Longland could see was a snow-swept circle of twenty or thirty yards. His snow-goggles quickly filled with snow. He took them off, 'only to find that eyelids and eyelashes coated up as well, forming an opaque film which had to be rubbed away every few minutes' before he could peer out and get a glimpse of the next few yards.[63] The wind came in terrifying gusts, forcing the men to cling or cower against the rocks to avoid being blown bodily away. Longland's description of his harrowing route-finding predicament appeared in 1940 as a book chapter titled 'Caught in an Everest Blizzard':

> We had a moment's respite in the lee of a small cliff, where we happened on the tattered remains of a green tent. It must have been the old Camp VI from which Mallory and Irvine left in 1924 for their attempt on the summit, and were never seen again. For a minute or two the least tired porters rummaged among the wreckage. One brought out a candle lantern and another an electric torch – the kind that worked with a press-button. Even after nine years of storm and cold the torch still worked, so we pushed on rather heartened by these signs of human occupation, many years old as they were.
>
> But the finding of the 1924 tent gave me my nastiest moment. I had a photograph in my pocket on which the position of Mallory's camp was marked. I was going to use it to mark accurately for Smythe and Shipton, who were to follow up Harris and Wager if the first attempt failed, the position of our own new Camp VI. I pulled the photograph out of my pocket now, and discovered to my horror that Mallory's camp was marked as being not on the main north ridge at all, but on a subsidiary spur further east. This must mean that, in spite of all my care, we were not on the main

ridge, and more than that, this second spur ran out on appallingly steep ice slopes overhanging the East Rongbuk Glacier thousands of feet below. If I led the party on to these slopes there was no escape – it would at best have meant a night in the open and to spend a night out at this height, even without a storm, would have been fatal.

I had to think desperately quickly – and it was a problem I couldn't possibly share with the porters, though if I went wrong they were equally involved in an unpleasant death … [64]

Longland remembered the last part of the descent as 'all slipping and staggering down icy screes and round little snowed-up cliffs'. Then, suddenly, squinting down through the blizzard he spotted a little patch of green, a cluster of four tents: Camp V and safety. The descent through the storm had taken only two hours, but they were the longest two hours of Longland's life. He wrote: 'I seemed to have crowded a lifetime of fear and struggle and responsibility into that short time.'[65]

Although three other members of the expedition later reached about 28,100 feet (8,565 metres), the mountain remained unclimbed. Yet Jack Longland's retreat became famous, and from then onwards press reports involving him would invariably introduce him to the reader as 'Mr Longland, the Mount Everest climber'.

*

Two stone lighter and fresh from the daring but expensive adventure, which had been open only to an invited few, Longland arrived back to a county still blighted by unemployment and poverty, two issues that would dominate most of the 1930s, until pushed sharply aside by the question of world peace.

In July 1933, a month or so after Longland's nerve-wracking retreat from Everest, Kurt Hahn in Germany made a different sort of a retreat from danger. As a Jewish intellectual, who had been bold enough publicly to defend his educational beliefs and methods against Nazi interference, his position had become precarious. He had been described as 'a decadent Jewish corrupter of German youth'.[66] At 2am on 11 March, Nazi storm-troopers surrounded Salem school. They arbitrarily arrested Hahn and took him to Überlingen gaol. He was released on 16 March but was ousted from the headship of his school and was exiled from the state of Baden. Geoffrey Young's wife Len hurried out to Salem, collected some of Hahn's secret papers, and spirited them out of Germany. Hahn decided to leave Germany. He arrived in Britain on 12 July.[67]

While Hahn, helped by Geoffrey Young, was picking up the pieces to start a new life and a new school, Longland in Durham resumed his lecturing sideline, mainly giving illustrated talks on the Everest expedition but also occasionally on subjects like 'The Craft of Mountaineering'.[68] On 31 January 1934 in Durham Town Hall he gave a lecture in aid of a local charity, the Durham House Settlement. The lecture, delivered twice in the one evening, attracted large audiences and inspired one admirer to describe Longland as 'one of the most popular men in the University of Durham, successful lecturer in English, a fine rugby footballer, and a thoroughly good fellow'.[69]

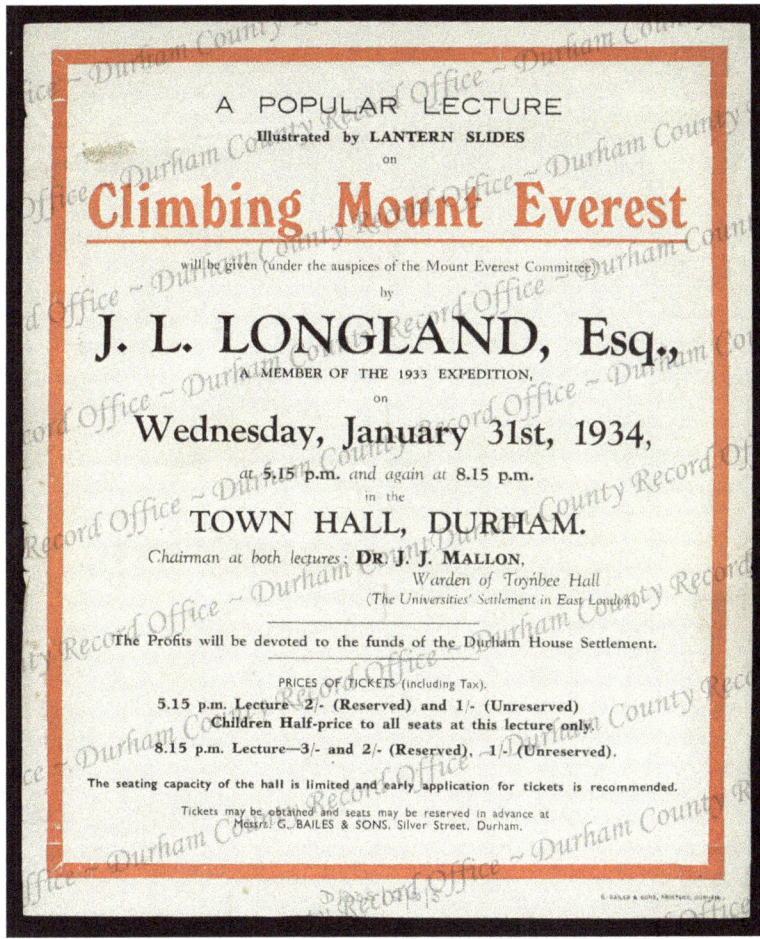

Poster advertising an illustrated public lecture by Jack Longland, 1934.

Before the Everest expedition, Longland, had he wanted to, could have got married in Durham without any people except his family and close friends being aware of it. But after Everest, his name began to become known to the masses. His life changed in a way that one might nowadays associate with a minor celebrity of popular culture. In June 1934 he married Peggy Harrison, a local girl, and the event reached the newspapers in columns with headings like 'Brancepeth Bride for Everest Climber' and 'Arch of Ice-axes at Wedding'.[70] After the reception, 'Mr and Mrs Longland left by motor for a honeymoon in the Isle of Skye, the bride wearing a costume of turquoise blue with hat to match'.[71]

The following summer, Peggy again accompanied her husband on a summer holiday, this time to Greenland. Jim Perrin, who probably had some inside knowledge, called Longland's 1935 visit to Greenland 'a light-hearted trip'.[72] In comparison to the Everest 1933 expedition, it probably was. However, the light-heartedness did include, for Longland and five companions, a 110-mile sledge journey across unexplored mountains and glaciers. At one stage, Longland found himself 'wondering … whether there were not more rational ways of exploring these mountains than this eternal pulling of sledges up inclines of snow like granulated sugar'.[73]

The team of six reached the summit of the highest mountain in the Watkins range. Nowadays, the mountain – Gunnbjørn Fjeld (3,694 m) – is not often climbed, and when it is, access is usually by helicopter or ski-equipped plane from Iceland.

*

When we look back at Longland's life, 1933 stands out clearly as the peak of his active climbing. As if to fill a hole, however, the period 1934–5 provides us with glimpses of a new Longland, one who – although barely thirty years old – enters confidently and with a mind of his own into the intrigue and manoeuvring of climbing politics, an area that grabs at his principles and sucks him in and which would benefit from his incisiveness and occasional artfulness for over forty years.

In 1934 the BMC did not exist. The unofficial voice of British mountaineering was the Alpine Club, based far away from the hills and top-heavy with well-connected professional gentlemen but conveniently close, for efficient public relations, to Fleet Street and the Houses of Parliament. In charge of coordinating and financing successive British Everest expeditions was the Mount Everest Committee, a body formed in 1921 by the Alpine Club and the Royal Geographical Society.[74]

The Mount Everest Committee obtained permission from Tibet to attempt Everest again in 1935 and 1936, but a controversy arose over who should be invited to lead the 1936 expedition. The committee favoured Hugh Ruttledge, the diffident and mild-mannered ex-commissioner of the Indian civil service who had led the 1933 expedition. A handful of younger climbers proposed Colin Crawford, another colonial administrator, for the role. Longland was in this group of dissidents, who jointly thought that the whole business of climbing Everest was being grossly mismanaged.[75] He considered Ruttledge to be insufficiently experienced in mountaineering and indecisive. 'It is difficult to overemphasize the frustration felt by young climbers in the mid-nineteen thirties,' he wrote many years later, 'believing, as they did, that the conduct both of the [Alpine] Club and of Everest affairs was largely in the hands of people who had not been near a serious climb for years.'[76]

On 28 March 1935 the Alpine Club old guard narrowly won this particular engagement, by a chairman's casting vote for Ruttledge and in an atmosphere of spiteful skulduggery.

Before the dust had settled, Crawford was controversially kicked off the Mount Everest Committee. Longland, C F Meade, Graham Brown and Crawford resigned from the Alpine Club committee (but not from the club; Longland served as its president for the three years 1974–6).[77]

The Everest Committee excluded Crawford from the 1936 team. Being unwilling to unconditionally support Ruttledge, a decent but ineffectual man, Longland was not invited onto the 1936 expedition.

The 1933 Everest team, while including Longland, had excluded several of the other top British rock climbers of the period, such as Colin Kirkus and Maurice Linnell. The politics involved, in which Longland had become embroiled, are palpable when you read Ruttledge's reported comment: 'I am coming more and more to the opinion that we must beware of the north British school of rock-climbers if we are to succeed on Everest. Individually they are probably good men, but they are a close corporation, with, it seems to me, a contempt for every one outside their own clan.'[78]

In private, Longland would not have tolerated this statement. He knew and respected several of the top northern climbers. He had achieved his big breakthrough – Longland's Climb on Clogwyn du'r Arddu – in an impromptu combined team of two climbers from Cambridge and three from Manchester. In 1930 he and Ivan Waller had partnered the Manchester climber Alf Bridge on Bridge's first ascent of the futuristic Lean Man's Superdirect at Black Rocks.[79] Longland's sharper side did not brook prejudice or pomposity. Faced with such attitudes, he was very capable of denouncing them. Whether there is any record of his responding on this occasion, either in public or in private, I have yet to discover.

Years later the Scottish climber Tom Patey lampooned the Alpine Club's Himalayan recruitment principles, focusing on the class-based bias that was still rigid enough, in 1953, to keep Joe Brown out of John Hunt's Everest team:

> Our climbing leaders are no fools
> They went to the very best Public Schools
> You'll never go wrong with Everest Men
> So we select them again and again
> Again and again and again and again[80]

*

In March 1936, Longland's career changed direction. Had he not made this change, White Hall Centre might never have happened. Saying a decisive goodbye to Shakespeare's iambic pentameters, he left academia to join the Community Service Council for Durham County, a body that had been formed in May 1935 to promote the development of voluntary social service, primarily for the unemployed (30 per cent of County Durham's workforce) and secondly for the community as a whole.[81] Initially Longland was the education officer and deputy to the director, John Newsom. A newspaper article approved of Longland's appointment:

> He is a young man of widespread experience who will be a great acquisition to the forces of this new movement, which is casting an influence over the whole face of the county.
> It was six years ago that Mr Longland first descended upon Durham, and he has accomplished brilliant work at the University. He feels he will have a greater opportunity in this new and important task in the Durham coalfield.[82]

Longland continued to give lectures to the public and to local organisations, which remained popular. The range of subjects branched out to include education and social policy, revealing a critical edge to his beliefs that may not have surfaced in his Everest and climbing lectures.

Addressing some Workers' Educational Association students in March 1936, he discussed 'waste' in higher education. In his view, 'a great deal of the university education of [that time] as practised was so remote from the lives, homes, and families of the students that it was a wonder they carried away anything at all'.[83]

In July 1937 John Newsom left the Community Service Council for Durham County to become the liaison officer for the National Council of Physical Training and Recreation. Longland succeeded him as director. A newspaper reported that

> Mr Longland has made a close study of conditions in the County, and during the past 18 months has mingled among the unemployed in the colliery villages. Mr Longland had a promising career as a University of Durham lecturer in English, but he placed it to one side in order to give himself to the welfare of the unemployed.[84]

In about September, three months after Longland's step-up to the directorship, Bill Tilman invited him to join the 1938 Everest expedition. The director of the National Council for Social Services refused him leave of absence, saying: 'No, I see no reason at all why we should give you leave to go.'[85] Although very disappointed, Longland took his job seriously and could not afford to lose it.[86]

On 6 January 1938, in an address to the Sunderland Rotary Club, Longland called for a long-term government social-service policy for Durham and counties like it:

> In the South of England, said Mr Longland, one found an inconceivable ignorance of conditions existing in a mining village or a shipyard town in Durham. People in the south seemed unwilling to realize the changing conditions which set in north of the Trent – to realize that in Durham there are many villages with no proper shop, a derelict chapel, no priest, no doctor, and with the dwellings consisting of only a few rows of houses which ought to have been condemned 30 years ago.[87]

He was not exaggerating. Nationally, during the 1930s depression – the hungry thirties – the average daily calorie intake of the poorest 10 per cent of the population was 2,317 calories per head per day.[88] The British Medical Association's nutrition committee said that an 'average' man required 3,400 calories per day (though this figure was disputed).[89] In February 1936, after the publication of *Food, Health and Income* by John Boyd Orr, *The Times* said that 'one-half of the population is living on a diet insufficient or ill-designed to maintain health'.[90]

Medical inspections of children carried out annually in the 1930s showed that in Durham 22.5 per cent of children were undernourished. In the town of Jarrow the proportion undernourished was 29.6 per cent.[91] We know that Longland joined the Labour Party at some point during his years in Durham; perhaps this was that point. He never concealed his allegiance to Labour, of which he would remain a member until the early 1980s.[92]

The social-service movement in Durham, which had begun in the early 1930s, was local in origin. By 1938 there were eighty centres, run on independent democratic lines, and about 20,000 members. In April 1938, Longland reported that a gradual industrial recovery had reduced the number of unemployed men from 90,000 in 1935 to 56,000 in March 1938.[93]

The late 1930s saw the beginnings of Longland's participation in radio broadcasts. A search of Genome, the Radio Times database, indicates that the first five programmes he took part in were probably the following, which were all connected with mountaineering or the countryside: *This Time Last Year: Among Mountains – A Climber's Holiday* (22 June 1936); *Northern Cockpit: Afforestation in the Lake District* (17 Mar 1937); *Up Against It: Caught in an Everest Blizzard* (22 July 1938); *Three Mountains: Pillar and Pillar Rock* (23 Aug 1938); and *Climbing Hut* (2 June 1939). Over the rest of his lifetime, Longland would take part in well over a thousand radio documentaries or shows.

By 1938, with the possibility of war increasing, people's minds were turning away from the needs of the unemployed to think instead about the uncertain future. At the annual meeting of Lambton Street Boys' Fellowship Centre, Longland expressed concern that in the face of the campaign for national service, the importance of community service would be underestimated. Many people were saying that social service efforts must be curtailed or even abandoned because money was needed for other purposes. Longland argued that the country could not afford to curtail its social services.[94]

The year 1939 was his last full year in Durham. At 4.45am on 1 September 1939, the *Luftwaffe* attacked several targets in Poland. Two days later Neville Chamberlain announced on BBC radio that Britain was at war with Germany.

By July 1940 Longland had spent over four years in social-service roles in Durham, a seminal period of his life. Having acquired an enduring concern for the less privileged, he moved into educational administration, which would occupy him for the rest of his professional career. A member of the Community Service Council said: 'While we cannot quarrel with his decision, we feel that he is leaving in the work of the Council a most difficult gap to fill.'[95]

Hertfordshire and Dorset

At the end of July 1940, Longland left Durham to take up the position of deputy to John Newsom, his old boss and now the county education officer for Hertfordshire. Newsom, still only twenty-nine and a man of deeply humanitarian ideals and progressive ideas, had been appointed to the directorship in April that year. He has been described as 'the leading county administrator of the moment'[96] and as 'undoubtedly idiosyncratic in his management of educational affairs'.[97] Newsom shared Longland's concern for social disadvantage.[98]

According to Peter Lloyd, Longland never made a show of his caring idealistic side. But in an address Longland gave in 1970, he said why he had entered the business of presiding over local-authority education:

> I came into educational administration at the end of the squalid and hungry 1930s after some years working with unemployed Durham miners and their families. I think those underfed children, their fathers on the scrapheap, and the mean houses under the tip, all the casual products of a selfishly irresponsible society, have coloured my thinking ever since. They were one main cause of my entering the statutory education business. I had been shunting about in social sidings for long enough, helping men to move mountains with little shovels. I wanted the mainline express to a new world and fair shares all round.[99]

As well as possessing flair and enthusiasm, John Newsom was a skilled manipulator inside county hall; some of this talent may have rubbed off on Jack Longland.[100] The role of county education officer (also called chief education officer) in the 1940s was different from what it is today. David Parker, in his biography of Newsom, touches upon this aspect: '[Newsom] was an independently minded and decisive leader who was badly needed at the time, and for whom there would be no place in the highly centralised and controlled world of education today.'[101]

The move to Hertfordshire presented Longland with the opportunity to adopt an idea that Kurt Hahn had been developing since
arriving in Britain. Before we join Longland in Hertfordshire, we need
to digress briefly to find out what Hahn had been up to in Morayshire, where he now lived. As mentioned earlier, Hahn had fled from
Germany to Britain in July 1933, leaving Salem School to serve the
educational requirements of the Third Reich. (The young Prince Philip
of Greece, who joined Salem in September 1933 and stayed for two
terms, had experienced a nazified institution in which there was much
heel-clicking, and shouts of '*Heil Hitler*' were compulsory for German
nationals.[102])

In 1934, with the help of Geoffrey Young, of Young's circle of establishment contacts, and of other British well-wishers and benefactors,
Hahn had created a company called British Salem Schools Ltd. This
had led to the establishing in May 1934 of Gordonstoun School, a
public (ie, fee-charging) boarding school near Elgin on the Moray Firth.
The site was chosen because it was close to the sea and the mountains,
thus providing opportunities for adventurous outdoor pursuits. For
Hahn, the activities were of equal importance to the academic work.
He believed that in tackling the activities, the pupils would meet difficulties, and that in overcoming those difficulties the pupils would
develop holistically. The school's director of activities revelled in an
equal status to the director of studies. The outdoor pursuits included
cycling, walking, climbing, skiing and camping. The first cutter, for
sailing, came into use in 1935. In time, seamanship would become the
'senior' activity at Gordonstoun.[103]

Gordonstoun retained many of the distinctive features of Salem.[104]
'Fewer hours [were] spent in the classroom than [happened] at a normal
grammar school.'[105] The aim was for all-round development and for
character building or character training. (Both these terms had been
common since at least the late 19th century. Some people used the
two terms to mean slightly different things; this distinction was never
widely adopted.[106])

Prince Philip returned from Germany and in autumn 1934 joined
Gordonstoun, becoming its third pupil and thriving on two cold showers a day, summer and winter. 'Although many traditionalists dismissed
Hahn's experiment as a somewhat Spartan fad – even by the notoriously
harsh standards of the British boarding school – Philip proved that,
for the right kind of pupil, it offered everything a growing boy could
require, both physically and intellectually.'[107]

Important elements of Gordonstoun's unorthodox curriculum included service to the community, athletics, swimming, walking and sailing. Hahn set levels of proficiency for different age groups. Success in meeting these challenges earned the Gordonstoun Badge. In 1936 this badge scheme was expanded to become available to all boys over fourteen in Morayshire and to boys and girls of Elgin Academy.[108] The Moray Badge involved three challenges: athletics (throwing, jumping and running), swimming and adventurous expeditioning. At the beginning of the second world war, the Moray Badge gained national status, becoming the County Badge and acquiring a project element and a service element (such as working as a beach lifeguard or a coastguard or a firefighter).

By now, the number of pupils at Gordonstoun had risen to 150. Longland's friend Geoffrey Young chaired the board of governors, and so Longland will probably have been well informed on these developments.

Morayshire was within easy striking distance from German-occupied Norway. In June 1940, Gordonstoun moved to mid-Wales temporarily, as a wartime precaution. From 14 August to 6 September, an experimental summer school took place there, and Longland visited this course to deliver a lecture on Everest.[109] It seems that Kurt Hahn was present (at least for part of the time) during this summer school, because he first met Jim Hogan during it; so it seems likely that Longland and Hahn will have met there.[110]

Also in August 1940, a few weeks after Longland arrived in Hertfordshire, the *Times Educational Supplement* published a main article that 'estimated, not by wild hopes, but on solid calculations, that a million boys could be trained under the County Badge scheme within a year.'[111] Later in the year, *The Times* carried a series of optimistic letters supporting the scheme.

The year 1941, however, was not a time for such a scheme to prosper. The priorities of the moment were issues connected with air-raid shelters, black-out sheets, evacuations, emergency schools, the land army, food shortages, conscription and all the other realities of wartime. In autumn 1941, Newsom and Longland were awarded annual bonuses in recognition of their organising inflow of 25,000 evacuated children, which included procuring over 200 extra buildings and 140 feeding centres.[112]

Most local education authorities put the County Badge scheme on hold. The Hertfordshire county youth committee was the only local

authority committee to engage in the badge scheme with commitment
and vigour. Longland was the guiding force. Each year about 200
children across the county took part. 'Success came in those schools
where teachers were prepared to plan a curriculum based less on rigid
subject divisions and more on practical activities straddling a range of
subjects.'[113] Some of these teachers used the badge requirements as
opportunities to link field studies – including map-reading, compass
work and camp-craft – to a range of normal curriculum subjects.

The badge scheme had its critics. Some schools were wary of over-
loading the curriculum, interfering with the teaching of basic subjects
and overworking the staff.[114]

Hertfordshire's experiment lasted for seven years. Some folk considered it a great success.[115] Recalling this situation, Jim Hogan picked
out one other County Badge experiment worthy of a mention. This was
the work of E G Simm at Derby School, which in 1941 was occupying a former camp school in the Hope Valley, the pupils having been
evacuated from Derby.[116] (Another school that introduced the County
Badge was the training ship HMS *Conway*.)

The existence of the County Badge scheme was a factor in the origins
of Outward Bound. One of Hahn's purposes in starting Aberdovey
OBSS in October 1941 was to demonstrate the effectiveness of the
fourfold-achievement scheme in a short-term community as opposed
to in a long-term community such as a boarding school.[117] A successful demonstration would, he hoped, bring about the extension of the
scheme to day pupils in maintained schools as against fee-paying pupils
in residential public schools.

The County Badge Experimental Committee, a national group, stuck
to its task and prepared a scheme booklet. The individuals responsible
for Hertfordshire's version of the scheme gave valuable help. The booklet was published in 1942. Section III, titled 'The Fourfold Achievement', was virtually a reproduction of Hertfordshire's plan.[118] The four
pillars were a project, an expedition, a service and sporting achievements. The inclusion of Section VII, 'The Training of Girls', reflected
Hertfordshire's desire that the training scheme should be open to girls
as well as boys. Section VIII explained why the County Badge plan kept
clear of religion. In the booklet's concluding pages, the writers expressed
the hope that other local authorities would follow the example of
Hertfordshire in initiating and guiding experiments in their area.[119]

The scheme's avoidance of any religious content contrasted with
the approaches of some of the other youth movements. Morning

prayers and a Bible reading had quickly become a routine part of courses at Aberdovey OBSS and would remain so for a number of years. In 1953 Spencer Summers, the chairman of the Outward Bound Trust, wrote to *The Times* about the spiritual bankruptcy of young people: 'Materialism and indeed, paganism, may be widespread, but in seeking to substitute Christianity as the motive force in society let us aim high and demand much. God's creatures are still made in His own image.'[120]

The experimental committee's grand design immediately landed on a wartime shelf, to become an unrealised idea, but it still contained the

The County Badge or the Fourfold Achievement, a booklet produced by the County Badge Experimental Committee in 1942.

seeds that, twenty years later, would grow into the successful and prestigious Duke of Edinburgh's Award. Expedition training courses for young folk seeking this award would eventually become regular features of White Hall Centre's annual programme. Looking back from 2000, Tom Price called Kurt Hahn 'a kind of latter-day Baden-Powell' who 'loved certificates and badges'.[121] The passage of time suggests that in recognising the place for such things in the lives of some young people, Hahn knew what made some young people tick.

*

One further point about Longland's time in Hertfordshire remains to be made: John Newsom believed strongly in school camps and particularly in school camps in which informality was the order of the day. He encouraged 'a corporate camp spirit of collegial activity, friendship, help and enjoyment between the children, and between the children and the staff'.[122] It seems reasonable for us to see a direct connection between the informal ethos of Newsom's school camps and the very similar atmosphere that developed at Longland's White Hall.

Newsom was confident that school camps would eventually 'become part of the normal privileges of every child'.[123] This was another Newsom idea that probably influenced Longland.

On 31 July 1942, after two years in Hertfordshire, Longland was appointed county education officer for Dorset. He was thirty-seven. Thirty-five people had applied for the job, and three had been interviewed.

An article in the *Western Gazette* reported his appointment and listed the gist of his curriculum vitae, distilled into eight or nine dense column inches of accomplishments. The subheading of the article was SCHOLAR, ATHLETE AND MOUNTAINEER; he had given talks on BBC radio but he was not yet a broadcaster well known nationally.

*

In 1943 Longland contributed to an obituary for the climber Colin Kirkus who had served in the Royal Air Force and had been 'presumed killed' after not returning from a raid on Bremen. Much of the obituary dwelt on Kirkus's climbing ability and achievements, which were remarkable but are outside the scope of this book. However, a few sections of Longland's tribute tell us that in 1943, seven years before White Hall opened, Longland already had ideas and concerns about some aspects and issues of teaching climbing.

Firstly, there is a paragraph that praises Kirkus's book *Come Climbing*. Longland celebrated Kirkus's power of expression and conviction, which would transmit to ordinary readers his deep and simple affection for the hills. The book

> made the specialised attraction of mountains seem real and impor-
> tant and of general application, and so … will take its place with
> that very small collection of volumes which have actually turned
> non-climbers into climbers, and brought walkers in the flat lands
> and even those who before had not walked at all into a world of
> new experience … It is safe to prophesy that it will bring many
> new recruits to climbing, and that, with the rest of the book, it will
> go a long way to ensure that they come with a sound grounding
> in attitude and technique.[124]

As well as advocating the promotion of the sport of rock climbing, which he favoured provided that the instructing was done well, Longland also discussed the existence of a growing number of climbers, a situation with an unstoppable momentum, and the problem of who would teach the beginners:

> From inclination, as well as perhaps partly from circumstance, Colin turned more and more in the last few years of his life to the task of introducing other people to the pleasures which he had found in mountain climbing. Weekend after weekend he was to be found patiently and carefully coaching novices up Welsh climbs, and thereby adding immeasurably to the happiness of those who had found their way to the threshold of adventure, which but for him they would never have tasted. And here again, without need for moralising, he had something of a lesson for the rest of us. Perhaps the biggest problem facing climbers today is to find means, without giving ourselves airs, of sharing what we have ourselves been taught of good and safe mountain-craft, among the thousands who are coming into the hills and who want to make themselves into climbers. Neither individually, nor in the somewhat self-satisfied communities which are our climbing clubs, have we done much to tackle this big new demand.[125]

These thoughts, expressed so clearly in Longland's tribute to Colin Kirkus, would greatly influence his reasons for setting up White Hall Centre.

Kirkus's example may still have been in Longland's mind when, in April 1944, he took time off to instruct on a ten-day mountaincraft course for army cadets. This course originated in a request from the War Office to the Alpine Club. The course was held in north Wales and had character training as one of its aims. With Longland, Ivan Waller, Alf Bridge and Alan Hargreaves among the instructors, it seems likely that the sheer enjoyment of climbing might have pushed explicit character building to one side. Apparently the course was very successful. (Chapter 6 will include a more detailed look at this course.)

Also in 1944, Longland found himself being inexorably drawn into the national organisation and internal politics of climbing. Back in 1907, Geoffrey Young had raised the idea of a having a single organisation to represent all the mountaineers in Britain. But this had never happened. At the end of 1943, the Alpine Club was still performing that role, a job it had assumed in the 19th century. Young was the club's president from 1941 to 1943. With his valedictory address in December 1943, he persuaded most, but not all, of the members of the Alpine

Club that their club was no longer the right body to represent British mountaineers. In February 1944 he organised a conference attended by twenty-three representatives of all the main British clubs. Among his arguments for setting up a national representative body was the need, as he saw it, to make the collective experience of the clubs available to the large number of young people then starting to climb.[126]

The inaugural meeting of the BMC took place on 2 December 1944. Thirty-two representatives of twenty-three clubs, representing about 7,000 mountaineers, were present.

A few members of the Alpine Club gerontocracy continued to oppose this development. Longland, an increasingly respected and influential voice within British mountaineering, became heavily involved in what he called 'the dogfight' in the Alpine Club. This was no gentlemanly airing of differences. In a private letter, Longland mentioned that he was going to speak at an Alpine Club committee meeting 'in order to try and do down Eaton, Spenser, Strutt and the other ex-Everest rats who have crawled out of their holes.'[127] He crafted a powerful speech and delivered it to the club's committee on 10 April 1945. 'This carefully orchestrated broadside proved to be the final nail in the coffin for the uprising.'[128] The mood of the times was against the few 'privileged die-hards who regarded the hills as their private playground and preserve'.[129]

An article in the *Manchester Guardian* in August 1945 listed some of the BMC's aims:

> Its chief objects are to encourage the sport of mountaineering and to make it more widely known that it is by no means expensive; to give advice and help on clothes, equipment, bivouacking, food, and the best climbing centres; to put climbers in touch with local clubs and leading mountaineers; and to provide instructors for training leaders for recreational organisations, for whom there is already a considerable demand.[130]

The article added that the council would work to protect mountain scenery and to advance the cause of national parks. The council was also concerned that 'expeditions into the mountains by inexperienced and ill-equipped persons may be a menace not only to their own lives but also to the lives of those called upon to go to their rescue'.

*

During this period of Longland's career, he was in frequent contact with Joan Simon, the assistant to the editor of the *Times Educational Supplement*. She described the Dorset years:

> Although not yet 40 Jack soon gained his own directorship – Dorset – and was to stick to administration to the last despite offers of various jobs at home and abroad. There was quite enough to do in England, he wrote me in 1946: 'God help us if they raised the leaving age to 16 before we'd got a few senior schools built.' By then he had had three years of bitter struggles with the chairman of his education committee who had blocked the county development plan under the Education Act. It was that chairman's last act. Jack engineered his removal – in the end by 38 votes to 4 – 'The first time I think it's ever been done in county history, without a complete political landslide.' With his own choice in the chair, reform was under way and the education office staff circulated 'with expressions of bewildered joy on their faces'.[131]

Jim Perrin, one of the most outstanding and authoritative writers on climbing and climbers, knew both sides of Longland's personality: 'He is a man of true, strong principles, great intelligence and devastating wit, who can stomach neither fools nor pomposity and is quite capable of savaging either when they cross his path. The idealist in him is so urgent a creature as still occasionally to become choleric.'[132]

In November 1949, Longland was appointed director of education for Derbyshire. He was forty-three years old. We have followed him through these years. We know something about him. He understood the pure joy of climbing. He was interested both in promoting the sport of climbing and in helping beginners to learn its techniques and to avoid accidents caused by inexperience. His time in Durham had heightened his concern for the underprivileged. The educational ideas and enthusiasms of his older friend, mentor and occasional climbing partner, Geoffrey Young, had influenced him. So too had the beliefs of his old boss John Newsom and the passionate pedagogic theories of Kurt Hahn. Newsom, for example, had strongly promoted Hahn's County Badge scheme. However, whereas Aberdovey OBSS already existed, White Hall Centre had yet to appear, and nobody knew in 1949 how similar to or different from each other these two places would be.

I have said little, so far, about Derbyshire, the county he is heading for and in which he will set up an outdoor pursuits centre. What is the

Derbyshire terrain like? When did rock climbing start there? What other outdoor pursuits take place there? Was anyone, before Longland arrived there, already arranging opportunities for Derbyshire's young people to take up outdoor pursuits? What effect did the second world war have on the sport of climbing?

To answer these questions I will leave Longland poised to take up his new job and I will step back half a century to set the scene for his arrival.

Four of the sixteen members of the 1933 Everest team, on board the mail-ship *Comorin* at Tilbury, bound for India, 20 January 1933. L to R: Jack Longland (27), Hugh Ruttledge (48), Colin Crawford and Eric Shipton (25). A portentous photograph that provides some visual background to the Everest leadership disagreement of 1935.

Daily Mail, 22 March 1933, p. 8.

250-MILES TREK TO EVEREST BEGINS

ALL CLIMBERS IN TIBET

———

BAGGAGE PROBLEMS

———

OXEN TO RELIEVE MULES

From Our Own Correspondent

KALIMPONG, North Bengal,
Tuesday.

ALL the members of the Mount Everest climbing expedition under the leadership of Mr. Ruttledge are now in Tibet, where the weather is fine but the visibility poor.

(c) Royal Geographical Society (with IBG) S0001289.

Jack Longland demonstrates pole-vaulting, using a long bamboo pole, at Tengkye Dzong in Tibet during the approach march to Everest in 1933. A photograph taken by Frank Smythe.

Notes

1   Hugh Ruttledge, *Everest, 1933*, 5th edn (London: Hodder & Stoughton, May 1936), p. 24.

2   Ibid., p. 85.

3   Richard Williams, 'Cambridge Night Climbing History' (21 Oct 2009) <http://www.insectnation.org/cambridge-night-climbing-history.pdf> [accessed 28 Oct 2014].

4   Michael Westmacott, 'Obituary: Sir Jack Longland', Independent (4 Dec 1993) <http://www.independent.co.uk/news/people/obituary-sir-jack-longland-1465146.html> [accessed 22 July 2014].

5   Jim Perrin, *Menlove: The Life of John Menlove Edwards* (1985; repr. Holyhead: Ernest Press, 1993), p. 41.

6   B R Mitchell, *British Historical Statistics* (Cambridge: Cambridge University Press, 1988), p. 557. Also Statista, 'Number of cars on the road in the United Kingdom (UK) between 2000 and 2015 (in millions)' (2015) <http://www.statista.com/statistics/299972/average-age-of-cars-on-the-road-in-the-united-kingdom/> [accessed 5 Mar 2015].

7   William Hillcourt and Olave Baden-Powell, *Baden-Powell: The Two Lives of a Hero* (London: Heinemann, 1964), pp. 223–226.

8   Geoffrey Winthrop Young, *The Grace of Forgetting* (London: Country Life, 1953), p. 28.

9   Allen Warren, 'Powell, Robert Stephenson Smyth Baden, first Baron BadenPowell (1857–1941)', in *Oxford Dictionary of National Biography* (May 2008) <http://www.oxforddnb.com.ezdunedin.kotui.org.nz/view/article/30520> [accessed 14 Jan 2015].

10 Alan Hankinson, *Geoffrey Winthrop Young: Poet, Educator, Mountaineer* (London: Hodder and Stoughton, 1995), pp. 62, 93.

11 Ken C Ogilvie, *Roots and Wings: A History of Outdoor Education and Outdoor Learning in the UK* (Lyme Regis, UK: Russell House Publishing, 2013), p. 187.

12 Alan Hankinson, *Geoffrey Winthrop Young: Poet, Educator, Mountaineer* (London: Hodder and Stoughton, 1995), p. 226.

13 Lynn Cook, 'Outdoor Education: Its Origins and Institutionalisation in Schools with Particular Reference to the West Riding of Yorkshire Since 1945' (PhD thesis, University of Leeds, 2000), p. 67.

14 Geoffrey Winthrop Young, *Mountains with a Difference* (London: Eyre and Spottiswoode, 1951), p. 129.

15 Simon Thompson, *Unjustifiable Risk? The Story of British Climbing* (Milnthorpe, UK: Cicerone, 2010), p. 126.

16 Geoffrey Winthrop Young, 'The Message of the Mountains', in *Outward Bound*, ed. by David James (London: Routledge and Kegan Paul, 1957), pp. 98–107 (p. 101).

17 Adam Arnold-Brown, *Unfolding Character: The Impact of Gordonstoun* (London: Routledge and Kegan Paul, 1962), pp. xi, 9.

18 Nick Veevers and Pete Allison, *Kurt Hahn: Inspirational, Visionary, Outdoor and Experiential Educator* (Rotterdam: Sense Publishers, 2011), pp. 1–2, 16.

19 'Character Builder', *Observer*, 13 Nov 1960, p. 13.

20 Jim Perrin, 'The Essential Jack Longland', *Mountain*, no. 123 (Sept–Oct 1988), pp. 26–29.

21 Jim Perrin, 'Sir John Laurence ('Jack') Longland: 1905–1993', *Climbers' Club Journal: 1993,* 21, no. 3 (new series) (1994), pp. 79–83 (p. 80).

22 Jim Perrin, 'The Essential Jack Longland', *Mountain*, no. 123 (Sept–Oct 1988), pp. 26–29.

23 George Wedell, 'Hahn, Kurt Matthias Robert Martin (1886–1974)', in *Oxford Dictionary of National Biography* (Oct 2006) <http://www.oxforddnb.com./view/article/31187> [accessed 20 Dec 2014].

24 Thomas James, 'Kurt Hahn and the Aims of Education' (2000) <http://www.kurthahn.org/writings/james.pdf> [accessed 22 May 2015].

25 Nick Veevers and Pete Allison, *Kurt Hahn: Inspirational, Visionary, Outdoor and Experiential Educator* (Rotterdam: Sense Publishers, 2011), pp. 1–4, 76.

26 Anna Crutchley, Archives, Jesus College, Email to P McDonald, subject 'John Lawrence Longland', 3 June 2015 [Email].

27 Alan Hankinson, *Geoffrey Winthrop Young: Poet, Educator, Mountaineer* (London: Hodder and Stoughton, 1995), p. 241.

28 Jim Perrin, 'The Essential Jack Longland', *Mountain*, no. 123 (Sept–Oct 1988), pp. 26–29 (p. 27).

29 Jim Perrin, *Shipton and Tilman: The Great Decade of Himalayan Exploration* (London: Hutchinson, 2013), p. 96.

30 Alan Hankinson, *Geoffrey Winthrop Young: Poet, Educator, Mountaineer* (London: Hodder and Stoughton, 1995), p. 210.

31 Jim Perrin, 'The Essential Jack Longland', *Mountain*, no. 123 (Sept–Oct 1988), pp. 26–29 (p. 27).

32 J L Longland, '1925–1930', *Climbers' Club Journal: 1948,* 8, no. 3 (new series) (1948), pp. 255–265 (p. 260).

33 Ibid. (p. 262).

34 *The Oxford Illustrated History of Britain,* ed. by Kenneth O Morgan (Oxford: Oxford University Press, 1986), p. 539.

35 Peter Lloyd, John Hunt and Charles Warren, 'Sir Jack Longland 1905–1993', *Alpine Journal,* 99 (1994), pp. 336–341 (p. 336).

36 Peter Harding, 'Ivan Mark Waller 1906–1996', *Alpine Journal,* 102 (1997), pp. 353–354.

37 Peter Lloyd, John Hunt and Charles Warren, 'Sir Jack Longland 1905–1993', *Alpine Journal,* 99 (1994), pp. 336–341 (p. 336).

38 Peter H Hansen, 'Young, Geoffrey Winthrop (1876–1958)', in *Oxford Dictionary of National Biography* (Jan 2011) <http://www.oxforddnb.com./view/article/37073> [accessed 1 Sep 2014].

39 Alan Hankinson, *Geoffrey Winthrop Young: Poet, Educator, Mountaineer* (London: Hodder and Stoughton, 1995), pp. 263–264.

40 Ken C Ogilvie, *Roots and Wings: A History of Outdoor Education and Outdoor Learning in the UK* (Lyme Regis, UK: Russell House Publishing, 2013), p. 238.

41 Thomas Alexander and Beryl Parker, *The New Education in the German Republic* (London: Williams & Norgate, 1930), p. 53.

42   'Sir Jack Longland', *The Times*, 2 Dec 1993, p. 23. Also Jim Perrin, 'Sir John Laurence ('Jack') Longland: 1905–1993', *Climbers' Club Journal: 1993*, 21, no. 3 (new series) (1994), pp. 79–83.

43   Quoted in Jack Soper, Ken Wilson and Peter Crew, *The Black Cliff: The History of Rock Climbing on Clogwyn du'r Arddu* (London: Kaye and Ward, 1971), p. 24.

44   Ibid., pp. 24–26.

45   Kurt Hahn, 'The Seven Laws of Salem', Schule Schloss Salem (1930) <http://www.salem-net.de/en/about-us/history/the-seven-laws-of-salem.html> [accessed 3 June 2015].

46   Alan Hankinson, *Geoffrey Winthrop Young: Poet, Educator, Mountaineer* (London: Hodder and Stoughton, 1995), p. 264.

47   E H Cookridge, *From Battenberg to Mountbatten* (London: Arthur Barker, 1966), p. 254.

48   Jonathan Petropoulos, *Royals and the Reich: The Princes von Hessen in Nazi Germany* (London: Oxford University Press, 2009), p. 93.

49   Jim Perrin, 'Sir John Laurence ('Jack') Longland: 1905–1993', *Climbers' Club Journal: 1993*, 21, no. 3 (new series) (1994), pp. 79–83.

50   R A Smith, 'The Development of Equipment to Reduce Risk in Climbing', *Sports Engineering*, 1, no. 1 (Sept 1998), pp. 27–39 (pp. 27–28).

51   Ivan Waller, 'Cat among the Pigeons', *Fell and Rock Journal*, 23, no. 1 (1978), pp. 1–5 (p. 2).

52   Raymond Chesterfield, 'The Growth and Expansion of the Durham Miner's Association – History of the D.M.A. Part Two', Durham in Time (no date) <http://www.durhamintime.org.uk/durham_miner/growth_dum.pdf> [accessed 28 Nov 2014].

53   'Durham University Posts', *Yorkshire Post*, 1 July 1930, p. 4.

54   'Everest Climber to Lecture', *Sunderland Daily Echo*, 5 May 1933, p. 9.

55   'Mount Everest Climber', *Sunderland Daily Echo*, 19 Nov 1935, p. 2. Also 'The Literature of Mountaineering', *Sunderland Daily Echo*, 1 Mar 1935, p. 2.

56   'Mount Everest Climber', *Sunderland Daily Echo*, 19 Nov 1935, p. 2.

57   Jim Perrin, 'Sir John Laurence ('Jack') Longland: 1905–1993', *Climbers' Club Journal: 1993*, 21, no. 3 (new series) (1994), pp. 79–83 (p. 83).

58   Editor, 'Club Report', *New Durham*, 2, no. 2 (Epiphany 1933), p. 74.

59   'Mr Lawrence Housman', *Sunderland Daily Echo*, 25 Nov 1932, p. 11.

60   J L Longland, '1925–1930', *Climbers' Club Journal: 1948*, 8, no. 3 (new series) (1948), pp. 255–265 (p. 261).

61   Walt Unsworth, *Everest: The Mountaineering History*, 3rd edn (London: Bâton Wicks, 2000), p. 163.

62   *Everest: The Best Writing and Pictures from Seventy Years of Human Endeavour*, ed. by Peter Gillman (London: Little, Brown, 1993), pp. 202–204.

63   J L Longland, 'Caught in an Everest Blizzard', in *Tight Corners*, ed. by Alan Cobham (London: Allen and Unwin, 1940), pp. 17–30 (p. 26).

64   Ibid. (pp. 26–27).

65   Ibid. (p. 29).

66   Quoted in E H Cookridge, *From Battenberg to Mountbatten* (London: Arthur Barker, 1966), p. 255.

67   Alan Hankinson, *Geoffrey Winthrop Young: Poet, Educator, Mountaineer* (London: Hodder and Stoughton, 1995), pp. 266–269.

68   'Seaham Oddfellows' Pride', *Sunderland Daily Echo,* 21 Jan 1935, p. 3.

69   'Famous Climber's Visit', *Sunderland Daily Echo,* 1 Feb 1934, p. 2.

70   'Arch of Ice-axes at Wedding', *Yorkshire Post,* 29 June 1934, p. 4.

71   'Brancepeth Bride for Everest Climber', *Sunderland Daily Echo,* 28 June 1934, p. 3.

72   Jim Perrin, 'Sir John Laurence ('Jack') Longland: 1905–1993', *Climbers' Club Journal: 1993,* 21, no. 3 (new series) (1994), pp. 79–83 (p. 81).

73   J L Longland, 'The Watkins Mountains', *Alpine Journal,* 48 (1936), pp. 40–57 (p. 49).

74   Walt Unsworth, *Everest: The Mountaineering History,* 3rd edn (London: Bâton Wicks, 2000), p. 30.

75   Ibid., p. 185.

76   Quoted in ibid., p. 186.

77   Ibid., pp. 187–191. Also Glyn Hughes, Email to P McDonald, subject 'Re: Alpine Journal 48 (1936), pp. 40-57', 19 Dec 2014 [Email].

78   Quoted in Simon Thompson, *Unjustifiable Risk? The Story of British Climbing* (Milnthorpe, UK: Cicerone, 2010), p. 181.

79   Phil Kelly, Graham Hoey and Giles Barker, *Peak Rock: The History, The Routes, The Climbers* (Sheffield: Vertebrate Publishing, 2013), pp. 48–49.

80   Tom Patey, *One Man's Mountains* (1971; repr. Edinburgh: Canongate, 2005), p. 263.

81   'Durham Rural Community Council (Ref: D/DRCC)', Durham County Record Office (19 Jan 2012) <http://www.durhamrecordoffice.org.uk/Pages/AdvancedSearchCatalogue.aspx> [accessed 7 Dec 2014].

82   'Community Service "Recruit"', *Sunderland Daily Echo,* 30 Mar 1936, p. 2.

83   'Education System "Waste"', *Sunderland Daily Echo,* 30 Mar 1936, p. 7.

84   'Climbed Everest', *Sunderland Daily Echo,* 1 July 1937, p. 2.

85   Jim Perrin, 'The Essential Jack Longland', *Mountain,* no. 123 (Sept–Oct 1988), pp. 26–29 (p. 29).

86   Walt Unsworth, *Everest: The Mountaineering History,* 3rd edn (London: Bâton Wicks, 2000), pp. 212–213.

87   'Social Service Need', *Sunderland Daily Echo,* 6 Jan 1938, p. 7.

88   K Theodore Hoppen, *The Mid-Victorian Generation 1846–1886,* The New Oxford History of England (Oxford: Oxford University Press, 1998), p. 85.

89   D J Oddy, 'Food, Drink and Nutrition', in *The Cambridge Social History of Britain 1750–1950,* ed. by F M L Thompson, 3 vols (Cambridge: Cambridge University Press, 1990), vol. 2, pp. 251–278 (pp. 273–274).

90   'Diet and Maintenance', *The Times,* 13 Feb 1936, p. 13.

91   D J Oddy, 'Food, Drink and Nutrition', in *The Cambridge Social History of Britain 1750–1950,* ed. by F M L Thompson, 3 vols (Cambridge: Cambridge University Press, 1990), vol. 2, pp. 251–278 (p. 277).

92   'Sir Jack Longland', *The Times,* 2 Dec 1993, p. 23.

93   'Tribute to Durham's Unemployed', *Northern Daily Mail,* 27 Apr 1938, p. 6.

94 'Plea for Social Service', *Sunderland Daily Echo*, 25 Oct 1938, p. 7.

95 'Director Resigns', *Sunderland Echo*, 25 July 1940, p. 2.

96 'Longland, School Champion', *Guardian*, 4 Dec 1993, p. 30.

97 David Parker, *John Newsom: A Hertfordshire Educationist* (Hatfield, Hertfordshire: University of Hertfordshire Press, 2005), p. 2.

98 Stuart Maclure, 'Newsom, Sir John Hubert (1910–1971)', in *Oxford Dictionary of National Biography* (Jan 2004) <http://www.oxforddnb.com.ezproxy.otago.ac.nz/view/article/31495> [accessed 8 Dec 2014].

99 Peter Lloyd, John Hunt and Charles Warren, 'Sir Jack Longland 1905–1993', *Alpine Journal*, 99 (1994), pp. 336–341 (pp. 337–338).

100 Stuart Maclure, 'Newsom, Sir John Hubert (1910–1971)', in *Oxford Dictionary of National Biography* (Jan 2004) <http://www.oxforddnb.com.ezproxy.otago.ac.nz/view/article/31495> [accessed 8 Dec 2014].

101 David Parker, *John Newsom: A Hertfordshire Educationist* (Hatfield, Hertfordshire: University of Hertfordshire Press, 2005), rear cover.

102 John Parker, *Prince Philip: A Critical Biography* (London: Sidgwick and Jackson, 1990), p. 53.

103 Nick Veevers and Pete Allison, *Kurt Hahn: Inspirational, Visionary, Outdoor and Experiential Educator* (Rotterdam: Sense Publishers, 2011), pp. 22, 26–27, 31, 73.

104 George Wedell, 'Hahn, Kurt Matthias Robert Martin (1886–1974)', in *Oxford Dictionary of National Biography* (Oct 2006) <http://www.oxforddnb.com./view/article/31187> [accessed 20 Dec 2014].

105 'A Public School on the Moray Firth', *Times Educational Supplement*, 16 Sept 1949, p. 633.

106 Tom Price, 'Some Aspects of Character-building', in *Kurt Hahn*, ed. by H Röhrs and H Tunstall-Behrens (London: Routledge & Kegan Paul, 1970), pp. 81–91 (pp. 86–87).

107 'Prince Philip, the Duke of Edinburgh: Part 1 of 4', The Royal Report; Britain Express (2001) <http://www.britainexpress.com/royals/philip.htm> [accessed 2 Jan 2015].

108 Nick Veevers and Pete Allison, *Kurt Hahn: Inspirational, Visionary, Outdoor and Experiential Educator* (Rotterdam: Sense Publishers, 2011), pp. 38–40.

109 I. S., 'The Summer Course', *Gordonstoun Record: Christmas 1939 – Easter 1941*, no. 5 (1941), pp. 16–19.

110 James Martin Hogan, 'The Establishment of the First Outward Bound School at Aberdovey, Merionethshire', in *Kurt Hahn*, ed. by H Röhrs and H Tunstall-Behrens (London: Routledge & Kegan Paul, 1970), pp. 60–66.

111 'The County Badge Scheme: Training 1,000,000 Boys a Year', *Times Educational Supplement*, 17 Aug 1940, p. 319.

112 David Parker, *John Newsom: A Hertfordshire Educationist* (Hatfield, Hertfordshire: University of Hertfordshire Press, 2005), p. 38.

113 Ibid., pp. 48–49.

114 Ibid., p. 49.

115 Kurt Hahn, 'Origins of the Outward Bound Trust', in *Outward Bound*, ed. by David James (London: Routledge and Kegan Paul, 1957), pp. 1–17 (p. 9).

116 James Martin Hogan, *Impelled into Experiences: The Story of the Outward Bound Schools* (Wakefield, UK: Educational Productions, 1968), p. 21.

117 Nick Veevers and Pete Allison, *Kurt Hahn: Inspirational, Visionary, Outdoor and Experiential Educator* (Rotterdam: Sense Publishers, 2011), p. 56.

118 County Badge Experimental Committee, *The County Badge or the Fourfold Achievement* (London: Oxford University Press, 1942), p. 9. Also 'Youth Service Squads in Hertfordshire', *Times Educational Supplement*, 5 Jan 1941, p. 37.

119 County Badge Experimental Committee, *The County Badge or the Fourfold Achievement* (London: Oxford University Press, 1942), p. 28.

120 G Spencer Summers, 'Roots of Crime', *The Times,* 24 Jan 1953, p. 7.

121 Tom Price, *Travail So Gladly Spent* (Ty Croes, Wales: Ernest Press, 2000), p. 183.

122 David Parker, *John Newsom: A Hertfordshire Educationist* (Hatfield, Hertfordshire: University of Hertfordshire Press, 2005), pp. 32–33.

123 Ibid., p. 33.

124 J L Longland, 'In Memoriam: Colin Fletcher Kirkus', *Climbers' Club Journal: 1943,* 7, no. 2 (new series) (1943), pp. 173–181 (p. 180).

125 Ibid., (p. 180).

126 *The First Fifty Years of the British Mountaineering Council,* ed. by Geoff Milburn, Derek Walker and Ken Wilson (Manchester: British Mountaineering Council, 1997), p. 3.

127 Quoted in ibid., p. 280.

128 Ibid., pp. 280–284.

129 Ken C Ogilvie, *Roots and Wings: A History of Outdoor Education and Outdoor Learning in the UK* (Lyme Regis, UK: Russell House Publishing, 2013), pp. 255–256.

130 'Mountaineering: A British Council', *Manchester Guardian,* 7 Aug 1945, p. 3.

131 'Longland, School Champion', *Guardian,* 4 Dec 1993, p. 30.

132 Jim Perrin, 'The Essential Jack Longland', *Mountain,* no. 123 (Sept–Oct 1988), pp. 26–29 (p. 26).

2. Peak District Backstory, 1900–49

The classic study of early-20th-century outdoor recreation in the Peak District was Ernest Baker's *Moors, Crags and Caves of the High Peak and Neighbourhood* (1903). The title of his book provides three of the subjects that this chapter needs to cover: walking, climbing and caving. Also taking place in Derbyshire in 1903 were the sports of cycling, canoeing and dinghy sailing. Although the overall structure of this book is chronological, I have decided to introduce the six recreational activities separately, as six sub-themes from the first half of the 20th century. This chapter will look at the first four, the hill sports. It will also acknowledge the place of camping, which was sometimes an end in itself and sometimes a necessary part of one of the pursuits. Chapter 3 will look at canoeing and dinghy sailing, the water sports. Both these chapters will focus on adult participation in the activities. Chapter 4 will examine school-pupil participation in them. (In case you're wondering, I will offer a definition of outdoor recreation later, but not until Chapter 24.)

Walking and Camping, 1900–49

Baker led the Derby contingent of the Kyndwr Club, a group of Sheffield and Derby walkers and climbers, founded in 1900. His book describes the club's regular trespasses over Kinder Scout and Bleaklow, often enlivened by dodging the gamekeepers.

Baker mentions none of his companions by name. Some readers have criticised his accounts of walking and climbing as egotistical; others have interpreted them more kindly. He does seem to have envied Jim Puttrell, a superior climber.[1] An obituary in the *Derbyshire Advertiser* stated: 'Baker was autocratic and intolerant of incompetence or indolence in either work or recreation, and did not seek to obtain popularity with the average man.'[2] On the balance of evidence he was probably an early example of what for many of us is an intuitive truth: taking part in adventurous sports does not necessarily endow someone with endearing character traits.

Be that as it may, he left some fine writing that still today captures what makes the Peak District so alluring:

> The very place-names have the same savour of romance and antiquity, that the philologist relishes with so much gusto in such moorland names as Fairbrook Naze, Ladybower, Wildboar Clough, Ouzleden, and Featherbed Moss. Throstle Bank, Dimpus, the Roych, Ollerenshaw, Black Edge are just as full of suggestion and romantic sound. To pick them out on the map is, to a lover of old picturesque words, like finding plums in a pudding.[3]

Baker was one of the first people to latch onto the population aspect of the Peak District's geographical position, which made recreational access to land an important issue: 'Right in the centre of England, midway between Sheffield and Manchester, at the threshold of the world's most populous cluster of manufacturing towns, there lies this broad area of wild country, as lone and untamed as any south of Cheviot.'[4]

For the inhabitants of those towns, it was wonderful to have the Peak District so close, except for one snag: much of the elevated moorland plateau, the southern end of the Pennines, was privately owned, and many of the landowners declined requests from walkers for access.

Skiers near Buxton, November 1912.

Topical Press Agency / Getty Images

Before the first world war, walkers tolerated the access problems by remaining on public footpaths or they knowingly trespassed, ignoring minor repercussions. The number of individuals involved was relatively small. However, by 1914 the number of motor cars in the UK had grown to 150,000, and motor transport began to effect a rediscovery of the countryside. One other statistic to bear in mind is that in 1914, out of the total UK population aged over twenty years, only three out of ten were registered to vote. Democracy was far from flowing in full flood.[5]

After the war, the Representation of the People Act (1918) brought about universal male suffrage and the right to vote for women over thirty years. In 1919–20, some seven million workers in Britain obtained cuts in working hours averaging six and a half hours a week; the normal working week was reduced from fifty-four hours to forty-eight.[6] As the number of ramblers and climbers grew in the 1920s and 30s, so too did the number of access difficulties and incidents.

In 1924, Ernest Baker self-published an essay *The Forbidden Land: A Plea for Public Access to Mountains, Moors, and Other Waste Lands in Great Britain.* In a section on England and Wales, he pinpointed the area where the access problem was most acute: 'The trouble has been … particularly with the great stretches of moorland from the Peak of Derbyshire to the Border, large parts of it contiguous to our densest population.'[7]

For hundreds of years, access on foot had not been a problem: 'the moorlands [had] remained waste lands out and out and nobody troubled much about them. So far as access was concerned, no let or hindrance [had been] interposed by heedless landowners. Those who wanted to could cross [the moorlands] where they pleased from village to village'. Then,

> one unlucky day, grouse-shooting became a pastime with the idle rich, and the policy of shutting up the open wild gradually began. Nobody was as yet alive enough to the charm of these solitudes to raise objections. Only in the last few decades have the public realised the seriousness of their loss. Now, however, it is becoming at length an obvious fact, and we wonder how our fathers could have failed to appreciate it, that the open spaces of the Pennines are the back garden, the recreation ground, for the crowded millions of workers in the adjoining towns.[8]

By 1925 there were 693,000 cars in the UK.[9] We have already met, in Chapter 1, Jack Longland and Ivan Waller in 1925, snatching a week-end in north Wales by driving through the night. At the same time, for many people unemployment was creating undesired leisure time. Carless inhabitants of the towns close to the Peak District, employed and unemployed, began to use their leisure time in outings by bus or train into the countryside, often benefitting from cheap bus or train fares.

Not everyone could afford the bus fare. A Manchester scoutmaster, Harold Bee, recalled:

> In 1926 I had a pack of 26 Cubs in Newton Heath. Two of their fathers were working, four were on unemployment pay and the rest were on relief. If we wanted to take a trip, I had to plan the journey so that they didn't have to spend more than 3s. each on travelling expenses. A trip to Edale in Derbyshire was five or six bob. They just couldn't do it.[10]

Perhaps this was just as well. The regular influx of townees did not please some Peak District locals. In April 1928 a resident of Edale called for the press and the Ramblers' Federation 'to educate the crowds who now infest the Derbyshire valleys'. According to this person, the ramblers of a few years earlier had formed 'a very fine class', but the last few years had brought 'thousands of the childish type who delight to wear a multi-coloured béret and render Sunday hideous with singing and ukelele playing'.[11]

Unsurprisingly, protests from residents failed to silence the singers. In 1931 the songwriter Ralph Butler added another song to the ramblers' repertoire, 'I'm Happy When I'm Hiking'.

The access problems in the Peak District culminated on 24 April 1932 when the grouse moorland of Kinder Scout hosted what became known as the mass trespass. Benny Rothman, the trespass's prime mover, 'was a 20-year-old Manchester communist in the motor trade – Jewish by descent, tiny in stature and fiery in rhetoric'.[12] Five hundred people advanced onto the moor. As they marched they sang the 'Red Flag' and the 'Internationale'. A report in the *Manchester Guardian* began:

> Four or five hundred ramblers, mostly from Manchester, trespassed in mass on Kinder Scout to-day. They fought a brief but vigorous hand-to-hand struggle with a number of keepers specially enrolled for the occasion. This they won with ease, and

then marched to Ashop Head, where they held a meeting before
returning in triumph to Hayfield. Their triumph was short-lived,
for there the police met them, halted them, combed their ranks
for suspects, and detained five men.[13]

The trespass gave rise to Ewan MacColl's 1932 song 'The Manchester
Rambler', the lyrics of which put out a defiant political message. Access
to some areas in the Peak District would remain a problem into the
1950s, as White Hall's first warden, Peter Mosedale, would discover.
In time, however, the trespass would come to be regarded as a model
of effective civil disobedience. In 2007, at the seventy-fifth anniversary
of the trespass, the veteran politician Roy Hattersley would be able,
justifiably, to describe the trespass as the most successful direct action
in British history.[14]

By 1933, there were 1,313,000 cars on the roads in the UK – cars
were becoming a common middle-class possession – but in many
neighbourhoods the soup kitchens of the Great Depression were in
constant use.[15] While Jack Longland was on his way to Everest, a growing number of city-dwellers from outside the Peak District caught the
bus or train on a Friday night or a Saturday or Sunday morning, heading for a day or two's walking over the windswept moors or through
the sublime limestone dales. A new word, 'hitchhike', arrived from
America (where the first known occurrence of it was in 1923); hitchhiking became a way of travelling to the hills for people with plenty
of time but little money. (It would still be a common practice in 1956,
when the BBC television film *Climbing* was shot.)

In the depressed industrial towns, numerous local clubs emerged,
including rambling, camping, cycling, cross-country running, caving
and gymnastic clubs. This period also saw the starts of several important
national countryside movements: the Council for the Preservation of
Rural England (1926), the Youth Hostels Association (1930) and the
Ramblers' Association (1935).

The Youth Hostels Association was the right idea at the right time.
From its beginning it emphasised the potential educative value of
outdoor travel and outdoor recreation. In October 1936, an article in
the *Derby Evening Telegraph* summarised the progress that had been
made in just six years:

There has been a steady increase in week-end hiking, and expectations are that this will continue. Derbyshire has contributed a

large share to the popularity of the [Youth Hostel] movement, for during the past year the development of the youth hostels in the county has been astonishing. There are now 11 of them in the chain extending over the best area of rambling country. Figures cannot truly express the great work of the movement, but they show the vitality of an organisation which is growing stronger year by year.[16]

This article also announced that winter would no longer be a closed season for hikers. For the first time, all the Derbyshire hostels would remain open during the coming winter. It was expected that they would be among the most heavily used in the country.

Youth hostels were cheap because they had minimal staffing. This arrangement required several regulations that contributed to the uniqueness of a hostelling holiday. A writer in the *Sunday Times* summarised the main ones:

> Rules ordain that you must arrive not later than seven p.m. and be away, unless it is pouring, by 10; that anyone arriving after 10 at night is liable to be repulsed, but if you are plausible enough to get by the doorkeeper, you must pay an extra shilling; that you must not smoke in the sleeping quarters, but anywhere else [is OK]; that you must leave your dog outside, unless special permission is given; that you must shake and fold your blankets before you go, and that if you have broken anything you must report it.[17]

Ramblers began to organise themselves nationally in 1931, when six regional federations representing walkers from all over Britain joined to create the National Council of Ramblers' Federations.[18] Once a month, the *Manchester Guardian* published news from ramblers' federations around the country. On 11 April 1932, for example, these news reports occupied about thirty-six column inches of tiny type.[19] Local newspapers quickly followed suit. On 10 March 1933 the *Derby Evening Telegraph* started 'A Rambler's Note-book', to appear every Friday.[20] This column continued throughout the 1930s. The *Nottingham Evening Post*, the *Lancashire Evening Post* and the *Yorkshire Evening Post* all had their regular 'Rambling Notes'.

According to Simon Thompson, but never mentioned in the newspapers' ramblers' notes, nude bathing was the norm on both climbing and hiking expeditions. Even the all-female Pinnacle Club engaged in mass naked swims.[21]

For many people in the 1930s, camping was an end in itself, a cheap way of enjoying the countryside. In July 1933 the *Nottingham Evening Post* reported on this 'sport':

> It is an established fact that the healthy sport of camping has now reached a popularity never before achieved, and although its adherents are drawn from a variety of out-of-doors organisations, some thousands have been enlisted from the ranks of the ramblers. No matter where one walks nowadays, a tent is to be seen, either by the river, near the farmstead, or nestling in the bosom of the hills. Wherever a track has been made the hiker-campers have gone exploring.[22]

The Ramblers' Association (RA) was created on 1 January 1935. In June that year, Tom Stephenson, the open-air columnist for the *Daily Herald* who was a keen rambler, wrote an article proposing a high-level long-distance walk along the whole length of the Pennines; pushing this forwards from an idea to reality would take Stephenson and the Ramblers' Association thirty years.[23]

One other new national organisation of relevance to outdoor pursuits appeared in 1935. From the midst of economic gloom, to fill a pressing need, emerged the Central Council of Recreative Physical Training, sponsored by two leading physical education bodies. Its object was to help to improve the physical and mental health of the community through the development of facilities for recreative physical activities.[24] The council aimed to coordinate the efforts of the voluntary organisations identified with physical culture and recreation. At the inaugural meeting, Lord Astor emphasised that 'physical training' included every form of indoor and outdoor activity. In 1937 the Physical Training and Recreation Act made two million pounds available for the expansion of facilities for sport and recreation. Competitive sports still dominated the sport and leisure scene, but further legislation in 1939 and policy changes began to recognise the existence and needs of recreational outdoor pursuits, preparing the way for postwar developments.[25]

Caverns Measureless to Man, 1850–1949

The caves of the White Peak have produced widespread archaeological traces of early man and associated animals, and here and there, such

as in Poole's Cavern in Buxton, the Romans left evidence of their speleological excursions. After the Romans had left Britain, lead-mining
became the backbone of the wealth of the Peak District for over 1,500
years.[26] In many places, lead-miners broke into natural caves. By the
mid-19th century, tourists had appeared on the scene. Speedwell Cavern
had been enrolled among the Wonders of the Peak. An 1837 guidebook
described its so-called Bottomless Pit as 'a terrific void … as vast as
Milton's palace of Pandemonium, and filled with impenetrable darkness'.[27] Poole's Cavern in Buxton, a rival Wonder of the Peak, opened
as a show cave in 1853.

By the end of the 19th century, lead-mining had almost ended. A
few men of leisure began to take an interest in Derbyshire's caves and
abandoned mines. They went about their exploring in a gentlemanly
way, allotting due importance to the preliminaries, such as handshaking
and taking tea and posing for photographs. The following newspaper
report illustrates some of the niceties of a caving trip in 1902:

Exploration of the Peak Cavern
The exploration of the caverns of Castleton is being continued,
and last Saturday a visit was made by members of the Kyndwr
Club to the Peak Cavern with highly satisfactory results. The
party included Messrs J W Puttrell, G F R Freeman, S.A.C.,
and W J Watson from Sheffield, Mr McCrumm from Castleton,
and Messrs A Bemrose, M.A., F.G.S., E. A. Baker, M.A., Dr
Jameson, etc., etc., from Derby. Mr F Bamforth, photographer,
from Holmfirth, with searchlight and camera was in attendance.
The Derby contingent arrived at Castleton at 8.30, and after
hearty handshaking with their Sheffield comrades, and a change
into working clothes, sat down to a good tea provided by Mrs.
Johnstone, at the Peak Hotel. The party then, after having been
photographed, set out for 'Cave Dale' armed with iron bars, ropes,
etc., under the leadership of Mr. Puttrell. Here … they saw the
mouth of a hole, and were informed that Messrs Freeman and
McCrumm were going to lower Mr. J. W. Puttrell down, and if
the remainder of the party would follow Mr. Watson, he would
guide them to 'The Great Cave' in the Peak Cavern, to await if
successful the arrival of the daring pioneer. Fifteen minutes later
Mr. Puttrell was roped up, and after crawling into the hole some
fifteen feet was followed by Messrs Freeman and McCrumm.
Here the size of the chimney was 1 ft. 4 in. by 2 ft., and after a

'good luck, old man' from his friends, Mr Puttrell started on his
downward journey of 115 ft. In half an hour the party in the
Great Cave set up a cheer: Mr. Puttrell had reached the cave –
and the first descent from Cave Dale into the Peak Cavern was
an accomplished fact.[28]

DCC: Buxton Museum and Art Gallery – Douglas collection.

James Puttrell and friends caving in Derbyshire in the early 1900s. Puttrell enjoyed
both climbing and caving. Many White Hall instructors have had this dual interest.

These early cavers sometimes tackled vertical descents by being lowered while sitting in a bosun's chair, a plank or canvas seat long used
by mariners. Alternatively, rope ladders were used, borrowed from the
shipping industry or home-made. Lead-miners frequently fixed pieces
of wood called 'stemples' into the walls on both sides of a shaft, thus
making a crude ladder.[29] In mined shafts, these footholds were often
still available to the new explorers, if they dared to use them.

Much of the exploration was, in fact, re-exploration, a process that
still continues today. In September 1913, J W Puttrell described some
recent exploring in Speedwell Mine:

We came across evidences of old lead-mining operations, namely
wooden stemples, stone walls and a welcome well-trod path which
we followed to the end, or in local mining phraseology, to 't'owd
man'. Here, indeed, the miner of a century ago had stopped fol-

lowing the 'vein', and his final efforts with the pick were as fresh in appearance as though they were only of yesterday.[30]

After the first world war, a new generation of cavers emerged and restarted the search for new passages and new caves. Yet the number of serious cavers involved was very small. Travel difficulties and the logistics of organising enough cavers, with bulky rope ladders and other kit, limited the frequency of trips.

By the mid-1930s, however, more people were venturing under-ground for their recreation. This growth in the popularity of the sport of caving coincided with an expansion of scientific interest in caves. 'The reputation of the Peak's tourist and bone caves attracted the inaugural meeting of the British Speleological Association to Buxton in 1936, and scientific speleology in Britain can be said to date from then.'[31]

A notable Derbyshire discovery by sporting cavers before the second world war was Nettle Pot, dug out by the Derbyshire Pennine Club in the 1930s. People were often attracted by the sport's unique physical challenges, summarised by one newspaper in one sentence: 'Worming a way among holes, rocks and waterfalls under the earth seems the most forbidding of pastimes, as bad as rock-climbing for precariousness, coal-mining for gloom, and hauling a herring-net for damp discom-fort.'[32] For the first time in caving, accidents began to happen. One of the earliest, in October 1934, involved a caver with a broken leg in Gingling Hole in Yorkshire.

An article in the *Yorkshire Post* described the dilemma that accom-panied the rise in the popularity of caving: 'Motoring, cycling and walking bring strangers to the holes every week-end, and many have been seen to attempt apparently easy descents without any guidance or any knowledge of the sheer falls beneath them. Pot-holing clubs have also grown in membership until the ideal of experienced personal supervision for every descent is hard to maintain.'[33]

These concerns reappeared, intensified, after the second world war, when caving underwent a sudden, almost explosive growth in popular-ity. The worries about accidents caused by inexperience were similar to those expressed in connection with climbing and hillwalking. Caving was a great sport, with the potential to benefit a person's physical and mental health, and therefore was worth promoting to young men and women, but only if adequate guidance was also available.

About a third of the Peak District national park is composed of lime-stones; this area of gently rolling hills sliced by deep dales is known as the White Peak. The rest of the national park is composed of millstone grit, which forms bleak peat moorlands, known as the Dark Peak.

The limestone part is one of the main caving areas in the British Isles, the other main ones being in the Yorkshire Dales, in South Wales and in the Mendips. The sport of caving would arguably become White Hall's most reliable group activity and would be especially useful on schools' courses in the winter.

Going Out for a Bike Ride, 1870–1949

In its early years and through the 1870s, the bicycle was mainly the preserve of men of leisure and adequate wealth. On 5 August 1878, fifty of them met in Harrogate and formed the Bicycle Touring Club. The annual subscription was fixed at half a crown. The club's objects were 'to promote touring by bicycle'. It was the first bicycle touring club in the world. In 1883 it changed its name to Cyclists' Touring Club.[34]

The emergence of the safety bicycle in 1885, followed in 1888 by the addition of pneumatic tyres, boosted the attractiveness of cycling.[35] Women of leisure joined the wheelmen.

One day in March 1891, an editorial in the *Manchester Guardian* noted the rise of a movement that was reconnecting young townspeople with the countryside: 'For the richer section of society cycling clubs are doing good service by drawing boys and young men away from the towns and into pure air, and it is satisfactory to see that so pleasant a means of obtaining both exercise and amusement is rapidly being brought within reach of persons who are by no means well-to-do.'[36]

By the early 1890s, cycling was attracting members of the lower middle class. *The Cyclist* of 13 August 1892 said: 'The two sections of the community which form the majority of "wheelmen" are the great clerk class and the great shop assistant class.'[37] Even so, for most workers, paid holidays had not yet arrived, nor had youth hostels. Many less-well-off cyclists saw no need to join a touring club. Most members of the Cyclists' Touring Club were still business men, doctors, lawyers, parsons and civil servants.[38]

In March 1893 the *Manchester Guardian* began a weekly column called Cycling Notes. (Previously cycling had appeared under 'Athletics and Cycling'.) The cycling notes quickly evolved into a roughly equal mix of news on cycle racing and on cycle touring. The notes reported on rides ranging over Derbyshire, Lancashire, Cheshire, Staffordshire and Yorkshire.

On Monday 6 August 1894, part of a bank-holiday weekend, the cycling correspondent reported on his weekend's ride, two days in the countryside. This ride probably typified the trips of thousands of other cyclists over that weekend, some of them perhaps equipped with the relevant sheet of Bartholomew's 4-miles-to-an-inch *Tourist's and Cyclist's Road Map of England and Wales*, which was published that year:

> It often happens that those who leave Manchester in bad weather are well repaid for the hazard, and so it ultimately proved on this occasion.
>
> My destination was Ludchurch, a pretty spot, but very little known, being on the extreme northern border of Staffordshire … The cleft cut out of the moorland, which is Ludchurch, is said to have been a retreat of the Luddites …
>
> On the way to Ludchurch I had one of the finest mountain rides I can remember. The first stage of the journey was to Buxton … By dodging to the right of Stockport all that is unpleasant in the run may be avoided … [He stayed overnight in Buxton.]
>
> The morning was gloriously bright, and I was on the road before the town was fairly awake. My way lay first by the coach road to Macclesfield, but at Burbage the left hand branch had to be taken in the direction of Leek. The gradient is a rising one … As we rise ranges of hills farther and farther off come into view, and the grey point of Chrome [Hill] appears conspicuous among them …
>
> Just after passing the Travellers' Rest … we take the right-hand road for Flash … Leave your machine at Flash … To walk the last three miles to Ludchurch is by far the more enjoyable plan.[39]

On 3 May 1897 the *Guardian*'s cycling notes occupied two full columns of dense type – about forty column inches or a quarter of the broadsheet page. 'New clubs [were] still springing up,' said the writer. Many cycling clubs were now mixed sex.[40] Saturday 1 May had featured the annual Royal May Day fair in Knutsford. A fixture list showed that there were seventy-five club runs in that part of Cheshire and Lancashire on that day, forty-seven of which were bound for Knutsford. The writer estimated that 'Manchester alone must have sent about three thousand [cyclists]. Never has the old Chester Road been better lit than it was by their homecoming … a seemingly endless procession of swiftly moving lights'.[41]

In 1896 the automobile speed limit had been raised from 4 mph to 12 mph[42], but motor cars had yet to appear in large numbers; cyclists in 1897 shared the serene countryside with an occasional bewildered creature, one of Britain's 1,526,000 horses.[43] For many adults, bicycles were affordable. They served as practical transport and as recreational equipment. They emancipated women. Manufacturing and selling bicycles and accessories was a sizeable industry. The *Manchester Guardian* had recognised cyclists as in important group of newspaper readers. Cycling was huge. Membership of the Cyclists' Touring Club grew from 14,166 in 1894 to 60,499 in 1899.[44] The 60,499 included about 20,000 women. Dave Horton, an academic who now writes almost exclusively about cycling, has argued that 'the bicycle powerfully enabled the expansion in the geographical, social and political horizons of both feminists and socialists at the turn of the twentieth century'.[45]

By 1903, all the sheets of Bartholomew's 2-miles-to-an-inch maps for tourists and cyclists had been published and had become almost instantly popular at a price of 1s. 0d. (paper folded) or 2s. 0d. (cloth folded).[46] Half an inch to the mile was an ideal scale for showing all country lanes; cyclists and horses were still the main users of these roads, but the end of this cyclists' utopia was in sight. In 1903 the speed limit for motor cars was raised to 20 mph.[47]

After the first world war, a new generation of wanderers on two wheels arrived: ordinary working people.[48] Cycle touring remained popular throughout the 1920s and 30s. Around 1925, manufacturers began making lightweight bicycles for touring. During the years of economic slump and uncertainty, cycling provided an escape from factories, shops and offices to the countryside and fresh air. Legislation reduced the numbers of working hours for many workers. Many also gained improved arrangements for holidays with pay.[49]

In 1919 the Cyclists' Touring Club (CTC) launched a junior membership scheme. In 1927 the club extended its affiliation arrangements to include 'Boy Scouts, Girl Guides, similar organisations, and any group of scholars at a responsible school'.[50] As well as welcoming new young cyclists, in 1936 the CTC added a concern for their safety by creating a cycling proficiency scheme. In 1946 the club extended the benefits of junior membership to include the club's monthly magazine, the *CTC Gazette*. This CTC embracing of young cyclists contrasted sharply with the more selective and guarded approach to young novice climbers taken by many of the older climbing clubs at that time.

Sheffield Clarion Cycling Club members camping at Dovedale, 1925.

Picture Sheffield v01723.

Cycle touring in 1929.

Frank Patterson.

Out for a bike ride, at Ashopton post office, 1936. The village of Ashopton is now under Ladybower Reservoir.

Frank Patterson

A tandem, climbing up from Sparrowpit, Derbyshire, 1935.

Manchester Daily Express / Getty Images 90760830.

A group of cyclists on the road past Mam Tor, October 1939. Cycle touring had been a popular pastime for adults since the 1890s. Although some touring took place off the roads, such as on bridleways, most cycle tourists remained on roads.

Throughout the 1920s and 30s, the *CTC Gazette* vigorously defended cyclists against repeated attempts by motoring interests to encroach on their freedom and welfare. It encouraged and inspired the club's members to resist all attempts, by government and motoring bodies, to restrict cyclists' free use of the roads, and to impose on them compulsory rear lights, taxation, number plates and licences.[51]

Despite its potential, recreational cycling received scant recognition in the physical training provision of many schools for the first half of the 20th century. But searching of newspaper databases does reveal occasional exceptions: examples of school pupils undertaking ambitious cycling tours, either organised by teachers or on the pupils' own initiatives. A few random examples of these cycling trips appear in Chapter 4.

In 1946 a bicycle frame-builder began a cycle shop called Mercian Cycles in London Road, Derby. Hand-built Mercian bikes became recognised worldwide for their quality of workmanship. Mercian Cycles is still supplying custom-built bicycles today.

From 1950 onwards, the activity of recreational cycling would be ignored by most LEA residential outdoor pursuits centres. White Hall's first programme of courses, produced in December 1950, listed cyclists as among those young people who would be catered for, but not until 1991 would White Hall Centre buy bicycles.

Perhaps recreational cycling was always destined to be an enigmatic member of the set of things known as adventurous outdoor pursuits, because it took place, until relatively recently, mainly on roads, albeit often on rural ones. A few keen cycle tourists followed bridleways on ordinary road bikes but they were a small minority. In competing for a young person's attention, cycling was at a disadvantage compared to activities that took him or her deeper into the countryside or onto rivers and lakes or into the wilderness.

Outcrop Exploration, 1880–1949

In Britain in the 1880s, many wage-earners worked a nine-hour day for six days a week (fifty-four hours a week).[52] Many of them also felt obliged to attend church on Sundays. They had limited leisure time. Walter Haskett Smith, however, was the son of a wealthy landowner, had been educated at Eton and Oxford, and led a life of travel and scholarly inquiry, sustained by his private income.[53] He was an all-round athlete, very daring, self-confident and strongly individualistic. He also discovered that climbing rocks could be fun, especially without a rope. Geoffrey Young described Haskett Smith as 'the first notable instance of the successful athlete in whom the passion for climbing competed with, and surpassed in the end, the passion for orthodox games'.[54]

This led to a key point in the development of British rock climbing. In 1886 Haskett Smith climbed Napes Needle, a photogenic rock pinnacle on the side of Great Gable in the Lake District. Photographs and accounts of subsequent ascents received wide publicity, which helped to establish rock climbing in Britain as a sport, something to do solely for the pleasure involved. Before this time, climbing in Wales and the Lakes and Scotland had often been thought of as merely a means to an end, as training for more demanding and worthwhile outings in the Alps and elsewhere.[55]

As commonly happens with climbers, Haskett Smith's devotion to rock was limited to particular types. Peak District rock did not captivate him. He wrote:

> Derbyshire is well endowed in point of rock scenery, but it is not really a climber's country. The rocks are of two kinds – the Limestone, of which Dovedale may be taken as a type, and the Millstone Grit, which prevails further north. The former shows many a sharp pinnacle and many a sheer cliff, but is often dangerously rotten, while the latter assumes strange, grotesque forms, and, when it does offer a climb, ends it off abruptly, just as one thinks the enjoyment is about to begin.[56]

By 1900 the total number of rock climbs in the Lake District had reached about a hundred.[57] Half the population of Britain lived in towns and cities. The small community of Britain's rock climbers – previously a handful of professional men with comfortable incomes – had diversified to include people in lower-middle-class occupations. Climbing was not yet a poor man's sport, participation was still restricted to those with some money and leisure; but neither in Britain was rock climbing ever exclusively a rich man's sport. 'Especially in the Lake District, the sport came to be dominated by northern manufacturers, shopkeepers and teachers, some of whom came from working-class family backgrounds.'[58]

More men climbed than women, yet there are many accounts of women climbing. On 31 March 1890, Miss D J Koecher became the first woman to climb Napes Needle, four years after Haskett Smith's first ascent. Her achievement was part of a long slow social change that had started in the 19th century. Frequently mentioned influences or events include the activities of the alpinist Henriette d'Angeville in the 1820s, a number of 19th-century English women alpinists such as Lucy Walker, the development of the safety bicycle in the 1880s, and the wearing of what was called rational clothing.

Between 1886 and 1900, a few trailblazers ignored Haskett Smith and climbed on the millstone grit outcrops of the southern Pennines, without catching the attention of the British climbing scene of that time. Haskett Smith had underestimated the importance of gritstone. After 1900, the leading gritstone-trained climbers began to unleash their technical skills and muscular strength on the mountain crags of north Wales and the Lakes, with impressive results. Gritstone climbing would remain a centre (some would say *the* centre) of British climbing throughout the 20th century. The gritstone outcrops are scattered around Derbyshire, Staffordshire, Yorkshire and Lancashire. The Peak District, of which a large chunk of Derbyshire is the main constituent, has the lion's share of these dark-brown layered rocks, composed of coarse sandstone and pebbles formed under an estuary many millions of years ago. Pre-eminent among royal company reigns the long escarpment of Stanage Edge, personified recently as 'the queen of grit, this sumptuous of all mistresses'.[59]

Jim Puttrell, the manager of the Sheffield silversmiths Mappin & Webb, has been called the inventor of gritstone climbing, in recognition of his early routes on Wharncliffe Crags, about seven miles north of the city centre. He climbed most of these in the 1880s and 90s. Earlier in this chapter, the cycling section included an account of a bike ride undertaken on the bank-holiday weekend of 4–5 August 1894. It is quite possible that while the *Guardian* correspondent was pedalling to Ludchurch (now Luds Church), Jim Puttrell may have been enjoying two or three days of exploring the gritstone crags on the opposite side of the Peak District, within reach of Sheffield. He might have even used a bicycle to get there.

As time passed, Puttrell ventured further afield:

By the turn of the century a growing band of followers around Sheffield had formed themselves into the Kyndwr Club, and Puttrell began to climb more regularly outside the Peak District. In many respects, Puttrell was the prototype 'hard-man' trained on grit before transferring his athletic climbing style to the bigger crags in the Lakes and Scotland.[60]

James W Puttrell on a climb at Wharncliffe, near Sheffield, from a 1904 postcard.

Richard Holt. National Archives. Copy 1/474/68.

In 1907 the Ladies Alpine Club was founded, followed by the Ladies Scottish Climbing Club in 1908.

In the years leading up to the first world war, two outcrop-trained climbers dominated Lake District climbing. Fred Botterill, a school teacher based in Leeds, honed his skills on Yorkshire gritstone. Siegfried Herford started climbing while studying at Manchester University, closer to Derbyshire. During his final year at university in 1912, he spent 100 days on the crags, a level of activity easier to achieve on short local outcrops than on remote mountain cliffs.[61] As a result of this training, he climbed at a higher grade than any of his contemporaries. On 20 April 1914, Herford led Central Buttress on Scafell, the biggest ever breakthrough in the standard of Lake District climbing. On

22 May, about two months before the outbreak of the war, an article in the *Daily Mail* announced that 'within the next few days hundreds of rock-climbers will meet in the Lake District. The difficult sport of rock-climbing will see an immense increase of popularity this year.'[62]

By the time Jack Longland was a teenager, at the end of the first world war, millstone grit outcrops were a well-recognised forcing ground for British rock climbing. The most popular crags were Almscliff in Yorkshire, Wharncliffe Edge, Laddow Rocks to the north of Crowden, and Black Rocks near Cromford. For a while, these developments were controversial, perhaps not in keeping with climbing's cherished status as an amateur sport. 'The idea of climbing small outcrops was often ridiculed by the mountaineering establishment as demeaning, reducing the sport to the level of cheap stunts, gymnastics and showmanship.'[63]

This debate was one that the reactionaries could not win, not without banning climbing on gritstone. Some exclusion did occur, but for other reasons. Many gritstone outcrops were on private land, typically grouse-shooting moorland. Some landowners refused to allow climbers access to these crags. Confrontation between climbers and gamekeepers happened frequently.

Another postwar development, more of a national one than a Derbyshire one, was the start of another club for women rock climbers, the Pinnacle Club, which was formed on 26 March 1921. Geoffrey Young's wife Eleanor was its president. In a letter to the *Manchester Guardian* she said that the last decade had witnessed a notable increase in the number of women who were devoted to the pursuit of rock climbing.[64]

On 5 April 1926, in an article headed 'Pillar Rock Girls', the *Daily Mail* reported that the previous day most of the 600 members of the Fell and Rock Climbing Club had met at Pillar Rock to celebrate the centenary of the first recorded ascent of that crag. We learn from this article that 'the girl climbers were neat and trim and dainty in appearance' and that 'they made a pretty picture as they slung or straightened the rope on projecting rocks'. Two cragswomen earned a mention for their coolness, but several men retained conspicuous possession of the lead roles, walking unroped 'up the old crest to the rock summit … with their hands in their pockets as though precipices were non-existent'.[65]

Further afield, in the late 1920s, an American woman climber of outstanding ability, Miriam O'Brien, advanced women's climbing by deciding to try some climbs not only guideless but 'really manless'.[66]

ROCK·CLIMBING FOR WOMEN

To the Editor of the Manchester Guardian.

Sir,—The last decade has witnessed a notable increase in the number of women who are de- voted to the pursuit of rock-climbing. For some time it has been felt that women climbers required some organisation which would· con- cern itself with their special interests, and serve the double purpose of promoting the in- dependent development of the climbing art amongst women and of bringing into touch with one another those who are already united by the bond of a common love for a noble sport.

To this end a club has been formed called the Pinnacle Club. The inaugural meeting was held at Pen-y-Gwryd on March 26, and the club already possesses 41 members.

Any women who are interested in the objects of the new club are requested to communicate with Mrs. H. M. Kelly, at 29, Fountain Street, Manchester, from whom full particulars may be obtained.—Yours, &c.,

ELEANOR WINTHROP-YOUNG, President.
M. E. KELLY, Hon. Secretary,
Pinnacle Club.

Letter to the *Manchester Guardian*, 2 April 1921.

In Britain, the climbing fraternity continued to broaden. In 1936 and 1937, the Workers' Travel Association ran rock climbing holidays at Langdale, Capel Curig and Glen Brittle and alpine climbing holidays at Chamonix, Zermatt and several places in Austria. All these ventures were 'designed for those with limited means and leisure'.[67]

By the late 1930s, the number of accidents happening to climbers and hillwalkers in all the mountainous areas of Britain, including the Pennines, was becoming a matter of alarmed concern for experienced observers of the sports. William T Palmer, a Lake District guide-book author and founder member of the Fell and Rock Climbing Club, wrote to *The Times*:

Perils of Rock-climbing
Sir,—Every rock face in Britain in turn is getting its 'blood-bath', and the repute of mountaineering as a sport is sadly dimmed.

After every holiday there is a cumulative list of injuries as well as fatalities. At least two deaths on Great Gable, in Cumberland, and one on the snows of Ben Nevis, in Scotland, together with a non-fatal accident on Bow Fell, in Westmorland, are the Easter toll of the heights …

To-day the best-known rock faces are often crowded with novices, half of them unequipped, rarely in [the] charge of experienced leaders, often defiant of any advice, and impertinent of any offer of suggestion. Many are unable to read a map, or to recognize the foot or top of a described rock climb. The danger of Easter will be multiplied in the more popular holidays which follow.

Rock-climbing as a sport can never become tame, but the present holocaust of life and limb by irresponsible, untrained, and badly equipped parties among dangerous and difficult crags can neither be excused nor justified.

I am, &c.,

W. T. PALMER.[68]

Jack Longland, living and working in Durham at this time, and familiar with the skills needed to stay alive high on Everest, might have been thinking the same thing.

By the start of the second world war in 1939, outcrop climbing on millstone grit had produced a succession of leading climbers for forty years. New routes were appearing regularly, but the production of guidebooks had yet to catch up with them. (The only recent Peak District climbing guidebooks were *A Guide to Laddow* and *Wharncliffe Crags*, both published in 1934.) The characteristics of gritstone were well understood. It has excellent friction but few in-cut holds. Climbing on grit requires and develops balance, agility and strength. Many outcrops are close to urban areas, allowing regular weekend climbing and – for those people close enough – unforgettable summer evenings. Most outcrops are low enough to provide single-pitch climbing, which, while allowing concentration on technical difficulties if required, also suits novice climbers. (Pennine limestone was considered a waste of time, too loose for rock climbing; but its time would come.)

After the war, the leading of rock climbs was as serious a pastime as it had ever been. When Dennis Gray started climbing, in 1947, 'few climbers understood the use of running belays, mainly because of the lack of karabiners on the market'. The prevalent attitude was still that the leader should never fall.[69]

When Longland arrived in Derbyshire in late 1949, the Peak District National Park was about to be created. Just a couple of months before, on 4 September, an unknown young climber from Manchester had made the first ascents, with audacious ease, of Right Unconquerable and Left Unconquerable on Stanage Edge; Joe Brown, later known as the Baron, the human fly and, most appositely, Curly Legs, was poised to keep gritstone at the centre of British climbing. The population of Derbyshire was about 820,000.[70] Young folk growing up in Derby lived about half an hour's drive from the edge of the planned national park. The Peak District had no Snowdon Horseshoe and no Ullswater but the idea of setting up an outdoor pursuits centre out of the county probably never entered Longland's head. A centre in the Peak District would be very relevant to the lives of Derbyshire's young people. The only question was, where? Chapter 5 will tell how a vacant abode high on Long Hill came to be chosen.

Notes

1   Ernest A Baker, *Moors, Crags and Caves of the High Peak and Neighbourhood*, Facsimile of 1st (1903) edn (Tiverton, Devon: Halsgrove, 2002), pp. 2–5. Also Phil Kelly, Graham Hoey and Giles Barker, *Peak Rock: The History, The Routes, The Climbers* (Sheffield: Vertebrate Publishing, 2013), pp. 21–22.

2   Quoted on dust jacket of Ernest A Baker, *Moors, Crags and Caves of the High Peak and Neighbourhood*, Facsimile of 1st (1903) edn (Tiverton, Devon: Halsgrove, 2002).

3   Ibid., p. 59.

4   Ibid., p. 9.

5   François Bédarida, *A Social History of England 1851–1990*, 2nd edn (London: Routledge, 1991), p. 141–142.

6   H Cunningham, 'Leisure and Culture', in *The Cambridge Social History of Britain 1750–1950*, ed. by F M L Thompson, 3 vols (Cambridge: Cambridge University Press, 1990), vol. 2, pp. 279–339 (p. 282).

7   Ernest A Baker, *The Forbidden Land: A Plea for Public Access to Mountains, Moors, and Other Waste Lands in Great Britain* (1924), p. 23.

8   Ibid., pp. 25–26.

9   Sean O'Connell, 'The Social and Cultural Impact of the Car in Interwar Britain' (PhD thesis, University of Warwick, 1995), p. 5.

10   Richard West, 'In the Tracks of B-P', *Sunday Times*, 16 Feb 1964, p. 6 [S].

11   'The Wrong Kind of Rambler', *Manchester Guardian*, 26 Apr 1928, p. 20.

12   Jim Perrin, 'Benny Rothman: Inspirational Figure Who Led the Kinder Scout Mass Trespass in Its Fight for Open Access', Guardian (25 Jan 2002) <http://www.theguardian.com/news/2002/jan/25/guardianobituaries> [accessed 15 Jan 2015].

13   'Mass Trespass on Kinder Scout', *Manchester Guardian*, 25 Apr 1932, p. 9.

14   'Archive Marks Kinder Mass Trespass Anniversary', BBC (8 Mar 2012) <http://www.bbc.com/news/uk-england-derbyshire-17304410> [accessed 18 Jan 2015].

15   Sean O'Connell, 'The Social and Cultural Impact of the Car in Interwar Britain' (PhD thesis, University of Warwick, 1995), p. 5.

16   'Winter Rambles in Derbyshire', *Derby Evening Telegraph*, 15 Oct 1936, p. 10.

17   E V Lucas, 'A Wanderer's Note Book', *Sunday Times*, 31 Mar 1935, p. 16.

18   'Our History', Ramblers (2015) <http://www.ramblers.org.uk/about-us/our-history.aspx> [accessed 3 Feb 2015].

19   'The Doings and Plans of the Ramblers' Federations', *Manchester Guardian*, 11 Apr 1932, p. 5.

20   'A Rambler's Notebook', *Derby Evening Telegraph*, 10 Mar 1933, p. 3.

21   Simon Thompson, *Unjustifiable Risk? The Story of British Climbing* (Milnthorpe, UK: Cicerone, 2010), p. 131.

22   'Rambling Notes', *Nottingham Evening Post*, 7 July 1933, p. 10.

23   Tom Stephenson, *Forbidden Land: The Struggle for Access to Mountain and Moorland*, ed. by Ann Holt (Manchester: Manchester University Press, 1989), p. 70 note.

24   'The Training of Youth', *The Times*, 18 June 1935, p. 13.

25   Ken C Ogilvie, *Roots and Wings: A History of Outdoor Education and Outdoor Learning in the UK* (Lyme Regis, UK: Russell House Publishing, 2013), pp. 228–231.

26   Trevor D Ford and J H Rieuwerts, *Lead Mining in the Peak District*, 2nd edn (Bakewell: Peak Park Joint Planning Board, 1975), p. iii.

27   Quoted in Ernest A Baker, *Moors, Crags and Caves of the High Peak and Neighbourhood*, Facsimile of 1st (1903) edn (Tiverton, Devon: Halsgrove, 2002), p. 163.

28   'Exploration of the Peak Cavern', *Derbyshire Courier*, 8 Mar 1902, p. 5.

29   Trevor D Ford and J H Rieuwerts, *Lead Mining in the Peak District*, 2nd edn (Bakewell: Peak Park Joint Planning Board, 1975), pp. 24–25.

30   'The Speedwell Mine', *Yorkshire Telegraph*, 18 Sept 1913, p. 4.

31   *Limestones and Caves of the Peak District*, ed. by Trevor D Ford (Norwich: Geo Abstracts, 1977), p. 14.

32   'Pot-hole Dangers', *Yorkshire Post*, 5 Feb 1935, p. 10.

33   Ibid.

34   William Oakley, *Winged Wheel: The History of the First Hundred Years of the Cyclists' Touring Club* (Godalming, UK: Cyclists' Touring Club, 1977), pp. 3–6.

35   James McGurn, *On Your Bicycle: An Illustrated History of Cycling* (London: John Murray, 1987), pp. 86–90.

36   'Editorial Article 7', *Manchester Guardian*, 9 Mar 1891, p. 5.

37   Quoted in James McGurn, *On Your Bicycle: An Illustrated History of Cycling* (London: John Murray, 1987), pp. 90–91.

38   William Oakley, *Winged Wheel: The History of the First Hundred Years of the Cyclists' Touring Club* (Godalming, UK: Cyclists' Touring Club, 1977), p. 19.

39   'Cycling Notes', *Manchester Guardian*, 6 Aug 1894, p. 7.

40   James McGurn, *On Your Bicycle: An Illustrated History of Cycling* (London: John Murray, 1987), p. 93.

41   'Cycling Notes', *Manchester Guardian*, 3 May 1897, p. 7.

42   James McGurn, *On Your Bicycle: An Illustrated History of Cycling* (London: John Murray, 1987), p. 139.

43   B R Mitchell, *British Historical Statistics* (Cambridge: Cambridge University Press, 1988), p. 202.

44   William Oakley, *Winged Wheel: The History of the First Hundred Years of the Cyclists' Touring Club* (Godalming, UK: Cyclists' Touring Club, 1977), pp. 8, 12.

45   Dave Horton, 'Social Movements and the Bicycle' (Nov 2009) <https://thinkingaboutcycling.files.wordpress.com/2009/11/social-movements-and-the-bicycle.pdf> [accessed 30 Mar 2015], p. 1.

46   Ken Winch, 'A Brief Guide to Dating Bartholomew Maps' (no date) <http://www.cartography.org.uk/downloads/MCT_BartsMaps.pdf> [accessed 7 Apr 2015].

47   James McGurn, *On Your Bicycle: An Illustrated History of Cycling* (London: John Murray, 1987), p. 140.

48   William Oakley, *Winged Wheel: The History of the First Hundred Years of the Cyclists' Touring Club* (Godalming, UK: Cyclists' Touring Club, 1977), pp. 27–30.

49   James McGurn, *On Your Bicycle: An Illustrated History of Cycling* (London: John Murray, 1987), pp. 144–145.

50   William Oakley, *Winged Wheel: The History of the First Hundred Years of the Cyclists' Touring Club* (Godalming, UK: Cyclists' Touring Club, 1977), p. 43.

51   Ibid., pp. 29, 46.

52   H Cunningham, 'Leisure and Culture', in *The Cambridge Social History of Britain 1750–1950*, ed. by F M L Thompson, 3 vols (Cambridge: Cambridge University Press, 1990), vol. 2, pp. 279–339 (280–281).

53   Chris Williams, 'Smith, Walter Parry Haskett (1859–1946)', in *Oxford Dictionary of National Biography* (Jan 2004) <http://0-www.oxforddnb.com.www.elgar.govt.nz/view/article/62423> [accessed 17 Feb 2015].

54   Geoffrey Winthrop Young, 'In Memoriam: W P Haskett-Smith', *Fell and Rock Journal*, 14, no. 3 (1946), pp. 268–271.

55   Ronald W Clark, *A Picture History of Mountaineering* (London: Hulton Press, 1956), plates 186, 199.

56   W P Haskett Smith, *Climbing in the British Isles* (London: Longman, Green and Co, 1894), vol. 1 - England, p. 35.

57   Trevor Jones and Geoff Milburn, *Cumbrian Rock: 100 Years of Climbing in the Lake District* (Glossop, UK: Pic Publications, 1988), p. 35.

58   Simon Thompson, *Unjustifiable Risk? The Story of British Climbing* (Milnthorpe, UK: Cicerone, 2010), pp. 53–55.

59   David Simmonite, 'Around the Bloc: Stanage Apparent North', Climber (no date) <http://climber.co.uk/articles/bouldering/apparent-north-stanage-edge.html> [accessed 6 Nov 2016].

60   Simon Thompson, *Unjustifiable Risk? The Story of British Climbing* (Milnthorpe, UK: Cicerone, 2010), p. 105.

61   Ibid., pp. 90–91.

62   William T Palmer, 'The World's Best Rock-climbing', *Daily Mail*, 22 May 1914, p. 6.

63   Simon Thompson, *Unjustifiable Risk? The Story of British Climbing* (Milnthorpe, UK: Cicerone, 2010), p. 106.

64   Eleanor Winthrop-Young and M E Kelly, 'Rock-climbing for Women', *Manchester Guardian*, 2 Apr 1921, p. 12.

65   'Pillar Rock Girls', *Daily Mail*, 5 Apr 1926, p. 7.

66   Miriam Underhill, *Give Me the Hills* (London: Methuen & Co, 1956), pp. 150–151.

67   'Climbing Holidays', *Sunday Times*, 26 Apr 1936, p. 30. Also 'Climbers!', *Sunday Times*, 4 July 1937, p. 33.

68   W T Palmer, 'Perils of Rock-climbing', *The Times*, 18 Apr 1939, p. 10.

69   Dennis Gray, *Rope Boy* (London: Victor Gollancz: 1970), pp. 16–18.

70   University of Portsmouth, 'Total Population', A Vision of Britain through Time (no date) <http://www.visionofbritain.org.uk/unit/10061428/cube/TOT_POP> [accessed 12 Feb 2015].

3. Messing about in Boats, 1865–1949

Chapter 2 dealt with four activities that I called the hill sports; it looked at adult participation in these sports during the fifty years before White Hall Centre existed. This chapter covers canoeing and sailing, the water sports; again it looks at adult involvement, but from slightly further back, about the 1860s.

Robin Weaver / Alamy BHRA67.

The Hanson log boat, a Derbyshire link with the canoeists of the past. The Bronze Age dugout was found in 1998 in a gravel pit in Shardlow, a village near the River Trent. The boat is on display in Derby Museum and Art Gallery.

Recreational Canoeing, 1865–1949

Canoeing in the British Isles dates from prehistory, but purpose-built recreational craft have only appeared in relatively recent times. In 1830 a Mr Canham from London crossed from Cherbourg to Alderney in a canoe 'much like an Icelander's caiak, consisting of a light wooden framework some ten feet by two feet, covered with tarred canvas …

The owner, sitting in the centre was protected from spray by a covering of tarred canvas'.[1]

The credit for popularising the sport of canoeing goes to a remarkable Scot, John MacGregor, an energetic and eccentric London barrister. In 1865 a London boatbuilder built for him his first canoe, an all-wood clinker-built craft that he named Rob Roy. In 1866 he published an account of a long journey, *A Thousand Miles in the Rob Roy Canoe on Rivers and Lakes of Europe*. If we judge from this book's illustrations, he always wore a jacket and boater.

'Fixed on the Fall'. An engraving from John MacGregor's 1866 account of canoeing down the River Aar in Switzerland.

The book sparked an upsurge of recreational canoeing. Numerous reprints or new editions were required to meet the demand. (The nineteenth edition was published in 1892.) MacGregor's story has inspired paddlers from the Victorians to today's canoe campers and sea kayakers.

Also in 1866, the Canoe Club was formed, nine years after the Alpine Club and nine years before the Yacht Racing Association. Branches of the Canoe Club were formed on the Humber, on the Mersey and in Cambridge. From 1873 onwards the Canoe Club was allowed to call itself the Royal Canoe Club. Canoeing, at least with this particular club, was a gentleman's sport, undertaken in white plimsolls, white flannels and blue caps.

As well as yacht clubs and canoe clubs, there were boat clubs. Boat-club events often included both rowing and canoeing. In 1869, a Sudbury newspaper reported that

> the ardour for aquatics and boat-racing appears contagious … and has led Boat Clubs to send and receive challenges, thus frequently introducing all the concomitants of laudable rivalry, training, practising, &c., in towns which can boast a river wide enough to allow play for a pair of sculls … The River Stour, at Sudbury, is on a

summer evening quite alive with divers crafts including punts, canoes, long rowing boats, ordinary skiffs … [2]

The following year, a Cambridge newspaper carried a more sobering story headed 'Melancholy Case of Drowning'. An undergraduate had drowned while canoeing on the River Cam at Grantchester. The coroner remarked that he had held twelve inquests on deaths by drowning on that river from 1855 to 1869. 'In the majority of cases the persons who venture[d] up a somewhat rapid, winding, and deep stream in extremely light and ticklish craft, [were] unable to swim.'

A witness described the river: 'I have been accustomed to the river, and the only dangerous part of it is the overhanging trees – they hang half over the river in a great many places. There are sudden curves in the stream, and trees hang over there, making it more dangerous.'

The dead man had hired the canoe from a boatbuilder who had twenty canoes available for hire. A question arose about whether the boatbuilder was legally obliged to check that a client could swim. The coroner, discussing this point, said 'a person who let a horse and gig was not actually bound to inquire whether the hirer was able to drive. So in the same manner, a person who let boats was not bound to ask whether the person could manage the boat he took.'[3]

Narrowing our focus to Derbyshire, we find the River Derwent hosting a fair amount of boating and canoeing, accompanied – perhaps less regularly than the River Cam – by occasional melancholy.

An accident on the Derwent in 1877 involved another Cambridge undergraduate, 'a young gentleman … aged 19, son of the Rev. T. L. Garland'. He capsized and was seen being swept downstream towards Darley Paper Mills. 'All at once Mr. Garland went under the water, and never rose to the surface again. Immediately afterwards the canoe struck the piles of Darley-bridge, and was split up.'[4]

In 1887 the British Canoe Association was formed. It was concerned mainly with touring rather than with competition or canoe sport. It lasted about thirty years.

In the 1890s most of the Derbyshire reservoirs that are now valued venues for flat-water canoeing had yet to be built. The River Derwent, which in its original, natural state would have offered attractive canoeing, suffered from numerous snags, especially problematic in flimsy wooden canoes. In *The Derwent and Its Tributaries* (1895), Edward Bradbury wrote:

The Derwent is only here and there navigable, and that for short distances, and for pleasure skiffs only ... Mr MacGregor could not sail his 'Rob Roy' canoe in the Peak, unless he indulged in a sort of aquatic steeplechasing over water-hurdles, for the stream is broken up by a succession of weirs to supply mills with motive power ... But the Derwent is just such a stream as the Rev. Charles Kingsley loved ... [for] it is everywhere fishable.[5]

Over a century later, many kayakers and canoeists would now relish the aquatic steeplechasing, were it not for PRIVATE notices, barbed wire and the legal consequences of the Derwent's evident fishability.

I have found few newspaper accounts of canoeing in Derbyshire in the first half of the 20th century. In 1923 Edith Cameron of Grantham wrote *Our Canoe Trip*, a 'most readable and interesting little account' of a 'thoroughly enjoyable' tour that included sections of the Grantham Canal, the River Trent, the Derby Canal and the River Derwent. As with newspaper reports of rock climbing, canoeing accidents received far more coverage than uneventful trips. In September 1931, 'an adventure in a folding canoe on the River Derwent nearly ended in disaster'. The two-seater canoe overturned at the top of one of the weirs at Calver. The occupants were thrown out and carried over the weir. Bystanders pulled them from the water.[6]

Canoe on the bank of the River Trent, Rugeley, Staffordshire, 1919.

Illustrated London News.

H R H The Prince of Wales (future King Edward VIII) in the bows of the leading canoe on the River Nipigon while on holiday in Ontario, 1919.

Sueddeutsche Zeitung Photo / Alamy CPJB9F.

A folding canoe at an exhibition in Germany in 1934. In the early 1930s, elegant folding canoes were seen in hundreds on German rivers.

A 1939 advertisement.

The start of a British Canoe Union weekend meet on the River Ouzel near Newport Pagnell in June 1944. A folding canoe is being assembled.

In March 1936, representatives of the canoe section of the Camping Club of Great Britain, Clyde Canoe Club, Manchester Canoe Club and the Royal Canoe Club formed the British Canoe Union (BCU).[7] The different branches of canoeing continued to evolve. They included sprint racing, sailing canoes, slalom, wild water racing, long distance racing, canoe polo, touring and sea kayaking. In 1939 the first British slalom took place at Trevor Rocks on the River Dee in Wales. In Derbyshire the most prominent branch in the 1940s was probably canoe racing. In 1948, Midland canoeists persuaded the Canoe Camping Club to break with precedent and to allow them to stage the 1949 championships at Trent Lock.[8]

By the end of the second world war, the CCPR had been engaged for ten years in promoting physical and mental health through all forms of physical activity. In April 1946 the council opened Bisham Abbey, the first National Recreation Centre, set in Berkshire alongside a stretch of the Thames ideal for canoeing, sailing and rowing. Bisham Abbey became an important centre for training coaches and for providing young people with expert instruction in water sports and at least eight other sports.[9]

A BCU committee began to develop proficiency tests in the late 1940s. In 1949 the BCU and the CCPR discussed the need for a coaching scheme, although ten years were to pass before this idea came to fruition.[10]

Also in the late 1940s, the canoeist and writer Percy Blandford began designing and making wood-and-canvas canoes, his first being the PBK 10 (Percy Blandford Kayak 10 foot). He then produced instructions and full-size drawings, which he sold to do-it-yourself enthusiasts.[11] Thousands of home-built PBK canoes would appear in the 1950s, including a dozen or so at White Hall Centre. Apart from swimming, canoeing was the cheapest way to get onto the water and take pleasure from it.

Dinghy Sailing, 1875–1949

If antiquity is a merit for a sport, yachting more than rivals mountaineering. King Charles II liked messing about in boats, so much so that he built at least twenty-six luxury yachts for his own use, saying, 'God would not damn a man for a little irregular pleasure.'[12] (The king is said to have expressed the same thoughts about Nell Gwyn.) For about two hundred years, 1660–1851, yachting was well served by the definition 'the use of pleasure vessels by private gentlemen'. On 17 November 1875 thirty-five of these men formed the Yacht Racing Association.

Membership was open to 'former and present owners of racing yachts of and above 10 tons Thames measurement and such other gentlemen as the Committee may elect'.[13]

The subject of weather will crop up regularly throughout this book, in connection with many outdoor activities. Few activities, though, are more weather dependent than sailing. The words 'sailing' and 'wind' are frequent companions. It should come as no surprise to us, therefore, that in the 1850s Admiral Robert FitzRoy pioneered daily weather predictions, which he called by a new name of his own invention: 'forecasts'. Before this, fishermen, farmers and others who worked outside had to rely on weather wisdom, such as the appearance of clouds or the behaviour of animals, to tell them what was coming. Despite FitzRoy's scientific efforts, 'the belief persisted among many that weather was completely chaotic. When one MP suggested in the Commons in 1854 that recent advances in scientific theory might soon allow them to know the weather in London "twenty-four hours beforehand", the House roared with laughter.'[14]

FitzRoy persevered. Following a particularly successful forecast, the satirical magazine *Punch* suggested he should henceforth be known as 'The First Admiral of the Blew'. But his forecasts, calculated by hand and with minimal data, were often awry. Faced with continuing criticism, he grew depressed. His last forecast was published on 29 April 1865. The following morning, FitzRoy killed himself. In fact, he was ahead of his time, not mistaken or eccentric but at the start of a very long journey.[15] Knowing about isobars and occluded fronts and cumulonimbus remains an important part of an instructor's range of skills today.

Towards the end of the 19th century, as yacht racing became excessively expensive, people began to use smaller boats for sport and recreational sailing, built either exactly to one design or to an open formula that allowed wide variations within a few overall restrictions.

In October 1904, Mrs H G Allan, the owner of not one but two yachts, was elected as a member of the Yacht Racing Association, the first woman member. But yachting remained essentially a male preserve.[16]

Locally, the history of sailing and sailing clubs in Derbyshire and in neighbouring parts of the surrounding counties has some similarities to the story of climbing and climbing clubs. Both stories feature the gradual influence, over many decades, of a growing middle class with rising amounts of leisure time and disposable income. Two of the local sailing clubs were formed more than a century ago. Trent Valley Sailing Club, near Long Eaton and fifteen miles from Derby, began in 1886 and is one of the oldest inland sailing clubs in Britain. Burton Sailing Club began in 1902. Both these clubs sailed on the River Trent, which marked the Derbyshire border (their clubhouses may have been in the neighbouring counties). Most of the area's reservoirs had yet to be built; sailing on Derbyshire reservoirs would not develop until the second half of the 20th century.

In 1907 the *Nottingham Evening Post* reported that the Trent Valley Sailing Club had 'survived the critical years after the early novelty had worn off and [had survived] again when the design and build of the racing machines … became so high-class that only a very few could spare time or money for the sport'.[17]

This newspaper allocated a weekly column, 'Riverside Jottings', to the affairs of the Trent Valley Sailing Club. In August 1910, under 'Riverside Jottings: Sailing as a Sport for Ladies', the newspaper reported that the fleet of sailing boats at Trent Bridge was likely to have an addition, a boat owned and sailed by a lady. The correspondent wrote: 'For a girl of pluck and initiative there is certainly no more delightful or fascinating sport, and with ordinary care there is no more danger in sailing than in any other pastime on the river.'[18] This local example of a woman taking up dinghy sailing matched a slow national trend that is apparent in the following 1920 newspaper extract:

WOMEN COMPETITORS IN SAILING RACES AT HORNING

Fritillary sailed by a crew of three women.

Mere man assisting in the management of a boat.

The start of the women's sailing race at Horning, Norfolk.

A feature of the Horning Town Sailing Club's last meeting was a handicap race for boats steered by women.—(*Daily Mirror* photographs.)

Daily Mirror, 24 July 1920, p. 7.

Dinghy racing, with women at the helms, at Horning in Norfolk, July 1920. These women were pioneers, breaking into a male domain.

Dinghies of Burton Sailing Club on the River Trent in 1912. The club was formed in 1902.

Dinghies of Burton Sailing Club racing on the River Trent in 1912.

Burton Sailing Club evidently folded at some point (but would be re-established in 1935).[19]

In February 1923 the Yacht Racing Association, a little behind on gender issues, issued an open invitation 'to all men associated with [dinghy sailing]' to a meeting to discuss that branch of the sport. Yachting had an image problem, frankly recognised by an article in the *Observer*:

Among vast numbers of people there is a deep-rooted idea that yachting in any form is a sport that can only appeal to the wealthiest classes. At Wednesday's meeting, however, we shall hear discussion upon small types of boats, some costing no more than £50, which are recognised as international class boats …

This [meeting] should help to dispel the notion still extant in many quarters that yachting is an exclusive hobby, and that yachtsmen are a close corporation …

For many years past it has been customary to chronicle the performances of our big racing craft at Cowes and a few other important regattas, while ignoring the existence of hundreds of enthusiastic small-boat sailors around our coasts. Hence, it is hardly surprising that those lacking an intimate knowledge of the sport only think of it as a prohibitively expensive pastime. We recognise county cricket as the highest form of this game, but we are not unmindful of the fact that our schools and village greens are nurseries for the game. Yachtsmen want to see a similar all-round recognition of sailing.[20]

In the 1920s and 1930s Uffa Fox, a boat designer and 'one of the last genuine English eccentrics', contributed to the design of many new classes of dinghy.[21] He also introduced hull shapes that could plane, a major advance popularised in the 1930s.

In the 1930s, the international 14-foot dinghies were hugely popular but at £100 to £150 for a new racing 14-footer were considered by many yachtsmen to have unnecessary costly sophistications.[22] Converting old prices into present-day equivalents is a refined pastime of economists; for what it's worth, using the cumulative historical UK inflation rate, something that cost £150 in 1934 would have cost £9,700 in 2016.

This chapter and the last have looked at adults' participation in hill and water sports. Chapter 4 will look at the involvement of school pupils in these adventurous recreational pursuits.

Courtesy of Burton Sailing Club.

Members of Burton Sailing Club in a race on the River Trent in about 1949 or 1950. The boats are National 12s. Number N711 was built in 1949 and was once owned by a rector at Burton-upon-Trent. Burton Sailing Club is now based at Foremark Reservoir, near Swadlincote, Derbyshire.

Catharine M Loader

Sailing instruction on Loch Morlich during a Glenmore Lodge course in June 1950.

Notes

1   Quoted in *The British Canoe Union Canoe and Kayak Handbook*, ed. by Franco Ferrero, 3rd edn (Bangor, Wales: Pesda Press, 2002), pp. 8–9.

2   'Sudbury: Boat Races on the Stour', *Bury and Norwich Post*, 14 Sept 1869, p. 8.

3   'Melancholy Case of Drowning', *Cambridge Chronicle and University Journal*, 28 May 1870, p. 7.

4   'Fatal Canoe Accident', *The Times*, 6 Jan 1877, p. 6.

5   Edward Bradbury, 'The Derwent and Its Tributaries', *Derbyshire Times and Chesterfield Herald*, 3 Aug 1895, p. 6.

6   'Man and Woman Carried over Weir', *Dundee Evening Telegraph*, 7 Sept 1931, p. 4.

7   *The British Canoe Union Canoe and Kayak Handbook*, ed. by Franco Ferrero, 3rd edn (Bangor, Wales: Pesda Press, 2002), p. 9.

8   'Canoe Races on the Trent', *Nottingham Evening Post*, 29 Dec 1948, p. 3. Also 'Copenhagen', *Nottingham Evening Post*, 6 July 1950, p. 4.

9   Phyllis C Colson, 'National Recreation Centres', *Physical Recreation*, 6, no. 2 (Apr–June 1954), pp. 8–13.

10 British Canoe Union, 'History of Canoeing' (no date) <http://www.bcu.org.uk/files/history%20of%20canoeing.pdf> [accessed 20 Mar 2015]. No longer available at this location.

11 'Percy Blandford – Obituary', Telegraph (22 Jan 2014) <http://www.telegraph.co.uk/news/obituaries/10590350/Percy-Blandford-obituary.html> [accessed 25 Mar 2015].

12 John Rousmaniere, *The Golden Pastime: A New History of Yachting* (New York: W W Norton, 1986), p. 16.

13 Gordon Fairley, *Minute by Minute: The Story of the Royal Yachting Association (1875–1982)* (Woking, UK: Royal Yachting Association, 1983), p. 1.

14 Peter Moore, 'The Birth of the Weather Forecast', BBC (30 Apr 2015) <http://www.bbc.com/news/magazine-32483678> [accessed 3 Jan 2017].

15 Ibid.

16 Gordon Fairley, *Minute by Minute: The Story of the Royal Yachting Association (1875–1982)* (Woking, UK: Royal Yachting Association, 1983), p. 35.

17 'Sailing in Notts', *Nottingham Evening Post*, 26 July 1907, p. 5.

18 'Riverside Jottings: Sailing as a Sport for Ladies', *Nottingham Evening Post*, 13 Aug 1910, p. 7.

19 *History of the County of Stafford: Volume 9, Burton-upon-Trent*, ed. by Nigel J Tringham, The Victoria History of the Counties of England (Woodbridge, Suffolk: Boydell and Brewer, 2003), p. 149.

20 'This Year's Yachting', *Observer*, 11 Feb 1923, p. 18.

21 June Dixon, *Uffa Fox: A Personal Biography* (Brighton: Angus and Robertson, 1978), dust jacket.

22 'Yachting: The Prince of Wales Cup', *The Times*, 25 July 1930, p. 6.

4. Boy-centred Adventure, 1880–1949

Chapter 2 looked mostly at a limited geographical area – the Peak District – and at the general population of adult walkers, cyclists, campers, cavers and climbers. Chapter 3, on water sports, by necessity looked further afield but again at adult participants.

How involved were Derbyshire school pupils in these pursuits, particularly in the Peak District, before 1950? Because of the diminutive number of recorded examples, this question is difficult to answer. However, by expanding the area to Britain and the Alps and other mountains and by looking at the outdoor activities of pupils from any schools, some concrete examples become available to provide a vague idea of what was occurring nationally.

The Best of British Pluck, 1880–1949

We saw in Chapter 3 that in 1866 John MacGregor reconnected adults with an antediluvian activity, canoeing. In Chapter 2, we saw that in 1885 the emergence of the safety bicycle increased the popularity of a very new activity, cycling. Interest in these activities and other outdoor pursuits spread to young people, slowly for some activities, more rapidly for others. One notable influence on the spreading was the *Boy's Own Paper*. The place of the *Boy's Own Paper* and that of the *Girl's Own Paper* in children's literature have been the subjects of much historical research. Writers have drawn attention to the differences between the two middle-class magazines and to the questionable assumptions behind those differences. Social historians have examined the magazines' aims of inculcating gender-differentiated social and cultural values. Both magazines enjoyed enduring success. Copies can still be found in libraries all over the English-speaking world. Of particular relevance to the origins of boys' outdoor recreation is the frequent emphasis the *BOP* put on outdoor escapades: 'The *BOP* was full of tales of derring-do and encouraged boys both literally and figuratively to expand their horizons by taking up healthy outdoor pursuits, under-taking scientific experiments, and thinking about life and adventure in the further reaches of the Empire.'[1]

Published by the Religious Tract Society, the *Boy's Own Paper* came into existence in 1879, announcing itself to be 'pure and entertaining reading'. It was priced at one penny with the express intention of counteracting the sensationalist 'penny dreadfuls' that were targeted at young people. It soon found room for an article about how to make a boat, appropriately placed immediately after 'How I Swam the Channel' by Captain Webb.[2] The home-made boat could be rowed or paddled. This was the start of a long-lasting *BOP* interest in canoeing. Several issues of the *BOP* in the 1880s contained do-it-yourself articles on making a canoe and another boat.

Also in the 1880s, the *BOP* included an occasional cycling column. Bicycles were continually improving in design. In September 1887 the *BOP* published a comprehensive update on the types of bicycle that were available.[3] The Rev G Herbert informed his readers that the safety bicycle was supplanting the ordinary bicycle (penny-farthing bicycle). Safety bicycles offered the advantage of

> immunity from what are known as 'croppers'. This somewhat vulgar piece of cycling phraseology refers to the throwing of the rider forward over the handles of his bicycle. It is an accident to which a bicyclist is very liable in descending hills, and when meeting an obstacle.[4]

Herbert concluded his article: 'I think my young friends of the B.O.P. will now have some idea of the leading features of the safety machines at present so popular.'

In December 1889 the *BOP* contained an article about Ordnance Survey maps. The magazine told its readers (middle-class boys): 'About half a million are sold every year, and no boy should be contented until he has at least an inch [to the mile] sheet of the neighbourhood in which he lives.'[5]

In June 1890 at Abbotsholme school, 'with the coming of summer new possibilities were explored, such as haymaking, bathing, boating, fishing, and bicycling expeditions'.[6]

The accounts of pupils taking part in school-organised outdoor pursuits in 1900–50 speak mainly of boys rather than girls and often feature a schoolmaster who himself enjoys the outdoor activity. A fair amount of hillwalking and camping and cycling took place, sometimes with a school club or a school scout troop. Rather less school canoeing and dinghy sailing happened; when it did, boys were the main beneficiaries. An indication of the boy-centred influences at work is that Percy Blandford, whose 1950s canoe designs spread throughout the world, learnt much of his canoe handling skills and canoe design knowhow from the *Boy's Own Paper*:

> Like many others I learned much of my early canoeing and boating skill almost literally with the paddle or tiller in one hand and the *B.O.P.* in the other. Much of my earlier training in canoe building came from a long out of print *B.O.P.* book called *Canoes, Dinghies and Sailing Punts*.[7]

Most schools never contemplated introducing their pupils to rock climbing. The instances of pupils rock climbing or mountaineering with their teachers during this period are rare exceptions.

Karl Neumann. In *Abbotsholme 1889–1899* (1900), by Cecil Reddie.

Cecil Reddie, the founder of Abbotsholme school, picnicking with a group in 1893 or slightly earlier. They are below Lion Rock in the lower Churnet valley (now the site of a climb called The Pride).

Boys on the Hills

I have collected some random examples of school pupils camping or hillwalking with their teachers; finding these was relatively easy. Also findable are reports of young people cycle touring, either with their teachers or with the Scouts or on their own initiative. The examples below, ordered chronologically, also include a few mentions of teachers taking their pupils rock climbing; these isolated antecedents were more difficult to find.

19th-century writings include some concerns about the safety of teenage mountaineers. In the late 1860s, the Reverend A G Girdlestone, an allegedly reckless and bumbling alpinist, came under fire from the Alpine Club for sometimes taking boys of sixteen and seventeen on his inept adventures in Switzerland. 'Those who knew him must have expected to read of his death with three or four innocents any time during any season.'[8] F Crawford Grove, a widely experienced climber, raised the matter in the Alpine Club in a paper read in June 1870. Grove's main objective was to save Girdlestone's young companions from sudden death. The Alpine Club concluded that Girdlestone had 'not taken proper precautions, [and] that if his example were generally followed (*i.e.*, such slipshod methods used) the result would be a frightful increase of accidents'.[9]

The overall picture gained from newspaper reports is slanted because news of adventurous pursuits that ended in misadventure or grief invariably reached the newspapers, whereas smooth-running successful days often went unrecorded.

Boys on the Hills, 1900–20

The magazine of Bootham School in York has many accounts of school summer camps under canvas, starting in 1903 (which was four years before Baden-Powell's experimental camp on Brownsea Island). The origins of Bootham School were linked to a Quaker, William Tuke. The philanthropist Joseph Rowntree (senior) was instrumental in the school's foundation and governance. The school valued leisure pursuits and the development of the whole individual.

On the first camp, several pupils and masters and two Bootham old boys took twelve youths 'from a lads' club' in Leeds to the coast near Filey. The days were filled with playing football and cricket on the sands, plunging into the sea, walking along the coast, hunting for mushrooms, fetching water, collecting fire wood and tending the campfire. 'It was perhaps the first healthy sea-side holiday they [the lads from Leeds] had ever had.'[10]

This first camp set a pattern for the following years, the Bootham school camps being run partly as an altruistic service to the community, providing a holiday for city boys. By 1906 the number of campers had risen to twelve from Bootham school and about twenty-two city lads.[11]

At a meeting of the Old York Scholars' Association in 1909, one of the teachers described the Bootham annual camp as 'an important institution, highly educational, as well as highly enjoyable to all who take part. Present boys and masters, to the number of some 16, act as leaders and hosts, at once controlling and entertaining some 30 York boys drawn from the poorest quarters of the City.' When a vote was taken on a motion to spend £20 on camping equipment, 'the proposal received a large measure of support, larger, indeed, than any financial proposal of recent years'.[12]

Boys from Bootham School, York, on a summer camp at Robin Hood's Bay, 1913. Top: general view. Btm: washing up.

Boys from Bootham School getting ready for a swim during
their school camp, 1915.

Another innovator of school camps, concurrently with Bootham
school, was Manchester Grammar School. In 1892 the Student Volunteer Missionary Union had started a movement called the Universities' Camps for Public Schools. The object of the movement was 'the
advancement of Christ's Kingdom among boys, and the promotion
of true and practical Christianity in life at home and at school ... by
the establishment of holiday camps, or other means'.[13] Through this
organisation, a few boys from Manchester Grammar School had taken
part in camping and rambling. In 1904 the idea really caught on when
John Lewis Paton, the high master of the school, organised a school
camp at Alderley Edge in Cheshire. He believed in the physical benefits
of spending a week or two in the open air. Forty-seven boys took part.
This Whitsuntide camp was popular and was followed a few weeks later
by a camp at Grasmere. 'Soon hundreds of boys were in camp every
holiday'.[14] At the Grasmere camp, the main activity became walking;
in 1910, despite over eighty years of railway building and despite the
growing presence of omnibuses and motor cars, for most people human
bipedal locomotion was still a basic human activity, 'that singular system
of movement that amounts to going forward by falling from foot to
foot'.[15] Reflecting on these school camps in July 1924, a correspondent
to the *Manchester Guardian* said: 'Manchester Grammar School can
claim that it has worked out the idea [of school camps] more fully and
more fruitfully than any other school in the country.'[16]

Some validity may have lain behind this claim, yet other people could
reasonably have added other perspectives. In 1913 George Mallory,
another climbing protégé of Geoffrey Young, was a young teacher at
Charterhouse in Surrey. At Easter he took three of the Charterhouse

boys climbing in north Wales.[17] Again at Easter 1920, after the war, he took another group of Charterhouse boys to Pen y Pass. Also he wrote down his ideas about the ideal school of the future. He wanted to reduce the stress laid on the importance of organised games and to extend the encouragement of outdoor pursuits and crafts.[18] About thirty years and one war later, Jack Longland would be saying something similar.

Between 1915 and 1923 (and for some time afterwards) Thomas Cowlishaw, the headmaster of Eccles Secondary School in Manchester, 'organised a good many parties of his senior boys for the purposes of fell-walking and mild rock-climbing. These parties usually went to the Gritstone districts of Derbyshire.'[19]

Rowntree boys at the halfway house while climbing Skiddaw, Cumbria, in 1909. The group numbers about sixty. The boys were thirteen- or fourteen-year-old apprentices of the Rowntree company.

Rowntree boys assemble by their tents near Coniston, Cumbria, summer 1913.

Boys on the Hills, 1920s

In May 1921, fourteen boys from the Leeds Modern School scout troop, under the guidance of two masters, trekked thirty-five miles through the Pyrenees.[20]

In summer 1921, the Duke of York (later King George VI) sponsored a holiday camp for 400 young men aged from seventeen to nineteen. Half of them were industrial workers, selected from employees of member firms of the Industrial Welfare Society. The other half were boys from public schools. Under the heading 'Factory Lads Chum with Public-school Boys', the *Daily Mail* reported that the boys 'sat at luncheon at the Royal Mews, Buckingham Palace … before setting out for a holiday camp at the old Littlestone Aerodrome, near New Romney, Kent, which the Duke has established with the object of bringing together young men of different classes.'[21]

The Duke of York's camp became an annual event that would continue until 1939. The handbook that was presented to each camper contained only one rule, borrowed from public schools, 'play the game'. An unwritten rule stipulated the wearing of shorts and an open-neck shirt. A further unwritten rule applied to speeches given by visiting industrialists and educationists: there was a time limit of three minutes, and if a speaker exceeded that, a pistol was fired to end the speech.[22]

Kurt Hahn regarded the Duke of York's camps as the forerunners to Outward Bound courses.[23]

In April 1924 about thirty Birmingham schoolboys, accompanied by a sixty-year-old teacher, undertook a six-day walking tour across mid-Wales, finishing at Aberystwyth. (You can view a news-clip about this walk on the British Pathé website.[24])

British Pathé. Film 338.11. Still 44.

A group of about thirty Birmingham schoolboys climb a hillside during a six-day walk across Wales to Aberystwyth in 1924. They followed country roads and farmtracks, accompanied by a sixty-year-old teacher.

In August 1924, thirty boys from Manchester Grammar School camped at Voss in Norway and climbed the Lonehorgen, a mountain of 4,670 feet.[25] Three years later another party from this school – thirty-two boys and two masters – went 'on trek' through Norway, their most memorable day being a twenty-two-mile hike to reach and camp at the snowline.[26]

In August 1925, eighteen Scouts and Rover Scouts, mainly from Southall, London, attempted to climb the Breithorn in the Pennine Alps. The party was led by Lieutenant Colonel G S Hutchinson and was accompanied by a photographer and several guides. Most of the party reached a point within 1,500 feet of the summit and then retreated in thickening cloud and a rising wind. 'The storm, which had been slowly gathering, broke a short while afterwards with full force. With a weird high whistle an ice-cold wind struck our faces like a whip, and, as we bent our bodies to escape the full blast, its force seemed to increase, carrying with it a horizontal blast of snow, hail and ice … The guide who was leading us walked almost on all fours.'[27] The party reached the shelter of a hut.

In the same month, ten boys from Fettes College, Edinburgh, and a teacher from the school's modern languages department climbed Mont Blanc. The boys' ages ranged from fifteen and a half to nineteen.[28] This ascent was repeated in 1927 by three boys from Lincoln School, their headmaster and another schoolmaster.[29]

In September 1926, six Scouts from London took the steamer to Dundee and then cycled 300 miles through the Scottish Highlands.[30] In 1931 two secondary school boys from Newport, aged sixteen and eighteen, cycled 1,500 miles through France, Switzerland, Germany and Belgium, a journey that included many hours of riding on cobbles.[31]

Manchester Grammar School Archives

Boys and masters of Manchester Grammar School on a trek in the Savoy Alps in 1928.

A boy or master from Manchester Grammar School bouldering in the Lake District in 1929.

Boys from Manchester Grammar School on Striding Edge, Helvellyn, 1929

Boys on the Hills, 1930s

In July 1930 the *Boy's Own Paper* gave half a page to 'Tips for Ramblers and Climbers'. Arthur Sharp informed his readers that 'the boy or young man who desires to know something of the out-of-the-way places must go on foot … the delights of the stony bypaths, the unmapped sheep-tracks over the wide moors, the heathy ascents of the hills, and the boulder-strewn mountain footways are only for the sturdy walker and the intrepid climber.'[32] On cue, the 1930s editions of Arthur Mee's *Children's Encyclopedia* contained a twelve-page article about the hills of England, focusing mainly on their aesthetic and recreational appeal. The young readers of this article learnt that 'the Earth has no mountains on an equal area excelling [those of the Lake District] in variety and beauty'.[33]

One day in December 1932 a group of ten boys and several masters from Stretford Grammar School, Manchester went for a walk over Kinder Scout. While following the steep track up Jacobs Ladder, 'one of the lads lost his foothold and started to roll down the slope. He collided with two others, and all rolled a considerable distance.' One suffered concussion and was carried down the hill on a gate.[34]

In March 1933 a schoolmaster in Westmorland failed to follow the adage 'the leader must not fall':

Master Saved by Boy
A science master at Windermere Grammar School, Mr. L. W. Brown, had a narrow escape from death while climbing in Lakeland [yesterday]. He owes his life to a 14-year-old pupil at the school, Morris Dixon …
    The two were climbing Dow Crags, Coniston, and were ascending the famous Easter Gully. Mr Brown was leading and Dixon had him belayed with the rope around a rock. When only a few feet from the top of the pitch he was climbing, the master slipped and fell about 40 feet.
    Dixon, taking in the situation at a glance, steeled himself for the jolt, and then for nearly a quarter of an hour held on against the heavy load, until climbers in the next gully came to the rescue.[35]

One weekend in August 1934, a boy in a group from Manchester Grammar School fell while walking down Cader Idris. A farmer and some farmhands rescued him from a precarious position, difficult to reach. According to a newspaper report, the group on the walk comprised about forty pupils and three masters.[36]
    Also in August 1934, a party of boys from Ryhope Secondary School in Sunderland, accompanied by one of the masters, took part in a fortnight's cycling tour in Holland.[37]
    Bentley Beetham, a member of the 1924 Everest expedition, had a long association with Barnard Castle School in County Durham, firstly as a pupil and later as a master. A school rock climbing club was formed in June 1929. In 1930 one of the boys climbed Napes Needle.[38] During the 1930s, Beetham regularly took groups of pupils climbing or bouldering on the gritstone outcrops at Goldsborough, above Baldersdale, to the west of Barnard Castle. The club became known as the Goldsborough Club. In 1936 the Goldsborough Club acquired the lease of a hut near Rosthwaite in the Lake District. A need to avoid the overcrowded established crags led to Beetham and the boys climbing more than fifty new routes in the Borrowdale area.[39] The Goldsborough Club flourished for twenty years until Beetham retired from teaching. None of Beetham's pupils had an accident while rock climbing.[40]

Bentley Beetham and a pupil from Barnard Castle School climbing in Borrowdale in the 1930s.

By the mid-1930s, for over fifty years the *Boy's Own Paper* had been carrying occasional stories or articles about camping, hiking, cycling, canoeing and sailing. It had also provided mountaineering stories but had seldom allocated any space to British rock climbing. The mid-1930s brought a noticeable change. The paper still supplied its readers with stirring tales of gallant endeavour, but with a less colonial flavour than before. Someone decided that it was time to tell boys about British rock climbing. Four full stories or instructional articles about climbing appeared in 1935–8. The coloured cover of the March 1937 issue featured a picture of two boys climbing, with the caption: '"Yo Heave Ho!" See E. P. Olney's grand CRAG-CLIMBING ARTICLE inside'. The florid account, by a writer who called himself 'paterfamilias', was illustrated with three photographs. In April 1938, Sydney Moorhouse titled his article 'Climb, Boys! Climb' and told his readers that 'there is no doubt that climbing is a splendid tonic and a sport that comes within the reach of us all.'[41] In September 1938 Percy Longhurst wrote that 'to learn how to climb one must climb'. He added: 'Climbing is a splendid exercise; it gets one into the open air (where all exercise ought to be taken), and it brings into play far more muscles than the novice is likely to suspect.'[42]

Another juvenile publication, *The Children's Newspaper*, joined the *Boy's Own Paper* by publishing occasional photographs of rock climbers, including one of two boys under instruction in July 1935.[43]

The cover of the annual bound volume of the *Boy's Own Paper* for 1934–5.

R H Evens / Boy's Own Paper.

A drawing from a 1935 *Boy's Own Paper* story about an ascent of Snowdon.

The Children's Newspaper, 27 July 1935.

An illustration from *The Children's Newspaper*, 1935. The original caption was: 'Learning to be cragsmen – these boys of the Lake District are learning to scale crags near Grasmere under the instruction of skilled climbers.'

Cover of the *Boy's Own Paper*, March 1937. E P Olney's
article describes rock climbing on Little Tryfan, 'an excellent
practice ground for initiating a junior party into the use
and misuse of the rope'.

Lynn Cook observed that while many school trips in the 1920s and
30s followed well-worn routes, 'some masters led their charges into
little known places on exploratory and geographical expeditions of
considerable adventure and daring'.[44] The Public Schools' Exploring
Society was founded in 1932. It organised annual ventures to Arctic or
sub-Arctic regions, with the aim of 'allowing young people to manage
real experiences and to learn through doing'.[45]

In summer 1935, in the midst of economic distress and great unemployment, fifty public schoolboys took part in an expedition to Newfoundland. Most were under the age of eighteen. Their object was 'to
explore as much of the little-known interior … as could conveniently
and safely be done in the time at our disposal'. A large area of unmapped
country was traversed for the first time.[46]

In April 1936, sixteen London schoolboys aged from fourteen to seventeen, accompanied by one schoolmaster, were caught in a heavy snowstorm while walking up the Watkin track on Snowdon. 'They hoped to seek shelter in the hotel, but found it closed. To descend by the steep slopes by which they had come was too dangerous, as they had no ropes or ice axes. They were, however, able to reach safety by following the Llanberis Mountain Railway Track, and had to cling to the rails … to prevent being swept off their feet by the wind.' In keeping with the nonjudgmental tendency of those times, *The Times* described the incident as 'a feat of mountaineering'.[47]

One day in July 1936, twenty-one boys and four masters from Wirral Grammar School climbed Scafell in the Lake District. During the walk down, F Allen, the classics master, slipped and fell about thirty feet. His head struck a rock, causing injuries from which he died an hour later. 'The boys, working in relays, carried him on an improvised stretcher to a small farm.'[48]

Manchester Grammar School continued to develop its outdoor programmes. In the mid-1930s a master and four old boys from the school formed a syndicate to buy a barn and campsite at Grasmere. Manchester Grammar School also developed annual treks in Scotland and the Alps, during which the boys carried their tents and equipment. In August 1938 a large party from the school visited the Dauphiné in southeast France. One of them wrote: 'Sixty of us, boys and masters … tramped through some of the finest and wildest mountain scenery in France'. The trip was notable for arduous climbs and magnificent views.[49]

Boys and masters of Manchester Grammar School on a Dolomite summit in 1933.

Manchester Grammar School Archives

Manchester Grammar School Archives

Boys and masters of Manchester Grammar School
on a trek in the Dolomites in 1933.

In summer 1939 a Gordonstoun teacher took ten pupils aged
between fifteen and nineteen on an expedition to Lapland. The group
skied between huts, using sleds (which they hauled) and reindeer to
transport their equipment.[50]

On 4 August 1939, the *Manchester Guardian* carried a sizeable article titled 'Trekking and Camping at Home and Abroad: Lancashire
Schoolboys' Holidays'. Treks, camps, and other organised holidays with
a more or less energetic open-air character, the article said, were 'now
familiar features of extra-curricular life in the larger Lancashire boys'
schools'. The article listed fourteen schools and the outdoor pursuits
planned by each of them. A dozen boys from Oulton High School in
Liverpool were to take part in a 'Senior Hiking Expedition … into the
wilds of Derbyshire'. Twenty boys from Preston Grammar School were
to camp at the old village schoolroom at Nether Wasdale, their base

for climbing and fell-walking. Rossall School had already run end-of-term outings that had included 'the option of climbing the Pillar Rock, Scafell, or Crinkle Crags'.[51]

Richard Leared, a pupil from Abbotsholme school, on the Cork Stone, Stanton Moor, in the Peak District, 1935.

The Cork Stone, Stanton Moor, Peak District.

Camp Schools Act 1939

If you reverse the term 'school camp', the result is 'camp school'. The term 'school camp' usually referred to a group of pupils living in tents erected for a week or two, a transient arrangement, often taking place in the holidays. The term 'camp school' usually meant something more permanent, but the distinction could be fuzzy. Pupils attended camp schools for weeks or for several months or even years. Many camp schools began between the wars. Some used heavy-duty canvas tents and some used huts. Although the aims and curriculums of camp schools varied greatly, the health benefits of the outdoors formed a common theme.

Carlton Camp in north Yorkshire was one example of a camp school. In the late 1920s William Wilson Clark, the headmaster of Ward Jackson Junior School in Hartlepool, began to take children from his school camping in the Cleveland Hills. With several other individuals he formed a charity to raise funds. In October 1931 the trustees bought a field in the village of Carlton-in-Cleveland. All the facilities were under canvas until 1935.[52] This camp school eventually became Carlton Outdoor Education Centre, which still exists today.

Before the Camp Schools Act of 1939, the growth in popularity of school camps and permanent camp schools occurred in an arbitrary and scattered way, often being dependent on the enthusiasm and drive of an individual teacher. Some moral support, if not financial, came from Board of Education pamphlets and teachers' journals, which throughout the 1930s expounded the merits of active participation (rather than those of passive reception, known as chalk and talk) and the benefits to be derived from taking children out of doors.[53]

By 1939 about twenty camp schools existed, many of them aiming to improve children's health by outdoor work and play. The Camp Schools Act of 1939 foresaw the building of fifty more permanent camp schools, which if necessary could be used to house evacuees.

One of the new camp schools was Amber Valley Camp School in Derbyshire, built in 1939 to house 250 children. The huts were set among spacious lawns near the River Amber. In 1940 this camp became home to children evacuated from Derby and Nottingham. (In 1958 the valley was flooded to create Ogston Reservoir. The dining hall of the school camp became the clubhouse for Ogston Sailing Club.)

By 1948, thirty new camp schools had been built under the Camp Schools Act, in the form of Canadian cedar-wood huts sitting on concrete foundations and roofed with wooden shingles.[54] School children occupied these camps for between nine and eleven months of the year. The average number of children at each camp during the year ended 31 March 1948 was 177.[55]

Boys on the Hills, 1940s
In August 1948, pupils of Clapham College, London, climbed in the Lake District with a party of senior boys from various districts in France. It was reported that 'the Clapham College pupils have had considerable summer and winter experience on the Lakeland fells and crags, where they are familiar with leading rock climbs of a severe technical standard'.[56] (One of those pupils, Michael Nichols, informed me that 'the Clapham College climbing club was never the same after the death of a boy who fell and died on Scafell in the late 1950s … it was amazing it started in the first place when you realise that we were a London inner city school 200 miles from the nearest outcrop of

rock, climbing was such a "foreign" sport and transport out was erratic, indirect and expensive.'[57])

In August 1949, Herbert Carr – the headmaster of Harrogate Grammar School and a future president of the Climbers' Club (1954–7) – and his friend D D Payne led a party of twelve teenagers, aged between fifteen and nineteen, over most of the High Level Route between Chamonix and Zermatt. In a letter to the *Times Educational Supplement*, Carr wrote: 'Visits to the High Alps by British boys and girls have been organized both in summer and in winter ever since the pioneer days of mountaineering. References to school parties may be found in the "classic" Alpine literature of the last century …'[58]

No doubt Carr was correct. He acknowledged, though, that taking school pupils to the Alps raised 'critical questions of age, number, ratio of juvenile to adult members, character and length of the expeditions planned, occupation of mountain huts, employment of professional guides, insurance against accident, and so on.'[59]

The final word in this random sample of examples of boys on the hills belongs to Manchester Grammar School. Graham and Phythian, in their 1965 history of the school, write that between 1904 and 1965 'hundreds of masters and thousands of boys … together explored large areas of the British Isles and Europe'.[60]

Boys Underground, 1920–49

Before 1950, very few schools in Britain provided or encouraged the sport of caving, either as part of the curriculum or as an optional extra. However, some of the exceptions – typically independent schools located in caving areas – possessed notably active caving clubs as early as the 1920s. Some of these school caving clubs still exist today.

Some Clifton College boys may have been interested in caving as early as 1913. By then, an old boy of the school, Harry Savory, had become a pioneer of Mendip caving. He was also an accomplished underground photographer. In 1913 he delivered a lecture on caving, illustrated by lantern slides, to Clifton College Scientific Society.[61]

In summer 1923, Cecil Reddie and some Abbotsholme boys escorted fifteen Danish scouts on a tour of the Peak District that included a trip down Speedwell lead mine.[62] Whether this trip was as tourists in the show cave or as independent unguided cavers is not known.

In Yorkshire, the magazine of Sedbergh School for June 1927 described an 'Ingleton expedition' involving eighty pupils and teachers who 'thoroughly explored and photographed' Yordas Cave.[63] A similar trip took place in June 1937. This time twenty-six boys and teachers visited Yordas and 'were thankful for the coolness of the cave'. Two members of the party 'discovered a new way out of the cave by way of a narrow underground tunnel and a long slit in the rock (in many places only nine inches wide) which led upwards to the sunlight above'.[64]

The main forcing ground for schoolboy caving, however, was not Derbyshire or Yorkshire but the West Country. By 1926, Sidcot School, a few miles from Goatchurch Cavern in the Mendips, had a thriving speleological society. A S Griffin, writing in a *Boy's Own Paper* article headed 'A Unique School Club', said: 'There is probably only one school in Great Britain that has a cave-exploring club – in swagger phrase, a speleological society ... To explore [Goatchurch Cavern] and similar caves is the ambition of many of the senior boys of Sidcot School ... Under certain conditions, and subsequent to their parents' consent, some of the seniors are granted "Speleo-Leave".'[65]

For over fifty years, the Sidcot School cavers explored the Somerset caves, recording their findings in about twenty-five logbooks, often without adult input. The logbooks, covering from 1929 to 1978, are available online.[66]

Members of Sidcot School Speleological Society, Somerset, 1937.

Sidcot School, Somerset / MCRA.

Other school caving clubs that were active in the Mendips in the 1930s included those of Wells Cathedral School, Bristol Grammar School and Clifton College.[67]

The Clifton College archives hold a 'Caving Book', a handwritten log of caving trips written from 1938 onwards by boys of South Town (Day Boy House). On the weekend of 25–26 June 1938, for example, a Clifton College party of fifteen (including an ex-headmaster and another adult) camped in the Burrington area 'to explore as fully as possible not only Goatchurch and Sidcot caves, but also the numerous other smaller and lesser known openings'. Their equipment was 'both scarce and comparatively simple'.[68]

Boys from Clifton College were still caving regularly in the late 1940s. On school holidays 'there [was] frequently a small party hitch-hiking to the hills in oldest clothes and nailed boots, with a coil of rope, a bag of candles, and with or without a master'. Caving was considered to be a good sport for the adventurous, demanding skill and endurance.[69]

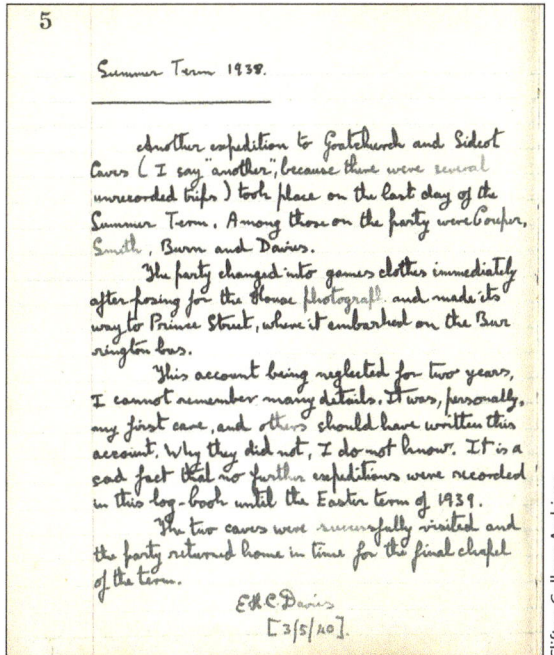

A page from the Clifton College Caving Book. This page records a visit in 1938 to Goatchurch Cavern and Sidcot Swallet, after which 'the party returned home in time for the final chapel of the term'.

In November 1949 the *Times Educational Supplement* published a full-page illustrated account of a trip into GB Cave by boys from Clifton College. The report successfully caught the essence of novice caving trips, including the difference between perceived risk and real risk:

> It is true that rock forms underground in ways of great beauty, takes on grotesque shapes, and pleases the eye with contrasts and subdued colour; but for most cavers, especially boys, the expedition is chiefly an adventure and the rewards are the satisfaction of a difficult task accomplished, the spice of danger which appears convincingly to be much greater than it is, and the lure of penetrating where no man has been before, which even in a cave is seldom the case but [is] always easy to imagine.[70]

A carefully posed photograph of boys on a visit to Bagshawe Cavern, 1936. This cave became a frequent destination for White Hall caving groups in the mid-1950s.

Boys on the Water, 1880–1949

Canoeing and Rowing

In December 1885 the *BOP* published plans for building a canvas-covered wooden-framed canoe.[71] Considerable wood-working skills were required; it seems likely that more boys then had these skills to the required level than would do so now. Subsequent issues of the magazine over many years contained occasional letters about 'the B.O.P. canoe'. One satisfied builder wrote: 'I have made a canoe from the "B.O.P." instructions, and it is a complete success … It is a splendid sea boat, and I have been out in some pretty heavy seas, without being upset once.'[72]

Abbotsholme school, fronting onto nearly a mile of the River Dove, may have been one of the first schools in the UK to use boating and canoeing for educational purposes. In *Abbotsholme* (1900), Reddie mentions that some of the boys' parents had 'lately had sent from Canada several splendid canoes'. The school also had some canoes built by the boys and a homemade rowing punt.[73] Patrick Geddes, while visiting Abbotsholme in 1904, noticed one or two boys repairing and painting the canoes.[74]

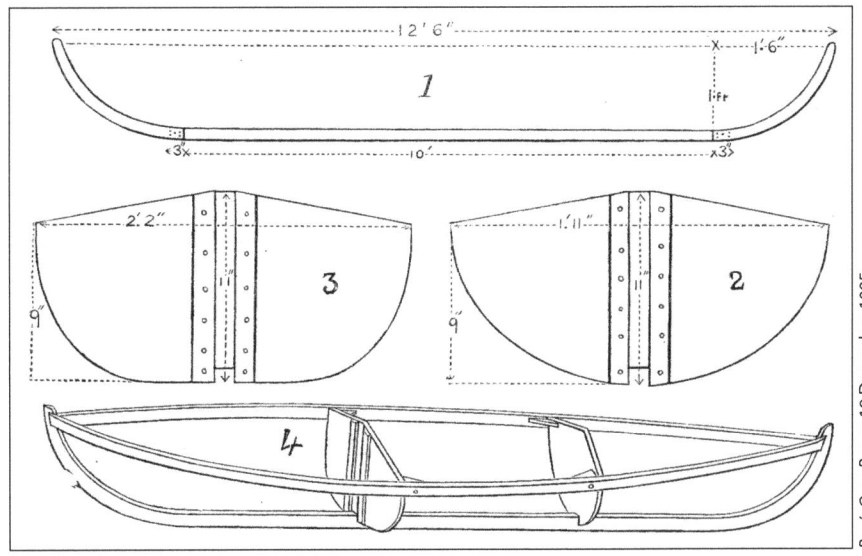

Boy's Own Paper, 19 December 1885.

Illustrations from an 1885 *Boy's Own Paper* article on how to make a canvas-covered wooden-framed canoe.

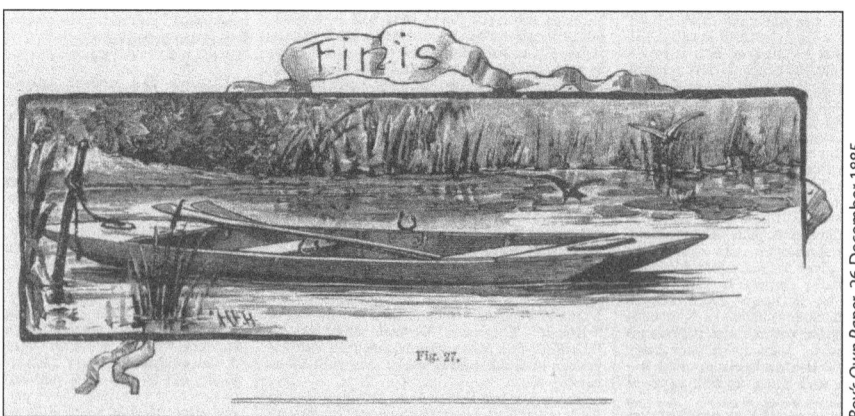

HOW TO MAKE A CANVAS CANOE.

BY E. T. LITTLEWOOD, M.A.,

Peterhouse Boat Club, Cambridge, and Medway Rowing Club.

PART II.

Boy's Own Paper, 26 December 1885.

Fig. 27.

Boy's Own Paper, 26 December 1885.

An illustration of a rowing punt, from an 1891 *Boy's Own Paper* article on how to make a boat.

Karl Neumann. In *Abbotsholme 1889–1899* (1900), by Cecil Reddie.

Abbotsholme boys and their home-made boat on the River Dove, summer 1892. Possibly a rowing punt based (with adaptations) on plans published in three issues of the *Boy's Own Paper* in 1891.

Some boys at Repton school, another Derbyshire public school, were also building canoes at this time. In September 1904 one of them, William Chalmers, having left school to become a naval cadet, used his Repton canoe to paddle with a friend twenty miles down the River Duisk and River Stinchar in south Ayrshire. They passed numerous fishermen, 'who were extremely astonished at the unusual spectacle of a boat on the river'.[75]

The canoe designer Percy Blandford was born in 1912. In 1946 he recalled his youth:

Two of us youngsters built a rigid canvas-covered two-seater canoe, using packing case wood and other second-hand timber for the frame and an old shop blind for the skin. The whole cost was not much over £1. During a summer holiday we sent the canoe, packed with camping kit to Glasbury-on-Wye by goods train. From there we journeyed down the Wye, camping at night and thoroughly enjoying ourselves: most of the time far away from civilisation and in close touch with nature. The rapids on this river are not dangerous, but they gave us plenty of thrills. To negotiate a rapid, with the boiling water surging around you and spray flying over the decks, then to glide into the slack water below, is a thrill which must be experienced to be appreciated.[76]

Some other accounts tell a different tale. If we judge from the newspaper reports, the story of boys' canoeing throughout the first half of the 20th century is one long list of drownings. Some typical headings read: 'Holiday Accidents … Capsized Canoe: Two Boys Drowned Near Dublin' (1913)[77]; 'Hampshire Canoe Accident' (1927)[78]; 'Boys Found Clinging to Canoe: Lake Windermere Rescue' (1930)[79]; 'Bathing and Canoe Tragedies' (1934)[80]; 'Canoe Capsizes: Bridlington Girls Rescued by Boy Scout' (1935)[81]; 'Boy Drowned: Home-made Canoe Tragedy' (1936)[82]; 'Boy Missing in Canoe: Adrift in Mersey' (1938)[83]; 'Mersey Canoe Tragedy: Boy Drowned' (1939)[84]; and 'Richmond A.T.C. Cadet Drowned' (1945)[85].

This alarming picture of the sport of canoeing lacks the many trips that went smoothly. It distorts the true situation. Stories of boys' well-ordered canoeing accomplishments only occasionally reached the newspapers.

Sometimes the accounts featured dramatic adventures with happy endings. In September 1941, five French boys paddled two small Canadian canoes down a river to reach the English Channel on a Tuesday evening. Adverse currents prevented them crossing the Channel that night. For the whole of the next day they were occupied avoiding being seen by German soldiers. On the Wednesday night they headed across the Channel. They landed at Eastbourne on the Thursday morning, three of them having to swim ashore after hitting a rock.[86]

In the five years before White Hall opened, 1945–9, the canoe designer Percy Blandford sold 3,000 plans of rigid canoes, folding canoes, single-seat and double-seat canoes. According to the *Daily Mirror*, Blandford said that for an outlay of £6 10s for materials – and less than two months' hard labour – a man could build a canoe which would take him almost anywhere, provided that he followed the instructions to the last spot of synthetic glue.[87] It is likely that some of the plans that Blandford distributed went not to men but to schoolboys, and it is almost certain that a few of his plans for double-seat canoes reached White Hall soon after it opened.

Mark Goebel / Getty Images.

Sheer fun on 1 January 1933. (Not UK, but does it matter!)

Sailing

Chapter 3, when discussing adult sailing, mentioned that near the end of the 19th century, people began to use smaller and cheaper boats for sport and recreational sailing. This development soon filtered down to bring sailing within reach of some boys. In 1899–1900 the *Boy's Own Paper* carried a three-part article on how to construct a fourteen-foot clinker-built sailing dinghy.[88] The author, D F McLachlan, viewed the growing popularity of sailing dinghies as an important development: 'Of late years, small-boat sailing has secured a great hold among those who take an interest in yachting, and nothing has done more to effect this than the sailing dinghy, besides placing practical yachting within the reach of those whose limited incomes would otherwise have prevented them taking any interest in it.'[89]

D F McLachlan. From *Boy's Own Paper*, 18 November 1899.

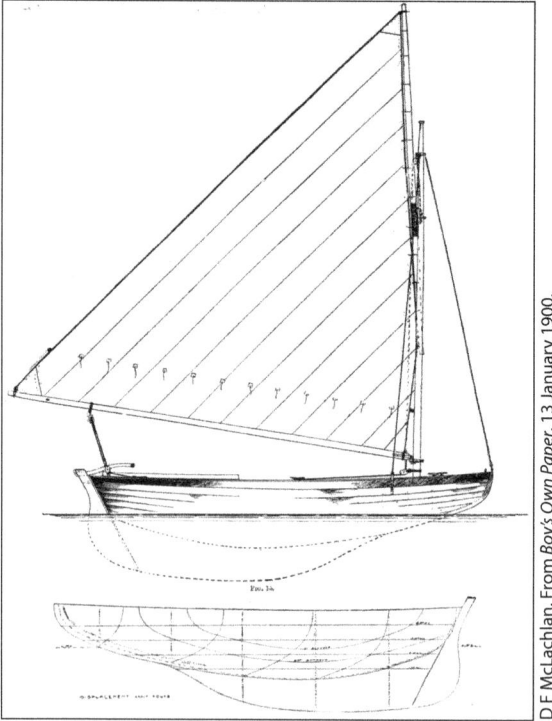

D F McLachlan. From *Boy's Own Paper*, 13 January 1900.

Illustrations from an 1899–1900 *Boy's Own Paper* plan for making a dinghy. This was a far more sophisticated vessel than the *BOP* canoe of 1885 and the *BOP* rowing punt of 1891.

There are occasional accounts of young people in Britain learning to sail in the years between the two world wars. Uffa Fox himself, known to his friends as a bit of a character, featured infamously on one of these occasions, taking ten Sea Scouts across the English Channel in a thirty-foot whaleboat, having led the boys' parents to believe that the group would just be camping in the Solent area. 'He thought it wiser not to let the parents know for they would only worry or perhaps even forbid the voyage.' They set off from the Solent at 7.20pm on Saturday 30 July 1921, without their passports or any ship's paper. Forty hours later, after a combination of rowing (with heavy fifteen-foot oars) and sailing, they entered the harbour at Le Havre. The return journey, a week or two later, was uneventful. There were repercussions when the parents discovered the truth about the boys' summer holiday.[90]

In May 1930, thirty years after its first foray into dinghy design, the *Boy's Own Paper* delivered instructions for building another B.O.P. sailing dinghy, a little craft of ten and a half feet in length, small enough to build in a shed or room.

Photographs of boys taking part in dinghy racing appeared occasionally in *The Children's Newspaper*.[91] On 16 September 1933 this newspaper included a photograph of schoolboys in 14-foot dinghies racing off Southampton, accompanied by an adult 'assistant' in each boat.[92]

The Children's Newspaper, 16 Sept 1933.

Schoolboys in 14-foot dinghies rounding the first buoy during a race off Southampton, September 1933. From *The Children's Newspaper*.

Such examples as this, however, were isolated instances, usually involving a privileged few, as we might deduce from a 1934 newspaper column in *The Times*:

A race open to Public School boys will take place on September 1 off Hythe Pier, Southampton. The race is open to boys on the books of a Public School, and is to be sailed in Royal Southern [Yacht Club] 14ft. dinghies. The boy is to steer, but to carry one skilled yachtsman, who should interfere as little as possible.[93]

One day in August 1934, the *Daily Mail* published a dramatic photograph of two boys taking part in a race for boys under eleven years old at Burnham-on-Crouch.[94]

As well as dinghy sailing, there is another type of sailing that now takes place at some coastal outdoor centres or on ships operated by sail-training organisations: the crewing of traditional types of craft that date from the days of sail and whose designs evolved over centuries of use in essential trading or travel. These boats vary from cutters and sloops to large traditionally rigged sailing vessels, sometimes called tall ships.

The Boy Scouts Association formed a Sea Scouts branch in October 1910. On 4 August 1912 nine Scouts drowned off Leysdown, Kent, as a result of a sudden squall that struck and capsized an ex-naval thirty-foot sailing cutter conveying twenty-three Scouts and five adults to camp. A witness at the inquest said there had been good discipline in the boat and that none of the sails had been made fast. The cutter was in every respect seaworthy. He put down the accident to a big squall striking the boat when it had lost way while changing tack. The jury returned a verdict of 'accidentally drowned'.[95]

Watersports had been the first love of Geoffrey Young, the mountaineer and inspector of schools. In 1912 the Admiralty asked him to inspect the Royal Naval Colleges at Osborne and Dartmouth. The atmosphere of these places impressed him compared to Eton and Harrow. He attributed the vitality and initiative to the adventure of the sea. The visits strengthened his belief in the educational benefits of adventure.[96]

The educational use of boating was further pioneered in Finland and Germany. In 1925 two teachers from Salem took about twenty pupils on a demanding month's expedition sailing four or five open barges, which needed rowing, across the lakes of Finland. Four years later, Spetzgart, a branch of Salem School, began regular sailing and other watersports on the Bodensee (Lake Constance).[97]

In Britain, at Gordonstoun the boys' first voyage of any significance took place in June 1935. The boys took their cutter, the *Mansfield Cum-*

ming, across the Moray Firth to Dornoch.[98] The two Gordonstoun cutters could be sailed or rowed.

Unattributed. From Arnold-Brown, Adam, *Unfolding Character: The Impact of Gordonstoun.*

The Gordonstoun cutter *Mansfield Cumming* entering Hopeman harbour in 1934. On seamanship afternoons, the boys cycled the three miles from the school to the village.

The main vessel at Aberdovey OBSS in 1942 was the *Prince Louis*, a sixty-ton two-masted schooner, crewed by about twelve boys and a captain, a mate, a bosun and an engineer. According to a feature in the *Picture Post*, Lawrence Holt said the sea school's purpose was 'to enable youths that wish to adventure upon the sea to get in the quickest time experience of the physical training and vocational discipline necessary for success'.[99] Other sources have made the point that Holt also believed that training through the sea could benefit people in all walks of life.[100]

In June 1948, fourteen boys from the Dover College sailing club did a double crossing of the English Channel in two whalers. The boats were under the charge of the headmaster and the modern-languages master. They were accompanied by an ex-Brixham trawler that developed a defect and had to return to Dover.[101]

Dinghy sailing in the UK would boom in the 1960s. The subject will reappear in this story when White Hall school groups start sailing, in about 1970.

Dipping-lug sailing cutter sailed by a watch from Aberdovey
Outward Bound Sea School. Date unknown. 1950s or 60s?

Outdoor Girls, 1890–1949

Until the 1880s, most girls' schools avoided physical education because
of the lack of any effective and widely accepted system.[102] In these
circumstances, before the growth of physical training for girls (in the
form of the Swedish Ling system of exercises), it is not surprising that
few girls were introduced to adventurous outdoor pursuits. The *Girl's
Own Paper*, which began in 1880, merely reinforced the status quo.
While the boys were narrowly escaping from pirates or were grappling
with grizzlies, the girls' magazine 'sought to combine spirituality with
domestic advice and to rehearse girls and young women for future
roles as wives and mothers'.[103] The *Girl's Own Paper* directed its readers towards domestic interests such as cooking, embroidery, knitting,
dressmaking and gardening.

In combination, then, the two magazines gave the impression that
adventurous pursuits in the outdoors were for boys only. But motivated
and assertive individuals sometimes ignored this gender-based demar-

cation. In some homes, there was nothing to stop sisters and mothers (or fathers) from reading the weekly boys' newspaper and being inspired by it. In about 1890 a girl in Blackpool built a canoe based on plans published in the *Boy's Own Paper*. In May 1891 her mother, Mrs Reaney, wrote to the newspaper:

> I really feel *tempted* to send you, as a curiosity, a photograph of my daughter, in a canoe made entirely by her own hands after the plan given in the 'B.O.P.' but with improvements suggestive of *sea*-paddling.
>
> She spent many an hour upon the open sea last year in this canoe. The photograph does not do the small craft justice. It is, however, suggestive of what a girl of energy can accomplish. Her workshop was a cellar, and no one saw the boat until it was nearing its later stages of completion. Her tools were very few in number.[104]

Mrs Reaney, in encouraging her energetic daughter to ignore discriminatory social boundaries, was ahead of her time but she was not alone. In June 1894 the *Girl's Own Paper* carried an article titled 'On Recreations for Girls', written by the eminent physician Sir Benjamin Ward Richardson. He wrote that 'within a very short space of time, within my own recollection, certainly, a change has been effected in respect to the cultivation of physical exercise amongst women'.[105] Richardson was careful, however, to remind his readers that women must continue to 'undertake special maternal duties, and that for home to be home they must ... display domestic talents, and do domestic work which comes exclusively under their control.'[106]

Walking earned Richardson's professional approval as a suitable exercise for women, subject to the understanding that 'neither man nor woman is destined to walk more than four miles per hour, and the woman who achieves three and a half miles does well ... The head should be kept erect, but some freedom of motion in the upper limbs should be permitted.'[107]

In 1896 the *Girl's Own Paper* reported cautiously and impartially on the suitability of cycling for young women. While the tricycle was 'obviously a safe and useful machine for the exercise of ladies', the bicycle raised 'as many objections as spokes in its wheels'. The writer, a doctor, recognised the physical benefits of cycling, but when 'consulted by young ladies with their mothers' he dared not propose cycling, as the activity 'was hardly ... within the bounds of propriety'.[108]

In later chapters, much space is given to discussing the idea of character training, and particularly the sort of narrow and conservative character training designed to instil obedient conformity to the values of the trainer. An example from an 1896 *Daily Mail* reveals the extent to which character training was used to reinforce a status quo rather than to subject a social norm to independent critical thought:

> Character Building
> Lady Charlotte
> For character building the foundation stones must, of course, be the principles of religious truth, whilst a voluntary obedience to the law of duty should be the ultimate object of all moral training ... Duty, like charity, begins at home.
> A girl should be taught that her part is to make the sunshine of the home, to bring cheer and joyousness into it. She should especially be led to recognise her obligations to her father, whose love provides for her comfort and happiness, with untiring devotion and unremitting effort.[109]

We shall stick with the *Daily Mail* for a moment, to give it a chance to redeem itself. The *Daily Mail* has always prided itself on its large number of female readers. In January 1907 it asked its readers: what is the best outdoor exercise for women? Three days later it reported on the results. Although the original question was about exercises for women rather than for girls, the activities suggested by readers could equally have suited girls, and so this *Daily Mail* article will serve as a start to a look at girls' participation in outdoor pursuits before 1950.

The newspaper had received many letters, advocating every variety of sport. All sorts of claims had been made. Croquet encouraged companionship and induced a sweet and equable temper. Hunting would keep you free of headaches and rheumatism. Many delicate girls had gained considerably in health by playing hockey. Bicycling was a delightful and health-giving exercise, provided that women stayed in fairly level country. Skipping, women ought to know, was once popular in the Navy. Above all else, one correspondent said, wear a rational system of clothing. But far more letters were received in favour of walking than of any other form of exercise.[110]

The Indoor Girl or the Outdoor Girl—Which?
READERS DECLARE WALKING TO BE THE BEST EXERCISE FOR WOMEN.

What is the real secret of happiness—outdoor exercise or indoor enjoyment, or a combination of both?

THE INDOOR GIRL.

THE OUTDOOR GIRL.

Daily Mail, 2 February 1907.

An illustration from the *Daily Mail*, 2 February 1907. An article a few days earlier had asked readers to respond to the question: 'What is the best outdoor exercise for women?' This drawing accompanied the results of the survey. Far more letters were received in favour of walking than of any other activity.

Climbing did gain a mention, with some ringing assertions to match the claimed benefits of the other sports:

> Sir,– I am emboldened to write and suggest that far too few girls attempt to discover how exhilarating [rock]climbing is … Climbing is very good for the heart and lungs, and excellent for the nerves. It also fosters women's powers of resistance under stress …, makes them resourceful in emergencies and cool in judgment.
> D. MACFARLANE
> Glasgow

Perhaps unintentionally, this letter acknowledged climbing's status as a minority sport for women (as well as for men).

If we were to judge from the *Daily Mail*'s findings, we would expect a search for accounts of girls participating in outdoor pursuits before 1950 to be dominated by rambling or hillwalking. To some extent this expectation would prove correct. But also, another activity would appear: camping.

By 1909, following the success of the Boy Scout movement, many girls were asking to join. Baden-Powell, looking back, wrote: 'Now the girls were coming forward of their own volition to get the same adventure as their brothers. This is the accepted thing in 1932; it was a big innovation in 1909.'[111] The Girl Guides Association was formed in 1910. Baden-Powell agreed to the production of a separate training manual for girls, in association with his sister Agnes. The resulting book, *How Girls Can Help to Build Up the Empire* (1912), disappeared even faster than the Empire. (A more successful manual, *Girl Guiding: A Handbook for Guidelets, Guides, Senior Guides, and Guiders*, would appear in 1918.)

In 1913, Dr Mabel Barker, an unconventional and liberated teacher and outdoor enthusiast, organised a camping trip to Seathwaite in Borrowdale for about twenty-five girls from Saffron Walden College. This was one of the earliest all-girls outdoor-pursuits initiatives.[112]

Despite the war, the Girl Guides movement grew strongly. In April 1919, nearly 900 Cambridgeshire guides attended a rally in Cambridge, described as 'a magnificent success'.[113]

In August 1923 the *Aberdeen Journal* reported that

> there has been this year a remarkable increase in the number of associations devoted to the training and welfare of the young – Boys Brigades, Boy Scouts, and Girl Guides – members of which have been able to spend a week or two under canvas; and there has probably been no previous season in local history when so many of these organisations have succeeded in putting in a week (and in a few cases even a fortnight) in some rural retreat.

The writer estimated that about 3,000 boys and girls had been under canvas in various parts of Aberdeenshire and Kincardineshire during July, 'enjoying the open-air life' and at the same time 'receiving valuable lessons in good citizenship and other manly and womanly virtues'.[114]

In the same month, down in Wales, ten Girl Guides from Staffordshire and Birmingham climbed Cader Idris one night, to see the next morning's sunrise. They reached the summit at 1am in heavy rain and a gale.[115]

An oblique reference to the cultural change under way appeared in the *Daily Express* in July 1927, in a brief item headed 'Women Doing

Less Needlework: Outdoor Pursuits Preferred'. At the annual meeting of shareholders, the chairman of the English Sewing Machine
Company had said: 'Shareholders will not be surprised to hear that
our turnover in the home market shows a slight fall. The habit of art
needlework … still shows a decline. The increased participation of
women in outdoor pursuits and indoor entertainments is no doubt
principally responsible.'[116]

To keep the degree of this progress in perspective, bear in mind that
thousands of London's half a million children had never seen the River
Thames. In 1928, on a school journey, seventeen girls from the top class
of a school in a poor district of London saw the sea for the first time.
Five of them saw a live cow for the first time.[117]

On every year from 1927 to 1935 (except 1928), groups of Chesterfield schoolgirls took part in a summer camp in or close to the Peak
District. Two schools were involved: Grassmoor Central Girls' School
and North Wingfield Girls' School. The campsites used were Grove
Farm, Old Brampton (1927); Hope (1929); Hopping Farm, Youlgreave
(1930); Lea Hill Farm, near Lea (1931); unknown (1932); Bradbourne
Mill, Bradbourne (1933); Rowsley, near Bakewell (1934); Hartington
Hall (1935) and Roston (1935). Photograph albums, exercise books
and newspaper clippings from these camps, donated by J R Cresswell,
the honorary secretary of the Derbyshire branch of the School Journey
Association, are held at the National Trust Museum of Childhood.

Girls from North Wingfield Girls' School (near Chesterfield), camping at
Lea Hill Farm, near Lea, Derbyshire, 1931.

National Trust Museum of Childhood 995752.

Girls from North Wingfield Girls' School (near Chesterfield), camping at Lea Hill Farm, near Lea, Derbyshire,
1931.

National Trust Museum of Childhood 671385.

Girls from Grassmoor Central Girls' School, Alfreton, on a walk during
a camp near Rowsley, Derbyshire, 1934.

Ward / Getty Images.

Twelve-year-old Irene Jackson of Barrow-in-Furness on Dow Crag in the
Lake District, 7 April1933. Prewar photographs of young people climbing
are rare.

In May 1934 a *Daily Mirror* article promoting the Girl Guides
movement spoke of clean air, simple food and laughter, and of 'all the
excitement of pitching tents, getting fires lighted, and the reward of
sitting down to one's meal with a well-whetted appetite'.[118]

Also in 1934, Stanley Watson, a key figure in the popularising of
rock climbing in the 1930s, made *High Hazard*, a film about climbing
in the Lake District. This film included footage of nine-year-old Vivian Verity climbing Napes Needle.[119] (W G Milligan, the president
of the Fell and Rock Climbing Club, disapproved: 'As a club, we are
opposed to the making of films of this kind. We dislike the publicity

which they attract, and … we deplore the exploitation of the sport for money-making purposes.'[120])

Nine-year-old Vivian Verity climbing Napes Needle in 1934, from Stanley Watson's film *High Hazard*.

Merlyn Severn / Getty Images.

Abseiling at Harrisons Rocks, Kent. Published as part of a double-page spread on rock climbing in the *Picture Post*, 17 August 1946. In 1948 the average weekly sales of the *Picture Post* were 1,229,788.

A girl (centre) climbing at Creag a' Chalamain
Gap during a Glenmore Lodge course in July
1949.

I will finish this section by returning to the main pre-1950 progressive schools and outdoor centres. Which took girls as well as boys?
Abbotsholme had been a boys' school since its founding in 1889; Cecil
Reddie was 'always unalterably opposed to co-education'.[121] (Abbotsholme would become coeducational in 1969). Salem was coeducational
from its beginning. Gordonstoun was for boys only (it would become
coeducational in 1972). The Gordonstoun badge scheme was for boys
only. Apparently Kurt Hahn wanted to avoid being labelled 'progressive',[122] but in the avoidance, in the opinion of one critic, he 'rendered
women invisible'.[123] However, Hahn did at one point contemplate
opening a house near Gordonstoun and using it for short courses for
girls. The derivatives of the Gordonstoun badge scheme – the Moray
badge, the County badge, and the Duke of Edinburgh's Award – were
for all young people.

Aberdovey OBSS was for boys only, although Jim Hogan 'twice
arranged rather limited courses for girls [in the early 1940s]. These
two courses were organised in conjunction with the Sea Ranger branch
of the Girl Guides Association.' Hogan met some resistance from his

naval officers: 'The seamen viewed the whole undertaking as amusing or irresponsible. The captain refused to take the girls to sea on the grounds that they would be incapable of handling sail and in indifferent weather would constitute a serious liability.'[124]

As things turned out, the girls caused these words to be swallowed. The captain grudgingly agreed to give the girls a full day at sea in the ketch. He returned enthusiastic about their performance. However, Rhowniar, the first Outward Bound school for girls, would not be opened until July 1963. Two years later, while chairing a discussion panel at an Outward Bound conference, Jack Longland, who valued the qualities of coeducational courses, would raise one of the main differences between Outward Bound schools and LEA residential outdoor centres, asking: 'Why does Outward Bound separate the sexes? Outward Bound is unusual in doing so.'[125]

Glenmore Lodge, which opened in summer 1948, took boys or girls or mixed groups from the beginning. The CCPR administered Glenmore Lodge on behalf of the Scottish Education Department.[126] In February–March 1950, forty schoolgirls from Glasgow secondary schools attended 'a month's course of character building' at Glenmore Lodge. The outdoor activities included skiing, climbing, map-reading and surveying. Indoor lessons covered basketwork, knitting and cookery.[127] A similar course took place in March 1951. Photographs from this course appeared in the *Times Educational Supplement* under the heading 'A Commando Course for Girls'.[128]

Chapter 7 will look at some 1950s statements on the purpose of White Hall. Several of them declared clearly that White Hall would be for girls as well as boys. Two pieces of evidence showing that mixed groups quickly became the norm are a TV film from 1957 and a TV news-clip from 1958.[129]

Notes

1   Alison Enever, 'Boys Should Be Boys and Girls Should Be Wives: The Construction of a Gendered Identity in the "Boy's Own Paper" and "Girl's Own Paper"', *Emergence: University of Southampton Humanities Graduate School Research Journal*, 4 (Autumn 2012), pp. 32–36.

2   James Macaulay, ed., 'My Boat, and How I Made It', *Boy's Own Paper*, 1 Feb 1879.

3   G Herbert, Rev, 'Safety Bicycles', in *The Boy's Own Annual: 1886–1887* (London: Boy's Own Paper Office, 1887), pp. 508–510, 524.

4   Ibid., p. 508.

5   G A Hutchison, ed., 'Ordnance Maps, and How They Are Made', in *The Boy's Own Annual: 1889–1890* (London: Boy's Own Paper Office, 1890), vol. 12, pp. 203–204.

6   B M Ward, *Reddie of Abbotsholme* (London: George Allen and Unwin, 1934), p. 64.

7   Percy W Blandford, *Canoes and Canoeing* (London: Lutterworth Press, 1962), p. 9.

8   R S T Chorley, 'Some Mountaineering Controversies', *Fell and Rock Journal,* 8, no. 3 (1930), pp. 293–303 (p. 300).

9   Quoted in ibid. (p. 301).

10   F Sturge, 'A Few Days under Canvas', *Bootham: The Magazine of Bootham School, York,* 1, no. 5 (Oct 1903), pp. 418–420.

11   F H Knight, 'Bootham School Camp, 1906', *Bootham: The Magazine of Bootham School, York,* 3, no. 2 (Sept 1906), pp. 159–160.

12   R O Mennell, 'O.Y.S.A. Business Meeting', *Bootham: The Magazine of Bootham School, York,* 4, no. 5 (Oct 1909), pp. 325–330.

13   Special Collections Department of the University of Birmingham, 'Records of the Student Christian Movement' (Aug 2011) <http://calmview.bham.ac.uk/GetDocument.ashx?db=Catalog&fname=Student+Christian+Movement+1.pdf> [accessed 26 Aug 2015].

14   J A Graham and B A Phythian, *The Manchester Grammar School, 1515–1965* (Manchester: University of Manchester, 1965), pp. 100, 146–148.

15   Joseph A Amato, *On Foot: A History of Walking* (New York: New York University Press, 2004), p. 5.

16   'The Grammar School Camps and Treks', *Manchester Guardian,* 31 July 1924, p. 11.

17   Dudley Green, *Because It's There: The Life of George Mallory* (Stroud, UK: Tempus Publishing, 2005), p. 63.

18   Ibid., 82–83.

19   Arthur Chambers, 'T I Cowlishaw', *Fell and Rock Journal,* 15, no. 1 (1947), p. 95.

20   'English Boy Scouts in the Pyrenees', *Manchester Guardian,* 26 May 1921, p. 4.

21   '"All-sorts" Camp', *Daily Mail,* 1 Aug 1921, p. 8.

22   'Young Guests of the King', *The Times,* 28 July 1938, p. 11.

23   David Hopkins and Roger Putnam, *Personal Growth through Adventure* (London: David Fulton Publishers, 1993), p. 26.

24   'A Healthy Holiday 1924', British Pathé (no date) <http://www.britishpathe.com/video/a-healthy-holiday-1/query/33811> [accessed 27 Nov 2015].

25   'Grammar School Boys in Norway', *Manchester Guardian,* 29 Aug 1924, p. 9.

26   'Grammar School Boys in Norway', *Manchester Guardian,* 19 Aug 1927, p. 11.

27   'London Scouts' Alpine Experience', *Manchester Guardian,* 15 Aug 1925, p. 14. Also *British Boy Scouts 1925*. British Pathé archive film ID 418.07 [News-clip]. British Pathé. 1925.

28   'Scottish Schoolboys Scale Mont Blanc', *The Courier and Argus [Dundee],* 18 Aug 1925, p. 7.

29   C E Young, 'Mountaineering Trials and Thrills', *Lincolnshire Echo,* 19 Dec 1931, p. 3.

30   '300 Miles Cycle Tour', *Courier and Advertiser [Dundee]*, 9 Sept 1926, p. 4.

31   'Island Schoolboys' Tour', *Portsmouth Evening News*, 4 Sept 1931, p. 9.

32   Arthur Sharp, 'Tips for Ramblers and Climbers', in *The Boy's Own Annual: 1929–1930* (London: Boy's Own Paper Office, 1930), vol. 52, p. 719.

33   [Anon.], 'Our Great and Little Hills', in *The Children's Encyclopedia*, ed. by Arthur Mee, 10 vols (London: Educational Book Company, 1930s), vol. 1, pp. 461–473 (p. 463).

34   'Kinder Scout Mystery', *Nottingham Evening Post*, 23 Dec 1932, p. 12.

35   'Master Saved by Boy', *Yorkshire Evening Post*, 14 Mar 1933, p. 11.

36   'Fell over Precipice', *Citizen [Gloucester]*, 7 Aug 1934, p. 5.

37   'Cycling in Holland', *Sunderland Daily Echo*, 2 Aug 1934, p. 11.

38   Michael D Lowes, *Lure of the Mountains: The Life of Bentley Beetham 1924 Everest Expedition Mountaineer* (Sheffield: Vertebrate Publishing, 2014), pp. 119–120.

39   Bentley Beetham, 'An Interim Report from Borrowdale', *Fell and Rock Journal*, 14, no. 3 (1946), pp. 179–194 (p. 179).

40   Michael D Lowes, *Lure of the Mountains: The Life of Bentley Beetham 1924 Everest Expedition Mountaineer* (Sheffield: Vertebrate Publishing, 2014), p. 139.

41   Sydney Moorhouse, 'Climb, Boys! Climb', in *The Boy's Own Annual: 1937–1938* (London: Boy's Own Paper Office, 1938), vol. 60, p. 337.

42   Percy Longhurst, 'The Way to Fitness: Climbing', in *The Boy's Own Annual: 1937–1938* (London: Boy's Own Paper Office, 1938), vol. 60, p. 612.

43   'A Daring Rock Climb [Picture]', *Children's Newspaper*, 24 Nov 1934, p. 3. 'Young Cragsmen [Picture]', *Children's Newspaper*, 27 July 1935, p. 3. 'Rock Climbers [Picture]', *Children's Newspaper*, 17 June 1939, p. 3. ·

44   Lynn Cook, 'Outdoor Education: Its Origins and Institutionalisation in Schools with Particular Reference to the West Riding of Yorkshire Since 1945' (PhD thesis, University of Leeds, 2000), p. 61.

45   Quoted in ibid., p. 61.

46   Philip Stockil, 'Schoolboys in Newfoundland', *Yorkshire Post and Leeds Intelligencer*, 8 Jan 1936, p. 6.

47   'Schoolboys in Snowstorm on Snowdon', *The Times*, 22 Apr 1936, p. 16.

48   'Schoolmaster Killed in Lakeland', *Courier and Advertiser [Dundee]*, 31 July 1936, p. 3.

49   'Manchester Grammar School Holiday Treks', *Manchester Guardian*, 22 Aug 1938, p. 11.

50   Nick Veevers and Pete Allison, *Kurt Hahn: Inspirational, Visionary, Outdoor and Experiential Educator* (Rotterdam: Sense Publishers, 2011), p. 23.

51   'Trekking and Camping at Home and Abroad', *Manchester Guardian*, 4 Aug 1939, p. 6.

52   Carlton Outdoor Education Centre, 'History of Carlton Outdoor Education Centre' (no date) <http://www.carltonoutdoors.org/carlton_history.php> [accessed 14 Feb 2015].

53   G A N Lowndes, *The Silent Social Revolution*, 2nd edn (London: Oxford University Press, 1969), pp. 132–133, 137–140.

54   Lynn Cook, 'Outdoor Education: Its Origins and Institutionalisation in Schools with Particular Reference to the West Riding of Yorkshire Since 1945' (PhD thesis, University of Leeds, 2000), pp. 109–113.

55   'Thirty School Camps in Use', *Times Educational Supplement,* 10 July 1948, p. 392.

56   'Young Mountaineers', *Times Educational Supplement,* 5 June 1948.

57   Michael Nichols, Email to P McDonald, subject 'Climbing Details', 10 Dec 2014 [Email].

58   'Schoolboys in the High Alps', *Times Educational Supplement,* 23 Sept 1949, p. 655.

59   Ibid.

60   J A Graham and B A Phythian, *The Manchester Grammar School, 1515–1965* (Manchester: University of Manchester, 1965), p. 146.

61   Harry Savory, *A Man Deep in Mendip: The Caving Diaries of Harry Savory 1910–1921* (Gloucester: Alan Sutton, 1989), p. 63.

62   B M Ward, *Reddie of Abbotsholme* (London: George Allen and Unwin, 1934), p. 109.

63   'Sedgwick Society', *The Sedberghian,* June 1927, pp. 100–101.

64   'Sedgwick Society', *The Sedberghian,* July 1937, pp. 134–135.

65   A Sercombe Griffin, 'A Unique School Club: Sidcot's Speleological Society', in *The Boy's Own Annual: 1926–1927* (London: Boy's Own Paper Office, 1927), vol. 49, pp. 53–54.

66   'MCRA Logbooks: Sidcot School SS 1929-1978', Mendip Cave Registry and Archive (no date) <http://www.mcra.org.uk/logbooks/?dir=SSSS> [accessed 7 Oct 2015].

67   Peter Johnson, *The History of Mendip Caving* (Newton Abbot, Devon: David & Charles, 1967), p. 44.

68   Clifton College Archives (Bristol), Caving Book for South Town (Day Boy House) covering 1938–1950s, p. 6.

69   'Down a Mendip Cave', *Times Educational Supplement,* 25 Nov 1949, p. 822.

70   Ibid.

71   E T Littlewood, 'How to Make a Canvas Canoe', in *The Boy's Own Annual: 1885–1886* (London: Boy's Own Paper Office, 1886), vol. 8, pp. 185–186, 201.

72   A Benyon, 'The "B.O.P." Canoe', *Boy's Own Paper,* 19 Sept 1891.

73   Cecil Reddie, *Abbotsholme 1889–1899* (London: George Allen, 1900), p. 302.

74   Patrick Geddes, 'The School at Abbotsholme, Conducted by Dr. Cecil Reddie', *The Elementary School Teacher,* 5, no. 6 (Feb 1905), pp. 321–333, 396–407 (p. 329).

75   'Daring Boy Navigators', *Manchester Guardian,* 7 Sept 1904, p. 10.

76   Percy W Blandford, *Canoeing To-day: A Fascinating Pastime Fully Explained* (London: Vawser & Wiles, 1946), p. 3.

77   'Holiday Accidents', *Manchester Guardian,* 25 Mar 1913, p. 12.

78   'Survivor's Evidence Rejected by Coroner: Hampshire Canoe Accident', *Manchester Guardian,* 24 Dec 1927, p. 5.

79   'Boys Found Clinging to Canoe', *Manchester Guardian,* 14 Apr 1930, p. 12.

80   'Bathing and Canoe Tragedies', *Yorkshire Post,* 23 July 1934, p. 9.

81 'Canoe Capsizes', *Manchester Guardian,* 6 July 1935, p. 18.

82 'Boy Drowned', *Manchester Guardian,* 7 Sept 1936, p. 16.

83 'Boy Missing in Canoe', *Manchester Guardian,* 28 Dec 1938, p. 9.

84 'Mersey Canoe Tragedy', *Manchester Guardian,* 20 Apr 1939, p. 15.

85 'Richmond A.T.C. Cadet Drowned', *Yorkshire Post,* 14 Aug 1945, p. 3.

86 'French Boys Canoe Over Channel', *Manchester Guardian,* 19 Sept 1941, p. 6.

87 '3,000 New Canoes Launched – Thanks to Mr. Blandford', *Daily Mirror,* 29 Dec 1950, p. 8.

88 D F McLachlan, 'A Sailing Dinghy and How to Build It', in *The Boy's Own Annual: 1899–1900* (London: Boy's Own Paper Office, 1900), vol. 22, pp. 108–110, 205–206, 236–238.

89 D F McLachlan, 'A Sailing Dinghy and How to Build It', *Boy's Own Paper,* 18 Nov 1899.

90 June Dixon, *Uffa Fox: A Personal Biography* (Brighton: Angus and Robertson, 1978), pp. 36–40.

91 'White Wings on the Thames [Picture]', *The Children's Newspaper,* 24 May 1930, p. 9. 'Sailing and Bailing [Picture]', *The Children's Newspaper,* 23 June 1934, p. 9.

92 'Boy Yachtsmen [Picture]', *The Children's Newspaper,* 16 Sept 1933, p. 3.

93 'Dinghy Sailing', *The Times,* 13 July 1934, p. 5.

94 'Schoolboy Yachtsmen [Picture]', *Daily Mail,* 17 Aug 1934.

95 'The Leysdown Disaster', *The Times,* 8 Aug 2012, p. 8.

96 Alan Hankinson, *Geoffrey Winthrop Young: Poet, Educator, Mountaineer* (London: Hodder and Stoughton, 1995), p. 131.

97 Nick Veevers and Pete Allison, *Kurt Hahn: Inspirational, Visionary, Outdoor and Experiential Educator* (Rotterdam: Sense Publishers, 2011), pp. 10–12, 97–98.

98 Adam Arnold-Brown, *Unfolding Character: The Impact of Gordonstoun* (London: Routledge and Kegan Paul, 1962), pp. 29–30. Some sources say that both cutters made the journey, accompanied by a yacht belonging to a group of teachers.

99 'Schoolboys Handle Their Own Schooner', *Picture Post,* 1 Aug 1942, pp. 11–13. Some sources say 100-ton.

100 Nick Veevers and Pete Allison, *Kurt Hahn: Inspirational, Visionary, Outdoor and Experiential Educator* (Rotterdam: Sense Publishers, 2011), pp. 55–56.

101 'Dover College's "Expeditions"', *Dover Express,* 25 June 1948, p. 7.

102 Ken C Ogilvie, *Roots and Wings: A History of Outdoor Education and Outdoor Learning in the UK* (Lyme Regis, UK: Russell House Publishing, 2013), p. 165.

103 Alison Enever, 'Boys Should Be Boys and Girls Should Be Wives: The Construction of a Gendered Identity in the "Boy's Own Paper" and "Girl's Own Paper"', *Emergence: University of Southampton Humanities Graduate School Research Journal,* 4 (Autumn 2012), pp. 32–36 (p. 32).

104 Mrs Reaney, 'A "B.O.P." Canoe', *Boy's Own Paper,* 30 May 1891.

105 Benjamin W Richardson, 'On Recreations for Girls', in *The Girl's Own Annual: 1893–1894* (London: Girl's Own Paper Office, 1894), vol. 15, pp. 545–547 (p. 545).

106 Ibid. (p. 546).

107 Ibid. (p. 546).

108 A T Schofield, 'The Cycling Craze', in *The Girl's Own Annual: 1895–1896* (London: Girl's Own Paper Office, 1896), vol. 17, pp. 185–186 (p. 185).

109 Lady Charlotte, 'Character Building', *Daily Mail*, 28 May 1896, p. 7.

110 'The Indoor Girl or the Outdoor Girl – Which?', *Daily Mail*, 2 Feb 1907, p. 9.

111 'Girl Guides', *The Times*, 21 May 1932, p. 11.

112 Ken C Ogilvie, *Roots and Wings: A History of Outdoor Education and Outdoor Learning in the UK* (Lyme Regis, UK: Russell House Publishing, 2013), p. 222.

113 'Girl Guides' Rally', *Cambridge Independent Press*, 11 Apr 1919, p. 6.

114 'July Camping', *Aberdeen Journal*, 2 Aug 1923, p. 5.

115 'Caught in Mountain Gale', *Aberdeen Journal*, 16 Aug 1923, p. 2.

116 'Women Doing Less Needlework: Outdoor Pursuits Preferred', *Daily Express*, 21 July 1927, p. 9.

117 G A N Lowndes, *The Silent Social Revolution*, 2nd edn (London: Oxford University Press, 1969), p. 137.

118 Pauline Patterson, 'Girl Guides and the Open-air Life', *Daily Mirror*, 5 May 1934, p. 25.

119 Mountain Heritage Trust, Penrith, Papers of Stanley Watson c.1920–2012, Ref. no. GB 3075 STW.

120 'Camera-man in Rope Cradle', *Manchester Guardian*, 14 Mar 1934, p. 10.

121 B M Ward, *Reddie of Abbotsholme* (London: George Allen and Unwin, 1934), p. 71.

122 Alan Hankinson, *Geoffrey Winthrop Young: Poet, Educator, Mountaineer* (London: Hodder and Stoughton, 1995), p. 283.

123 Quoted in Lynn Cook, 'Outdoor Education: Its Origins and Institutionalisation in Schools with Particular Reference to the West Riding of Yorkshire Since 1945' (PhD thesis, University of Leeds, 2000), p. 33.

124 James Martin Hogan, *Impelled into Experiences: The Story of the Outward Bound Schools* (Wakefield, UK: Educational Productions, 1968), pp. 90–91.

125 British Library, Question Time, in Outward Bound in the 60s and 70s: A Report on the Conference Held at Harrogate on May 8th and 9th 1965; UIN: BLL010114322536, pp. 4–6.

126 Catharine M Loader, *Cairngorm Adventure at Glenmore Lodge: Scottish Centre of Outdoor Training* (Edinburgh: W Brown, 1952), pp. 14, 34–38 & Plates 29–35.

127 'Schooling on the Hills', *Courier and Advertiser [Dundee]*, 3 Mar 1950, p. 5.

128 'A "Commando" Course for Girls', *Times Educational Supplement*, 6 Apr 1951, p. 261.

129 *Climbing*. Dir. Stanley Williamson. British Film Institute ref. no. N-117606 [Television]. BBC. 1957. Also *Midlands News: 21.11.1958: Duke of Edinburgh Visits Derbyshire*. Media Archive for Central England story no. 1525 [Television]. ATV. 1958.

5. Outdoor Recreation in 1940s Derbyshire

Although the last three chapters have looked at the hill and water sports up until 1949, they have only skimmed lightly over the last decade, 1939–49. This chapter will examine more closely the war years and the immediate postwar years, and in particular in Derbyshire.

Writers on the origins of outdoor education in the UK often single out Jack Longland as having been the driving force behind the establishing of White Hall Centre. There are sound reasons for this. Certainly in 1949–50, the two years before White Hall opened, he instigated the development with determination and conviction.

A less known facet of the origins of White Hall is the wartime and immediate postwar contribution of the Derbyshire county council youth service, between 1943 and 1948, before Longland arrived on the scene. But before we focus on the youth service, we can add some background by asking the question: did Derbyshire's young people take part in *any* outdoor recreation during the war?

Outdoor Recreation in Wartime Derbyshire

On 13 May 1940, Winston Churchill told parliament that he had 'nothing to offer but blood, toil, tears and sweat'. In *War Memories of a Teenager Living in Buxton*, an account written in the 1990s, Rosemary Clements recalled the summer and autumn of 1940, when wave after wave of German bombers droned over the Peak District at night, on their way to Manchester and Liverpool. (In Chorlton-on-Medlock in Manchester, a ten-year-old Joseph Brown used to cower under the dining table, listening to the sirens, the bangs and crashes.[1]) Describing the following year, 1941, she wrote:

> The war now settled down into an ongoing thing you had to live with. Once the evenings began to lengthen and the daylight hours increased, the bombing became less acute. In the summer Hitler

unexpectedly attacked Russia and the acute anxiety of standing alone against the enemy lessened. Gas masks were left at home, the siren ceased to sound (at least in our area) and we all carried on living our own lives as best we could.[2]

Throughout 1941, the outcome of the war was still uncertain. Despite the suspense, some Derbyshire youth clubs and other bodies managed to organise outdoor activities for young people. On 28–29 June 1941, led by Mr W E Hallam, a party of boys of Staveley Youth Club spent the week-end in camp in the Peak district. Sunday included rock climbing under the leadership of Mr Williams. According to the press report, these camps were open every weekend and there was no charge.[3]

In August–September 1941, Mr F Beeston, a probation officer for the Chesterfield county police division, took a dozen boys for a week's camping holiday at Leam Hall Hostel, Grindleford. The holiday was spent tramping on the moors, rock climbing and visiting Derbyshire beauty spots.[4]

Further afield, the wartime state of suspense did not prevent Kurt Hahn, James Hogan and Lawrence Holt – encouraged by Geoffrey Young – from conceiving and creating Aberdovey OBSS, whose first course began on 14 October 1941. The course consisted of eight boys from the Blue Funnel Line who stayed the full four weeks and eight each from HMS *Conway* sea-training school and Gordonstoun who changed over each Saturday. The school was staffed mainly by officers seconded from the ships of the Blue Funnel Line and paid by Alfred Holt and Company.[5] Lawrence Holt was a great believer in the virtue of sail-training. (The Outward Bound Trust had not yet been formed.) A year later, after twelve courses, Herbert W Richmond – admiral, educationist and master of Downing College, Cambridge – inspected the school and was particularly 'attracted by the training under sail, which engenders the qualities of initiative, resource, patience, and vigilance as vital as ever to the sailor of to-day yet more difficult for him to acquire in the modern man-of-war'.[6]

In October–November 1942 the Western Allies won the decisive second battle of El Alamein. For Rosemary Clements in Buxton, 'the atmosphere of the war seemed to change … from then on we began to look forward'.

It was about this time that Joseph Brown in Manchester, now twelve years old and already keen on the outdoors, joined his local Scout troop, only to be expelled a couple of months later for refusing to go on a church parade.[7] (Another Manchester lad, Donald Whillans, two years younger than Brown, joined the Scouts in 1945 and was more compliant than Brown, lasting for four years and thriving on the Peak District camping and walking.[8])

In 1943 Rosemary went on Youth Hostel holidays in the Lake District and Wales. These were probably walking holidays, as hostellers had to travel on foot or by bicycle or by canoe. Motorists were not allowed to use youth hostels. In seeking outdoor recreation, two years before the end of the war in Europe, Rosemary was not alone. Life all over Britain was beginning to inch back towards normality. Membership of the Cyclists' Touring Club, for example, revived in 1943 after two years of major decline, and would continue to increase each year until 1950.[9]

In August 1943, still ten months before the D-Day landings in Normandy, Derbyshire Education Committee ran or jointly ran several youth-leader courses that appear to have included cycling and walking in the Peak District.[10] In June 1944, less than two weeks after D-Day, the *Picture Post* featured an account of a recent BCU weekend meet at Newport Pagnell, during which sixteen kayakers toured for thirty miles along the River Ouzel.[11]

Youth Service Proposal, 1944

In August 1942 the president of the Board of Education had set up the Youth Advisory Council to advise him on questions relating to the youth service in England. In August 1943 this council completed its report, *The Youth Service after the War*.

One of several general points made in this report was that young people were not all alike. There were wide differences of temperament and interest in young people between the ages of fourteen and eighteen (which was the age range relevant to the youth service). For these years, the report argued, the widest possible variety of opportunities should be provided:

> There will always be some boys and girls who prefer a uniformed Corps to any other form of youth activity; there will always be some who would rather belong to an Old Scholars' Association than to anything else; there will be some who wish to spend their evenings in further education, in the more formal sense; there will be some who will want the companionship of a mixed Club … There are, further, some boys and girls, by no means the least interesting and valuable, who are not by temperament

attracted to communal activities, who find the life of a club or any other organised body of their contemporaries overwhelming and uncongenial ... There are others who are much more attracted by out-door forms of collective activity than by clubs or other in-door meetings. They prefer cycling, walking and camping. And they may well prefer to follow these pursuits outside any organisation. If they choose to spend their leisure alone or in the company of a few friends, rather than in any organised collective activity, we can see no reason why they should not be helped to do so. This would mean the encouragement of such associations as cycling clubs and holiday fellowships, the provision of camping sites, and of instruction and opportunity for those young people who wanted, for instance, to become mountain climbers. We mention these especially because their interests are apt to be overlooked in concentration upon bigger and more organised groups.[12]

The members of Derbyshire's youth service committee studied this report.[13] They may also have looked at the 1943 Norwood Report, *The Curriculum and Examinations in Secondary Schools*, which saw a place for the outdoors in education but with a character-training focus similar to that of Aberdovey OBSS: 'It is essential to bring boys and girls in touch with sea and mountain, and in open-air tasks and ventures to build up the moral strength and create the physical endurance that come from such contact ... Experience of war has shown that young people can respond to situations demanding courage and endurance.'[14]

With hindsight and lessons from the second half of the 20th century, many people would probably now keep their distance from the last two sentences. Interpretations of 'moral strength' might stretch all the way from the qualities and beliefs that underlie hierarchical naval discipline to those that precipitate conscientious objection to armed conflict. The response to situations demanding courage and endurance but also involving group dynamics is not always an onset of admirable behaviour. Even when it is, that behaviour might not transfer to other parts of a person's life.

During the year 1943–4, nearly seven years before White Hall Centre opened, Derbyshire's education committee accepted in principle a recommendation from a sub-committee that one or two houses should be secured to serve as residential centres for the youth service for use immediately after the war.[15]

To the north of Buxton lies an oblong of high moorland called Combs Moss. A broad and ill-defined spur drops northwestwards from Combs Moss, forming the watershed between the long Goyt Valley to the west and the small Combs valley to the northeast. Perched on a savagely exposed marshy flattening of this spur, at about 400 metres (1,300 feet) above sea level, is an isolated patch of spindly sycamores, which live short and battered lives before they succumb to winter gales. This location is a fine site for a wind turbine and it perfectly fits the stereotypic site for a Roman road. In the late 17th century or earlier, for reasons known

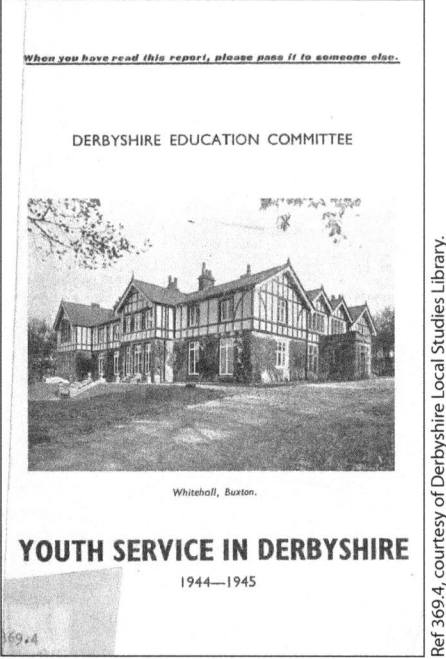

When you have read this report, please pass it to someone else.

DERBYSHIRE EDUCATION COMMITTEE

Whitehall, Buxton.

YOUTH SERVICE IN DERBYSHIRE
1944—1945

Ref 369.4, courtesy of Derbyshire Local Studies Library.

The document that led, later, to the purchase of White Hall.

only to themself but for which we are grateful, some hardy soul built a house here and called it White Hall. A later courageous person, probably in the mid-19th century, had a mock Tudor mansion constructed in dressed gritstone with a roof of Welsh slate.[16] Whether there were trees there at that time, I do not know.

During the war the evacuated pupils of Elizabeth College in Guernsey had occupied White Hall (a story in itself and the subject of two books[17]). In 1945 they returned to Guernsey, leaving White Hall empty. That year, Derbyshire county council entered into negotiations to buy the property.

An area youth officer, Jack Kilkenny, well-known locally, had much to do with the early stages. The primary purpose of White Hall, as then envisaged, was to be 'to provide a place where short training courses for leaders and members of youth organisations can be organised both by the sub-Committee and by voluntary bodies'.[18] These residential courses were to be for general youth service purposes, not necessarily outdoor activities. Some wishful thinking tidied the loose ends of this plan by saying that when not required for its primary purpose, the building would serve for youth service conferences, teachers' conferences and adult education.

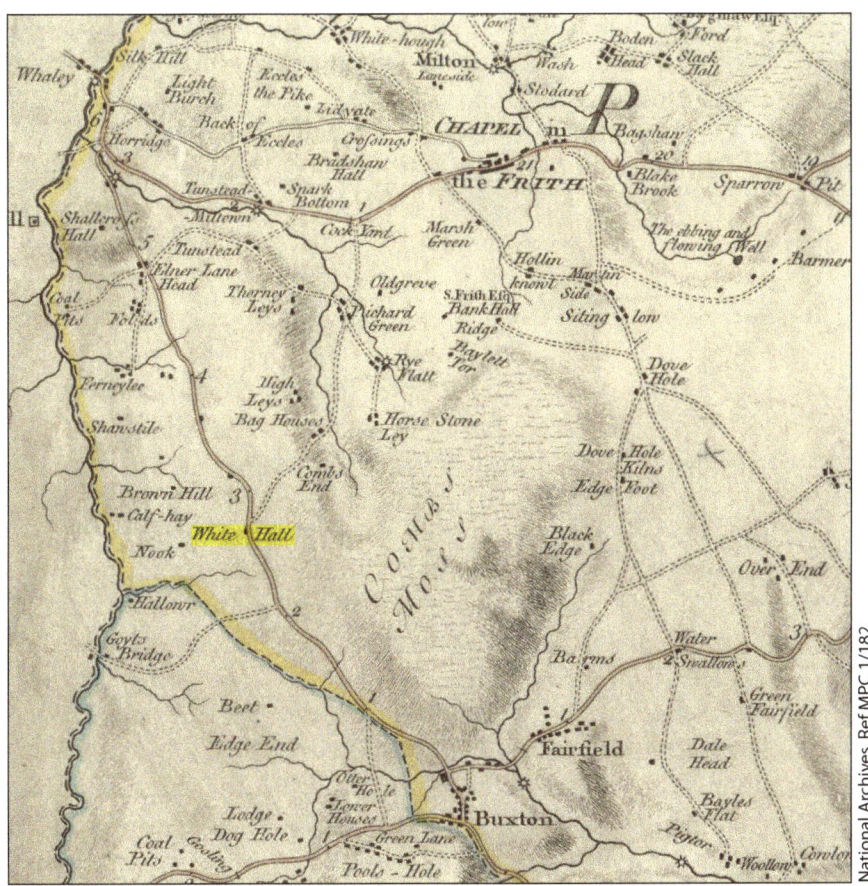

An extract from a 1791 edition of P P Burdett's 1 inch to 1 mile 1767 map of Derbyshire. The extract shows Combs Moss, White Hall and the old Long Hill road.

Nationally, the 1940s were a decade of optimism for the youth service. A government circular in 1939, 'In the Service of Youth', had raised the sector's status. In England, LEA-run youth centres saw prolific new growth. One enquiry published in 1949 estimated that 70 of 113 local authorities contacted had between them opened 900 youth centres.[19] In 1945 there was little to distinguish Kilkenny's planned centre from the many other residential youth centres.

The end of World War II in Europe was officially announced in Britain at 7.40pm on 7 May 1945. In July the Labour Party won the general election, gaining power with a large majority: 393 members (of whom 168 were of working-class origin) as against 213 Conservatives. 'This was an unequivocal popular mandate for the construction of a new world – just, egalitarian and peaceful.' The Labour government started with boundless ambition, foreseeing a total transformation of society. But postwar realities soon imposed an atmosphere of grey austerity, which would continue throughout Labour's term of office, 1945–51.[20]

On 27 July – 3 August 1946, Derbyshire Youth Committee ran a camp school in Bakewell for youth club leaders. The activities included outdoor interests such as camping, angling, rock climbing and exploration as well as music, drama, arts and crafts.[21]

By about 1947, people had realised that White Hall was badly sited for use for general youth service courses or as a conference centre, except perhaps for studying the extremes of English weather. The building was virtually unused. Despite various difficulties, however, Jack Kilkenny and a colleague ran several weekends there, sleeping in tents and storing equipment in out-buildings.[22]

Further afield, in London in October 1947, the *Picture Post* ran a feature on a Swiss climbing school at Rosenlaui, including photographs of clients under instruction. One of the article's contributors, Arnold Lunn, wrote: 'It is high time that we started a mountaineering school in Britain. The nucleus for such schools already exists in the excellent schools of mountain warfare started in the war.'[23] The average net weekly sales of the *Picture Post* in 1948 were 1,229,778.[24]

Up in Derbyshire, enter, on cue, Jack Longland, the charismatic ex-Everest mountaineer and broadcaster, determined perhaps not to let Glenmore Lodge grab all the action. On 17 November 1948 Longland was appointed to become Derbyshire's director of education.[25] He was the right man at the right time to select and adapt some of the ideas being pioneered by a few independent establishments (such as Abbotsholme School, Gordonstoun, Lakeside YMCA, Aberdovey OBSS and Brathay Hall Centre) and by one LEA centre (Denton House) and by Glenmore Lodge. With these ideas and his own, he would set up a residential centre that would serve all the young people in the entire county. This facility would greatly expand the promotion of outdoor pursuits in Derbyshire, and would eventually influence many other LEAs, especially in England and Wales.[26] But the development would need a special person with a strong nerve, abundant energy, irrepressible enthusiasm and a persuasive tongue. Longland was that rare individual. Looking back from the mid-1970s, Eric Langmuir wrote: 'From the beginning Jack Longland has been the most articulate spokesman for the whole Outdoor Education movement.'[27]

The initial initiative behind the setting-up of White Hall had come from Jack Kilkenny. The necessary drive and belief and influence were injected, crucially, by Longland.

He came along just in time. The house on the hill very nearly never became Longland's place. Some moves were afoot to sell it. Salford education authority had shown a marked interest in acquiring it.[28] On 10 May 1949, Derbyshire education committee agreed to buy a property in Buxton for use as a conference centre in place of White Hall. The committee also agreed to the opening of negotiations for the sale of White Hall to the Salford education committee.[29]

Centre for Open Country Pursuits, June 1949

Behind the scenes, there may have been some argument. At some point, Longland visited White Hall at the request of Jack Kilkenny, who had already seen the possibilities of the empty house.[30] As soon as Longland arrived at the building and saw its location, he too recognised its potential. On 7 June 1949 at a meeting of the Further Education Sub-Committee 'it was resolved to take no further action with regard to the negotiations for the sale of Whitehall … pending the submission of a report by the Director of Education regarding the possible use of the premises in connexion with open-country pursuits'.[31] The minute recording this decision is the earliest example I have found of the phrase 'open-country pursuits' being used in connection with White Hall.

A few days later, Longland found time to instruct in the Lake District on a five-day mountaineering course for teachers and youth leaders, held from 11 to 15 June. A press report described this as the first rock climbing course organised by the Ministry of Education.[32] The course was held under the leadership of Gilbert F Peaker, an inspector of schools who was also a member of the Alpine Club. An obituary in 1984 described Peaker as 'a man of brilliant mind and vigorous body', whose 'list of [alpine] climbs from 1923 to 1929, all guideless, would be considered very fine today, and in those years astonishing'.[33] (Peaker also had a few unlovable idiosyncrasies, encountered by Tom Price.[34]) Also instructing was David Bryson.

On 28 June 1949, when Britain was still deep in a period often remembered for its austerity, the education committee authorised Longland to inspect suitable properties in the county with a view to setting up a training centre for open country pursuits, including walking, camping, and climbing.[35]

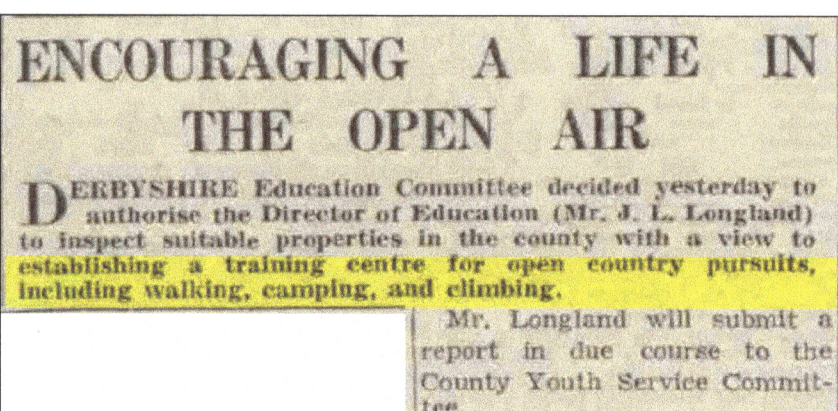

ENCOURAGING A LIFE IN THE OPEN AIR

DERBYSHIRE Education Committee decided yesterday to authorise the Director of Education (Mr. J. L. Longland) to inspect suitable properties in the county with a view to establishing a training centre for open country pursuits, including walking, camping, and climbing.

Mr. Longland will submit a report in due course to the County Youth Service Committee.

Press cutting from the *Derby Evening Telegraph*, 29 June 1949.

On 5 July 1949 the committee resolved to approve in principle the suggested scheme for the use of White Hall in connection with open country pursuits. The committee also approved Longland's proposals on staffing, organisation and essential adaptations. It agreed to ask the Ministry of Education to approve the estimated spending of £3,019 10s. 0d. on these adaptations.[36] From this moment on, the name 'Longland' appeared frequently in the press reports about White Hall. A newspaper article in August 1949 reported Longland saying that 'the centre would cater in the first place for 20 students (male and female), increasing in number to 30 or 40 over three years. Students would be recruited from youth organisations, senior pupils in schools, adult clubs, Youth Hostels Association members, [the] Ramblers' Association and individual sources.'[37]

There was a delay in receiving the go-ahead from the Ministry of Education, which led in January 1950 to a speculative *Buxton Advertiser* report titled 'Whitehall Plan "Axed"?' The circumstances may sound familiar: according to the newspaper, some of the work on alterations to the building had been held up by government cuts in spending.[38]

The name Kilkenny would pop up again much later, when he organised a Pennine Way course in July 1961. A B Afford, when mentioning this course, notes that Kilkenny had been in at the beginning, seventeen years earlier.[39]

In a letter to the *Derby Evening Telegraph* on 27 December 1950, Longland acknowledged the involvement of the previous director of education and of the youth service: 'I ought ... in justice to my predecessor to say, that the decision to establish a centre was taken nearly seven years ago'.[40]

For an LEA in 1950, Longland's open-country pursuits ideas were innovative and bold and not without their critics. For much of 1945–49, White Hall had been empty apart from during youth service gatherings. In some administrators' eyes it was a white elephant. The arrival of Longland greatly strengthened the influence of the pro-White Hall contingent. Even so, throughout the first wardenship, some critics would continue to describe White Hall as the white elephant of the county.[41] According to A B Afford, a notable achievement of the second warden, Geoff Sutton, would be in hosting the visit of the Duke of Edinburgh in November 1958, which would bring the white elephant under Royal patronage.[42]

In May 1950 the Derbyshire education committee invited applications for the post of warden of White Hall, described as an open country pursuits centre that would be used for short residential courses for young people in rambling, mountain-walking, rock climbing and camping.[43] It would be an advantage, the advertisement said, if the warden's wife could fill the post of housekeeper. According to a newspaper report ten days later, for the warden post the education committee required someone who was both a teacher and a mountaineer. Already a hundred hopefuls had applied for the job.[44] Longland appointed Peter Mosedale, aged thirty-two, and his wife Betty, to put the ambitious plans into practice – and austerity be damned!

DERBYSHIRE EDUCATION COMMITTEE. WHITE HALL, BUXTON : Open Country Pursuits Centre.—Applications are invited for the post of WARDEN. The Centre will be used for short residential courses for young people in rambling, mountain-walking, rock-climbing and camping. The Warden will act as Director. It will be an advantage if the Warden's wife can fill the post of Housekeeper. Salaries : Warden (A.P.T. V). £520 × £15 × £20 to £570 plus residence, value £120. Housekeeper : £250 × £10 to £350 plus residence, value £100.
Further particulars from J. L. LONGLAND, Esq., Director of Education, County Youth Service, 25, St. Mary's Gate, Derby.

The Times, 26 May 1950.

An advertisement for the post of warden, 26 May 1950.

Peter Mosedale was born on 20 September 1917 in Chilvers Coton, Warwickshire, a village where the Mosedale name ran through at least four generations. The village heritage centre has a Mosedale Room, where his grandfather once taught. Peter was educated at the High School, Worthing. He left school at fifteen, retook the London Matriculation by correspondence course, and was allowed back into the school. In April 1936 the eighteen-year-old Mosedale was elected to a special exhibition in history at University College, Oxford.[45]

He joined the Officers' Training Corps, ran for the college and became an active member of the Oxford University Mountaineering Club.[46] Because of the war, the OUMC did not publish any journals covering the climbing done in the years 1937 to 1946, and so we know nothing about any climbing Mosedale did while at Oxford. (In his 1975 monograph he mentions that OUMC members had developed practice climbs on the stone railway bridges at Horspath east of Oxford, but he may have been reporting a 1950s development.) He joined the Climbers' Club in 1939.

He graduated in July 1939. In September, at the outbreak of war, he was in Chamonix. He caught the last ferry to Newhaven and enlisted in the Royal Artillery. While awaiting his call-up, he returned to Oxford and gained the Special Certificate in Education in December 1939 and the Diploma in Education in July 1940. Commissioned in early 1941, he served with the West African Division and the Indian Artillery, rising from second lieutenant to major.[47]

After the war he joined the Colonial Office and spent about four years as an inspector of schools in the Gold Coast, which was then still a colony, part of British West Africa.[48] He was based at Tamale, the capital of the northern region. In the Gold Coast, government-sponsored secondary education had begun only after 1930. So Peter Mosedale just caught the last days of the Empire, inspecting new schools in an old colony, where the inspector probably still wore a white pith helmet or some other emblem of imperialness. (Gold Coast achieved independence as the Republic of Ghana in 1960.)

At some point, probably in 1949, ill health brought about a return to Britain, where he took up dairy farming in Pembrokeshire. In August 1949 his wife Betty gave birth to a daughter, Janet Rachel, in Cardigan, Wales.[49] Restored to health, in mid- or late 1950 Peter Mosedale was appointed to the job of warden of White Hall Centre.

It is a pity and in some ways surprising that whereas Mosedale eventually marshalled his outdoor-recreation thoughts into a systematic manuscript, Longland, despite his literary and historical bent, did not. As far as I know, the longest piece of Longland writing directly connected with outdoor centres is his chapter, 'Outward Bound Junior Courses', in the edited book *Outward Bound*. Longland led the busiest of lives. He served on numerous committees. He was in great demand as a lively lecturer, raconteur and after-dinner speaker. His contributions as a panellist on radio programmes such as *Any Questions?* were characterised by clarity of thought and wide human sympathy.[50] His writing was generally lean and businesslike, the routine faultless work of a top administrator. However, although commandingly articulate, he never had the time to gather his White Hall thoughts into a book. We are the poorer for it. But many pithy fragments have accumulated from Longland's reported statements and from his articles in and letters to newspapers and magazines and journals. They jointly form what is probably an accurate picture of his hopes and beliefs.

Notes

1   Joe Brown, *The Hard Years* (1967; repr. London: Penguin Books, 1975), p. 25.

2   Rosemary Clements, 'WW2 People's War: War Memories of a Teenager Living in Buxton', BBC (12 Aug 2003) <http://www.bbc.co.uk/history/ww2peopleswar/stories/09/a1141309.shtml> [accessed 25 May 2014].

3   'Staveley and Dist. Notes', *Derbyshire Times*, 4 July 1941, p. 6.

4   'Chesterfield Items', *Derbyshire Times*, 5 Sept 1941, p. 5.

5   G Spencer Summers, 'The History of the Trust', in *Outward Bound*, ed. by David James (London: Routledge and Kegan Paul, 1957), pp. 18–58 (p. 22).

6   H W Richmond, 'The Training Holiday', *The Times*, 30 Dec 1942, p. 5.

7   Joe Brown, *The Hard Years* (1967; repr. London: Penguin Books, 1975), p. 28.

8   Jim Perrin, *The Villain: The Life of Don Whillans* (London: Arrow, 2006), pp. 32–33.

9   William Oakley, *Winged Wheel: The History of the First Hundred Years of the Cyclists' Touring Club* (Godalming, UK: Cyclists' Touring Club, 1977), p. 65.

10   'Leaders of Youth in Training', *Derby Evening Telegraph*, 5 June 1943, p. 4.

11   'A Canoeing Week-end', *Picture Post*, 17 June 1944, pp. 21–23.

12   Youth Advisory Council of the Board of Education, *The Youth Service after the War* (London: H M Stationery Office, 1943), p. 13.

13   Eric Byne and Geoffrey Sutton, *High Peak: The Story of Walking and Climbing in the Peak District* (London: Secker and Warburg, 1966), p. 187.

14   Board of Education, *Report of the Committee of the Secondary School Examinations Council, Curriculum and Examinations in Secondary Schools*, Norwood Report (London: HMSO, 1943), Part III, Ch. 2, p. 83.

15   Derbyshire Local Studies Library, Derbyshire Record Office (Matlock, UK), Derbyshire Education Committee: Youth Service in Derbyshire 1944–1945, Section 4 – Whitehall, Buxton, Ref 369.4.

16   A B Afford, *The Story of White Hall Open Country Pursuits Centre; vol. 1* (Buxton, Derbyshire, UK: A B Afford, 1978), pp. 14–15.

17   Michael Marshall, *The Small Army* (London: Constable, 1957). Also V G Collenette, *Elizabeth College in Exile, 1940–1945* (Guernsey: Guernsey Press, c. 1960).

18   Derbyshire Local Studies Library, Derbyshire Record Office (Matlock, UK), Derbyshire Education Committee: Youth Service in Derbyshire 1944–1945, Section 4 – Whitehall, Buxton, Ref 369.4.

19   Bernard Davies, *From Voluntaryism to Welfare State: A History of the Youth Service in England: 1939–1979*, History of the Youth Service in England, 2 vols (Leicester: Youth Work Press, 1999), vol. 1, pp. 18, 26.

20   François Bédarida, *A Social History of England 1851–1990*, 2nd edn (London: Routledge, 1991), p. 191.

21   'Camp School for Youth Club Leaders', *Derby Evening Telegraph*, 11 May 1946, p. 4.

22   A B Afford, *The Story of White Hall Open Country Pursuits Centre; vol. 2* (Buxton, Derbyshire, UK: A B Afford, 1978), p. 1.

23   R H Dr Schloss and Arnold Lunn, 'Climbing School', *Picture Post*, 11 Oct 1947, pp. 8–11.

24   'Popular Newspapers during World War II', Adam Matthew Publications (2014) <http://www.ampltd.co.uk/digital_guides/popular_newspapers_world_war_2_parts_1_to_5/ABC-Net-Sales.aspx> [accessed 24 Nov 2014].

25   '[Appointment]', *Manchester Guardian*, 18 Nov 1948, p. 3.

26   Glenmore Lodge, administered at first by the Scottish arm of the Central Council of Physical Education in response to a request from the Scottish Education Department, would become a major influence in Scotland.

27   Letter, quoted in A B Afford, *The Story of White Hall Open Country Pursuits Centre; vol. 2* (Buxton, Derbyshire, UK: A B Afford, 1978), p. 20.

28   Ibid., p. 2.

29   Derbyshire Record Office, Education minute books, D919 C/1/17/29, 10 May 1949, no. 7315(c).

30   A B Afford, *The Story of White Hall Open Country Pursuits Centre; vol. 1* (Buxton, Derbyshire, UK: A B Afford, 1978), p. 39.

31   Derbyshire Record Office, Education minute books, D919 C/1/17/29, 7 June 1949, no. 7459.

32   'Teachers to Climb', *Daily Mail*, 11 May 1949, p. 2. Also 'Course in Mountaineering', *Manchester Guardian*, 31 May 1949, p. 6.

33   C Douglas Milner, 'Gilbert Fawcett Peaker CBE 1903–83', *Alpine Journal*, 89 (1984), pp. 264–266 (p. 264).

34   Tom Price, *Travail So Gladly Spent* (Ty Croes, Wales: Ernest Press, 2000), p. 61.

35   'Encouraging a Life in the Open Air', *Derby Evening Telegraph*, 29 June 1949, p. 7.

36 Derbyshire Record Office, Education minute books, D919 C/1/17/29, 5 July 1949, no. 7667.

37 '"Whitehall" May Be First Country Pursuits Centre', *Buxton Advertiser*, 27 Aug 1949, p. 3.

38 'Whitehall Plan "Axed"?', *Buxton Advertiser*, 14 Jan 1950.

39 A B Afford, *The Story of White Hall Open Country Pursuits Centre; vol. 2* (Buxton, Derbyshire, UK: A B Afford, 1978), pp. 1–2, 19–20.

40 'Needs of County's "Tragic Children"', *Derby Evening Telegraph*, 27 Dec 1950, p. 2.

41 A B Afford, *The Story of White Hall Open Country Pursuits Centre; vol. 2* (Buxton, Derbyshire, UK: A B Afford, 1978), p. 10.

42 Ibid., p. 14.

43 'Public Notices', *The Times*, 26 May 1950, p. 1.

44 'The Townsman in the Country', *Manchester Guardian*, 5 June 1950, p. 4.

45 'University News: Elections at University College, Oxford', *The Times*, 27 Apr 1936, p. 19.

46 Tom Mosedale, 'University College Oxford Record 2014 – Part 5: Obituaries' (Oct 2014) <https://issuu.com/univoxford/docs/record_2014_-_pt5_obituaries_etc> [accessed 11 May 2016].

47 Ibid.

48 Peter Haddington, 'Gateway to Adventure at the White Hall Centre for Open Country Pursuits, near Buxton', *Derbyshire Countryside*, 23, no. 5 (Sept 1958), pp. 30–33.

49 'Births', *The Times*, 8 Aug 1949, p. 1.

50 'Longland, School Champion', *Guardian*, 4 Dec 1993, p. 30.

6. Consequences of Training the Soldiers

On a TV show in 2004 the gardener and broadcaster Alan Titchmarsh estimated that during the second world war the armed services had used one-fifth of the British countryside for training purposes.[1] In 2010 George Gardner, who had served in the Parachute Regiment, recalled undergoing a four-week commando training course in Inveraray Castle, Argyllshire, followed by six weeks of 'training hell' based at Hardwick Hall in Derbyshire. The hell sounds like a scholarship version of an Outward Bound course of the 1950s: twenty-mile route marches, 'trotting with weapons at the trail', tree-scaling, assault courses and obstacle courses. 'There was one session when we were taken by transport to an unknown spot, given directions, and told to make our own way back to Hardwick Hall, avoiding capture en route by those wearing red armbands to denote them as "enemy"'.[2]

Some training of British soldiers in mountain warfare and cliff assault may have taken place in Derbyshire. Most of such training, however, took place in other areas of Britain, especially in Scotland, north Wales and Cornwall, and in various centres abroad.

A soldier from No. 1 Commando during training at Glencoe, 19 November 1941.

In May 1942 Major John Hunt, who later led the 1953 Everest expedition, ran a two-week toughening-up course in Snowdonia for an armoured unit of the Kings Royal Rifles. Twenty men of all ranks, from private to major, attended the course, based at the Climbers' Club hut Helyg. Hunt was helped by the climbers Wilfred Noyce and Alfred Bridge. The group chemistry impressed Hunt:

> We did some hair-raising things on that course; its success was a revelation to everyone who took part. Not least surprising at that time was the notion that all of us, ranging in rank from trooper to major, could happily share the crowded hospitality of a small mountain hut for a fortnight, eating, sleeping, sharing washing up and all the other chores together, with no detriment to essential discipline.[3]

This work with soldiers in mountain terrain led Hunt to think about the value of such an approach and setting for the training of leaders in the armed forces.[4] He sent a memorandum on this topic to Geoffrey Young, the president of the Alpine Club. Young may have seen the paper's relevance to the education of young people in general. He sent the paper on to Kurt Hahn. This connection would later lead to Hunt's involvement in the Duke of Edinburgh's Award.

On 1 December 1942 the Commando Mountain and Snow Warfare Training Camp was opened at Braemar in Scotland, with Hunt as the chief instructor.[5] Hundreds of men were introduced to the equipment and skills of rock climbing, of travelling on foot over rough terrain including snow and ice, and of load-carrying, skiing, abseiling, bivouacking and map-and-compass navigation.[6]

In about 1943 Geoffrey Rees-Jones spent a period in charge of cliff-assault training at St Ives in Cornwall. He recalled: 'We did demonstrations to a lot of bloody generals in the stupidest of places.' The accident rate at St Ives was high.[7]

In May 1944 the *Picture Post*, said to be read by half the population of the UK[8], published a two-page feature about the Middle East Mountain Warfare Training Centre in the foothills of the Lebanon mountains. Titled 'We Get Ready for Fighting in Mountain Country', the article included an explanation of the background to this development:

> An army is organised according to its geographical configuration and the tasks with which its soldiers are most likely to be con-

fronted. It was the countries with interests in the neighbourhood of the Alps, therefore, which devoted themselves to the problems of mountain troops, and built up crack units most intensively. In this way there arose the famous Tyrolese riflemen in Austria, the German Alpine Corps, the Chasseurs Alpins in France and …

Naturally, the British General Staff could not expect before the war that it would ever be confronted with highly trained German troops in mountainous districts. During the first world war, the Allies had at their disposal special French and Italian formations for fighting in mountain regions, and it was expected that the French would be available for the present war … France fell out of the war and the British army had to tackle the organisation, equipment and training of mountain troops as quickly as possible. This is a laborious and wearisome task, especially difficult when there is a shortage of instructors.[9]

A Belgian Commando descends a 35-metre cliff somewhere in Britain in 1945. In wartime, any method that got you efficiently up or down the cliff was acceptable. The ethics of the sport of rock climbing did not apply.

© Imperial War Museum D 23727.

A separate and different venture, which took place in 1944, was the army's use of mountaincraft courses as character training for army cadets. Army cadet battalions had been first formed in the 1880s to provide military training for boys under army age. Membership when war broke out in 1939 had been 43,000. By mid-1944 it had grown to 170,000, one-fifth of the eligible boy population.[10]

To solve the problem of the shortage of mountaincraft instructors, the War Office sought the help of the Alpine Club. (The BMC did not yet exist.) An experimental course for cadets of the Army Cadet Force was held in north Wales over ten days in April 1944. It was based at a military camp near Llanberis. The course also had the use of Helyg, the Climber's Club hut.

The cadets were not carefully picked. Their average age was barely seventeen, and most came from industrial towns. Among the team of Alpine Club or Climbers' Club members acting as instructors were Jack Longland (on leave from Dorset), his Cambridge mate Ivan Waller, the steeplejack Alf Bridge, Alan B Hargreaves, Peter Bicknell, Geoffrey Bartrum and Claude Elliott, the headmaster of Eton, who before his appointment to the headship had said: 'Well, thank God I have no damned theories about education'.[11] Elliott was also a governor of Gordonstoun.

The sheer sensuous pleasure of balancing on small footholds received generous attention: 'The Tryfan buttresses were all teeming with cadets almost daily, and it was here that some cadets led some rock climbs towards the end. Very nearly half of their available days were spent in rock climbing.' Other activities included compass games, a manhunt, and expeditions to the Cnicht and Silyn areas, Snowdon, the Glyders and the Carnedds.[12]

Hargreaves, a leading gritstone climber, later recalled this 1944 course, which was considered a great success:

> These cadets were an excellent mixture of 17-year-olds – some of them from public schools – who responded well to the daily activity on the hills, often in poor weather … we (the instructors) had with us on various climbs, the Army NCOs, who knew it all (!), but didn't. One or two of them were more of a problem than the boys! …
>
> The most frightening part of the whole 10 days was having to be driven around in army transport by young soldiers … Amongst

the top brass who came to see what was going on, was Geoffrey Winthrop Young.[13]

In September 1944, the government was planning to introduce, after the war, compulsory Cadet service for all boys. In the case of the Army Cadet Force, this service was to be from the age of fourteen to seventeen.[14]

In the following year, 1945, two more army-cadet training courses took place in Wales, based at Llanberis and staffed largely by members of the Climbers' Club. The second one involved a hundred boys.[15]

A few accounts of being an Army mountaineering instructor are available. Captain E A H Hamson, a member of the Climbers' Club, was posted to the Mountain Training Wing at Llanberis in June 1945. For him, 'the first day in the Welsh hills after being away for five years was one of the supreme moments of life … the sun shone on the slopes of the Glyders and the oak woods across the lake. The Snowdon massif was a dark silhouette with the light right behind it, and from the end of the village street one could see the actual top of Snowdon peeping over the cliffs of Clogwyn du'r Arddu.' By the end of June, a small group of instructors, maybe eight or nine, had assembled. Hamson writes: '[the] War Office who had so ably collected us had omitted for the moment to give us any particular instructions, so all we had to do was to go on climbing.' Most mornings in July found the lucky sinecurists 'driving out of Llanberis up the pass, and most evenings drinking tea in the kitchen with Miss Jones at Pen-y-Pass or Mrs. Williams at Ogwen Cottage'.[16]

Six years on from the 1944 army-cadet course, Longland, Waller and Bridge would all attend White Hall Centre's opening weekend. We can only speculate on whether they brought with them any ideas or lessons from 1944.

Writing about this wartime army-cadet character training in 1997, Bob Pettigrew raised the Alpine Club and Geoffrey Young to pre-eminence among the founders of residential outdoor education:

> There appears to be no doubt … that the principal driving force in the movement towards the use of mountains as an education medium and vehicle, which gathered such momentum as to be irresistible even to Government and programmes of legislation, was the Alpine Club led by the redoubtable Geoffrey Winthrop Young, doyen of Alpinists, Her Majesty's Inspector of Schools,

President of the Alpine Club and the British Mountaineering
Council, poet, visionary and educationist.[17]

Pettigrew was simplifying things to try to identify the core. I do not
think he meant to say that, by jointly organising a 1944 course for army
cadets, the Alpine Club and Young had invented outdoor education,
in all its infinite guises. How valid is Pettigrew's précis of the history?
His 1997 opinion carries weight. He had been close to developments
for forty-seven years, since White Hall's opening weekend in 1950. His
1954–5 Loughborough Training College thesis on outdoor activities
scrutinised the developments of the early 1950s. His instructing experience included running rock climbing evening classes in Nottingham
and alpine-climbing courses in France.[18] He had been the chief adviser
for outdoor education in Hampshire (1975), president of the BMC
(1976–9), chair of the MLTB (1987–93), and chair of the outdoor
pursuits division of the CCPR.

A different perspective than Pettigrew's might come in useful. The
history of LEA outdoor education in one of Derbyshire's neighbouring
counties provides one. In July 2000, Lynn Cook completed a doctoral
thesis on the origins of outdoor education and on its institutionalisation
in schools, particularly in the West Riding of Yorkshire. She looked
especially closely at the history of the long-established Bewerley Park
Outdoor Centre. Her exhaustively researched 338-page thesis does
not once mention the Alpine Club or Geoffrey Young and only once
mentions the BMC.[19]

There are just two possible explanations for the acutely different
perspectives of Pettigrew and Cook. Either one of them got things
horribly wrong. Or they were both correct, because not all LEA centres
were fashioned on the White Hall Centre model. Bewerley Park Outdoor Centre developed independently, from a camp school that firstly
changed into a junior field-study centre and then, under the influence
of Jim Hogan, became an outdoor pursuits centre. Furthermore, narrowing our focus back to Derbyshire, the centre that would evolve on a
windswept spur above Buxton would scrutinise the character-training
aims and claims of Young and others more suspiciously than the army
had done in 1944. Peter Mosedale's White Hall would not broadcast
any overt character-training message or claim. On the contrary, I will
suggest later that, under the influence of Mosedale, Arthur Afford,
Harold Drasdo and others, everyday conversation at White Hall in the
1950s and early 60s would avoid the term 'character training', leaving

a vacuum for a while, which was eventually filled by the term 'social and personal development'.

Pettigrew may have been correct in linking the Alpine Club and Young and the 1944 cadet course with the birth of White Hall Centre in 1950, but collectively they were just one of many influences on the spirit and approaches that evolved.

*

Although the whole point of training soldiers for mountain warfare was for confrontation and not recreation, the army's efforts to train mountain troops amounted to promotion of the sports of rock climbing and mountaineering on a massive scale. As well as boosting the number of skilled climbers, the needs of the armed services led to the development and manufacture of cheap and serviceable outdoor equipment, including camouflaged windproof anoraks and trousers, heavy-duty rucksacks, karabiners and – most importantly – laid nylon rope, with its revolutionary elasticity. These would become the staple equipment of a generation of postwar adventurers.[20]

There was every likelihood that some men would continue climbing when the war was over. And this is what happened. The Derbyshire moorlands and outcrops were just one of the areas in Britain where climbing and hillwalking flourished after the war. But this burgeoning popularity of adventurous outdoor pursuits became particularly evident in Derbyshire and in some fragments of neighbouring counties, which formed an island of upland, ringed by large towns and cities. Many millions of people lived within a forty-five-minute car or train journey from the Peak District. Northern Derbyshire was an obvious place in which to set up a pioneering residential outdoor pursuits centre, particularly one that would depend greatly on the help of voluntary instructors.

Notes

1   Ken C Ogilvie, *Roots and Wings: A History of Outdoor Education and Outdoor Learning in the UK* (Lyme Regis, UK: Russell House Publishing, 2013), p. 249.

2   George Gardner, 'Wartime Memories of the Late W Bro George Gardner', Provincial Grand Lodge of Gloucestershire (2010) <http://www.glosmasons.org.uk/LinkClick.aspx?fileticket=AkbINkoFo5c%3D&tabid=1890> [accessed 20 Jan 2015].

3   John Hunt, *Life Is Meeting* (London: Hodder & Stoughton, 1978), pp. 62–63.

4   *The First Fifty Years of the British Mountaineering Council*, ed. by Geoff Milburn, Derek Walker and Ken Wilson (Manchester: British Mountaineering Council, 1997), p. v.

5   Tim R Moreman, *British Commandos 1940–46* (Oxford: Osprey, 2006), p. 40.

6   John Hunt, *Life Is Meeting* (London: Hodder & Stoughton, 1978), pp. 62–64.

7   Telegraph Media Group, 'Geoffrey Rees-Jones' (4 Oct 2004) <http://www.telegraph.co.uk/news/obituaries/1473259/Geoffrey-Rees-Jones.html> [accessed 9 Mar 2015].

8   'Popular Newspapers during World War II', Adam Matthew Publications (2014) <http://www.ampltd.co.uk/digital_guides/popular_newspapers_world_war_2_parts_1_to_5/ABC-Net-Sales.aspx> [accessed 24 Nov 2014].

9   E Werth, 'We Get Ready for Fighting in Mountain Country', *Picture Post*, 13 May 1944, pp. 12–13.

10   'Growth of Army Cadet Force', *The Times*, 7 July 1944, p. 2.

11   Jack Longland, 'Claude Aurelius Elliott 1888–1973', *Alpine Journal*, 79 (1974), pp. 280–281.

12   T A Brocklebank, 'Army Cadet Force Mountain Course', *Alpine Journal*, 54 (1944), pp. 442–443.

13   *The First Fifty Years of the British Mountaineering Council*, ed. by Geoff Milburn, Derek Walker and Ken Wilson (Manchester: British Mountaineering Council, 1997), pp. 135–136.

14   'All Boys Will Be Cadets', *Daily Mail*, 21 Sept 1944, p. 1.

15   J L Longland, 'Annual Report', *Climbers' Club Journal: 1945–1946*, 8, no. 1 (new series) (1946), pp. 111–114 (p. 113).

16   E A H Hamson, 'Mountain Training Wing, Llanberis, 1945', *Climbers' Club Journal: 1947*, 8, no. 2 (new series) (1947), pp. 157–164.

17   *The First Fifty Years of the British Mountaineering Council*, ed. by Geoff Milburn, Derek Walker and Ken Wilson (Manchester: British Mountaineering Council, 1997), p. 136.

18   Doug Scott, *Up and About: The Hard Road to Everest* (Sheffield: Vertebrate Publishing, 2015), pp. 43, 79.

19   Lynn Cook, 'Outdoor Education: Its Origins and Institutionalisation in Schools with Particular Reference to the West Riding of Yorkshire Since 1945' (PhD thesis, University of Leeds, 2000).

20   David Hopkins and Roger Putnam, *Personal Growth through Adventure* (London: David Fulton Publishers, 1993), p. 27.

7. Purpose Statements, 1949–50

By 1950 the term 'open country' had a statutory meaning. The National Parks and Access to the Countryside Act 1949 had assumed that planning authorities in England and Wales would negotiate with private landowners to create access land, typically comprising open moorland rather than enclosed fields. In these agreed areas of uncultivated land the public would have the 'right to roam'. The negotiated areas were to be called 'open country'. They would consist wholly or predominantly of mountain, moor, heath, down, cliff or foreshore. For its first thirty-five years, White Hall had no formal written aims apart from what its full name implied: White Hall Centre for Open Country Pursuits. Until the mid-1980s, this name – helped by little more than the centre's evolving traditions and character – made the centre's purpose self-evident. It hard-wired adventurous outdoor pursuits into the centre's *raison d'être*.

Even so, I thought in 2014, it would be interesting to find something concrete on White Hall's purpose, dating from the start. So I began looking at newspapers and other writing from the late 1940s and early 1950s. An hour's research found several newspaper or magazine reports that carried the same message as the centre's long name, with added specifics and nuances. A day or two later, my collection of these newspaper and magazine extracts numbered thirteen, mainly from 1949–52, with three from 1958–61. Four of them were articles that quoted Longland, one was an article written by him and two were letters written by him. Some examples are reproduced in this chapter, scattered around. None of them were formal mission statements (the term didn't exist), many were mere mentions, but in total they clearly define the initial purposes of the house on the hill.

Further research unearthed two other purpose statements of types more official than press reports. Both of these came to light in 2014. One is a section of a printed annual course programme of the early 1950s. The other is an important paragraph in an article written by Cyril Machin in 1956; this paragraph appears to date from White

Hall's opening weekend and is virtually what some people would now call a mission statement or a statement of intent. Appendix 2 gathers more than twenty purpose statements and mentions, arranged chronologically.

Longland had been involved with and influenced by Kurt Hahn's County Badge scheme. He agreed with Hahn's view that it is the birthright of the normal child to be taught to run, to throw, to jump, to balance, to swim and to climb, in order to complement the acquisition of equally essential academic skills.[1] Then as now, however, people's ideas about adventurous outdoor pursuits varied, and Longland's view of the value of outdoor training might have differed slightly from the views of some his contemporaries.[2] Jim Perrin, who knew Longland well, wrote: 'Though inspired to some extent by his friendships with John Newsom, Geoffrey W Young and Kurt Hahn, his own idealism was the prime motive for [moving into educational administration]'.[3]

Longland Replies to Janus, June 1950

On 10 April 1950, the *Manchester Guardian* reported that Buxton Liberal Association had strongly criticised Derbyshire education committee's plans to set up 'a climbing school at "Whitehall", Longhill, Buxton … when normal schools were crying out for a mere hut to accommodate an increasing number of scholars'. The writer 'understood that the purchase price [of White Hall] was in the neighbourhood of £17,000'.[4] This exaggerated figure subsequently gained some prominence before being proved incorrect.

The Liberals' criticism might have been quickly forgotten had it not come to the attention of Wilson Harris, the long-serving editor of the *Spectator*, the Conservative-leaning weekly magazine of news and current affairs. The *Spectator* was widely known for its essays on political and literary issues. Harris was a witty and incisive commentator on public affairs, who for eighteen years had helped the *Spectator* to retain a greater influence than its circulation suggested.[5]

In the issue of 14 April 1950, writing under the pseudonym Janus, Harris supported the criticism of the Buxton Liberal Association and he added some further concerns:

> I am not surprised that the singular proposal of the Derbyshire Education Committee to establish a school for climbers in a mansion at Buxton purchased, it is said, for £17,000, should be severely criticised by the Buxton Liberal Association. The figure

mentioned is, of course, only the cost of acquiring the building. What the cost of running the school [is], and what its purpose [is], remain to be disclosed. On those points, it may be assumed, Derbyshire ratepayers will have enquiries to make. So, I should hope, will the Minister of Education. There may be some good explanation; the need for one is manifest.

JANUS.[6]

The word 'singular' has several meanings. Harris's use of it was pejorative, meaning 'odd' or 'strange'.

In the letters column of the next issue, a correspondent, W McG Eagar, wrote in support of Derbyshire education committee, provided that the White Hall Centre courses were of a certain type:

> … Derbyshire has enviable opportunities for the training of manhood. The value of mountaineering for building of character and inculcating intelligent interests, to say nothing of developing physical strength and dexterity, is great; the Outward Bound Trust has now established a Mountain School in Cumberland in addition to its Sea School at Aberdovey. Its purpose is to give a training holiday to boys employed in industry under conditions which challenge their spiritual as well as their physical ambitions. There are discipline, effort and some measure of hardship in the four weeks' course, but there is no shortage of boys anxious to take it … This should be enough to indicate that there is much more in the Derbyshire project than at first meets the eye, and will, I hope, encourage the Derbyshire Education Committee to make its own case good against criticism from any quarter.
> I am, Sir, yours &c. W. MCG. EAGAR.
> 2 South Square, Hampstead Garden Suburb, N.W.11.[7]

Waldo Mcgillicuddy Eagar had been a key figure in the forming of the National Association of Boys' Clubs.

The *Spectator* had now published two direct requests for Derbyshire education committee to explain the purpose of White Hall Centre. Four articles in northern newspapers had already said what that purpose was – in simple terms, at least – but this was probably of little comfort to Jack Longland. The Janus article and the letter deserved a comprehensive response. This need intensified on 26 May when Janus (Wilson Harris) renewed his disapproval:

In spite of a letter in last week's *Spectator*, I remain unconvinced that Derbyshire Education Committee is justified in spending £17,000 in the purchase of a mansion to be used as a school for rock-climbers. It is clear from reports in the local Press that in parts of Derbyshire, at any rate, buildings for schools for ordinary children from five to fifteen are badly needed. This £17,000 would help a good deal to provide them. A rock-climbing school may be an excellent thing in its way, but I should have thought its provision was the business of some national body, voluntary or official, not of a single county Education Committee.

JANUS.[8]

In questioning the place of climbing in education, Harris was running true to form. In April 1949 he had used his column to express the opinion that all guideless climbing in the Alps should be banned.[9] This suggestion had hardly been worth the trouble of responding to, but at least three readers took the bait, one of them remarking that 'to talk about the abandonment of Alpine climbing is grotesque, and, thank goodness, [a ban would not be] possible to enforce'.[10]

On 16 June 1950 the *Spectator* published Longland's responses to Harris's critical remarks and to Mr Eagar's ideas. Perhaps we should thank Harris for provoking Longland into action, because Longland's letter discussed the intended purpose of White Hall more deeply than any written explanation that had previously reached the public:

SIR,—The Derbyshire Education Committee's decision to establish, as part of their provision for the service of youth, a centre for open country pursuits, has been criticised in your columns as extravagant and as singular. I do not know on what authority Janus quotes £17,000 as the cost of acquiring the building only. In round figures White Hall, which is a good deal less than a mansion, cost £6,000; we have had to spend £1,500 on eradicating dry rot, and the Ministry of Education has approved the spending of £2,500 on repairs and conversion; new furniture and equipment will cost a further £1,000. The total initial cost is thus £11,000 – about half the cost of a gymnasium for a small secondary school. Of its running costs it is sufficient to say that it will work on the general lines of a first-rate Youth Hostel. A minimal domestic staff will provide the students with one cooked meal a day; for the rest, they will make their beds, their breakfasts and their sandwiches.

But this is no time to devise strange new ways of spending five-figure sums. What of the project's 'singularity'? The doctrine that the training of the human spirit is incomplete without the kind of physical discipline that is offered by hills and by the sea is not a new one. It is as old as Wordsworth. It is as old as Plato. The education of the *Republic* is aristocratic; I will, therefore, recall Bertrand Russell's argument that we shall not achieve a truly egalitarian society until all children are given the training for courage traditionally reserved for the ruling classes.

Nor is our proposal out of step with this generation. Mr. Eager [*sic*], who has most nobly stated much of our case for us, has reminded you of the sea school at Aberdovey and the mountain school in Eskdale. The background against which Aberdovey and Eskdale and White Hall are all to be seen, the foundation on which they are surely based, is much broader. It has found its expression in the snowball growth of the Youth Hostels move-ment, the clamant demand for access to mountains, the establish-ment of National Parks. White Hall stands in one of these parks; it is no small matter that this generation should learn their proper use and full enjoyment.

Janus's comment on May 26th raises an issue of principle. 'A rock-climbing school,' he says, 'may be an excellent thing in its way, but I should have thought its provision was the business of some national body, voluntary or official, not of a single county Education Committee.' Now the development of pioneer ideas has always been the province of local education authorities. It is, perhaps, their most significant national contribution. In this sense they *are* national bodies. Neither White Hall nor the ideas which it embodies will be reserved to the young people of this county. Yours faithfully, J. L. LONGLAND.
County Education Office, St. Mary's Gate, Derby.[11]

Three points are worth noting about this letter. Firstly, it is not Jack Longland speaking to locals at a Youth Hostels Association public meeting in Derby; it is the Cambridge scholar addressing the sub-scribers to and readers of the *Spectator*, using language and argument chosen for the occasion, and calling on a Greek thinker for support. Secondly, Longland's agreement with Mr Eagar's enthusiasm for Outward Bound is wholehearted and unqualified; his thoughts on the OB approach would later become more complex and somewhat guarded. Thirdly, Longland clearly views White Hall Centre as a trailblazer with the potential to influence ideas nationally rather than just locally. This is curiously similar to Kurt Hahn's hopes, in the late 1930s and early 1940s, that the Moray Badge scheme and Aberdovey OBSS would achieve expansion by demonstrating.[12]

Longland's letter was not the end of the *Spectator*'s exchange of views. A Derbyshire county councillor, R W P Cockerton, joined the discussion, which may have reminded Longland that his plans faced some opposition closer to home. Cockerton wrote:

> SIR,—As a Derbyshire County Councillor of some sixteen years' standing I was interested to read Mr. J. L. Longland's defence of the Derbyshire project, primarily devoted to rock-climbing—an art in which he himself excels. What puzzles me is that at the very time when this admittedly expensive scheme is being sponsored by him and his committee, that same committee has discontinued, upon grounds of economy, the very modest grants previously available to assist young people to go to outdoor camps of various sorts.
>
> Is rock-climbing exempt from the economy axe, which has fallen upon some of the other less spectacular but equally desirable outdoor activities for young people, or have the camping grants had to go by the board because the rock-climbing hostel is eating into the limited finances available for youth work? Some of us here in Derbyshire are not very happy about the expense of the White Hall project and its impact upon the finance of other youth work within the county.
> Yours faithfully, R. W. P. COCKERTON
> Burre House, Bakewell, Derbyshire.[13]

Letters to the editor that express opposing views are the lifeblood of magazines, but this particular argument ended six weeks later with another moan from the camping enthusiast, Mr Cockerton:

> SIR,—I notice that Mr. Longland has not replied through your correspondence columns to the questions which I put in my last letter. Since then I have elicited the fact that, though Whitehall was purchased in October, 1946, it has not, nearly four years later, been yet officially opened. In the meantime, apart from the capital

cost of £6,060, a sum of £2,565 has been spent upon maintenance, including the repair of dry rot. No young person has, as yet, had any benefit whatever during nearly four years except that one or two small parties have camped outside in the grounds at their own expense. Now we are told that a further £3,582 of capital must be spent (which includes £1,000 for furniture).

Meanwhile other outdoor activities for young people of established and proved worth in the County of Derby are being crippled through lack of finance, and grants hitherto available have been withdrawn or cut down on grounds of economy. Young people are being denied the 'physical discipline' (the words are Mr. Longland's own) of outdoor camping with the aid of camping equipment, grants towards which would cost very much less than half the cost of a gymnasium for a small secondary school which is, according to Mr. Longland's letter, to be regarded as a standard of reference when assessing the value of educational projects for youth.

Yours faithfully, R. W. P. COCKERTON.

Burre House, Bakewell, Derbyshire.[14]

This exchange of letters about an allegedly expensive scheme, costing either £11,000 or £17,000 depending on whose figures you prefer, took place from May to August 1950.

I do not know whether Longland replied to the allegation that the money spent on White Hall had been taken from existing provision for camping. He could justifiably have answered that the camping gear at White Hall would be used frequently for eight months each year, and that the total amount of camping undertaken by young people in Derbyshire would increase.

In the middle of this period, on 18 June 1950, the minister of education opened Eskdale OBMS. Newspapers reported that the Outward Bound Trust was appealing for donations of money to raise £100,000 with which to increase the number of Outward Bound schools until the demand for places was met.[15] Field-Marshal Lord Montgomery had launched this appeal in 1948.[16]

Most 1950 and '51 newspaper articles about the setting up of White Hall did not mention any opposition to the idea. Just three (that I have found) did so. An article in the *Sheffield Daily Telegraph* said that Longland had helped to establish White Hall in the face of much public opposition.[17] In March 1951, after the first two schools' courses, the

Buxton Advertiser reported on a meeting of the Derbyshire education committee at which two councillors had expressed contrasting views on White Hall. Councillor A Buchan claimed that 'the bulk of the young people who attended the course[s] were earning good money'. He must have been referring to a youth service course. He asked: 'Are we justified in spending money on such people?' In reply, alderman F A Gent declared that 'the natural development of young people could not be measured in £ s. and d.'[18]

Councillor Cockerton was a prominent local politician, active in the rough and tumble of county-council wrangling and policy-making. In November 1950, after a procedural disagreement between Cockerton and alderman C F White, the chairman of Derbyshire county council, White wrote in a letter to the *Derby Evening Telegraph*: 'When first I knew Councillor Cockerton I thought he was a paragon of infallibility. When I knew him a little better I thought he was an ubiquitous quidnunc – but when I saw him receiving instructions from his legal colleague … I had come to the conclusion he was an obsequious sycophant.'[19]

On 16 November 1951 the *Buxton Advertiser* reported that a questioner at a Workers' Educational Association lecture had criticised White Hall as 'an expensive project'. The mayor, presiding over the meeting, said in defence of White Hall that 'it gave people the opportunity to develop initiative, and was similar to the Outward Bound schools, which had not been criticised'.

It is an iron rule of history that what looks inevitable in hindsight may have been far from obvious at the time. In setting up White Hall Centre in 1949–51, Longland faced considerable opposition; few people would have predicted the high degree of success that the centre would enjoy or the galvanising influence that the centre would exert on other LEAs.

A Buxton Outward Bound School?

Two months before White Hall Centre opened, Longland spoke at a meeting of the Ilkeston Rotary Club. A press report of this speech quoted him frequently, indirectly or directly, and it tells us something of what was in his head. It seems that at one point he was planning to name the new centre 'White Hall Outward Bound School' or perhaps 'Buxton Outward Bound School'. The report is about 420 words – hardly a pedagogic dissertation – yet it is the fourth longest Longland statement of White Hall aims that I know of. These aims range over a wide spectrum. If read imaginatively, there's something for every shade of outdoor evangelist of today:

Derbyshire may soon have an Outward Bound School to teach young people how to understand the countryside, Mr. Jack Longland, Director of Education for Derbyshire, told Ilkeston Rotary Club yesterday.

Already two such schools are in operation – one on the Welsh coast, mainly to teach safety in sailing, and the other at Eskdale in Cumberland.

Mr. Longland said that, in order to provide a proper place for the youngsters to develop their own potentialities and to give them a legitimate outlet for adventure, courage and endurance, the Derbyshire Education Committee were hoping shortly to open a training centre at Whitehall, Buxton, which would be known as an Outward Bound School.

The aims of the schools, said Mr. Longland, are to get together a group of young girls and boys, preferably between the ages of 16 and 20, in as natural surroundings as possible and teach them to understand the countryside and appreciate its beauty.

'The countryside, like the jungle, is neutral; it is what you make of it that counts and it takes certain qualities to make it a success,' Mr. Longland continued.

He said that far too often young people out in the country became bored with their surroundings simply through not knowing what to look for, and often their ignorance put them in danger. The Outward Bound School, with a trained staff, could help the youngsters to understand the necessary fundamentals of safe recreation in the countryside, and provide an excellent place for developing in them resourcefulness and independence.

After a short period of training at the school the 'recruits', in batches, are given the task of finding their own way across an area of country, using the knowledge they have been given, and at the same time having a great chance of developing their own initiative.

'What would have been a dangerous and tricky journey without the coaching is turned into a chanceless outing and is thoroughly enjoyed by all,' Mr. Longland added.

He said that rock climbing would form only a small part of the training. Bird watching would be encouraged.

'The schools are useful to all types of youngsters,' Mr Longland commented. 'The particularly intelligent boy has a chance to make his body as powerful as his brain, and therefore becomes a more evenly-balanced person. The rebel, helped in the right direction, learns to adapt his natural capabilities to other, more useful things, than being a nuisance.[20]

In using the name 'outward bound school' in a generic way, like 'grammar school' or 'comprehensive school', Longland may have chosen it as a convenient label for an only half-developed idea, without necessarily anticipating any formal link with the Outward Bound Trust. His audience would have already been at least vaguely familiar with what went on at Aberdovey OBSS and at Eskdale OBMS. As the 1950s passed, to the lay observer, the Outward Bound schools and White Hall Centre would remain indistinguishable from each other. In reality, the two types of centre would differ in some important ways.

Outdoor Recreation Promotion

In 1949–50 a number of newspapers carried short articles about the setting-up of White Hall Centre. Most of these articles mentioned the purpose of the centre, briefly and in plain language. The dominant message, among several, was that White Hall would introduce young people to outdoor leisure activities such as walking, camping and climbing. A closely related aim would be to train leaders of these activities. The following press cutting from August 1949 typifies these newspaper reports:

> Derbyshire Education Committee is going ahead with plans to provide a training centre for open country pursuits, including walking, camping and climbing ... [The mansion] is considered to be an ideal site to provide accommodation for out-door activities in the Peak District.
>
> Mr. J. L. Longland, the County Director of Education, who was with the 1933 Everest expedition, instigated the scheme, and one of its main objects will be to show that climbing can be a cheap and safe sport.
>
> The mansion will be run on youth hostel lines and will accommodate about 20. Organised parties are expected to attend from schools, but there will also be opportunities for young men and women and for leaders of youth organisations.[21]

A similar newspaper report from the same week quoted Longland directly:

> Mr. J. L. Longland, 41 [years old] ... says: 'We mean to show climbing can be a cheap and safe sport for all. At present, there are too many unnecessary accidents.'[22]

Both of these newspaper pieces mention the education committee's need for Ministry of Education permission to spend £3,000 on converting the country house. The 1944 Education Act, one of the more influential acts in the history of education in the UK, may have helped Derbyshire to gain this approval. Section 53 of this act made it the duty of LEAs to ensure that the provision for primary, secondary and further education included 'adequate facilities for recreation and social and physical training'. In connection with this duty, with the approval of the minister an LEA could establish and manage 'camps, holiday classes, playing fields, play centres and other places' and could 'organise games, expeditions and other activities'.[23]

A press report in December 1950 kept to the same clear-cut description as the earlier reports. It quoted from the programme of courses for January to May 1951: 'The basis will be fell-walking or rambling and there will be opportunities to learn and practise some of the skills and techniques of hillcraft on which ... the enjoyment of wild country depends – walking, path-finding, outdoor cooking, rock-climbing, and the study of country life and work.'[24]

On several occasions Longland compared the attractions and benefits of outdoor adventurous pursuits with those of sports traditionally taught at schools. He thought that there was a place for both. This argument did not go unchallenged. In December 1950, three days before White Hall Centre opened, a harsh critic of Longland wrote to the *Derby Evening Telegraph*, disapproving the spending of money on establishing White Hall. Longland replied at length. He argued for a fair deal for outdoor pursuits, as a facet of – or an extension of – physical education:

> Large sums are spent annually on the gymnasia and playing fields required for physical exercises and national games and, whether or not it be true that Waterloo was won on such playing fields, nobody disputes the worth-whileness of this expenditure.

We ought not to overlook the fact that our wilder national play-grounds, like the High Peak, with their less artificial rules-of-the-game, offer disciplines of adventure and self-reliance which are of high educational value and which the young are, of themselves, seeking on an unprecedented scale. White Hall is a modest and experimental attempt to make the most of these opportunities.[25]

On Friday 29 December 1950, immediately before White Hall's opening weekend, the writer of an article in the *Daily Mirror* supported Longland's endeavours:

This is something to shout about! At last a county education authority has discovered that recreation means more than playing fields.

Town boys who can so easily learn how to be a footballer, how to clear a puck, or how to deal with a sticky wicket, have had to find their own way to the hills. Now Derbyshire has thrown a lot of hard work and £11,000 into the White Hall venture.[26]

In seeking in 1950 to broaden physical education in Derbyshire, and hence by example more generally, Longland was ahead of most tertiary PE faculties. Few had added outdoor pursuits to their programmes with any degree of commitment. One exception was the University of Birmingham's PE department, which had run an outdoor-activity camp at Hoathwaite beside Coniston Water in 1947. This had become an annual event. (Over the years this would develop from a six-week camp to a full-time enterprise with permanent buildings, the Priestley Centre.)

In the years that followed, Longland would repeat this argument many times, such as in a talk to the staff of the CCPR in 1955, when he spoke about there being 'too much concentration on teams games which only a few of the consumers will, in fact, play later on in life'.[27] According to Ken Ogilvie, in the mid-1950s the nation's PE colleges were still not really ready for outdoor pursuits. Adventurous outdoor recreation was still only a peripheral topic at Carnegie College of Physical Education and at Loughborough College of Physical Education.[28]

Writing in 1954–5, Bob Pettigrew lamented the lowly status of adventurous outdoor recreation within PE. He said that notwithstanding the obvious value of outdoor pursuits such as rock climbing and sailing as training agencies and as carry-over subjects from school into adult society, these forms of training remained the cinderella section of physical education both in specialist training colleges and in schools.

In 1956, Cyril Machin, a voluntary instructor and White Hall identity, much remembered for his likeable personality and for some wayward climbing habits, reiterated Longland's and Pettigrew's arguments:

> For generations the gymnasium and football fields have been essential features of English education, but the contribution which Open Country Pursuits have to make has not been so long, or so widely, recognised. A generation or two ago the hills were the particular preserve of a small and, for the most part, a relatively well-off handful of enthusiasts.
>
> To-day the Lake District, Snowdonia, the Scottish Highlands, and the Peak District are national playgrounds, and young people flock to them in thousands. Educational theory and practice are now trying to catch up with this development … Open Country Pursuits, with their more natural and less artificial rules-of-the-game, do offer disciplines of adventure and self-reliance which are no less important than the lessons to be learnt from our traditional national games.[29]

Seventeen years later, in the book *Outdoor Education*, Parker and Meldrum would say that residential outdoor pursuits centres were generally regarded as serving four aims, one of which was to introduce young people to a lasting and worthwhile recreation. They severely criticised this aim.[30] Whether that criticism itself has stood the test of time is debatable.

Accident Reduction

One strand of Longland's thinking, shared by the BMC of 1946, then two years old, was a concern for safety, allied to a belief that many of the climbing and mountaineering accidents that were happening were caused by inexperience. Before World War II, rock climbing had been mainly a middle- and upper middle-class activity characterised by protracted apprenticeships and insular old clubs. After the war, what had been the preserve of the middle class became far more egalitarian.[31] New provincial and regional groups were formed: 'From about 1944, pre-dating the Sound of Music by 15 years, the Derbyshire hills were full of the sound of climbing clubs being formed. This phenomenon was due in part to the vast post-war increase in the number of active climbers and the difficulty they had in gaining membership of one of the senior clubs.'[32] Longland later, in 1952, explained the reason for this nonadmittance: 'the established clubs, perhaps understandably, have been unwilling to open the floodgates to all who might wish to join lest their traditions be swept away'.[33] Reflecting on this in 1976, his story remained unchanged: 'We tried hard to persuade the established climbing clubs to open wide their gates to youngsters, and in general we failed.'[34] Elizabeth Coxhead, discussing the postwar surge in the popularity of climbing, probed the old traditions a little further than Longland: 'Responsibility for proper training was accepted by some of the existing climbing clubs, but by more it was evaded; the attitude too often was: "We don't want the rabble on the hills."'[35]

A writer in the *Derby Evening Telegraph* in April 1947 explained one of the reasons for the climbing boom:

> One week-end evening you may have for company in your favourite Peakland pub a company of husky men in windproof jackets, moss-stained flannels or knickerbockers, and clinkered boots; and their talk will contain unfamiliar words like 'abseiling', 'traverse belay', 'arete' and 'tricouni'. They are rock climbers – a coterie grown tenfold since so many, in their war training, discovered both a head and an aptitude for heights.[36]

The BMC empowered its secretary, J E Q Barford, to edit a book 'giving the technical information essential to any beginner … if he is to learn to hill-walk, or to rock-climb safely and efficiently'. The council estimated that at least nine out of ten mountain accidents in Britain were due to ignorance, or carelessness, or both.[37] *Climbing in Britain*, a Pelican book published in 1946 at a price of one shilling, sold 120,000 copies before it went out of print.[38]

Reading *Climbing in Britain* today reminds you of where climbing had reached just four years before White Hall Centre began. In 1946, the merits of laid nylon rope were still a matter for debate. Barford avoided taking sides: 'Until the outbreak of war the best ropes were considered to be of manila hemp, Italian hemp or flax. But experience in the services has shown the virtue of nylon and it is not improbable that soon this may become the standard rope. Meanwhile, I shall say nothing further here as to the respective merits.'[39] In reality nylon rope, the first rope to stretch like elastic, was far superior to hemp rope.

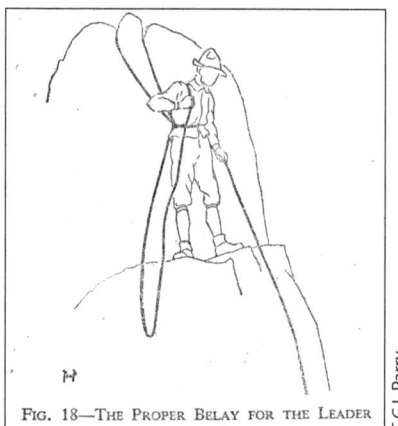

FIG. 18—THE PROPER BELAY FOR THE LEADER

T C L Parry.

A line drawing from *Climbing in Britain* (1946). This modest 160-page paperback met an urgent need for information on techniques.

Unattributed. From the *Boy's Own Paper*, April 1938.

A B Sutcliffe, a Lakeland guide, bringing up a young pupil during a lesson in climbing. This photograph was used to illustrate a *Boy's Own Paper* instructional article on rock climbing, April 1938.

Some young climbers became very good very quickly. Standards rose. But learning climbing techniques and ropework skills from a book, even from an accurate and informative book, rather than from experienced climbers, was fraught with snags. A sixteen-year-old Joe Brown learnt this lesson on the Kinder Downfall cliffs, shortly after reading Colin Kirkus's popular and commonsense book *Let's Go Climbing*.[40] Even after the publication of *Climbing in Britain*, inexperience remained a common factor in climbing accidents.

On 30 July 1948, the day before Glenmore Lodge opened as the Scottish Centre of Outdoor Training, a press report about it was headed 'Aim: Fewer Climbing Accidents'.[41] Lord Douglas-Hamilton later described Glenmore Lodge as 'the first Civilian Mountain School in Great-Britain'.[42]

Reflecting on the training aspect in 1975, Peter Mosedale wrote: 'One of the main arguments for the establishment of outdoor centres at public expense was that adequate training should be given in safety matters, not only directly to young people interested in taking up these pursuits, but also to leaders in organizations such as the Scouts and Guides, Colleges of Education, Youth Clubs and Secondary Schools generally, where members were taken on hill and water expeditions.'

Reservations about Character Training

Having now covered the promoting of outdoor recreation and the reducing of the occurrence of accidents, I have dealt with the two most straightforward reasons for White Hall's existence. They were frequently mentioned in writing, especially in newspaper reports, and were obvious roles for an outdoor-pursuits centre to undertake. The same could not be said of character training (or character building). The subject of character training – its merits, its faults, its believers, its critics – is not straightforward. But understanding the 1950s and 60s debate about character training is a necessary part of understanding what sort of place White Hall became.

I will show, over three chapters, that by 1957 a collective response from White Hall had amounted to a determined rejection of character training of the pre-war sort, the very foundation of Outward Bound and of Scouting and Guiding, and a central plank of Gordonstoun, the 1943 Norwood Report, and the War Office's mountaincraft courses for army cadets. The most important constituents of this rejection were Longland's cautious avoidance of the subject of character training, Mosedale's private scepticism about it and Drasdo's outspoken opposition to it (not put in writing until 1962). At least one other White Hall instructor, Arthur Afford, appears to have supported this rejection. Another individual with links to White Hall, Bob Pettigrew, was well aware of the negative baggage that the term 'character building' was beginning to carry. He wrote: 'I want to make it clear that I am not claiming for out-door activities powerful character building qualities.'

All this happened in White Hall's first seven years, before any other LEA outdoor-pursuits centre existed. In rejecting character training as one of its aims, the White Hall approach to residential courses involving adventurous pursuits departed significantly from what had gone before. If indeed White Hall was a pattern followed by many other LEA centres, as is commonly believed, the strength and importance of its influence on the development of British outdoor education may have been greater than has previously been recognised.

Finally, in discussing the place of character training, there is one other aspect, an apparent contradiction, that we need to understand: while something called 'character training' grew decidedly out of favour, something else called 'social and personal development' became a legitimate and meritorious goal.

*

Questions about moral training taxed the brains of Greek philoso-
phers.[43] In more recent times, in Britain, the idea of 'character training'
– a process closely related to moral training – dates from the public
school revival in the 19th century. A definition I found in an American dictionary of education published in 2003 is inclusively broad, or
perhaps hopelessly vague, and would have been equally suitable for
a British dictionary of education of 1903: character education is 'an
approach to education that focuses on developing students' character
and supporting their moral reasoning and development'.[44]

Among the influential headmasters who inspired new attitudes to
the development of character was a young Scottish academic, Cecil
Reddie, the founder in 1889 of Abbotsholme School, a progressive
public (fee charging) boarding school in rural south Derbyshire.[45] Reddie was a complex fellow who moved between two worlds: that of his
cherished boys and that of solemn educational theorists. Beyond these
two spheres, his manner towards his schoolmasters was autocratic and
his relationship with most of them was distant and sometimes riven
by strong disagreement. He has been described as a man of exalted
ideals, with exacting demands and a great intensity of purpose, but
who took life terribly seriously and showed little sense of humour.[46] In
1900, Abbotsholme had about sixty pupils, in the process of acquiring
'the manly bearing and independent habits which [would] fit them
peculiarly for life, and make them not merely students, but men.'[47] In
1902 the *Sheffield Daily Telegraph* reported:

> Derbyshire has from time almost immemorial been famous for
> its Great Public Schools. If they are not as celebrated as Eton and
> Harrow, Rugby and Winchester, they hold their own with other
> scholastic establishments. Ashbourne, Buxton, Denstone, Derby,
> Mackworth, Repton, Risley, and Trent are illustrations ready at
> hand … Another Derbyshire school that is coming to the front
> is Abbotsholme, between Rocester and Ashbourne.[48]

Reddie called Abbotsholme the 'New School'. It was novel in almost
every way, except in being for boys only, or more precisely – in Reddie's
own words – 'for English boys of eleven to eighteen belonging to the
directing classes'.[49] Reddie's mentors were Ruskinians, and 'Abbotsholme was inspired by Ruskin's disdain for the competitive society,
and his wish to replace undue bookishness with "learning by doing"
so as to foster co-operativeness'.[50] Reddie's strong belief in being close

to nature made natural science an obvious subject, with work on the estate providing the practical experience to match the theory. Vegetables were grown, harvested and cooked; classes were suspended during haymaking; digging, wood-chopping and fencing were perennial tasks and livestock and bees were cared for. Such a mixture of farm and school was unknown in England at that time.[51] The invention of Abbotsholme and other New Schools of that period has been called an attempt to 'rescue the upper classes from the stupefied overconformity of the Public Schools'.[52]

Pupils at Abbotsholme were given unusual freedom to wander in the countryside. Reddie devised a uniform of comfortable clothes (soft shirt, soft tie, Norfolk jacket of grey tweed and knee breeches of the same material) at a time when boys at public schools wore stiff collars and top hats.[53]

Other activities available, usually in the afternoons, were bicycling, fishing and boating.

Abbotsholme's patronage during the school's first fifty years had its ups and down, as also, in the wider educational world, did notions about character training and the development of morals.

In 1911 in a tetchy exchange of letters to the editor of the *Daily Mail*, five correspondents connected with teaching or the Scout movement disputed which institutions – elementary schools or Scouts – were the most effective builders of character. There was an implied acceptance that character building was not only a desirable but an essential part of education. One of the correspondents wrote: 'No teacher, man or woman, worthy of the name ever neglects character building. It is brought out in history, geography, literature, music, and in nearly all subjects taught. Character building is the foundation of any good teaching.'[54]

Another enthusiastic promoter of character training was Robert Baden-Powell, whose life has received prolonged and penetrating biographical revision. Some of the complexity is apparent in Robert MacDonald's suggestion that the Scout movement was a success because it was both progressive and reactionary. Its conservative, imperialist and militarist aspects appealed to some people; its liberal ideas in education and social theory appealed to others.[55] A common remark of Baden-Powell's contemporaries was that he 'had discovered the one thing which alone would make a youth movement successful: he remembered that boys loved adventure, and he had found a way to let them have fun in a world of their own.'[56]

The Scout movement, despite its phenomenal success, attracted several criticisms. One, of being militaristic (seen as a virtue by some people, a drawback by others) eventually died away, after gradual change and fresh scrutiny. Another criticism, about the practical ingredients of Scouting's character training, persisted. Ernest Reynolds, one of Baden-Powell's more benign biographers, explained Baden-Powell's use of the word 'character':

> B.-P. used the term 'character' in a special way; by itself the word simply means the sum of the qualities – good or bad – which go to make up a man's nature. To him the word came to have a more specific meaning; when he used it, he implied the character which makes a man a good member of society …

An example of Baden-Powell using the word 'character' in this way appeared in Part VI of the original edition of *Scouting for Boys*. Under the heading 'Hints to Instructors: Character', the advice was not so much a hint as a categorical statement of a basic principle: 'Keep before your mind in all your teaching that the whole ulterior object of this scheme is to form character in the boys – to make them manly, good citizens.'[57]

In attempting to clarify what Baden-Powell meant by the word 'character', Reynolds inadvertently revealed a basic predicament with the notion of character training: who decides the qualities of a good member of society?[58]

The Outward Bound schools, starting in 1941 with Aberdovey OBSS, became confident champions of character training, for a while.

One of the places where some individuals would view character training cautiously or uneasily or even sceptically, from the beginning in 1950, would be White Hall Centre. In a draft magazine article sent to the publishers two weeks before White Hall opened, Longland dealt slightly guardedly with character training: 'Without making an exaggerated claim about the value of walking and climbing in building character, it can safely be said that these pastimes can help to produce self-reliant people who trust and are trusted by their companions in difficulties and dangers and … '[59]

To collect more evidence of Longland's views, we need to briefly step further ahead into the 1950s. Longland's public statements on character training are conspicuous by their rarity, especially if we take into account that he was familiar with the theories and practices of Kurt Hahn. This quite revealing aspect may not have been noted by previous writers. Longland supported much that Hahn stood for. However, Longland was also capable of criticising specific aspects of Hahn's approach to schooling. In 1953 in a letter to Adam Arnold-Brown, Longland agreed that the Eskdale methods should not be allowed to be 'controlled too much ... by any mystique which may be thought to be part of the Tables and the Law handed down by Kurt Hahn'.[60]

Longland's views on character training surfaced in January 1955 in a frank talk given at a CCPR staff conference. He said that the traditional view that the value of team games lay in the formation of character had gradually become a bandwagon that all sorts of sports had crept onto. The basis of the character-training claims was a simple belief in transference. If you learnt unselfish behaviour in, say, a football team, then you would show the same qualities in your work-a-day life. However, he said, the transference notion had become a platitude of school speech days and an undisputed ingredient 'in autobiography after autobiography by famous sportsmen' and 'in propaganda for organisations like the Outward Bound Trust'.

> You have to ask, 'Is this theory [of transference] true?' 'Is character built up by transference from the games field into later life?' We are bound to answer 'No!' In no way is it completely true. And it is only true, if it is true at all, in a very indirect way ... Did Hillary get up Everest because of his indomitable character, or did he develop that character because he had made himself a mountaineer and so got up Everest? This theory of transference is altogether too slick and altogether too easy.[61]

What came next was a forerunner of points that would be repeated by some character-training sceptics of the 1960s and 70s. Longland was ahead of the crowd. He described three unnamed sportspeople (a rugby player and two climbers) whose admirable sporting personas were unfortunately absent in their daily lives. For Longland, a behavioural change that transferred from physical recreation to the rest of someone's life – if this did occasionally happen – was a by-product, a secondary result of taking part in an activity for enjoyment, a bonus for some individuals.[62]

According to Harold Drasdo, who was at White Hall in about 1956–7, Longland recognised value in Hahn's version of character training, but was well aware that the notion of character was a complex abstraction. He cautioned against setting desirable character traits by selecting whatever moral virtues happened to be institutional or national priorities: such as, for a young seaman, unerring obedience and solid religious beliefs.[63] Yet the Outward Bound Trust, a body Longland supported, had nailed its character-building colours high on the *Prince Louis's* mast and was widely seen as an organisation caring for the spiritual and moral wellbeing of young people.[64]

Longland's doubts about character training surfaced briefly again, indirectly, in 1957 in a chapter he wrote for an edited book. By then, the beliefs behind character training amounted to such a shaky and controversial edifice that Longland neatly avoided the subject by saying that he found character building to be too difficult a subject to write about.[65]

Peter Mosedale was a member of the Climbers' Club from 1939 until at least 1954. His involvement in climbing bridged the gap between Longland's hemp rope, tricounis and rubbers generation and the post-war nylon rope, Vibram soles and PAs era. Mosedale's thinking on outdoor pursuits closely matched Longland's in many respects. The two men may have privately discussed the moral assumptions, class values, religious influences and military imperatives that lay behind the term 'character training', and which led to some observers questioning the intentions of the character builders. But they did not discuss these issues openly in the early 1950s in a way that reached the general public, such as with visiting journalists.

Mosedale's reservations about the efficacy of using adventurous sports as agencies for character building, and about the propriety of using character building as a means of social control and as a stimulus for nationalism, did not appear in any newspaper reports or articles. He eventually expressed his doubts forcefully in writing but not until he wrote his manuscript of 1975, which was 'lost' until 2014. Mosedale harboured reservations about some particular versions of character training, especially the principle of character training through exacting exposure to an unfamiliar and hostile environment. Mosedale's manuscript, intended as the basis for a book, is quite short, just sixty-nine A4 pages (22,000 words). Yet it is the perfect partner for Arthur Afford's equally informative local history. The two works, although different in styles and scope, together tell us much about the thinking and intentions behind White Hall Centre.

You only need to reach as far as page six of the Mosedale manuscript to arrive at some deep reservations about character building. Writing

in 1975, he wanted nothing to do with some of the manifestations of
character training that had been fashionable in the first half of the 20th
century, intended to mass-produce decent, well-mannered chaps, good
sports who would always be ready to face a danger. He repeats these
doubts subsequently in several places. They had clearly influenced the
directions he had headed with White Hall. His first example dates back
to the 19th century. He questions upper-class claims linking adventure
on mountains with allegedly virtuous traits:

> Early expeditions, usually disguised as scientific explorations, gave
> way to the pursuit of adventure for its own sake as, increasingly,
> this type of person [the sort with the necessary wealth and free
> time] grew more remote from direct participation in industry
> and commerce. The fact that a mountain was there justified the
> climbing of it. Adventure for its own sake became acceptable.
> Exertion and regulated danger came to be seen as beneficial to
> the character and not only to the physique. The emotional impact
> of wild scenery handed down from the early Romantic poets and
> artists became alloyed with the puritanism and the arrogance of
> the active upper-class sportsmen.[66]

Staying on the character-training theories of privileged adventurers,
Mosedale then selects a 1922 Everest expeditioner, founding member
of the Alpine Ski Club and president of the Alpine Club, and is elo-
quently dismissive:

> A jump forward in time to 1918 reveals George Finch, for, exam-
> ple, arguing in his book *The Making of a Mountaineer*: 'Our youth
> is beginning to find the dancing floor, the tennis court and the
> playing fields of Great Britain too narrow, too lacking in scope,
> perhaps also a bit too soft, and the craving grows for wider fields
> and a sterner, freer pastime.' This, in its references to the recrea-
> tions of a privileged few and in its date of publication toward the
> end of the bloodiest war on record, is revealing. His claim, and
> others like it, can be traced in their course from the outer reaches
> of leisured society, through military training, into formal state and
> local authority provision for education.[67]

Finally, he dismantles some purple prose of Geoffrey Young, an elder
statesman of the climbing world, much admired for his first ascents in

the Alps before the first world war. For Young, and others of his generation, the youth of today were the soldiers of tomorrow. In March 1942,
when Britain faced starvation and ruin, Young, now sixty-five, wrote a
letter to *The Times* titled 'Stamina in War: Example of the Commandos'.
He seemed to claim that the process of becoming a mountaineer (but
only a British one) would imbue a person with desirable attributes and
behaviours that would be of use beyond mountaineering:

> … it is the men of our country who have made of mountain craft
> – as in the past centuries we have made of sailing and seaman-
> ship – a masterly process of training in self-knowledge and self-
> discipline, in individual hardihood, and in comradeship in service.

The letter then praised the County Badge scheme but insisted that 'the
training be begun early, at twelve years old, and that it contain those elements which toughen the moral as well as the physical fibre and which
can continue to provoke the individual to always sterner progress'.

It seems a fair assumption that Mosedale had first read this letter in
1942, when it was published. There is a possibility that as early as 1942,
eight years before he arrived at White Hall, he had been sceptical about
using the mountains to 'toughen the moral as well as the physical fibre'
of ordinary young people.

We cannot be sure of that. It is a matter of conjecture. But what
we know for certain is that when writing about this letter in 1975,
Mosedale rejected the wartime suggestion of using our mountains
to transform twelve-year-old boys into splendid fighting men who
would joyfully give up their lives. Perhaps Major Mosedale of the
Royal Artillery had seen a different sort of war than the war in which
Young, forty years older than he was, had lost a leg and been mentioned
in dispatches.[68] Mosedale picked out Young's jingoistic men-of-our-
country sentence and dismissed it concisely: 'This masterly use of emo-
tive language has sufficient power to hide the very doubtful accuracy
of its basic statement.'

These three Mosedale comments are very telling. George Finch was
a man of 'brilliance, determination and complexity'.[69] *The Making of
a Mountaineer* was a beautifully written influential classic, crafted to
inspire young people to take up mountaineering. Bob Pettigrew, writing
in 1997 about mountain training, praised Finch's contribution to the
richness and variety of our mountain literature.[70] Mosedale, in contrast,
had strongly rejected some traits of that written heritage.

Young was an eminent and respected mountaineer and poet and educationist. He had inspired Longland at Cambridge, and was an early advocate of mountain pursuits as an adjunct to education.[71] He had met Kurt Hahn in Germany in 1926, he had later become a founding member and the first chairman of Gordonstoun's board of governors, and he had helped Hahn to start the Outward Bound schools.[72] His book *On High Hills* (1927) had become a classic of mountaineering literature. He had climbed the Matterhorn eight times, on the last occasion, in 1928, with a wooden leg. Young had crafted his letter to *The Times* to stir the spontaneous and universal patriotism that was prevalent. Some people had admired the letter and credited him with anticipating the commando idea. In 1943–4, he had played a crucial role in the founding of the BMC. He died in 1958, aged eighty-one. Yet despite Young's formidable status and influence, Mosedale did not hesitate in exposing weaknesses in Young's arguments.

I have discovered little about Mosedale's wartime experiences, but a clue to the reasons for his distaste for the pre-war versions of character training may lie in a poem written by him and published in an Australian newspaper in 1974.[73] The poem also leaves one wondering about the impact on him of his post-White Hall stint working for the National Coal Board:

Britain at war
So was it all poor Tommy Atkins' fault
When mud and shellfire slowed him to a halt,
When, hurled in thousands at the uncut wire,
Whole armies reeled and Britain felt the fire?

And was it that the quiet-voiced young men
From city, village street and lonely lane
Accepted all the blame, just smiling when,
In failure bleak and nights of fear and pain
As yet another generation fell,
Their leaders claimed all could and would be well?

When Britain reels from lost industrial health
In peace that is but war for power and wealth,
Is it the rank and file whose will to win
Has failed and let the jackals in?

Is it poor Tommy Atkins' fault this time
As Britain still slips down while others climb,
Or is it that his leaders once again
Have all been planning for the wrong campaign?

By 1975, Mosedale had had twenty-five years to mull over the various examples of character training that had been identifiable halfway
through the 20th century. His manuscript's sceptical references to
character training of a narrow, upper-crust pre-war sort – a tool of
the Establishment – amount to a comprehensive questioning of the
1940s–50s Outward Bound ethos. In describing the transformation of
the role of outdoor recreation in society that had taken place by 1940,
he scorns the influence of a minority who saw outdoor recreation as a
means to an end, linked to the necessities of national survival in the war:

> Whereas the majority of enthusiasts were attracted by the oppor-
> tunities given by outdoor recreation to complete themselves as
> persons, to escape from manmade deprivation into the fresh air
> and contact with a more natural world, there was still the more
> puritanical and masochistic element, especially among those in
> authority, which saw the main human and educational value of
> such enterprise in terms of courage and hardship and struggle.
> And it was but a step further to those who saw the benefits in
> terms of race, eugenics and open elitism.[74]

The growth of one's character, in Mosedale's view, involved – among
other things – emotional, intellectual and physical education:

> Particularly in such fields as the teaching of outdoor sports,
> because of their history, there is still strong support for the belief
> that education is concerned with the formation of character and
> the production of 'good' individuals who will contribute well-
> balanced activity and practical effort to society. And educational
> justification for so considerable an effort in outdoor recreation
> may need to be found in Britain in this characteristic concern,
> in which emotional, intellectual and physical education are all
> necessarily involved.[75]

In Mosedale's opinion, the influence most likely to produce these
rounded citizens was a liberal education, and even that could be a

relatively slight force compared to someone's family background and life outside school:

> It is unfortunate, however, that opportunities for emotional education in Britain through outdoor recreation appear so often to be restricted to links which tie up with an over-riding and rather illiberal concern for character education in a narrow sense. Much more could be done to cultivate emotional education through the eyes, the ears and the hands, through art, through music, through crafts and an appreciation of local cultures. Judgement and character depend, in the opinions of many, on a liberal education in which outdoor activities and experiences can play a valid even if a minor role. They depend even more – to keep the matter in perspective – on the family life and the experiences of the young outside school or college.[76]

That's enough on character training, for the time being. Keep in mind one thing: Mosedale's ideas lay on a library shelf, unread, until 2014. His criticism of Geoffrey Young's interpretation of character training has yet to meet widespread scrutiny. There are other views on Young, the bohemian and louche figure who influenced generation after generation of young climbers. Writing in 1997, Bob Pettigrew portrayed Young as a faultless influence on the use of the mountains as an educational medium and for character training.[77] The subject of character training will return in Chapter 8, under 'Veering Away from Outward Bound'.

The Countryside

'I hate the outdoors. To me the outdoors is where the car is.' So said Will Durst, an American writer and political satirist. In about 1996 Bill Bryson walked the Appalachian Trail with Katz, one of his oldest friends but not the easiest of companions. Mostly, for Katz, 'hiking was a tiring dirty, pointless slog between distantly spaced comfort zones'.[78] It takes all sorts to make a world. The school-pupil Will Dursts of this world probably know their own young minds well enough to keep far away from outdoor-pursuits centres and sheep tracks. But many young people who live in towns and cities have never or seldom visited the countryside; they have not yet formed views and attitudes on the outdoors or on the strange idea of using one's legs to walk across the landscape or on the even more weird idea of sleeping on the ground, using a folded jersey for a pillow. In the case of Derbyshire, these slightly curious don't-knowers need introducing to the rolling villaged uplands of the White Peak, the heather and groughs of the Dark Peak, the gritstone edges, the public footpaths and bridleways, the caves and reservoirs, and the rivers and streams and the famous warm spring. The different landscapes, at different seasons, in different weather. The copses, woods and plantations. The country lanes. The disused railway lines. The stone circles, the Roman roads, the Saxon crosses, the Norman churches, the stone farmhouses, the great mansions.

Few explicit mentions of these things appear in the purpose statements that I have collected from the late 1940s and the 1950s. The word 'environment' had not yet begun the surge in usage that later would spread it densely through everyday English. The terms 'environmental appreciation' and 'environmental education' had yet to become common. People talked about liking the countryside and about nature studies and field studies; there is a light scattering of these phrases in my collection of purpose statements. A few mentions of country codes occur. The main reference to the landscape was in Longland's reported speech to Ilkeston Rotary Club, in which he talked about teaching boys and girls 'to understand the countryside and appreciate its beauty'.

Part of the reason for the infrequency of specific references to appreciation of the countryside may have been that the writers were taking it for granted that the awareness of landscape and a knowledge of things rural would develop as automatic adjuncts to the outdoor pursuits. An article in the *Daily Mirror* discussed this very point:

> A Derbyshire County spokesman told me:
> 'I don't think that printed countryside codes are much use.' (I couldn't agree more.)
> 'We've got to *show* city people that leaving a gate open in the country can be as destructive as throwing sand into a turbine. The "students" at White Hall will be a mixed lot … from clubs and factories and grammar schools.'[79]

Another part of the reason for the infrequency of references to countryside enlightenment may be that the writers thought that many schools already offered field studies, either at school or at residential field-studies centres. Field studies, furthermore, had a century's start on outdoor pursuits in becoming a normal part of schooling. At Bootham School in York, for example, the Natural History Society had been formed in 1834 and its members had taken part in many excursions.[80]

Mountaineering has been called a way to recapture 'the euphoric satisfaction and extraordinary empowerment of reconnecting with nature and each other'.[81] The sport contains a fluid mix of muscular, environmental and social elements. A day spent as a member of a group on outdoor pursuits in the Peak District is a similar and equally complicated cocktail. A range of scholars and academics have spent over sixty years delving into the contents of this cocktail: what goes on at residential outdoor centres. In 1973 in one of the earliest books on outdoor education, Parker and Meldrum singled out countryside appreciation for special status, outsparkling the other valid, but lesser, reasons for outdoor centres to exist.[82] Maybe they had a point. John Muir, the Scottish-born conservationist and naturalist, would have agreed with them. He offered this advice to a companion in North America: 'Keep close to Nature's heart ... and break clear away, once in a while, and climb a mountain or spend a week in the woods. Wash your spirit clean.'[83]

Opening-weekend Aims Declaration

In 1956 Cyril Machin wrote an article titled 'The Educational Value of Open Country Pursuits', which was published in the *Journal of the Midland Association of Mountaineers*. Three paragraphs in the middle of this article declared the aims of White Hall Centre. Although Machin did not show any of the text as being direct quotation, the introduction implied official origins: ' ... at the inauguration [30–31 December 1950] the Director of Education, Jack Longland, supported by the Warden of the Centre, Peter Mosedale, stated their aims. These included ... '

The language that followed, in the first of the three paragraphs, is formal and sounds authentic, as if Machin had copied the text from an original official document. It seems safe to interpret this paragraph as closely matching what Longland had said during the opening weekend:

> ... stated their aims. These included the provision of basic training in hillcraft in all weathers and in the allied sports of climbing, caving, camping, canoeing, and ski-ing wherever conditions are suitable; to set before those coming to the Centre a vision of greatness in Nature and in Man, to inspire them with it and to persuade them to approach it in humility. This involves the training of self-reliance, the discipline of living together, the opportunity for the boy and girl to use their abundant physical and nervous energies in activities which can do nothing but good. It involves

an uplifting of the spirit and a challenge to the whole personality. It provides natural penalties, sharper than a referee's whistle, for inefficiency, slackness and selfishness. All these advantages can be gained without overtaxing strength, providing the work is continuously adjusted to the age and condition of the student and to the weather.

The last sentence highlights an aspect that comes across strongly in the next chapter and particularly in Peter Mosedale's accounts: the need for flexibility, keeping things in proportion, not overdoing things, pragmatism rather than any one narrow educational philosophy.

Earlier in the article, Machin remarked that the Lake District, Snowdonia, the Scottish Highlands and the Peak District had become national playgrounds and that young people were flocking to them in thousands. In response to this, he said, educational theory and practice were trying to catch up with the developments. The second and third paragraphs of his article's section on aims seem to be Machin's own words, written in 1956, attempting to state the approach and ambitions of White Hall in a way that would be consistent with educational theory and practice:

> Everything taught, no matter how elementary, is based on sound principles and practice, so that any part of the teaching will serve as a foundation for further training and experience to build on.
>
> The Centre does not aim at producing an expert in any activity, its aim is to start the beginner on the right road, the safe road, the most rewarding road. Educationally there are two main ambitions. The first is to extend physical education in the broadest sense to the out-door world [and] to deal similarly, but to a lesser degree, with other matters such as geography and natural history. The second is to give young people experience of living and taking responsibility in a very energetic small community, to improve their knowledge of each other and of themselves, and to encourage them to regard life as an adventure in which the most satisfying rewards come to those who put most into it. The desire is to make those who come to the Centre more aware of the importance of high standards at work, at play, and in their service to the community.[84]

One can speculate on what prompted Machin to write this article. We cannot say for sure. But the above two paragraphs could be an early example of a writer seeking to express the purpose of an LEA outdoor centre in terms that would satisfy educationists and lead to authoritative approval of the money being spent on it.

A week after White Hall's opening weekend, while at the North of England Education Conference in Stockport, Longland returned to the theme of a fair deal for outdoor pursuits:

> Mr. J. L. Longland, Director of Education, Derbyshire, said that in physical training in schools we had concentrated too much on sports which were later enjoyed by only a few. The focus should be on a wider and more relevant renewal of physical activities after schooldays than we had yet conceived.[85]

This argument would later become self-evident to many hillwalkers and climbers and kayakers and dinghy sailors and yachtsmen. In 1950 it was a small but progressive siege weapon, aimed at the solid conservative battlements of traditional physical education; it was underpowered for the task, but was deployed by enthusiasts determined to persevere. Longland would still be setting forth this argument fifteen years later. Ironically, some of the opposition to the running of courses in climbing and mountaineering for young people would come not from conservative forces in physical education but from reactionaries in mountain sports.[86] The arrival of the Mountain Leadership Certificate (MLC) in 1964 would further complicate this situation.

Aims Statement from an Annual Programme

White Hall's annual printed programmes in the 1950s and 60s included a short section explaining the centre's aims. Until Mosedale's manuscript turned up, the earliest known example of such a section in a programme came from the one for April–September 1961.[87] Mosedale takes us back another decade, quoting a statement that appeared in some of the annual programmes of the early 1950s:

> [The centre] is intended for young people of both sexes who are interested in open country pursuits. It is for those who have already discovered the hills. It is also – and equally – for the complete beginner.

On the hills, as at sea, the beginner has much to learn. White Hall is a place where young people may learn and practise the skills of hill-craft which will equip them to go into mountain country with enterprise and confidence. It is a place where they may discover the joy, the challenge, the invigoration and the special comradeship which the hills offer. And it is a place where the beginner will meet experienced mountaineers and fell-walkers, not only as instructors but as friends.[88]

*

In this chapter we have discussed two purposes – recreation promotion and accident reduction – that Longland briefly but explicitly prescribed for White Hall on numerous occasions. A third purpose, character training, appeared occasionally – but with doubtful origins – in newspaper articles about White Hall. A fourth purpose, he mentioned at least once: teaching boys and girls to understand the countryside and to appreciate landscapes. To this fourth one we could add seascapes.

To some observers, the first two ambitions – recreation promotion and accident reduction – seemed to be obvious and straightforward responses to needs that had arisen, especially in rock climbing. Yet behind the good intentions lay the seeds of a baffling and potentially divisive dilemma. By improving the training of novice climbers, and hence enhancing their technical skills and their understanding of risk, a dangerous sport could be made less risky. But climbing could never be made completely safe, especially at the time we are talking about, the late 1940s – early 1950s. Climbing was (and in some of its forms still is) a philosophically complicated sport, with unwritten rules, vulnerable traditions and an alluring mix of the rational and the irrational. Was it a suitable sport for young people to take up? Would their parents understand it? Some climbers were convinced that parents would not understand the sport and that climbing should not be promoted at all.

Tom Price summed up the dilemma: 'We are, of course, inclined to want to have our cake and eat it. We say: "Give our children thrilling adventures and make absolutely certain nothing untoward happens."'[89] Trying to meet both of these requirements results in a feeling of discomfort; this tension or anxiety is a state that psychologists call cognitive dissonance. The mind always tries to reduce the dissonance. But, in this particular example, if you believe deeply in both the value of adventure and the need for safety, it is difficult to resolve the inconsistency.

In 1951 the journalist and author Ronald W Clark, writing about climbing and hillwalking accidents, raised other aspects of the same dilemma:

> There is another problem, even more difficult [than the shortage of mountaineering instructors] because it is a psychological one. Mountaineering is an art or craft as well as a sport. It has been described as 'a way of looking at life', and it is not infrequently described as a religion. Whatever one may think of such definitions, it is certain that [mountaineering] does not lend itself to systematisation, to control, to gradings. And, however flexibly any national training scheme were organised, it would seem to many people that the bright glory of the day had been put in shadow, that the business was somehow degenerating to mountaineering by numbers. This would not necessarily be so, but there is a widespread and genuine fear of such a development.[90]

We now know that two perspectives were heading for a philosophical collision; the expectations of an increasingly risk-averse society would collide with the determination of mountaineers to retain total control of the way their sport was practised.

*

In his monumental history of outdoor education, Ken Ogilvie says that some poorly informed people wrongly see outdoor education as primarily one of three types: physical in character (activity oriented); or environmental in character (field studies-ecology oriented); or social in character (personal and social education). In practice, he points out, 'in the real world of a group working in the outdoors, all three elements [are] in fact present in varying degrees whatever the declared intention or emphasis for the day might be.'[91]

On this point, I fully intend to be guilty of repetition. I said something similar to it in some writing in the mid-1990s: 'A list can mislead, for in showing separate Aims it neglects to show that they're linked. In each of us the strands coexist: our personalities, recreational passions and need to touch the Earth grow together, threads from an earthy past.'[92] The White Hall aims statements quoted in this chapter, mainly from 1949–50, have included all three main aspects.

Fitting into the physical aspect, we have had understanding the fundamentals of safe recreation in the countryside; introducing young people to open country pursuits, including walking, camping and climb-ing; and developing endurance.

Belonging in the environmental area, there was Longland's talk to the Ilkeston Rotary Club, about understanding the countryside and appreciating its beauty.

Examples of parts of social and personal education were references to developing resourcefulness, independence, initiative, self-reliance, and courage. Also mentioned were living as a member of a small group and taking responsibility.

At some point (it is not clear when), White Hall teaching staff began writing individual course reports for all pupils on schools' courses. These reports were expansive in content, virtually open-ended. Any personal characteristics worth mentioning, especially positive ones, appeared in print. As a side benefit, perhaps unintended, the regular task of report-writing helped the teaching staff to maintain a broad interpretation of the centre's aims.

*

Out of Doors magazine was published six times a year from 1944 (and possibly earlier) to 1955. In November 1949 it described itself as 'of especial interest to walkers, cyclists, mountaineers, campers, and all nature-lovers'.[93] In 1950 *Out of Doors* absorbed a similar magazine, *Countrygoer*.[94] My research had led me to believe that Jack Longland had contributed writing to *Out of Doors* at some time before 1952. In about May 2015 an old schoolfriend of mine had visited the Bodleian library in Oxford, searching *Out of Doors* for any Longland articles, but without success. I had then abandoned this line of enquiry.

One day in January 2016, I am working on Chapter 19 of this book when an email arrives from Mark Lambert, who is writing a biography of Jack Longland. Our projects overlap. He has helped me greatly by reading my draft. The email carries an attachment, a copy of a private paper containing an article that Longland had submitted to *Out of Doors* magazine on 13 December 1950.[95] The filename is WhyProvideMtn-TrainingCentres.docx. I open the document. The writing fills three A4 pages (1,900 words). I glance through it. Gotcha! The Bakewell Scrolls! With incontestable origins. This is an organised statement of White Hall's aims, submitted to a magazine two weeks before White Hall opened. It was written before later trailblazers developed different interpretations of outdoor education, leading to different denomina-tions. It is exactly what I had started looking for two years earlier.

The article describes the main purposes of White Hall methodically and effortlessly, in straightforward language. It could have served as a summary of this chapter. Everything is there: promoting outdoor recreation, understanding the countryside, reducing the number of accidents caused by inexperience, and a brief and restrained – almost apologetic – mention of character training.

The article may or may not have been published, I am still trying to find this out; what seems certain is that the article had remained virtually unknown for sixty-five years. Had it become widely known, outdoor educators would have recognised it long ago as the earliest clear and authoritative statement on White Hall's *raison d'être* (except for short press reports). It is therefore important historically, both locally and nationally.

Twenty-two years were to pass before anyone expanded Longland's systematic analysis – Harold Drasdo would do so, in *Education and the Mountain Centres* (1972) – and Drasdo was another person with connections to White Hall.

Although our focus will now shift firstly onto Peter Mosedale and then onto his successors, Longland will never be far away and will reappear occasionally. He had more on his mind than just White Hall Centre. He saw White Hall as part of several broader unfoldings. In Byne and Sutton's *High Peak*, it was probably Sutton who wrote: 'Jack Longland ... saw the project as one part of a wider development which included, among other elements, the establishment of the National Parks, the growth of Youth Hostelling, the demand for access to mountains, and the founding of other types of centres by the Outward Bound Trust, the Central Council of Physical Recreation (CCPR), and similar bodies.'[96]

Notes

1   Sir Jack Longland, 'Letters: In Defence of Educational Climbing', *Mountain*, no. 52 (1976), p. 45.

2   Lynn Cook, 'Outdoor Education: Its Origins and Institutionalisation in Schools with Particular Reference to the West Riding of Yorkshire Since 1945' (PhD thesis, University of Leeds, 2000), pp. 128–140, 215–231, 297–301.

3   Jim Perrin, 'Sir John Laurence ('Jack') Longland: 1905–1993', *Climbers' Club Journal: 1993*, 21, no. 3 (new series) (1994), pp. 79–83.

4   'Mansion into School for Climbers: Derbyshire Plan Attacked', *Manchester Guardian*, 10 Apr 1950, p. 10.

5   'Obituary: Mr. Wilson Harris', *The Times*, 13 Jan 1955, p. 11.

6   Janus, 'A Spectator's Notebook', *The Spectator*, 14 Apr 1950, p. 488.

7   W McG Eagar, 'A School for Climbers', *The Spectator*, 19 May 1950, pp. 686, 688.

8   Janus, 'A Spectator's Notebook', *The Spectator*, 26 May 1950, p. 713.

9   Janus, 'A Spectator's Notebook', *The Spectator*, 19 Aug 1949, p. 224.

10   C A Milward, 'Alpine Accidents', *The Spectator*, 26 Aug 1949, p. 267.

11   J L Longland, 'The Derbyshire Hostel', *The Spectator*, 16 June 1950, p. 823.

12   Nick Veevers and Pete Allison, *Kurt Hahn: Inspirational, Visionary, Outdoor and Experiential Educator* (Rotterdam: Sense Publishers, 2011), pp. 66–68.

13   R W P Cockerton, 'A Derbyshire Hostel', *The Spectator*, 23 June 1950, p. 858.

14   R W P Cockerton, 'The Derbyshire Hostel', *The Spectator*, 4 Aug 1950, pp. 147–148.

15   'Character and Friendship through Hardship', *Times Educational Supplement*, 16 June 1950, p. 474. Also 'Outward Bound Trust: New Mountain School', *The Times*, 17 June 1950, p. 6.

16   'New Outward Bound School: Mountain Training', *The Times*, 25 Mar 1950, p. 7.

17   'Boy of 14 to Train Tough Climbers', *Sheffield Daily Telegraph*, 28 Dec 1950, p. 3.

18   'Whitehall: "Can't Be Measured in £ s. d."', *Buxton Advertiser*, 24 Mar 1951.

19   Chas F White, 'Ald. C. F. White Replies to Coun. Cockerton', *Derby Evening Telegraph*, 11 Nov 1950, p. 7.

20   'Countryside Teaching Plan: Outward Bound School in Peak', *Derby Evening Telegraph*, 24 Oct 1950, p. 7.

21   'Training Centre', *Derby Evening Telegraph*, 26 Aug 1949, p. 3.

22   'School for Climbers: £3,000 Project for Buxton', *Nottingham Evening Post*, 23 Aug 1949, p. 5.

23   Lynn Cook, 'Outdoor Education: Its Origins and Institutionalisation in Schools with Particular Reference to the West Riding of Yorkshire Since 1945' (PhD thesis, University of Leeds, 2000), pp. 78–79.

24   'Country Pursuits Centre', *Derby Evening Telegraph*, 27 Dec 1950, p. 4. Also Derbyshire Record Office, Programme for January to May, 1951: White Hall Centre for Open Country Pursuits, D7786/BOX/1/Bundle 6.

25   'Needs of County's "Tragic Children"', *Derby Evening Telegraph*, 27 Dec 1950, p. 2.

26   Grant Scrimgeour, 'The Anti-vandal War', *Daily Mirror*, 29 Dec 1950, p. 8.

27   J L Longland, 'Physical Recreation and Character', *Physical Recreation*, 7, no. 2 (Apr 1955), pp. 7–11 (p. 11).

28   Ken C Ogilvie, *Roots and Wings: A History of Outdoor Education and Outdoor Learning in the UK* (Lyme Regis, UK: Russell House Publishing, 2013), pp. 281–282.

29   Cyril B Machin, 'The Educational Value of Open Country Pursuits', *Journal of the Midland Association of Mountaineers*, 3, no. 1 (1956), pp. 16–18.

30   T M Parker and K I Meldrum, *Outdoor Education* (London: J M Dent and Sons, 1973), pp. 87–89.

31   Doug Scott, *Up and About: The Hard Road to Everest* (Sheffield: Vertebrate Publishing, 2015), p. 43.

32   'In the Beginning 1949–1953', Oread Mountaineering Club (no date) <oread. co.uk/images/pdf/49to53pub.pdf> [accessed 15 July 2014], p. 7.

33   J L Longland, 'Mountain Risks and Remedies', *Observer*, 13 Apr 1952, p. 4.

34   Sir Jack Longland, 'Letters: In Defence of Educational Climbing', *Mountain*, no. 52 (1976), p. 45.

35   Elizabeth Coxhead, 'Sporting Aspect: Taking to the Rocks', *The Spectator*, 12 Mar 1954, pp. 294–295.

36   'Those Who Know Fat Man's Chimney', *Derby Evening Telegraph*, 22 Apr 1947, p. 3.

37   *Climbing in Britain*, ed. by J E Q Barford (Harmondsworth: Pelican Books, 1946), p. 12.

38   'Climbers in Council', *The Times*, 15 Oct 1956, p. 11.

39   *Climbing in Britain*, ed. by J E Q Barford (Harmondsworth: Pelican Books, 1946), p. 23.

40   Joe Brown, *The Hard Years* (1967; repr. London: Penguin Books, 1975), pp. 31–32.

41   'Aim: Fewer Climbing Accidents', *Aberdeen Journal*, 30 July 1948, p. 4.

42   Catharine M Loader, *Cairngorm Adventure at Glenmore Lodge: Scottish Centre of Outdoor Training* (Edinburgh: W Brown, 1952), p. 8.

43   'Mr. Bryce on Moral Training', *The Times*, 6 Feb 1907, p. 3.

44   John W Collins and Patricia Nancy O'Brien, *The Greenwood Dictionary of Education* (Westport, Connecticut: Greenwood Press, 2003), pp. 51–52.

45   David Hopkins and Roger Putnam, *Personal Growth through Adventure* (London: David Fulton Publishers, 1993), p. 23.

46   B M Ward, *Reddie of Abbotsholme* (London: George Allen and Unwin, 1934), pp. 14–16, 31.

47   Cecil Reddie, *Abbotsholme 1889–1899* (London: George Allen, 1900), p. 22.

48   'Current Topics', *Sheffield Daily Telegraph*, 6 Dec 1902, p. 8.

49   Cecil Reddie, *Abbotsholme 1889–1899* (London: George Allen, 1900), p. iv.

50   Peter Searby, 'Reddie, Cecil (1858–1932)', in *Oxford Dictionary of National Biography* (May 2005) <http://0-www.oxforddnb.com.www.elgar.govt.nz/view/article/46697> [accessed 23 May 2015].

51   Abbotsholme School, 'Abbotsholme: Our History' (no date) <http://www.abbotsholme.co.uk/Abbotsholmes-History> [accessed 15 Feb 2015].

52   Frank Musgrove, *School and the Social Order* (Chichester: John Wiley and Sons, 1979), p. 84.

53   B M Ward, *Reddie of Abbotsholme* (London: George Allen and Unwin, 1934), p. 27.

54   A Schoolmaster, 'Character Building in Schools', *Daily Mail*, 11 July 1911, p. 4.

55   Robert H MacDonald, *Sons of the Empire: The Frontier and the Boy Scout Movement 1890–1918* (Toronto: University of Toronto Press, 1993), p. 26.

56   Ibid., p. 117.

57   Robert S S Baden-Powell, *Scouting for Boys: A Handbook for Instruction in Good Citizenship*, Reprint of six-part (1908) edn (Oxford: Oxford University Press, 2005), p. 317.

58   E E Reynolds, *Baden-Powell: A Biography of Lord Baden-Powell of Gilwell*
     (London: Oxford University Press, 1942), p. 155.

59   'Why provide mountain training centres?', in private papers of Jack Longland,
     sent to *Out of Doors*, 13 Dec 1950.

60   Cambridge University Library, Longland to Arnold-Brown, 13 June 1953,
     in Correspondence and papers of Arnold-Brown relating to OBMS after his
     departure, MS Add.8270/21/2.

61   J L Longland, 'Physical Recreation and Character', *Physical Recreation*, 7, no. 2
     (Apr 1955), pp. 7–11 (pp. 7–8).

62   Ibid. (pp. 9–11).

63   Harold Drasdo, 'The Character Builders', *Anarchy*, no. 11 (Jan 1962), pp. 25–28.

64   'Mountain-craft School', *The Times*, 21 July 1949, p. 3.

65   Jack L Longland, 'Outward Bound Junior Courses', in *Outward Bound*, ed. by
     David James (London: Routledge and Kegan Paul, 1957), pp. 174–187 (p. 187).

66   Derbyshire Record Office, Monograph: Hill and Water Sports in British
     Education: Peter Mosedale, 1975, D7786/BOX/1/Bundle 5.

67   Ibid., p. 6.

68   Alan Hankinson, *Geoffrey Winthrop Young: Poet, Educator, Mountaineer* (London:
     Hodder and Stoughton, 1995), p. 168.

69   Robert Wainwright, *The Maverick Mountaineer: The Remarkable Life of George
     Ingle Finch: Climber, Scientist, Inventor* (London: Allen and Unwin, 2016), p. 405.

70   *The First Fifty Years of the British Mountaineering Council*, ed. by Geoff Milburn,
     Derek Walker and Ken Wilson (Manchester: British Mountaineering Council,
     1997), p. 134.

71   Michael Westmacott, 'Obituary: Sir Jack Longland', *Independent*, 4 December
     1993.

72   Alan Hankinson, *Geoffrey Winthrop Young: Poet, Educator, Mountaineer* (London:
     Hodder and Stoughton, 1995), pp. 263, 283.

73   Peter Mosedale, 'Britain at War [Poem]', *Canberra Times*, 9 Mar 1974, p. 11.

74   Derbyshire Record Office, Monograph: Hill and Water Sports in British
     Education: Peter Mosedale, 1975, D7786/BOX/1/Bundle 5.

75   Ibid., p. 46.

76   Ibid., p. 47.

77   *The First Fifty Years of the British Mountaineering Council*, ed. by Geoff Milburn,
     Derek Walker and Ken Wilson (Manchester: British Mountaineering Council,
     1997), pp. 136–137.

78   Bill Bryson, *A Walk in the Woods* (London: Black Swan, 1998), p. 112.

79   Grant Scrimgeour, 'The Anti-vandal War', *Daily Mirror*, 29 Dec 1950, p. 8.

80   Jenny Orwin, Bootham School, Email to P McDonald, subject 'Photographs
     Sought', 12 June 2015 [Email].

81   Quoted in Doug Scott, *Up and About: The Hard Road to Everest* (Sheffield:
     Vertebrate Publishing, 2015), p. 224.

82   T M Parker and K I Meldrum, *Outdoor Education* (London: J M Dent and Sons,
     1973), p. 89.

83   Quoted in Samuel Hall Young, *Alaska Days with John Muir* (New York: Fleming
     H Revell, 1915), pp. 216–217.

84   Cyril B Machin, 'The Educational Value of Open Country Pursuits', *Journal of the Midland Association of Mountaineers,* 3, no. 1 (1956), pp. 16–18.

85   'Work – A Pleasure or a Hardship? Plain Speaking at Southport Conference', *Manchester Guardian,* 6 Jan 1950, p. 2.

86   Ken C Ogilvie, *Roots and Wings: A History of Outdoor Education and Outdoor Learning in the UK* (Lyme Regis, UK: Russell House Publishing, 2013), pp. 339–340.

87   A B Afford, *The Story of White Hall Open Country Pursuits Centre; vol. 2* (Buxton, Derbyshire, UK: A B Afford, 1978), pp. 17–18.

88   Quoted in Derbyshire Record Office, Monograph: Hill and Water Sports in British Education: Peter Mosedale, 1975, D7786/BOX/1/Bundle 5.

89   Tom Price, 'Adventure by Numbers', *Mountain,* no. 38 (1974), pp. 17–19.

90   Ronald W Clark, 'Mountain Tragedies', *The Spectator,* 20 Apr 1951, pp. 516–517.

91   Ken C Ogilvie, *Roots and Wings: A History of Outdoor Education and Outdoor Learning in the UK* (Lyme Regis, UK: Russell House Publishing, 2013), p. 469.

92   Pete McDonald, *Climbing Lessons: Inside Outdoor Education* (Kaikohe, NZ: Pete McDonald, 1997), pp. 295–296.

93   'Out-of-Doors: The Open-air Magazine', *Manchester Guardian,* 3 Nov 1949, p. 1.

94   'Magazine for Walkers', *Manchester Guardian,* 31 Mar 1950, p. 6.

95   'Why provide mountain training centres?', in private papers of Jack Longland, sent to *Out of Doors,* 13 Dec 1950.

96   Eric Byne and Geoffrey Sutton, *High Peak: The Story of Walking and Climbing in the Peak District* (London: Secker and Warburg, 1966), p. 189.

Part Two:
The Formative Years, 1950–70

8. Peter Mosedale and Bandits, 1950–5

One day in June 2014, I am pleasantly occupied collecting material for a proposed White Hall Centre archive when I come across the name Peter Mosedale. I know nothing about him, except that he was the first warden of White Hall. Subsequent searches of databases find some scraps of information about him, but no hints of anything more substantial, such as an academic paper by him or a book mentioning him. He receives only one passing mention in Ogilvie's immensely detailed *Roots and Wings*, and that is connected with his attending a conference, not with his pioneering stint in Derbyshire. The almost complete blank surprises me. Sutton, Langmuir and Meldrum, the next White Hall bosses after Mosedale, all wrote books directly or indirectly connected with outdoor pursuits. The crucial part played by Jack Longland is widely recognised. The ideas of Hahn, Holt and Hogan, the visionaries behind Aberdovey OBSS, are conveniently covered by education texts and several biographies (as well as, for Hahn and Hogan, by their own writing). Dozens of other people's names became household names within outdoor education. Mosedale ran White Hall for nearly five years. How could he disappear so completely?

As a last resort I search for 'Mosedale' and 'education' on WorldCat. org. Up pops *Hill and Water Sports in British Education*. A link takes me to the library of the University of Canberra. The library record, on both catalogues, is unusually skimpy, slightly intriguing.

About a month later, I pick up the interloan from Dunedin public library. Instead of a published book, I find a hardback manuscript, neatly typewritten and professionally bound. Peter Mosedale has been little more than a name on my list of persons of interest, not entirely forgotten – allocated about five pages in A B Afford's *The Story of White Hall Open Country Pursuits Centre* (1978) – but elusive. Suddenly I am holding in my hands Mosedale's account of five years spent on the treeline, just below Combs Moss, which is one part of his examination of outdoor recreation in Britain, an analysis consisting of a brief historical scene-setting followed by a scrutiny of 1950–75. At a local-history level – that of outdoor education in Derbyshire – my finding this neglected study is ample reason for a visit, later that day, to Filadelfio's pizza restaurant and bar.

*

The manuscript is 22,600 words long, enough writing for a short book. Mosedale wrote it in 1975. Since then, in a more logical world a published version of his writing would have been available in Britain, on the library shelves close to two other small books, Hogan's *Impelled into Experiences* (1968) and Drasdo's *Education and the Mountain Centres* (1972). Instead, *Hill and Water Sports in British Education* lay on a library shelf in Australia for thirty-nine years, unpublished, jettisoned, almost unknown and a long way from home.

The manuscript's deliberately precise and descriptive title is compelling evidence of the founding purpose of White Hall Centre for Open Country Pursuits. Mosedale's book title reinforces the message given by the centre's full name. Furthermore, if we bear in mind the consensus that White Hall was a model imitated, at least to some extent, by many later LEA residential outdoor pursuits centres, Mosedale's emphasis demands wide recognition.

At first sight it seems strange that such an important fragment of the history of British outdoor education could remain undiscovered or ignored for thirty-nine years. But an examination of the manuscript's minimal library record half explains how this happened. A database search for such terms as 'outdoor pursuits', 'outdoor activities', 'outdoor education' and 'outdoor learning', but without the name 'Mosedale', does not find this manuscript. In 1955 Peter Mosedale's career path took him out of the world of outdoor-pursuits centres; despite his success at White Hall, his name almost vanished from the records. I may have been the first researcher to search library catalogues for the words 'education' and 'Mosedale'.

There seems little doubt that Mosedale intended his manuscript to be the basis of a published book but did not find a publisher. At the age of about fifty-seven and in the peace and quiet of a study-leave he had sorted out and recorded the ideas of half a lifetime. The Canberra copy appeared to be the only one in existence. A check of the British Library catalogue and COPAC did not bring up any copies. Had he been asked to in 1975, Jack Longland – I'm sure – would have happily contributed an enthusiastic foreword to the Mosedale manuscript. Instead, the manuscript carries a slightly forlorn note consigning it to obscurity: 'This monograph … has not been pruned for commercial publication – the market is too limited apparently – but [the manuscript] may be of interest and utility as it stands'.

We would like to know more. How hard did he look for a publisher? One explanation could be that Canberra or London publishers rejected a submission and that Mosedale decided not to take things any further, rather than to self-publish from Australia. Bear in mind that one of the two books mentioned earlier, Drasdo's, was self-published (and we are glad that it was). In the age before computers and page-layout software, much self-publishing attracted the label of 'vanity publishing'; someone once called it an introspective extravagance for rich dilettantes. Academics will have been acutely aware of this stigma.

Still today, 'scholarly research monograph publishing is very much, but not exclusively, the domain of arts and humanities disciplines … The monograph remains the gold standard … Career progress over the years is measured to [a] considerable extent in terms of books authored.'[1]

One thing seems certain: the Mosedale manuscript came to be deposited silently and placidly and far from its natural resting place. When discovered in June 2014, Mosedale's manuscript might never have reached the UK. Furthermore, it tells the story of the early years at White Hall without ever mentioning the author's leading role.

His role deserves recognition. This chapter will try to provide it. As for his ideas, they are part of the history of outdoor education, and I will compensate for the manuscript's long wait by reproducing some lengthy extracts from it.

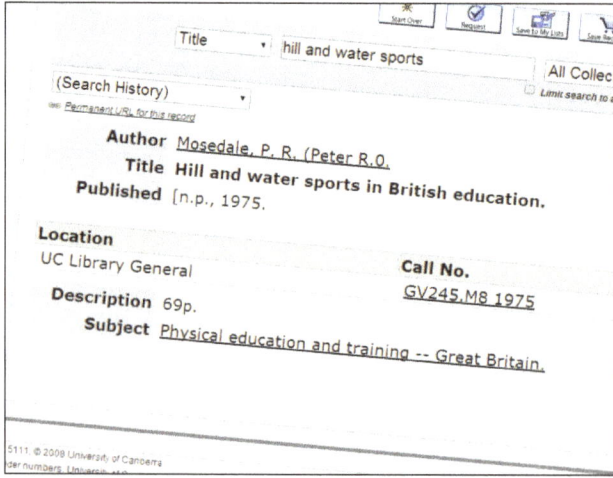

The library record (in 2014) for Peter Mosedale's 1975 manuscript, on the catalogue of the University of Canberra.

In a letter written in the mid-1970s, Mosedale recalled the first few months in his new job, a hectic round of exploration, planning, decision-making and decorating: 'I arrived in White Hall in October 1950 while it was still being reconstructed and spent two months getting to know the district and developing ideas on courses which were to be, in the beginning, for youth service clubs and societies of all kinds.'

Two weeks before White Hall opened, the county council was still advertising vacancies for a married couple for cooking and housework for a weekly salary of £4/7/- each, less 23/- each for board and accommodation. 'Residential post very suitable for people fond of moorland country and young people. Comfortable accom. but no room for children.'[2]

Mosedale's letter continues:

> We had a tremendous job to make the place habitable for the first weekend course at the end of December – I remember staining upstairs floors on the day it began – and the very first weekend revealed many difficulties in aim and organisation which had to be settled straight away. I met with the local H.M.I., and Mr Boon, P.E. Adviser from London after this, and argued the case for extending our work to senior schools as part of the general effort in P.E. and outdoor education.[3]

Already, then, after one weekend, Mosedale and other managers were taking steps to widen the centre's role from that of a facility primarily for youth-club members aged from fourteen to eighteen to a facility both for secondary-school pupils and for youth-club members. Annual programmes in the 1960s stipulated a minimum age of thirteen years for pupils on standard schools' courses. It is likely that this lower age limit applied since 1950. It would remain in place, casually if not explicitly, until the 1990s.

Opening Weekend: Informal and Collaborative

One of the course members who arrived on the evening of Friday 29 December 1950, the day before White Hall's opening weekend, was Ken Oldham, a teacher with an interest in outdoor pursuits. Describing that first evening, he wrote:

> Peter Mosedale met us in the lounge and with his outstretched hand and welcoming smile he made himself known and assured

us of a pleasant weekend ahead. For a while we sat in the pulpit seats alongside the huge log-fire that dominated the lounge. I can't remember very much what went on that evening except that it was an evening of introductions, all very pleasant and centred round an excellent meal at which we were introduced to Betty Mosedale, who, as the Warden's wife, organised the whole of the domestic arrangements. The evening was consolidated by a lecture, concerning the prospects offered. Discussion continued around the log fire until late when we retired for a self-service supper.[4]

One press report adds that snow dripping into the lounge caused Peter Mosedale to apologise for the air of decay.

Ken Oldham's accounts are notable for mentioning the role of Betty Mosedale. In a letter looking back from the 1970s, he said:

Peter and Betty Mosedale were invaluable assets to White Hall. I cannot recall a visit when welcome wasn't permeating the air. They had the happy knack of being able to converse genially with everybody and would guide or persuade the visitors and voluntary instructors into the wide variety of activities that enriched the courses. There was always a general discussion (briefing) after breakfast to decide upon the various activities and these were related to the staff available, the conditions prevailing and the choice of course members. This was done in a friendly and informal fashion.[5]

Another of the voluntary instructors on the opening weekend was Bob Pettigrew, a member of an RAF mountain rescue unit based at Harpur Hill, Buxton, a 'National Serviceman with a mop of black hair, already full of the enthusiasm that was to make him a successful leader of expeditions to arctic Norway and the Himalayas.'[6] When Peter Mosedale came to write his manuscript twenty-five years later, he added a note of thanks for the use of Pettigrew's 1954–5 thesis on outdoor activities. By then, 1975, Pettigrew was the chief adviser for outdoor education in Hampshire.[7] He remembers Mosedale as 'a charming man and an inspired and gentle educationist, like his cousin Sir Jack Longland'.[8] (Pettigrew was partly wrong on the last point; Mosedale and Longland were not related.) In time, Longland and Pettigrew would each serve a term as president of the BMC.

Also present on the first weekend, as voluntary instructors, were Alf Bridge, Ivan Waller, Eric Byne, Ronald Townsend and Norman Kershaw.[9] Jack Longland's fourteen-year-old son John, already a capable climber, attended as another voluntary instructor. An assortment of twenty-seven 'students, from 16 to 25 years of age, clerks, factory workers and apprentices of all kinds, came from all parts of Derbyshire'.[10] (A *Sheffield Daily Telegraph* report of 28 December 1950 had said that the first pupils at White Hall would be twenty-five county grammar school boys aged fifteen years and over. This appears to have been incorrect.) The weekend included the Monday, New Year's Day.

Jack Longland and his son John, aged fourteen, at White Hall's opening weekend, 30–31 December 1950. John had done his first roped climb at the age of six.

Early on Saturday 30 December 1950, a *Manchester Guardian* special correspondent travelled from Manchester to White Hall Centre to observe and join in the activities on White Hall's opening day. Hitchhiking featured essentially:

White Hall, standing alone on the edge of Combs Moss at 1,350 feet, commands a good deal of the Peak National Park. Situated some way off the bus route, it is not too easy to get to from the Manchester end. The stretch requiring the greatest resource (and hillcraft) in snowy weather, and if you are on foot, is the five miles or so of Long Hill, the road winding up the edge of Combs Moss.

The only transport available in the snowy season may well be, as on this occasion, a slow-moving roadman's lorry from the back of which three elderly men with shovels scatter cinders in their wake with broad, resigned gestures. One keeps pace with it hopefully until the cargo has been dealt with. Then one is invited, with a friendly word, to make oneself at home in the back, windswept as it may be, while the working party contrives to get into the front cab with the driver. The company is cheery enough and one arrives, but it does not seem a service to be relied on. Perhaps one should recommend the Buxton bus and the long way round [ie, travel from Manchester to Buxton and then back northwards to White Hall].

The more adventurous way of travel does at least, in some measure, prepare one in body and spirit for the atmosphere which one finds at White Hall, and the zest to get out of doors especially, it seems, when it looks uncomfortable.[11]

Hitchhiking to White Hall became common in the 1950s. Some course members and other visitors used to arrive in Buxton by bus or train and then walk three miles up Long Hill to White Hall, finishing via the old road.

Among the activities during the opening weekend was a walk up Kinder Scout on the Saturday, accompanied by Jack Longland and Peter Mosedale. 'Seven students braved a blinding snowstorm and did remarkably well … although at times they were waist-deep in snow drifts.'

The First Schools' Course

The first White Hall schools' course took place from Monday 26 February to Friday 2 March 1951. One of the schools involved was Spring Bank School, New Mills.[12] This was a school that in 1943 had been crowded with evacuees who had fled the Manchester bombing. To one of the wartime teachers, some of the families in New Mills had seemed disturbingly impoverished. At Spring Bank School in 1943, 'there was a lot of malnutrition and scabies was rife. The "Nit" nurse had a busy time … and the district medical officer was well occupied.

One pair of twins … were so malnourished they were too tiny to sit at a proper desk.'[13]

These difficult years were still recent history when ten second- to fourth-year boys from Spring Bank School spent five days at White Hall, exploring the Peak District on foot. A teacher from the school, Ken Oldham, accompanied them and appears to have filled four roles: visiting teacher, sole instructor, photographer and diarist. By choosing to work with a group of ten, he may have influenced the adoption of an activity-group size that preceded the minibus and became standard for White Hall and which would remain unchanged for forty years.

Oldham kept a diary as a written record for the school's headmaster. This was forwarded to Jack Longland. Its location is now unknown, but A B Afford had access to it while writing his Part Two. This enabled Afford to convey an account of the first schools' course:

> Map reading, compass work and field study occupied them fully. 'The boys had become quick and eager to find things out: they were gaining a new confidence in their own ability; and they had the grand satisfaction of a good day's work well done.'
>
> Evenings they returned to the house where hot baths and mealtime were followed by singing, table tennis, colour slides and work on the notebooks they each kept on the things they had discovered. There was a great sense of occasion, they were conscious that they were chosen for an experience of great importance. This was reinforced by the whole school and Headmaster Mr. Birkby and other staff who visited and helped them. Some of these boys came back to White Hall, others took up outdoor life on their own but none of them ever forgot this first course, the first experiment had succeeded.[14]

Map-reading immediately became a core skill at White Hall on all basic schools' courses. You could even argue that the ability to read a map and navigate is *the* core skill of outdoor pursuits. Pupils could be led over Kinder Scout but they gained more from leading the way themselves. Unaccompanied expeditions, even in relatively sheltered farming areas of the White Peak, could not take place without maps.

In allocating such importance to map-reading, White Hall was merely repeating what the Scout movement had been doing for forty years. Baden-Powell recognised the absolute necessity of map-reading when in 1908 he wrote: 'You should on all occasions take a map with

you, and find your way by it, as far as possible, without having to ask
the way of passers-by.'[15] Within a year or two, thousands of boys and
a few girls were busily setting their maps to north.

Boys using a baseplate compass at Glenmore Lodge
in January 1951.

In 1951 the fees paid by young people for the White Hall courses
and accommodation ranged from about 7s 6d for a short weekend to
about 30s for a week.[16]

Ken Oldham was twenty-seven years old, just six years younger than
Peter Mosedale. During the war, he had trained as a bomber pilot.[17]
We shall meet him again a year later, when he makes a lack of transport
into a blessing.

If Longland and Mosedale had merely adapted the 1940s Aberdovey OBSS approach to suit slightly younger pupils, this first schools'
course would have been different in some small but important respects:
it would have included some sort of uniform, equivalent to the navy-
blue Aberdovey sweaters; it also would have featured parading before
the Union Jack and rigorous early-morning runs and cold showers

and somewhat formal staff-pupil relationships. Instead, from the very beginning Longland and Mosedale prioritised informality and enjoyment. Part of this approach probably stemmed from John Newsom's influence on Longland ten years earlier in Durham and Hertfordshire.

Wally Blake instructed at Devon Outward Bound School and at White Hall, in the 1960s. In 2016, after reading the manuscript for this book, he offered another perspective on the subject of character building:

> I still wonder if the actual experience differed so very much between the Outward Bound schools and the later LEA centres … Yes, there were morning prayers, and cold showers [at Outward Bound schools], but I never remember giving that much thought at any other time of the day. Of course, high expectations were heaped on the boys, but participation was always encouraged, never forced on reluctant students. There was undoubtedly, moral pressure, but I believe that is always present in any group situation. A reluctant student, unwilling to abseil, for instance, would be treated at Outward Bound in a similar way to a student in the same situation at White Hall.[18]

I agree with some of Blake's points, especially in the context of the 1960s. However, as I see it, although the differences between White Hall and Aberdovey OBSS in 1951 were individually small, they were collectively significant. They reflected differences in staff expectations and priorities. There were three main aspects to them: the degree of formality in staff-pupil relationships; the amount of importance attached to enjoyment; and the level of commitment to character building.

We shall see in Chapter 10 that Peter Mosedale's successor, Geoff Sutton, would continue and strengthen White Hall's relaxed approach. Doug Scott remembers the White Hall of 1955–7: 'White Hall was such a friendly place to be, like one big family. Its ethos was quite different from the strict, somewhat regimented Outward Bound centres. White Hall had been created to interest a much younger age group. The courses were designed to last for either a weekend or at most a week; there was less emphasis on character building and more on enjoyment.'[19]

In time, the friendly and cooperative White Hall spirit would permeate much of the LEA sector. You could argue that there is an unmistakeable difference between a cold shower and a hot one.

Photographs from White Hall's first schools' course, 1951.

The photographs on this page and on the next six pages show pupils on White Hall's first schools' course, which took place on 26 February – 2 March 1951 and was attended by ten second- to fourth-year boys from Spring Bank School, New Mills. Ken Oldham, one of their teachers, accompanied the boys. It seems likely that he took all these photographs, which are from an album of fifty-three. I have reproduced the original minimal captions (in quotation marks).

D836 C/EA 18/1, courtesy of Derbyshire Record Office.

'Leaving school.' Monday 26 February 1951. The distinctive stone gateposts and iron railings are those of the old office entrance to Spring Bank School. The man standing between the gateposts may have been the headmaster, Mr Birkby, who had encouraged Ken Oldham to take the boys to White Hall.

D836 C/EA 18/5, courtesy of Derbyshire Record Office.

'Leaving Old Dam.' Near the village of Peak Forest. February–March 1951.

'Towards Peak Forest.' February–March 1951.

D836 C/EA 18/6, courtesy of Derbyshire Record Office.

'Heading for Combs.' February–March 1951.

D836 C/EA 18/8, courtesy of Derbyshire Record Office.

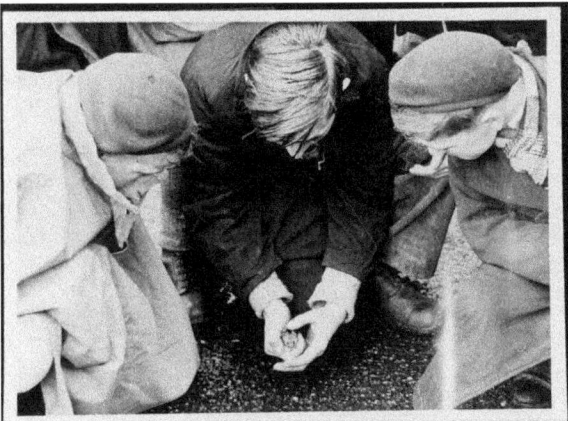

'Field mouse at Combs.' February–March 1951.

D836 C/EA 18/9, courtesy of Derbyshire Record Office.

'Checking by compass and map.' February–March 1951.

'Parts of a sheep.' February–March 1951.

'Two groups meet near Chapel Milton.' February–March 1951.

'Testing the snow.' February–March 1951.

'Rock strata exposed – Shooters' Clough.' February–March 1951.

'Dying forest – Shooters' Clough.' February–March 1951.

'Approaching the Winnats.' February–March 1951.

'Limestone at Winnats.' February–March 1951.

'On Winnats.' February–March 1951.

'Entrance to a cave in Winnats.' Horseshoe Cave, Feb–March 1951.

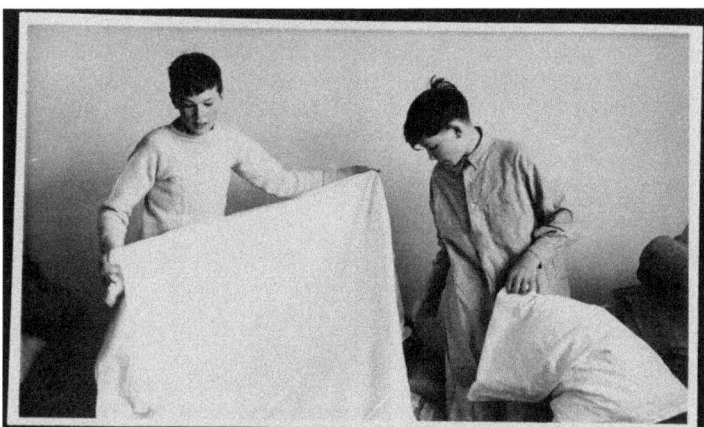

'First job.' February–March 1951.

'Breakfast is served.' February–March 1951.

D836 C/EA 18/51, courtesy of Derbyshire Record Office.

[No caption.] February–March 1951.

D836 C/EA 18/52, courtesy of Derbyshire Record Office.

[No caption.] February–March 1951.

D836 C/EA 18/23, courtesy of Derbyshire Record Office.

[No caption.] February–March 1951.

D836 C/EA 18/24, courtesy of Derbyshire Record Office.

'Leaving White Hall.' This is the back lane, heading northeastwards down to the hamlet of Combs. February–March 1951.

Education (Councils & Education Press)
26 January 1951, p. 157.

" Enjoy the Hills "—Derbyshire Centre

Derbyshire Education Committee have acquired White Hall, a country house on the edge of Combs Moss, some three miles from Buxton, and have opened it as "a place where young people of a specially adventurous spirit may practise the techniques of hill-walking, of camping and cooking, of where and where not to ski, of rock-climbing—in short a place where young people may learn to enjoy the hills without unnecessary danger or discomfort." The fees for the various courses and accommodation range from 7s. 6d. for a short week-end to 30s. for a week. Students from outside Derbyshire are charged more than this, but they will find comfortable accommodation with central heating, drying rooms, and libraries of books and of films.

Staffing, Transport and Equipment

Three months after White Hall opened, Jack Longland reported to the education committee that 'the continuous courses were a great strain on the warden and his wife, who were the only professional staff'.[20] Longland said he hoped it might be possible to obtain teachers from Derbyshire schools to help at White Hall.

Some time passed before it became possible to employ two permanent instructors to share the continual load Peter and Betty Mosedale carried.[21] The long hours lasted throughout Mosedale's wardenship: 'Even when Donald Blair and then John Hird (Killamarsh) were seconded from the teaching service we used to be on duty from 7.30 a.m. until 11 p.m. including, usually, a full stint out of doors.'[22]

Requests for courses came from a wide range of organisations: from youth clubs and schools, as had been expected, and also from colleges of education, Scout and Guide troops, and industrial organisations, which hadn't been planned for. The range of teachers who showed an interest and became involved was wider than had been expected. Many requests for courses arrived from individuals. Mosedale, Blair and Hird had to design courses to meet disparate needs ranging from sheer enjoyment through new experiences right up to leadership training at a general or specialist level.[23] A youth-service week in July 1955, for example, as well as providing opportunities for caving and climbing, included 'theatre visits and evenings for dancing at Buxton'.

It is not known whether Mosedale had a secretary. He might not have even had a typewriter, initially.

People who remember the White Hall of the 1980s and 90s may remember defying the elements. The climate on the exposed spur below Combs Edge will not have changed much over the years. Most staff who have lived in will recollect the shifting dunes of powder snow that commandeered the front drive during January blizzards. There's no better place than at White Hall to feel on your cheeks the bite of a starry frost on an enchanting February night.

These people may also recall the presence of three busy minibuses. Mosedale, if he were still with us, would not remember any centre vehicles; at first, there were none:

> … local cliffs were used intensively for climbing, local moorland and hills were used for route finding, lightweight camping, hill-walking and skiing. Much work was done on the geography and ecology of the local district. Canoeing was introduced. Every effort was made to exploit the area within walking distance. Expeditions further afield, to the cliffs of the Roaches near Leek, or to Bleaklow in the north, were based on walking and bivouacking, sometimes in tents but often under boulders or in the barns of cooperative farmers.[24]

Mosedale used his car to transport course members.[25] Voluntary instructors also helped as necessary by using their cars. Later in Mosedale's time, the centre obtained a Land Rover and trailer.

In England in 1951, hardly one household in fifteen had a television.[26] Eighty-six per cent of households in the UK had no regular access to a car.[27] I was only four years old, too young to remember much. But I do remember the relatively car-free streets of Wallasey, Merseyside from about 1953 onwards. Boy Scouts, as they had done for decades before the war, used trek carts, even on the main roads. Wallasey scouts piled their camping equipment onto the carts and wheeled them six miles out from the terraced streets to Overchurch campsite, on the urban fringe, while singing 'Hitler Has Only Got One Ball'.

For a while after the end of the second world war, army surplus gear was for many people an improvement on what had been available during the war. But this was relative. There were only six or seven shops in the country specialising in climbing equipment: Ellis Brigham in a tiny shop on Conran Street in Manchester, Robert Lawrie and Benjamin

Edgington in London and several branches of Black's of Greenock. 'The availability of equipment after the end of the war was dire. There had been no imports or home manufacture for public use. Everything was in short supply … to make matters worse the Government off-loaded enormous stocks of cheap surplus mountaineering equipment which was little short of useless, if not dangerous.'[28]

Even so, for many hillwalkers and climbers in 1950, army surplus stores were the outfitters of choice. In Nottingham, 22s 6d would buy an army rucksack. In Derby, for 45 shillings you could obtain a kapok-filled cotton sleeping bag. Kapok, also known as Java cotton, was the material traditionally used for filling cushions. An ex-War Department kapok-filled sleeping bag was a technical advance on a woollen blanket, until it got wet. White Hall used these sleeping bags for camping and bivouacking.[29]

Most of the boots in White Hall's equipment store will probably have had nailed leather soles rather than Vibram soles. In a letter to Adam Arnold-Brown in January 1950, Jack Longland warned him about the limitations of rubber soles on greasy rock. Longland recommended that all Eskdale students should 'learn safe mountain walking and scrambling in nailed boots', which would cost about five guineas a pair.[30]

One area of postwar improvement was the production of climbing guidebooks. Between 1948 and 1951, five new Peak District guidebooks were published.[31]

The wartime rationing remained in place for some food. Eggs were not de-rationed until March 1953; sugar not until September 1953; butter, cheese, margarine and cooking fats not until May 1954; and meat not until June 1954.[32]

Advertisements for hiking and camping gear at two army-surplus stores in Nottingham in July 1950.

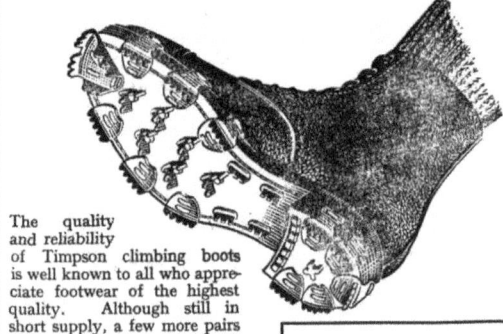

TIMPSON Boots
for Climbers

The quality
and reliability
of Timpson climbing boots
is well known to all who appreciate footwear of the highest
quality. Although still in
short supply, a few more pairs
will be available and we shall
be glad to have your enquiries.

Post your Repairs to the

TIMPSON
Shoe Shops

91-93, Corporation Street,
BIRMINGHAM 3.

Empiric House, Gt. Ducie Street,
MANCHESTER 3.

Your Boots Repaired & Re-nailed

Timpson craftsmen give
new life to your climb-
ing boots. Through
Sole and Heel, re-nail-
ing, re-welting and new
middles.

Prompt Service

Journal of the Midland Association of Mountaineers, 2, no. 3 (1951).

A 1951 advertisement.

A group at the old back door of the mansion, 1953.

Voluntary Instructors

Mosedale's manuscript provides a first-hand insight into the managerial challenges of the early years of White Hall. We can see here the foundations of the centre's character and spirit, which became its traditions and its usual approaches.

One of these foundations was the reliance on and the frequent use of voluntary instructors (VIs), especially at weekends:

> In the early years the policy was to employ a very small permanent teaching staff and to rely on the cooperation of voluntary instructors to make up the balance. There was, and is, much to be said for this policy – and it is discussed later – even when the major reason for its implementation lies in financial stringency. The support of specialist clubs throughout the area of central England had been won, to an extraordinary extent, by a campaign of publicity and public relations. Applications to act as instructors were handled originally by these clubs. Those who gave their services were paid travel expenses and provided with food and simple accommodation by the Centre. Valuable connexions were thus established with many serious climbing and caving clubs and outdoor societies and, in some cases, the experience of assisting at the centre proved to be very beneficial to the clubs themselves.[33]

Most of the voluntary instructors came from the newer, postwar clubs. One or two may have come from older clubs such as Manchester's Rucksack Club. 'From the old and new club world [Mosedale] found the voluntary instructors who played such a valuable and fascinating part in the practicalities of the original concepts.'[34]

High Peak adds some further background: 'In its first experimental stage it was not considered wise to spend too much on the new Centre, and its success or failure therefore depended on the local mountaineering clubs. Jack Longland issued an appeal to the Oread, Stonnis, Valkyrie, Innominate, Polaris, Peak, Sheffield University and other clubs, for voluntary instructors to assist the newly appointed warden … The response was heartening in the extreme.'[35] An Oread newsletter records that 'when Jack Longland, supported by Alf Bridge, outlined his objectives for [White Hall] in 1950 before an invited audience, mainly comprising Peak District climbers, his proposal that local mountaineering clubs would provide a core of voluntary instructors was enthusiastically received.'[36]

The backing of Alf Bridge, then about forty-eight and a hugely experienced climber and endurance walker, will have helped considerably. Writing a year earlier, Bridge had recalled the help he had received as a novice in the mid-1920s. In 1949, such tutoring from experienced climbers was no longer available to most beginners: 'How very different it is now when there is too much talk of training the youngsters in the principles of our craft and too little done'.[37]

As a young Manchester steeplejack 'with unusually prehensile fingers, and a great strength of arms, shoulders and legs', Bridge had been introduced to climbing one day in 1926 at the Roaches, where he had led Via Dolorosa (graded Very Severe).[38] Standing on scaffolding, however, had not taught him to coax the maximum help out of small toeholds. 'He used to wear out the tops of his gym shoes, trailing his legs behind him like a mermaid.' Ivan Waller and Jack Longland subsequently persuaded him to use his feet as well as his hands, and he had become a very good climber.[39] Bridge met Maurice Linnell at Cratcliffe in 1929, and so began a powerful partnership.

In the early 1930s, the running belay had yet to be developed, so Bridge, very sensibly, started to practise the technique of jumping from a height, thus entering climbing's mythology. The facts and fictions of Bridge and the art of falling are difficult to separate. Apparently, he argued that if a leader was in danger of falling, he should turn and leap for a suitable landing spot. Bridge's deliberate and controlled falls of thirty feet and over on such climbs as Christmas Crack at Stanage were unforgettable.[40] We should recognise him as one of the originators of extreme sports.

In May 1942, Bridge had helped as a civilian mountaineer on an army mountain training course in north Wales. Major John Hunt, who ran this course, wrote that 'Alf Bridge … belonged to a select côterie of outstanding rock climbers who were in the van of working-class interest in the sport. Tough, uncompromising and intensely loyal to his friends, he talked the language of the soldiers and fired them with his passionate love of the hills.'[41]

Montage of photographs of White Hall course members on various activities. Reproduced in the *Journal of the Midland Association of Mountaineers*, 3, no. 1 (1956).

Access to Land

On the day before the *Guardian* correspondent hitchhiked up Long Hill, in London Sir Patrick Duff, the chairman of the National Parks Commission, signed the designation order for the Peak District National Park. This was the first order to be made under the National Parks and Access to the Countryside Act, which had been passed on 16 December 1949.[42]

The mere act of designation meant no change. The land remained in the hands of the then owners. The intention was that later there would be access agreements and, if necessary, access orders, to allow public passage over land in the park. The first negotiated access agreement in the Peak District National Park would not come into force until 16 April 1954.[43]

Peter Mosedale's pioneering role would have been demanding enough without there being a new national park. Longland and Mosedale stuck their necks out a long way. Introducing other people's children to risky sports was not, in 1950, the exhaustively analysed trade or art that it is today. Norman Dobson has pointed out that Longland was 'rather pushing at open doors at that time, for discussion about education was still fairly fluid'.[44] Even so, most other LEAs except Cumberland just watched White Hall and waited for eight or more years before setting up their own residential outdoor-pursuits centres. Some quarters of the education establishment perceived the outdoor movement as a group of mavericks.

A few bold innovators had taken British school pupils rock climbing before 30 December 1950. Chapter 4 mentioned examples of schoolteachers taking pupils climbing in 1913, 1915–23, 1920, 1929–49 (the Goldsborough Club at Barnard Castle School), 1933, 1939 and 1948. Glenmore Lodge had opened in summer 1948, and some of its courses for school groups had included rock climbing.[45] One weekend in March 1950, the climbing guide Charlie Wilson had run a climbing course for young people, based at a youth centre in Keswick.[46] But on the organisation and skills involved in introducing thirty pupils to climbing each week, much remained to be learnt. And the same could be said of caving, kayaking, sailing and other adventurous outdoor activities.

The creation of the Peak District National Park, with a mass of new legislation behind it, added complications to Mosedale's job that nobody anywhere in Britain had dealt with before. Relations between walkers or climbers and some of the Peak District landowners had been difficult for decades; the extra level of government bureaucracy and the new planning controls did not necessarily bring outdoor recreators and farmers immediately together.

Two gritstone edges – Castle Naze and Windgather Rocks – were within walking distance from White Hall. In 1948, Windgather, on the Derbyshire-Cheshire border, was one of several favourite edges of an eighteen-year-old novice climber by the name of Joseph Brown. He later described some of the peculiarities of climbing there:

At Windgather we had to keep a sharp lookout for the farmer who owned the grazing rights to the land surrounding the rocks. He had gone to extraordinary lengths to rid himself of 'climbing pests'. He had poured tar over sections of the crag that he regarded as popular. He had chipped off holds, not realising that there were probably more holds on this crag than any other in Britain. A few less was no bad thing! If he caught you on the rock face it was quite normal for him to stand at the bottom, throw stones with a notable lack of accuracy and deliver a torrent of abuse, until you fell off or scrambled to the top and ran away.[47]

Joe Brown in 1948, short and muscular and exceptionally agile, was about to add a quiet cunning and an almost infallible judgment to his make-up, to become the most well-known British climber of the 1950s and perhaps the most celebrated of the century. He will reappear in Chapter 11.

In a letter to A B Afford, Mosedale remembered the problems faced in the early 1950s in accessing White Hall's closest moorland and crag: 'Outside we had many problems over access – especially to Combs Moss and Castle Naze.' Meldrum and Parker, writing in 1973, referred to the same obstacle: 'Although situated on the edge of the Peak District National Park, Whitehall Centre does not have access to the hills immediately dominating the centre. Ideally when they leave [a] centre for an expedition students should experience a feeling of freedom rather than one of constraint.'[48] As things turned out, despite the intention of the National Parks and Access to the Countryside Act, about fifty years would pass before the public would enjoy the legal right to walk on Combs Moss, the moor above White Hall.

Another no-go area, for a while, was the Roaches. In the 1990s, in the climbing-equipment store at White Hall, hung an old notice said to have come from the Roaches, probably in the 1960s: CLIMBING IS DANGEROUS AND IS FORBIDDEN. Yet Ernest Baker, in 1903, had very clearly recognised the recreational importance of the Staffordshire outcrops:

> There is nothing in Derbyshire so closely resembling a miniature range of mountains as the Roaches, the lofty gritstone ridge that dominates the borders of smoky Staffordshire, and supports a group of rocky peaks within full view of the chimney-stacks and dingy warehouses of Leek. We have here a bit of real highland scenery – cliffy hill-tops and heathery braes, with woods of pine underneath, and a solitude that is all the more delectable because we are only a few miles from a dense manufacturing population.[49]

Negotiations were sometimes successful. Mosedale 'used the Roaches regularly after negotiations with Colonel Brocklehurst over his wild wallabies; walking to and fro and bivouacking close to the cows in the farm at the back of the rocks.' Mosedale discussed the same issue in his manuscript, saying that in practice the warden of an outdoor centre must expend considerable effort in trying to reconcile the interests of his students with those of local residents and officials.[50]

From the beginning, despite access difficulties, and despite food rationing and poor ex-army equipment, White Hall groups camped all over the place. Mosedale particularly recalled a bleak camp on ice above Kinder Downfall with some lads from Heanor Grammar School at a New Year.[51] Bob Pettigrew wrote that 'there [were] many barns in the vicinity of the popular crags offering central heating from the cows beneath the hay loft'.

In January 1954, the first national park warden in the UK, Tom Tomlinson, was appointed. Tomlinson was the warden of Edale Youth Hostel. A couple of months later, on Good Friday, a hundred ramblers gathered in Edale to hear the first access land in the Peak District National Park formally declared open. Negotiations with landowners had opened up about six thousand acres of Kinder Scout.[52]

In *Hill and Water Sports in British Education*, Mosedale discusses several aspects of recreational access to land, including the need for close rural-urban relations:

> Another problem is to integrate the outdoor centre with its imme-
> diate environment and community. Even though these centres
> teach activities which are specialist and largely urban – in that
> their followers are usually urban rather than country dwellers –
> part of their educational value must still be in introducing students
> to the countryside, to ideas on the interdependence of country and
> town, of farm and manufacturing industry, the ways in which local
> farmers make a living, in which forest and hill land is utilized.[53]

In 1950 the work of outdoor centres in educating the urban recreator and particularly the walk-leaders was only just starting. Progress would sometimes be slow. In November or early December 1962, a party of more than 100 Sheffield schoolchildren, accompanied by only one master, set off on a midnight hike over Kinder Scout.[54]

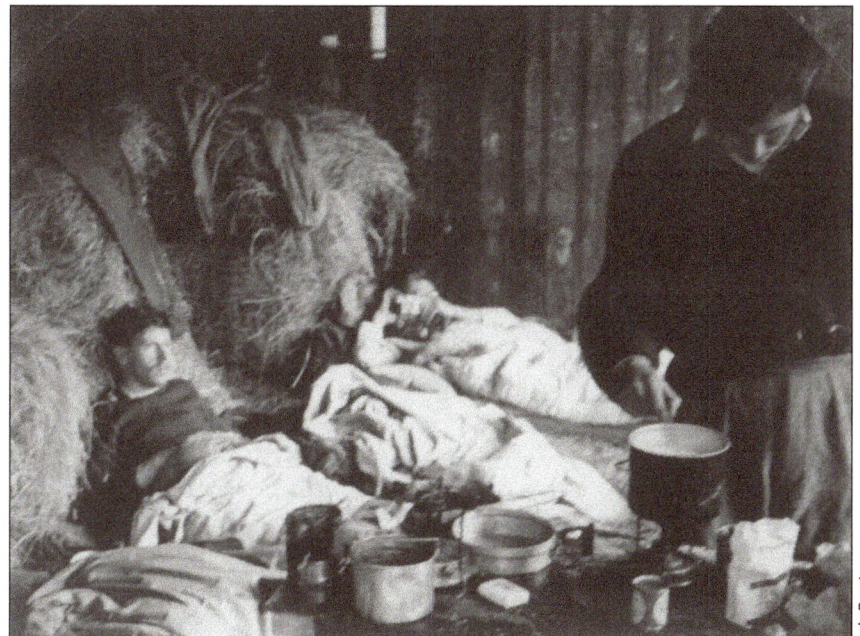

White Hall course members bivouacking in a hay barn, about 1954.

Sign said to be from The Roaches.

Veering Away from Outward Bound

Nationally, White Hall Centre was the pattern most commonly followed, with variations, by other LEA centres. Had Mosedale's manuscript been published in 1975, it might possibly have earned a niche in the general history of outdoor education in the UK. Now it is forty years 'out of date'. But who better to tell the story of the beginning of LEA outdoor centres than the guy who ran White Hall for its first five years?

Mosedale's writing is central to our understanding of his objection to
character building of a partial, illiberal sort, an objection that influenced
the approaches that evolved at White Hall. Despite its importance,
what he said was unpublished; for this reason, I quoted him frequently
in Chapter 7 and will continue to do so, in one place at some length.

On the day before White Hall had opened, a writer in the *Daily
Mirror* had said: 'Derbyshire has given the lead. Will the other local
authorities have the good sense to follow?'[55]

They would, but not immediately. Mosedale's position was a lonely
and vulnerable one. One other LEA outdoor pursuits centre seems to
have existed, although without having been declared to be such a facility.
Cumberland education authority (later a part of Cumbria education
authority) had opened a residential county youth centre in Keswick
in about April 1948. The early history of this centre is discussed in
Appendix 1.

Other LEAs were slow to follow Cumberland's and Derbyshire's
leads. West Bromwich (later renamed Sandwell) education authority
opened Plas Gwynant in 1958. Ron James, Trevor Jones and Tony
Mason-Hornby opened Ogwen Cottage as a mountaineering school in
1959 but The Cott, as it was known, was not purchased by Birmingham
city council until 1964. The most rapid expansion of outdoor education
occurred in the 1960s.[56]

If we interpret the term 'outdoor centre' loosely, by 1973 the UK had
over three hundred outdoor centres of varying sorts. About 140 of these
were primarily outdoor pursuits centres, owned by LEAs, other local
and central government agencies, charitable trusts, industrial firms, and
private individuals.[57] Mosedale overviews the whole range and then
scrutinises two particular centres. The first was a place he had known
well: White Hall, a mountain-based centre, run by an LEA. While
writing his manuscript in 1975, Mosedale revisited White Hall, and
the place 'still seem[ed] the same'.[58] The second was the National Sailing Centre at Cowes, a water-based centre, administered by the Sports
Council in consultation with the Royal Yachting Association (RYA).

Evoking his memories of a time of 'gross overwork and under-
financing', Mosedale recalls the on-the-fly development of White
Hall's flexible and informal approach to working with young people.
In 1950, necessity was the mother of invention, helped by intuition and
spontaneous decision-making. Telling this story embroils Mosedale
almost immediately in a comparison with Outward Bound's approach
and philosophy, as stated by the then chairman of the Outward Bound

Trust and quoted by Mosedale within the following extract from his manuscript:

> White Hall, Buxton, was set up by Derbyshire County Council in 1950 as a result of a recommendation coming from its Youth Service and Education Committee which concluded that, instead of waiting for large scale provision to be made nationally, it was desirable to cater for that minority of adventurous young people who wished to learn how to travel and camp and climb in hill country … It was felt that a centre could be formed to provide training in appropriate skills in surroundings of natural beauty, could provide for social experience in small residential groups and for individual enterprise in conditions of inspiring natural surroundings and solitude outside the centre …
>
> The house itself was bought for some £6,000[59] after the war but conversion and repairs were lengthy and costly and the new Centre did not open until December 28[60], 1950, shortly after the Outward Bound Trust had opened a mountain school at Eskdale in the Lake District, to supplement the work done by their first sea-school at Aberdovey. A letter from the Chairman of that Trust, Spencer Summers, in *The Times* of March 1, 1950, is interesting in view of White Hall's start as a service to the youth movement in Derbyshire: 'What is required for youth work is leadership by boys whose adventurous qualities have been directed into the right channels by proper training … We seek to project, into all kinds of youth and social work, boys between the ages of 15½–18½, who have undergone short term character training courses at the sea-school at Aberdovey and the mountain school in Cumberland … ' This was and is the philosophical justification behind the Outward Bound Movement, and the 1973 leaflet for the Ullswater Mountain School, for example, is headed 'Self-discovery through Adventure' and states in its introductory paragraph: 'The purpose of the School is not specifically to train mountaineers. It is designed to challenge the qualities of its boys in adventure; the adventure of coming together as strangers and building a purposeful community; the adventure of conquering ordeals and difficulties while living in the mountains. Comparable difficulties come to everyone at some time in life and Outward Bound training seeks to encourage a boy to discover that a clear head and a common sense approach will reduce formidable problems to rea-

sonable proportions. It also accustoms him to hard effort, makes him physically fit, resilient, mentally and spiritually alert and brings a comprehension of inner power, a greater confidence in himself and a closer understanding of and respect for his fellows.'

Many criticisms have been made of this claim, with its apparent dependence on the training of character, its reliance on transfer of this training from one sphere of life to another, its pragmatic approach to problems which indicate a basic acceptance of the status quo in society and its somewhat patronising tone which places it fairly in the school of thought which sees education as concerned primarily with the teaching of cultural and moral values. It has the advantage, however, of being a plain statement of policy, even though begging many questions, and its appeal, like the Scout Movement, to what might be called the biological memory of man's experience in sterner times, defines a clear-cut British concept of the educational value of outdoor recreation which continues to attract strong support.

The difficulty for staff at White Hall lay in the absence of such a clear philosophy which was so easily saleable to those in positions of authority. Yet the problem of working out its own policy in terms which could be justified on educational grounds, and thus used to encourage increased support from a local government education authority, was faced squarely from the beginning.[61]

So, here we have a picture of Mosedale, twenty-five years after opening White Hall, deep in thought about the pros and cons of the 1950s Outward Bound version of outdoor training, but also informed by a 1973 leaflet. A little-known piece of that picture is that, as we saw in Chapter 7, two months before White Hall opened, Jack Longland had referred to the planned centre as an Outward Bound School.[62] In the event, not only did he name it distinctly differently, but also it would acquire a different philosophy.

The difference between White Hall and the Outward Bound schools showed up clearly in early press reports. On 16 June 1950 the *Times Educational Supplement* published a full-page article about Eskdale OBMS, which was to be officially opened on 18 June.[63] The heading, 'Character and Friendship through Hardship', was an accurate title for the article that followed, correctly catching the character-building spirit of the Outward Bound movement, as it was then. Despite the expertly imposed hardships, a few participants were smitten by the outdoor pursuits, like Michael Fisher at Eskdale in 1952:

> Friday 27th June
> After dinner I got a long climb in with Eddy McGaul and Mr Lagoe on Arrowhead Ridge. Mr Lagoe said it was graded 'moderate' but he judged it to be 'difficult'. The rock was cold and wet to the touch … I led up the first pitch and belayed to a convenient rock spike, then brought Mr Lagoe up … He went ahead and when he had taken his belay I brought Eddy up to me. At this point the weather cleared, the mist parted and the view down into Wasdale was spectacular. The scree below us fell away in a long sweep of some 1600 feet down to the waters of the lake which then stretched away for three miles towards the distant sea. The sense of exposure was immense. I loved it. I had never been so high and so precariously perched above such a tremendous drop in all my life. If this was rock-climbing, I was sold on it![64]

Six months after Eskdale OBMS opened, White Hall opened. A quite detailed *Manchester Guardian* article appeared under the heading 'Learning Hillcraft in Comfort: New Derbyshire Centre for Young People'. This heading accurately reflected the tone of the article that followed, which talked about young people learning 'to enjoy the hills without unnecessary danger or discomfort'.[65] The accent was on enjoyment rather than on needless Spartanism, both outdoors and indoors: 'There is more than ordinary camp comfort, with central heating, drying rooms, armchairs, and big fireplaces aiming to encourage the most newly adventurous spirit'. The article did not mention character training. However, it is undeniable that despite the central heating and the minimising of hardship and the emphasis on outdoor pursuits and education for leisure, much valuable social and personal development was an automatic and unavoidable side benefit of a weekend or week at White Hall.

Mosedale's short but eloquent account of the strengths and weaknesses of Outward Bound, written in retrospect twenty-five years later, and read thirty-nine years later again, reveals a man harbouring some concerns about the moralistic parts of the Outward Bound approach, while appreciating the advantage in having a plain statement of policy, as the Boy Scout movement had.

Here and there, Mosedale employs the forgotten art of the long sentence. In the lengthy extract reproduced earlier, the penultimate paragraph, beginning 'Many criticisms have ... ', flows like poetry. The final paragraph is profound. In acknowledging that White Hall lacked the sort of very clear policies that steered Outward Bound and Scouting, and which met the approval of some educationists, Mosedale latched onto a matter that would occupy the sharpest minds in outdoor education for years and years.

On the other hand, as the man in charge of a new enterprise, unconstrained by any detailed written doctrine of a high-profile sort, Mosedale – with the help of his voluntary instructors – could follow his instincts to head in whatever direction suited the abilities and interests of the students. This autonomy would become a long-standing feature of White Hall's operations.

In Chapter 9, Mosedale and Longland will help us to compare White Hall and one particular Outward Bound school, but Longland will cautiously sidestep the subject of character training. In Chapter 12, Harold Drasdo will confront it head on.

Morning assembly at Aberdovey Outward Bound Sea School, 1940s or 1950s.

Towards Flexibility and Pragmatism

Shortly after discussing the pros and cons of the Outward Bound approach, Mosedale launches into another flowing paragraph, this time describing the different path taken, deliberately, by White Hall. This direction differed from that of the Outward Bound schools. And it was plural, a number of approaches to suit varying needs:

> It was not only legitimate but necessary to see White Hall as teaching mountain and water activities for their own value and in their own right, and not because they provided a convenient arena in which character training could proceed. Yet it had to be more than an instructional centre for the rigorous and serious activities connected with hills and mountains. Its responsibility was to cater also for those who were most interested in its countryside, in camping, in photography, in sketching, in gentle hill walking and the investigation of wild life, to meet the needs of those who found satisfaction in tickling trout in a local stream and sleeping out under the stars as well as those who wanted to learn rock climbing and serious mountaineering. And, within each interest, it needed to try to allow for the physically strong and the comparatively weak, the driven, the leisurely, those attracted to the hills mainly through emotional pulls and those seeing them as presenting opportunities primarily for physical action.[66]

Numerous press reports of the 1950s and 60s reflect the importance attached to outdoor recreation by Longland and Mosedale and his successors. Many of these newspaper articles also acknowledge – perhaps not in these words – the social and personal development aspects of residential courses in outdoor pursuits. For some people the term 'character development' had acquired mildly pejorative undertones; but for others, 'character development' remained a respectable label for a desirable aim. It cropped up occasionally. A journalist who visited White Hall in 1958 wrote that the teaching staff 'reckon that on the longer courses they can start to do a little character-building of the type for which Outward Bound schools are famous'.[67] In March 1961 a *Guardian* reporter spent a day with a White Hall group that was climbing at the Roaches. At the end of a longish article he summed up the centre's purposes: 'Although rock climbing, caving, camping, walking, and so on, were becoming increasingly popular, many young people, it was felt, were trying them out without learning the basic principles.

The centre was established to show them how to look after themselves and, incidentally, but not less in importance, to develop character.'[68]

A B Afford was more circumspect: 'The enjoyment of a sport or skill was accepted from the start and friendly relationships were natural in this terrain … The effect on character and leadership qualities was also recognised and channelled but never with the obvious emphasis used in the Forces or O.B. movement where the "challenge" was all important.'[69]

Peter Mosedale's rather stronger reservations about character training, expressed earlier under 'Veering away from Outward Bound', may have reflected a general postwar trend. In some quarters nationally, the distaste for the term 'character building' and some of the ideas historically associated with that term became evident. 'After World War II, "character building" came to be thought of [in some quarters] as sinister, comical or simply archaic'.[70] It is easy, though, to find examples of uncritical acceptance of the term and its ideas. In March 1950, for instance, Dundee's *Courier and Advertiser* reported that 'forty schoolgirls from Glasgow secondary schools [were] halfway through a month's course of character building under Glasgow School Welfare Department's scheme of residential education, based at Glenmore Lodge'.[71]

The overwhelming feeling from much of Mosedale's writing is of a pragmatism that senses the needs of individuals, combined with a desire to meet those needs: 'We were all concerned at first to cater for everyone as far as possible and to make experiences enjoyable – even if only in retrospect – as well as a challenge. For this reason I developed wide games and orienteering quite early. Our day games were normally on Wild Moor and we had several night navigation games for Combs Moss.'[72] These local wide games included Hare and Hounds, Night Rescue and Hunt the Light.

The most ambitious wide game, called Bandits, took place over Kinder Scout and Bleaklow. Sending unaccompanied fifteen-year-olds across Kinder and Bleaklow required meticulous planning and management. The potential seriousness of these moors can suddenly become real and can catch people out. Paul Nunn knew the moorlands well:

Most hills have moods, subtleties and nuances, whose scope is too diverse to be absorbed in a single day's experience. Kinder Scout is no exception. This ambivalent plateau, as large in area as many a Munro, is a hub of the northern Peak District, claiming the admiration and fascination of thousands of visitors … The plateau is a land of mercurial mood and playful chicanery. Once understood, it seems friendly, but it can be merciless to the care-less. Hazy summer afternoons swiftly boil into nimbus in the west, and sudden gusts of wind carry drenching pillars of rain up the Kinder Ravine.[73]

In his developing of wide games, Mosedale adapted the idea from Scouting, which itself had modified a manhunt game organised at Seatoller House in Borrowdale by Geoffrey Young in June 1898.[74] Wide games were one Geoffrey Young idea that Mosedale embraced wholeheartedly.

The Seatoller manhunt of 1898 originated in a conversation between Young and his friend George Macaulay Trevelyan. During a walking tour of Cornwall in the spring of 1898, they had discussed Robert Louis Stevenson's *Kidnapped*, which contains a description of English red-coat soldiers chasing two fugitives across the Highlands. They had subsequently devised a game designed to re-create the excitement of that chase. It was also a mountainous modification of Hunt the Hare, played in English schools since the 16th century, and of cross-country running, a late-1860s development.

In June, sixteen Cambridge undergraduates, including Young and Trevelyan, spent four days manhunting across the central mountains of the Lake District. Twelve acted as hounds and four as hares. A touch of the hand was a capture. Trevelyan described one near-capture as 'the most exciting five minutes I have ever had in my life'.[75]

The game, sometimes called the Trevelyan manhunt, became an annual event. After the 1908 Whitsun hunt, Young wrote: 'The Lake Hunt delightful. More convivial than usual … The 10th anniversary of our old joke! … Good weather and long hunts. George [Trevelyan] hunted me for three hours, and I got away; pleasant not to be too old yet.'[76]

The centennial hunt took place in 1998, at the same time as the explosion of a 'new' idea that sometimes involved outdoor games spread across extensive areas and which came to be known as reality television.

Unattributed. From Hankinson, Alan, *Geoffrey Winthrop Young: Poet, Educator, Mountaineer* (1995).

Geoffrey Young and Charles Trevelyan at Seatoller House in 1914 wearing the red sashes that denote them as hares for the day's manhunt across the Lake District, held annually since its invention in1898 by Young and George Macaulay Trevelyan.

Shanks's Pony and Map-reading

Sometime in 1951 Ken Oldham moved on from Spring Bank School to take charge of science and rural studies at Longdendale School in Hollingworth, which is at the bottom of Longdendale, about four kilometres northwest of Glossop. When all the circumstances were perfect, Oldham, like Mosedale, liked to give young people the chance to tackle more than average physical challenges. In 1952 he accompanied a group of twelve boys on a ten-day course at White Hall. (Hollingworth was in Cheshire, but, as Doug Scott has noted, there was so much positive feedback from Derbyshire schools that students from other authorities were invited.[77])

Before we look at that course, a word about gender bias. Boys had dominated many references to education in the outdoors during the first half of the 20th century. But many of the earliest references to the purpose of White Hall Centre, in 1945–51, spoke of boys and girls or young men and young women. The phrase 'boys and girls' appeared three times in Longland's 1950 *Out of Doors* article. Some gender bias, however, lingered on into the 1950s and is apparent in some of the quotations from those years. The two Ken Oldham groups that I have written about happened to be all boys. I have not discovered any detailed information about the numbers of each sex attending schools' courses in the 1950s. In the 1957 television film *Climbing*, the group of White Hall pupils filmed at Windgather Rocks was mixed. When the Duke of Edinburgh visited White Hall in 1958, he met boys and girls. Mixed groups became by far the most common arrangement for White Hall's schools' courses. Looking back at this situation from 2017, I wonder if a seldom recognised achievement of Jack Longland and the 1950s White Hall staff was their contribution to Girl Power.

The 1952 course was a residential extension of classroom work. Again Oldham kept a detailed diary, which was printed in full for circulation to official quarters, but whose location again is unknown.[78] Recalling the programme twenty-four years later, he described some of the most memorable parts:

> The first day of the course involved trekking the twenty miles to the centre as a map reading and field observation exercise (we had no money for transport, nor was it desired!). For the record, six boys were fourth year, four were third year and the remaining two, second year pupils. The route to White Hall was divided into four stages and three boys were to lead the party along each section. Roads were to be avoided and the choice of route restricted to footpaths. The children were thus thrust into situations of responsibility from the start and the remainder of the course followed the same pattern of placing them into situations which demanded their full participation.
>
> … the introduction to climbing and caving proved to be the highlights of the course. None had climbed before and as the instructors demonstrated the knots and rope drill and the very necessary safety precautions, [the boys] became completely absorbed in the task and profited greatly from their experience … It was an exhilarating and wonderful exercise. All appreciated the value of the right equipment and clothing for the task, as well as the courtesy and teamwork that climbing demands. The choice of routes by the instructors was first rate and although the later climbs fully extended the boys, none of them was too difficult. The boys were singing on the way back to White Hall in a jubilant manner that I had never observed in them before.[79]

On the final day the boys set off homewards, again – as ten days earlier – using their own legs as a means of transport. In three groups of four they went by way of Kinder Scout, about a twenty-mile trek. A snow storm swept across the high moor and each group safely navigated by various routes to Glossop, the final checkpoint.[80] As for the first schools' course the previous year, map-reading was again an essential part of this course.

In August 1952 a group of seven boys from Longdendale School, aged thirteen to fourteen, traversed the whole 270 miles of the Pennine Way (thirteen years before the long-distance way was officially opened); this group may have been the first school party to do so. In April 1955, Ken Oldham moved to Lancashire to become the headmaster of Whitehough Camp School (established in 1938), a post he held for thirty-two years until his retirement in 1987.[81] He is regarded as one of the trailblazers of British outdoor education.

Oxbridge, Redbrick and Stalybridge

Adventurous sports like climbing and caving can be great levellers, if participation is open to all. Rock climbers do sometimes fall out with each other, but usually the arguments take place in writing, such as in letters to climbing magazines, or, if spoken, indoors. Scattered through climbing literature are occasional accounts of mountaineers feuding during climbs; a 1961 expedition to Nuptse became notorious for the 'personality conflicts' (ie, punch-ups) that took place on it.[82] Often, though, friends made through climbing remain friends for life.

Many of the voluntary instructors upon whom White Hall relied in the 1950s and 60s came from relatively new clubs and groups such as Derby's Oread Mountaineering Club (formed in 1949 in Burton-upon-Trent) and Birmingham's Cave and Crag Club (formed in 1947). This belonging to new clubs, however, was not universal. Some volunteers came from clubs that were neither new arrivals nor 19th-century pioneers. Cyril Machin's club, the Midland Association of Mountaineers (formed in 1922), came into this category.

A few of the club members were manual tradesmen; some were white-collar clerical workers and some were professional people with redbrick degrees. When instructing for White Hall, all the volunteers worked as equals with each other and with a succession of wardens shaped by Oxbridge and by the traditions of senior clubs like the Climbers' Club (formed in 1898). The White Hall of the 1950s and early 1960s blended people from different backgrounds. Looking even casually at that period opens up a who's who of the Climbers' Club, the Oread and other climbing and caving clubs. This story would be incomplete without a few legendary characters from that most exclusive of clubs, Manchester's Rock and Ice; Messrs Brown (The Baron) and Whillans (The Villain) both make appearances at White Hall, and not to repair the roof or to mend the plumbing.

In 1952 the class structure of British climbing was perhaps fraying at the edges but was still quite strong in some areas of the centre. Mount Everest was climbed on 29 May 1953, the ascent serving as 'a leitmotif for the new Elizabethan age … [and] at a stroke making a risky activity seem highly respectable in official eyes'.[83] John Hunt, whom we met earlier running a mountaincraft course in north Wales, was thrown into prominence and knighted.

Joe Brown should possibly have been on that Everest expedition, but the argument about this is inconclusive, as he hadn't climbed in the Alps. He was not invited to join the Everest team. Talking about this in 1961, he reportedly said: 'Everest wasn't for the likes of me. Only University men or Army officers or people with money were invited.'[84]

Picture the scene, firstly, in Chamonix in summer 1953. Don Cowan, Don Whillans and Joe Brown of the Rock and Ice, and Whillans's girlfriend Audrey, have travelled to the Alps on two motorbikes. It is Whillans's second trip to the Alps, Brown's first. The three men are enjoying a rest day after climbing the East Ridge of the Dent du Crocodile. They meet Geoff Sutton and Bob Downes at the Bar Nationale.[85]

Whillans (20), short and muscular, has survived a pugnacious childhood on the narrow cobbled streets of Adelphi in Salford, Manchester. He is now an apprentice plumber and general handyman who, when at home, is required to work on Saturday mornings.[86] Brown (22), similar in stature and agility to Whillans but opposite in temperament, has grown up happily in a very small terrace house in the middle of a large slum area in Ardwick, Manchester.[87] He is a jobbing builder. Cowan works on the railways as a locomotive fitter. Sutton (23) and Downes (21) are undergraduates at Cambridge University. Sutton has attended Harrow School (until being invited to leave), speaks fluent French and is president of Cambridge University Mountaineering Club (CUMC).[88] Downes is a product of Perse School (upper-school fees now, in 2017, £16,032 a year excluding lunches) and he has served as an officer in the Royal Corps of Signals. He is on his way to gaining a 2:1 in history and is a future president of the CUMC.[89] Sutton later described him as 'small and puckish; his slanting eyes and pointed ears and scarred cheek gave the air of a sardonic yet twinkling elf'.[90]

Sutton knows the Chamonix Aiguilles well. He is full of energy and enthusiasm. Physically he is tall and burly rather than wiry, but he can lead quite hard routes for the time, whether delicate or strenuous, with perfect control.[91] He teams up with the Manchester pair and the Sheffielder Cowan to attempt the west face of the Aiguille de Blaitière, which is the only climb in the guidebook with a rock pitch graded VIb (ie, very hard, and therefore considered suitable for Brown's third alpine route). They are unsuccessful, but the builder, the plumber and the railway man have now climbed with – in Whillans's words – one of the 'university wallahs'. Whillans considers Sutton and Downes to be 'university types but not standard issue'.[92]

Whillans's memoirs, *Don Whillans: Portrait of a Mountaineer,* co-written with Alick Ormerod, have been called highly unreliable. But the book's reported Whillans comments about university students are characteristically blunt and they ring true. Before meeting Sutton and Downes at an Alpine Climbing Group dinner in April 1953,[93] Whillans, already a fledgling anti-hero, had never had much time for university climbers. He and Joe had enjoyed some laughs at the expense of the varsity types:

> I remember one weekend when we were at the Roaches and a whole coach-load of blokes arrived from Oxford University Mountaineering Club. You should have seen them. They were capurtling off all over the place. We were just walking along the foot of the crags when one of those lads crunched down just in front of us. I turned to Joe.
>
> 'Bloody hell, Joe,' I said, 'I wonder how many they write off every weekend?'[94]

Brown adds some similar but more analytic observations, from a day on the Idwal Slabs in north Wales at Christmas 1947:

> It was snowing and we were wearing gym shoes. Near by a party of Oxford types stretched out in Javelin Gully was having a difference of opinion about the merits of climbing in gym shoes in the prevailing conditions. In a high voice the leader was ordering one of his companions to get off the rope because he was wearing gym shoes. The conversation between them was most unfriendly.

We wondered if this sort of conduct was normal in climbing relationships because it was the opposite to our behaviour with each other.

Of the five climbers I've named – Sutton, Downes, Brown, Whillans and Cowan – some may have heard of White Hall Centre (by 1953), but as far as can be ascertained none of them had been there. In the following ten years, three of them would join the White Hall staff: Sutton (warden), Downes (assistant warden) and Brown (instructor). Whillans too would turn up at White Hall once or twice, on climbing business.

In summer 1954 Brown and Whillans climbed the West Face of the Petit Dru in a fast time, an achievement that helped Brown to gain an invitation to join the 1955 expedition to Kangchenjunga, the highest unclimbed peak in the world. The invitation alone represented a significant weakening of the class barrier in British mountaineering; Brown's subsequent first ascent of Kangchenjunga with George Band, a geologist and petroleum engineer, further opened up the Himalayas to everyman. Brown credited Charles Evans for this change: 'Evans had chosen his team as a dependable body of climbers and for an ability to get on with each other … That one person might be a professor and another a labourer had no relevance to climbing a mountain.'[95]

Now imagine the scenes in Derbyshire and in the Alps in summer 1955. In Derbyshire, Longland, clever and multi-talented, even by Cambridge standards, is hovering in the White Hall background, inextricably involved with the wider scheme of things nationally, particularly with the training of novices and outdoor leaders and with accident reduction. Mosedale, the Oxford-educated inaugural warden, has steered White Hall safely past all the early obstacles, has allowed clear (but unwritten) directions to gradually evolve, and is in his last four months of non-stop labour at the house on the hill. In the Alps, three other, younger men, all Cambridge chums, probably familiar with climbing drainpipes at night – Geoff Sutton, Bob Downes and Eric Langmuir – join Alan Blackshaw, an Oxford climber, to climb together. They visit the Bregaglia and the Mont Blanc area. The team of four makes a scholarly ascent of the north-east face of the Piz Badile, then considered to be one of the harder routes in the Alps. Their ascent is part of a postwar renaissance of British alpine climbing, and it introduces to this book another future White Hall boss, Eric Langmuir.

Three months later, in autumn 1955, Peter and Betty Mosedale head north to Scotland, and Geoff and Ann Sutton take their place as White

Hall warden and housekeeper. To further reinforce the intelligentsia, a Nottingham teacher Harold Drasdo (another climber and writer-to-be) arrives, and then Bob Downes joins the team, in preference to a career in the Colonial Service. The staffroom whiffs of Oxbridge erudition, Climbers' Club tradition, Robert Lawrie stockings, and the superior newsprint and sentence structure of *The Times*.

At the same time, voluntary instructors (VIs) from Derbyshire towns and further afield join the proceedings each weekend. They come from all walks of life. The class differences are more subtle and multifaceted than simply south and north, or public school and state school. The climbing VIs from Nottingham tend to be working class, whereas the Oreads of Derby come from the professional middle classes.[96] Some of the volunteers wear Army and Navy Store camouflage anoraks and trousers. Some come armed with prismatic compasses no longer needed by the Eighth Army. The anoraks are paper-thin cotton, designed for hot climates. It is said that if there had been no war, British climbers would have had to go naked.

Some of the volunteers arrive wearing tricouni-nailed boots, well worn, while others have Vibram-soled boots, newish looking and still uncomfortable; the relative merits of nails and rubber are much discussed every weekend. A few are smoking cigarettes; 80 per cent of British men are smokers. One or two bring along pocket-size climbing guidebooks and French karabiners and black or white gym pumps marked 'Empire Made'. There's a copy of the *Derby Evening Telegraph* going around, picked up on the way out of town. Some of the volunteers have come by bus.

One such is a bespectacled fourteen-year-old Nottingham youth, Douglas Scott, who had started climbing at Black Rocks earlier that year, had then attended a White Hall schools' course, and is returning as a trainee instructor.[97] He already has his eyes on bigger hills than Combs Moss. White Hall is an official stopping place for the X2 Nottingham–Manchester express bus. It dropped him off at the South Lodge.

Another is much older, about forty-five, the guidebook writer, historian of Peak District climbing and Oread member Eric Byne, who probably has more friends among climbers than any man of his generation.[98] Reflecting later on his years of climbing, Byne supplies another angle to the story of voluntary instructing: 'However, my rapidly declining standard on rock could no longer be denied. But my ego received a boost at this critical period. First I took over the Organisation of

Meets for the M.A.M. [Midland Association of Mountaineers]. Then White Hall was opened and I was able to exhibit my remaining talents to complete novices.'[99]

Jack Longland, not present on these autumn weekends in 1955 but kept informed on general developments, is pleased to learn that Byne is still involved. Just five years older than Byne, Longland has been long aware of Byne's influence on the sport. He would later write: 'Eric Byne was the living link who brought together the two main groups in British climbing, those from an academic, professional, traditionally leisured background, and those from the cities and industrial towns who had to learn their craft during evenings and snatched weekends in the nearest climbing ground.'[100]

By 1956 Bob Downes, a shy man with a quiet humour, and Don Whillans, famously laconic and temperamental, have had four years to learn to understand each other's vernacular. There's mutual respect, as well as a shared interest in pitons and nylon slings. In late 1956, Downes offers Whillans, the flawed genius, a place on the Rucksack Club's expedition to Masherbrum.[101] At this particular time in Whillans's climbing career, this opportunity is an important step forward. The expedition holds its first meeting at White Hall.[102] Ann Sutton makes all the down gear for Masherbrum. Climbing, the great leveller, has flattened some of the class barriers in one of the most class-ridden of societies. By November 1958, voluntary instructors number over 150 from dozens of climbing and caving clubs.[103]

An idea of the importance of the voluntary instructors and a hint of the quality of the grounding received from them – in all its aspects – can be gained from the following thank-you letter, written by a course member and addressed directly to the Oread Mountaineering Club:

Dear Sir,

I am writing as a student of White Hall, and would like to send an appreciation of the instructors who, I believe are Oreads. I arrived in Buxton on Feb. 26th with another student and two instructors. One was an Oread but the other would not identify himself. We were soon installed in a Spanish bar, and hours later we arrived at White Hall to the jingle of bottles. Saturday found three inches of snow outside, and parties were quickly dispersed to Shale Gully and to skiing. I was in the Gully Party. One member wore a boater which stopped falling stones from hitting the last man. In the afternoon we went skiing. The least said the better.

In the evening a slide show by Messrs. Brown and Falkner was followed by a social evening. Stan Moore and Dick Brown did a complete traverse on the wall of the lounge. Sunday proved amusing to the Gully Party. An instructor went crampons (sic) over balaclava down the Gully but was not hurt. He said it was a controlled glissade. Over lunch certain Oreads gave imitations of penguins which were very good – at least everyone had indigestion that afternoon. I should like to thank the members of the Oread concerned for some very useful instructions throughout the weekend.

D.R. Hammond[104]

Among the voluntary instructors of the 1950s were Charlie Abelthorpe, Alf Bridge, Maurice Buckley, Derrick Burgess, Eric Byne, Byron Connelly, Chuck Cook, Les Corfield, Bill Curzon, Norman Dobson, Peter Evans, Des Hadlam, Frank Hall, Mike Handley, Geoff Hayes, Hugh Jordan, George Kitchin, 'Larry' Lambe, Cyril Machin, Don Morrison, Ken Oldham, Bob Pettigrew, Ernie Phillips, John Philpot, John Plowes, Joe Porter, Harry Pretty, Norman Rimmer, Frank Salt, Doug Scott, Ron Townsend, Bill Vale, William Walker, Ken Wall, Ivan Waller, Wilf White, N 'Plum' Worrall, and Peter Wright. (This list is very incomplete.)

Alf Bridge and Ivan Waller had climbed with Jack Longland more than twenty years before White Hall Centre existed. Here is Waller, recording his first ascent of Fallen Block Crack, in Wales, a hard climb of its time (1927): 'My second-man was unable to follow. I had never seen him before, and I have never seen him since.'

It seems likely that most of the other voluntary instructors knew Longland or were at least aware of his name and reputation. Some of them were themselves already part of British climbing history. Most of them probably owned a copy of Barford's *Climbing in Britain* and may have peer reviewed its line drawings. One or two will have been founts of information on every crag between the Tissington Spires and Ravenstones. But few of them, except those who were teachers, will have known much about the 1944 Education Act – nor did they need to, however far-reaching it was. How many of them had heard of Kurt Hahn is difficult to tell. Hahn was a public figure, with a penchant for currying the favour of powerful men.[105] In the period 1940–60, Hahn's name appeared in the *Manchester Guardian* about as often as Longland's.[106]

A few voluntary instructors gain a special mention in the written accounts. For a time, Cyril Machin took up residence and did valuable work. (It is not clear whether this was paid or voluntary.)[107] Sutton and Byne later described him as a man who was 'completely tireless despite his sixty years, whose climbing was only just coming to its best, and who seemed to gather legends around him as a boulder gathers moss'.[108]

Eric Byne knew Machin well and remembered offering him some advice:

> As his skill improved, his recklessness increased. He was in a tearing hurry to get everything in, and in order to do more than one climb in a day would without thought run out 120-foot lengths without belays or safeguards; he never seemed to worry about his Second's feelings. We climbed together leading through on some hard routes and I had to browbeat him into shorter leads and runners. He was often at his limit … He was nevertheless a remarkable man, tough, impervious to weather …
>
> His character seemed to change when he went to White Hall. He became gentler, more thoughtful for others and himself, and lost that fierce, reckless determination. His friends became legion and his reputation legendary. We laughed about his past misdemeanours and joked in front of him about his past reckless days – and with a twinkle in his eye he would relate some closely guarded tale of one of his misadventures.[109]

Peter Mosedale tells a similar story, having encountered one of those awkward snags that occasionally arises in climbing, even with the finest of companions. Let's call it a weakness in technique. When he required a sound belay, Machin was something of an illusionist. Mosedale wrote: 'I was in Skye with Cyril Machin over the Coronation holiday. He was a terrifying abseiler, putting the rope round a stone with his foot on top, and I was hardly surprised when he so sadly came off at Castle Naze. I still remember taking him in the ambulance to Manchester, groaning all the way in spite of the heavy morphine.'[110]

This serious accident happened on 9 May 1954. 'It [was] believed that the rope slipped over the belay.' Machin sustained injuries to his back. After a long spell in hospital he recovered but was encumbered by metal braces for the remainder of his life.[111] (Which raises a question that I will not try to answer: are we better off nowadays, when such an accident often triggers off – sometimes justifiably and sometimes

not – a carnival of investigation, interrogation, allegation, recrimina-
tion and litigation?)

Machin was a prominent member of the Midland Association of
Mountaineers. A fellow member wrote of 'Cyril's boundless energy,
much of it devoted to introducing novices to the pursuits that meant
so much to him.' Showell Styles wrote: 'I don't think I ever heard Cyril
speak of his love for mountains, but you had only to spend a day on
the hills with him to know that he was utterly at one with them.'[112]

Machin served on the Gritstone Guidebook Committee (inaugu-
rated in November 1962), and was secretary of the Peak District Committee of the BMC. He also served on the Peak Park Planning Board.

Burgess, Connelly and Walker gave up their time weekend after
weekend. Walker had learnt a trick or two while wandering over Italy
for months as an escaped prisoner of war. Now he fascinated groups of
schoolboys as they watched him gather sodden heather in the pouring
rain and set fire to it with one match.[113]

We will see later that Eric Langmuir, when recalling his time at
White Hall, would pick out the presence of voluntary instructors as
being the most important influence on the character of the place. Voluntary instructors would continue to arrive in considerable numbers
throughout the 1960s and 70s.

This chapter has drawn on several eyewitness accounts from the
period 1950–5, including Peter Mosedale's manuscript, Ken Oldham's
papers and A B Afford's history. One other source, Bob Pettigrew's
1954–5 thesis, demands our attention. In 1954–5 Pettigrew was attending Loughborough Training College, studying for the Supplementary
Certificate in Physical Education of the University of Nottingham. For
his research topic he examined the general history of several adventurous outdoor activities and then their specific roles at White Hall Centre.

Two-thirds of Pettigrew's thesis – Chapters IV, V and VI – looks
explicitly at the teaching of outdoor activities at White Hall, including
hill walking, navigating, camping, bivouacking, caving, rock climbing,
skiing, woodcraft and estate work, and first aid and mountain rescue.
Once you get past the chuckling and gurgling streams and the other
affected prose of a young writer bent on matching Wordsworth, this
thesis reinforces and sometimes expands upon what we already know
about the period. It includes a sequence of about twenty-seven photographs taken during a climbing session at Castle Naze.

Bob Pettigrew

Pupils from Shepshed, Leicestershire, at Castle Naze, about 1954 or 1955.

Bob Pettigrew

A pupil from Shepshed pays out the rope to the leader on Studio Climb at Castle Naze, about 1954 or 1955.

The belayer is on Studio Climb, the leader is on
The Nithen, Castle Naze, about 1954 or 1955.

A lunch break at Castle Naze, about 1954 or 1955.

D7786/BOX/1/6, courtesy of Derbyshire Record Office.

White Hall course members on Studio Climb on Castle Naze in 1954 or 1955.

Caving and Canoeing and Away Courses

Caving

Caving is arguably the supreme group activity for an outdoor pursuits centre. (Let's not quarrel over whether an underground activity is outdoor.) Caving was added to White Hall's range of activities in 1952. Arthur Afford, at that time a voluntary instructor, had some experience of lying in mud and exploring Stygian chambers but Mosedale and the other two permanent staff members probably had none. At first, help from local cavers was essential, not an optional extra:

> In 1952 came Plowes and his men from the Caving Clubs. They introduced a whole new activity to us and Blair, Hird, Machin and I began to use regularly Giant's Hole, Eldon and Bagshawe. We used Bagshawe a lot, including the tight crawl (8 inches between planes – you know it?) in which I was rashly stuck wearing a sweater and Machin and party left me! Cyril used to encourage

students to slide down a slippery incline there when they didn't
know there was a deep unseen pool at the bottom. One of our parties discovered a new cave near Buxton Reservoir, down a rabbit
hole, in late 1953 I think. We explored it. It was a frightening one
and I felt in danger of potential flooding – Plowes found a green
grass line high up in the first cavern much to his horror – and
they may have stopped using it.[114] [John Plowes was a member
of the Orpheus Caving Club. In 1952 he became the secretary of
the newly formed Derbyshire Cave Rescue Organisation.]

Bagshawe Cavern is a mainly natural system that was entered by lead-
miners in the 18th century.[115] Exploring cavers have extended it. Ernest
Baker wrote an account of a 1902 exploratory trip into Bagshawe, lit by
hurricane lamps and candles: 'On we went again, now walking upright
through high-roofed corridors, now going on hands and knees over
sharp boulders that cut our legs severely, and now wriggling under low
rocks on our breasts.'[116]

In being a rock climber who adapted himself enthusiastically to
caving, perhaps partly as something different – and a great sport – for
winter, Mosedale was the first of many White Hall staff members who
were climbers firstly but who then acquired considerable competence
in caving. The dual interest is quite common among people who live
in or near caving areas. Ernest Baker was one such person, and in 1903
he compared the peculiarities of the two sports:

> Climbing is the most exhilarating of sports, the joys of cave wan-
> dering are won in defiance of all that seems gloomy and depress-
> ing. Nor as an exercise is it equal to climbing in the open air. The
> exertion is often far more arduous; there are few kinds of physical
> discipline more trying than to crawl on your stomach over sharp
> rocks, with no space to lift your head for hundreds of yards per-
> haps, and one arm cramped with holding a flaring candle out in
> front, which keeps burning your fingers.[117]

Several accounts of White Hall's caving of the early 1950s talk of using
candles. Bob Pettigrew, for example, wrote in 1954–5 that 'general
illumination is provided by candles which give an efficient, all-round
illumination'. At some point, candles became confined to the emergency kits. Thereafter, the lighting on White Hall caving trips was by
carbide lamps, which fitted into brackets on the helmets. The helmets

were a standard industrial type, made for coalminers. Much caving equipment was still home-made. You can gain an idea of the technology of the period from the comprehensive book *British Caving: An Introduction to Speleology*, published in 1953. The science of clothing had not yet progressed much beyond wool and cotton:

> The following garments are suggested as a minimum for either sex; ankle-length under-pants, half-sleeved vest, bathing trunks or costume, woollen shirt, a pair of shorts or trousers, a long-sleeved and high-necked sweater, waterproof or semi-waterproof golfing jacket or smock, and the whole covered by one-piece [cotton] overalls. The last item is expensive, but for anyone contemplating many caving trips it is well worth the money.[118]

Novice cavers who lacked overalls were recommended to ask elderly relatives for cast-off woollen underwear. For outer garments, an old jacket and pair of trousers would serve. Over these, if obtainable, a discarded raincoat would complete the outfit, with the skirt cut off about three inches above the knees.[119]

On the subject of general equipment, the book described nylon rope as the best type of rope but 'expensive and therefore beyond the means of the average caver or small club'. Vertical caving was by ladder and

D7786/BOX/1/6, courtesy of Derbyshire Record Office.

White Hall course members at the resurgence entrance to Lathkill Head Cave in 1954 or 1955, during a dry period.

lifeline; the advice about ladders was that 'most clubs make their own rope ladders. It is cheaper and makes the members realise the work involved, so that they are more likely to handle them carefully.' Wire ladders with alloy rungs, called electron ladders, had become almost universal in French caving, but were only gradually coming into use in Britain.[120]

Canoeing

We saw in Chapter 3 that the most prominent type of canoeing in Derbyshire in the 1940s had probably been canoe racing, particularly at Trent Lock, Long Eaton. The River Trent is one of England's longest rivers. A Trent branch of the Canoe Camping Club had been formed in about 1946 or 1947. From this branch, in November 1951, evolved the Midland Canoe Club, which would come to be regarded as one of the Midland's premier canoe clubs, with members reaching high levels of competitive and noncompetitive canoeing and kayaking, on rivers and the sea. Sometime after the 1952 Olympics, a clubhouse behind the then Fisherman's Rest pub at Trent Lock became the club's headquarters.[121]

Canoeing was introduced at White Hall near the end of the Mosedale wardenship. 'We began to develop canoe-camping towards the end. The canoes were old-fashioned Blandford designs built by ourselves [canvas and wood]. We used the Whaley Bridge canal terminus mostly and used to camp overnight down on the Macclesfield branch. Then we used Toddbrook reservoir for training and had an ex-ships lifeboat as safety boat.'[122]

Blandford, P, *Canoes and Canoeing* (London: Lutterworth Press, 1962).

Boys fixing the bottom stringers on a Kittiwake canoe designed by Percy Blandford. (Location unknown.)

White Hall course members in canvas-covered wooden-framed kayaks on Todd-brook Reservoir, 1954 or 1955. Later White Hall photographs, taken in 1958, show the canoeists wearing life jackets.

Away Courses

Mosedale and his instructors also ran several longer expeditions to the Lake District and north Wales, staying at a youth centre in St Johns in the Vale and at the Midland Association of Mountaineers hut at Ogwen. These away courses were the forerunners of many.

Some ambitious plans did not reach fruition. In 1954 Ken Oldham was teaching at Longdendale School in Cheshire but he still had strong connections with White Hall. He encountered a difficulty reconciling his own enthusiasm for the outdoors with the different priorities of his school's governors, a frustration that many teachers have since come to know:

> The ultimate development of the outdoor activities was to be an ambitious climbing holiday in the Dolomites organised by Cyril Machin, [an] Assistant Warden [at] White Hall in 1954. The party comprised fifty seven Derbyshire children and thirteen from Longdendale [School, Cheshire]. Naturally Derbyshire fixed the dates, and the three week venture involved overstaying the local midsummer holiday period by three days. Leave of absence was officially requested and refused. 'The group must return on time

– the holidays were long enough'. Unless the groups travelled as a unit there would be no travel price concession and there was no option. The governors of the school decided that the children should be left in the Dolomites with the Derbyshire party and I should return alone to take up my duties on schedule at the school!

This was totally unacceptable but before the situation could be resolved, the Dolomites Expedition was cancelled because of a serious climbing accident to Cyril Machin. A four and a half week cycling and rambling tour covering eight hundred miles of Scotland from Arran to the Cairngorms was arranged as a substitute programme for a small group of boys …

The failure of the governing body to accept that all these exploits involved considerable work and were of educational value led to my search for a new post. At the year end I regretfully resigned my position in order to return to Derbyshire where outdoor education was developing steadily as part and parcel of the normal education.

Mountain and Cave Rescue – Mosedale Period

For the rock climbers and mountaineers of the 19th century, at the heart of mountain rescue lay self-reliance. When accidents happened, the nearest able-bodied volunteers – often a mixture of climbers and farmers – worked together to carry injured climbers off the hills, improvising stretchers or splints when necessary.

Organised mountain rescue in Britain, in a prepared and systematic way, can be traced back to a climbing accident on Scafell Pinnacle in September 1903, when a rope of four men fell the length of the crag, tied together. When found, perhaps an hour later, three were dead and one was badly injured but still conscious. Evacuating the injured man was a prolonged process, making use of a hurdle brought up the hill by dalesmen. He died on the way. The Scafell disaster was the worst that British rock climbing had known. An account written shortly after the accident remarked that 'they were all such uncommonly first rate fellows'.[123]

A shocked climbing community began to consider the rising accident toll and the paucity of rescue resources available. Within a year, first aid and mountain rescue equipment began to appear in key areas, such as the Gorffwysfa Hotel at Pen-y-Pass in Snowdonia.[124]

An accident in 1928 at Laddow Rocks and the great difficulty encountered by the rescuers led to Wilson Hey, a consultant surgeon, campaigning for the formation of an organised mountain rescue service with the provision of morphia.[125]

By August 1948 the Mountain Rescue Committee (MRC) had been formed. Twenty-seven MRC rescue posts had been created throughout Britain's mountains and moorlands, each equipped with mountain stretchers, medical supplies and the means of keeping a casualty warm.[126] Only one of these posts was in Derbyshire. This was in Hope, near Castleton. It comprised a Neil Robertson stretcher and two rucksacks of equipment.[127] In December 1949 the Home Office agreed to the supply of morphia to mountain rescue posts.

Between 1951 and about 1970, all four White Hall wardens or principals were involved occasionally in the planning and development of mountain rescue in the region. As well as this administrative involvement, they and other staff members took part practically in searches or evacuations.

When White Hall opened in 1950 it was not yet a mountain rescue post. It became one during Peter Mosedale's wardenship. A letter from Mosedale informed A B Afford: '[In your research] you may also come across Wilson Hey's name, the Manchester surgeon, who lived at Fernilee and helped us to set up a rescue post and get a good stretcher.'[128] Fernilee is less than two miles from White Hall. Apparently Hey, a climber and mountaineer himself and a key figure in the history of mountain rescue, visited the centre regularly. He died in 1956 at the age of seventy-three.

*

Cave rescues in Derbyshire had occurred occasionally for centuries, in lead mines that often combined excavated passages and natural limestone caves. By the end of the 19th century, lead-mining had almost ended. A few early cavers began to take an interest in Derbyshire's caves and abandoned mines. Most of the cave rescues that took place in Derbyshire in the first half of the 20th century were short or relatively easy. Cavers summoned to help usually handled any difficulties successfully.

Interest in caving increased after the second world war, and caving accidents began to happen more often. In May 1952, the Derbyshire Cave Rescue Organisation (DCRO) was formed. I do not know whether any White Hall staff involved themselves in cave rescues at this time. However, as we have already seen, experienced cavers like John Plowes, the DCRO's first secretary, were White Hall's main source of caving expertise.

A glimpse of the state of cave rescue in 1952 further illustrates the era that Peter Mosedale was working in: 'The original DCRO was woefully inadequate and its response time was incredibly slow because few members lived nearer to the caves than Sheffield, Manchester, Nottingham or Derby, few of them were on the phone and hardly any of them had transport.' In Derby, there was no police vehicle available to transport rescuers; policemen travelled mostly on foot or by bicycle. At one point, it seemed to the Derby-based cave-rescue personnel that the most reliable way for them to turn out on a rescue was by public transport.[129]

National Developments – Mosedale Period

All White Hall wardens and principals have been involved, to different extents, in regional or national issues during their terms in charge. In 1950–70 this happened despite the ubiquitous Jack Longland dominating the scene, seemingly chairing every conference and every committee that had anything to do with the mountaineering aspects of what would eventually become known, imprecisely, as outdoor education.

Peter Mosedale, fully occupied with letter-writing and inspecting dormitories and filling teapots and coiling ropes, together with regional mountain-rescue developments, had enough to do without also becoming involved in national matters. He was probably thankful that Longland was toiling in the upper echelons, at the centre of national developments. The more you discover about Longland's life, the harder it becomes to understand how he found the time to do his main job, overseeing the administration of several hundred primary and secondary schools.

Starting in January 1950, Longland was occasionally involved in advising Adam Arnold-Brown, the warden of Eskdale OBMS, on mountaineering. This advice included recommendations on equipment, notes on the suitability of various people for employment as instructors, comments on an accident involving an Eskdale student, and detailed thoughts about the possibility of boys leading rock climbs during a proposed Eskdale follow-up course.[130]

At Easter 1951, Longland was in north Wales, taking a break from committee meetings. On Sunday 25 March, Snowdon was sheathed in snow and ice. Longland's old climbing friend, Ivan Waller, was in the area, enjoying some skiing. Longland, now forty-five but still slim and agile, was probably looking forwards to a day on the mountain in rare alpine conditions, requiring cramponing or some step-cutting.

Instead, in a series of accidents, all on Snowdon, three climbers were killed and four injured. The three deaths were separate incidents and all featured slips on ice. Four rescue parties were needed. Longland was in the thick of it, sheltering with twenty-one people overnight at the Snowdon summit hotel, until conditions allowed a safe descent.[131]

On 8 April 1951, delegates at the annual conference of the national council of the Ramblers' Association unanimously passed a resolution calling for a national conference of outdoor organisations to discuss the problem of mountain accidents.[132]

On 11 April 1951, the *Manchester Guardian* reported another death on Snowdon, thought to have been caused by a collapsing cornice. It was the eighth fatal climbing or hillwalking accident in Snowdonia that year.[133] There had also been at least five deaths in the Lakes.[134]

Inexperience and inadequate equipment were factors in many of the accidents. Longland didn't need the Snowdon experience to know this. He and others had been concerned about it since 1945 or earlier.

In a long article in the *Observer* in April 1952, Longland wrote: 'What we have to persuade the young walker or climber is that he has much to learn, and that he will live a much more full and interesting life as well as a safer one if he does take the trouble to learn. These are the lessons which are being successfully taught at the courses of the Mountaineering Association, at the Outward Bound Mountain School, at the C.C.P.R. mountain centre in the Cairngorms, and at our own Derbyshire training centre on the moors above Buxton.'[135] (The mention of the Cairngorms reminds me to add that in 1952 Catharine Loader's book *Cairngorm Adventure at Glenmore Lodge* was published. It is now a noteworthy historical record.)

A year later the CCPR, on the advice of its Outdoor Activity Advisory Committee, organised a conference to discuss standards in mountain training. Because of the growing numbers taking up hillwalking, rock climbing and mountaineering, the question of training was an urgent issue. Forty-six people from over twenty governing bodies attended this conference. Longland chaired it. Eric Shipton of Eskdale OBMS and Peter Mosedale spoke to the assembly, cautiously exploring a subject not previously discussed by such a mixed gathering.[136] Mosedale spoke about 'the type of qualifications instructors must possess and gave some arguments both for and against the compilation of a central register of people who had been found satisfactory'[137].

This conference, held at the Alpine Club on 2 May 1953, was an important first step along a long and potholed road.

'An open discussion showed certain divergencies of view about train-ing methods and the length of training required – particularly of the value of week-end courses – but complete unanimity about the value of training as one of the safeguards against mountain accidents.'[138] Eleven years would pass before the first meeting of the Mountain Leadership Training Board.

Also in 1953, after the ascent of Everest, the demand for climbing courses rose nationally. The *Yorkshire Evening Post* reported:

> Inspired, no doubt, by the recent conquest of Mount Everest, West Riding Youth Club members continue to demand rock-climbing courses.
>
> To meet this demand the Central Council of Physical Recrea-tion, in conjunction with the Yorkshire Mountaineering Club, has arranged yet another course for beginners at Highfield House, Ilkley, during the weekend July 11 and 12.[139]

In the early 1950s, Longland – despite his many roles – found the time to contribute articles to the magazine *Out of Doors and Countrygoer*, published six times a year. He also found the necessary versatility to contribute a chapter on climbing and mountaineering to *The Boys' Country Book* (1955), described by a reviewer as: 'A magnificent Christ-mas present. Just as suitable for girls as boys.'[140] His description of the pleasures of rock climbing has not dated much:

> There's the pleasure of stepping as delicately as a dancer up a steep slab on tiny holds you would hardly balance a shilling on; there's the different pleasure of fighting your way inch by inch up an overhanging crack, that tries all the time to shoulder you off into space; there's standing on a small ledge, about the size of the top of a box of biscuits, with two hundred foot of rock-wall dropping so sheer beyond your boot toes that the first thing you see is the rucksack you left at the foot of the climb, and a steep wall rising another hundred feet or so behind your back up which you have still got to go; there's pulling up the last little bit, and the sense of relaxed triumph as you sprawl on a grass ledge at the top, all tension forgotten in the moment when the mountain and the clouds chasing across the sky and every remembered foot of the climb are all yours.[141]

*

In April 1951 Hugh Dalton, the Minister of Local Government and Planning, confirmed the designation order for the Peak District National Park, thus completing the formal process of establishing Britain's first national park. Seven others followed during Mosedale's wardenship: the Lake District (1951), Snowdonia (1951), Dartmoor (1951), Pembrokeshire Coast (1952), North York Moors (1952), Yorkshire Dales (1954) and Exmoor (1954).

On 5 July 1951, Dalton officially approved the route for the Pennine Way, intended for walkers and for riders on horseback. It was the first long-distance route approved under the National Parks and Access to the Countryside Act 1949. A press report reproduced an official summary of the route:

> It runs through the Cheviots, along the Roman Wall, over Cross Fell, through the wildest and loneliest crossing of the Pennines by Birkdale and Maize Beck to High Cup Nick, along the Tees past two magnificent waterfalls at Cauldron Snout and High Force, along the western ridge of the Pennines, cutting between the industrial regions of Lancashire and Yorkshire, then through the Peak National Park and over the moors of Black Hill, Bleaklow and Kinder Scout.[142]

In April 1955 the CCPR opened Plas y Brenin, giving it the title The Snowdonia National Recreation Centre. At Plas y Brenin, the chief instructor John Disley imported orienteering from Scandinavia, laying on Britain's first event, which was held in the forest across the river from the centre. In the 1930s, orienteers in Sweden had developed the Silva baseplate compass with a liquid-damped capsule. After the arrival of orienteering in Britain, these compasses become popular for navigation on the hills as well as for the sport of orienteering, but it is not known whether White Hall possessed Silva baseplate compasses in Mosedale's time. It may have done. There is a 1951 photograph of boys at Glenmore Lodge using what looks very like a Silva compass.[143]

White Hall was now nearly five years old. Mosedale and his instructors had avoided any serious accidents happening to course members and had built up an optimistic, but not yet universal, enthusiasm. They had learnt how to make the most of the feeble sun of a short December day. They had accumulated a shared local knowledge, ranging from an awareness of the presence of precarious scree on the decaying top of Castle Naze to delicate but improving acquaintances with landowners.

The UK had emerged from World War II as a military victor but with a debilitated manufacturing base. Postwar recovery had been slow (and would remain so). Mosedale had achieved much on minimal funds, and against the background of the Korean War (1950–3) and the 1953–4 recession that accompanied the winding-down of that war.

The world was changing fast. On 2 June 1953 the Coronation of Queen Elizabeth II had taken place at Westminster Abbey. I had watched it, in a large group of kids gathered around one of the first televisions to arrive in our neighbourhood. On 11 January 1954, the first televised weather forecast had taken place, advancing a development begun in the 1850s by Admiral Robert FitzRoy. By the mid-1950s, in California a number of surfers had invented skateboards and in Germany a company had invented kernmantel rope, which used fine nylon strands running the length of the rope, the kern, protected from abrasion by a braided sheaf, the mantel. As well as more entertaining weather forecasts and skateboarding and improved climbing ropes, major social change was coming.

The front entrance, August 2015. Several accounts from the 1950s record that pupils were not allowed to use this entrance until they had demonstrated the ability to climb up the outside of the front porch.

White Hall Centre

	PROGRAMME FOR COURSE 197 (ABOUT 1955)		
DAY	9am–10am	MORNING	AFTERNOON	EVENING
Monday Duty: JL H			Arrive and settle in. First bell – introduction to Course 197. 4pm–5pm: Tea. Help yourself and wash up.	5pm–6pm: Walk. 6.15pm: Hot meal in dining room. Duties after. 7.15pm: Either out or north Derbyshire colour slides. 9pm: Supper. 10pm: Lights out.
Tuesday Duty: PRM	9am (whistle): Room inspection. Stand by your beds. 9.10am: Briefing: clothing for the hills; routes for today.	10am–4.30pm: Somercotes: map routes, cooking soup on wood fires, moorland walking, collection of leaves, grasses, mosses, fungi. Castle Grisley: map reading. 4pm–5pm: Tea.		5.30pm: Writing up the day's log. 6.15pm: Hot meal. 7.15pm–9pm: If fine, night game. Or Tales from the Jungle.
Wednesday Duty: JLH	9am: Room inspection. 9.10am: Briefing: hill walking.	10am–4.30pm: Somercotes: bus to Earl Sterndale. Upper Dove Valley – Axe Edge – White Hall. Castle Grisley: as above. 4pm–5pm: Tea.		5.30pm: Writing up the day's log. 6.15pm: Hot meal. 7.15pm: Skiing film. Country dancing.

Continued on the next page.

PROGRAMME FOR COURSE 197 (ABOUT 1955)

DAY	9am–10am	MORNING	AFTERNOON	EVENING
Thursday Duty: PRM	9am: Room inspection. 9.10am: Briefing for today.	9.30am–5.15pm: Kinder Scout hillwalking. Including a small party to Edale Youth Hostel, returning on the next day (Mr Fisher). 5pm–5.30pm: Cup of tea.		6.15pm: Hot meal. 7.15pm: Writing up the day's log 7.45pm: Filmstrips: country code and map-reading.
Friday Duty: JLH	9am: Room inspection. 9.10am: Briefing for today.	A – Canoe instruction and repair. B – Light camping instruction and compass course instruction. C – Temperature and altitude: graphs. D – Map of types of tree in the Goyt Valley. 4pm–5.30pm: Tea.		5.30pm: Day's log. 6.15pm: Hot meal. 7.15pm: To be announced.
Saturday Duty: PRM	9am: Room inspection. 9.10am: Briefing: British mountains; where are they?	A – Canoe instruction and repair. B – Easy rockclimbing. C – Combs Edge: scrambling. D – Light canoeing instruction and compass course instruction.		5.30pm: Day's log. 6.15pm: Hot meal. 7.15pm: Film. Dancing.
Sunday	9am: Room inspection. 9.10am: Sunday service. 9.30am: Briefing.	Parties to be arranged later.		Meal to suit time of departure. End of course.

Source: Pettigrew, Robert G, 'A Short History of Some Outdoor Activities and Their Application in the Current Work of a Typical Centre – White Hall' (Supp. Cert. in PE thesis, Loughborough Training College, 1954–5), between pp. 71 and 72.

Notes

1   'Open Access Monographs', Oasis (2014) <http://www.openoasis.org/index.
    php?option=com_content&view=article&id=348&Itemid=381> [accessed 4 Aug
    2014].

2   'Vacancies', *Derby Evening Telegraph,* 15 Dec 1950, p. 10.

3   Letter, quoted in A B Afford, *The Story of White Hall Open Country Pursuits
    Centre; vol. 2* (Buxton, Derbyshire, UK: A B Afford, 1978), p. 3.

4   Quoted in ibid., p. 4.

5   Letter, quoted in ibid., p. 5.

6   Eric Byne and Geoffrey Sutton, *High Peak: The Story of Walking and Climbing in
    the Peak District* (London: Secker and Warburg, 1966), p.188.

7   Jim Perrin, *The Villain: The Life of Don Whillans* (London: Arrow, 2006), p. 301.

8   Bob Pettigrew, Email to P McDonald, subject 'A Book in Search of Authors', 18
    Feb 2015 [Email].

9   Eric Byne and Geoffrey Sutton, *High Peak: The Story of Walking and Climbing in
    the Peak District* (London: Secker and Warburg, 1966), p. 188.

10 'College for Climbers: Students' First Week-end at White Hall', *Buxton Herald,*
    5 Jan 1951, p. 8.

11 'Learning Hillcraft in Comfort', *Manchester Guardian,* 2 January 1951, p. 3.

12 Several schools may have sent groups to this first schools' course. According to
    a newspaper report in 2001, a group from Long Eaton School attended White
    Hall's first schools' course in 1951. 'Reunion to Mark Activity Centre's Half-
    century', *Derby Evening Telegraph,* 26 Feb 2001.

13 'Education in New Mills as I Remember It', New Mills Local History Society:
    Newsletter 31 (Autumn 2003) <http://newmillshistory.org.uk/pdf/nl31>
    [accessed 2 Aug 2014], pp. 12–13.

14 A B Afford, *The Story of White Hall Open Country Pursuits Centre; vol. 2* (Buxton,
    Derbyshire, UK: A B Afford, 1978), pp. 4–5.

15 Robert S S Baden-Powell, *Scouting for Boys: A Handbook for Instruction in Good
    Citizenship,* Reprint of six-part (1908) edn (Oxford: Oxford University Press,
    2005), p. 155.

16 'Learning Hillcraft in Comfort', *Manchester Guardian,* 2 January 1951, p. 3.

17 Alistair Macdonald, 'Kenneth Oldham: Introducing Children to the Great
    Outdoors', Guardian (14 Apr 2004) <http://www.theguardian.com/news/2004/
    apr/14/guardianobituaries.schools> [accessed 18 Aug 2014].

18 Wally Blake, Email to P McDonald, subject 'White Hall Centre', 24 Mar 2016
    [Email].

19 Doug Scott, *Up and About: The Hard Road to Everest* (Sheffield: Vertebrate
    Publishing, 2015), p. 62.

20 'Whitehall: "Can't Be Measured in £ s. d."', *Buxton Advertiser,* 24 Mar 1951.

21 A B Afford, *The Story of White Hall Open Country Pursuits Centre; vol. 1* (Buxton,
    Derbyshire, UK: A B Afford, 1978), p. 34.

22 Letter, quoted in A B Afford, *The Story of White Hall Open Country Pursuits
    Centre; vol. 2* (Buxton, Derbyshire, UK: A B Afford, 1978), p. 5.

23 Ibid., p. 9.

24   Derbyshire Record Office, Monograph: Hill and Water Sports in British
      Education: Peter Mosedale, 1975, D7786/BOX/1/Bundle 5.

25   A B Afford, *The Story of White Hall Open Country Pursuits Centre; vol. 2* (Buxton,
      Derbyshire, UK: A B Afford, 1978), p. 13.

26   François Bédarida, *A Social History of England 1851–1990*, 2nd edn (London:
      Routledge, 1991), p. 256.

27   Craig Lindsay, 'A Century of Labour Market Change: 1900 to 2000', *Labour
      Market Trends,* (Mar 2003), pp. 133–144 (p. 141).

28   *The First Fifty Years of the British Mountaineering Council,* ed. by Geoff Milburn,
      Derek Walker and Ken Wilson (Manchester: British Mountaineering Council,
      1997), p. 17.

29   Bob Pettigrew, Email to P McDonald, subject 'Book Project', 19 Feb 2015
      [Email].

30   Cambridge University Library, Longland to Arnold-Brown, 23 Jan 1950, in
      Miscellaneous confidential administrative correspondence and papers, MS
      Add.8270/12/4.

31   George Bridge, *Rock Climbing in the British Isles 1894–1970: A Bibliography of
      Guidebooks* (Reading: West Col Productions, 1971), pp. 19–20.

32   'Rationing in Britain During the Second World War', Imperial War Museum
      (no date) <http://archive.iwm.org.uk/server/show/ConWebDoc.2498> [accessed
      1 Aug 2014].

33   Derbyshire Record Office, Monograph: Hill and Water Sports in British
      Education: Peter Mosedale, 1975, D7786/BOX/1/Bundle 5.

34   A B Afford, *The Story of White Hall Open Country Pursuits Centre; vol. 1* (Buxton,
      Derbyshire, UK: A B Afford, 1978), p. 39.

35   Eric Byne and Geoffrey Sutton, *High Peak: The Story of Walking and Climbing in
      the Peak District* (London: Secker and Warburg, 1966), p. 188.

36   'In the Beginning 1949–1953', Oread Mountaineering Club (no date) <oread.
      co.uk/images/pdf/49to53pub.pdf> [accessed 15 July 2014], p. 9.

37   A W Bridge, 'Prelude', *Climbers' Club Journal: 1949,* 9, no. 1 (1949), pp. 84–89 (p.
      84).

38   Ibid. (pp. 84–85).

39   Ivan Waller, 'Cat among the Pigeons', *Fell and Rock Journal,* 23, no. 1 (1978), pp.
      1–5.

40   Eric Byne and Geoffrey Sutton, *High Peak: The Story of Walking and Climbing in
      the Peak District* (London: Secker and Warburg, 1966), p. 126.

41   John Hunt, *Life Is Meeting* (London: Hodder & Stoughton, 1978), pp. 62–63.

42   'The First National Park', *Manchester Guardian,* 29 Dec 1950, p. 3.

43   'Ramblers on Kinder Scout No Longer Trespassers', *Manchester Guardian,* 17
      Apr 1954, p. 10.

44   Norman William Dobson, 'Influences on the Development of Outdoor Pursuits
      in French Children's Education' (PhD thesis, University of Leicester, 1999), p.
      132.

45   'Country Pursuits at Glenmore', *Times Educational Supplement,* 27 Jan 1950, p.
      58.

46   Frederick P Knowlson, 'Climbing in Lakeland', *Yorkshire Post,* 13 Mar 1950, p. 1.

47   Joe Brown, *The Hard Years* (1967; repr. London: Penguin Books, 1975), p. 40.

48   T M Parker and K I Meldrum, *Outdoor Education* (London: J M Dent and Sons, 1973), p. 83.

49   Ernest A Baker, *Moors, Crags and Caves of the High Peak and Neighbourhood*, Facsimile of 1st (1903) edn (Tiverton, Devon: Halsgrove, 2002), p. 120.

50   Derbyshire Record Office, Monograph: Hill and Water Sports in British Education: Peter Mosedale, 1975, D7786/BOX/1/Bundle 5.

51   A B Afford, *The Story of White Hall Open Country Pursuits Centre; vol. 2* (Buxton, Derbyshire, UK: A B Afford, 1978), p. 6.

52   'Ramblers on Kinder Scout No Longer Trespassers', *Manchester Guardian*, 17 Apr 1954, p. 10.

53   Derbyshire Record Office, Monograph: Hill and Water Sports in British Education: Peter Mosedale, 1975, D7786/BOX/1/Bundle 5.

54   'Shadow across the National Parks', *The Times*, 8 Dec 1962, p. 9.

55   Grant Scrimgeour, 'The Anti-vandal War', *Daily Mirror*, 29 Dec 1950, p. 8.

56   David Hopkins and Roger Putnam, *Personal Growth through Adventure* (London: David Fulton Publishers, 1993), p. 42.

57   Ken C Ogilvie, *Roots and Wings: A History of Outdoor Education and Outdoor Learning in the UK* (Lyme Regis, UK: Russell House Publishing, 2013), pp.383–385.

58   A B Afford, *The Story of White Hall Open Country Pursuits Centre; vol. 2* (Buxton, Derbyshire, UK: A B Afford, 1978), p. 35.

59   A different source gives a purchase price of £5,000, see 'The Townsman in the Country', *Manchester Guardian*, 5 June 1950, p. 4. The costs of conversion and repair appeared in J L Longland, 'The Derbyshire Hostel', *The Spectator*, 16 June 1950, p. 823.

60   Press reports say that White Hall opened on Saturday 30 December 1950. 'The Alpine Touch to Open Centre', *Derby Evening Telegraph*, 30 Dec 1950, p. 7. Some of the course members arrived and were welcomed on the Friday evening.

61   Derbyshire Record Office, Monograph: Hill and Water Sports in British Education: Peter Mosedale, 1975, D7786/BOX/1/Bundle 5.

62   'Countryside Teaching Plan: Outward Bound School in Peak', *Derby Evening Telegraph*, 24 Oct 1950, p. 7.

63   'Character and Friendship through Hardship', *Times Educational Supplement*, 16 June 1950, p. 474.

64   Michael Fisher, 'Michael Fisher', The Outward Bound Trust (June 1952) <http://www.outwardboundgenerations.org.uk/story/michael-fisher> [accessed 2 Mar 2015].

65   'Learning Hillcraft in Comfort', *Manchester Guardian*, 2 January 1951, p. 3.

66   Derbyshire Record Office, Monograph: Hill and Water Sports in British Education: Peter Mosedale, 1975, D7786/BOX/1/Bundle 5.

67   'Rock-climbing, Ski-ing and Caving for the Young', *Manchester Guardian*, 17 Feb 1958, p. 5.

68   'Getting a Firm Foothold in Open-country Skills', *Guardian*, 6 Mar 1961, p. 19.

69   A B Afford, *The Story of White Hall Open Country Pursuits Centre; vol. 2* (Buxton, Derbyshire, UK: A B Afford, 1978), p. 9.

70   Quoted in Ken C Ogilvie, *Roots and Wings: A History of Outdoor Education and Outdoor Learning in the UK* (Lyme Regis, UK: Russell House Publishing, 2013), p. 487.

71   'Schooling on the Hills', *Courier and Advertiser [Dundee]*, 3 Mar 1950, p. 5.

72   A B Afford, *The Story of White Hall Open Country Pursuits Centre; vol. 2* (Buxton, Derbyshire, UK: A B Afford, 1978), p. 6.

73   Nunn, Paul, 'Kinder Scout Plateau [?]', *Mountain*, no. 34 (1974). Reproduced in Paul Nunn, *At the Sharp End* (London: Unwin Hyman, 1988), pp. 27–29.

74   Alan Hankinson, *Geoffrey Winthrop Young: Poet, Educator, Mountaineer* (London: Hodder and Stoughton, 1995), pp. 46–47.

75   Quoted in ibid., p. 46.

76   Quoted in ibid., pp. 97–98.

77   Doug Scott, *Up and About: The Hard Road to Everest* (Sheffield: Vertebrate Publishing, 2015), p. 42.

78   Kenneth Oldham, 'Outdoor Education: A Personal Involvement Spanning Thirty Years: Part 1' (unpublished paper, July 1976), p. 8.

79   Ibid., pp. 6–7.

80   Ibid., pp. 7–8.

81   Kenneth Oldham, 'Whitehough Camp School: Outline History of the School' (unpublished paper, c. 1988, Rev. Feb 2001).

82   Jim Perrin, *The Villain: The Life of Don Whillans* (London: Arrow, 2006), p. 214.

83   *The First Fifty Years of the British Mountaineering Council*, ed. by Geoff Milburn, Derek Walker and Ken Wilson (Manchester: British Mountaineering Council, 1997), p. ii.

84   Vincent Mulchrone, 'Are We Too Class Conscious to Salute Joe Brown?', *Daily Mail*, 9 Sept 1961, p. 6.

85   Don Whillans and Alick Ormerod, *Don Whillans: Portrait of a Mountaineer* (London: William Heinemann, 1971), p. 60. Jim Perrin, *The Villain: The Life of Don Whillans* (London: Arrow, 2006), p. 132.

86   Joe Brown, *The Hard Years* (1967; repr. London: Penguin Books, 1975), p. 66.

87   Ibid., p. 21.

88   Harold Drasdo, 'Geoffrey Byrne-Sutton: 1930 (1952–1967) – 2000', *Climbers' Club Journal: 1999–2000*, 23, no. 3 (new series) (2001), pp. 144–147 (p. 145).

89   Ian Wall, 'The R O Downes Hut', Climbers' Club (no date) <http://www. climbers-club.co.uk/cms/wp-content/uploads/2013/05/Downes.pdf> [accessed 19 Aug 2014]. Also 'Mr. R. O. Downes: A Young Climber of Distinction', *The Times*, 29 Aug 1957, p. 10.

90   G J Sutton, 'R. O. Downes', *Climbers' Club Journal: 1958*, 12, no. 2 (new series) (1958), pp. 266–269 (p. 266).

91   Harold Drasdo, 'Geoffrey Byrne-Sutton: 1930 (1952–1967) – 2000', *Climbers' Club Journal: 1999–2000*, 23, no. 3 (new series) (2001), pp. 144–147 (p. 145).

92   Don Whillans and Alick Ormerod, *Don Whillans: Portrait of a Mountaineer* (London: William Heinemann, 1971), p. 53.

93   Jim Perrin, *The Villain: The Life of Don Whillans* (London: Arrow, 2006), p. 135.

94   Don Whillans and Alick Ormerod, *Don Whillans: Portrait of a Mountaineer* (London: William Heinemann, 1971), p. 53.

95   Joe Brown, *The Hard Years* (1967; repr. London: Penguin Books, 1975), p. 109.

96   Doug Scott, *Up and About: The Hard Road to Everest* (Sheffield: Vertebrate Publishing, 2015).

97   Ibid., pp. 41–43, 62.

98   J L Longland, 'Eric Byne', *Alpine Journal,* 73 (1968), pp. 266–267.

99   'Golden Oldies – Consolidation 1953–1958 [pub3]', Oread Mountaineering Club (no date) <http://oread.co.uk/images/pdf/53to58pub3.pdf> [accessed 15 July 2014], p. 82.

100 J L Longland, 'Eric Byne', *Alpine Journal,* 73 (1968), pp. 266–267.

101 Don Whillans and Alick Ormerod, *Don Whillans: Portrait of a Mountaineer* (London: William Heinemann, 1971), p. 125.

102 Ibid., p. 126.

103 A B Afford, *The Story of White Hall Open Country Pursuits Centre; vol. 2* (Buxton, Derbyshire, UK: A B Afford, 1978), p. 15. The 1963 HMI report on White Hall gives the number of voluntary instructors as 'over 150'.

104 'In the Beginning 1949–1953', Oread Mountaineering Club (no date) <oread. co.uk/images/pdf/49to53pub.pdf> [accessed 15 July 2014], p. 9.

105 Thomas James, 'Kurt Hahn and the Aims of Education' (2000) <http://www. kurthahn.org/writings/james.pdf> [accessed 22 May 2015].

106 A search of the 1940–60 *Manchester Guardians* for 'Longland AND Jack' found 28 occurrences. A search for 'Hahn AND Kurt' found 27.

107 Eric Byne and Geoffrey Sutton, *High Peak: The Story of Walking and Climbing in the Peak District* (London: Secker and Warburg, 1966), p. 189.

108 Ibid., p. 180.

109 Showell Styles, Eric Byne and others, 'C B M: A Symposium', *Journal of the Midland Association of Mountaineers,* (1964), pp. 26–31 (p. 30).

110 Letter, quoted in A B Afford, *The Story of White Hall Open Country Pursuits Centre; vol. 2* (Buxton, Derbyshire, UK: A B Afford, 1978), p. 8.

111 'Golden Oldies – Consolidation 1953–1958 [pub2]', Oriad Mountaineering Club (no date) <http://oread.co.uk/images/pdf/53to58pub2.pdf> [accessed 15 July 2014], p. 44.

112 Showell Styles, Eric Byne and others, 'C B M: A Symposium', *Journal of the Midland Association of Mountaineers,* (1964), pp. 26–31.

113 Eric Byne and Geoffrey Sutton, *High Peak: The Story of Walking and Climbing in the Peak District* (London: Secker and Warburg, 1966), p. 189.

114 A B Afford, *The Story of White Hall Open Country Pursuits Centre; vol. 2* (Buxton, Derbyshire, UK: A B Afford, 1978), p. 7.

115 *Limestones and Caves of the Peak District,* ed. by Trevor D Ford (Norwich: Geo Abstracts, 1977), p. 351.

116 Ernest A Baker, *Moors, Crags and Caves of the High Peak and Neighbourhood,* Facsimile of 1st (1903) edn (Tiverton, Devon: Halsgrove, 2002), p. 197.

117 Ibid., pp. 205–206.

118 *British Caving: An Introduction to Speleology,* ed. by C H D Cullingford (London: Routeledge and Kegan Paul, 1953), p. 321.

119 Ibid., p. 321.

120 Ibid., pp. 325–327.

121 Midland Canoe Club, 'History of the Midland Canoe Club' (2015) <http://www.derbycanoeclub.co.uk/> [accessed 24 Mar 2015].

122 Derbyshire Record Office, Monograph: Hill and Water Sports in British Education: Peter Mosedale, 1975, D7786/BOX/1/Bundle 5.

123 YRC Committee, 'The Disaster on Scafell Crags', *Yorkshire Ramblers' Club Journal*, 2, no. 5 (1903), pp. 75–78.

124 Judy Whiteside, 'From the Mountains to Mountain Rescue – The Birth of Mountain Rescue', Mountain Rescue England and Wales (31 Jan 2010) <http://www.mountain.rescue.org.uk/information-centre/the-oracle/history-and-people> [accessed 27 Aug 2014], p. 2.

125 Ibid., p. 3.

126 'Growing Toll of Mountain Accidents', *Manchester Guardian*, 19 Aug 1948, p. 3.

127 *Climbing in Britain*, ed. by J E Q Barford (Harmondsworth: Pelican Books, 1946), pp. 147–154.

128 A B Afford, *The Story of White Hall Open Country Pursuits Centre; vol. 2* (Buxton, Derbyshire, UK: A B Afford, 1978), p. 8.

129 Bill Whitehouse, 'The History of Cave Rescue before the 1959 "Neil Moss Tragedy"' (30 Oct 2012) <www.mountain.rescue.org.uk/assets/.../CaveRescueBeforeNeilMoss.pdf> [accessed 10 Apr 2015].

130 Cambridge University Library, Longland to Arnold-Brown, & other letters, 1951–2, in Miscellaneous confidential administrative correspondence and papers, MS Add.8270/12/4, 5, 6, 7, 28, 73, 78.

131 'Three More Deaths on Snowdon', *Manchester Guardian*, 26 Mar 1951, p. 5.

132 'Ramblers to Discuss Mountain Accidents', *Yorkshire Post*, 9 Apr 1951, p. 1.

133 'Climber Found Dead', *Manchester Guardian*, 11 Apr 1951, p. 5.

134 *The First Fifty Years of the British Mountaineering Council*, ed. by Geoff Milburn, Derek Walker and Ken Wilson (Manchester: British Mountaineering Council, 1997), pp. 296–300.

135 J L Longland, 'Mountain Risks and Remedies', *Observer*, 13 Apr 1952, p. 4.

136 H Justin Evans, *Service to Sport: The Story of the CCPR – 1935–1972* (London: Pelham Books in association with the Sports Council, 1974), p. 82.

137 H Justin Evans, 'Mountain Training: A National Conference at the Alpine Club', *Physical Recreation*, 5, no. 3 (July–Sept 1953), pp. 24–25.

138 'Mountain Training Methods', *The Times*, 4 May 1953, p. 5.

139 'Climbing Course', *Yorkshire Evening Post*, 17 June 1953, p. 3.

140 *The Boys' Country Book*, ed. by John Moore (London: Collins, 1955).

141 *The Boys' Country Book*, ed. by John Moore, 2nd edn (London: Collins, 1961), p. 67.

142 'Mr. Dalton Approves Pennine Way Route', *Yorkshire Post and Leeds Mercury*, 7 July 1951, p. 1.

143 Catharine M Loader, *Cairngorm Adventure at Glenmore Lodge: Scottish Centre of Outdoor Training* (Edinburgh: W Brown, 1952), Plate 36.

9. Different from Outward Bound

Peter Mosedale left White Hall in autumn 1955 and headed for Scotland to run the National Coal Board Residential Training Centre in Clackmannanshire. Of his hectic pioneering time at White Hall, he later wrote: '[Alf Bridge] was one of the few people who understood the physical strain of running the place. Certainly none of us would ever have worked so hard afterwards.'[1] A typical course programme dating from about 1955 shows Mosedale and John Hird each doing three duty nights during a seven-day schools' course.

Mosedale and Fifteen-year-olds

Later that year, the Outward Bound Mountain School at Ullswater began to trial some junior courses, working with secondary-school boys who were two or three or four years younger than the sixteen- to eighteen-year-olds who normally attended Outward Bound courses. The educational correspondent for *The Times* wrote an article revealing that 'the experiment [had] already set the staff of the school some searching problems'.[2] Several letters to the editor followed promptly, discussing the abilities of fourteen- and fifteen-year-old boys.[3] An assumption underlying the letters was that little was known about running adventurous courses for the younger age group. Peter Mosedale, having just spent five years often working with exactly such teenagers, and with much success, added his thoughts to the debate. The second part of his letter to *The Times*, about one particular wide game, provides another glimpse of the White Hall of the 1950s.[4] To play Bandits, you needed attackers and defenders, messages hidden under rocks, and a big hill like Bleaklow. 'Intermediate messages were left under rocks on Kinder. Enormous distances were travelled at great speed and a bivouac was involved.'[5] In 1958, three years after Mosedale had left White Hall, the troops were still trying to recapture a strongly guarded bridge in the Goyt Valley.[6]

The essence of Mosedale's message was that a *motivated* fourteen- or fifteen-year-old may be capable of a great deal, as shown by the following two examples from the 1920s.

In August 1927, two fifteen-year-old boys from Aberdeen Grammar School cycled sixty-one miles (ninety-eight kilometres) to Inverey, a hamlet at the foot of the Cairngorms, five miles west of Braemar. They towed a homemade cart loaded with their camping gear and food for two weeks. From their camp at Inverey, over a week or so they climbed Ben Macdhui, Cairn Toul, Braeriach and Cairngorm. One of them swam across Loch Avon. Then they cycled home:

> They returned at length, via Braemar, wild, unkempt creatures with gym shoes on their stockingless feet. Needless to say, they created a stir, but they went blithely on their way, and spun home to Aberdeen ... with the wheels of the coffin-like cart humming in their relief from the weight of the vanished stores.[7]

In the summer of 1928, Kenneth Wormald, a fifteen-year-old from Birmingham, reached the summit of the Dent Blanche 'in eddying mist and intermittent snowstorms'. He was in a guided party.[8] The Dent Blanche is one of the highest peaks in the Alps.

In 1957 Jack Longland joined this conversation publicly by contributing a chapter, 'Outward Bound Junior Courses', to the edited book *Outward Bound*. He wrote frankly and perceptively about the fourteen- to fifteen-year-old adolescents on the experimental junior courses at Ullswater OBMS:

> They are plunged for four weeks into an atmosphere and tradition of near-adult ideas such as self-discipline, self-reliance, unselfish team-work, endurance up to and beyond the limit, and service to others whom they have never regarded as their responsibility, including strayed fell-walkers and foundering mariners. And if one dares generalize about the characteristics which they bring with them, it can only be said that they seem to be made up of most bewildering and frustrating contradictions. Boys and girls in their early middle teens are by turns (and sometimes simultaneously) selfish and altruistic, energetic and deeply idle, capable of feats of endurance but prone to alarmingly sudden collapse, passionately absorbed and comprehensively bored, gregarious but sometimes intent only on retreating to the loneliest corner, serious

beyond the verge of priggishness and yet magnificently impervious to moral exhortations! No wonder the Outward Bound staff dealing for the first time with these strange animals felt that they needed – and deserved – a long holiday at the end of it.[9]

As regards what teaching styles might suit the strange animals, Longland added a few dos and dont's:

> In the more enlightened secondary schools, there are very few prolonged sessions of 'chalk and talk' … Though [14- and 15-year-olds] are mostly polite enough to sit still and quiet, they have an immense capacity for abstracting their attention completely from what is being said. If you doubt that try questioning the average secondary schoolboy about the theme of the speech he has just heard from any eminent Bishop at Prize Day! Our first Warden at our own Derbyshire Mountain Training Centre, Peter Mosedale, who had to deal mainly with youngsters of exactly the same age, had a very good rule of never letting any talk or homily last for more than fifteen minutes. The one exception was for talks illustrated by films or lantern slides, which have the obvious advantage that the eye may still catch what the ear has long ceased to listen to.[10]

Towards the end of this down-to-earth essay, Longland gently hinted at the root cause of the difficulties encountered on the experimental courses:

> It is hard to resist the conclusion that one thing that our admirable Outward Bound staffs lacked when running these first junior courses was a little old-fashioned practice in handling, and leading and inspiring boys of this precise age and this particular school background. It would be absurd to suggest that for future courses our staffs should be recruited only from among trained and practising teachers. For one thing, even the best schools have their limitations and inhibitions. For another, a specialized kind of enthusiasm and missionary spirit is required in Outward Bound staff, whatever the age of the boys they are leading. But it does seem sensible to suggest that on each of these courses there should be added to the staff one or two of the best and most enlightened teachers our day schools can produce.[11]

Mosedale, Longland and Character Training

Longland ended this tactful course critique by deftly dodging the potentially controversial issue of character building. At this time, 1957, he was not yet on the council of the Outward Bound Trust, so he was in the delicate role of commenting as an invited outsider. (He would be appointed to the council in 1961 and would serve for thirteen years.) Always the diplomat, he avoided taxing his split loyalties, but in doing so he revealed them clearly:

> I have also said little directly about the opportunities which junior courses may provide for building character and for starting these boys on the road that they may themselves follow to become better men. This is because I find character-building difficult to write about, as it is difficult to pursue, since, like happiness, it is a by-product of right activity and not a target you can aim at directly. But I hope that what I have written does not obscure my own belief in the shining importance of character, and in the need to see that its foundations are laid down in these dangerous and hopeful years of early adolescence.[12]

Longland was writing here as a contributing author to an important book about Outward Bound. Hahn himself also contributed a chapter. For Longland, this was an obvious opportunity to publicly state his support for Hahn's character-building ideas. He chose not to. But neither did he criticise those ideas. He could have avoided the topic by steering clear of the term 'character building'. Instead, he pointed the reader directly at a Pandora's box of controversy, without actually opening it. My feeling is that Longland was caught between the passionate pre-war conviction of Hahn and Young (much older men) and the sceptical postwar reservations of Mosedale and Drasdo (the younger generation), the first of whom had steered White Hall through its remarkably successful first five years.

A brief eyewitness account, relating back to 1950 and 1951, appeared in 1999 and suggests that Longland shared Mosedale's eschewal of overt character-training claims. Norman Dobson, who had represented Great Britain in the 1,000 metres kayak singles at the 1948 Olympics, was a voluntary instructor at White Hall during those first two years. Nearly fifty years later in a doctoral thesis he wrote expressly about Longland's rejection of character training as a focus for White Hall: 'There were some people who equated White Hall courses with

Outward Bound experiences and talked of character development but Longland dissociated himself and White Hall from that idea.' On one occasion Dobson heard Longland say words to the effect: 'We have umpteen schools where people learn to work but now we have one where they can learn to play.'[13] Dobson stated that 'Longland never believed in ODP [adventurous outdoor pursuits] baldly being "good for character" though he believed people should have the chance to experience them.'[14]

Robert Baden-Powell and Kurt Hahn both sought the development of the whole person, physically, mentally and spiritually. The two men spent long periods of their lives promoting ways to achieve this end. 'Baden-Powell's scheme, complete with charts and diagrams, was designed to eliminate every major and minor ailment of Edwardian life, from drunkenness and unemployment to illegitimacy and flat feet.'[15] Both men believed that taking part in outdoor pursuits, in conjunction with camping or a residential centre, could very effectively bring about the all-round growth. In connection with this growth, Baden-Powell used the term 'character training' enthusiastically and confidently. The same term came to be associated with Kurt Hahn; on 13 November 1960 in the *Observer*, a substantial profile of Hahn, aged seventy-four, was titled 'Character Builder'.

An exemplary version of character training, aimed at producing young people who were physically fit, alert in mind, and independent and generous in spirit, would have needed to recognise and foster numerous social and personal qualities that were generally considered to be 'right' for western democratic society. In practice, however, for many instructors of outdoor pursuits in the 1950s and 60s, the term 'character training' (or 'character building') came to be associated not with the desirable development of the whole person, which was its meaning when used by Baden-Powell and Hahn, but with something more sinister. By 1955, when Mosedale left White Hall, the term carried with it, for many people, definite old-fashioned undertones, redolent of 'Onward, Christian Soldiers'. There was a feeling that for half a century character training had been socially conservative, focused narrowly on endorsing behaviour and attitudes that moulded young people to fit obediently into an authoritarian society, and especially into manufacturing industry, the merchant marine and the armed forces. In postwar Britain, development of the whole person remained a legitimate aim, but the process needed a new name. Hence the arrival, gradually, of social and personal development. Peter Mosedale had done his bit to influence that change. But it was unfinished business. The subject of character training will resurge, again, in Chapter 12.

Mosedale and Enjoyment

Mosedale's message in his 1955 letter to *The Times* was not only that fourteen- and fifteen-year-olds could achieve a surprising amount, but also that the achieving could and should be fun. Sometimes, for the instructor with local knowledge who is conducting a routine activity, running on automatic is all that is required to guarantee that his or her group enjoy themselves. Often, however, filling a day successfully and safely can demand much forethought that takes into account numerous factors. Peter Mosedale had set the agenda that prioritised informality and enjoyment, and it is no surprise that he said, after leaving White Hall, that he would never work so hard again.

Having fun was not, in 1955, a characteristic that was always apparent in groups of youths undertaking Outward Bound expeditions.

In about 1956 Outward Bound changed the whole system and curriculum of its junior courses to make them suit the younger age group.[16] Wide games made an appearance, as suggested by Peter Mosedale.

Outward Bound's traditional courses, for young people aged between 16½ and 19½, were also to change, eventually. To some extent, each school evolved under the influence of a succession of wardens. Some UK Outward Bound schools were slow to adapt their approaches and courses to respond to social change and to meet new demands.

In the mid-1970s, Eric Langmuir, reflecting on twenty years of growth of outdoor education, wrote:

> There must be now dozens of residential outdoor centres who owe at least something of their programme, building, administration, staffing and so on to the White Hall mould.
>
> I think another thing that is interesting is that the White Hall mould was very different from the Outward Bound, with all credit to it and to those who fashioned it.[17]

Peter Mosedale had been the first of these fashioners. Sutton and Byne, writing in *High Peak*, emphasised his achievements: 'Peter Mosedale did an amazing job at White Hall, building up the Centre with strictly limited resources and a spirit of inventiveness, charming everyone and getting them to give of their best.' A B Afford was equally applauding: '[Mosedale] was the pioneer who made the empty shell into a living organism, borrowing ideas from elsewhere such as Outward Bound, Boy Scouts and the Youth Hostels Association. He managed to create from the start a unique atmosphere, a strange mix of efficiency, friendliness, enjoyment and instruction that became a basic hallmark persisting to this day [mid-1970s] throughout all the changing influences'.[18]

The character and atmosphere of a place like White Hall is influenced both by the ambitions of the founder and by the practical labours of the management and other staff. Jack Longland is widely and rightly recognised as the main instigator behind the setting-up of White Hall. Peter Mosedale turned the ideas into reality, a process that demanded wisdom and sound judgment. The 1950s White Hall approach evolved for eight years before another LEA residential outdoor centre appeared (except for Keswick Youth Centre). During those years virtually alone, the centre's self-belief matured, its reputation flourished and its influence widened. Mosedale's achievements and impact deserve a wide recognition.

After his work in Scotland, he was head of the Department of English and General Studies at the Cambridge College of Art and Technology. In 1969 he became head of the School of Liberal Studies at the Canberra College of Advanced Education, Australia. On retirement in 1978, he became an emeritus professor of Canberra University. He was very proud of his pioneering work at White Hall Centre and his contribution to outdoor education. He died on 29 May 2014 aged ninety-six. A copy of his manuscript was repatriated to Derbyshire in August 2014. Perhaps now is the time also to re-introduce Bandits.

Letters to *The Times* Discussing the Abilities of 14- and 15-year-old Boys

The Times, 19 December 1955, p. 8.

OUTWARD BOUND EXPERIMENT

YOUNGER BOYS FIND THE GOING HARD

FROM OUR EDUCATIONAL CORRESPONDENT

Ordinarily, the members of an Outward Bound training course are young workers in industry and boys from the upper forms of public and grammar schools. This month and next, however, the new mountain school at Ullswater, opened last September, is running experimentally two courses for secondary modern schoolboys.

This means that the average age of the members is at least two years below that of a normal course. Of the 63 boys sent by 20 local education authorities (and one or two other bodies) to the December course, 29 were between 14 and 15, and only three had passed their sixteenth birthday.

The experiment has already set the staff of the school some searching problems. These younger boys – who are typically representative of the senior forms of good secondary modern schools – have shown themselves to be quite a different kettle-of-fish from the 17–18-year-old apprentices and sixth-formers.

NO NATURAL LEADERS

They are very cheerful and willing – almost too willing at the outset of a task. They do readily the household chore demanded of them, and for their age they excel their seniors in the athletics exercises, the walking, running, jumping, and throwing which form an integral part of every Outward Bound course.

But they do not seem to possess the initiative, judgment, sense of responsibility, and capacity for sustained endurance which come out so abundantly in the older boys. They need much more supervision, and they have as yet thrown up no natural leaders: This is in spite of the fact that the more extreme rigours of the school's programme have been excised or modified for them.

They do no rock-climbing, for example, and when they go on one of the canoeing or walking expeditions which last several days they are expected to bivouac only one night; the other nights they sleep in huts. Nevertheless, they tend to wilt by the end of the day, and they are very slow in getting away the next morning.

MATURITY FACTOR

Perhaps all this was to be expected; possibly too much is still being demanded of too tender an age. The question has to be faced (as it is being at Ullswater) whether the full benefit of Outward Bound training can be assimilated unless a boy has attained a certain degree of maturity – mental as well as physical.

'Everyone at some time in life faces problems which may demand self-discipline, endurance, courage, and exceptional willpower for their solution.' It is the aim of the Outward Bound Schools, by means of a brief intensive period of severe training, in which Nature offers the challenges and provides the ultimate tests, to give boys between the ages of 15 and 19 added strength and resolution to overcome such problems. It has yet to be proved whether the aim can be achieved with boys below the age of 15.

The Times, 22 December 1955, p. 7.

OUTWARD BOUND EXPERIMENT

TO THE EDITOR OF THE TIMES

Sir,–We are grateful to your Educational Correspondent for his understanding comments, in your issue of December 19, on the experimental courses for secondary modern schoolboys being held at the Outward Bound Mountain School, Ullswater. His article however, gives the impression that because the boys are manifestly less mature they may not be able to profit as much from Outward Bound training as do their seniors.

It is of course natural to compare the reactions of the younger boys with those two years older, but it may prove wiser to consider the experiment in isolation. During their last year at school many need additional stimulus to fit them for the imminent change which life holds for them and it was in response to this demand that junior courses were arranged. It was felt that the experience of working away from home with contemporaries who were strange to them, in strange conditions, doing unfamiliar things under unusual leaders, would present a challenge from which they could hardly fail to benefit.

Boys of 14 to 16 years should not be expected to possess the qualities of leadership, initiative, and endurance found in those of 16 to 18 years and so their reactions to even the modified training may well be different. It was, and still is, believed that seeds may be sown which later will fructify and that a quickening of the spirit would result through an experience which can only be obtained on a residential basis.

The question we have to answer is not 'Could we safely and wisely do in a modified form for juniors just what we do for seniors?' but 'Can a month's residential training be evolved, based on the Outward Bound principle of challenge, from which secondary modern schoolboys can really benefit?' We and those who have collaborated with us believe that it can.

As yet only one junior course has been held. No doubt the training can and will be improved, but at least when the boys left on December 17 they were obviously thrilled by their experience and all wanted to come back. It is much to be hoped that final judgment will be withheld until two more courses have taken place and the experience of each applied to its successor. Yours faithfully,

G. SPENCER SUMMERS, Chairman, Management Committee, Outward Bound Trust.
123, Victoria Street, S.W.1.

The Times, 24 December 1955, p. 7.
OUTWARD BOUND EXPERIMENT
TO THE EDITOR OF THE TIMES

Sir,–The article by your Educational Correspondent in your issue of December 19 on the Outward Bound courses at Ullswater for young men instances the difficulty of finding leaders among boys of 14 to 15 years of age. There can be no doubt that there are potential leaders among such boys as there is no lack of them when boys of 16 and above attend Outward Bound schools. Does this not indicate that courses for the younger boys are too advanced and that they have not reached the age when they can cope with difficult conditions on their own? If this is so should not the conditions of courses for younger boys be less intensive and exacting, and more time be given to training under instructors in the development of personal character?
Yours, &c.,
W. H. C. RAMSDEN,
R. J. SPRINGHALL
Little Manor, Fritwell, Oxfordshire.

The Times, 29 December 1955, p. 7.
OUTWARD BOUND EXPERIMENT
TO THE EDITOR OF THE TIMES

Sir,–The problems posed by outdoor adventure courses for lads of 14 or 15 may be new to Outward Bound, but several organizations have already accumulated much relevant experience which might be used to good effect. For example, for the past five years I have run, for the Derbyshire Education Committee, very many short residential courses for boys from all types of secondary school.

Three principles seem to be worthy of mention. First, younger boys react far better to natural challenges, under good leadership, than to any self-conscious appeal to achieve personal toughness or betterment. Second, they benefit more from attempting sports like rock climbing and skiing, which involve skill and daring, than they do from mountain 'slogging,' and they should never be expected to carry heavy packs efficiently. Third, the best results in personal achievement are often obtained from rather fanciful wide games, with small groups of boys working to instructions under very remote control.

Provided imagination is fired, lads of 14 can produce astonishing performances, without being aware of the fact. I shall never forget one game during which three boys of 14 from a Chesterfield secondary technical school went from Buxton to the north edge of Kinder Scout the first afternoon, slept out by themselves, cooked breakfast at 5 a.m., and set off north again in search of the 'bandits' at 6 a.m., found their trail and chased them at a gallop all over Bleaklow, caught one of them about midday, and then decided to walk all the way back to Buxton from Bleaklow top. Those of your readers who are fell-walkers may like to try this round for themselves.
Yours faithfully,
PETER MOSEDALE, Principal, National Coal Board Residential Training Centre, Sauchie, Alloa, Clackmannanshire.

Notes

1   Letter, quoted in A B Afford, *The Story of White Hall Open Country Pursuits Centre; vol. 2* (Buxton, Derbyshire, UK: A B Afford, 1978), p. 8.

2   'Outward Bound Experiment', *The Times,* 19 Dec 1955, p. 8.

3   G Spencer Summers, 'Outward Bound Experiment: To the Editor of the Times', *The Times,* 22 Dec 1955, p. 7. And W H C Ramsden and R J Springhall, 'Outward Bound Experiment: To the Editor of the Times', *The Times,* 24 Dec 1955, p. 7.

4   Peter Mosedale, 'Outward Bound Experiment: To the Editor of the Times', *The Times,* 29 Dec 1955, p. 7.

5   Letter, quoted in A B Afford, *The Story of White Hall Open Country Pursuits Centre; vol. 2* (Buxton, Derbyshire, UK: A B Afford, 1978), p. 6.

6   Peter Haddington, 'Gateway to Adventure at the White Hall Centre for Open Country Pursuits, near Buxton', *Derbyshire Countryside,* 23, no. 5 (Sept 1958), pp. 30–33 (p. 31).

7   'Two Boys in the Cairngorm Mountains', *Aberdeen Press and Journal,* 24 Sept 1927, p. 5.

8   'Boy's 14,000 Feet Alpine Climb', *Nottingham Evening Post,* 6 Sept 1928, p. 5.

9   Jack L Longland, 'Outward Bound Junior Courses', in *Outward Bound,* ed. by David James (London: Routledge and Kegan Paul, 1957), pp. 174–187 (p. 177).

10   Ibid. (pp. 179–180).

11   Ibid. (p. 185).

12   Ibid. (p. 187).

13   Norman William Dobson, 'Influences on the Development of Outdoor Pursuits in French Children's Education' (PhD thesis, University of Leicester, 1999), p. 236.

14   Ibid., p. 232.

15   Michael Rosenthal, *The Character Factory: Baden-Powell and the Origins of the Boy Scout Movement* (New York: Pantheon Books, 1984), dust jacket.

16   G Spencer Summers, 'The History of the Trust', in *Outward Bound,* ed. by David James (London: Routledge and Kegan Paul, 1957), pp. 18–58 (pp. 42–43).

17   Quoted in A B Afford, *The Story of White Hall Open Country Pursuits Centre; vol. 2* (Buxton, Derbyshire, UK: A B Afford, 1978), p. 20.

18   A B Afford, *The Story of White Hall Open Country Pursuits Centre; vol. 1* (Buxton, Derbyshire, UK: A B Afford, 1978), p. 39.

10. Geoff Sutton and Public Relations, 1955–9

By 1955, although Longland and Mosedale had borrowed some ideas from earlier times, they had done so selectively. Robert Baden-Powell (1857), Geoffrey Young (1876) and Kurt Hahn (1886) were from older generations. Longland (1905) and Mosedale (1917) were younger and had ideas of their own. The two men had set White Hall in a direction in keeping with those ideas.

White Hall Centre had veered away from Baden-Powell and social conservatism; away from Young and training for 'Stamina in War'; away from Hahn – that is to say, away from any operational approach overtly influenced by the belief that 'storm is the weather that hardens the tree', even if the instructors partly agreed with that sentiment; away from the War Office and character training for military service; away from Hogan – or, at least, away from the title of his book *Impelled into Experiences*. 'Impel' means 'to urge or force (a person) to an action'. 'Impel' is not as strong a word as 'compel', but it was too strong a word to describe the White Hall approach to activities. A more suitable word would be 'encourage'. (Incidentally, the contents of Hogan's book are more restrained than the strident rhetoric of its title.)

Where was White Hall heading? It was involved in what Mosedale later summarised as 'hill and water sports in British education'. It was already on course to contribute to what Longland later described as 'an astonishing drift of the whole range of subjects which we call physical education towards outdoor pursuits, towards mountains and moors and rivers, lakes and the sea.'[1] The new warden, Geoff Sutton, could probably have altered that direction, had he wanted to. In the event, he approved it and reinforced it.

Climbing and canoeing and hillwalking and caving, however, were never the whole story. The phrase 'character training', on the occasions when it had reached the White Hall staffroom, had met reactions ranging from polite uninterest to summary rejection; but no objections would ever be raised to its replacement, connoting a far more general aim, social and personal development. The importance given to social and personal development would become evident at White Hall in the form of course reports, a practice whose starting date has proved difficult to discover but which would be deeply engrained throughout the 1970s and 80s. As regards a challenging activity like abseiling or rock climbing, the White Hall approach would always be that of patient and helpful, but not suffocating, encouragement.

*

Geoffrey Sutton[2], born in Bristol, was nine years old when the German army invaded Poland, starting the second world war. He spent the war years in Canada with an aunt and then 'he returned to Britain where his further education at Harrow ended abruptly in expulsion (out of bounds, riding a motor-bike, and with a girl on the back)'.[3] Undaunted and while still a schoolboy, in about March in 1947 he drove his bike up to Wales. One lovely spring afternoon, riding up the Nant Ffrancon valley, he picked up a hitchhiker, a young woman carrying a climbing rope. This person was Gwen Goddard, who had started climbing in early 1946 and is better known by her later name, Gwen Moffat. In the days that followed, she took Sutton up his first climbs, on the Milestone Buttress. 'He was a slim, dark youth,' she recalled, 'in appearance in his early twenties, but actually about seventeen or eighteen. He was full of charm and enthusiasm.'[4] (It was Sutton who later first suggested to the elegant climber Gwen Moffat that she become a qualified climbing and mountaineering guide.[5])

After some overseas travel, the climbing bug began to bite and he seized every opportunity to climb in north Wales and in the Avon Gorge. He did his national service as a subaltern in the Somaliland Scouts. The year 1951[6] saw him at Cambridge studying for the English tripos and beginning to engage in serious climbing, particularly in the Alps. In the early and mid-1950s, 'Geoff took part in ascents of a fair number of those routes in the Western Alps most highly prized by British climbers'.[7]

Although not at the cutting edge of contemporary rock climbing, he could lead quite hard routes for the time, whether delicate or strenuous, with perfect control.[8] Another Cambridge climber of the same period, John Turner, was strongly influenced by Sutton's 'deep love of rock and the mountains' and by his 'appreciation of style and quality, rather than difficulty'. Jim Perrin considered Sutton to be 'a pivotal figure in the

British climbing scene of the 1950s, and a hugely influential one in post-war writing about the sport.'[9]

Sutton graduated in June 1954. He taught in Bristol for a while and then worked as an instructor at Brathay Hall, before arriving at White Hall in November 1955. Records list him – and Gwen Moffat, Johnnie Lees and Bob Downes – as all qualifying as BMC guides in March 1956.[10] Sutton, Moffat and Downes were also members of the Alpine Climbing Group, an elite association formed to encourage mountaineering of the highest standard.

Sutton is now well-known among climbers as a writer and translator. At the start of his time at White Hall, most of his writing had yet to come. Two pieces of his writing would appear during his White Hall wardenship: *Mont Blanc to Everest* (1956, a translation of a book by Gaston Rébuffat), and a section of *Snowdon Biography* (1957). The latter moved Jim Perrin to write: 'Sutton's account of rock-climbing in Wales from 1927 to 1957 remains the finest historical essay on rock-climbing ever written.'[11]

In coming to White Hall, says A B Afford, 'Geoff Sutton took on a job that could be compared to the military consolidation of a bridge-head prior to a fresh advance.'[12] The other half of the joint appointment, his wife Ann, was more than qualified for the role of housekeeper; she was both a doctor and one of the most competent woman rock climbers of the 50s.[13] In late 1955 the two of them left their mark on Dartmoor's Haytor, with two new routes, Honeymoon Corner and Ann. She joined in many climbing rescues and schools' course expeditions. A magazine article in 1958 reported that '[Mr Sutton's] wife Ann helps with the running of the centre (besides looking after their baby daughter, Fiona), though the permanent staff includes a cook, a caretaker, and a cleaner'.[14]

The pair carried on where the Mosedales had left off, building the centre's distinctive informality. 'Sutton's strong interest in people, his lively curiosity and his huge enjoyment of get-togethers in newly discovered pubs broke down barriers.'[15] Doug Scott recalls arriving at White Hall on a Friday evening: 'Invariably, the warden Geoff Sutton, tall, broad-shouldered and usually wearing thigh-length sealskin boots from a Greenland expedition, was there to greet us and invite us into the kitchen. His charming wife Anne would cook us delicious, garlic-flavoured omelettes for supper as we sat listening to stories told by permanent staff members Harold Drasdo and Andrew Maxfield.'[16] The arrival of Gordon Mansell onto the staff, in about 1957, added music: 'Gordon Mansell strummed his guitar and regaled us with songs, backed up by his beautiful wife Maureen … People like Geoff, Harold and Gordon were all larger than life characters, so full of infectious enthusiasm for the climbing life. They were all highly individual but had one thing in common – they made me, and everyone who came to White Hall, feel at home.'[17]

An idea of the casual but productive relations between the four permanent instructors and the many voluntary instructors can be gained from the following extract from a 1957 Oread newsletter. White Hall Rocks is a rotten and repulsive outcrop on Combs Edge, a short walk from the centre. The writer is George Sutton, no relation to Geoff:

White Hall Rocks
All this waffle about which Sutton did the White Hall rocks guide – let me reveal the horrid truth. That indefatigable writer of guide books, Uncle Eric [Byne], despatched the inevitable wad of notes to Geoff Sutton, who asked me what I thought about them. When I had exhausted my full range of blasphemous comment, having but recently rescued the then President of the Oread … from a dilemma on these same cliffs, we decided on a fateful evening just to have a look at the crag again. Of course, the first climb Eric told us about in Mosedale's day was up a detached buttress (this, of course, is not unusual on White Hall Rocks, since nothing is attached very firmly to anything else). By sitting on the main crag, six of us put our feet against the detached buttress and pushed, thus erasing one climb in entirety from any future guide book. It was some hours before Eric deigned to speak to us again … On this fateful evening, I just missed Geoff Sutton's head by knocking a rock out of a V.S. which I was imprudent enough to climb (on a top rope). Several other near misses occurred. Eventually we gave up. If Geoff has since been on these cliffs, he is madder than I thought – they should be blown up!
George Sutton[18]

Initially the permanent instructors who worked with Sutton were Harold Drasdo, Geoff Roberts and Bob Downes. On the schools' courses, there were usually thirty pupils.

Drasdo was a member of a small coherent group known as the 'Bradford Lads', which included several of the leading Lake District climbers of the 1950s. According to one of the group, Dennis Gray, the Bradford Lads' working-class credentials didn't quite match the revered tradesman origins of the Rock and Ice, as Gray himself and Drasdo and one or two fellow members were grammar-school boys.[19] However, the Yorkshiremen were individualistic, radical in outlook, and opposed to everything that smacked of authority.[20] The Bradford Lads were England's watered-down version of Glasgow's Creagh Dhu Mountaineering Club, a gang notorious for the anti-establishment behaviour of some of its postwar members.[21] The Yorkshiremen rejected the British climbing establishment, but less violently than their formidably pugilistic Glaswegian counterparts. Suspicious of the gentlemanly characteristics of the established climbing clubs, the Bradford Lads deliberately chose a different approach, climbing hard but with no formal club structure at all.

The zenith of the Bradford Lads had been the years 1950-3.[22] In September 1952 Drasdo had led the first ascent of North Crag Eliminate on Castle Rock, which would become one of just eleven Lake District climbs selected for inclusion in Ken Wilson's book *Hard Rock*. Drasdo became a prolific essayist, considered by Trevor Jones to be 'one of the best of rock-climbing writers'[23]. In 1997 Mick Ward expanded a little on this, reporting Drasdo's book *The Ordinary Route* to be 'very good indeed' but describing its author as an enigmatic figure whose writing had previously been panned by the critics and been condemned to literary extinction.[24] Drasdo himself, in 1997, added another consideration to this divided opinion by saying: 'I'm the kind of writer who'd like to disown most earlier work.'[25]

By 1956, Bob Downes, 'at twenty four, an age when many of the greatest have hardly begun, and having known none but the worst conditions in the Alps, ... was already one of the very finest and most accomplished British Alpinists'.[26] He was equally at home on rock, ice or mixed terrain. In August 1956, Whillans and Downes made the first ascent of Centurion on Carn Dearg Buttress, Ben Nevis. It quickly became a great classic climb.

In October 1956, Geoff and Ann Sutton, Drasdo and Downes spent four days on the granite of the Poisoned Glen in north Donegal. Drasdo and Downes made the second ascent of Spillikin Ridge, then the hardest route in Ireland.[27]

In about January 1957, Geoff Roberts left White Hall, being replaced by Gordon Mansell.

In July 1957, just nine months after the Donegal trip, Downes died of pneumonia at Camp VI on Masherbrum. Lung infections at 24,000 feet are unforgiving. We are now more alert to this danger. He was just twenty-five years old. 'He was, beneath a shy, almost forbidding exterior, the perfect companion, undeterred by mishaps, and bringing to every situation a quiet humour which eased the burden.'[28] The Climbers' Club set up a memorial fund. The R O Downes Memorial Hut at Froggatt in Derbyshire was officially opened on 29 April 1961.[29]

Bob Downes on Diagonal, Dinas Mot, north Wales, mid-1950s.

Also in 1957, Geoff Sutton and Drasdo returned to the Poisoned Glen, making the first ascent of Hammer and Sickle.[30] In August 1958, Drasdo, already a qualified teacher, moved on from White Hall to undertake a special year of English in Derby, being replaced by Arthur ('AB') Afford.

Sutton and Drasdo crossed over again to the Poisoned Glen in 1959, this time with Eric Langmuir and Andrew Maxfield, and they found a number of fine new lines.[31] (Mansell and Maxfield appear frequently in Drasdo's 1997 reminiscences, *The Ordinary Route*.)

An interview with the Yorkshire climber Allan Austin, conducted in the late 1980s by Alan Hankinson, revealed the extent to which White Hall had been a hive of climbing activity, a source of information on local and national developments. Mountain Heritage Trust, the mountaineering archive in Cumbria, has a recording of the interview. In the 1950s there were no climbing magazines. (*Mountain Craft* was the in-house magazine of the Mountaineering Association. *Climber and Rambler*, the first commercial magazine for climbers, began in November 1962.) Information about new routes and new equipment went from person to person. In the interview, the subject of 1950s footwear came up. Austin explained how he found out about the new French rock shoes called PAs (after Pierre Allain) and known as 'magic boots':

> AA: We bought Vibram boots [for our climbing] … well, we used to climb at Almscliff at Christmas in nails.
> AH: Yeah, and later on did you get the kind of PA [inaudible] … ?
> AA: Went down to Buxton, er, White Hall. Geoff Sutton used to run courses and he would invite all sorts of folk down … and during the winter all sorts of people went down. It was really worth going (AH – mm) Erm, because there was no magazine. The information that was available at White Hall was unique. You couldn't find out anywhere else how hard this route was, how so-and-so … (AH – yeah) there was always someone there who knew. (AH – yeah) They're all there now, and there were [Bob Downes] and Geoff and, er, Harold Drasdo all with these new PAs that they'd got in, er, Paris (AH – yeah) so he gave us the address and we sent off for some.[32]

Seeking Respectability

When Geoff Sutton arrived at White Hall, there were still a few voices in Derbyshire saying that the old mansion perched on a windy spur was a white elephant. 'In those early days a good many people in the county were doubtful of White Hall's educational value, and whether public money was being well spent.'[33] Partly to counter this negativity, Sutton started lobbying for constructive publicity. He did so in a deliberate and organised way, intensifying a process that Longland and

Mosedale had started. In an area of education that subsequently had always to battle to gain and maintain a place in the curriculum, Sutton headed this way before most other LEA centres existed.

In 1956–7 Sutton was the key figure in organising some early BBC radio and television features on climbing. One of his intentions was to attract publicity, recognition and support for White Hall.[34] He will have been aware that a documentary about Aberdovey OBSS had been shot in the summer of 1955. Called *Blue Peter*, this film was showing countrywide in Rank cinemas.[35] Another of Sutton's intentions was to promote the sport of climbing and to improve the public's understanding of the curious games climbers play.

The latter intention was more complicated than it sounds, even with the help of radio, television and cinema. Asking nonclimbers to understand and accept the sport of climbing had the potential to be a self-defeating endeavour; the more the nonclimber learnt about the sport, the clearer became its undeniable risks. Looking back in 1993 at his life of climbing, Dennis Gray's third autobiographical book *Tight Rope: The Fun of Climbing* was a densely anecdotal compendium of memories. It lived up to its title in the best traditions of ripping yarns. Still today some nonclimbers would enjoy reading about the amusements and contests and rivalries and mischiefs and merrymakings that Gray romps through, until jerked back to reality by a mention, on page 137, of 'the misfortunes that have befallen many of my climbing friends over the years, with over 50 of them killed, and others badly injured.' Climbers become inured to the deaths (or they give up climbing); the parents and other relatives of each victim do not.

In the case of radio, Sutton may have benefitted from some of Longland's experience and contacts. Longland's participation in radio broadcasting, begun in the late 1930s, had continued sporadically during the war. The frequency of his involvement had increased greatly after 19 January 1947; on this day he had taken part in *Country Questions*, a series that subsequently ran for about 300 episodes, many featuring Longland as question-master. After his move to Derbyshire in 1949, he had continued to take part frequently in this programme. His involvement with radio had further intensified when he had joined the panel of *Any Questions?* on 16 January 1949, to contribute 'always a voice of reason and sanity'.[36]

On several occasions, Longland had taken the opportunity to link a radio show with White Hall, thus gaining publicity for the centre. In November 1951, for example, he had chaired an episode of *The*

Younger Generation Question Time that was recorded at White Hall. In June 1953 he was involved in an episode of *Summer Parade* that included recordings of a White Hall student making his first climb at Windgather Rocks.[37]

In about 1956, Sutton teamed up with Stanley Williamson, 'a writer and BBC documentary producer of remarkable range, covering subjects as diverse as the music of Vaughan Williams and modern Japan'. Williamson loved the hills of northern England. After taking up rock climbing in the early 1950s, he had recorded what he claimed was 'the first live running commentary from a rock climb'. To achieve this, he had followed the well-known climber Rusty Westmorland up a route on Shepherds Crag, armed with 'a copper-rimmed moving-coil microphone with a cable running back to an engineers' van on the roadside below', linked by telephone to Broadcasting House in Manchester.[38]

At least four BBC radio programmes on climbing, broadcast in 1957–9, list Williamson and Sutton in the credits, together with a sprinkling of names of well-known climbers. The title of the first of these programmes exactly reflected the message that Sutton wanted to send out: *In Praise of Climbing*. A second programme covered climbing techniques. A third described some climbing areas in Britain and Europe. A fourth, in a series called *People Today*, examined Sutton himself; the listing in the *Radio Times* described him as 'climber, potholer, explorer, ex-merchant seaman, translator, biographer, poet and Warden of Centre for Open Country Pursuits'.[39]

The Williamson–Sutton partnership also resulted in a pioneering climbing documentary for television. It was filmed in 1956–7 as an episode of a series called Eye to Eye. The half-hour programme, titled *Climbing*, was designed to show a range of difficulty from easy beginners' climbs on short outcrops to more serious and demanding routes on mountain crags. Williamson and Sutton tailored it both to inform and to entertain.

The filming of rock climbing for television posed technical and organisational challenges that may not have been unique but which were certainly unusual. Ways had to be found to deliver heavy equipment to remote cliffs and then to position the cameramen safely in exposed positions. This required coordinating a sizeable group of climbers and technicians to go into action exactly when required to do so, always subject to the weather and light allowing the climbing and filming to proceed successfully.

The finished programme compressed about seventy years of English and Welsh climbing history into thirty minutes. The main ingredients were simple: two historic climbs from different periods; three old identities from memory lane and two well-known young men, fresh from Kangchenjunga; two female role models, in the vanguard of women's climbing; and a group of beginners at Windgather Rocks. A few supporting characters hovered around in minor roles. This mixture was wonderfully effective. Even the hitchhiking looks genuine, with Harold Drasdo and Geoff Roberts acting roles much practised. The film is now a rich historical resource, a reminder of the helmet-free years, of shoulder belays, of tying on with a bowline and of nylon or hemp waistlines. The climbers wore cotton shirts, woollen jerseys, floppy cotton trousers or voluminous breeches. Some wore cotton anoraks. On their feet were boots or noticeably tattered PAs or gym pumps.

In the Lake District, the 71-year-old Rusty Westmorland and Monica Jackson climb Napes Needle, where, some say, British rock climbing began in 1886. Perhaps Westmorland's Tyrolean hat is a deliberate addition, to take us back to those times. In 1956 Jackson had led a women's expedition to the Himalayas. The *Manchester Guardian* had reported that 'Mrs Monica Jackson, leader of the first all-woman expedition to the Himalayas, is small and fragile-looking – a dainty little person, who at five foot one tops Mme Claude Kogan, "the world's highest woman", by an inch.'[40]

Also in the Lakes, George Abraham, one of the famous photographer brothers and now about eighty-five, has swapped his camera for a paintbrush and watercolours, and sits quietly in his studio, working on a landscape.

In north Wales, in the warmth of the Pen-y-Gwryd Hotel (which reportedly was still, in 2015, uncomplicated, eccentric and timeless), the octogenarian Geoffrey W Young discusses what he calls 'the three elements of mountaineering'. His moustache is still intact, his bow-tie a little the worse for wear, his voice clipped. He chooses his words carefully, speaking slowly and deliberately and precisely, as if he were reciting one of his poems. In 1939 he had become a pioneer performer on television.[41] He knows that there won't be many more of these TV moments. He has prepared well for the camera.

Young had been born in an age of letter-writing and diary-keeping, of poetry and prose, not film and television. Now nearing the end of an extraordinary life, he was still regularly recording his thoughts in writing. The footage of Young for the television programme was taken in May 1957 during the Alpine Club's centenary meet. Young's diary tells us more than the film:

> The Pen-Y-Gwryd and crowds. Arnold Lunn and Geoffrey Bartrum of the old school. The Hunts also, and the Olympic runners Brasher and Disley, nice boys. We drove about, and to the coast. I made up my mind at last about the immense change to the new climbing world. No use bridging any gap. It is a new and different mind, as well as approach. Joe Brown and the colossal new 'tigers' doing their rock tricks for television. I was kept a whole morning to record a three-minute introduction. And I had to repeat it, owing to a camera break.[42]

From the Pen-y-Gwryd Hotel, the film moves to Idwal. The inspirational Gwen Moffat, the first woman mountain guide in Britain, leads a climb on the Idwal Slabs, wearing Vibram-soled boots. She is seconded by her husband Johnnie Lees, a lanky RAF mountain rescue team leader. His boots have tricouni nails.

A young George Band, who with Joe Brown in 1955 had made the first ascent of Kangchenjunga, answers the question: how does rock climbing in Britain compare after climbing in the Himalayas? A geologist and petroleum engineer by profession, Cambridge educated, ex-president of Cambridge University Mountaineering Club, his credentials perfectly fit the Climbers' Club genteel template.

Joe Brown talks about why people climb. He weighs his words, in a Mancunian accent and without using the personal pronoun 'one'. He makes the point that 'climbs don't 'av t'be difficult t'be enjoyed'.

The film also includes footage of Geoff Sutton and Gordon Mansell teaching a group of novices some basic climbing techniques at Windgather Rocks. This is a place, the commentator says, where children can take their first steps in perfect safety.

The film ends with shots of Brown – strong in the arms and shoulders, supple at the hips and knees – leading Suicide Wall at Idwal, a route that had been a break-through in climbing difficulty when first climbed in 1945. He wears a borrowed white pullover for the camera.[43] The first running belay is miles up the pitch. He hangs beside it on a straight arm, relaxed. The vague spike will accommodate only a thin nylon loop; it looks like Number 1 three-strand line, about six millimetres thick. Missing the first attempt to clip the karabiner doesn't bother him. In 1956 the route was arguably still the hardest in north Wales.

Edited out of this part of the film are some finer details: the plan had been for George Band to second Brown; 'in the event, despite wearing rock-shoes, Band had to retreat, and Lees, in boots intended for nothing more technical than mountain-walking, eased his way up the tiny holds of the vertical face, in front of the cameras, with complete aplomb.'[44]

The commentator was – who else but – Jack Longland, the lucky owner of a cut-glass accent that was perfect for the BBC of the 1950s. And perfectly at ease quoting Byron.

BBC Eye to Eye – Ep 8 Climbing TX23/08/57.

Geoff Sutton and his group arrive at Windgather Rocks. 1956 or '57.

BBC Eye to Eye – Ep 8 Climbing TX23/08/57.

Windgather Rocks, 1956 or '57.

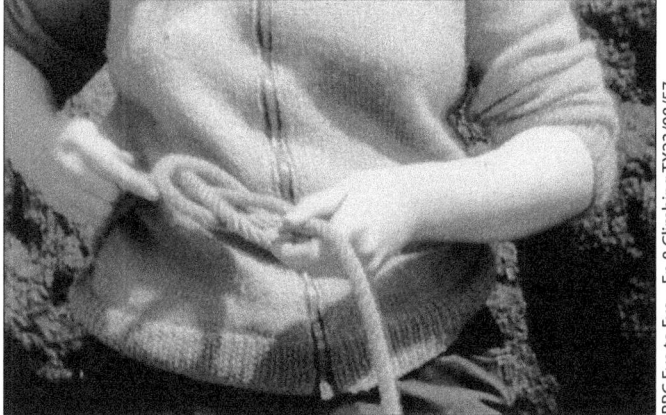

Learning the bowline knot. 1956 or '57.

On her first rock climb. 1956 or '57.

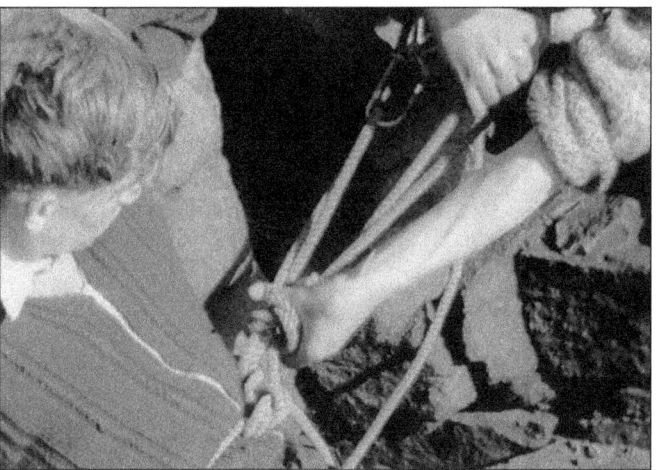

More knots. 1956 or '57.

Using a shoulder belay. 1956 or '57.

Sutton's drive for increased recognition and a helpful status included giving talks and slide shows to schools and clubs. White Hall also made a habit of welcoming visitors, especially county councillors and other influential people. One weekend in April 1958, Sutton and Long-land took Nancy Spain climbing on Windgather Rocks. Spain was a senior free-range *Daily Express* columnist, adept at addressing a mass readership. Her story about climbing spread across five columns of the newspaper. She was a complete beginner and, at her own admission, was more at home in a 'lovely, over-heated Paris dress salon' than on a windy Derbyshire hill:

> Jack lashed me into a rope with a genuine bowline and two half hitches, and then to my annoyance took away my gym shoes and made me put on his daughter Joe's … It seems that my gym shoes were O.K. for tennis but too thick in the sole for climbing. 'You need nice thin rubber soles,' said Jack, 'so that your toes can feel the little roughnesses of the rock.'
>
> … From time to time our photographer (a sadist if ever I met one) suggested that Miss Spain might lean away from the rock more so that he could photograph beautiful Derbyshire beyond and under her. Then I arrived at the top, smugly thinking my wounds were honourable ones.[45]

Longland and Sutton's indirect message to the public was: if Nancy Spain can climb, anyone can.

The public-relations campaign, directed at educationists as a whole and the general public, culminated in a visit by the Duke of Edinburgh on Friday 21 November 1958, reported on ATV Midlands television news and in local and national newspapers including the *Illustrated London News*.

A B Afford, who was there that day, describes the Duke's visit in detail, allocating it an importance that is not obvious in the newspaper reports:

> This event was undoubtedly a crucial turning point in a success story, everyone was impressed by the Duke's obvious real inter-est and knowledge of the situation and also that White Hall was deemed worthy for inclusion between visits to organisations of technological importance.
>
> There is not the space here to explain the real reasons behind the visit except to refer to the facts that in the progressive outdoor movement there were links between the Royal Family, Kurt Hahn, Jack Longland and many others with a particular outcome in the County Badge Scheme, the Duke of Edinburgh Award Scheme, Gordonstoun, Abbotsholme, Outward Bound, Brathay Hall and now White Hall.[46]

Afford's not explaining the 'real reasons behind the visit' may have resulted partly from his reluctance to discuss potentially sensitive issues. He leaves us to speculate on what those issues, if they existed, might have been. At the risk of guessing wrongly, I am left wondering whether Longland and Sutton thought that the London Establishment's obvi-ous status-boosting support for Gordonstoun and Outward Bound – and for the Duke's award scheme, which the Duke himself had launched in February 1956 – ought to be matched by equally enthu-siastic approval of the new kid on the block, a local-authority-funded centre. In this connection, I searched some 1940s and early-1950s copies of several London-based national newspapers for references to these outdoor centres.

In the 1940s *The Times* was sometimes dubbed 'the gazette of the ruling class'. Institutionally it projected an 'aura of running the uni-verse'.[47] Before and during the war, *The Times* had allocated a gener-ous amount of space to the projects that Kurt Hahn had launched. The editor Robin Barrington-Ward and Hahn were old friends from their Oxford days.[48] Hahn also had connections with the influential

Times Educational Supplement. (Donald McLachlan, the *TES* editor in 1939–40, later contributed a chapter to *Kurt Hahn*, the 1970 biography edited by H Röhrs and H Tunstall-Behrens.)

Were Hahn's Fleet Street connections still productive after the war? The *Times Educational Supplement* published at least five Outward Bound articles or photographs in 1949–51, including a substantial feature on the Eskdale OBMS. It also found space in this period for a main article on Gordonstoun (and for three sizeable articles about Glenmore Lodge). The *Picture Post* published features about Aberdovey OBSS in August 1942, December 1948 and June 1949. The *Illustrated London News* gave a whole page to Eskdale OBMS in July 1950. A rudimentary search for mentions of White Hall Centre in the same late-1940s and early-1950s newspapers found no occurrences.

Many family, academic and establishment connections linked Abbotsholme, Salem, Gordonstoun, the Outward Bound movement and the Duke of Edinburgh's Award scheme. One of the three Abbotsholme boys with Kurt Hahn in the Dolomites in summer 1903 had been Robert Arnold-Brown. His son, Adam Arnold-Brown, had been one of the first pupils at Gordonstoun, joining in September 1934.[49] In 1950 Adam Arnold-Brown had become the first warden of Eskdale OBMS. Jack Longland had helped him with some mountaineering aspects of his new job: 'Jack Longland … gave me an entrée to the climbing world and much down-to-earth advice. For some time I felt that the climbing fraternity were a little critical of my appointment for I was an indifferent rock climber and it was not at once appreciated that we did not set up to be a climbing school, but a character-training school based on mountaineering.'[50]

The royal recognition of White Hall Centre was of more than local importance. It could be interpreted, and probably was interpreted, as Establishment approval of the whole idea of LEA residential outdoor pursuits centres. It gave the green light to the expansion of such centres that was about to occur.

Over the following decade, although the number of residential outdoor centres nationally would expand rapidly – thanks to the success of the pioneer centres, the influence of several reports and education acts, and the end of postwar austerity – the desire and search for recognition and acceptance would gradually become a common concern. Eventually this concern would lead to adjustments in the names of outdoor centres and in the terminology used to describe what they did and who did it.

'Warden' would be the first word to go, vanishing suddenly to be replaced by 'principal'. (At White Hall, this would first happen in an advertisement for Geoff Sutton's successor in May 1959.[51]) The job title 'chief instructor' would, somewhat less urgently, become 'deputy principal'. (John Cheesmond joined the instructional staff at White Hall in 1963 and became the chief instructor in about 1967. He left in early 1969. The advertisement for his replacement sought a deputy principal.[52])

Lagging further behind, the more numerous inhabitants of centre staffrooms would eventually lose their 'instructor' label to become 'teachers' or 'outdoor educators'. From the late 1960s, only qualified teachers would be appointed to the vacancies for permanent instructors. (In December 1972 an advertisement for a vacancy on the White Hall staff sought a teacher/instructor.[53])

In the late 1960s, the term 'outdoor education' would become common. The more specific terms 'outdoor pursuits', 'outdoor activities', 'open-country pursuits' and 'wild-country pursuits' would remain but would appear less often. Yet the widespread adoption of 'outdoor education', often shortened to OE, would not end the semantic arguments. Although it would perhaps help to cultivate a more helpful image among some educationists, its infuriating vagueness would cause confusion and controversy.

High Peak News

All agaze, below the ramparts of Castle Naze. Jack Longland, the Duke of Edinburgh and Geoff Sutton, 21 November 1958.

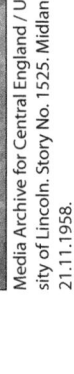

Media Archive for Central England / University of Lincoln. Story No. 1525. Midland News: 21.11.1958.

Performing for royalty. Castle Naze, 21 November 1958.

Derby Telegraph.

'We're sure you could do it, Philip.' Jack Longland (left), the Duke of Edinburgh and Geoff Sutton below Castle Naze, 21 November 1958.

http://whitehall.derbyshire-outdoors.org/gallery/

'I wonder if I could climb that in these borrowed wellies.'The Duke of Edinburgh and Jack Longland at Castle Naze, 21 November 1958.

http://whitehall.derbyshire-outdoors.org/gallery/

'That's right. You can't beat a good bowline!'

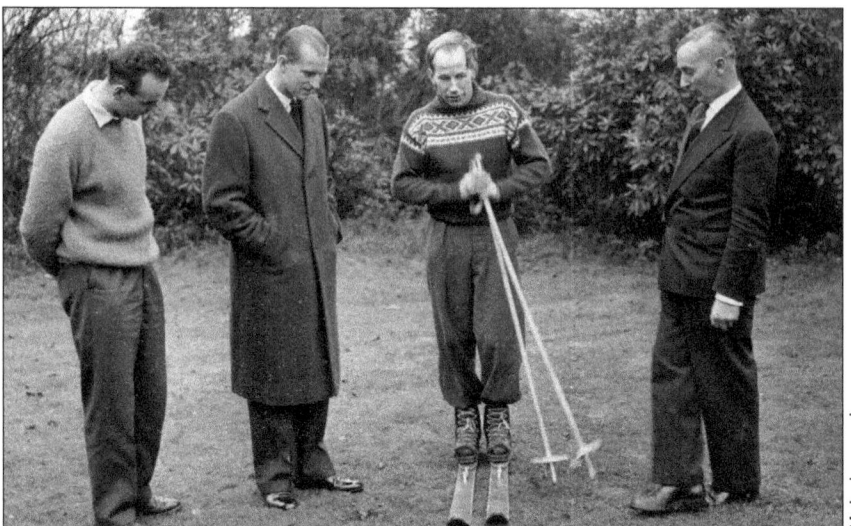

'We teach the Austrian method, but we go Norwegian for the après-ski.' Geoff
Sutton, the Duke of Edinburgh (before swapping the Royal shoes for wellies), Eric
Langmuir and Jack Longland, 21 November 1958.

'I'll have some snow sent down from Balmoral.' The Duke of Edinburgh at White Hall
Centre, 21 November 1958. Jack Longland on the left.

D7786/BOX/1/Bundle 6/14th group, courtesy of Derbyshire Record Office.

White Hall pony trekkers meet the Duke of Edinburgh, 21 November 1958. Pony-trekking was an optional extra chosen by some pupils. They paid a surcharge on the standard course fee.

Daily Mirror

A SORE POINT?

ANNE DUDGALE (above) of Macclesfield, leans forward in her saddle to catch a question by the Duke of Edinburgh. She had just given a riding lesson to eight boys who had never been on a horse before. And the Duke wanted to know :" Is it a case of riding for one day and being sore for a week ? "

The Duke was visiting the White Hall Training Centre for Outward Pursuits near Buxton, Derbyshire, yesterday. He also saw boys at the centre being trained in rock climbing (story below).

D7786/BOX/1/Bundle 6/10th group, courtesy of Derbyshire Record Office.

White Hall pony trekkers meet the Duke of Edinburgh, 21 November 1958.

A Typical Schools' Course, 1958

In late summer 1958, Peter Haddington visited White Hall. His account of the centre appeared in *Derbyshire Countryside*. It includes a useful third-party description of a typical Monday–Sunday schools' course:

> Let us take a look at the programme for a typical secondary school party of thirty boys with their teacher. The boys are very excited as they arrive on the Monday afternoon for a week's course during term time, for they are looking forward to these unusual 'lessons'. First they let off steam with an evening game of stalking, an objective such as Goyt's Bridge being chosen. Mr Sutton splits them into 'attackers' and 'defenders', the intention being to place marks on the strongly-guarded bridge. The defenders, however, are allowed to bring down the 'aggressors' as roughly as they like (with girl parties it's more gentle!).
>
> Tuesday morning is devoted to lectures and map reading, and this instruction is put into practice with an afternoon outdoor exercise. Evening brings another lecture and possibly some films, though if the weather is good a mountain rescue exercise may be held outdoors with the rescue stretcher.
>
> Wednesday's fare usually consists of a lengthy ramble, after which the boys are taught how to use a primus stove and pitch a tent. The great adventure, however, starts on Thursday, when the party leaves for an overnight camp. Tents are used unless the weather is extremely good, in which case the expedition might sleep in bivouac style or in caves on Stanage Edge or Harboro' Rocks near Brassington. In bad weather, on the other hand, a mountain hut may be used. This is often the first time a pupil has slept outdoors.
>
> On Friday afternoon the party returns to White Hall, following a brief introduction to climbing or caving (in summer some parties enjoy canoe camping on the River Derwent). With the arrival for the week-end of volunteer instructors, the boys elect to take specialist instruction in such things as climbing, canoeing or caving to complete their course. The choice is entirely their own, since there is no compulsion to take part in any one activity.
>
> No article on White Hall, however, would be complete without a description of the specialist activities …
>
> Climbing is one of the most popular activities, and instruction is usually given at Castle Naze, on Combs Moss, or on Wind-

gather Rocks at Kettleshulme. The Staffordshire Roaches are also visited by 'bus, and for more experienced pupils climbs like Stanage Edge at Hathersage, or Froggatt Edge and Gardom's Edge, near Baslow, are tackled. Caving attracts fewer enthusiasts, though the warden claims that half of those who take a course find they like this sport and subsequently join caving clubs. Instruction is given at a number of places, including potholes on Stanley Moor and Axe Edge, near Buxton, and around Castleton and Mam Tor. Bagshaw Cavern, at Bradwell, and the fearsome Eldon Hole and Oxlow Pot on Eldon Hill are other favourites.

The mountain terrain around White Hall affords excellent ski-ing in snowy conditions, so pupils do not have to go far for their sports … Fell walking is popular, too, and favourite weekend regions include Kinder Scout, Bleaklow and Dovedale. Yet another activity has recently been added to White Hall's syllabus. Arrangements have been completed with the owners of local stables for the hire of ponies for a cross-country pony trekking course.[54]

The standard schools' courses finished late on the Sunday afternoons, after the two option days. The daily charge for each pupil in September 1958 was 3s. 6d. According to Haddington, as well as accommodation and instruction, this covered the provision of breakfast, a packed lunch, high tea and supper. It is likely that Sutton had invited Haddington to observe a course, as part of the push for helpful publicity.

Courtesy Frank Shaw / www.picturethepast.org.uk
DCHQ002645

A group of boys at White Hall, 1959.

Staff Training and Improved Equipment

As well as consolidating the programmes and routines of the Mosedale era, Sutton and his teaching staff pushed forwards into new areas, improving and widening their own skills, developing and applying new standards in instruction, and upgrading the centre's stock of outdoor clothing and equipment.

The permanent staff, all climbers, learnt to ski, kayak and cave. We have already seen that voluntary instructors greatly influenced the White Hall community socially. These volunteers were amateurs in the true sense of that word but were often essential authorities – the experts – technically:

> Some V.I.s were indispensable because they were experts in other areas [who] were able to train the permanent staff, who were previously climbers. A good example is in caving which also had become a 'growth' sport in which the specialist clubs became the only people with knowledge of new discoveries, techniques and equipment. Dave Allsop, a founder member of the Eldon Pothole Club in Buxton [was] one such, an invaluable friend from the start and eventually a professional …
>
> There were many other clubs involved, since White Hall depended not only on the cavers. Ski-ing and canoeing instructors were also necessary to maintain multi-activity centres especially before training establishments had been set up on a national basis, to train the trainers.[55]

According to one 1958 account, the voluntary instructors were mostly under thirty years old and came from all over the country, even as far away as London and Bristol. White Hall paid their travelling expenses for distances as far as Birmingham, but beyond that the volunteers met their own costs. Sutton said their keenness in overcoming obstacles to reach the centre was sometimes fantastic. Nearly every weekend, about eight volunteers arrived. They were accommodated in the old chapel (which later became an indoor climbing wall).[56]

In a letter to Arthur Afford in about 1978, Eric Langmuir wrote:

> Looking back on White Hall days now, I am struck by the marvellous balance between professional and amateur staff, between discipline and relaxed enjoyment, between adventure and safety and so on. It all seemed to happen so naturally and that's a real

tribute to the staff – a very remarkable bunch! Perhaps it showed itself best in the system of voluntary instructors which worked so well. White Hall would not have been the same without them, nor would its influence have spread out into the climbing and caving world of the clubs and beyond.[57]

Throughout Sutton's wardenship, in their spare time he and one or two of his assistants – Downes and Drasdo at first, then Mansell and Andrew Maxfield – often wandered around the crags of the Peak District for pleasure. Downes's main contributions to UK climbing were on mountain crags but he 'added several connoisseur's pieces to the Peakland repertoire at Shelf Benches on Bleaklow and at Five Clouds below the Roaches'.

Drasdo, slim and wiry, was among the first people to realise the climbing potential of Chee Dale's limestone buttresses. In the early 1950s, the advice to newcomers had been that 'the rock climber studiously eschews the dangerously loose limestone of the dales'.[58] In 1955 Drasdo and Mansell climbed The Stalk on Plum Buttress and in doing so contributed to an increasing focus on the bulgy black-streaked cliffs of the valley.[59]

Sutton found neglected gaps to fill in at Mow Cop, Cratcliffe, the Roaches, Bamford Edge, Derwent Edge, Stanage and Froggatt.[60]

Perhaps the main advantage enjoyed by the White Hall staff in those days, compared to the staff who came after them, was that they could enjoy their private climbing and kayaking and caving and skiing without also having to continually be working towards or revalidating numerous national instructing qualifications.

*

By the mid-1950s, Italian boots and French climbing hardware and footwear had begun to appear in a small number of UK outdoor shops.[61] By the late 1950s, outdoor clothing and equipment had stepped onto the bottom of a technological staircase that is still heading inexorably upwards today. The starting-point, though, had hardly been touched by science.

Army surplus gear, not necessarily designed for the British climate, was gradually replaced by superior clothing and equipment. Wartime snap-links (early karabiners) of crude design and doubtful strength were no longer considered adequate. An understanding of the importance of waterproof outer shells began to spread, often too slowly, from the Royal Navy to the mountaineering and sailing fraternities. Cavers continued to construct ladders at home, but these ladders would occasionally fail and come under scrutiny. Sailing and canoeing organisations introduced improved standards for lifejackets and buoyancy aids. People began to make canoes out of fibreglass-reinforced resins laid by hand in two moulds, producing two halves that were then connected together. This method of canoe construction did not require a frame and it allowed improved hull shapes. The method was a revolution in canoe construction.

White Hall kept up with these technological advances adequately. The county council increased the amount of money available for equipment. Compared to the restrictions that Mosedale had faced, 'it was comparatively easy for his successor, Geoffrey Sutton, to ask the county authorities for more finance'.[62] A visitor to the centre in 1958 observed the results:

> Perhaps the most interesting corner of White Hall is the store room, packed with equipment purchased with an annual grant from the County Council. A mountainous pile of rucksacks rears up on one hand, while tier upon tier of wooden shelves are crammed with rambling and climbing boots of every size and type. Here are stocks of caving lights run on carbide, not to mention caving ladders and other tackle. Skis and ski-sticks stand to attention in one corner; ice-axes, climbing ropes, rolled-up tents and sleeping bags are well in evidence. Indeed a sight to make every outdoor sportsman envious![63]

Sleeping bags were not yet universal. In 1958, as an eleven-year-old Scout, whenever I went to camp I improvised a sleeping bag out of a woollen blanket, held together with blanket pins, a technique about which the August 1919 issue of *Popular Science Monthly* contained a dense treatise.

As a result of the expanding stock of equipment, an improved store-room became a high priority. Also, a need for better maintenance of equipment was recognised.

A Widening Range of Courses

Introductory schools courses remained at the core of White Hall's annual calendar. But the centre also provided courses at higher technical levels for teachers and youth leaders who wanted to run their own outdoor activities. Programmes were also developed at intermediate levels. In the case of climbing, when pupils reached an adequate stage of competence at seconding, the White Hall instructors supervised their transition to leading. Many of the Peak District's short climbs on gritstone were ideal for this purpose. Doug Scott takes us back to about 1956: 'The instructors at White Hall took us out to local crags such as Windgather and Castle Naze where they showed us how to belay properly. When they thought we could cope, they put us into the lead, helping us realise our full potential.'[64]

The centre also devised programmes for older members of various organisations including colleges of education, Ranger Scouts, Ranger Guides and the police. 'An experiment with Borstal boys proved highly successful and led the Home Office to organise similar training courses of its own.'[65]

The number of away courses rose. A B Afford's mention of the away courses of the late 1950s is brief but adequate: 'The winter trips to the Cairngorms, and the summer trip to Skye led to unforgettable experiences.'

In winter 1957–8 the centre held a most successful two-week skiing course at Braemar in the Cairngorms.

Doug Scott remembers a summer 1957 trip to Arran with Mick Garside, Gordon Mansell, and Maureen and Harold Drasdo:

> Mick and I were lucky enough to travel to the Isle of Arran as volunteers on a White Hall trip. On a break from instructing, we set off with Harold and Gordon to climb the South Ridge Direct on the Rosa Pinnacle of Cìr Mhòr, the splendid, symmetrical peak in the centre of the island. It was the longest route I'd yet done. I was pushed into the lead, spurred on by these luminaries watching from below, feeding my ego as I made short work of the layback crux. The rock was just wonderful, the setting superb and the company always inspiring.[66]

A fascinating account of a 1957 twelve-day summer course arrived in my email inbox one morning in May 2016. Brian Sharp's memories, which I have lightly edited, are wonderfully clear, fifty-nine years after the course:

> I was 13 when I first visited White Hall in 1957. I was one of 15 to 20 boys from Castle School in Hadfield in the top northwest corner of Derbyshire. We went on a 12-day course. The staff at

that time were Geoff Sutton (warden), Gordon Mansell, 'Max' Maxfield, Arthur Afford and Harold Drasdo.

We climbed on Castle Naze and Windgather, all within reasonable walking distance of the centre. I think at that time there was only one Land Rover. Map reading was quickly learned and was put into practice in the Goyt valley. We also did some caving (Carlswark Cavern in Stoney Middleton) and some canoeing on the canal in Whaley Bridge and on Combs Reservoir not far from the centre.

After 6 days at White Hall we went up to the Yorkshire Dales. We were all issued with sleeping bags and ex-army commando rucksacks with horrible metal frames. We went up to Clapham on the train. I remember changing trains in Manchester, all of us in single file with all our gear walking through the rush hour from Piccadilly to Victoria Station.

We camped in a field at Clapham. We were split up into 2 groups for ease of transport. From there we walked up Ingleborough in the mist. Next day we did Gaping Gill cave.

We were then sent off on a two-day walk without an instructor. I was appointed leader of a group. I was given sealed instructions to be opened when we were under way. We had tents, sleeping bags, primus stoves and enough food for the two days. It rained a lot! I can't remember what sort of anoraks we had but I remember being wet most of the time. We set off from the campsite and I opened the envelope. I was instructed to lead the group over Ingleborough then on to another peak called Pen-y-ghent and down into Ribblehead and up to a third peak called Whernside. We were to be picked up by Land Rover at a placed called Chapel-le-Dale. We did the first two peaks and planned to camp but the farmer took pity on us and offered us to sleep in his barn. Next day it rained again! Progress was slow so we didn't make it up Whernside. (This walk is now called the Yorkshire Three Peaks route.)

Next day one of the boys (Chris Butler I think) from the other group who were doing Gaping Gill [Bar Pot] fell and injured his head. There was a big cave rescue and the BBC came up and interviewed some of the group.

Brian Sharp ('Sharpey') returned to White Hall as storeman in 1965, staying until 1969. He then lived in Switzerland for forty-one years and he now lives in Bavaria, southern Germany.

Accident in Bar Pot

The caving accident mentioned by Brian Sharp took place in Bar Pot, a part of the Gaping Gill system, on the night of Sunday 23 June 1957. My research for this book initially discovered little about the circumstances, just two short press reports. So I was very grateful to Mary Wilde, the librarian of the British Cave Research Association, when she found an informative and revealing Cave Rescue Organisation call-out report in the *Journal of the Craven Pothole Club*.

Five boys were descending the cave. At least one instructor accompanied them. The party had ladders and a rope. According to one newspaper report, which may have been incorrect, the boys were equipped with candles, the instructors with 'headlights', presumably carbide lamps.[67]

The call-out report describes the route taken:

[The] party ... had descended the first pitch (40ft.), the long scramble, and the second pitch (100ft.) down one of the avens, into the S.E. Passage of Gaping Gill, beyond the S.E. (Flood Exit) Pot. They then traversed round the latter into the Main Chamber. On the way back a brief halt was made at T Junction and, in spite of warnings, one of the lads [fourteen-year-old Chris Butler] wandered off ahead ... The lad walked over the edge, rolled about 20 feet and then dropped a sheer 70ft. onto the wide ledge in S.E. Pot.[68]

Chris Butler sustained severe head injuries and a broken arm. The call-out report continues and it reminds us that the technology of communication in the 1950s was very basic:

The call for assistance went out a little earlier than usual, and by 7.10 p.m. the Police had put out the white sheet around the tree outside Settle Police Station – thus catching many members of various clubs homeward bound, from individual motor cyclists to the Burnley Pothole Club Bus.[69]

The first group of rescuers reached Bar Pot at about 7.30pm. The rescue took over seven hours. 'At one time 30 men were below ground while

80 more stood by.'[70] Chris Butler was brought out on a stretcher at 3am on the Monday. 'Fortunately, miraculously, [he] survived the ordeal.'[71] He reportedly recovered completely.[72]

In the second half of the call-out report, the anonymous author discussed whether the accident could have been avoided. Without mentioning any names, he pointed out – correctly, in my view – that the transfer of skills and techniques and attitudes from rock climbing to caving, although considerable, has limitations:

> I am sure it is a fact that certain trained mountaineers who have not much experience of potholing, tend to think that, because we use ladders and ropes from the top of the pitch, the job is a cake walk. It should be, of course, normally, but should there be a change in the weather, or a mishap, however slight, or tiredness leading to exposure, the results down a pothole can be far more serious than on an exposed mountain top. For this reason, I feel, that parties of inexperienced people should not be taken down potholes with pitches over 50 feet or so, and not more than two pitches. Lead them down Long Churn, by all means, or, if they have to have pitches, Calf Holes or Sel Gill.[73]

Secondly, the report raised the question of instructor-pupil ratios. Although these ratios were an appropriate subject, the intimation in this section of the report seems to stray into Utopia:

> The proportion of experienced potholers to novices in a party has an important bearing on the problem. Rock climbers of experience, if they take a novice [climbing], put him in the middle of [a rope of] three – two experienced to one novice. The Bar Pot party were tackling the equivalent of a mild severe climb, not with a party of a ratio of two [instructors] to one [novice] but of a ratio of … one [instructor] to five [novices]. By all means encourage one's friends to come potholing but in ones and twos, not in sightseeing trips.[74]

Suffice to say that there is a gigantic difference between an instructor-pupil ratio of 1:5 and the suggested one of 2:1, an imaginary ideal, totally unrealistic for novice caving with groups of school pupils. Had this extreme recommendation been adopted, it would have ruled out caving as an activity at LEA outdoor pursuits centres. In the years to come, the staff-pupil ratio for White Hall's novice caving would eventually settle down to 3:10, the three being two instructors and one visiting teacher.

Thirdly, the report raised the matter of the spacing between the rungs on a caving ladder. Chris Butler's plunge down South East Pot had nothing to do with ladders, but ladders were a controversial issue of the time. The report says that the ladders used in Bar Pot had rungs spaced twelve inches apart, which was too far. Ladders with a rung spacing of ten inches or eight inches would have been easier for novices.

What is interesting about these three issues is that two of them – staff-pupil ratios and ladder rung spacing – would reappear at White Hall ten years later, after two fatal caving accidents.

The report did not mention the lighting aspect: caving partly by candlelight, like 18th-century lead miners, implied in the *Daily Mail* article. This newspaper's reference to the boys using candles may have been wrong. Brian Sharp was in a different group of five boys, who had done the same trip on the day before the day of the accident. Asked recently about the lighting, he said: 'As far as I can remember we all had Carbide lamps which needed a lot of attention. I can remember climbing down two pitches in Bar Pot. Doing that with candles would have been a horror. I have been on a lot of caving trips with Whitehall … late 50s, early 60s and they have never used candles.'[75]

Despite working at White Hall for sixteen years, I never heard a mention of the Bar Pot near-fatality of 1957. The accident had happened in the middle of Geoff Sutton's public-relations campaign. Negative publicity could have derailed this campaign. Luckily the episode had a happy ending and was perhaps quickly forgotten. You wonder, had it been a death, whether the rapid expansion of LEA centres that started with Plas Gwynant Centre in 1958 would have been quite so rapid.

Canoeing with White Hall

Another development of the late 1950s was the beginning of away canoeing courses. In about 1954, shortly before Geoff Sutton's arrival, White Hall had built up a collection of wood-and-canvas Percy Bland-ford (PBK) two-seater kayaks. Apparently, Peter Mosedale and others had built these canoes themselves. No photographs have been found that show this White Hall boat-building, but the practice was common in British secondary schools and in organisations like the Sea Scouts. (The British Pathé film archive has a 1956 news-clip showing teenagers building wooden-framed canoes at Woolwich Recreational Institute.[76])

Groups used these two-seater kayaks on Toddbrook Reservoir and on Combs Reservoir, which were both feeder reservoirs for the Peak Forest Canal. Groups also canoed on sections of the canal itself, between Whaley Bridge and Marple and on the Macclesfield branch. Oral history, yet to be verified, says that White Hall groups also canoed on the attractive upper reaches of the River Derwent, enjoying the best of Derbyshire's rather nondescript moving water; this part of the Derwent, whose water was often a peaty colour but was otherwise clean and fresh, later became legally inaccessible.

At this stage in the development of canoeing in Britain, seats were often crude or nonexistent. Many canoes lacked knee rests and foot rests. Frequently, even competitive slalomists had to make their own knee rests and foot rests.[77]

The White Hall canoes were transported in an ingenious all-metal trailer, said by Haddington to have been made at the centre for less than £10[78] but by Afford to have been built by Weston Brothers in Buxton.[79] The centre's Land Rover did the towing. Kayaking became a reliable and popular activity on the programmes. This was about fifteen years before dinghy sailing arrived on the programme.

In 1956–7 the first glass-reinforced plastic (GRP) canoes appeared on the market. People referred to these loosely as being fibreglass canoes.

One of White Hall's most ambitious projects in 1958 was a twelve-day canoe camping holiday down the River Wye on the Welsh border.[80]

A B Afford mentions that White Hall's wood-and-canvas PBKs were battered to bits on rocky rivers; by about 1959 they had been replaced by hard-shell two-seater fibreglass kayaks.[81]

Several more flat-water canoeing sites would come into use much later, in the 1970s and 80s. Also, starting in the 1970s, the venues for away canoeing courses would change from rivers to the sea.

Media Archive for Central England / University of Lincoln.
Story No. 1525. Midland News: 21.11.1958.

Canoeing on Combs Reservoir during the Duke of
Edinburgh's visit on 21 November 1958. The boats are
wood-and-canvas Percy Blandford kayaks (PBKs), hard
chine with a distinctive square back to the cockpit.

http://whitehall.derbyshire-outdoors.org/gallery/

'You look a bit cold. Reminds me of bloody Gordonstoun.' Canoeing on
Combs Reservoir during the Duke of Edinburgh's visit.

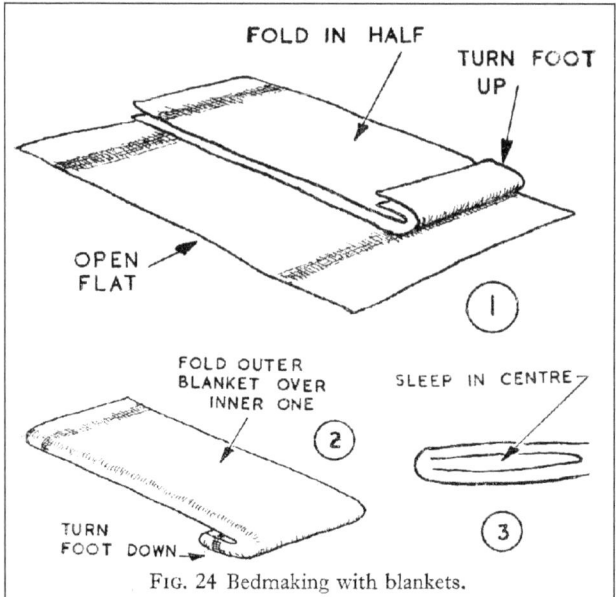

FIG. 24 Bedmaking with blankets.

Instructions for making a blanket bed for canoe camping.
From Percy Blandford's 1946 book, *Canoeing To-day*.

The Mansion House and Transport

Despite regular stoking of the fireplaces and boiler, some aspects of the old mansion that had opened in December 1950 were still spartan, like the early youth hostels. During Sutton's wardenship, a gradual process of improvement began, aiming to upgrade the building to a comfortable and efficient residential centre. 'Endless persuasion and publicity ensued in efforts to convince the sceptics that more support and investment must be forthcoming to make all these changes possible.'[82]

The house was redecorated. Some building alterations were undertaken. A television appeared in the staffroom (where the *Manchester Guardian* was now more in evidence than *The Times*). Old kitchen fittings were replaced.

The Mosedales had carried the full burden of domestic work with occasional help from schoolgirls from Cavendish Grammar School on a rota, two at a time. Now, a resident full-time cook, Mrs Margerison, was appointed. Her husband Bill became driver-handyman. There was already a caretaker and boilerman, Fred Gartland.

By 1958 a visitor was able to report:

An essential part of the centre is the lecture room, with its magnificent cinematographic equipment, for here pupils are briefed in map and compass reading and shown films on the sports they are studying. The kitchens possess up-to-date cookers for preparing meals both swiftly and cleanly, while another room is set aside for the depositing of wet or dirty clothes after a hard day on the hills. Bathrooms which include showers complete ideal facilities.[83]

In actuality, the improving would continue for many years.

The centre bought a long-chassis Land Rover, which extended the variety of sites that groups could visit. Permanent and voluntary instructors continued to use their own cars when necessary. For the away courses to Scotland, Wales and the Lakes, the centre sometimes borrowed Land Rovers and trailers from High Peak Borough Council.[84] The combination of the centre's own Land Rover and borrowed ones enabled the development of a more ambitious annual programme of courses.

Mountain and Cave Rescue – Sutton Period

By the time that Geoff Sutton arrived, White Hall had acquired a reputation as a place staffed by skilled mountaineers and cavers. In 1956 Sutton offered the services of the White Hall staff to help in mountain rescue.[85] They became regularly involved in rescues and searches. In March 1959 the White Hall staff were one of the first units to be called out to an accident in Peak Cavern, where Neil Moss, a young potholer, was jammed in a crevice nearly a mile from the cave entrance. Sutton spent twelve and a half hours underground on the rescue attempt.[86]

Moss was stuck in a very tight passage, so there was an obvious need for slim but strong rescuers. A *Daily Mail* front-page report on this accident reminds us of a far wider issue than cave rescue – the oppression of women by men. In the late 1950s, if gender dynamics were an irresistible force, traditional attitudes were an almost immoveable object:

Girls Offer to Go Down But Are Refused
Fifteen girl volunteers were told by police: 'No girls will be allowed to try to reach Moss. No matter how small they are. The job is too dangerous for women.'[87]

In spite of the immense efforts of rescuers, Neil Moss died. The tragedy was widely reported overseas as well as in Britain and it had important repercussions for cave rescue and training.

Cavers in Peak Cavern, Castleton, during or shortly after the attemped rescue of Neil Moss in March 1959. Geoff Sutton spent twelve and a half hours underground on this desperately difficult struggle to save a life, which ultimately failed.

National Developments – Sutton Period

The pilot programmes for the BBC radio quiz *My Word!* were broadcast in 1956. The first proper episode went out on 1 January 1957, and Longland – this extraordinarily versatile man – joined the show as host on 5 August 1957.[88] Blessed with wide interests and a sense of humour, 'he did a fine job of keeping up with [Frank] Muir and [Denis] Norden's flights of fancy'.[89] He would stick with the show for twenty years and would become known in Bakewell, where he lived, as 'Broadcasting Jack'.

In summer 1957 Longland was appointed to the Wolfenden Committee to examine games, sports and outdoor activities. The CCPR set up the committee in response to a concern that sport in Britain was in a poor state. The CCPR's balance sheet for the year ended 31 March 1957 had shown a deficit of £24,659 on a total spending of £192,000. The council's honorary treasurer said that the government should take a greater share of the responsibility for financing the work of the council in helping those over school age to take part in games, sports and outdoor activities.[90]

The White Hall Centre archive has several photographs of Longland with the Duke of Edinburgh during the duke's visit to White Hall one day in November 1958. For Longland, this might have been a rare day out of a busy office in Matlock. (County Hall moved from Derby to Matlock in April 1956.) As a member of the Wolfenden Committee, in November 1958 Longland became involved in a consultation with every possible interest group in the United Kingdom, which would last for about two and a half years.

Also, in the month of the duke's visit, the Ministry of Education set up the Albemarle Committee to report on the youth service in England and Wales. The concern this time was about the meagre funding of the youth service by the Ministry of Education and about the consequential poor image that the youth service had acquired.

Sutton left White Hall just before the national scene became a crowded festival of important conferences and far-reaching committee reports. The Wolfenden Report and the Albemarle Report did not become available until Eric Langmuir's principalship, and so I will look at them later, in their chronological place.

*

What other developments had taken place nationally? In February 1956 the Duke of Edinburgh's Award scheme had been launched, with its origins in the County Badge scheme but with John Hunt in charge to ensure that Hahn's ideas 'were suitably adapted to the temperament and needs of young people in Britain'.[91] The first Duke of Edinburgh's Award ceremony was held later that year.

Ironically, at this time the British element of a much older scheme for young people was experiencing a cyclic downturn. Between 1913 and 1938, the number of Scouts in England had risen from 152,000 to 438,000.[92] Robert Baden-Powell had died in 1942, lauded as a figure of global significance. But in the 1950s there was a decline in the number of British Boy Scouts. Many boys in their mid-teens were leaving. In August 1957, in an article in the *Observer*, Jack Longland ranged over the origins of the Boy Scout movement, its status as 'the largest, the most widespread, and the most successful youth organisation in the world', and the current problems of the British branch.[93] (He might more accurately have talked about the two most successful youth organisations, Boy Scouts and Girl Guides.)

Scouting, he said, was a very remarkable achievement, and one that stemmed from the inspiration of a single man. The old complaint that the movement was militaristic no longer stood up to scrutiny. But scouting was 'passing through a most interesting crisis of conscience'. The difficulties, Longland thought, were deep-rooted in the personality of the movement's founder:

> Baden-Powell remained a young boy to the end of his life, with all the virtues, but also many of the disadvantages, which that state entails. He imported from a colonial empire … a passionate admiration for the pioneers, scouts and explorers in jungle, bush and forest. His *Scouting for Boys* is the oddest book ever to become the bible of a great international movement. It is badly organised, jumping rapidly from principle to minute detail, prodigal of advice which is sometimes downright dangerous … and yet a rich quarry full of knowledge of the very young and of the best ways to handle them.
>
> I have written 'knowledge of the very young' with deliberation. We live in a shrunken world, and Britain, at least, is poor in jungle, bush and forest. B. P. himself cheerfully went on seeing buffaloes roaming in Kensington Gardens … to the end of his life. But this kind of magnificent make-believe is a quality of the very young, and disappears with adolescence. There is, I think, a causal connection between the naive boyishness of the first Chief Scout and the fact that the Movement he founded loses so many of its members in their middle teens.[94]

The basic reason for the decline, in Longland's opinion, was a failure to change to tackle 'the mid-twentieth-century malaise which makes the growing youngster increasingly unwilling to follow the advice and example of the adults who have made such a mess of the world which he is to inherit'.[95]

What Longland did not say in this national newspaper was that at Derbyshire's White Hall Centre, fifteen-year-olds were responding enthusiastically to residential courses in outdoor pursuits. The mid-teens were exactly the age group with which White Hall was having resounding success, some of which was attributable to wide games such as Bandits, borrowed from Scouting.

Nationally, the pre-war neglect of outdoor pursuits for girls was beginning to be remedied. In August 1956, Nottinghamshire county council ran a week's experimental course for girls aged between fifteen and twenty, with the object of stimulating a taste for the outdoor life and adventure. The fifteen participants came from grammar schools, factories and offices. They stayed at Leam Hall Youth Hostel, near Grindleford. The activities included rock climbing, canoeing and swimming.[96]

While Sutton and his staff forged ahead at White Hall, the late 1950s at the Outward Bound Trust were years of considerable managerial disagreement, centred on practices that had previously enjoyed an unchallenged place in the Outward Bound concept. John Lagoe, the young warden of Eskdale OBMS, vigorously questioned the badge scheme, an Outward Bound sacred cow since 1941. He also called for the daily athletics, such as the high jump, to be replaced by endurance training. Lagoe pushed through fundamental changes despite the combined conservative fervour of Hahn, Freddie Fuller and Jim Hogan.[97]

The Outward Bound Trust had not yet opened any Outward Bound schools for girls. Looking back at this later, Harold Drasdo wrote:

> There is something quite hilarious about the accounts of the crises that have shaken the [Outward Bound] movement. It seems odd, for instance, that the suggestion that the activities might be offered to young women caused such head-shaking and such torturing uncertainties. It is touching to read of the simple pleasure and positive self-congratulation of those concerned after this intimidating step was taken and the girls proved that arduous mountain and sea expeditions were not beyond them. Everyone outside Outward Bound and interested in climbing or sailing knew this already: but the promoters of these courses seem to have felt that they had made an important discovery.[98]

*

Two more national parks were created during Sutton's time at White Hall: Northumberland in 1956 and the Brecon Beacons in 1957. A total of ten national parks had been designated in seven years. The UK's first motorway, the M6 Preston Bypass, was opened on 5 December 1958.

When founded in 1944, as a representative body for mountaineers, the BMC had twenty-five member clubs. By 1958 there were sixty-nine member clubs, with an average of one new one joining each month.[99] Jack Longland wrote a 3,300-word article for *Mountain*, describing the British climbing milieu of the late 1950s. Climbers hitchhiked or rode motorbikes, stayed in tents and barns rather than hotels, and 'no climber [was] complete without his festoon of slings, the badge of his trade'.[100]

PGL, a private provider of activity holidays for children, arrived in 1956. The Army Training Camp at Towyn opened in 1957. Inverclyde National Watersports Centre opened in 1958. A fifth Outward Bound school, Ashburton, opened in 1959. Just one other LEA residential outdoor centre appeared during Sutton's wardenship, being Plas Gwynant in 1958. The most rapid period of expansion of LEA centres was imminent.

Geoffrey Winthrop Young died on 6 September 1958, aged eighty-one, after a life spent climbing, saving lives (he ran a wartime ambulance unit), educating, writing and mixing with more than a few personages from *Who's Who* and *Debrett's Peerage*. In 1959, Wilfrid Noyce acknowledged Young's work for Outward Bound. Noyce also touched upon a concern that some climbers had about outdoor pursuits centres:

> In the wide field of boyhood adventure [Young] joined with Kurt Hahn and others in realising the scheme now known as the Outward Bound Movement, himself becoming chairman of the Trust. For he believed passionately in adventure on hill and sea as a character-forming element in education; and whatever climbers, who tend to be individualists, may think privately of organised and collective adventure, they must admit that the scheme has succeeded beyond the dreams of its originators – and has borne fruit in others, such as the Duke of Edinburgh's Award.[101]

The climbers' concerns that Noyce mentioned had not affected Young's involvement in Outward Bound, but they would emerge forcefully in the late 1970s to embroil Jack Longland in a bitter controversy.

In September 1959, White Hall was nearly ten years old. Its staff had jointly made steady progress in every facet they had any influence or control over. However, like everything else in those days, the handful of outdoor centres scattered around Britain operated in a simpler world than later times, with no Mountain Leadership Training Board, no Mountain Leadership Certificate, no BCU Senior Instructor qualification, no Whernside Manor caving centre, no Cave Instructor qualification, no Sparklets,[102] no Association of Wardens of Mountain Centres, no National Association for Outdoor Education, no Cowes National Sailing Centre, no Holme Pierrepont National Water Sports Centre, no *Mountain Leadership* (Langmuir), no *Safety in Outdoor Pursuits* (Department of Education and Science), and no *Education and the Mountain Centres* (Drasdo). These bodies and qualifications and books were just a few of the developments that were still in the future. We did have some of the best maps in the world, but these did not yet show public rights of way. The term 'outdoor education' had seldom appeared in British writing, although it was becoming common in North America.

The bleakest years of postwar austerity were behind. In July 1957 the prime minister Harold Macmillan, an Etonian and member of a wealthy publishing family, had told a large meeting: 'Let us be frank about it: most of our people have never had it so good.'[103] History had been made in October 1957 when the Soviet Union had launched Sputnik 1. More national and global change was coming. But first, at White Hall, it was time for a changing of the guard.

*

After leaving White Hall in September 1959, Geoff and Ann Sutton settled in Geneva, where Geoff occupied a series of prestigious posts involving languages and translating.[104] In the 1960s he translated autobiographies of leading continental alpinists. He also wrote or contributed to the books *Samson: The Life and Writings of Menlove Edwards* and *Artificial Aids in Mountaineering* and *High Peak: The Story of Walking and Climbing in the Peak District*.

The dust jacket of *High Peak* (1966) proclaimed: 'There is no doubt that [this book] will remain the definitive work in its field, and it appears opportunely at the moment when exploration is nearing completion.' *High Peak* was a seminal account, combining Eric Byne's thirty years of research with Geoff Sutton's fluent story-telling. In 2005 Jim Perrin summarised it as 'a marvellously rich and stylish regional outdoor history, now a much-sought-after collector's item.'[105] The first dust-jacket prediction proved correct for forty-seven years, until the publication of *Peak Rock* in 2013. As for exploration being nearly finished, the book itself boosted the everlasting search for unclimbed rock.

The best known of Sutton's climbs is Poor Man's Peuterey at Tremadog. He continued climbing, canoeing and sailing for a while and skiing and walking throughout his life.

Sutton's love of literature never withered. 'In a letter written six weeks before his death, he remarked that he had been re-reading Pushkin, Tsvetaeva, Blok, Pasternak, Akhmatova and Mandelstam "as much for instruction as for pleasure".'[106]

Notes

1   Quoted in *The First Fifty Years of the British Mountaineering Council*, ed. by Geoff Milburn, Derek Walker and Ken Wilson (Manchester: British Mountaineering Council, 1997), p. 141.

2   Born 21 Jan 1930, Geoffrey Joannes Sutton, mother's surname Byrne. Middle name in University of Cambridge records is John. Surname in later use was Byrne-Sutton.

3   Harold Drasdo, 'Geoffrey Byrne-Sutton: 1930 (1952–1967) – 2000', *Climbers' Club Journal: 1999–2000*, 23, no. 3 (new series) (2001), pp. 144–147 (p. 144).

4   Gwen Moffat, *Space below My Feet* (London: Hodder and Stoughton, 1961), pp. 61–63.

5   Ibid., p. 183.

6   Enrolled on 1 Nov 1951, having been admitted to Peterhouse. J Cox, University Archives, University of Cambridge, Email to P McDonald, subject 'Geoffrey J Sutton', 8 Sept 2014 [Email].

7   Harold Drasdo, 'Geoffrey Byrne-Sutton: 1930 (1952–1967) – 2000', *Climbers' Club Journal: 1999–2000*, 23, no. 3 (new series) (2001), pp. 144–147 (p. 145).

8   Ibid. (p. 145).

9   Jim Perrin, *The Villain: The Life of Don Whillans* (London: Arrow, 2006), p. 132.

10 *The First Fifty Years of the British Mountaineering Council*, ed. by Geoff Milburn, Derek Walker and Ken Wilson (Manchester: British Mountaineering Council, 1997), p. 224.

11 Jim Perrin, *The Villain: The Life of Don Whillans* (London: Arrow, 2006), p. 340.

12 A B Afford, *The Story of White Hall Open Country Pursuits Centre; vol. 2* (Buxton, Derbyshire, UK: A B Afford, 1978), p. 10.

13 Harold Drasdo, 'Geoffrey Byrne-Sutton: 1930 (1952–1967) – 2000', *Climbers' Club Journal: 1999–2000*, 23, no. 3 (new series) (2001), pp. 144–147 (p. 146).

14 Peter Haddington, 'Gateway to Adventure at the White Hall Centre for Open Country Pursuits, near Buxton', *Derbyshire Countryside*, 23, no. 5 (Sept 1958), pp. 30–33.

15 Harold Drasdo, 'Geoffrey Byrne-Sutton: 1930 (1952–1967) – 2000', *Climbers' Club Journal: 1999–2000*, 23, no. 3 (new series) (2001), pp. 144–147 (p. 146).

16 Doug Scott, *Up and About: The Hard Road to Everest* (Sheffield: Vertebrate Publishing, 2015), p. 62.

17 Ibid., p. 64.

18 'Golden Oldies – Consolidation 1953–1958 [pub3]', Oread Mountaineering Club (no date) <http://oread.co.uk/images/pdf/53to58pub3.pdf> [accessed 15 July 2014], p. 85.

19 Dennis Gray, *Tight Rope! The Fun of Climbing* (Holyhead, Wales: Ernest Press, 1993), p. 41.

20 Dennis Gray, *Rope Boy* (London: Victor Gollancz: 1970), p. 22.

21 Jeff Connor, *Creagh Dhu Climber: The Life and Times of John Cunningham* (no place given: Ernest Press, 1999), pp. 55–61.

22 Harold Drasdo, *The Ordinary Route* (Ty Croes, Wales: Ernest Press, 1997), p. 45.

23 Trevor Jones and Geoff Milburn, *Cumbrian Rock: 100 Years of Climbing in the Lake District* (Glossop, UK: Pic Publications, 1988), 143–144, 159.

24   Michael Ward, 'No Ordinary Man', *Climber*, (Aug 1997), pp. 82–83.

25   Harold Drasdo, *The Ordinary Route* (Ty Croes, Wales: Ernest Press, 1997), p. 2.

26   G J Sutton, 'R. O. Downes', *Climbers' Club Journal: 1958*, 12, no. 2 (new series) (1958), pp. 266–269 (pp. 267–268).

27   R O Downes, 'Ireland: Wicklow', *Climbers' Club Journal: 1957*, 12, no. 1 (new series) (1957), pp. 92–93.

28   'Mr. R. O. Downes: A Young Climber of Distinction', *The Times*, 29 Aug 1957, p. 10.

29   Ian Wall, 'The R O Downes Hut', Climbers' Club (no date) <http://www.climbers-club.co.uk/cms/wp-content/uploads/2013/05/Downes.pdf> [accessed 19 Aug 2014].

30   A Blackshaw, 'Notes on Climbing in the British Isles 1957–9', *Alpine Journal*, 65 (1960), pp. 101–108.

31   Ibid.

32   Mountain Heritage Trust (Penrith), Alan Hankinson Collection, GB 3075 AHA 3/2/1 c. 1988/89 [Audio].

33   Eric Byne and Geoffrey Sutton, *High Peak: The Story of Walking and Climbing in the Peak District* (London: Secker and Warburg, 1966), p. 188.

34   A B Afford, *The Story of White Hall Open Country Pursuits Centre; vol. 2* (Buxton, Derbyshire, UK: A B Afford, 1978), p. 13.

35   G Spencer Summers, 'The History of the Trust', in *Outward Bound*, ed. by David James (London: Routledge and Kegan Paul, 1957), pp. 18–58 (p. 36).

36   'Genome Beta: Radio Times 1923–2009', BBC (2014) <http://genome.ch.bbc.co.uk/> [accessed 8 Dec 2014]. Also 'Longland, School Champion', *Guardian*, 4 Dec 1993, p. 30.

37   'The Younger Generation Question Time', *Radio Times*, 11 Nov 1951, p. 33. 'Summer Parade', *Radio Times*, 12 June 1953, p. 31. 'The Younger Generation Question Time', *Radio Times*, 12 Mar 1954, p. 37.

38   Quoted in 'Stanley Williamson', Telegraph (5 Nov 2010) <http://www.telegraph.co.uk/news/obituaries/culture-obituaries/tv-radio-obituaries/8113633/Stanley-Williamson.html> [accessed 4 Dec 2014].

39   'In Praise of Climbing', *Radio Times*, 6 Sept 1957, p. 48. 'Time Out of Doors: Climbing Technique', *Radio Times*, 28 Feb 1958, p. 42. 'Time Out of Doors: Climbing', *Radio Times*, 21 Nov 1958, p. 46. 'People Today: Geoffrey Sutton', *Radio Times*, 24 July 1959, p. 26.

40   'Our London Correspondence', *Manchester Guardian*, 15 Nov 1956, p. 10.

41   Alan Hankinson, *Geoffrey Winthrop Young: Poet, Educator, Mountaineer* (London: Hodder and Stoughton, 1995), p. 290.

42   Quoted in ibid., p. 349.

43   Nea Morin, *A Woman's Reach: Mountaineering Memoirs* (London: Eyre & Spottiswoode, 1968), p. 156.

44   Jim Perrin, 'Johnnie Lees', Guardian (24 Aug 2002) <http://www.theguardian.com/news/2002/aug/24/guardianobituaries> [accessed 27 Jan 2015].

45   'Yes, Now She's Up the Peak!', *Daily Express*, 28 Apr 1958, p. 6.

46   A B Afford, *The Story of White Hall Open Country Pursuits Centre; vol. 2* (Buxton, Derbyshire, UK: A B Afford, 1978), pp. 14–15.

47   Joan Simon, 'Promoting Educational Reform on the Home Front: *The TES* and *The Times* 1940–1944', *History of Education: Journal of the History of Education Society,* 18, no. 3 (1989), pp. 195–211 (pp. 195, 200).

48   Donald McLachlan, 'Hahn', in *Kurt Hahn,* ed. by H Röhrs and H Tunstall-Behrens (London: Routledge & Kegan Paul, 1970), pp. 1–13 (pp. 1–2).

49   Adam Arnold-Brown, *Unfolding Character: The Impact of Gordonstoun* (London: Routledge and Kegan Paul, 1962), p. 16.

50   Ibid., p. 151.

51   'Derbyshire Education Committee: White Hall Open Country Pursuits Centre [vacancy]', *The Times,* 11 May 1959, p. 1.

52   'Derbyshire Education Committee: White Hall [vacancy]', *The Times,* 27 June 1969, p. 30.

53   'Classified Ad 13', *Guardian,* 12 Dec 1972, p. 18.

54   Peter Haddington, 'Gateway to Adventure at the White Hall Centre for Open Country Pursuits, near Buxton', *Derbyshire Countryside,* 23, no. 5 (Sept 1958), pp. 30–33.

55   A B Afford, *The Story of White Hall Open Country Pursuits Centre; vol. 2* (Buxton, Derbyshire, UK: A B Afford, 1978), pp. 11–12.

56   Peter Haddington, 'Gateway to Adventure at the White Hall Centre for Open Country Pursuits, near Buxton', *Derbyshire Countryside,* 23, no. 5 (Sept 1958), pp. 30–33.

57   Letter, quoted in A B Afford, *The Story of White Hall Open Country Pursuits Centre; vol. 2* (Buxton, Derbyshire, UK: A B Afford, 1978), p. 21.

58   'Those Who Know Fat Man's Chimney', *Derby Evening Telegraph,* 22 Apr 1947, p. 3.

59   Meldrum gives a date of 1957 for this first ascent. K I Meldrum, 'Reviews: High Peak', *Climbers' Club Journal: 1967,* 15, no. 2 (new series) (1967), pp. 276–277.

60   Eric Byne and Geoffrey Sutton, *High Peak: The Story of Walking and Climbing in the Peak District* (London: Secker and Warburg, 1966), pp. 190, 226.

61   'The History of Ellis Brigham Mountain Sports' (2013) <http://www.ellis-brigham.com/advice-inspiration/about-us/history-of-eb> [accessed 30 Aug 2014].

62   Eric Byne and Geoffrey Sutton, *High Peak: The Story of Walking and Climbing in the Peak District* (London: Secker and Warburg, 1966), p. 189.

63   Peter Haddington, 'Gateway to Adventure at the White Hall Centre for Open Country Pursuits, near Buxton', *Derbyshire Countryside,* 23, no. 5 (Sept 1958), pp. 30–33.

64   Doug Scott, *Up and About: The Hard Road to Everest* (Sheffield: Vertebrate Publishing, 2015), p. 43.

65   Eric Byne and Geoffrey Sutton, *High Peak: The Story of Walking and Climbing in the Peak District* (London: Secker and Warburg, 1966), p. 189.

66   Doug Scott, *Up and About: The Hard Road to Everest* (Sheffield: Vertebrate Publishing, 2015), pp. 63–64.

67   '3 am: Rescue Teams Get Boy from Pothole', *Daily Mail,* 24 June 1957, p. 1.

68   [Anon.], '1957 C.R.O. Call-outs: Bar Pot', *Journal of the Craven Pothole Club,* 2, no. 3 (1957), pp. 187–188 (p. 187).

69   Ibid. (p. 187).

70   'Paper Clue to "Lost" Parents', *Manchester Guardian,* 25 June 1957, p. 1.

71   [Anon.], '1957 C.R.O. Call-outs: Bar Pot', *Journal of the Craven Pothole Club,* 2, no. 3 (1957), pp. 187–188 (p. 188).

72   Derbyshire Cave Rescue Organisation (Buxton, UK), Report of the Board of Inquiry Set Up by the Derbyshire Education Committee [c. May 1967], Ref. 279.

73   [Anon.], '1957 C.R.O. Call-outs: Bar Pot', *Journal of the Craven Pothole Club,* 2, no. 3 (1957), pp. 187–188 (p. 188).

74   Ibid. (p. 188).

75   Brian Sharp, Email to P McDonald, subject 'Candles', 5 June 2016 [Email].

76   *Boy Canoe Makers 1956.* British Pathé archive film ID 43.10 [News-clip]. British Pathé. 1956.

77   British Canoe Union, 'History of Canoeing' (no date) <http://www.bcu.org.uk/files/history%20of%20canoeing.pdf> [accessed 20 Mar 2015].

78   Peter Haddington, 'Gateway to Adventure at the White Hall Centre for Open Country Pursuits, near Buxton', *Derbyshire Countryside,* 23, no. 5 (Sept 1958), pp. 30–33.

79   A B Afford, *The Story of White Hall Open Country Pursuits Centre; vol. 2* (Buxton, Derbyshire, UK: A B Afford, 1978), p. 13.

80   Peter Haddington, 'Gateway to Adventure at the White Hall Centre for Open Country Pursuits, near Buxton', *Derbyshire Countryside,* 23, no. 5 (Sept 1958), pp. 30–33.

81   A B Afford, *The Story of White Hall Open Country Pursuits Centre; vol. 2* (Buxton, Derbyshire, UK: A B Afford, 1978), p. 15.

82   A B Afford, *The Story of White Hall Open Country Pursuits Centre; vol. 1* (Buxton, Derbyshire, UK: A B Afford, 1978), p. 40.

83   Peter Haddington, 'Gateway to Adventure at the White Hall Centre for Open Country Pursuits, near Buxton', *Derbyshire Countryside,* 23, no. 5 (Sept 1958), pp. 30–33.

84   A B Afford, *The Story of White Hall Open Country Pursuits Centre; vol. 2* (Buxton, Derbyshire, UK: A B Afford, 1978), pp. 12–13.

85   Roger Bennett and Ian Hurst, *Mountain Rescue: History and Development in the Peak District, 1920s-Present Day* (Stroud: Tempus Publishing, 2007).

86   'Corkscrew Trap', *Daily Mail,* 24 Mar 1959, pp. 1, 5.

87   Ibid.

88   'Genome Beta: Radio Times 1923–2009', BBC (2014) <http://genome.ch.bbc.co.uk/> [accessed 8 Dec 2014].

89   'Comedy: My Word!', BBC (28 Oct 2014) <http://www.bbc.co.uk/comedy/myword/> [accessed 2 Dec 2014].

90   'Outlook on Sport', *Observer,* 3 Nov 1957, p. 23.

91   John Hunt, *Life Is Meeting* (London: Hodder & Stoughton, 1978), p. 131.

92   Bernard Davies, *From Voluntaryism to Welfare State: A History of the Youth Service in England: 1939–1979,* History of the Youth Service in England, 2 vols (Leicester: Youth Work Press, 1999), vol. 1, p. 14.

93   Jack Longland, 'The Boy Scouts Face a Challenge', *Observer,* 4 Aug 1957, p. 6.

94 Ibid.

95 Ibid.

96 'Outdoor Course for 15 Girls', *The Times*, 20 Aug 1956, p. 10.

97 James Martin Hogan, *Impelled into Experiences: The Story of the Outward Bound Schools* (Wakefield, UK: Educational Productions, 1968), pp. 96–104.

98 Harold Drasdo, *Education and the Mountain Centres*, 2nd edn (1972, 1973; repr. Penrith: Association for Outdoor Learning, 1998), p. 28.

99 *The First Fifty Years of the British Mountaineering Council*, ed. by Geoff Milburn, Derek Walker and Ken Wilson (Manchester: British Mountaineering Council, 1997), pp. 4–6, 22.

100 Reproduced in ibid., pp. 304–311.

101 Wilfrid Noyce, 'In Memoriam: Geoffrey Winthrop Young', *Climbers' Club Journal: 1959*, 12, no. 3 (new series) (1959), pp. 413–415.

102 Holders of the Post Graduate Certificate of Education (outdoor activities option) of the University College of North Wales in Bangor. The outdoor activities option was run by Barbara Spark (later Roscoe).

103 'More Production "The Only Answer" To Inflation', *The Times*, 22 July 1957, p. 4.

104 Harold Drasdo, 'Geoffrey Byrne-Sutton: 1930 (1952–1967) – 2000', *Climbers' Club Journal: 1999–2000*, 23, no. 3 (new series) (2001), pp. 144–147 (p. 146).

105 Jim Perrin, *The Villain: The Life of Don Whillans* (London: Arrow, 2006), p. 338.

106 Harold Drasdo, 'Geoffrey Byrne-Sutton: 1930 (1952–1967) – 2000', *Climbers' Club Journal: 1999–2000*, 23, no. 3 (new series) (2001), pp. 144–147 (p. 147).

11. Eric Langmuir and Skills, 1959–63

Eric Langmuir was born in Glasgow on 3 May 1931. After being evacuated during the war he moved on to Fettes College, Edinburgh (1943–50). He did national service in the Royal Artillery. During this he won the army cross-country championship, presaging a lifetime's interest in orienteering, as an addition to his rock climbing, alpine mountaineering and skiing. He went up to Peterhouse, Cambridge in 1952 and graduated in 1955 with an honours degree in Natural Sciences.[1] While at Cambridge he took part in the exploration of the Trilleachan Slabs above Loch Etive; in June 1954 he led the first ascent of Spartan Slab, which became a popular classic.

Eric and Maureen Langmuir arrived at White Hall in the autumn of 1959. In December the Crowther Report reminded the educational world that the people of England and Wales were marrying earlier, were having smaller families and a longer education, were better housed and were living longer than ever before.[2] 'It has hardly yet been generally realised how sharply the average standard of living has risen in the fourteen years since the end of the war.' Obesity in children was attracting as much attention as under-nutrition.[3] Unknown to Eric Langmuir in 1959, the 1960s would be the boom years for LEA residential outdoor education, with many new centres appearing. White Hall had a ten-year lead on most of them. The challenge to Langmuir was to continue to consolidate the successful aspects of the centre's modus operandi while at the same time identifying areas for further improvement or innovation. He inherited the staff trio of Gordon Mansell, Andrew Maxfield and Arthur Afford, thanks to whom, in honour of his Scottish heritage, he soon became affectionately known behind his back as 'the Laird'. Officially, he was the principal, a title more indicative of the professional responsibilities of the role than the old 'warden' label.

In March 1961, a year and a half into the Lairdship, a *Guardian* journalist visited White Hall on the final day of a six-day schools' course. Thirty pupils from Tibshelf County Secondary School, near Chesterfield, were in residence. A detailed and perceptive article subsequently appeared, which included the information: 'So popular has the centre become that Mr Langmuir receives five times as many applications as there are places, which goes to show that there is plenty of room in the country for much more in the way of facilities.'[4] If there were still doubters around – the white elephant accusers of the early 1950s – they appeared to be losing the debate.

The journalist observed a climbing session at the Roaches. Detailed descriptions of an activity on a schools' course, written in the 1950s or 60s, are uncommon. The *Guardian* article captured the spirit of a typical White Hall introduction to climbing:

> With the [fifteen] school children at the foot of the Roaches were five instructors, including the principal of the centre, Mr E. D. G. Langmuir; all of them were men who know the Roaches well enough almost to walk up in their sleep …
>
> Instructor A. J. Maxfield led the way … Anthea – after a minor struggle to get past a tree growing in a low crevice – began her climb, followed by her friend Carol, who had had a little previous experience; and an hour later she was shouting from the top that she had enjoyed it very much. And even if she had used her knees to push herself up in places, she had, her instructor said, done very well.
>
> By the time Anthea and Carol had reached the top, some of the pupils were waiting for a second climb, and by lunch-time the rock face was looking more like an assault course, with people dotted all along the length of it in various stages on their climbs. Feet inched into narrow footholds, fingers clutched at skimpy cracks, heaving, pushing, and reaching to instructions – 'Try that one to the left; you'll have to reach for it'; 'don't spreadeagle yourself like that, you can't see the footholds'; 'Hang on to that'; 'Now move round to your left'.
>
> At the end of it all there was general praise for the pupils at the way they had tackled the climbs: and the boys and girls were promising themselves that this would not be their last rock climb.[5]

An added bonus to some days at the Roaches, always attention grabbing, was the sighting of a wallaby, one of a small number descending from five that escaped from a private zoo at Roaches Hall during the second world war.[6] Michael Foulke, a voluntary instructor in the 1960s, once topped out at Windgather Rocks to come face to face with one.[7]

Courses Offered in April–September 1961

The county council or the White Hall office routinely printed six-month or one-year programmes that contained a list of courses. These programmes also contained information about the centre, which makes them a useful historical source. The programmes for part of 1951 and for 1967–68 and 1975–76 have survived. Also, Arthur Afford reproduced several large extracts from the programmes for part of 1961 and for 1969–70. The programme for summer 1961 explained the main ideas behind the weekend courses and the school courses, and it listed seventeen courses:

> There are two main kinds of course. Week-end courses cater for those whose work only allows them freedom at such times, and provide both elementary and advanced training, at the choice of the student in fell-walking, map-reading, rock-climbing, caving and canoeing in summer, and skiing when there is snow. Other activities such as light camping can be provided by arrangement. School courses are of a week or longer, and provide a more comprehensive scheme of training, including emphasis on self-reliance, comradeship and living in a community. More specialised courses are indicated on the programme, and the Principal is always ready to discuss suggestions for such courses to suit the requirements of particular organisations.[8]

Course List from Programme for April–September 1961

Course	Type of Course	Comment
467	One week	Training colleges
468	Week-end	Youth Service Spec.1
469	One week	Schools or training colleges
470	One week	Schools
471	Long week-end	General
472	12 days	Schools – Scotland
473	Week-end	Youth Service Spec.2
474	One week	Schools

475	10 days	Schools – Lake District
476	Week-end	Youth Service Spec.3
477	One week	Schools
478	Week-end	General
479	One week	Schools
The Centre will be closed during August		
480	10 days	Rangers
481	Week-end	General
482	10 days	Schools – Canoeing
An additional course will be held in July for Youth Service members – The Pennine Way.		

The standard schools' courses in 1961 followed a pattern of activities that was fairly similar to that described earlier for a 1958 schools' course. On most courses the participants came from three or more schools, 'with non-selective pupils in the majority' (whatever that means). When inspected in 1963, White Hall could accommodate a maximum of thirty students. Boys usually formed two-thirds to four-fifths of the total.

The purpose of the schools' courses of the early 1960s remained unchanged from ten years earlier. In March 1961 a newspaper account reproduced part of an official description of the centre:

> Our students learn to walk, to read a map, to steer a compass course in cloud or darkness, to camp and cook in the open, and to acquire the basic skills of some open-air sports. Our youngsters … get cheerfully wet and muddy exploring the limestone caves, develop from tumbling novices to quite accomplished skiers on the nursery slopes of the Combs Valley, learn to use their own canoes and explore the countryside on horseback.
>
> They emerge, after only a week's course, not only with a wealth of valuable new experience, but also more alive, more self-reliant, and with the humility that comes from pitting yourself against natural obstacles much larger than the ordinary human scale.[9]

Further details of the schools' courses are available in a 1963 report by Her Majesty's Inspectorate (HMI).[10] The report's description of

White Hall's follow-up courses for school pupils summarised what these amounted to in 1963:

> One form of 'follow-up' is provided by the special[ist] schools' courses held away from the centre. There are usually two of these in the summer, one, which lasts a fortnight, in Scotland, the other probably in the Lake District, and also one in winter, a ski-ing week in Scotland (or Norway). These courses are held under canvas (except the winter one) and give opportunity for students to practise more advanced techniques. Places are in large measure taken by pupils who have already been on the basic course.[11]

The Pennine Way course in summer 1961 seems to have been a one-off. It was organised by Jack Kilkenny. The *Guardian* reported that

> boys aged between 16 and 21 in Derbyshire are being invited to walk the 260 miles of the Pennine Way from the Scottish border to Edale as one of the youth projects organised for this summer by the county education committee. The walk is expected to take three weeks – from July 21 to August 12 – and toughening-up courses will be held in advance at the committee's White Hall Open Country Pursuits Centre, near Buxton.
>   The boys are warned in a leaflet that the journey with daily walking distances ranging from 16 to more than twenty miles, will be strenuous and exciting. Only those who are fit enough and experienced in fell walking will be accepted.[12]

The youth service specialist courses available in the early 1960s had evolved over ten years. They were progressive training courses at two levels, called members' level and leaders' level. Each course comprised three weekends. The minimum age for entry to these courses was sixteen for members' level and eighteen for leaders' level.

By 1963 much thought had gone into designing and running these weekends. To fully illustrate this fact, here is the whole of the relevant section of the HMI report:

> On the Youth Service Specialist Courses everyone normally starts with the members' Hillcraft Course. A general introductory talk is given and working groups are arranged on the first evening of the first weekend. Saturday morning is spent on equipment and

tentage, and map and compass work; a fell-walking exercise takes place in the afternoon and the evening is given over to first aid and a mountain safety film. The second weekend is spent either in the Lake District or Wales. Members meet at the centre on Friday evening, are kitted out and are transported to their camp site early on Saturday morning. Here they spend Saturday on a fell-walking exercise, and return to their site in the early evening. On Sunday morning they strike camp and set out on another exercise, at the end of which they are met and transported back to the centre. At their third weekend members sit a simple theoretical paper and then carry out a practical exercise, usually in mountain rescue, designed to test them in the skills and activities to which they have been introduced during the course.

The Leaders' Course in Hillcraft is run on similar lines but is more detailed and more intensive, and higher standards are expected throughout.

The Specialist Courses in Climbing, Caving and Canoeing follow a similar pattern to the Hillcraft course but are devoted entirely to a single skill. In each case Friday evenings are introductory – the course is explained, reading matter recommended and so on – and Saturday mornings are concerned with equipment, techniques and safety. From the first Saturday afternoon much time is given to carefully graded and progressive practice in each skill. The climbers start on Birchens Edge or the Roaches, spend their second weekend on faces in North Wales or the Lakes and finish the course in Derbyshire with a theory paper and on cliff rescue, leading practice, artificial climbing or perhaps snow and ice work. The cavers start their practice at Carlswark Cave, then tackle Hillocks Mine or the Stanley Moor Caves, spend their second weekend in Yorkshire or Mendip caves, and finish their course with a weekend which includes a theory paper and rescue drill. The canoeists follow a similar routine; the start their practice on the canal and the Derwent, spend a weekend away on the Dove or the Wye [*Afon Gwy*] and finish with a theory paper and rescue drill.

The emphasis throughout the members' proficiency level courses is on techniques and safety. Much else is done, students are encouraged to read up their special activity, to interest themselves generally in the countryside and all it offers and to extend their experience beyond their weekends at the centre. They are also clearly briefed not only on what the centre can offer them in the future, but on other local and national opportunities which will help them to become expert in their chosen skills and pursuits. Those who return for leadership level courses follow a roughly similar routine but at a considerably higher standard. The aim is to produce responsible leaders with the knowledge and qualities required to take charge of a party and get the best out of it.[13]

Remembering these courses, Eric Langmuir wrote in 1978: 'I believe our series of Week-end Youth Leadership Courses were in some way the fore-runners of the Mountain Leadership Certificate and as you know I was very much involved with Jack Longland and John Jackson [on that] … in 1962, I think.'[14]

The report's mention of canoeing on the River Dove is a rare reference to this river as a canoeing venue. It also returns us to the subject of Abbotsholme school. In 1955 the Quaker educationist and mountaineer Robin Hodgkin became the headmaster of Abbotsholme, having been encouraged to apply for the job by his friend Jack Longland. Through Longland and Hodgkin, there was a natural link between Abbotsholme and White Hall. Derek Sederman, who taught at Abbotsholme for nearly forty years, recalled the early 1960s:

> Elite rock climbing and mountaineering took hold at Abbotsholme with the appointment of Robin Hodgkin as Headmaster … I started teaching at Abbotsholme in 1960 and the extent of my mountaineering was one Easter in the Ogwen Valley in North Wales and three weeks surveying a Norwegian Glacier. As PE Master I was introduced to something very new and challenging as I remember outings to the grit stone edges with Robin, Eric Langmuir and Joe Brown. Eric and Joe would bring canoeing parties from Whitehall down the River Dove, camping on the Games Fields at Abbotsholme which bordered The Dove. Not only were we fortunate in having top class enthusiasts leading us but we also had exceptional budding climbers in the School in Nick Longland, Mark Vallance and others.[15]

There are very few other references to White Hall groups canoeing on the Dove. In the late 1960s the upper Dove was patrolled by an infamous bailiff who, legend has it, once waded across the river and kicked a hole into the side of someone's canvas-covered canoe.

Jack Longland eventually became chairman of the Abbotsholme school council.

Joe Brown

Joe Brown joined the White Hall permanent staff in September 1961, after returning from a filming assignment in the Elburz mountains, northwest of Tehran. He was thirty-one (a few days after starting). He already had connections with White Hall, having worked with Geoff Sutton and Gordon Mansell on a climbing film for television in 1956–7. Of his appointment, he later said: 'I was not qualified as a teacher but in outdoor activities it was thought that I could hold my own.'[16]

Mansell too was not a qualified teacher. Mansell had studied at several colleges of art and was a talented artist. (Years later, he supplied the line drawings for Harold Drasdo's book, *The Ordinary Route*.) Eric Langmuir believed that the best teachers did not necessarily make the best instructors. He 'was adamant that an innate ability to imbue children with a love of outdoor sports was as important, if not more so, than formal qualifications.' Many years later, Langmuir rated Joe Brown, Gordon Mansell and John Cunningham (the Glaswegian ship-yard worker and renowned climber) as the best instructors he had ever known.[17]

Geoff Sutton viewed the appointments of Brown and Mansell as 'a sign of recognition by an enlightened Education Authority that a teacher is something more than a bundle of paper qualifications'. He said it was pleasant to know that each of them had been an outstanding success. Brown's success as a teacher, Sutton said, was due to his innate sincerity, enthusiasm, and poker-faced sense of humour.[18]

Because they lacked teaching qualifications, at first Brown and Man-sell were paid less than instructors who were qualified teachers. The HMI report of 1963 referred to this 'rather delicate matter of salaries'. Their salaries, the inspectors said, did not seem to be commensurate with their skill and responsibilities. This pay-scales anomaly was a national issue arising from centres like White Hall being still com-paratively rare, although their number was increasing.[19]

The willingness of Geoff Sutton and Eric Langmuir to appoint instructors without teaching qualifications was not an approach taken by all centre wardens. I remember one centre warden declaring, in the late 1960s, that he would never appoint a non-teacher to be an instructor.

Brown's prolific record of first ascents of rock climbs in Britain, along with his Alpine and Himalayan successes and his appearances in televised climbs, had made him into the climber most well known to, and admired by, the British public. His presence on the White Hall staff became a frequent ingredient of press reports or publicity connected with the centre. Parents who knew little about climbing – and perhaps some administrators and local politicians – may have been reassured to hear that such an immensely experienced and respected climber was overseeing the White Hall novices.

White Hall remained a stopping-off place for prominent climbers. Dennis Gray called there a few times in the early 1960s to see Joe and Valerie Brown, old friends. On a couple of occasions he accompanied Joe out with a group to Windgather and Castle Naze. Gray knew or came to know numerous people connected with White Hall, including Harold Drasdo, Geoff Sutton, Eric Langmuir, Lyn Noble, Jack Longland, Arthur Afford, and Bob Pettigrew.[20] Nobody would have anticipated that a decade later several of these climbers would be on opposite sides of the mountain training dispute.

The atmosphere of the early 1960s also comes across strongly in some remarks of Dennis Green, a member of the Cave and Crag club, looking back from 2015. In the early 1960s, Green and his wife were renting a cottage on a farm near Windgather Rocks. While out climbing one day, Green met A B Afford and his group. They talked, and Afford invited Green over to White Hall. Before long, Green found himself packing a Land Rover with food, equipment and his dog, and heading for Scotland to join the White Hall skiing course in the Cairngorms:

> We were camping on the road to the ski area. The second night we had a blizzard where the weight of the snow and the wind blew the tent away. I asked Eric Langmuir … if we could come down and stay at the hostel with them. He said, 'Yes, definitely.' So we moved in with them.
>
> The ski instructor was Frith Finlayson … We had a great week skiing and broken ribs to prove it. This was the time that the Austrian ski instructors moved into Scotland. The Austrians were winning all the medals in ski racing, so their skiing style was very popular.
>
> Joe Brown was not really into these fancy turns going downhill. His idea of skiing was to point the skis downhill and go for it. At times I think he must have reached about 40 miles an hour.

After a week's skiing I went home.

At White Hall they had a dance. We went over to the dance and most of the Rock and Ice Club were there. My wife said that dancing with Don Whillans was like dancing with a tornado – it was Rock and Roll in those days.[21]

For Joe Brown, life at the house on the hill met some dilemmas that probably made him unique among his peer group of instructors. As a high-profile professional, he frequently received requests for his presence on filming or mountaineering expeditions. 'In fact I was offered trips on so many expeditions during this period that I could have been away almost continuously for two years.'

In late 1961, soon after he arrived at White Hall, he was asked to join a proposed expedition to attempt the unclimbed Aiguille Poincenot in the Fitzroy group in Patagonia. But he could not obtain the necessary leave from his new job. He had to turn down the offer.[22]

He wrote to the organiser of one of the expeditions: 'We'll have to do the job in a fortnight, or I'll be taking the record for the shortest-lived instructor at White Hall.'[23]

In his autobiography *Hard Rock*, he mentioned some of the pros and cons of White Hall and of instructing in general. Here is Brown the climbing coach:

One of the advantages of White Hall over most centres is its ideal position. A lot of the climbing is on gritstone which is much better than Welsh or Lakeland volcanic rock for teaching beginners how to climb. For one thing you can look after parties much more easily because the crags are small, but the main point is that you can teach particular techniques more easily. For instance, if a lad isn't too good at jamming or laybacking, then on gritstone you can find a climb which has to be tackled by these techniques.[24]

And here is Brown the career adviser:

My first opportunity to work and live in the hills came with a job as an instructor at the White Hall Centre for Outdoor Pursuits. At first the life was terrific, with plenty of interesting things to do spread over most of the British Isles. But the disadvantages soon appeared: there is little compensation for being in the hills if you still have to work and cannot make the best of the position. Of course it is pleasant just to be there, but in some respects one tends not to appreciate the surroundings so much as during a normal weekend when one has spent the previous week working at a desk in a city, or, as in my case, doing property repairs in Manchester.[25]

The demands of full-time instructing do not appear to have curtailed Brown's pioneering. In 1961 he and Eric Langmuir found time to explore the wings of Dinas Mot in the Llanberis Pass, creating a fine route, The Mole. In 1964–5 John Cheesmond provided the transport for quite frequents trips to Wales. John accompanied Joe on a number of new routes at Tremadog and on Anglesey and on one new route on Clogwyn du'r Arddu.[26] Cheesmond recalls this period: 'While I'm sure Joe's "serious" climbing career would in all probability have been more active in that period if he had continued in his building business, his instructional climbing was far from completely unrewarding. I recall him waxing lyrical to me about various routes he had done with students on a number of occasions (South West Route on Rosa Pinnacle on Arran, as an example).'

Several innovations at this time stemmed from Joe's inventiveness and ingenuity. The first was the Chapel Traverse, which is a Derbyshire version of Wasdale's Barn Door Traverse. In the early 1960s, before the shower block was built, all four exterior walls of the chapel were accessible. Brown, 'through constant practice, was able to complete seven complete rounds wearing bedroom slippers and smoking a cigarette – few could do one traverse wearing the proper equipment'.[27]

The next Brown innovation was the development of an improvised weight-drop machine:

> For two days Joe hung in slings thirty feet up a tree drilling holes through the trunk. From the platform that eventually appeared we all played about, dropping weights to simulate falling leaders. We did this mainly to test Joe's advocacy of the shoulder belay. Pete Crew was beguiled into an argument over the relative merits of waist and shoulder belays and was persuaded to try the machine. The man-weight falling stone left both of them writhing on the platform: Pete in surprise and pain and Joe in hysterical laughter.[28]

Weight-drop machines are used in industry for many different investigations. In the climbing context, you can use them to simulate a falling climber, either to practise belaying or to test the strength of equipment.

In the days of the waist belay and before sports climbing, practice on a weight-drop machine was a valuable exercise. Brown's improvised weight-drop was one of the earliest of such things but not the first. A climber had experimented with a falling weight in 1909, and had found 'that 10 stone dropping 10 feet would break a belayed rope, if the belay were less than 8 inches diameter'.[29] In the late 1940s, after Ken Tarbuck had invented a shock-absorbing knot, he subjected his system to fifty experimental drops.[30] In the 1960s at Glenmore Lodge, the improvised weight-drop arrangement sometimes took the form of a sack of rocks and a real cliff and a pair of thick gloves.

The reactions of the belayer during weight-dropping were not always amusing. A student belayed at the top of an early Glenmore Lodge climbing tower, and attempting to hold a falling sack, sustained a broken leg, a situation that required a complicated stretcher lower from the belay platform.[31]

Plas-y-Brenin gained a purpose-built weight drop in the 1960s. One based on the Plas-y-Brenin design was built at White Hall by Dave Edwards in the late 1970s.

Another Joe Brown project was a programme of building fibreglass kayaks, which led to his fabricating a fibreglass canoeing helmet, which was then modified to become a climbing helmet. Making one helmet at a time was slow and tedious, and so he made some moulds. Before long he was making twelve helmets at a time, a boost in productivity unusual in British industry of that era. According to Kim Meldrum, it was soon after Joe discovered that he had made fifty helmets that he decided to move to Llanberis and open his shop.[32] He left White Hall in December 1965, just in time to join a small select group, picking off the untouched plums at Gogarth.[33]

In the mid-1970s, long after Brown's four years of instructing in Derbyshire, White Hall groups were still occasionally using the whole or parts of his cleverly thought-out 1960s map and compass course that circled the Goyt and Combs valleys for thirty kilometres. No preparation of checkpoints was required, because each of the twenty-one checkpoints comprised about six numbers carved into stone, usually on a wall, each number being about four centimetres high. Sometimes the numbers were a six-figure grid reference of the next checkpoint. Sometimes they were a grid compass bearing and a distance in yards to the next checkpoint. No checkpoint was more than about an hour and a half's walk from White Hall. This distorted oblong, a demanding day's walk for fit hillwalkers, was known as Joe's carved-number circuit.

Chatting in 2016 to John Cheesmond about this circuit, Joe thought that, while he was at White Hall, no course member or members ever completed it in a single day, although one group of mid-teenage boys came very close to doing so.[34]

By the late 1970s, even for capable secondary pupils, easier map and compass courses and exercises had replaced Joe's circuit. Nowadays, White Hall does not promote or facilitate the use of the circuit. It was an educational facility, never intended for public usage. However, the circuit has proved vulnerable to rediscovery by the occasional connoisseur. Much of the circuit is still accessible, being open-access land.

Today, despite intense scrutiny, Brown's reputation as the colossus of 1950s climbing remains as strong as ever, having never suffered anything more damaging than the recognition that his legs were too short for running.[35]

Chapel Traverse, west wall, sometime between 1961 and 1969. On the left is Dave Allsop ('Soppy'), on the right is Keith Worsencroft ('Worm'). Both were voluntary instructors. They were members of the Eldon Pothole Club and were better known as cavers than climbers. Keith's son Mike comments: 'Never seen my dad that far off the ground in daylight, he must have had his eyes closed.'

Manchester Daily Mail.

Joe Brown instructing rock climbing at Windgather Rocks. Sometime in 1961–5.

HMI Inspection, 1963

Her Majesty's Inspectors for schools looked closely at White Hall in the summer of 1963. The inspectors' report expressed much confidence in the centre and particularly in all the staff – teaching and domestic.

The inspectors noted that voluntary instructors numbered over 150. They wrote that 'the mere existence of such an army of volunteers speaks volumes for the spirit of White Hall and the loyalty and enthusiasm which the Principal has inspired. It is a very real measure of the achievement of the centre in its first twelve and a half years.'[36]

In describing the purpose of the centre, the inspectors contented themselves with three lines, quoted from the annual course programme: the centre was a place 'where young people could learn the skills of living and moving with safety in hilly country, and in doing so learn to master themselves and their environment'.

Underlying the encouraging tone of the report was the premise that the techniques of living and moving safely in the hills were educationally desirable abilities. The inspectors took this for granted. Reading this report today, it comes across as delightfully lacking in sophisticated theoretical exposition.

The report said little about field studies (or environmental studies). Its only allusion to this area of education was brief and, in part, tentative: 'There is also much to be said for including in the programme, particularly in the hillcraft exercises, more systematic practice than is now given in observation of the weather, the rocks and vegetation and so forth. A case might even be made for asking students to produce a simple, informal record of such matters on paper.' This issue will crop up again in the 1970s, in Chapter 18.

The HMI report briefly mentions report-writing. Whether individual reports were written for pupils on standard schools' courses in the Langmuir period is not known. But they were certainly being written for the course members on youth service specialist courses: 'Each instructor is in charge of the same group throughout each stage. He lives with them, works with them, corrects their theory papers and writes a brief report on each member at the end of the course. Successful members receive a certificate at the completion of each stage of their training.'[37] (Later, on schools' courses in the Meldrum period, short individual reports were compiled by Kim Meldrum, with input from the instructors. On schools' course in the 1970s and 80s, each White Hall group instructor wrote a course report for each of his or her ten pupils.)

The inspectors mentioned that all the White Hall canoes were fibreglass, but that the fleet had been put to demanding use on the rocky River Derwent and needed replacing. In a rare reference to a technical matter, the inspectors reported that the canoes had barely enough buoyancy.

Some remarks on the inspectors' description of the buildings will appear in the next section.

The involvement of Her Majesty's Inspectorate in outdoor activities went back a long way. Earlier in the century, one or two individual HMIs, such as Geoffrey Winthrop Young, had personally promoted the value of activities like camping and sailing. After the 1963 inspection of White Hall, for nearly thirty years members of HMI would contribute frequently and valuably to the development of outdoor education. Their involvement would include committee work, advising, surveying, developing curricula, inspecting outdoor centres, speaking at conferences and initiating all manner of meetings. This would end in 1992 with the disbanding of HMI and its replacement, for schools in England and Wales, by the Office for Standards in Education (Ofsted).

The Mansion House and Transport

As well as endorsing Eric Langmuir's leadership and teaching skills, the inspectors in summer 1963 wrote that '[the principal's] wife holds the position of housekeeper, a post which brings with it unusual demands and difficulties in a centre such as this. She has met them all with skill and imperturbable good humour and has contributed not a little to the delightful spirit of White Hall.'[38] Arthur Afford records that Maureen Langmuir was a great influence in the White Hall community both as the housekeeper and as an expedition member on occasions. Also, the presence in the house of firstly the Sutton children and then the Langmuir children added to the family atmosphere.

Catriona, Moira and Roddy Langmuir on the front lawn, early 1960s.

White Hall at this time was still taking groups of a maximum of thirty. (In the late 1960s this total rose to forty, and at some point a full-time housekeeper was appointed.)

Of the non-teaching staff of this period, George Stone and Tom Round became legends. Bert and Doris Heathcote arrived about 1963–4. Bert was a charismatic addition to the White Hall populace, never short of a word and irrepressibly generous with trinkets of inside information.

By the end of 1962, nearly every room in the house and in the older stable-yard building was in use. Things were settling down. The basic division of the house into dormitories, student lounge, briefing room, office, staff quarters, kitchen, drying room, storeroom and workshop was nearly complete, but some of the furniture and fittings needed replacing.

Only one room was still empty and unused. In 1963 this room, in the stable block, was converted into a space for ten students, in an arrangement similar to the interior of an alpine hut, with a wide communal bunk. This room, an outpost away from the main house, became the base for the Mobile Unit, run by Afford and described by the inspectors later in the year as 'a project with many interesting possibilities'.

Each mobile course, of four or five days, would spend one or two nights here and the other nights away camping. The inspectors may not have been familiar with the sleeping platform of alpine huts. They said: 'This is acceptable in these unusual circumstances for one or at most two nights, but only if numbers are kept down to eight, all, as goes without saying, of one sex, and if the present small window is enlarged to provide something better than the present quite inadequate ventilation.'[39]

The inspectors' report listed many inadequacies of the main building:

> A nineteenth century manor house has certain advantages as a centre for training young people but it is also likely to need a good deal of modification if it is to be really satisfactory ... sleeping is in service-type double-tiered bunks which are now reaching the end of their life and should be replaced by furniture designed for the purpose ... the least satisfactory feature of the domestic arrangements is the provision for bathing. There are at the present day only two baths for instructors, and two baths and three ancient showers for students ... the whole [bath and shower] arrangement requires redesigning ... [also] it is suggested that a complete investigation of the sewage disposal system should be undertaken

... it is also suggested that there should be an investigation of the methods used for purification of the domestic water supply ...

Since the centre has abundantly proved its value and clearly ought to continue it should be given facilities properly designed for the purpose.[40]

These improvements, the inspectors acknowledged, would entail considerable expense. They suggested that it could be economical in the long run to extend the student accommodation from thirty to forty.

In about 1963, White Hall acquired a Safari long-wheelbase diesel Land Rover. It now had two Land Rovers. The inspectors' report commented briefly on transport: 'It is essential that the centre should have its own transport for taking students to the scenes of their activities. This is provided by two standard trucks with four-wheel drive. So arduous are the conditions under which they operate that their useful life is relatively short. It might be sound policy to replace one, in due course, with a larger vehicle.'[41] The Age of the Minibus was still some years away.

Arthur B ('AB') Afford

AB joined the White Hall permanent teaching staff in 1958. It is likely that he had worked previously as a voluntary instructor at weekends. He left White Hall in 1965. So he saw the end of Sutton's wardenship, the whole of Langmuir's and the start of Meldrum's. But his introducing young people to the outdoors had begun before White Hall Centre existed.

Arthur Bernard Afford was born in 1915 in Kings Norton, Birmingham. In about 1929, at the age of fourteen, he joined the Cyclists' Touring Club. Before the war he trained in pharmacy and was employed in social work.

Afford was about fifteen years older than his later White Hall colleagues. Thus, he was of the Peter Mosedale generation, whose young men went to war. He was in the Royal Army Medical Corps from 1940 to 1945, serving as a nursing orderly and pathology laboratory assistant. On 15 April 1945, the British army liberated the concentration camp Bergen-Belsen. Afford spent the late spring and summer assigned to the General Hospital at Belsen Camp.[42] Over 35,000 prisoners had died between January and mid-April. Another 28,000 prisoners died in the weeks after liberation.

He joined Birmingham's Cave and Crag Club in 1947 or 1948. In April 2013, Roy Morgan, a member of that club, contributed a few memories to the club's newsletter. Roy's recollections stretched elastically back to a time before White Hall Centre existed. In them we glimpse Arthur Afford and his – probably much loved – bicycle:

> First Meeting with A B Afford
> Early in 1947 when Brian Hogan and I were 11 years old together with some members of our little gang, we became interested in natural history, caterpillars and other creepy crawlies. After school we would set off on expeditions around the neighbourhood, searching in people's gardens and hedges for our prey.
>
> One evening upon our return to our home territory we met with another of our gang who was talking to a man on a bike. We stopped and were introduced to Arthur who was at that time connected to the local scout troop. He asked us what we'd got in our jam jars and after a poke around in the greenery within, promptly identified our collection. We chatted for a while then finally he said he would take us for a hike in the countryside but we first of all must obtain our parents' permission. This accomplished we were introduced to the footpaths and country lanes of Warwickshire the following Saturday.
>
> This chance meeting with A B Afford resulted in an early meeting with the Birmingham Cave and Crag Club with visits to Dave (Digger) Williams's parents' house where we helped to manufacture and assemble rope ladders for use in caving and of course our visits to Wetton and the Gateham dig.
>
> Brian and I are the only two of our little gang who, at attaining the age of eighteen became members of the Cave and Crag and are still active today …[43]

Roy Morgan's account shows that Afford was introducing young people to the outdoors as early as 1947. Andy Hemsted, the club's newsletter editor, added a fraction more to the picture: 'Though I'm a relatively new arrival in the Cave & Crag, the name of AB Afford comes up often when our older members are reminiscing. I don't think that he took a large part in club organising, but he certainly steered youngsters in the direction of the coach trips which were run at weekends by the club.'

At least two of those young people, Roy Morgan and Brian Hogan – and possibly many others – had enjoyed a lifetime of hillwalking and climbing or caving, thanks partly or even wholly to Afford's spotting and encouraging their budding interests.

There are several mentions of Afford caving in south Wales in the early 1950s. The Rawl Series of large chambers above the stream passage in Ogof Ffynnon Ddu was named after the four people who were present at its discovery in 1950: Railton, Afford, Wild and Little.[44] Afford also took part in exploration at Ffrydiau Twrch in south Wales in 1951[45] and 1954.[46]

After the war, he trained to be a teacher and then spent eleven years teaching in Manchester and Birmingham before moving to White Hall in 1958.[47] The HMI report of 1963 listed his outdoor experience as walking, caving, climbing and canoeing.[48] Harold Drasdo later called him an 'elder statesman and guru' of the Cave & Crag Club.[49]

The following eloquent tribute from *High Peak* (1966) bears the stamp of Geoff Sutton:

> [Arthur Afford] is a kind of genius with young people, to whom his life has been entirely devoted. His genuine affection for hordes of youngsters entirely as individual personalities, his Rabelaisian sense of humour, his musical gifts, his immense energy and yet his essential loneliness all found a setting and a means of expression at White Hall. After two or three years as an Assistant Warden he was given the authorisation to develop his own idea of a mobile-unit course separate from though based on White Hall.[50]

In 2014, Frank Salt, who was a member of the Cave and Crag Club in the 1950s, retained clear memories of AB:

> AB had a love of the outdoors and a dynamic urge to help young people escape to the mountains but at the same time was a very solitary person who could be reclusive. In hindsight many of his ways, reactions and lifestyle would today be regarded as typical post-traumatic stress symptoms … AB never spoke of his life before the Cave and Crag Club in 1947.
>
> One tale about him concerned the decoration of his room at White Hall which was carried out whilst he was away on holiday. Eric Langmuir selected a sample pattern of wall paper for his room, in his absence, little realising that the small sheet of colour was actually only a small section of a mass of coloured and angled rectangles. The end effect made the walls look like they

were sloping and leaning in. One of the other instructors, who was also an artist [Gordon Mansell] found the effect so disturbing that he couldn't stay in the room for any length of time. AB came back from holiday and didn't even notice that his room had been redecorated. My guess is that AB saw only the contents, not the box. Something that he did with people as well as rooms.

He was a great and lovely person.[51]

Afford left White Hall in 1964 to teach in Buxton. Mark Lambert, who knew him well, recalls the effect: 'I remember thinking that his departure from White Hall to what was then Kents Bank School was a great loss to the place and I seem to remember that Kim felt the same.'[52]

White Hall's loss was Buxton's gain, as Afford made a characteristic impact back in the classroom, which Mike Worsencroft makes clear:

AB was the most popular teacher in the school [Buxton College] and no kid was a lost cause with AB, he had time for them all and as I remember spent much of his own time introducing kids to the outdoors. Even the most disruptive of kids had time and respect for AB and he was something of a legend as I remember. On saying that though, I don't think he stood any messing. Treated the kids well and expected the same in return … I seem to remember him … having a few stress related issues … I think he had suffered some misfortune in the past … From what I remember though he was a real character and would be remembered very fondly by all the kids of Buxton College.[53]

Afford retired in about 1975. In 1978 he self-published *The Story of White Hall Open Country Pursuits Centre* (in two parts). This account cleverly put together the written contributions of five White Hall wardens or principals. It has become a significant historical source.

Mountain and Cave Rescue – Langmuir Period

In October 1962, White Hall hosted the first conference organised by the Mountain Rescue Committee, to which rescue-post supervisors from all over Britain were invited.

At some point in his principalship, Langmuir suggested to one of his instructors, Howard Hodgkinson, that a more formal rescue team be set up in Buxton using the expertise of some of the White Hall staff. This conversation led to the formation of Buxton Mountain Rescue Team, which was operational by mid-1963, with Hodgkinson as its first team leader. At this early stage, the team used the equipment from the White Hall rescue post.[54]

National Developments – Langmuir Period

On 3 February 1960 the Albemarle Committee reported on the needs of the youth service in England and Wales. The report described the youth service as in a critical condition, held back by economic restrictions. Furthermore, the end of national service in 1960 was expected to return an estimated 200,000 men aged between eighteen and twenty to civilian life. The report recommended an expansion in both voluntary and paid workers and in buildings and facilities for sport.[55]

The Albemarle Report explicitly recognised the value of challenge for young people, thus helping to establish a basic rationale for adventure education: 'Some of the most arousing challenges to individual achievement come from enterprises which have to be corporately met, as in exploration or mountaineering, for then the individual satisfies his [or her] own longing to achieve something worth while by contributing to the group effort.'[56] The government accepted the committee's recommendations. Jack Longland later said that the report's emphasis on challenge and adventure training had affected activities in the youth service and in schools.[57]

In September 1960 the Wolfenden Committee released its report on games, sport and outdoor activities. Longland and all but one of the other committee members all held full-time and responsible positions in other work, 'yet for over two and a half years they [had] spent what must have seemed endless hours absorbing immense piles of circulated evidence and attending meetings on 58 days.'[58]

The creation of a Sports Development Council was the committee's main recommendation. The report praised the work of the CCPR. The committee found a shortage of facilities in each of the three main groups. Facilities for outdoor activities were mainly provided by nature in mountains, rivers, the open country and the sea. Restrictions on their use, the committee said, should be reduced.[59]

On the subject of outdoor activities, the committee's remarks had 'Longland' written all over them:

> We can no longer look to ... the well-established clubs to guide the steps of all those who, trained or not, are determined to have a go at one or other outdoor pursuit. And there is difficulty and danger here. In most other sports beginners can at wish or at need teach themselves by simply trying and practising. Coaching will probably help them to learn more quickly and with fewer mistakes, but trial and error will not usually lead to disaster. But in many outdoor activities there is an element of danger. In fact this element may be not only integral to the sport, but part of the attraction to those who wish to pursue it. It is not that actual danger is enjoyed for its own sake; its presence usually means that the situation has got out of control. What is clear is that the means of mastering potential dangers is to be found only in technique and applied experience ...
>
> An important point is that many outdoor activities, unlike some other sports and games, demand a high proportion of coaches to learners. For this reason, we express the hope that many more of the most experienced and active participants will find the time and the enthusiasm to coach those who are just beginning.[60]

In some outdoor pursuits, this was beginning to happen. In 1959 and 1960, John Dudderidge, a BCU representative, toured the country selecting people upon whom to build a coaching scheme. In September 1961 the BCU set up its national coaching committee.[61]

The Wolfenden Committee's main recommendation was ignored until the Labour Party, having pledged to create a sports council, won the October 1964 general election.[62]

Longland's services, and his personal charm, remained in demand. In 1961 he chaired a CCPR conference on using reservoirs and other restricted waters for recreational purposes. In December 1961 he was appointed to the council of the Outward Bound Trust, a position he would hold until February 1974 (when he would become a vice-president of the trust).[63]

He also found time to write a forward to Gwen Moffat's autobiographical account *Space Below My Feet*, an uninhibited story whose importance has increased with age. Moffat, according to one recent interpretation, 'took the pre-war construal of a woman mountaineer as a donnish, wealthy, leisured woman and ripped it to shreds, re-defining women mountaineers and the mountaineering world within the cultural and social context of the post-war period.'[64]

March 1962 saw a rare dent in the Longland charisma. In the heat of an unscripted discussion during *Any Questions?*, Longland and another panel member, Lord Boothby, criticised several staff members of Beaverbrook Newspapers 'in an intemperate manner'. In July, after action in the high court, Longland and Boothby paid substantial damages to the Beaverbrook journalists.[65]

Later that year, Chris Bonington and Ian Clough made the first British ascent of the north face of the Eiger, an event that propelled Bonington – and climbing in general – into the media spotlight.

A third report, the Newsom Report on the education of pupils aged from 13 to16 and of average or below average ability was published on 17 October 1963. This was a couple of months after Eric Langmuir had left White Hall, but I will include it here to keep the three reports together.

John Newsom was a former county education officer for Hertfordshire (1940–57). In 1940–2, when Jack Longland was Newsom's deputy, Hertfordshire had been the only LEA to embrace wholeheartedly Hahn's County Badge scheme. Also on the Newsom Committee was Alec Clegg, chief education officer for the West Riding (1945–74) and described by Lynn Cook as a man for whom 'the substance of education in the secondary school was the development of the total personality which, all too readily, he thought, tended to give way to the measurable.' Clegg believed that 'outdoor activities could motivate and "bolster" children, enhance pupil-teacher relationships, facilitate learning through the environment and ultimately enable children to become responsible members of society'.[66]

In a radical move, the Newsom Report interpreted the word 'education' to include extra-curricular activities. The report applauded the value of residential experience for all pupils towards the end of their compulsory schooling. The committee had seen much evidence confirming the value of living away from home for a short period, in a fairly small and intimate group, and in a novel environment:

This is variously achieved through school journeys and expeditions, camps, or residential courses of different types, lasting, generally, anything from a weekend to a month ... we noted with admiration the enterprise of many schools in this respect.

The residential courses ... take many forms. Some of them lay great stress on strenuous, outdoor, physical activity: some schools successfully combine courses of this kind with work in school for the Duke of Edinburgh's award scheme; and one school known to us in Scotland integrates an 'adventure course' with its normal curriculum. Other courses are based on field studies of local plant and animal life, geography, geology, or history ... Variety is to be welcomed. Not all pupils' needs or interests are the same, and there would be nothing at all to be gained from uniformity.

By introducing boys and girls to fresh surroundings, and helping them to acquire new knowledge or try their hand at new skills, they provide a general educational stimulus. Many pupils, including some who were far from successful in normal school work, seem to come back with a new zest for everything they do: one headmaster described girls returning from a three-weeks' residential course as 'having a sort of glow about them' ... There is little doubt that many pupils benefit from these experiences in their personal and social development.[67]

Lynn Cook has commented in general and individually on the Albemarle, Wolfenden and Newsom reports. Referring to all three, she linked some of the influences behind them with the social conditions of the early 1960s, when a large increase in the number of fifteen-year-olds leaving school was anticipated:

The various initiatives recommended in the reports appear to suggest that outdoor activities are a corrective for some of the perceived 'ills' of society, especially insofar as young people were held to be directly responsible for them. The initiatives need to be seen in the context of an enduring preoccupation of politicians, educationists and welfare workers with the way in which young people, particularly working-class boys, occupied their leisure time.[68]

Looking at the recommendations of each of these reports, Cook suggests that the Albemarle Report promoted outdoor activities mainly as a means of making character-building activities more widely available, the Wolfenden Report as a response to the demand for increased leisure facilities in the outdoors, and the Newsom Report as a response to social needs. All three reports assumed, she says, that the behaviour of adolescents could be moulded by the intervention of adults in order that their 'characters and energies' be channelled into 'new and potentially more positive directions'.[69]

These three reports of the early 1960s amounted, collectively, to a significant promotion of outdoor education. However, as we have seen, White Hall Centre had already distanced itself from character building. Chapter 12 will show that, as the 1960s passed, the terms 'character training' and 'character building' would come under increasing scrutiny nationally.

*

Before arriving at White Hall, Eric Langmuir had spent a year teaching science at Wimbledon Independent Grammar School, and before that he had worked in Canada for about three years as a field exploration geologist. Unlike Longland, he hadn't been involved in the 1953 conference at the Alpine Club, at which delegates discussed standards in mountain training. Nor had he taken part, as far as I know, in any subsequent national debate on the matter. But a year in charge at White Hall changed that. Concerned about the growing number of accidents happening to school hillwalking parties and uneasy about climbing accidents caused by inexperience, in about August 1960 he raised the issues in *Mountaineering*, the bulletin of the BMC:

> … the appalling increase in the number of [rock climbing] accidents – the average this season in North Wales alone has been one every eight days … What are we doing to tackle this problem? Obviously the answer is not for bigger and better Rescue Organisations. We must examine the roots of the question which lie in the training and leadership of the thousands of young people who are now taking to the hills.

The article also mentioned that in the ten years since White Hall had opened, almost 15,000 students had attended courses there without a single serious accident. This article marked the beginning of Langmuir's years of working to improve the training of novices and to lift the skills of instructors and leaders.[70]

In 1961 the CCPR published its booklet *Safety on Mountains*, written by the staff of Plas y Brenin and illustrated by the White Hall instructor Gordon Mansell. (Still in print and now published by the BMC, the latest edition being 2010.)

An illustration from the booklet *Safety on Mountains*, written by the staff of Plas y Brenin, illustrated by the White Hall instructor Gordon Mansell, and first published by the CCPR in 1961. It met a need and went through several print runs.

On 5 October 1962, EMI Studios released the Beatles' first single, 'Love Me Do'; massive social change was imminent. On 15–16 October 1962, Longland and Langmuir both attended the first conference of the mountain centres, held at Plas y Brenin. Longland, as president of the BMC, chaired the assembly. Langmuir also took a prominent role, sitting on a panel of heads from four different types of centre. This conference, with fifty-three official attendees, was the first organised gathering of the scattered outdoor professionals.[71]

Delegates discussed the growing number of mountain accidents involving schoolchildren. There was widespread agreement that inadequate leadership was the primary factor in the cause of most of these accidents. Too many children were taken to the mountains by teachers who had too little experience. The delegates were divided on how the accident rate could be reduced. 'Jack Longland … said that during the past few years there had been "an explosion" of young people into the mountains. Education authorities and youth organisations had a responsibility to meet that challenge.'[72]

This conference now occupies a notable place in the history of UK outdoor education. Ken Ogilvie has summed this up: 'This milestone conference was hugely important for a number of reasons. It met two newly arisen needs – a network for the centre wardens and tentative support for some kind of mountain activities training scheme.'[73]

At White Hall four months later, Langmuir hosted an informal meeting of wardens to discuss setting up a wardens' group. The wardens needed to be able to communicate with others in similar situations, share information and give mutual support. The group decided to call itself the Association of Wardens of Mountain Centres (AWMC).[74]

Both Longland and Langmuir were now involved in national committee work, at the heart of pioneering developments, as well as coping with the everyday demands of their main jobs. This would continue for years, involving successive White Hall principals.

*

It is now August 1963. What stage have maps and equipment reached?

For some parts of the UK in 1963, there are now inch-to-the-mile topographic maps that show rights of way, mainly public footpaths and bridleways. The first sheet had been published in 1959.[75]

1963 is the centenary of the tent manufacturer and outdoor equipment company Thomas Black and Sons (Greenock). The firm's turnover has increased by five times in the last ten years.[76]

The use of nylon rope in climbing has led to changes in belaying technique. Many climbers are now using a hemp waist line to which the end of the climbing rope is attached by a karabiner. The shoulder belay is well on the way out; the waist belay, using controlled sliding friction, is becoming the normal method. It is several years since Kenneth Tarbuck, a knot inventor and advocate of the new methods, ran a staff-training session at White Hall. However, on White Hall schools' courses, attaching oneself to the end of a climbing rope is still achieved using a bowline knot. (Nylon-webbing waistbelts are under development, harnesses have not yet been invented.) Nearly all rock climbing by school pupils takes place wearing walking boots. In the White Hall store, sixty pairs of boots are available for students, but a bigger stock is needed, to cope with both school pupils and adults.

On White Hall courses, caving is still done using carbide lights and wearing woollen grots (old jerseys) and cotton boiler-suits.

Wool is still the unrivalled fibre for underwear, shirts and jerseys. Polypropylene and fleecewear are some years away. Anoraks are cotton. (In 1964 the fourth edition of *Safety on Mountains* suggested that 'a plastic mackintosh … can be invaluable for wearing over the anorak in a heavy downpour'.) Overtrousers are seldom seen. Helly-Hansen heavy PVC-on-cotton sailing jackets and overtrousers have not yet arrived from Norway. Waterproofed nylon cloth is under development.

Up in Penrith, the pupils of Ullswater School have had the use of an indoor climbing wall for three years, Britain's first purpose-built wall having been constructed there in 1960.[77] (A photograph in *Artificial Climbing Walls* shows a mainly-blank wall with a few protruding or missing bricks, certainly nothing to match the Cambridge classics, such as the complex South Face of Caius.)

*

In August 1963 the Langmuirs moved to Scotland, Eric to run Glenmore Lodge. He played a prominent part – at times a crucial diplomatic role – in the formation of the Scottish MLTB.[78] In 1969 the first edition of his book *Mountain Leadership* was published. It has since dominated its particular niche in the market; in 2013 a fourth edition came out.

At Glenmore he became frequently involved in mountain rescue, chaired the Scottish Mountain Rescue Committee and researched the properties and behaviour of avalanches. In January 1968 his work on the mechanical characteristics of snow gained an extra empirical element when he and three companions were swept 300 feet down Cairngorm, one man being buried seriously enough to lose consciousness.[79] In 1970, Moray House College of Education in Edinburgh appointed him specifically to lecture on outdoor education, the college's first such appointment.[80] In 1972 he became senior lecturer for a one-year post-graduate course in outdoor activities and environmental studies. In 1986 he was appointed MBE for his mountain-rescue work and his avalanche research.

Notes

1   Michael J O'Hara, 'Eric Duncan Grant Langmuir', Royal Society of Edinburgh (2006) <http://www.royalsoced.org.uk/cms/files/fellows/obits_alpha/Langmuir_e.pdf> [accessed 31 Aug 2014].

2   Geoffrey Crowther, *15 to 18: A Report of the Central Advisory Council for Education (England)*, 2 vols (London: HMSO, 1959), vol. 1, pp. 28–47.

3   Ibid., pp. 45–46.

4   'Getting a Firm Foothold in Open-country Skills', *Guardian*, 6 Mar 1961, p. 19.

5   Ibid.

6   'Wallabies and Yaks' (2014) <http://www.roaches.org.uk/wallabies.htm> [accessed 4 Feb 2015].

7   Robert Foulke, Email to P McDonald, subject 'The Story of White Hall Centre', 4 Feb 2015 [Email].

8   A B Afford, *The Story of White Hall Open Country Pursuits Centre; vol. 2* (Buxton, Derbyshire, UK: A B Afford, 1978), p. 19.

9   'Getting a Firm Foothold in Open-country Skills', *Guardian*, 6 Mar 1961, p. 19.

10   H M Inspectors, *Report by H. M. Inspectors on White Hall Centre for Open Count[r]y Pursuits, Buxton, Derbyshire* (London: Ministry of Education, 1963), pp. 6–10.

11   Ibid., p. 7.

12   'Boys Invited on 260-mile Walk', *Guardian*, 23 Mar 1961, p. 7.

13   H M Inspectors, *Report by H. M. Inspectors on White Hall Centre for Open Count[r]y Pursuits, Buxton, Derbyshire* (London: Ministry of Education, 1963), pp. 8–9.

14   A B Afford, *The Story of White Hall Open Country Pursuits Centre; vol. 2* (Buxton, Derbyshire, UK: A B Afford, 1978), p. 21.

15   Derek Sederman, Email to P McDonald, subject 'McDonald P 2015 05 18', 18 May 2015 [Email].

16   Joe Brown, *The Hard Years* (1967; repr. London: Penguin Books, 1975), 147–148.

17   Jeff Connor, *Creagh Dhu Climber: The Life and Times of John Cunningham* (no place given: Ernest Press, 1999), pp. 172–173.

18   Eric Byne and Geoffrey Sutton, *High Peak: The Story of Walking and Climbing in the Peak District* (London: Secker and Warburg, 1966), p. 191.

19   H M Inspectors, *Report by H. M. Inspectors on White Hall Centre for Open Count[r]y Pursuits, Buxton, Derbyshire* (London: Ministry of Education, 1963), pp. 3, 17.

20   Dennis Gray, Email to P McDonald, subject 'White Hall Centre Archive', 19 Aug 2014 [Email].

21   Dennis Green, Email to A Hemsted, subject 'White Hall Memories', 25 Apr 2015 [Email].

22   Jim Perrin, *The Villain: The Life of Don Whillans* (London: Arrow, 2006), pp. 221–222.

23   Joe Brown, *The Hard Years* (1967; repr. London: Penguin Books, 1975), p. 148.

24   Ibid., p. 226.

25   Ibid., p. 11.

26   John Cheesmond, Email to P McDonald, subject 'Impact of the Outdoors', 9 June 2016 [Email].

27   Kim Meldrum and Brian Royle, *Artificial Climbing Walls* (London: Pelham Books, 1970), p. 51.

28   K I Meldrum, 'White Hell Pursuing Centre', *Climbers' Club Journal: 1966*, 15, no. 1 (new series) (1966), pp. 61–67 (p. 63).

29   T C Ormiston-Chant, 'The Rope in Climbing', *Sunday Times*, 10 Oct 1909, p. 13.

30   *The First Fifty Years of the British Mountaineering Council*, ed. by Geoff Milburn, Derek Walker and Ken Wilson (Manchester: British Mountaineering Council, 1997), pp. 287–289.

31   Steve Mitchell, Email to P McDonald, subject 'Sack-dropping', 28 Oct 2014 [Email].

32   K I Meldrum, 'White Hell Pursuing Centre', *Climbers' Club Journal: 1966*, 15, no. 1 (new series) (1966), pp. 61–67 (pp. 65–66).

33   Peter Gillman, 'A Dinosaur in Wales', *Sunday Times*, 22 Jan 1967, p. 18.

34   John Cheesmond, Email to P McDonald, subject 'White Hall', 8 Feb 2016 [Email].

35   Dennis Gray, *Tight Rope! The Fun of Climbing* (Holyhead, Wales: Ernest Press, 1993), pp. 47–51, 61.

36   H M Inspectors, *Report by H. M. Inspectors on White Hall Centre for Open Count[r]y Pursuits, Buxton, Derbyshire* (London: Ministry of Education, 1963), p. 3.

37   Ibid., p. 10.

38   Ibid., pp. 2–3.

39   Ibid., pp. 4–5.

40   Ibid., pp.4–5.

41   Ibid., p. 5.

42   'KZ Lager Concentration Camp Items', Snyder's Treasures – Premium Militaria Collectables (no date) <http://snyderstreasures.com/pages/kz.htm> [accessed 21 Apr 2015].

43   Roy Morgan, 'Cave and Crag News: April 2013: Roy Morgan Sends These Memories' (Apr 2013) <http://www.caveandcrag.co.uk/blog/wp-content/uploads/bsk-pdf-manager/1_Newsletter-April-2013.pdf> [accessed 17 June 2014].

44   Peter I W Harvey, 'Ogof Ffynnon Ddu: Continued Exploration 1947-53', South Wales Caving Club (Mar 2009) <http://www.swcc.org.uk/aboutswcc/history/members/piwh_1/furtherexplorationofdl.php> [accessed 21 Apr 2015].

45   'South Wales Caving Club: Newsletter No. 1: May 1952' (May 1952) <http://www.swcc.org.uk/aboutswcc/newslett/archive/No_01.pdf> [accessed 21 June 2014].

46   'South Wales Caving Club: Newsletter No. 10: October 1954' (Oct 1954) <http://www.swcc.org.uk/aboutswcc/newslett/archive/No_10.pdf> [accessed 21 June 2014].

47   H M Inspectors, *Report by H. M. Inspectors on White Hall Centre for Open Count[r]y Pursuits, Buxton, Derbyshire* (London: Ministry of Education, 1963), p. 18.

48   Ibid., p. 18.

49   Harold Drasdo, *The Ordinary Route* (Ty Croes, Wales: Ernest Press, 1997), p. 102.

50   Eric Byne and Geoffrey Sutton, *High Peak: The Story of Walking and Climbing in the Peak District* (London: Secker and Warburg, 1966), pp. 190–191.

51   Frank Salt, Email to P McDonald, subject 'A B Afford', 21 Apr 2015 [Email].

52   Mark Lambert, Email to P McDonald, subject 'AB Afford', 31 Jan 2016 [Email].

53   Mike Worsencroft, Email to P McDonald, subject 'AB Afford', 25 Jan 2016 [Email].

54   Roger Bennett and Ian Hurst, *Mountain Rescue: History and Development in the Peak District, 1920s-Present Day* (Stroud: Tempus Publishing, 2007).

55   'Youth Service to Be Expanded', *Guardian*, 4 Feb 1960, p. 6.

56 Ministry of Education, *The Youth Service in England and Wales: Report of the Committee Appointed by the Minister of Education in November, 1958 [Albemarle report]* (London: H.M.S.O., 1960), p. 61.

57 Ken C Ogilvie, *Roots and Wings: A History of Outdoor Education and Outdoor Learning in the UK* (Lyme Regis, UK: Russell House Publishing, 2013), p. 295.

58 H Justin Evans, *Service to Sport: The Story of the CCPR – 1935–1972* (London: Pelham Books in association with the Sports Council, 1974), p. 152.

59 'Committee Propose "New Deal" for Sport', *The Times*, 29 Sept 1960, p. 3.

60 Wolfenden Committee on Sport, *Sport and the Community: The Report of the Wolfenden Committee on Sport* (London: Central Council of Physical Recreation, 1960), pp. 50–51.

61 British Canoe Union, 'History of Canoeing' (no date) <http://www.bcu.org.uk/files/history%20of%20canoeing.pdf> [accessed 20 Mar 2015].

62 H Justin Evans, *Service to Sport: The Story of the CCPR – 1935–1972* (London: Pelham Books in association with the Sports Council, 1974), pp. 154–168.

63 Francesca Scott, Email to P McDonald, subject 'Sir Jack Longland', 15 July 2015 [Email].

64 Karen Stockham, "'It went down into the very form and fabric of myself'": Women's Mountaineering Life-writing 1808–1960' (PhD thesis, University of Exeter, 2012), p. 192.

65 'Expressmen Get Apology and Substantial Damages', *Daily Express*, 12 July 1962, p. 1.

66 Lynn Cook, 'Outdoor Education: Its Origins and Institutionalisation in Schools with Particular Reference to the West Riding of Yorkshire Since 1945' (PhD thesis, University of Leeds, 2000), pp. 99–100.

67 John Newsom, *Half Our Future: A Report of the Central Advisory Council for Education (England)* (London: Her Majesty's Stationery Office, 1963), p. 49.

68 Lynn Cook, 'Outdoor Education: Its Origins and Institutionalisation in Schools with Particular Reference to the West Riding of Yorkshire Since 1945' (PhD thesis, University of Leeds, 2000), p. 160.

69 Ibid., p. 161.

70 Eric Langmuir, 'White Hall', *Mountaineering*, 3, no. 8 (Aug 1960), p. 21. Quoted in Ken C Ogilvie, *Roots and Wings: A History of Outdoor Education and Outdoor Learning in the UK* (Lyme Regis, UK: Russell House Publishing, 2013), p. 329.

71 Ken C Ogilvie, *Roots and Wings: A History of Outdoor Education and Outdoor Learning in the UK* (Lyme Regis, UK: Russell House Publishing, 2013), pp. 331–333.

72 'Climbing Hints for Teachers', *Guardian*, 16 Oct 1962, p. 2.

73 Ken C Ogilvie, *Roots and Wings: A History of Outdoor Education and Outdoor Learning in the UK* (Lyme Regis, UK: Russell House Publishing, 2013), p. 333.

74 Ibid., p. 352.

75 *A History of the Ordnance Survey*, ed. by W A Seymour and John H Andrews (Folkestone, England: Wm Dawson and Sons, 1980), p. 302.

76 Grace's Guide: British Industrial History, 'Thomas Black and Sons (Greenock)' (2014) <http://www.gracesguide.co.uk/Thomas_Black_and_Sons_(Greenock)> [accessed 27 Jun 2015].

77   Kim Meldrum and Brian Royle, *Artificial Climbing Walls* (London: Pelham Books, 1970), plate 9, & pp. 30–31.

78   Tom Price, 'What Led to the Leaders', *High Magazine*, no. 46 (Sept 1986), pp. 38–42 (p. 39).

79   'Mountain Team Buried in Avalanche', *Daily Mail,* 5 Jan 1968, p. 3.

80   Neville Crowther, John Cheesmond and Peter Higgins, 'A History of Outdoor Education at Dunfermline College of Physical Education and Moray House College and Institute of Education, Edinburgh – 1970–2000' (2000) <http://www.docs.hss.ed.ac.uk/education/outdoored/crowther_cheesmond_higgins_history.pdf> [accessed 1 Jul 2014].

12. Harold Drasdo and Tom Price on Enjoyment

Chapters 7, 8 and 9 devoted much space to discussion about character building. They included evidence to suggest that Jack Longland and Peter Mosedale had misgivings about character building from day one of White Hall. Chapter 9 showed that in the early 1950s both of them abstained from making any character-building claims for White Hall courses. It also showed that, after Mosedale had left White Hall, and with the added influence of Harold Drasdo, by the late 1950s the White Hall reservations about character training had become an instinctive rejection of this purpose, a rejection that was fundamental to the formative years of White Hall and perhaps to the formative years of British outdoor education in general.

You might be fed up of hearing about character building, but you are about to hear more (unless you choose to skip this chapter). After Mosedale left the scene, it is possible that the term 'character training' may have occasionally entered the conversation at White Hall, but my impression from reading press reports and other writings about the White Hall of the late 1950s and the 1960s is that the explicit subject of character training did not crop up often. Nationally within the outdoor centres, some discussion about Outward Bound and character training continued. This chapter will examine that discussion and will bring the subject of character training to a close.

From Naval Discipline to the Swinging Sixties

Two other people who left us some thoughts about the Outward Bound schools of the 1950s were Geoffrey Young and John Hunt. Young, aged 74 in 1950, was comfortable with the military flavour of Aberdovey OBSS and he approved of the sea school being staffed by officers of the merchant marine. Early photographs of morning parade at the school show rows of uniformed boys holding themselves upright and station-ary, like some sort of rehearsal for military service. 'Naval terminology, inspection of quarters, marching in formation, morning prayers, flag raising, and "sir-ing" of officers were the order of the day.'[1]

Jim Hogan, writing about his Aberdovey staff of 1943, describes the experience of standing 'between two powerful forces – the stolidity of the Captains, many of whom were charming men, and the dynamic force of a young officer [Freddie Fuller] who regarded most established institutions with scant respect'.[2]

Looking back from 1978, John Hunt saw the 1950s OB schools as a natural development from the commando, snow warfare and cliff-assault schools of the war years:

> For quite a while the regimes at the Outward Bound schools retained the same strong accent on rigorous training and discipline; at the end of the course a commonly held view was that it was an experience worth having, but not a pastime to be pursued voluntarily.
>
> Such was my impression in 1952, on first visiting the Outward Bound school in Eskdale … The regime has long since been considerably relaxed and the sense of enjoyment enhanced accordingly.[3]

The relaxation happened slowly, stretching over the 1950s and 60s. Eskdale OBMS, under the progressive young warden John Lagoe and then under Tom Price, appears to have led the way. During the planning of Eskdale OBMS, Geoffrey Young had been concerned that this mountain school would have to depend mainly on climbers as instructors, who would be enthusiastic but 'without professional training or any collective tradition of service discipline'.[4] But times were changing. Lagoe favoured informal relationships between instructors and course members, as he explained in 1958: 'Our prime task is to put the boys at ease, to make them feel at home, to get them to regard their Instructors as friends rather than remote superiors; and it's amazing how the mere use of Christian names breaks down barriers.' Lagoe also increased the emphasis on enjoyment.[5] The young Eskdale instructors of the late 1960s and onwards would cope well, without having done any military service.

Aberdovey OBSS also changed, but more slowly. Speaking to a special correspondent from *The Times* in 1965, Captain Fuller, the warden, said the accent had changed since the sea school was founded in 1941. There was no longer a cultural compulsion to face the course challenges.[6] But the regime at the school, despite the efforts of the deputy warden Ian Fothergill, remained somewhat militaristic and male-dominated, even through the massive social changes of the swinging sixties. At least, this was my impression from instructing there in 1970, albeit only on one course. The vestiges of uniform remained, in the form of a navy-blue sweater. We still paraded before the flag, although no longer with any explicit religious ingredient in the ceremony. In contrast, the cultures of many LEA outdoor centres from their beginnings were casual and affable and mixed sex.[7]

Libertarian and Authoritarian Influences

In the early 1960s an ex-White Hall staff member, Harold Drasdo, applied his mind to the subject of character building. We saw in Chapter 10 that Drasdo was one of the Bradford Lads, described by Dennis Gray as a close-knit group of radicals, inimical to anything that smelt of authority. Gray, as a teenager, had reacted against a secondary education that bore the hallmarks of a conservative variety of character training: 'Slowly it was dawning on me that school was just one part of a huge system, a sausage-machine for turning out a certain type of person, a conventional being who would do as he was told without question, swallow society's values whole, take up a profession that was "safe and respectable", believe that all was well with the world, that change would be bad, and the rest of it.'[8]

Gray and Drasdo were kindred spirits.

After teaching in Nottingham, Drasdo had instructed at White Hall for slightly over two years, in 1956–8. He recalls the arrangement: 'By what was called a gentleman's agreement my post had been offered for not less than one year, not more than three, it being felt then that work in outdoor education could only be regarded as a short and privileged sabbatical from real teaching.'[9] In 1957 many of his days off work saw him heading north to the Lake District to work on the Eastern Crags volume for the Third Series of Lakeland guidebooks. In 1964 he became chief instructor of The Towers, Wolverhampton education authority's residential outdoor centre in north Wales. He later became warden and remained there until 1983. Like Mosedale, he questioned the authoritarian version of character building that people associated, validly or mistakenly, with the Outward Bound Trust. He preferred a more libertarian approach.

Writing in January 1962 about character building, Drasdo began by saying that since the war, instruction in the informal sports – camping, mountaineering, sailing, and their derivatives – which were normally non-competitive activities, had become involved with public and private money through the setting up of permanent centres by the Outward Bound Trust, the CCPR, several LEAs, and other interested bodies. Already, he said, you could distinguish libertarian and authoritarian attitudes at work:

> Of these ventures the Outward Bound Trust is the most publicised and makes claims for its four-week courses different in kind from those made by the other centres. It has indirect liaisons with the Services and the Churches. A glance at any literature about the work of the Trust will help to identify its position provisionally. The vocabulary is characteristic: relating to its aims – spiritual awareness, leadership, loyalty, character training, self-discipline, clean living; [and] to its methods – competition, supreme exertion, shock treatment, honours and merit badges. It doesn't seem essential to outline the whole mystique of Outward Bound here but you can see immediately that there must be points for discussion in this idea.[10]

Drasdo discussed these points and then used White Hall as an example of a less regimented approach than that of Outward Bound. This Drasdo article is important and little known. I will quote a lengthy section:

> Whilst none of the other experiments has been based on professedly libertarian principles, some of them do stand at a noticeable remove from the authoritarianism of Outward Bound. The Derbyshire Education Committee's centre at Buxton, which has been running for more than ten years now, is amongst these. Its establishment was to the credit of the Director of Education for Derbyshire, Jack Longland, whose influence in this field has been very considerable and entirely to the good. He has, it is true, inevitably become involved in Outward Bound affairs but has, at the same time, firmly rejected facile theories of character-transference – the playing fields of Eton stuff. He has drawn attention to the loose identification of 'character' and 'morals'. And he has exercised a nice restraint, suggesting gently that the whole

concept of character is a more elusive and complex subject than the more exuberant of the outdoor educationists seem to assume. The following notes, however, don't pretend to represent official policy but simply a few aspects of the working rules evolved at White Hall.

The consideration which underlies all others is safety. It might not seem necessary to state this but it's worth mentioning since some of the ends and means we criticise operate against it. Where others' lives are concerned no-one has the right even to think about so-called 'calculated' risks. This said, the obvious first principle is that the youngsters and adults who visit the centre should enjoy themselves. The obvious test is whether they want to come again or not. The aim is the stimulation of a permanent interest in any of the activities. We are persuaded that we have been very successful with this approach and this success must largely result from the general absence of pressure. In detail, there is almost always complete freedom of choice as to which of the specialised activities – rock-climbing, canoeing, caving, and so on are taken and if anyone wishes he can just go fell-walking instead. We do not assume that everyone must like these pastimes. No-one is pressed to do anything he finds difficult or alarming. There is no element of competition and, accordingly, there is no obstacle to the co-educational course which is common. Potential leaders are not sought and relations between instructors and pupils are nearly informal. Indeed, the atmosphere at the centre has always been so friendly that there has been no difficulty in securing the assistance of as many unpaid volunteer instructors as has been thought useful every weekend since the centre was opened. Some of these instructors first came to the centre as novices. The cost of running this kind of service is not exorbitant in comparison with the sums spent on large playing fields for formal games and athletics. Many of us feel that such centres present the ideal forms of physical education and that where geographically possible – almost everywhere – whatever sorts of natural facilities are available ought to be used.[11]

This 1962 article, titled 'The Character Builders', is now old stuff. But in 1962 it was bold stuff. Unknown to Drasdo at that time, claims and counter-claims about character training's all-embracing successors –

social and personal development – would occupy outdoor education's academics for decades.

There was one aspect of the 1950s Outward Bound notion of character training that Drasdo did not discuss: few if any plausible methods existed to measure its impact. Mark Freeman has listed the limited research that did take place. He also summarised the complications faced: 'Even if systematic studies had been carried out, they were open to many objections, not least the difficulty of establishing a control group of young people who had not attended an Outward Bound course. More fundamentally, the nature of the impact of character training was such that it eluded statistical measurement.'[12]

For both LEA centres and Outward Bound centres, the difficulty in quantifying the effects of their courses contributed to two completely opposite concerns. The first was that potential customers and sponsors – industry or schools – would not be convinced of the value of the courses. The second was that the centres would exaggerate the impact of the courses. The latter situation was a concern, not of his making, for Tom Price when he was warden of Eskdale OBMS:

> Extravagant claims were made, especially by the Trust's P.R. man, Val Lunnon, whose selling line sometimes made me squirm with embarrassment, but there was no doubt that the course was a broadening and enlarging experience for most.[13]

There may have been no doubt in Price's mind and in the minds of many others, but obtaining academically acceptable evidence of the full impact of residential courses based on adventurous outdoor pursuits remains a controversial area today.

Drasdo on Enjoyment

Drasdo's article appeared in the literary journal *Anarchy*, a periodical whose title was more dramatic than most of its contents. The viewpoints he put forward seem (to me) measured and mainstream. Drasdo knew White Hall's approach. In stating that a basic principle at White Hall was that the students should enjoy themselves, he was merely underlining similar statements made ten years earlier, such as the item in a January 1951 issue of *Education* titled '"Enjoy the Hills" – Derbyshire Centre':

... a place where young people ... may practise the techniques of hill-walking, of camping and cooking, of where and where not to ski, of rock-climbing – in short a place where young people may learn to enjoy the hills without unnecessary danger or discomfort.[14]

Arthur Afford touched on part of the reason for the emphasis on enjoyment, pointing out that whereas going to school was compulsory whether pupils enjoyed it or not, attending White Hall courses was voluntary; to attract young people, the courses had to be enjoyable and the atmosphere informal, with seldom any need to resort to sharp reprimands or authoritarian discipline.[15]

Drasdo criticised two particular traits of Outward Bound courses, as they were in 1962.

It appears that, aside from any disagreement about what defines character, we can now make two major criticisms of the work of the Trust. Firstly, owing to the stress on extreme fitness, competition, the 'conquering of self', and so forth, it seems that in many activities the youngsters are pressed far past the point of enjoyment. Anyone who has talked to a number of unaccompanied Outward Bound parties on the fells will agree that, even allowing for temporary despondencies forgotten in retrospect and for the astonishing resilience of youngsters, a proportion of the boys is disenchanted forever with these pastimes. What proportion this may be it would be very difficult to determine but (of the 'conscripts' from industry, at any rate) some estimates put it at a majority. And if you believe that the activities are good in themselves and not simply as means there is an unanswerable failure here.

Secondly, for normal adolescents even these neutral pastimes may be given distasteful and irrelevant associations by the clumsily overt emphasis on 'character' and example. Youngsters tend to judge a sport by its practitioners and the way they talk. In mitigation of these criticisms it is important to add that when one is in unspoiled country a sense of freedom is often conspicuously present and a resistance to authority and its precepts may be encouraged by contrast; if the trainees are sent out unchaperoned, Nature subverts the intentions of the character builders at every step. Nonetheless, it seems certain that the basic merits of the activities are in many cases, if not negated, at least severely limited by this general approach.[16]

Tucked away in a literary journal, Drasdo's article may not have reached the staffrooms of the outdoor centres.

Geoff Roberts and Harold Drasdo (thumbing) in the 1957 BBC TV documentary *Climbing*.

This will be a tight squeeze. Forty years later, in his book *The Ordinary Route*, Drasdo allocated nearly a whole chapter to the subject of hitchhiking.

An Attempted Vindication

A loyal defence of character training arrived in August 1962 in the form of an autobiography by Adam Arnold-Brown, the Gordonstoun-educated ex-warden of Eskdale OBMS. The title of his book made the main subject clear: *Unfolding Character: The Impact of Gordonstoun*. Looking back at this book in 2013, Ken Ogilvie thought it an 'excellent book for gaining an insight into the way OB practice developed'.[17] Several of the book's reviewers in 1962 were less than enthusiastic about character training. Kenneth Allsop, writing in the *Daily Mail*, talked about a 'rigorous and controversial public school'. Allsop did not share Arnold-Brown's alarm about the sexual activities of adolescent boys:

> Misgivings deepen when he [Arnold-Brown] deplores the menace of sex to the adolescent – 'that energy-sapping, distracting, all-powerful interest in sex which can fill the vacant mind.' After leaving Gordonstoun, says Mr Arnold-Brown: 'I retreated further into my shell, regarding sex as a dangerous infection.'[18]

Another reviewer had similar misgivings:

> He demands 'absorbing activity to prevent morose preoccupation with sex'. Shades of Arnold and all that? He writes so often on stilts of propriety that it comes as a welcome surprise when he shows uninhibited enthusiasm for 'Anna and the King of Siam'.[19]

The *Guardian*'s reviewer wrote that Arnold-Brown 'gives a clear if oddly anxious and impersonal account of Kurt Hahn's curiously compounded philosophy. (Eton, Dr Arnold and Plato all went into the pot.)'[20]

Those reviews happened over fifty years ago. Perhaps Arnold-Brown's book should remain on the library shelves as a 1950s British manual of civilian and military character training.

Sceptical Climbing Fraternity

At the first conference of mountain centres in October 1962, about two months after the publication of Arnold-Brown's book, 'there was disagreement as to how far "character building" should be the purpose of a mountain centre, but it was accepted that experience of mountain activities did affect the character and outlook of those who took part in them'.[21]

I am reminded of a remark made in 1969 by the climber and Sheffield Polytechnic lecturer Paul Nunn: 'It is good to see the young on the crags, though what the climbing community will do to their characters I shudder to anticipate.'[22]

Climbers had always had a well-deserved reputation for wild and reckless behaviour, often anti-establishment and sometimes romantically anarchic. The sport had always attracted an odd and eclectic bunch of heroes and vagabonds. But during the 1960s, 'high spirits and youthful exuberance more frequently gave way to outright lawlessness, particularly in the Alps. Shoplifting was endemic among British climbers in the 1960s and 70s.'[23] The alcohol- and drug-induced drunken revelry of this period probably eclipsed any excesses of climbing's earlier countercultures.

Jack Longland was well aware of these ungodly developments. In his valedictory address to the Alpine Club in December 1976, he spoke out strongly against the decline in manners and moral standards among some young and disturbingly shameless British mountaineers. Among his concerns was the reputation of British climbers in Chamonix: 'Thanks to a small minority of cheats and thieves and layabouts, who have thieved from the shops and gardens, stolen other people's equipment and brawled in the pubs, the British name still stinks.'[24]

In his book on the history of British climbing, Simon Thompson ridiculed the idea that the sport of climbing would better a young person's character:

> Perversely, just as the morals of the climbing community were descending to new lows, the idea of outdoor education became popular ...
>
> The purported character-building benefits of outdoor education have their origins in the romantic idea of the moral superiority of the simple, rural life as compared with the corruption to be found in the cities. As the popularity of mountaineering spread, many people who perhaps should have known better started to believe that taking young people from the inner cities to the mountains for a few days would somehow reform their characters ... The idea that dangling a feckless youth from the end of a rope for an afternoon will transform his life chances is clearly ridiculous.[25]

Dennis Gray, writing in 1970, two years before becoming the national officer of the BMC, was equally blunt, if a little behind the developments in outdoor education:

> It is unfortunate that the educators have seized upon climbing as a way of making the man out of the boy, of character building, of implanting or testing courage. I cannot see how such claims can be justified. Undoubtably mountaineering is still rich in characters, but not of the type talked about by official bodies. Some climbers in my experience have been anti-social, some criminal; the outdoor community as a whole has been no more inclined to be virtuous and self-sacrificing than the non-climber, yet from such a premise as the character-building one, meaning I suppose producing people of high moral values, has come much of the impetus which has made these bodies favour mountaineering for training purposes.[26]

Another character-building sceptic, twelve years later, was the climber Peter Boardman, who was well-informed on outdoor education (he was a Sparklet) as well as on the latest developments in the major ranges. Writing about the effects of Himalayan mountaineering on the behaviour of expedition members, he said: 'Outward Bound, and other outdoor-education philosophies would have one believe that mountain climbing develops character, courage, resourcefulness and team work. That may be so, but it is also true that mountaineering expeditions can develop selfishness, fanaticism, glory-seeking and cunning.'[27]

Vocabulary: Out with the Old, In with the New

In May 1965, during a two-day Outward Bound conference at Harrogate, 'the younger leaders [of Outward Bound] such as Tom Price were joined by key figures from the wider educational world, notably Jack Longland, Alec Clegg and Bernard Davies … in questioning the "character-training" rhetoric of Outward Bound'.[28] Jack Longland, drawing on his eight years of anchoring radio's *My Word*, exclaimed: 'What a difficult word character is! We should look at that word again and decide what we mean by it'. He wondered 'whether Outward Bound needs a brand new vocabulary'.[29]

In some LEA residential outdoor centres, avoidance of some terms had already begun. Staff at White Hall, such as Peter Mosedale and Arthur Afford, had been alert to the connotations of 'character training' since the 1950s (in Mosedale's case since 1950). In the late 1960s, the language of Outward Bound began to change. People consciously avoided using the terms 'character training' and 'character building'. Another word that became passé was 'leadership'. Alternative, softer terms came into use, such as 'self-discovery' and 'personal growth'.[30]

Even the arch-Hahnians, Adam Arnold-Brown and Spencer Summers, could now see the semantic quandary. In 1959 Arnold-Brown had agreed that the term 'character training' had a 'distasteful connotation – it smacks of Pavlov, of the Hitler Youth, of Brave New World and authoritarianism'.[31] At the Harrogate conference, Spencer Summers, previously a vocal champion of character training, said that 'character training' was a 'misleading phrase'.[32]

In his 1968 book *Education, Physical Education and Personality Development*, P J Arnold listed some of the ingredients that contribute to the whole person. His socially oriented qualities included kindness, unselfishness, friendliness, truthfulness, justice, honesty, thoughtfulness, courtesy, helpfulness, tolerance, cheerfulness, loyalty, co-operation and a general consideration for others. His personal qualities were courage, ingenuity, initiative, decision making, perseverance, determination, self-reliance, self-control, self-restraint, thoroughness, enthusiasm, reliability and resourcefulness.[33] At White Hall in the 1970s, this ensemble became the veteran instructor's vocabulary of report-writing, in combination with words relating more specifically to the outdoor activities, such as agility, skill and strength.

In 1970 an English edition was published of the 1966 German book *Kurt Hahn*, edited by Hermann Röhrs. A piece of writing in this book may have contributed to a growing rejection of the terms 'character training' and 'character building', consigning them to the lexicographic class 'archaic'. What was special about 'Some Aspects of Character-building' was that it came not from the sceptical pen of someone from the LEA sector of outdoor education but from Tom Price, who had been the warden of Eskdale OBMS from 1961 to about 1968.

In eleven pages, Price summarised some main parts of the history of Outward Bound: the original aims and ideas that, he thought, underlay the setting-up of Aberdovey OBMS; the subsequent adjustments to the original concept; the growing diversity between the then six UK Outward Bound schools; and the development of courses that provided 'a memorable month of new experience, a mental and physical shake-up and tonic'.[34]

Price's perspective on enjoyment, viewing OB courses from the inside, differed considerably from Drasdo's impressions, which were those of an informed onlooker. Price said that OB training was presented to trainees as a hard challenge, whose main object was work and discovery, not a holiday, but that the training was full of incidental enjoyment. Price was happy to use the word 'impel'.[35]

His essay then considered several reservations that outsiders might have had about OB courses. Some of these doubts he viewed as misconceptions. There was, he said, no cult of toughness. Formal discipline was kept to a minimum and rules were few. There was nothing narrowly puritanical and restrictive about OB courses. However, he conceded that the phrase 'character training' could be interpreted to imply an attempt to mould opinions and to impose behaviour patterns. He wrote:

> I do not like the term 'character-training' … But in any case 'character-training' as a term has now been discarded. Character-building is preferred, and character development. But in my view the word 'character' itself is objectionable: it is at once too imprecise and too narrow for our purposes.[36]

You may view this change as merely semantic, a revision of the vocabulary. Or you might interpret it as a departure from the original concept of Outward Bound. Either way, Tom Price's frankly expressed dislike of the terms 'character training' and 'character building' was a significant happening. Looking back at Eskdale OBMS in 2000, he wrote: 'Hahn's views were tested in the field and hotly debated, interpretations of what we were trying to achieve varied considerably, and our enthusiasm for the work was tempered by a healthy scepticism.'[37]

The period about which Price was writing was his wardenship, 1961–8. His dissatisfaction with the terms 'character training' and 'character building' reflected a general trend, one that has also been noted by Lynn Cook who remarked that the two terms 'character building' and 'leadership' are 'rarely associated with outdoor education in the literature of the late-1960s and 1970s'.[38]

Seven years after writing his *Anarchy* article, Drasdo shifted his analytic focus sideways to examine the delicate relationship between safety and the 'rules' of climbing. His essay 'Margins of Safety' attempted to show that climbers organised their games in a way that conserved danger.[39] In a separate article, Kim Meldrum provided some statistics that appeared to support this suggestion.[40] The subconscious adjustment of an individual's risk 'thermostat' is also known as risk compensation. Looking back at Drasdo's essay now, it seems to have been a harbinger of the trouble that was to come in the form of the mountain-training dispute of the 1970s, two main constituents of which were educational climbers' desire for safety and sporting climbers' acceptance of and need for a degree of danger.

In 1972 Drasdo injected a wee bit more wry scepticism into the thinkers' corners of outdoor education, in the form of *Education and the Mountain Centres*. This essay attempted to shed light on educational and philosophical aspects of the work of LEA residential outdoor education centres.

A New Generation of Outward Bound Teachers

By 1973 the OB schools were employing more people with teaching qualifications or other professional qualifications than had been the case in 1957, when Jack Longland had identified a lack of experienced teachers to be a weakness in the staffing of OB junior courses. A survey of six OB schools in about 1972 or 1973 found that forty of the seventy members of staff had attended either a college of education or a university.[41] Writing in 1972, Harold Drasdo acknowledged the changes: 'Still, when all is said, something good and original may come out of Outward Bound yet. There is a new generation of teachers in the [Outward Bound] schools now, not quite so shackled, perhaps, by the obsessions of Kurt Hahn.'[42]

Mosedale and Longland and Price and Drasdo himself had helped to loosen those shackles. I'm not sure that Drasdo's part in this has been recognised. In 1993, David Hopkins, a University of Cambridge tutor who had once worked as an Outward Bound instructor, and Roger Putnam, an ex-principal of Outward Bound Eskdale, described Drasdo as 'essentially a romantic and a subversive'.[43] Maybe they had in mind his essay, *Trespasser's Guide to the Conwy Valley*.

An added complication in understanding the currents involved in this period is the question of whether all of Hahn's frequently quoted statements accurately represented his detailed beliefs. Hahn had a flair for the English language, with a talent for constructing pithy sayings and eloquent statements that sounded like verses from the King James Bible or lines from the libraries of Edwardian Oxford: 'It is the sin of the soul to force young people into opinions – indoctrination is of the devil – but it is culpable neglect not to impel young people into experiences.'[44] Boys were to meet failure as well as success and then were to defeat their defeatism. Expeditions were to be 'conquests without the humiliation of the conquered'.[45] His rich aphorisms may have tended to dominate and distort some people's perceptions of his ideas. Renate Wilson, in her book *Inside Outward Bound*, argued that much of what Hahn stood for was misunderstood, misinterpreted or misquoted.[46] Many of the references to his beliefs came from transcripts of lectures he gave.[47] It was sometimes difficult to distinguish between what Hahn actually said, what he was reported to have said, and what other people said about him. Similarly, Nick Veevers and Pete Allison detected a frequent absence of a sound grasp of Hahn's ideas.[48]

This Is All Now Ancient History

Outward Bound schools in the UK have altered beyond recognition since the times described in this chapter, as some LEA centres also have done. In 1968 the Ullswater OBMS was still making the best of canvas-covered kayaks, whereas Howtown Outdoor Pursuits Centre, the well-funded LEA centre across the lake from it, had a fibreglass fleet.

Howtown, belonging to Durham education authority, was a centre very much in the White Hall mould. But events in the 1990s added dramatically different chapters to this Ullswater history. In 1994, Durham decided that it could no longer afford to run Howtown. The centre changed from an LEA-run centre to a privately run centre. The *Journal of Adventure Education and Outdoor Leadership* saw the move as 'a lesson in survival, dedication, achievement and determination'.[49] But Howtown Outdoor Centre Ltd had a limited life. In February 2008, Howtown Outward Bound opened, in the building that for many years had been the LEA outdoor centre. If we judge from the Howtown website – which may not be the entire story – this six-year-old Outward Bound centre appears (in 2017) not only to have occupied the building once operated by Durham County Council education committee but also to have appropriated many of the approaches pioneered and developed by LEA centres. If you agree that the story of outdoor education has been one of gradual evolution, then the appearance of Howtown Outward Bound is your miracle of adaptation. The irony adds a twist to the story of the decline of state-funded residential outdoor centres.

Another LEA centre, Ogwen Cottage, recently underwent changes similar to Howtown's. In July 2014, Birmingham city council decided to shut Ogwen Cottage to cut costs. In October 2014 the National Trust bought the buildings. Ogwen Cottage reopened in 2015 as an

Outward Bound centre, run by the National Trust and the Outward Bound Trust in partnership.

If we look back from 2017 at the ups and downs of the UK Outward Bound schools over seventy years, Aberdovey, Ullswater, Eskdale and Loch Eil emerge as hardy survivors.

Nowadays, if you were to use the term 'character builders' in Britain, many people would think you were talking about an upmarket construction company. Over the centuries, moral training – to many people the term is just another name for character training – has wavered in and out of fashion. In the United States, public concern about a moral decline in society and the break-up of families led to the re-emergence of character education in the 1980s.[50] In 1997 Gloria Solomon, an assistant professor of kinesiology and physical education at Texas Christian University, closed a journal article with the statement:

> It is clear that recent research on character development in physical education demonstrates that the organized physical activity context is ripe for positive moral growth. Furthermore, evidence indicates that unless character development is directly addressed, the moral maturation process will not likely occur. Therefore, the physical educator has the responsibility and opportunity to create situations that will enhance the character development of children in their care.[51]

An academic scrutiny of character building is available in a paper by Andrew Brookes in the *Journal of Adventure Education and Outdoor Learning*, 3, no. 1 (2003), pp. 49-62.

According to Mark Freeman, character education had reappeared in the UK by 2010.[52]

Harold Drasdo wrote and climbed all his life until a balance problem in his late seventies ended the climbing.

Notes

1   Renate Wilson, *Inside Outward Bound* (Charlotte, NC: East Woods Press, 1981), p. 24.

2   James Martin Hogan, *Impelled into Experiences: The Story of the Outward Bound Schools* (Wakefield, UK: Educational Productions, 1968), p. 62.

3   John Hunt, *Life Is Meeting* (London: Hodder & Stoughton, 1978), pp. 128–129.

4   Geoffrey Winthrop Young, 'The Message of the Mountains', in *Outward Bound*, ed. by David James (London: Routledge and Kegan Paul, 1957), pp. 98–107 (pp. 103–104).

5   John Lagoe, 'Outward Bound in the Lake District', *Fell and Rock Journal*, 18, no. 2 (1958), pp. 156–161 (p. 157).

6   'Education Through Adventure', *The Times*, 8 May 1965, p. 9.

7   Pete McDonald, *Climbing Lessons: Inside Outdoor Education* (Kaikohe, NZ: Pete McDonald, 1997), pp. 56–57.

8   Dennis Gray, *Rope Boy* (London: Victor Gollancz: 1970), p. 20.

9   Harold Drasdo, *The Ordinary Route* (Ty Croes, Wales: Ernest Press, 1997), pp. 111–112.

10   Harold Drasdo, 'The Character Builders', *Anarchy*, no. 11 (Jan 1962), pp. 25–28.

11   Ibid.

12   Mark Freeman, 'From 'Character-training' to 'Personal Growth': The Early History of Outward Bound 1941–1965', *History of Education: Journal of the History of Education Society*, 40, no. 1 (Jan 2011), pp. 21–43 (pp. 35–36).

13   Tom Price, *Travail So Gladly Spent* (Ty Croes, Wales: Ernest Press, 2000), p. 180.

14   '"Enjoy the Hills" – Derbyshire Centre', *Education*, 26 Jan 1951, p. 157.

15   A B Afford, *The Story of White Hall Open Country Pursuits Centre; vol. 2* (Buxton, Derbyshire, UK: A B Afford, 1978), pp. 19–20.

16   Harold Drasdo, 'The Character Builders', *Anarchy*, no. 11 (Jan 1962), pp. 25–28.

17   Ken C Ogilvie, *Roots and Wings: A History of Outdoor Education and Outdoor Learning in the UK* (Lyme Regis, UK: Russell House Publishing, 2013), p. 289.

18   Kenneth Allsop, 'The Great Gordonstoun Mystery', *Daily Mail*, 24 Aug 1962, p. 6.

19   John Garrett, 'Eyes on Gordonstoun', *Sunday Times*, 26 Aug 1962, p. 21.

20   Edward Blishen, 'Character or Characters?', *Guardian*, 24 Aug 1962, p. 4.

21   Ken C Ogilvie, *Roots and Wings: A History of Outdoor Education and Outdoor Learning in the UK* (Lyme Regis, UK: Russell House Publishing, 2013), p. 332.

22   Paul Nunn, *At the Sharp End* (London: Unwin Hyman, 1988), p. 44.

23   Simon Thompson, *Unjustifiable Risk? The Story of British Climbing* (Milnthorpe, UK: Cicerone, 2010), p. 201.

24   Jack Longland, 'Valedictory Address: Jack Longland', *Alpine Journal*, 82 (1977), pp. 3–12 (p. 8).

25   Simon Thompson, *Unjustifiable Risk? The Story of British Climbing* (Milnthorpe, UK: Cicerone, 2010), pp. 203–204.

26   Dennis Gray, *Rope Boy* (London: Victor Gollancz: 1970), p. 312.

27   Peter Boardman, *Sacred Summits: A Climber's Year* (London: Hodder and Stoughton, 1982), p. 114.

28   Mark Freeman, 'From 'Character-training' to 'Personal Growth': The Early History of Outward Bound 1941–1965', *History of Education: Journal of the History of Education Society*, 40, no. 1 (Jan 2011), pp. 21–43 (pp. 38–39).

29   British Library, Question Time, in Outward Bound in the 60s and 70s: A Report on the Conference Held at Harrogate on May 8th and 9th 1965; UIN: BLL010114322536, pp. 4–6.

30   Mark Freeman, 'From 'Character-training' to 'Personal Growth': The Early
      History of Outward Bound 1941–1965', *History of Education: Journal of the
      History of Education Society,* 40, no. 1 (Jan 2011), pp. 21–43 (pp. 39–42).

31   Cambridge University Library, Talk on Outward Bound to Staff of Dept of
      Education, 1959, in Correspondence and papers of Arnold-Brown relating to
      OBMS after his departure, MS Add.8270/21/25.

32   British Library, Outward Bound in the 60s and 70s: A Report on
      the Conference Held at Harrogate on May 8th and 9th 1965; UIN:
      BLL01014322536, p. 17.

33   P J Arnold, *Education, Physical Education and Personality Development* (London:
      Heinemann, 1968), pp. 104–105.

34   Tom Price, 'Some Aspects of Character-building', in *Kurt Hahn,* ed. by H Röhrs
      and H Tunstall-Behrens (London: Routledge & Kegan Paul, 1970), pp. 81–91
      (p. 84).

35   Ibid. (p. 83).

36   Ibid. (pp. 86–87).

37   Tom Price, *Travail So Gladly Spent* (Ty Croes, Wales: Ernest Press, 2000), p. 181.

38   Lynn Cook, 'Outdoor Education: Its Origins and Institutionalisation in Schools
      with Particular Reference to the West Riding of Yorkshire Since 1945' (PhD
      thesis, University of Leeds, 2000), p. 215.

39   Harold Drasdo, 'Margins of Safety', *Alpine Journal,* 74 (1969), pp. 159–168.

40   K I Meldrum, 'Does Improved Equipment and Technique Reduce Accidents?',
      Alpine Journal, 74 (1969), pp. 308–309.

41   T M Parker and K I Meldrum, *Outdoor Education* (London: J M Dent and Sons,
      1973), p. 114.

42   Harold Drasdo, *Education and the Mountain Centres,* 2nd edn (1972, 1973; repr.
      Penrith: Association for Outdoor Learning, 1998), p. 29.

43   David Hopkins and Roger Putnam, *Personal Growth through Adventure* (London:
      David Fulton Publishers, 1993), p. 57.

44   Kurt Hahn, 'Kurt Hahn Quotes' (c1930) <http://kurthahn.org/quotes/quote4.
      html> [accessed 3 June 2015]. Arnold-Brown quotes a simpler version of this
      Kurt Hahn belief, Adam Arnold-Brown, *Unfolding Character: The Impact of
      Gordonstoun* (London: Routledge and Kegan Paul, 1962), p. 30.

45   Quoted in Nick Veevers and Pete Allison, *Kurt Hahn: Inspirational, Visionary,
      Outdoor and Experiential Educator* (Rotterdam: Sense Publishers, 2011), pp.
      68–70.

46   Renate Wilson, *Inside Outward Bound* (Charlotte, NC: East Woods Press, 1981),
      p. 16.

47   Nick Veevers and Pete Allison, *Kurt Hahn: Inspirational, Visionary, Outdoor and
      Experiential Educator* (Rotterdam: Sense Publishers, 2011), p. xvii.

48   Ibid., p. xvii.

49   Steve Mitchell, 'Howtown Outdoor Centre Ltd', *Journal of Adventure Education
      and Outdoor Leadership,* 13, no. 3 (Autumn 1996), p. 20.

50   *Encyclopedia of Education: Second Edition,* ed. by James W Guthrie, 8 vols (New
      York: Macmillan Reference USA, 2003), vol. 1, pp. 259–261.

51   Gloria Solomon, 'Does Physical Education Affect Character Development in Students?', *Journal of Physical Education, Recreation and Dance*, 68, no. 9 (Nov-Dec 1997), pp. 38–41 (p. 41).

52   Mark Freeman, 'From 'Character-training' to 'Personal Growth': The Early History of Outward Bound 1941–1965', *History of Education: Journal of the History of Education Society*, 40, no. 1 (Jan 2011), pp. 21–43 (p. 43).

13. Kim Meldrum and Risk, 1963–70

Keith Ian Meldrum was born in 1935 and was educated at Marlborough College (some sixty years after Geoffrey Winthrop Young). He joined the school mountaineering club when it restarted after the war. Frequent visits to the British hills whetted his appetite for greater things, further afield. On leaving school in summer 1954, and before doing national service in Germany, he hitchhiked through France and met a schoolmate Mike Gravina in Chamonix. Their holiday was memorable for a potentially serious route-finding error, not – as is normal and half expected – on an actual climb, but on the walk up to the Couvercle Hut.[1] The two young alpinists attempted to reach the hut without using the fixed iron ladders, an intention that could have been interpreted as an admirable desire for ethical purity but which was actually just a lapse into bumbledom.

The Alps were certainly greater things but not great enough, because 20 May 1957 saw Kim and Mike boarding a ship in Liverpool, on their way to Lima and the Cordillera Vilcabamba in Peru. The pair were two of three non-Cambridge members of the seven-man Cambridge Andean Expedition 1957. Also on the expedition was John Longland, Jack's oldest son. The expedition was notable for its young team (the oldest was twenty-four), its thorough organisation, and its big ambition: Pumasillo or the Puma's Claw, 20,490 feet. This striking peak, plastered in steep fluted snow and ice, was thought to be possibly the highest unclimbed mountain in the world outside Asia. A considerable prize, it was unattempted and virtually unknown.[2]

Pumasillo proved to be harder to find and harder to climb than anyone expected. Exploration of the approach route took nearly a month. Then, in five days, consummate teamwork overcame some steep ice and scary snow formations to put all seven climbers either onto the tiny summit, one at a time, or to within a rope-length of that snow pinnacle. The style of climbing was siege rather than alpine, but no porters were used.

Having survived the Alps, national service and this very successful expedition to the Andes, Meldrum then rounded off his education by going up to Oxford. An Oxbridge cv had become almost a conventional requirement for future White Hall principals of the 1950s and 60s.

Meldrum returned to Peru as leader of the Oxford Andean Expedition 1960, which made the first ascent of Allinccapac (19,250 feet) and of eight other peaks in the Cordillera Carabaya.[3]

Chapter 11 mentioned the HMI inspection that took place in summer 1963. Kim Meldrum arrived at White Hall shortly after the inspectors' report was received. During his principalship, all the recommendations were implemented.

Teaching-staff salaries were rationalised, lessening the concern about the pay of instructors who were not qualified teachers. A B Afford called this change an 'equalisation of status and salary'.[4] This remedy acknowledged that Joe Brown and Gordon Mansell, although not qualified teachers, possessed skills that deserved greater recognition than the Burnham pay scales allowed. (Behind the scenes, this issue may not have been entirely straightforward. As we saw earlier, in 1957 Jack Longland had discussed the experimental Outward Bound junior courses and had tentatively suggested that the presence of a few experienced schoolteachers would help Ullswater OBMS to adapt its approaches to better suit the younger age group.)

Gordon Mansell left White Hall in about August 1963. He was replaced by John Cheesmond, who would later become chief instructor. Arthur Afford left White Hall in about July 1964, which was roughly when Dick Wilkinson joined the staff.

Buxton Public Library

Kim and Barbara Meldrum at White Hall, about 1963.

Toddbrook Reservoir, about 1964. The canoes are single-seat glass-reinforced plastic (fibreglass) kayaks. They have replaced the 1950s two-seater wood-and-canvas kayaks.

D7786/BOX/1/Bundle6, courtesy of Derbyshire Record Office.

Toddbrook Reservoir, about 1964.

D7786/BOX/1/Bundle6, courtesy of Derbyshire Record Office.

Toddbrook Reservoir, about 1964. Kim Meldrum is on the slipway. (In sports jacket and flannels, perhaps he had been to a meeting.) On the water, in the rear kayak, is Joe Brown.

Toddbrook Reservoir, about 1964.

Meriel Evans

In summer 1965, the county council appointed White Hall's first female instructor, Meriel Evans. Meriel was twenty-three. She had done a three-year PE course at I M Marsh College of Physical Education, at the end of which, during a mountain-activities course at Glenmore Lodge in 1963, the well-known guide Molly Porter had introduced her to rock climbing.

Meriel had then spent two years teaching in Tewkesbury. While in Gloucestershire she had joined Gloucester Mountaineering Club, which had led to her climbing every weekend in Snowdonia or the Lake District. Immediately before the White Hall vacancy arose, she had her first alpine holiday, during which she climbed Mont Blanc. In 2016, Meriel recalled what happened next:

> I was then very fortunate in being in the right place at the right time, as in 1965 both White Hall & Plas y Brenin decided they needed a woman on their permanent staff; the White Hall interview was first, I was offered the job, and when I phoned Plas y Brenin to withdraw from their interview was pressurised to put White Hall on hold, and still look at the PyB job. However, at 23 I felt I did not really have the confidence to work teaching adults, and anyway, Joe Brown, a hero of mine, worked at White Hall! So, on my return from my first alpine holiday … I caught the train to Buxton, and so to White Hall. So as you see, rather a limited background for such a challenging job![5]

Nationally, this was a time of excited expansion of LEA outdoor centres, with a youthful workforce and a contagious optimism. In September 1965, Barbara Spark (later Roscoe) established a one-year Post Graduate Certificate in Education (PGCE) course for teachers of outdoor activities for the secondary school age group. It was obvious to observers of the outdoor-pursuits scene that the competition for instructing jobs in LEA centres would intensify and that paper qualifications in teaching would become essential. It was no coincidence that at exactly the same time, up in Glasgow the shipyard hand and accomplished climber John Cunningham began a two-year diploma course at Jordanhill College of Education, having become convinced (not entirely correctly) that 'he would never get a job without a bit of paper'.[6]

The White Hall of the mid-1960s may have challenged the values of a lone female instructor. One of the few references to Meriel (that I have found) is in Meldrum's satirical article of 1966, in which he questioned various national trends. One of those trends was the adoption of ski-instructor sweaters by the staff of Plas-y-Brenin and Glenmore Lodge. Meldrum wrote: 'The next and final step in the consolidation of outdoor activities is already happening. The introduction of uniforms. Perhaps it is the influence of our new instructress who is always criticising us for being shoddily dressed. It is possible to detect a certain resistance to this concept.'[7]

It is also possible to detect or imagine, in this extract, a male-dominated White Hall and an overtone slipped into the writing to suit the journal of an ancient men-only club. The Climbers' Club did not admit women members until 1975.[8]

As a schoolboy in the late 1960s, Mark Lambert visited White Hall several times. Now, just a sketchy memory of the offensive prejudices of that era remains in his head: 'I do remember the presence of a lady instructor, the subject of much smutty innuendo from some of the lads she taught on a weekend course I attended, but … she never actually taught me.'[9]

John Cheesmond, who was at White Hall throughout Meriel's four years, corroborates Lambert's recollections:

> On reflecting on our time there, I would say that Meriel experienced quite a bit of sexism in her dealings with other Centre staff and less consideration for her difficulties in adjusting to such a macho environment. With the experience of both running another centre after I left (Ogwen Cottage, near Bethesda) and twenty years of teaching OE at an institution in Edinburgh which, when I went there in 1972, was geared to an almost entirely female student body and with a mainly female staff including the Principal, I include myself in the maintenance of the sexist atmosphere at Whitehall. I'm sure it must be very different now, as it is everywhere, but it would be very interesting to hear from Meriel how she remembers that aspect of her working life at the Centre.[10]

Meriel recently recalled the situation she found herself in in 1965:

> I did not have a problem being the only woman in a staff of six permanent instructors … All the voluntary instructors were also men, but my time spent for the previous two years with the Gloucester Mountaineering Club was almost entirely as the only

woman, so I was perfectly at home! Even in the early 1960s I rarely came across other female climbers, although at Glenmore Lodge I was introduced to rock climbing by Molly Porter. Initially, I had a lot of free time at Whitehall, mainly because the job was residential, so meals, and everything else were provided … Obviously I spent time finding my way around the area, but also with Kim, teaching him how to use a sewing machine! I soon found that I could put my sewing skills to good use. I made waterproof stuff bags for the students' down sleeping bags when I realised how careless our students were over keeping down sleeping bags dry! I also helped Brian, the storeman with repairs to the clothing the students were kitted out in. At the time it did not occur to me that I might be setting a precedent (female skills?), and I do not know if my successors followed suit! As to Kim's comment that I found the other instructors scruffy, I have no recollection of that. However, at my specialist P.E. College, much was made of the importance of looking neat even in sports clothing, and so I myself did try to apply this personally when I was instructing at White Hall. I was also quite strict with the students when we were cleaning up after caving![11]

In 2016–17 Simon Beames interviewed White Hall's first six female instructors, whose tenures spread over the period from 1965 to 1993. Chapter 24 will include a mention of his study.

Other Staffing Developments

Alan Alldred, a caver, joined the staff in September 1965, at the same time as Meriel Evans. Alan, who had spent twelve years in the RAF, was one of the most technically able of all the staff of 1963–9, apart from Joe Brown. He could turn his hand to becoming capable in most spheres. His presence raised the kayaking and caving expertise of the staff.[12]

Fifty years later, recipients of Alan Alldred's technical advice were still appreciating its quality. In September 2015, a blogger on www.songofthepaddle.co.uk wrote:

A few weeks back a guy stopped outside my house as I was offloading a canoe from the van and introduced himself as a retired canoe instructor who was always on the lookout for someone to paddle with. Keeps his boat at Derwent Water and to give him a call if I fancied a paddle …

Some of you will almost certainly know Alan Allred … I had today off so we arranged to meet on Derwent Water this morning … The sun broke through as I arrived at Portinscale marina, met Alan and put my boat on the water. We spent the next hour paddling around near the marina and [with] me receiving probably the most intensive and useful coaching session I've had since the steep learning curve of my first ever days coaching.

D7786/BOX/1/Bundle6, courtesy of Derbyshire Record Office.

Alan Alldred on the Halton Rapids on the River Lune, late 1965. He is playing in a Sport Dipper slalom kayak, a state-of-the-art wooden-frame boat covered with PVC-coated canvas.

In January 1966, after Joe Brown moved on to Llanberis to open his climbing-equipment shop, Malcolm ('Wally') Blake arrived from Devon Outward Bound School. Another instructor for a year or two in the 1960s was Roy Byfleet, who had worked previously at Ullswater OBMS.

The help of voluntary instructors remained vital to White Hall's work, especially at weekends. No list of voluntary instructors of the 1960s exists, but they included Frank Hall, Frank Salt, Pete Olive, Jeremy Joel, Harold Lord, P Smith, Mark Lambert, Michael Foulke, John Davies, Mark Vallance, Keith Worsencroft and Dave Allsop.

In 1965 the appointment of a storeman, Brian Sharp, enabled instructors to devote more time to teaching. Brian was a founder member of Glossop Climbing Club and of Glossop Mountain Rescue Team. Photographs show that he sometimes helped with White Hall climbing and caving.

By 1966 the number of teaching staff had grown to six, being the principal and five instructors. In January 1966 they were Kim Meldrum, John Cheesmond, Alan Alldred, Malcolm ('Wally') Blake, Dick Wilkinson and Meriel Evans. All except Alan Alldred were resident staff; Alan lived with his family in Buxton. The increase from five to six may have very briefly reduced the reliance on the services of voluntary instructors, but only until the building's capacity rose from thirty beds to forty. In about 1967, a chief instructor role was created, with Cheesmond taking up the position. Also, more domestic staff were appointed.

The gradual upgrading of the premises, begun by Geoff Sutton and continued by Eric Langmuir, carried on under Meldrum. A new shower block and new furniture improved the building's attractiveness to students and to the growing number of visiting teachers. Audio-visual aids were improved. Less obviously but importantly, plumbers fitted water purification equipment, a sewage disposal unit and a sterilising sink. In about 1969, student accommodation rose from thirty to forty.[13]

Wally Blake and Meriel Evans left White Hall at the end of August 1969 and got married. Meriel obtained a lectureship in women's PE and outdoor education at Madeley College of Education. Like Joe Brown and Gordon Mansell before him, Wally was not a qualified teacher, and so he enrolled at Madeley as a mature student. In 1973 he was appointed to the post of deputy warden at Shropshire's field studies and outdoor education centre at Arthog on the Mawddach Estuary. Meriel and Wally spent fourteen years at Arthog, during the latter part of which Meriel was bursar and Wally was warden. In 1987 Wally became the outdoor education organiser for Shropshire.

Their love of the outdoors has never faltered. When I telephoned Meriel and Wally one Sunday evening in March 2016, while I was writing this book, they had just returned from a weekend in Glencoe. On that weekend, or on another trip a few weeks later, Wally climbed Tower Ridge on Ben Nevis in winter conditions.

Wally and Meriel were replaced at White Hall by Rick Scott and Janet Richards. Janet recalls that Jack Longland sat on the interview panel for these appointments, an indication of his continuing interest in the development of the centre.[14] She also remembers that her first course was a canoeing trip down the Spey from Newtonmore to Spey-mouth (a trip involving some sections over which legal-access arguments were about to rage for the following four years). Janet recently came across her first pay slip, for September 1969. Her annual salary was about £1000.[15] (Which reminds me that in 1969 I was working as an unqualified temporary instructor at Howtown Outdoor Activity Centre, having fun on the exiguous income of £1 a day.)

Towards the end of 1969, John Cheesmond left to take up the wardenship of Ogwen Cottage (1969–72), before moving on to join the outdoor-activities group at Dunfermline College of Physical Education, where he spent twenty years delivering outdoor-education programmes. Dave Draper replaced him; an advertisement for this position used the job title deputy principal instead of chief instructor.[16]

Wilfred Edmunds, Newsprints Ltd.

Kim Meldrum (right) and Frank Hall, a long-serving voluntary instructor, in the ski store, 1964. (The wooden skis with cable bindings were replaced in about 1978.)

Maturing Progression

The basic schools' courses continued under Kim Meldrum little changed apart from some modifications to ease the progression from basic schools' course to follow-up course.

Individual course reports formed an important part of the routine. The instructors wrote brief comments about the particular pupils with whom they had been on the overnight expedition (which in most weeks took place on Thursday night). These comments, along with others that had been made by colleagues, were used as the basis for short reports, written by Meldrum and then typed up by his secretary before being posted to the school principals.[17] The instructors continued the established practice of adding gradings to their notes on individuals, recommending some pupils for follow-up courses. The long follow-up courses, termed 'supplementary courses' and 'specialist courses', were open to applications from these selected students. Applicants for the summer ones needed to be aged sixteen or over and be capable of camping efficiently for nine or eleven days in Wales or the Lake District or Scotland, whatever the weather.[18]

Soon after White Hall had opened in 1950, Peter Mosedale had found that the demand for places from the formally organised section of the youth service, which was administered through the county council's education department, was considerably smaller than expected. This was still the case under Kim Meldrum. Rather than run under-used courses, he opened up the series of three youth service specialist weekends to a wider group, including individual school pupils and potential voluntary instructors.[19]

In response to the forming of the MLTB in July 1964 and to the running of the first mountain leader course at Plas y Brenin in December 1964, Meldrum set about developing more White Hall courses for teachers, particularly courses leading to formal qualifications in canoeing, caving, skiing, hillwalking and climbing.

Programme No. 31, September 1967 – September 1968.

Fees and Breakdown of Courses, Late 1960s

Programme 31, September 1967 – September 1968, includes a list of course fees:[20]

Type of Course	Fees for Derbyshire Students		Fees for All Other Students
	Under 18	18 and over	
Weekend (Fri–Sun)	£1 0s. 0d	£2 0s. 0d	£4 5s. 0d
Longer courses, per day	10s. 0d	£1 0s. 0d	£2 2s. 6d
Organised school parties, per day	6s. 0d		£2 2s. 6d

The travelling expenses, normally by bus route, of Derbyshire pupils who were members of school parties or were under eighteen and members of registered youth organisations were refunded in excess of five shillings. The travelling expenses of voluntary instructors and teachers accompanying organised school parties were repaid in full.

Special supplements were charged for away courses: £5 for Scotland; £2 10s 0d for Wales; and from £17 to £25 (all in) for Continental skiing.

In his history of the centre, A B Afford reproduced parts of Programme 33, September 1969 – September 1970. I have taken the following table from AB's history. The courses in the table are grouped in types rather than in date order. They ranged from two to eleven days in duration. The centre was closed for two weeks at Christmas and for a month in July and August 1970. Only two youth service weekends remained on the programme, a considerable change, especially if we look right back to the early 1950s. In 1969 the minimum age for the schools' open-country pursuits courses was thirteen.

OCP: Open Country Pursuits
MU: Mobile Unit
YS: Youth Service
MLC: Mountain Leadership Certificate

No. of Courses	Type	No. of days	Students
2	OCP general	W/E	YS
2		W/E	Sixth form
1			Exam. students

1		2	Colleges of education
1		2	Matlock College
1		1	Derbyshire PE teachers
5	Specialist courses	W/E	a.b.c. graded
8	MU	4	Schools
1	OCP	4	-
1	OCP	4	Exam. pupils
1	Instructor training		Derbyshire teachers
2	OCP	4	Special schools
1		4	Derbyshire teachers
1	Easter general course		
2	Navigation & camping	4	
9	OCP	6	Schools
1		6	Post exam. pupils
2	MLC intro. & assess.	6	
2	OCP	11	Schools
1	Canoeing	9	
1	Skiing Scotland	11	Aged 16 and over
1	Isle of Arran mountaineering	11	

Peter Watson campsite, beside the River Dane at Gradbach, in about 1960. White Hall groups occasionally used this fine Scout campsite.

A group on expedition in winter, climbing Grindsbrook, Kinder Scout, late 1960s. Brightly coloured cotton anoraks and canvas rucksacks have replaced the army-surplus gear of the 1950s.

A group on expedition, resting at Mam Nick, late 1960s.

Malcolm Blake

John Cheesmond and course members at Windgather Rocks in the late 1960s, before helmets became standard wear for instructed climbing.

Brian Sharp, the White Hall storeman, at Windgather Rocks in the late 1960s.

Malcolm Blake

Alan Alldred on Clough Brook in spate, Wildboarclough,1965 or 1966. He recalls
that a fraction of a second later, 'a rock needle pierced the fibre glass just in front
of my seat. I stayed lodged in position with Joe Brown on the bank in hysterics and
refusing to do anything until he had photos.'

John Cheesmond during an attempt with
Alan Alldred to climb Kilnsey Main Overhang,
late 1960s.

Alan Alldred and Dick Wilkinson on the ice of Pavey Ark, a staff-training day in the
late 1960s/early 1970s.

Infant Bureaucracy

In 1966 Kim Meldrum wrote a jocular article for the *Climbers' Club Journal*, questioning the proliferation of outdoor qualifications and satirising some of the consequences of society's disinclination to accept the existence of any risk in our lives:

> The Outdoor Pursuits scene is changing, changing very quickly as authorities realise the value of this sort of residential training … The whole field is tending to get bogged down in bureaucracy: Mountain Leadership Certificate, BMC Guides Certificate, Mountain Centres Instructors Certificate, First Aid Certificate, Life Saving Certificate, British Canoe Union Certificate, British Association of Professional Ski Instructor's Certificate … Without most of these, instructors are just non-starters: we've all joined the rat race.[21]

Later, there's an example of the paperwork:

> In spite of … advanced training methods, accidents still occur. Recently I had to write an accident report on a student who fell: ' … he fell and landed on the ground. He sustained a serious fracture to his right malleolus. At the time he was unroped. As he fell the instructor tried to grab him …'
> I fully expected the authority to make an issue over this and was looking forward to quoting from the *Kinder and Roaches Guide* which describes the Quarry traverse at Windgather as 'a 200 foot route never exceeding jumping distance from the ground' but was surprised that it went through without question.[22]

Until this point, the evolution of White Hall had mainly featured the excited optimism of successful trailblazing. The staff had solved or worked around all the teething problems. Mosedale had avoided the worst excesses of character building by steering steadily in several other directions, depending on the visitors' requirements. Sutton and Langmuir had concentrated on consolidation and course development. Meldrum's 'White Hell Pursuing Centre' rang an alarm bell that had not previously been heard much within the world of outdoor centres.

Meldrum wrote his essay at a time when the number of outdoor residential centres was expanding apace, when many wardens were contributing to the design phase of new qualifications, and just a year before he himself became involved in a national example of the growing bureaucracy (sitting on a subcommittee of the Association of Wardens of Mountain Centres). One essay, however amusing, was not going to turn this tide. The creeping bureaucracy and regulation affecting outdoor pursuits were the inevitable results of two closely related 20th-century changes in the world at large: the ever-increasing emphasis on safety and the permeating of society by risk aversion. The 'slough of certifications', as Meldrum called it, was a necessary evil.

The canoeing and sailing communities tolerated or just accepted or even welcomed these changes. Some climbers, however, considered the developments to be unnecessary evils. They were not convinced that climbing should be promoted at all.

Their objections, according to Simon Thompson, were not based on the efficacy of the training:

> Instead, they simply disliked the increasing popularisation and bureaucratisation of 'their' sport and worried about the impact of ever increasing numbers on the mountain experience. Despite the dramatic change in the social composition of the sport, many of their arguments would have sounded familiar to nineteenth-century members of the Alpine Club, with their concerns about the vulgarisation of the Alps, or the intellectual Pen-y-Pass set in the years before the First World War, with their preference for romantic reticence.[23]

The climbers' concerns about bureaucratisation of their pastime were shared by some cavers. Caving in the late-1960s was 'only slowly emerging from its old image as the pursuit of a few dirty cranks'.[24] The sport enjoyed and guarded an anti-organisation tradition that led to some cavers opposing instructed caving.

What was under way and was gathering momentum, however, was the start of the widest popularisation of the outdoors that Britain had known. Many influences were driving this phenomenon forwards. Individual objections from some climbers would not slow the expansion or prevent the changes any more than they would stop the use by climbers of chalk or Friends. Not that the growth of outdoor education would proceed completely unchecked. In the 1960s, outdoor education in Britain had yet to experience the repercussions of a multiple fatality, such as the Cairngorm tragedy that would take place in November 1971. Several shocks, too, were in store for White Hall Centre.

Meldrum's essay anticipated both the mountain training dispute of the 1970s and the unstoppable growth of risk aversion.

The Element of Danger

In a 1958 newspaper article about White Hall, a reporter wrote: 'They have had only two serious accidents in the history of the centre.'[25] One of the accidents the writer was referring to was probably the one in which the instructor Cyril Machin was the casualty, at Castle Naze on 9 May 1954. The other was a bad but not fatal caving accident in Bar Pot in Yorkshire on 23 June 1957, described in Chapter 10.

Nationally, the first fatal accident involving a member of an outdoor-centre group may have been one that occurred at Eskdale OBMS in the early 1960s. A boy succumbed to hypothermia while descending from a night's bivouac. The boy had a medical condition unknown to the Eskdale staff.[26]

The absence of fatalities from White Hall's record was brutally shattered in 1967 when two caving accidents in three weeks, in disparate circumstances, each involved the death of a course member.

Alum Pot, Yorkshire

The first death was violent and sudden and profoundly distressing in an immediate, destitute way. On Saturday 14 January 1967, a group of ten people on a White Hall specialist weekend set out to descend Alum Pot on Ingleborough in north Yorkshire. The course was the second of three progressive Youth Service weekends. Alum Pot and its associated caves, such as Long Churn, have been known for centuries. Guides were taking visitors through Long Churn in the 18th century.

The top of Alum Pot is a large open pothole about 60 metres (200 feet) deep, which was first descended in 1847. In the 1960s, before single-rope techniques revolutionised vertical caving, there were several ways to descend Alum Pot on wire caving ladders; the route taken by the White Hall group involved a ladder pitch of about 35 metres (115 feet) to an exposed ledge, quickly followed by a second ladder pitch, this time of 15 metres (50 feet).[27]

The group comprised one professional instructor, two voluntary instructors (Harold Lord and P Smith), one student instructor, and six students. The plan was for half of the group to descend Alum Pot, while the other half walked across the hillside to enter the system somewhere else. In overall charge was Dick Wilkinson, an experienced permanent member of the White Hall staff.

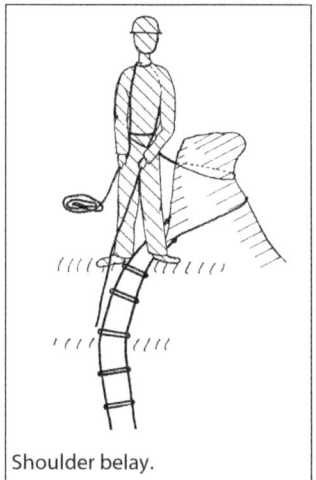

Shoulder belay.

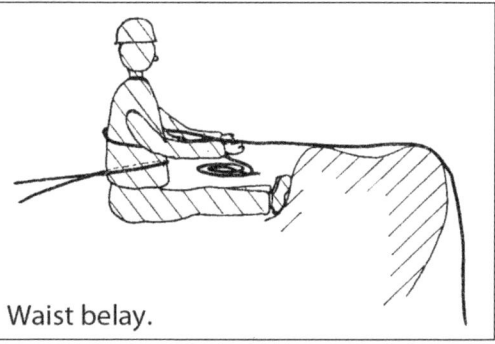

Waist belay.

Diagrams from *Manual of Caving Techniques* (1969) showing a caver controlling the lifeline at the top of a ladder pitch. On the left: belayed to a rock bollard and using a shoulder belay to hold the lifeline. On the right: belayed to something out of sight and using a waist belay to hold the lifeline.

Courtesy of Yorkshire Ramblers' Club, www.yrc.org.uk

First pitch of Alum Pot, Yorkshire, 1922.

The descent of Alum Pot began routinely. At 1pm the ladders were rigged on the first pitch. Dick then belayed himself to a tree about six metres back from the edge of the vertical drop. It was Dick's job to hold and control the lifeline, paying it out gradually as each caver descended the ladder. The way he held the rope is not entirely clear, but it was probably by wrapping the rope once around his waist, a method known as a waist belay.

At first, all went according to plan. Harold Lord descended the ladder, safeguarded by the lifeline held by Dick. Dick hauled the lifeline back to the surface, and then the student instructor, Alfred Dawson, descended without incident, again safeguarded by the lifeline.

The third person to descend was James Drummond, a twenty-two-year-old clerk-accountant from Ilkeston, Derbyshire. There is a knack to climbing down a vertical caving ladder, swinging around in mid-air, and novices have to learn that skill. Harold Lord, standing on the exposed ledge at the bottom of the first pitch and glancing up at the ladder, could see that James was having difficulty. Normally in these circumstances, the worst that could happen would see the tiring novice running out of arm strength and parting company with the ladder, to be held immediately by the lifeline. He or she would dangle in space on the lifeline. They would then be lowered the rest of the way on the lifeline. Instead, what happened must have been traumatic for Lord and Dawson: 'The next instant there was a thud and a crash on the ledge, and then a body fell off the ledge for a further 50 feet.' By chance, another party that was exploring the cave had just laddered the second pitch. Lord went down the pitch on these ladders and reached James within about a minute and a half.[28]

On reaching the body, Mr. Lord said, he did not see any signs of life. He checked Drummond's pulse which was rather weak, and then tried mouth-to-mouth resuscitation. Drummond started breathing again for about a quarter of an hour, but later ceased. The lifeline was still securely fastened to his waist and still led straight up to the surface. 'I shouted to the people at the surface, but the stream was rather high, and communication was nearly impossible,' he added.[29]

Members of the Settle and Ingleton Cave Rescue Organisation brought the body to the surface later that day.

The main part of the inquest was held in Settle on Friday 27 January. The coroner focused particularly on why the lifelining had failed. An important factor, among several, was that the tree belay was about six metres (twenty feet) back from the edge of the pothole, making it impossible for the lifeliner to see the person who was descending the ladder. A newspaper account of the inquest said:

> Mr. Wilkinson said that after Mr. Lord and Mr. Dawson had made the descent, he tied the lifeline to Drummond. He belayed the lifeline out for Drummond, and as he was doing so, the other members of the party set off to another entrance of the pothole.
>
> 'I was giving instructions to the man in charge of the other party, and suddenly I noticed the lifeline going out very fast. I tried to hold it, but did not manage it. The rope stopped going out, and as I was worried, I let go of the rope to go and see what was the matter.
>
> 'At this stage, the rest of the rope started to run out. I tried to grab hold of it, but did not manage to do so until all of it had run out. I then untied myself from the tree and went to the edge of the pot and I could see Drummond lying at the bottom.'
>
> Asked by the Coroner whether he considered this method of lifeline to be safe, Wilkinson said that in his experience, it had been safe until this occasion. It was a disadvantage, he said, if a person descending a pothole was out of view. 'If someone had been looking over the edge to watch the person climbing down and seen his progress this could have been a help.'
>
> Mr. Wilkinson said he had no doubts about Drummond's safety until the lifeline got out of control.[30]

The coroner said in his summing up that the course had apparently been carefully organised. For some reason, which still seemed to be in some doubt, the lifeline on which James Drummond depended failed to prevent his fall. There was no evidence to suggest anyone had been reckless or had ignored the lives and safety of others.

> The Coroner said that Mr. Wilkinson had given his evidence honestly and very fairly. 'It seems that he was unable to see the deceased from the position in which he himself was belayed to control the lifeline, and apparently he allowed the lifeline to go out in a condition which was not taut.

He seems to have considered [that] if the lifeline remained taut it might interfere with the freedom of action of the person who might have to depend on the lifeline. But by the fact of allowing the lifeline not to be taut, if a person falls from a ladder and is dependent on the lifeline, it seems there is at least an added reason that the lifeline cannot be held by the person who is controlling it.

'All the witnesses have considerable experience in the use of lifelines and all seem to be completely satisfied that the method adopted for controlling the lifeline and also that the materials used were completely satisfactory.

'Yet James Drummond is dead, and nobody suggested any method which could be used which would make the lifeline technique more effective in order to prevent a repetition of an accident of this kind,' the Coroner continued.

The Coroner went on to say that he was not an expert, and it might be dangerous for him and the jury to purport to tell people with considerable experience how a lifeline should be operated.

The jury returned a verdict of death by misadventure.

Much of the above information on the Alum Pot accident comes from two detailed newspaper reports, checked against a later inquiry report. I believe it to be reliable. A feature of many accidents is a combination of circumstances. The circumstances involved in this one seem to have been a beginner on the ladder, the ladder's 12-inch rung spaces, a breakdown in communications, a misunderstanding, possibly a moment of distraction, some slack in the lifeline, and the limitations of the waist belay.

In 1967 the waist belay was a common method of holding the lifeline. The basic principle of the waist belay used the friction of the rope wrapped around the lifeliner's body, with a twist around one arm, to help control the rope in a fall. The waist belay was later replaced by friction arrangements such as the Italian hitch or by mechanical brakes, which were less prone to failure.

Dick Wilkinson was still working at White Hall when I first worked there, in November 1973. A thoughtful and likeable guy who walked with a limp, Dick was full of stories about the 1960s, typically involving him and his group behind a dry stone wall, hiding from a landowner or gamekeeper. The 1967 Alum Pot accident was seldom mentioned either by Dick or by any of the other White Hall staff but it contributed towards a legacy in the form of a 1:3 staff-pupil ratio for caving, later modified to 3:10.

Carlswark Cavern

The second White Hall fatal caving accident happened in Carlswark Cavern at Stoney Middleton, Derbyshire. Carlswark Cavern is a cave system that has been frequently used by White Hall groups on schools' introductory courses, often as a half-day activity requiring about an hour and a half underground. The cave system, partly natural and partly mined for lead, is now in a Site of Special Scientific Interest.

Typically, parties of novices do Carlswark as a short through-trip, in one way and out by another. This involves a laddered descent of a ten-metre mineshaft, Eyam Dale Shaft, followed by a flat-out crawl to reach a low phreatic passage, Eyam Passage, formed naturally in solid limestone. You follow this water-dissolved passage mainly on hands and knees or by stooped walking. It is a sort of tube, roughly elliptical in shape. There are shallow pools of percolation water, but – unlike some other parts of the Carlswark system – Eyam Passage has no active streamway and it never floods. Towards the end of it you can stand and walk upright. The exit is by an easy scramble up a sloping lead-miners' entrance, called the Gin Entrance.

As well as White Hall, many other outdoor centres visit Carlswark with newcomers to caving. Thousands of young people have sampled Carlswark's damp crawls and have then scrambled up the Gin Entrance to finally clamber past tree roots and emerge back into daylight, soaking, muddy and grinning. The risks are minimal. But they are not zero, and unusual combinations of circumstances can arise to remind us of that.

Brian Sharp, the White Hall storeman, entering Carlswark Cavern by the Eyam Dale shaft. Late 1960s.

On Wednesday 1 February 1967 at about 11.30am, a White Hall group of five boys and one instructor, Malcolm ('Wally') Blake, began their Carlswark trip by descending the Eyam Dale Shaft on a caving ladder. Robert Fraser Macdonald, aged fourteen and from Taddington, asked several times to go first. Blake, who was lifelining the pupils, agreed to this request. Blake 'told everyone to wait at the bottom of the shaft until everyone was down'. There was a space here big enough for the whole group to assemble. (At the inquest, two of the boys said that Blake had repeated the instruction about three times.) But when the second boy reached the bottom, Macdonald had disappeared.[31] Blake assumed that Macdonald had made his way to the Gin Entrance alone, so he took the rest of the party through the cave and out by the Gin Entrance. But there was no sign of the missing boy.

Later that day, three White Hall instructors spent about three hours searching the cave. At about 8pm, members of the Derbyshire Cave Rescue Organisation began another search, concentrating on the cave's main sump (a water-filled passage at the bottom of the cave). Among the searchers were Dave Allsop, Keith Worsencroft and John Plowes, all of whom had worked occasionally at White Hall as voluntary instructors. Also present was Dr Hugh Kidd of Buxton, a future White Hall governor. About four and a half hours later, early on the Thursday morning, after thousands of gallons of water had been pumped from the sump, the boy's body was found in the sump.[32]

At the inquest, one of the boys told the coroner: 'He [Fraser Macdonald] was very keen and wanted to do well. He was always keen to be first.'[33] Fraser's father described his son as a healthy boy who was fond of outdoor life and outdoor sport. Fraser had wanted to go on the course. 'It was his own idea and I concurred', he said.[34]

Malcolm Blake said he had been an instructor at White Hall since January 1966. During the winter, he said, courses were given to school children, and parties numbered up to about ten. On this occasion there were five, and one instructor could cope with five. In answer to a question from the coroner, Blake 'said that he invariably went on his own with boys'.[35]

The verdict of the inquest was accidental death. Speaking to the jury, the coroner said: 'This young man was obviously keen, a good sportsman, and may have been a little adventurous. He was anxious to do that sport well and to go first and show what he could do … but in all such sports and activities, instructions must be fulfilled, as there [is] nothing more dangerous than when instructions [are] not obeyed.'[36]

No conclusion was reached on why Fraser had set off on his own.

Derbyshire education committee set up a five-man independent board of inquiry to look into the two caving deaths.[37] The members were A S Pigott, H K Hartley, C Hooley, J K Needham and J E Plowes. Alfred Pigott, the chairman, was a leading climber of the 1920s and 30s, Longland's forceful second during the first ascent of Longland's Climb, and later a recognised authority on mountain rescue – but was not a caver. Similarly, Herbert Hartley was secretary of the Mountain Rescue Committee but was not a caver. However, Charles ('Chuck') Hooley was both a caver and a climber, and in 1967 he had been the equipment officer of the Derbyshire Cave Rescue Organisation (DCRO) for seven years. John Needham too was a caver. In 1967 he had been the DCRO secretary for eight years. John Plowes, another caver and DCRO member, had helped White Hall develop its caving since 1952.

On the day of the inquiry, John Needham had been on another cave rescue all night long, had not exited the cave until 8.30am and hadn't had time to get home and change out of caving clothes. He arrived at the meeting wet through and covered in mud.[38]

In April 1967 this board reported on the circumstances of the accidents and it recommended new safety measures for White Hall's potholing. Two versions of the report exist. The first, sent to Longland on 3 April and signed by Pigott, is among Longland's private papers.[39] An apparently later version, retyped and unsigned, is held in the records of the Derbyshire Cave Rescue Organisation. Some of the wording of the second version has been changed. Most of the changes are minor.

The last sentence of the report forces me to digress. The first version included the phrase 'character building', a term that by then for many people had pejorative undertones that Longland was aware of: 'The Board accepts the fact that there is an element of danger in caving and mountaineering; against this must be set the educational and character building values of these activities.'[40] The final version crept slightly away from the outmoded term and slightly towards the more fashionable term, 'social and personal development': 'While the Board accepts that there is an element of danger in caving, it feels most strongly that rising to the challenges provided by nature can and does lead to personal development of character and ability and provides an individual with an increasing consciousness of group responsibilities.'[41]

In connection with the Alum Pot accident, the board recommended that the person operating the lifeline should be as near as possible to the edge of the shaft. If being close to the edge was impossible, another person should be in a suitable position to relay communications. The board also felt that ladders with 10-inch rung spaces would be preferable to ones with 12-inch rung spaces. It also recommended that a ladder pitch of 120 feet should not be undertaken by novices.

On the Carlswark accident, the board said that no blame could be attached to the instructor, Malcolm Blake. It recommended that all parties of cavers should have at least two instructors. In addition, the board recommended that there should be one instructor to every three pupils.[42] The question of what is an adequate staff-pupil ratio for caving had been first raised ten years earlier, after the near-fatality in Bar Pot.

In June 1967 the education committee approved the spending of £100 for the replacement of 12-inch rung-space caving ladders by 10-inch rung-space ladders, as recommended by the board's report.[43] This technical issue was another matter that had been discussed after the Bar Pot accident.

Another matter that came under review was the medical examination of pupils attending courses at the centre.[44] Also, some discussion took place about offering individual personal accident insurance for course members.[45]

Writing in 1978, reflecting on this difficult period in White Hall's history, Kim Meldrum remembered the fundamental questions that it had raised:

> During my last year at White Hall there were two fatal accidents –
> both were caving accidents and both were of a quite different char-
> acter. This led me to believe that however carefully programmes
> are devised and however stringently safety regulations are applied,
> accidents can always occur. It is the character of these activities
> that there should be a real element of danger – without danger
> the activities cease to offer any challenge. A mountaineering psy-
> chologist has said that fatalities are necessary. I began to ask myself
> whether it was right to introduce activities with these elements
> of danger to students who may not be sufficiently mature to be
> capable of recognising the hazards themselves. This perhaps is an
> issue which only other individuals can answer for themselves.[46]

A crucial thread in the ideas of Kurt Hahn was his belief in the value of adventure, despite the risks this might entail.[47] This was one Hahn tenet with which a succession of White Hall Centre staff had agreed. The accidents at Alum Pot and Carlswark Cavern must undoubtedly have precipitated a searching re-examination of the finer details of that belief, privately if not publicly.

In their book *Outdoor Education* (1973), Parker and Meldrum included some elementary and perhaps debatable statistics said to show that the accident risk in caving was considerably greater than in skiing, canoeing, climbing, walking and sailing.[48] The book gave no source for the figures used. The authors' conclusions may have reflected the happenings at White Hall, experienced by Meldrum, rather than the happenings in the sports as practised nationally by adults.

Ernest Baker had touched upon the same question as long ago as 1903, in a discussion on the sport of caving:

> … And this brings me to the attraction that may well be the keenest of all to some minds, namely, the danger. Not that cave exploration is to be ranked among the pastimes that involve a certain percentage of disasters; I do not think there has ever been a fatal accident placed to its account. Yet cave-work does belong to that masculine class of sports, of which mountaineering and rock-climbing are the type, which incessantly bring their followers into the presence of danger … The perils of rock-climbing are frank and open, those of cave-work are of an insidious and more intimidating kind.[49]

The first UK recreational caving fatality in the 20th century occurred in West Mine, Alderley Edge in May 1929, when two men failed to return from a Whit Sunday trip. Their bodies were found four months later in a little-known working of the mine.[50]

It would probably be a mistake to conclude from the happenings at White Hall that, in general, novice caving in the 1960s was more hazardous than novice climbing. So it is strange that White Hall's only other fatal accident – its third – would again take place on a caving trip (in May 1973). Stranger still, the only serious near-misses that I was personally involved in (in work time) during sixteen years at White Hall were two incidents that occurred on caving trips.[51]

Malcolm Blake

Caving group, Horseshoe Cave, Winnats Pass, late 1960s. They have miners' cap-lamps and Oldham lead-acid batteries, which have replaced the old acetylene cap-lamps. The boiler-suits are standard cotton industrial wear.

Mountain and Cave Rescue – Meldrum Period

Six months after Kim Meldrum arrived at White Hall, a rescue call-out occurred that subsequently led to his becoming influentially involved in mountain rescue. The forty-five-mile Four Inns Walk is a competition organised by the Scout Association and held annually. It was first held for Rover Scouts in 1957. The event is undertaken in teams of three or four. The route crosses the high moorlands of the northern Peak District, starting at Holmbridge and finishing in Buxton. Typically, times range from eight to sixteen hours.

At 6am on Saturday 14 March 1964, eighty-three three-man teams of Rover Scouts left Holmbridge at two-minute intervals to cover the forty-five miles to Buxton. Strong winds and cold driving rain battered the hikers, and poor visibility intensified the difficulties. Many teams dropped out. Four inches of snow fell on the Saturday night. White Hall staff took part in searches for missing competitors. Three Rover Scouts, aged nineteen, twenty-one and twenty-four, succumbed to the conditions, dying of hypothermia.[52] Only twenty-two of the field of about 240 competitors finished the event. Jack Longland and Kim Meldrum were asked to sit on a committee of inquiry with senior figures from the Scouts.[53]

Following this tragedy, Meldrum 'became a central figure in negotiations that led to the formation of the Peak District Mountain Rescue

Organisation. [He] chaired many of the early formative meetings held at the White Hall Centre and was eventually nominated as a member of the first mountain rescue search controllers' panel.'[54]

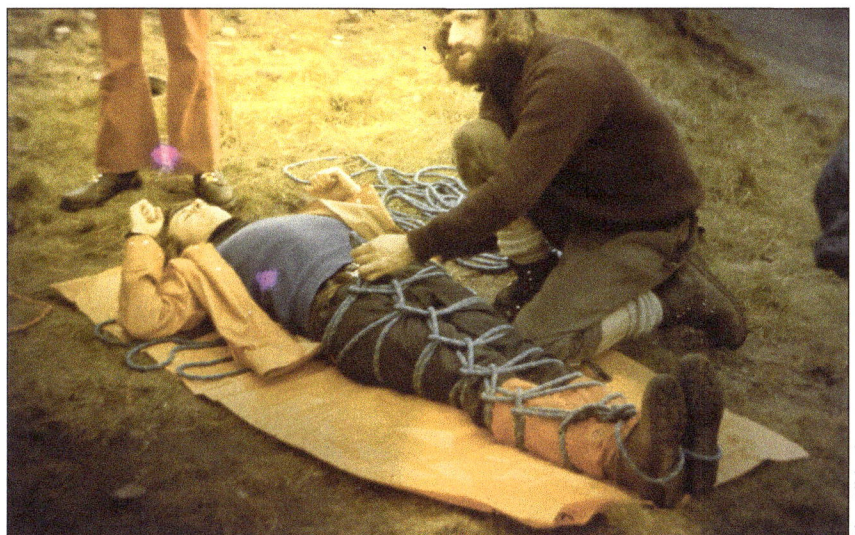

Improvised rescue. Alan Alldred shows the Glossop mountain rescue team how to tie an alpine basket, late 1960s/early 1970s.

Alan Alldred demonstrates an alpine basket lower.

Alan Alldred

Rick Scott (nearest) and Dave Draper (orange helmet) demonstrate a stretcher lower, early 1970s.

On 7 July 1965, a bizarre incident in Carlswark Cavern raised some concerns, in mountain- and cave-rescue circles at least, about the way that some sections of the army used adventurous sports. Sometimes there can be nothing more dangerous than obeying an instruction. An army cadet John Stevens, on an army initiative test, was ordered to dive into Carlswark's water-filled sump and to swim through it. (Jim Hogan's 1968 book comes to mind: *Impelled into Experience*. Hogan stressed, however, that the impellee should survive the impelling.) The sixteen-year-old was dressed in just jeans and a sweater, but he was a strong swimmer who swam for the army. Every morning, at the start of his training routine, he swam two lengths under water.

He obeyed the order. He swam along the flooded tunnel for twenty metres and then, miraculously, discovered an air pocket, just before running out of breath. There he remained, not risking either returning the way he had come or continuing on. Civilian rescuers spent thirteen hours pumping water from the sump, knowing full well that they were looking for a dead body. To everyone's astonishment, they found John alive and led him to safety.[55]

Thirty-six years later, in 2001, John Stevens returned to Carlswark during a reunion with his rescuers. He told the *Manchester Evening News*:

> Going down there brought back … the memories of exactly what happened. You forget the arrogance of the people who controlled us. The guy had to be off his trolley to send a 16-year-old boy down there. I had been in three times. I kept coming back to say that it was flooded and he said it couldn't be and to get back in there … There was an official enquiry, but I wasn't even invited. They paid for me to go away with my sister and when I got back I was transferred very quickly.[56]

By January 1966, Kim Meldrum was able to say, as chair of the Peak District Mountain Rescue Organisation, that it could now call on 600 rescuers and searchers: twenty teams with thirty members each. There had been five large-scale turn-outs since the organisation began.[57]

After about 1970, the involvement of White Hall staff members on mountain rescues diminished, as there were now enough local people experienced in hillwalking or mountaineering and able to devote their time to mountain rescue. Several White Hall instructors, particularly Dave Draper, remained involved in cave rescue, both in its administration and in rescues.

Malcolm Blake

Cliff rescue practice on Combs Edge, late 1965. Alan Aldred (standing) and a student.

National Developments – Meldrum Period

Nationally during White Hall's Meldrum era, the conferencing, committeeing and qualification-ing gathered pace and, sometimes, a little intrigue. Jack Longland was everywhere. In 1963, as well as being the BMC president, he was chairman of the CCPR's outdoor-activities advisory committee. According to the publisher and writer Ken Wilson, on 25 September 1963 Longland chaired a meeting of this committee that decided (quietly) that some sort of qualification was needed that lay between the BMC's Mountain Guide and the minimum qualifications the BMC circulated as necessary for schoolteachers venturing into the hills with children (Circular 326). Wilson, looking back in 1997, viewed this decision-making suspiciously: 'Major policy was decided, without warning and late at night at just one meeting. The background to the CCPR meeting is unclear. Was Jack Longland launching a completely personal initiative, or was he responding to some urgent Government "encouragement"?'[58]

With hindsight, we can now see, in the circumstances surrounding the advisory committee's meeting, the first tiny crack of a major rift that would open in 1973. However, until then the relations between the national organisations would remain harmonious enough to allow considerable progress.

In autumn 1963 Longland was present at the first 'Countryside in 1970' conference. He was one of the few people sufficiently influential and informed to straddle both environmental studies and outdoor activities.[59]

In late 1963 and early 1964 a CCPR working party met four times to discuss the proposed certificate. John Jackson (the warden of Plas y Brenin) and Eric Langmuir worked on the draft training syllabus.[60]

At a meeting in London on 17 July 1964, representatives of national bodies concerned with education, the youth service, and outdoor activities endorsed the detailed proposals for the certificate.

On 15 September 1964 the Mountain Leadership Training Board (MLTB) met formally for the first time. Longland was unanimously elected chairman, a position he would hold until 1980. Longland had been 'the prime mover in getting the scheme started ... and he had a talent for giving courteous regard to all views and for easing the ways of consultation and decision making'.[61] Two bodies had been behind a final three-year drive in 1961–4 to create the MLTB. One was the CCPR, and particularly its outdoor activity advisory committee, chaired by Longland.[62] The other was not the BMC (although the BMC was represented on the board); it was the Association of Wardens of Mountain Centres (AWMC). The term 'mountain centres' in this association's name was a slightly misleading generalisation; some of the wardens worked at centres more involved with the sea than the mountains.

The delegates at this inaugural meeting agreed to call themselves the Mountain Leadership Training Board (MLTB) and to call the qualification the Mountain Leadership Certificate.

In October 1964 Longland chaired the second conference of mountain centres. In a briefing he confirmed that the Mountain Leadership Training Board had been constituted. Its board comprised three representatives of the CCPR, three of the BMC, and several individuals appointed by the CCPR to serve in their personal capacities.[63]

Among the topics discussed at this conference were the Mountain Leader Certificate (MLC) and a proposed Mountaineering Instructor Certificate (MIC). The AWMC submitted a draft proposal for the latter.

By this time, Longland had reason to feel quietly proud of his achievement in setting up White Hall. When necessary he drew attention to the outdoor revolution that residential outdoor pursuits centres had contributed to, but he remained careful not to exaggerate. You wonder whether he had character training in mind when he said to the conference delegates that the case for residential outdoor centres was now proven, but warned them that excessive claims for intended effects might draw strong criticism.[64]

*

We saw in Chapter 7 that in the mid-1950s the colleges of physical education had, with one or two exceptions, not yet attached anything more than marginal recognition to outdoor pursuits. By the early 1960s, this uninterest had begun to give way to enthusiastic commitment, discoloured here and there with some pessimistic alarm. There had always been plenty of informal competition among climbers, but most hillwalking, climbing and mountaineering in the early 1960s was non-competitive in the sense that there were no written rules. (Still today, the BMC insists that it is a representational organisation, not a rule-making governing body.) For some older, senior PE lecturers, getting to grips with a sport that had no rules required a considerable mental adjustment. Also, part of the attraction of hillwalking and mountaineering involved an appreciation of landscapes, often accompanied by an element of romanticism and exaltation, encapsulated by the climber and scientist George Finch: 'I had made up my mind to see the world; to

see it from above, from the tops of mountains whence I could get that
wide and comprehensive view which is denied to those who observe
things from their own plane.'[65] If such aesthetics and transcendence
struck a PE lecturer as belonging somewhere other than in PE, then
for that person the adjustment in thinking was even greater.

In the *Physical Education Year Book* for 1963-4, John Disley, the
outdoor-activities adviser for Surrey county council, wrote that outdoor
pursuits were now firmly embedded in school programmes 'on their
own merits', irrespective of whether you believed that the pursuits were
character-building: 'Whatever the place outdoor activities have in the
school, it seems that they have come to stay ... It is far easier to justify
the teaching of outdoor activities to children than it is to defend the rest
of our conventional P. E. programme on educational grounds.'[66] Disley
believed that the merits included enjoyment and social development
and, for some pupils, the gaining of a lasting recreational interest. By
the mid-1960s, many colleges and universities that offered courses in
physical education were emphasising outdoor activities in their marketing literature and advertisements.[67] The word 'explosion' would not be
out of place. This widening of PE to include outdoor pursuits was one
part of a general postwar diversifying of PE to include a great variety
of activities and skills from games and sports and dance.[68]

While the PE colleges were waking up to outdoor pursuits, various
other tertiary institutions began to develop graduate or postgraduate
courses in outdoor education. Notable among these were I M Marsh
College (Liverpool), Moray House College (Edinburgh), Charlotte
Mason College (Ambleside), Bingley College (Yorkshire) and the
University College of North Wales (Bangor). Harold Drasdo, writing
in 1972, viewed the prospect of competition from younger writers as
more of a nuisance than a scholarly challenge: 'Centre Wardens are
plagued with questionnaires from students writing theses on outdoor
education and are forever having to decline the honour of contributing
a chapter or so on aims and purposes'.[69]

*

In 1950 Longland had recognised that White Hall Centre might
become an example that other LEAs would follow. There is little
doubt, anecdotally, that this happened. The geographical connections
in some cases were obvious. John W Cook, for example, a climber and
an enthusiast for outdoor education, was an assistant education officer
under Longland in Derbyshire. While there he acquired a knowledge
of White Hall. Then he moved to the West Riding LEA, where Jim

Hogan, an ex-warden of Aberdovey OBSS, was managing the transition of Bewerley Park from field-studies centre to outdoor-pursuits centre.[70] In 1964 John Cook, described by Longland as 'a first-class organiser'[71] and now possessing ideas both from White Hall and from Aberdovey OBSS, was appointed Lothian's deputy director of education. In 1966 he opened Benmore Centre, the first LEA residential outdoor-pursuits centre in Scotland.[72] Edinburgh owed much of its outdoor-education growth to John Cook.

As well as growing in number in the 1960s, outdoor centres also diversified, especially if you look beyond the LEA examples. Hafod Meurig, the Rainier Foundation's centre in north Wales, opened in September 1963 and pioneered the use of the outdoors for the intermediate treatment and rehabilitation of delinquent youths.[73] People's views vary on the success or otherwise of this sort of fairly ambitious enterprise. A frank account of the realities of working with sixteen- and seventeen-year-old tearaways appeared in Jeff Connor's biography of John Cunningham. While studying for a diploma in youth and community work in 1965–7, Cunningham discovered that 'some of the juvenile Dumbarton clientele proved stubbornly resistant to the charms of the great outdoors'.[74]

In December 1964 the first mountain leader training course took place at Plas y Brenin. The MLC was a reality. While the first young qualification-seekers presented themselves to be trained or assessed, in some quarter the hackles rose. In August 1965, Longland was already having to defend the MLTB against criticism of mountaineering courses in the climbing press. He replied staunchly.[75]

Also in 1965, Longland's three years as BMC president ended, and John Hunt took over. Tensions arose between Longland and Hunt over whether the MLTB or the BMC should run the proposed MIC scheme. Longland became chair of Plas y Brenin (the National Mountaineering Centre) management committee. He also became involved in a controversy over walking access in Wales.[76]

The Pennine Way was officially opened on 24 April 1965, thirty years after Tom Stephenson's *Daily Herald* article, 'Wanted – A Long Green Trail'.[77]

Harold Wilson's Labour Party had narrowly won the October 1964 general election. Acting on the recommendations of the Wolfenden report, in early 1965 the Labour government announced that it would establish a Sports Council to advise it on amateur sport and physical recreation and to encourage cooperation between the statutory authorities and voluntary organisations involved. The government transferred many of the CCPR's assets and operational staff into an interim body called the Advisory Sports Council.[78]

Also in 1965, the Department of Education and Science issued Circular 10/65, expanding a reform of secondary education that was already happening in some localities. The circular requested LEAs to prepare plans to reorganise secondary schooling on comprehensive lines and to end selection by examination at eleven-plus.[79]

In 1919–20, the working week for millions of workers had become forty-eight hours. But the next stage, the five-day forty-hour week, seeped in, drip by drip, over a long period. By 1964 even the retail and distributive trades had agreed 'a variety of alternative ways in which the five-day week could be operated, the central factor being that however it was done, there must be an additional full half-day of leisure'.[80]

In October 1965 the first-generation Ford Transit was introduced to Britain, heralding the Age of the Minibus. In August 1969, White Hall was running two Land Rovers and a twenty-seater bus. (One of the White Hall legends tells of a Land Rover overturning on the steep incline down into the Goyt Valley. I am indebted to Janet Davies for supplying the facts. The departure from an upright position took place in the winter of 1969–70. The cause was black ice, no-one was hurt, but the Land Rover needed one new wing mirror. The investigating police officer skidded out of control at exactly the same spot.[81]) From about 1970 onwards, minibuses would greatly influence the practicalities both of residential courses in outdoor pursuits and of school-based outdoor ventures.

Malcolm Blake

A White Hall Centre Land Rover, late 1960s.

Also in 1965 an American by the name of Sherman Popper invented the Snurfer (blending 'snow' and 'surfer'), now widely regarded as the first snowboard.

Into 1966, and the first of a string of safety conferences. In January, Longland was the main speaker at a University of Leeds conference on safety in outdoor pursuits. In July he might have grabbed a couple of hours to watch England win the World Cup. In April 1967 he contributed to a symposium on accidental hypothermia in cavers, hillwalkers and campers. Later that year he chaired a safety conference at Bedford College, where he spoke to an audience of over 400. In October 1969, he chaired an Imperial College conference on safety in mountains.[82]

Other national developments that took place during Kim Meldrum's time at White Hall included the publication of *Mountaineering* by Alan Blackshaw, the coming of the BCU Senior Instructor Certificate, the publication of the BMC's Mountain Code, the approval of the Cave Instructor Certificate, the publication of the first edition of Langmuir's *Mountain Leadership*, and the widespread adoption of the term 'outdoor education' (a change that is covered in the next chapter).

By 1969, after ten years of blissful expansion, the total number of outdoor centres of various sorts in England and Wales was at least 203 and was heading for 300, a number that would nearly be reached in 1973. The 1973 total would be 298, comprising 166 centres that were mainly for field studies and 132 centres providing mostly outdoor pursuits. The 132 outdoor pursuits centres were owned by LEAs and other bodies.[83]

The apparent large increase in just four years resulted partly from an initial under-recording. But it also reflected the difficulty in defining what was meant by a 'centre for outdoor education'. Regarding such terms as 'outdoor activities', 'outdoor studies', 'rural', 'experience', 'education' and 'centre', the authors of the *Directory of Centres for Outdoor Education in England and Wales* (1970) identified 'a rich and confused terminology with considerable semantic overlap, variety of interpretations and a tendency to give general terms a special meaning in particular contexts'.[84]

Some of the 132 outdoor pursuits centres saw their main work as being in the area of water activities, others as being in the area of mountain activities. Some claimed an equal emphasis on both areas. Water activities listed in the directory included sailing, canoeing, rowing, water skiing, subaqua, surfing, fishing and sea rescue. Mountain activities included general mountaineering, rock climbing, mountain leadership training, caving, camping and walking expeditions, mountain rescue, and mine shaft exploration. Other activities listed were gliding, horse riding, pony trekking, archery and skiing. Conspicuous by its absence was cycling, despite the Bicycle Touring Club having been formed in 1878 (later renamed the Cyclists' Touring Club).

About twelve LEAs had introduced various regulations to control the handling of groups of school pupils in the mountains. Some of these LEAs were insisting that the teacher in charge should hold the MLC. Others required their teachers to have gained approval from some appointed expert within the authority. Others had made no provision and appeared unlikely to do so in the immediate future.[85]

Nationally, some new concerns were emerging. There were complaints in the Lake District that the crags were becoming overcrowded. In an article titled 'How Many Climbers?', Kim Meldrum examined survey data in an attempt to inject some reliable numbers into this discussion. His conclusions substantiated the complaints.[86]

Robert Baden-Powell might have had something to do with that overcrowding. Despite its problems retaining boys in their mid-teens, the Boy Scout movement in 1963 still had 570,953 boys.[87] It had repulsed accusations of militarism and imperialism. The *Sunday Times* reflected on the organisation's resilience:

> The language and dress of the city boys pass through countless variations of ted, skiffle, trad, rock, beat and mod. The Scout uniform and law remain obstinately turn of the century. And that is the lasting paradox of the Boy Scouts. Why does the juke-box generation still hanker for camp-fire songs under an open sky?[88]

One of the reasons, the article suggested, was that the outdoor life was 'still one of the top charms of Scouting'. By 1967 in Britain, one adult in three had belonged to either the Boy Scouts or the Girl Guides.[89]

Scouting, invented by a diehard imperialist, a devotee of folk wisdom and colonial myth, was an irrepressible survivor. All over the Empire, however, the Union Jack was coming down. Somalia, Uganda, Tanzania, Malawi, Zambia, Botswana, Lesotho and Swaziland all gained independence between 1960 and 1968.

*

We have covered the immediate postwar years, 1945 to 1950, and the tenures of four White Hall wardens or principals, from December 1950 to late summer 1970. Before coming to White Hall, all four of these men had done national service, Mosedale during the war and the other three after the war. This period almost exactly matches Part Five of Ken Ogilvie's *Roots and Wings*, a section whose title sums up the twenty-five years metaphorically: 'Seeds Taking Root in the Pursuit of Freedom'.

Co-authoring *High Peak* in 1966, Eric Byne and Geoff Sutton glanced back at the seeds that had taken root at White Hall. You could argue all night about which seed most influenced the ethos that had evolved. Byne and Sutton, though, were certain of the answer: the joint appointments of married couples to the post of warden and housekeeper. They wrote: 'The real secret of the Centre's success, however, has always lain in the characters of Betty Mosedale, Ann Sutton, Maureen Langmuir and Barbara Meldrum, who have done ninety per cent of the necessary and unrewarding hard work while their husbands held the centre of the stage, in spite of which they have succeeded in conveying an atmosphere of homeliness and hospitality.'[90]

In 1970 Kim and Barbara Meldrum moved on to other pastures, hoping never again to have to deal with tragic and shocking events like those of January and February 1967. Also in 1970 Kim completed an MPhil thesis at the University of Nottingham[91] and with Brian Royle co-wrote *Artificial Climbing Walls*.[92] The latter book, which was once an up-to-date commentary on the purpose and types of exterior and indoor climbing walls, is now a historical source.

At some point the Meldrums headed north to Edinburgh, where in 1972 Kim took up a lecturing post at Moray House, working with Eric Langmuir on the post-graduate course in outdoor activities and environmental studies. He also teamed up with Terry Parker to write *Outdoor Education* (1973).

One section of this Parker-Meldrum book needs mentioning now, roughly in its chronological place. We saw in Chapter 7 that one of the purposes of White Hall, stated a number of times in print in 1949–50, was to promote outdoor recreation. Later, in 1963, the Newsom report welcomed the fact that adventurous outdoor pursuits could 'readily be carried forward into adult life'.[93] Ten years on from Newsom, Meldrum and Parke wrote that residential outdoor pursuits centres were generally regarded as serving four aims, one of which was to introduce young people to lasting leisure-time pursuits. But a crude cost-benefit analysis had led these two authors to conclude that spending public money on a centre for this reason would be totally inadvisable … if one further realizes that most mountain-eers cease their activities during their mid-twenties. Residential centres therefore cannot be regarded as viable if their principal aim is to provide young people with lasting leisure-time pursuits. In fact it would be difficult to find pursuits which were less suited to a lasting interest than rock climbing, canoeing and caving. Surveys have shown that other pursuits, such as sailing, camping, walking and skiing, are more susceptible to a lasting interest.[94]

How things change. Looking back from 2004, Derek Walker recalled that in the 1950s and 60s 'a lot of climbers … gave up climbing early, particularly when the pressures of family life weighed against a sport then potentially so much more dangerous than it is today'. In the 1950s, the average age of new members to one major club (for example) was twenty-four; by 2004 it had become forty-three. Except for the university clubs, people were joining clubs at a much later age and were continuing to climb for much longer. Climbing had become a sport for life.[95]

Even in the 1950s, although many climbers did give up climbing early, an unknown number did not. Peter Mosedale, writing in 1975, made this very point:

[The] advantages of these [hill and water] sports are that they can be continued throughout life – one of the pioneer instructors in the early 1950s [Cyril Machin] was a prominent member of the Midland Association of Mountaineers who did much of his best work and his best mountaineering after retirement – and that, because of their powerful emotional pull, they provide a focal point strong enough to encourage persistent physical training and general preparation over long periods. A climber may climb long Alpine routes only once a year on annual holiday, but this one serious mountaineering holiday is often sufficient to moti-vate him to take regular exercise and gear his life style towards healthy activity to use every local opportunity for climbing on rock outcrops. Even the Oxford University Mountaineering Club developed practice 'climbs' [in the early 1950s] on the stone-built railway bridges at Horspath east of Oxford.[96]

How intriguing, then, to see Meldrum and Mosedale, writing just two years apart, taking opposite views on this particular plank of White Hall's reason for existence.

Kim Meldrum's own life has demonstrated the possible longevity of an interest in mountaineering. In 1974 he moved back south, taking up a job in leisure and recreation in Greater Manchester. He was still climbing at the end of the century, visiting the Dauphiné in 1999 or 2000.[97] By this time his occasional articles in the *Fell and Rock Journal*, and in other climbing-club journals, stretched over forty-five years.

Martin Boysen has provided a more recent example of the lasting activity of some climbers. In 1963 he led the first ascent of Nexus on Dinas Mot, whose second pitch is one of the finest of its grade (E1) in Wales. In July 2013 he climbed it a second time.[98]

Even at the time the Parker-Meldrum book was published (1973), when the longevity argument was stronger than later, the straightforward conclusion that the authors drew from their cost-benefit analysis warranted some questioning. Over the 1960s, the residential outdoor-pursuits centres had contributed to an outdoor revolution, an explosion of young people into the mountains. Dozens of physical-education tertiary courses had been widened to include outdoor pursuits. By 1972 the mountain leader training scheme was one of the biggest training schemes in British sport.[99] Education authorities had a responsibility to recognise these developments in recreation and leisure.

Looking back today at the Parker-Meldrum rudimentary cost-benefit analysis, many authorities would now point out the extreme complexity of the issues involved, and especially the fiendish difficulty of measuring the salutary effects of a combination of a residential experience, an improved understanding of the countryside and an adventurous outdoor pursuit.[100]

The literature of mountaineering and sailing is packed with accounts of idyllic experiences in childhood or during teenage years influencing a person's whole life. The context in the books invariably involves some famous climber or sailor, but you do not have to be well known to remember an idyll, whether landscape or seascape; many grassroots climbers and sailors retain vivid memories of their first exploits on the rock or in boats. They may have perfect recall fifty years after their first, often hesitant, outings. The cause and effect, however, defy pedagogic attempts to link and quantify them (despite frequent claims to the contrary).

In 1969, Concorde made its maiden flight, Neil Armstrong stepped onto the surface of the moon, and in the UK the death penalty for murder was abolished. The number of private cars in Britain had risen from 2,258,000 in 1950 to 11,228,000.[101] Writing in 1965, Burton and Wibberley said that the single most important factor affecting the level of weekend recreation activity was the number of private cars in use. The car provided a degree of flexibility in the use of leisure time that could not be given by any other form of transport.[102] Easier travel and improved equipment had changed sports like climbing and canoeing, and would continue to do so, as Chapter 16 will relate. Recollecting the equipment of the late 1960s, Alan Alldred mentioned the 'superb Gannex anoraks' (a make of waterproof favoured by the prime minister, Harold Wilson).[103] More schoolteachers were taking pupils on outdoor pursuits. Physical education academics were beginning to view outdoor pursuits as a valuable part of the PE curriculum.[104] Society had become less authoritarian but was about to become more risk averse, nudged relentlessly in this direction by the influence of an unopposed alliance of statisticians, physicians, lawyers, journalists, politicians, administrators and other public-spirited citizens. Lyn and June Noble arrived at White Hall in autumn 1970 for what would become a stay of twenty-one years.[105]

Jack Longland retired from the job of director of education in August 1970, but he remained heavily involved with the Mountain Leadership Training Board throughout the 1970s, much of which was a period of growing controversy over mountain training. He continued in his radio role hosting *My Word* until about 1978. After Longland had left *My Word*, a radio and television columnist in *The Times* wrote: 'Because [*My Word*] is now something of a national institution, it matters a great deal how well the chairman of *My Word!* integrates with the witty quartet who make up the panel. Jack Longland was the perfect chairman, courteous, receptive, self-effacing and clearly well liked by the team.'[106]

Notes

1   K I Meldrum, 'A Warning to Nocturnal "Aquabats"', *Fell and Rock Journal*, 17, no. 2 (1955), pp. 169–172.

2   Simon Clark, *The Puma's Claw* (London: Hutchinson, 1959), pp. 19–24. Also K I Meldrum, 'The Ascent of Pumasillo', *Fell and Rock Journal*, 18, no. 2 (1958), pp. 125–133.

3   K I Meldrum, 'Climbs and Expeditions: Allinccapac, Cordillera Carabaya', *American Alpine Journal*, 12 (1961), pp. 398–400.

4   A B Afford, *The Story of White Hall Open Country Pursuits Centre; vol. 2* (Buxton, Derbyshire, UK: A B Afford, 1978), p. 24.

5   Meriel Blake, Email to P McDonald, subject 'White Hall Centre 1965', 18 Apr 2016 [Email].

6   Jeff Connor, *Creagh Dhu Climber: The Life and Times of John Cunningham* (no place given: Ernest Press, 1999), p. 164.

7   K I Meldrum, 'White Hell Pursuing Centre', *Climbers' Club Journal: 1966*, 15, no. 1 (new series) (1966), pp. 61–67 (p. 66).

8   Derek Walker, 'The Evolution of Climbing Clubs in Britain', *Alpine Journal*, 108 (2004), pp. 187–195.

9   Mark Lambert, Email to P McDonald, subject 'AB Afford', 31 Jan 2016 [Email].

10   John Cheesmond, Email to P McDonald, subject 'Impact of the Outdoors', 9 June 2016 [Email].

11   Meriel Blake, Email to P McDonald, subject 'White Hall Centre 1965', 18 Apr 2016 [Email].

12   John Cheesmond, Email to P McDonald, subject 'Impact of the Outdoors', 9 June 2016 [Email].

13   A B Afford, *The Story of White Hall Open Country Pursuits Centre; vol. 2* (Buxton, Derbyshire, UK: A B Afford, 1978), p. 22.

14   Janet Davies, Email to P McDonald, subject 'Women in outdoor education', 28 Feb 2016 [Email].

15   Janet Davies, Email to P McDonald, subject 'CfEE Directory of Centres', 3 Mar 2016 [Email].

16   'Derbyshire Education Committee: White Hall [vacancy]', *The Times*, 27 June 1969, p. 30.

17   John Cheesmond, Email to P McDonald, subject 'Minor Queries', 17 Dec 2015 [Email].

18   A B Afford, *The Story of White Hall Open Country Pursuits Centre; vol. 2* (Buxton, Derbyshire, UK: A B Afford, 1978), pp. 22–23.

19   Derbyshire Record Office, Monograph: Hill and Water Sports in British Education: Peter Mosedale, 1975, D7786/BOX/1/Bundle 5.

20   Derby Local Studies and Family History Library, White Hall Centre for Open Country Pursuits: programme no. 31 September 1967 - September 1968, LA369.4.

21   K I Meldrum, 'White Hell Pursuing Centre', *Climbers' Club Journal: 1966*, 15, no. 1 (new series) (1966), pp. 61–67 (p. 61).

22   Ibid. (p. 63).

23   Simon Thompson, *Unjustifiable Risk? The Story of British Climbing* (Milnthorpe, UK: Cicerone, 2010), p. 204.

24   Quoted in Ken C Ogilvie, *Roots and Wings: A History of Outdoor Education and Outdoor Learning in the UK* (Lyme Regis, UK: Russell House Publishing, 2013), pp. 348–349.

25   'Rock-climbing, Ski-ing and Caving for the Young', *Manchester Guardian*, 17 Feb 1958, p. 5.

26   Ken C Ogilvie, *Roots and Wings: A History of Outdoor Education and Outdoor Learning in the UK* (Lyme Regis, UK: Russell House Publishing, 2013), p. 329.

27   'Potholer Is Killed', *Craven Herald and Pioneer*, 20 Jan 1967, p. 8.

28   'Ill-fated Descent of Alum Pot', *Craven Herald and Pioneer*, 3 Feb 1967, p. 6 (?).

29   Ibid.

30   Ibid.

31   'Accidental Death in Pot-hole', *Buxton Advertiser & High Peak News*, 17 Feb 1967.

32   'Boy Drowns on Adventure Trip down Pothole', *Buxton Advertiser*, 10 Feb 1967.

33   'Boy Drowned in Pothole Ignored Order', *Guardian*, 14 Feb 1967, p. 3.

34   'Accidental Death in Pot-hole', *Buxton Advertiser & High Peak News*, 17 Feb 1967.

35   Ibid.

36   Ibid.

37   Derbyshire Record Office, Education minute books, D919 C/1/17/46, 7 Feb 1967, p. 444, no. 7895.

38   John Needham, Email to P McDonald, subject 'History of White Hall', 13 June 2016 [Email].

39   'Report of the Board of Inquiry Set Up by the Derbyshire Education Committee' and covering letter dated 3 Apr 1967, in private papers of Jack Longland.

40   Ibid.

41   Derbyshire Cave Rescue Organisation (Buxton, UK), Report of the Board of Inquiry Set Up by the Derbyshire Education Committee [c. May 1967], Ref. 279.

42   Ibid.

43   Derbyshire Record Office, Education minute books, D919 C/1/17/47, 20 Jun 1967, p. 95, no. 2, 3.

44   Derbyshire Record Office, Education minute books, D919 C/1/17/47, 23 May 1967, p. 47, no. 3.

45   Derbyshire Record Office, Education minute books, D919 C/1/17/47, 11 July 1967, p. 143, no. 460.

46   A B Afford, *The Story of White Hall Open Country Pursuits Centre; vol. 2* (Buxton, Derbyshire, UK: A B Afford, 1978), p. 24.

47   David Hopkins and Roger Putnam, *Personal Growth through Adventure* (London: David Fulton Publishers, 1993), p. 25.

48   T M Parker and K I Meldrum, *Outdoor Education* (London: J M Dent and Sons, 1973), pp. 104–105.

49   Ernest A Baker, *Moors, Crags and Caves of the High Peak and Neighbourhood*, Facsimile of 1st (1903) edn (Tiverton, Devon: Halsgrove, 2002), p. 205.

50   'List of UK Caving Fatalities' (6 Apr 2015) <https://en.wikipedia.org/wiki/List_of_UK_caving_fatalities> [accessed 24 June 2015].

51   Pete McDonald, *Climbing Lessons: Inside Outdoor Education* (Kaikohe, NZ: Pete McDonald, 1997), pp. 178–181, 284–286.

52   'One Scout Dead, Two Missing on 50-mile Walk', *Guardian*, 16 Mar 1964, p. 1 and back page.

53   'Inquiry on Scouts' Exercise', *Guardian*, 19 Mar 1964, p. 7.

54 Roger Bennett and Ian Hurst, *Mountain Rescue: History and Development in the Peak District, 1920s–Present Day* (Stroud: Tempus Publishing, 2007).

55 'Pot-luck of Boy Soldier Trapped in Cave', Manchester Evening News (2001) <http://www.manchestereveningnews.co.uk/news/greater-manchester-news/pot-luck-of-boy-soldier-trapped-in-cave-1189761> [accessed 5 Oct 2014].

56 Ibid.

57 'Mountain Rescue Tuition on Quarry Face', *Guardian*, 31 Jan 1966, p. 18.

58 *The First Fifty Years of the British Mountaineering Council,* ed. by Geoff Milburn, Derek Walker and Ken Wilson (Manchester: British Mountaineering Council, 1997), pp. 36–37.

59 Ken C Ogilvie, *Roots and Wings: A History of Outdoor Education and Outdoor Learning in the UK* (Lyme Regis, UK: Russell House Publishing, 2013), p. 366.

60 Ibid., p. 336.

61 Tom Price, quoted in ibid., p. 337.

62 Ibid., p. 338.

63 Ibid., p. 337.

64 Ibid., p. 333.

65 Quoted in Robert Wainwright, *The Maverick Mountaineer: The Remarkable Life of George Ingle Finch: Climber, Scientist, Inventor* (London: Allen and Unwin, 2016), p. 6.

66 *Physical Education Year Book: 1963–64* (London: Physical Education Association of Great Britain and Northern Ireland, 1964), p. 29.

67 Ibid., pp. 88–155.

68 P C McIntosh and others, *Landmarks in the History of Physical Education*, 3rd edn (London: Routledge and Kegan Paul, 1981), pp. 231–235.

69 Harold Drasdo, *Education and the Mountain Centres*, 2nd edn (1972, 1973; repr. Penrith: Association for Outdoor Learning, 1998), p. 6.

70 Lynn Cook, 'Outdoor Education: Its Origins and Institutionalisation in Schools with Particular Reference to the West Riding of Yorkshire Since 1945' (PhD thesis, University of Leeds, 2000), p. 145.

71 Cambridge University Library, Longland to Arnold-Brown, 21 Feb 1950, in Miscellaneous confidential administrative correspondence and papers, MS Add.8270/12/7.

72 Robbie Nicol, 'Outdoor Education for Sustainable Living? An Investigation into the Potential of Scottish Local Authority Residential Outdoor Education Centres to Deliver Programmes Relating to Sustainable Living' (PhD thesis, University of Edinburgh, 2001), p. 33.

73 Ken C Ogilvie, *Roots and Wings: A History of Outdoor Education and Outdoor Learning in the UK* (Lyme Regis, UK: Russell House Publishing, 2013), p. 474.

74 Jeff Connor, *Creagh Dhu Climber: The Life and Times of John Cunningham* (no place given: Ernest Press, 1999), p. 166.

75 Ken C Ogilvie, *Roots and Wings: A History of Outdoor Education and Outdoor Learning in the UK* (Lyme Regis, UK: Russell House Publishing, 2013), pp. 333–340.

76 Ibid., pp. 297, 330, 341.

77   Tom Stephenson, *Forbidden Land: The Struggle for Access to Mountain and Moorland*, ed. by Ann Holt (Manchester: Manchester University Press, 1989), p. 70 note.

78   Ken C Ogilvie, *Roots and Wings: A History of Outdoor Education and Outdoor Learning in the UK* (Lyme Regis, UK: Russell House Publishing, 2013), p. 294.

79   Clyde Chitty, 'The Role and Status of LEAs: Post-war Pride and Fin de Siècle Uncertainty', *Oxford Review of Education*, 28, no. 2 & 3 (2002), pp. 261–273 (pp. 264–265).

80   William Richardson, *A Union of Many Trades: The History of USDAW* (Manchester: Union of Shop, Distributive and Allied Workers, 1979), p. 242–245.

81   Janet Davies, Email to P McDonald, subject 'White Hall history: a date query', 27 Feb 2016 [Email].

82   Ken C Ogilvie, *Roots and Wings: A History of Outdoor Education and Outdoor Learning in the UK* (Lyme Regis, UK: Russell House Publishing, 2013), pp. 326–327.

83   Ibid., pp. 383–385.

84   Quoted in ibid., pp. 382–383.

85   T M Parker and K I Meldrum, *Outdoor Education* (London: J M Dent and Sons, 1973), pp. 100–102.

86   Kim Meldrum, 'How Many Climbers?', *Fell and Rock Journal*, 21, no. 1 (1968), pp. 16–19.

87   Richard West, 'In the Tracks of B-P', *Sunday Times*, 16 Feb 1964, p. 6 [S].

88   Ibid.

89   H Cunningham, 'Leisure and Culture', in *The Cambridge Social History of Britain 1750–1950*, ed. by F M L Thompson, 3 vols (Cambridge: Cambridge University Press, 1990), vol. 2, pp. 279–339 (p. 328).

90   Eric Byne and Geoffrey Sutton, *High Peak: The Story of Walking and Climbing in the Peak District* (London: Secker and Warburg, 1966), p. 191.

91   Keith Ian Meldrum, 'A Comparative Study of the Training Requirements and Certification of Teachers and Instructors of Mountain Activities in Selected Countries in Western Europe' (MPhil thesis, University of Nottingham, 1970). University of Nottingham, 1970

92   Kim Meldrum and Brian Royle, *Artificial Climbing Walls* (London: Pelham Books, 1970).

93   John Newsom, *Half Our Future: A Report of the Central Advisory Council for Education (England)* (London: Her Majesty's Stationery Office, 1963), p. 139.

94   T M Parker and K I Meldrum, *Outdoor Education* (London: J M Dent and Sons, 1973), p. 89.

95   Derek Walker, 'The Evolution of Climbing Clubs in Britain', *Alpine Journal*, 108 (2004), pp. 187–195 (p. 194).

96   Derbyshire Record Office, Monograph: Hill and Water Sports in British Education: Peter Mosedale, 1975, D7786/BOX/1/Bundle 5.

97   K I Meldrum, 'A Day (and a Half) in the Dauphiné', *Fell and Rock Journal*, 26, no. 3 (2000), pp. 559–560.

98   Martin Boysen, *Hanging On: A Life Inside British Climbing's Golden Age* (Sheffield: Vertebrate Publishing, 2014), p. 94 and Plate 64.

99   *The First Fifty Years of the British Mountaineering Council,* ed. by Geoff Milburn, Derek Walker and Ken Wilson (Manchester: British Mountaineering Council, 1997), pp. 44–45.

100   Pete Allison, 'When I Stop and Think about It ... Further Research Is Not Required', in *Proceedings from 3rd International Mountain and Outdoor Sports Conference, Hruba Skala, Czech Republic, 23–26 November 2006* (Czech Republic: IYNF, 2007), pp. 78–91 (pp. 78, 85).Hruba Skala, Czech Republic, 23–26 November 2006</style> (Czech Republic: IYNF, 2007

101   B R Mitchell, *British Historical Statistics* (Cambridge: Cambridge University Press, 1988), p. 558.

102   T L Burton and G P Wibberley, *Outdoor Recreation in the British Countryside,* Studies in Rural Land Use; Report No. 5 (Ashford, Kent: Department of Economics, Wye College, 1965), p. 41.

103   Alan Alldred, Email to P McDonald, subject 'White Hall OCPC', 30 Dec 2016 [Email].

104   Ken C Ogilvie, *Roots and Wings: A History of Outdoor Education and Outdoor Learning in the UK* (Lyme Regis, UK: Russell House Publishing, 2013), pp. 322–329.

105   [Anon.], 'New Whitehall Warden', *Climber and Rambler,* 9 (Nov 1970), p. 450.

106   Peter Davalle, 'Personal Choice', *The Times,* 3 Nov 1978, p. 33.

14. 'Outdoor education? Don't know what you mean!'

While Kim Meldrum oversaw an expanding White Hall, residential outdoor centres nationally multiplied and diversified. By the late 1960s, a new name for what these centres did had come into general use: outdoor education. Rather than chop the story of that name into pieces scattered chronologically through the book, I have left it intact, to be covered in this one chapter.

When Ken Ogilvie wrote *Roots and Wings* (2013), the earliest UK occurrence of the phrase 'outdoor education' that he had come across was in a 1962 draft MLC training programme. The second occurrence that he knew of was in 1965 (a year that also saw the first use in print of the term 'adventure education'). However, newspaper-archive databases are continually improving, and a recent search for 'outdoor education' dug up some earlier examples. They are isolated, independent applications of the term rather than indications of general use.

In 1907 the educationist J E G de Montmorency wrote a report for the Board of Education, *School Excursions and Vacation Schools*. The word 'outdoor' appears nine times in this report, but never combined with the word 'education'. However, a leading article in *The Times*, discussing this report, was titled 'Outdoor Education'. For the writer of this article, outdoor education was

> some hours in a hayfield, a ride in a country wagon, roaming aimlessly through woods, a game at cricket with village boys, watching the ways of birds, rabbits, or squirrels, a swim in the nearest river, a keen competition as to who shall see and name most birds, with no coddling and no overstuffing with useful or scientific information.

'Such experience,' he or she wrote, 'to a town-bred boy or girl is of incalculable value.'[1]

Ten years later, in 1917, a newspaper advertisement again used 'outdoor education' with a strongly rural connotation, but with a more specific, occupational meaning. The Children's Model Farm School in Crosby-on-Eden, Cumberland, was 'adapted for the outdoor education of Boys and Girls between the ages of 6 and 12 years'. As well as the normal school subjects, the school taught poultry farming, butter and cheese making, milking, bee-keeping, gardening, riding, swimming and carpentering.[2]

My third example of an early use of the term 'outdoor education' in British English is from a 1953 *Yorkshire Post and Leeds Mercury*. Richard Graham was a mountaineer who had been chosen for the Mount Everest expedition of 1924 (but had not been able to take part). Such was his passion for the outdoors that the following article was headed with the term we are interested in:

> Outdoor Education
> Mr. R. B. Graham, who has announced his decision to retire from the head mastership of Bradford Grammar School at the end of this year, is a firm believer in extramural activities for schoolboys. He encourages in them his own enthusiasm for games and the outdoor life.[3]

Before I return to Ogilvie's 1960s examples, I will briefly widen my mini survey to include American English. The term 'outdoor education' became common in the United States before it took hold in Britain. Often in the US, 'outdoor education' meant 'environmental education' or 'field studies'. For example, the *Training College Journal* for March 1961 has an article titled 'Outdoor Education in Winter'. It describes the programme of a school camp held in February 1960. The article lists twenty-three pamphlets that the pupils studied before and during the camp. The subjects are botanical (eg, Pioneer Plants), biological (eg, Along Came a Spider), geological (eg, Some Common Rocks and Minerals), astronomical (eg, A Universal Star Chart) and mathematical (eg, Formulae, the Poetry of Science).[4]

Bear in mind, however, that the US is a vast country, with educational policies decentralised across the individual states. One example does not prove uniformity.

The UK is a far smaller country, where you might have expected such uniformity. But no clear meaning was attached to the term 'outdoor education' in 1960s British English. On the contrary, people could not agree on what it meant. In November 1967 the AWMC set up a working committee to consider the formation of a professional association for teachers of outdoor pursuits. This committee first met in February 1968 (Kim Meldrum was a member). 'Although a definition of OE was needed because there was none in existence yet, it was decided to leave that difficult exercise until a later time.' On 4 October 1970, despite basic and unresolved disagreement over the meaning of 'outdoor education', the National Association for Outdoor Education was formally constituted.[5]

We are all familiar with name changes. Some happen abruptly; others slowly, by semantic creep. When I was at school, there was a subject called divinity. As time passed, it became religious studies or – more commonly – religious education. We did PT once a week, physical training. This became PE, physical education. Field studies became environmental education. In 1970 our centres for outdoor pursuits were becoming centres for outdoor education. The phrase 'character training', denoting a practice that had never received much respect in LEA centres, was becoming archaic as well as taboo; but 'social and personal development' was an authorised successor with flawless credentials. The instructors, in 1970, were still instructors but they would eventually turn into teachers or outdoor educators.

The old term 'outdoor pursuits' (or 'outdoor activities') had been accurately specific for many centres, and might have remained an effective label for some, but it had become too narrow for many other situations. Also, it lacked pedagogic clout. The new term 'outdoor education' was necessarily all-encompassing and nondiscriminating; it could stretch over every shade of outdoor centre. Furthermore, it had more gravitas than 'outdoor pursuits'; outdoor educators, living vulnerably on the extra-curricular margins of schooling, were seeking the approval and support of mainstream educationists, just as physical educators had always done. Yet one of the strengths of the new name, its flexibility, would also become its weakness. In many contexts the term 'outdoor education' would prove to be vague and unhelpful. Although the term had come into common usage, there were wide differences in what it meant, evidenced by strikingly dissimilar definitions both nationally and internationally.

In October 1970, at its inaugural AGM and conference, the NAOE ratified an expansive definition that would appeal to as wide a range of people as possible:

> [Outdoor education is] a means of approaching educational objectives through guided, direct experience of the outdoors, using as learning material the resources of rural and coastal environments.[6]

Ken Ogilvie has noted that the NAOE document setting out this definition contained 'no mention … of "personal and social development" possibly because it might have attracted the tarring of the Outward Bound "character building" brush which [the association] wished to avoid'.[7]

If this NAOE definition of outdoor education didn't grab you, a number of alternatives were becoming available, especially if you crossed back over the Atlantic. John J Kirk, a professor of environmental education and president of the American Camping Association, offered this one:

> Outdoor education is the method which utilises the out-of-doors to cultivate a reverence for life through an ecological exploration of the interdependence of all living things one on the other and to form a land ethic illustrating man's temporary stewardship of the land.[8]

The above two definitions are just samples of where people had got to, nationally and internationally, by the start of Lyn Noble's time at White Hall, in agreeing what outdoor education was all about. Locally, regarding the infiltration of the term 'outdoor education' into the White Hall culture, the centre's name was still White Hall Centre for Open Country Pursuits. This name worked tolerably well, there was little desire to change it, and it would remain unchanged throughout Lyn Noble's two decades.

Nationally, in the early 1970s some colleges of education and universities were including outdoor pursuits or outdoor education as curricular subjects, but the lack of a widely agreed definition of outdoor education 'created difficulties in the defining of aims and objectives thus making the job of gaining support quite difficult. Linking outdoor activities with environmental education sometimes helped the case.'[9]

A couple of years after moving on from White Hall, Kim Meldrum joined up with Terry Parker to write *Outdoor Education* (1973). Allocating the term 'outdoor education' as the title of a serious hardback put the seal of approval on the term, while the book itself, according to Ken Ogilvie, was a 'very informative and general work [that] looked at OE in a … factual and historical manner'. Meldrum and Parker endorsed the NAOE's broad and elastic definition of outdoor education.[10] But at least one reviewer found fault with the book's balance. His review, in *Geography*, gives us an insight into the continuing controversy, in the 1970s, over the meaning of 'outdoor education':

> The major disappointment, of what is a sound book on the physical aspects of outdoor studies, is the obvious lack of reference to the widening range of fieldwork which has formed an integral part of outdoor education for several decades. Surely outdoor education is all-embracing and should involve not only the physical educationist but also all who find the various environmental patterns, whether in an urban or rural setting, of direct value as a medium of instruction and leisure …
>
> Regrettably the book cannot truly reflect outdoor education because its specialism is so obviously physical.[11]

In the same month as this review was published (April 1974), Meldrum's successor at White Hall, Lyn Noble, presented a frank and penetrating discussion paper to the fifth annual conference of the NAOE. In his view, the NAOE was top heavy with 'academics and intellectuals who were ahead of their time and not fully in touch with member concerns. He suggested that the term "Outdoor Education" had been foisted on members before they were ready for it [and that they were] perhaps flattered by the respectable image it gave, but uncertain what the "OE bit" was and what they had been missing out on all this time.'[12]

Reflecting on this period, in 1991 Noble described several gradual changes, one of which was

> a move to establish outdoor opportunities firmly within the realm of education. The term 'outdoor education' appeared. I clearly remember Chris Phillips, then Director of Education for Derbyshire questioning its use … 'Outdoor education? Don't know what you mean!' In retrospect I'm not sure that many of us did. Indeed it seems to have taken the best part of 20 years to accept

that 'outdoor education' is no more than an umbrella covering a wide range of experiences, skills and disciplines. I now believe that Chris Phillips was right. It is not very helpful to use such a broad generic term for the sake of academic respectability.[13]

Helpful or not, by 1991 the old term was out and the new and unhelpful one was in. A clear illustration of the change exists in the story of the Department of Education and Science booklet *Safety in Outdoor Pursuits*, first published in 1972 with thirty-nine pages.[14] The second edition in 1977 and the third in 1979 retained the same title. In 1989 a revised version, extended to seventy-six pages, was retitled *Safety in Outdoor Education*.[15]

By the early 1990s, the term 'outdoor education' had been in widespread use in educational circles in Britain for twenty years. Yet it had not appeared in many dictionaries. Language works like that; it follows the will of the majority, and dictionaries always lag behind, perpetually revising to catch up with common usage.

There was some doubt as to whether the term 'outdoor education' would hang around long enough to earn a place in the dictionaries. Some organisations connected with outdoor education either by name or by image began to question whether 'outdoor education' was the most suitable label for their particular roles and what they stood for.

In 1992 the NAOE considered renaming itself. For the NAOE, the 'Outdoor Education' half of its name, far from being too generic, was not generic enough. The association's new-name debate bubbled intermittently until July 1998, when the NAOE became the Association for Outdoor Learning (AfOL).[16] In March and April 2001, a number of outdoor organisations, including the AfOL, merged to become the Institute for Outdoor Learning (IOL).[17]

In 2006 'outdoor education' achieved a place in the *Oxford Dictionary of Sports Science and Medicine*. The last eleven words of the definition illustrate the almost infinite elasticity of the term:

outdoor education: Education that takes place in the natural environment. It includes conventional field studies, outdoor pursuits, and any other educational activity which takes place in the open air.[18]

Despite this isolated lexicographic recognition, 'outdoor education' remained absent from most other dictionaries. The *Dictionary of Edu-*

cation (2009)[19], containing 1,250 terms, did not have room for it. At the time of writing (2016), it has not yet reached the *Oxford English Dictionary*, either as a headword or in the full text. It does not appear as a headword in the free online Collins, Macmillan, Cambridge and Longman's dictionaries.

'Outdoor education' is a noun phrase like 'indoor education' and 'black cat' (neither of which you will find in dictionaries) and like 'social media' and 'boomerang child' (both of which have recently appeared in some dictionaries). Teams of dictionary-makers base their inclusion or exclusion decisions on massive databases of spoken and written English. To be included, new words – or, as in this case, phrases – must be used frequently enough, by enough people, with a common meaning and over an extended period of time.

At present, it seems that 'outdoor education' is no more worthy of inclusion in dictionaries than 'indoor education' or 'black cat'. The phrase has been used often and for fifty years with specific meanings, in a way that 'indoor education' and 'black cat' have not. But it means different things to different people. If common definitions of outdoor education are difficult to achieve by consensus among outdoor educators, they should not be surprised when lexicographers of general dictionaries decide against inclusion.

In September 2016 the School of Education of Bangor University was still running its long-established and highly regarded Post Graduate Certificate in Education course for graduates who wanted to be involved in teaching out of doors. The name of the course remained 'PGCE (Secondary) Outdoor Activities'.

Changing terms used at White Hall Centre

	1950	1960	1970	1980	1990	2000
School subject	Open country pursuits or outdoor pursuits		Outdoor education			Outdoor education or outdoor learning
Head of centre	Warden			Principal		
Deputy head	(none)		Chief Inst.	Deputy principal		
Other teaching staff	Assistant wardens	Instructors of outdoor pursuits		Teachers/instructors of outdoor pursuits	Teachers of outdoor education	

Guardian, 23 April 1969, p. 14.

YOUTH SERVICE

OUTDOOR PURSUITS INSTRUCTORS

WHITE HALL CENTRE FOR OPEN COUNTRY PURSUITS
DERBYSHIRE EDUCATION COMMITTEE

Two instructors are required at White Hall, Buxton, for September, 1969. A wide knowledge of mountaineering and camping is an essential qualification together with experience of either caving or canoeing. Salary, Burnham Scale plus extraneous duties allowance of £300. One post will be filled by a woman who will have special responsibility for girl students. For the second post preference will be given to an instructor who can accept special responsibility for caving instruction. Both posts are residential. Application forms and further details may be obtained by sending s.a.e. to the undersigned, quoting Ref G C., to whom completed forms should be returned by 6th May. J. L. LONGLAND, Director of Education.

Guardian, 4 July 1972, p. 13.

Derbyshire Education Committee

White Hall Centre for Open Country Pursuits, Buxton

TEACHER OF OUTDOOR PURSUITS

Required as soon as possible. Single man for residential teaching post at the above centre. Applicants should have mountaineering and rock-climbing qualifications (preferably M.I.C.) and must be able to offer canoeing or caving to Senior Instructor to Cave Leaders standards respectively. Applicants must be concerned primarily with an integrated educational approach to outdoor activities.

Single bed-sitter available. Burnham Scale I plus an Extraneous Duties Allowance of £300 p.a., deduction of £225 for residents

Application forms and further details may be obtained by sending S.A.E. to the undersigned, to whom completed forms should be returned by July 17 1972.

H K FOWLER, Director of Education.
County Offices, Matlock.

These advertisements and those on the next two pages illustrate the changing job titles, from 'instructor' to 'teacher/instructor' and then to 'teacher of outdoor education'.

Guardian, 12 December 1972, p. 18.

Outdoor Pursuits

TEACHER/INSTRUCTOR

DERBYSHIRE EDUCATION COMMITTEE
WHITE HALL CENTRE FOR OPEN
COUNTRY PURSUITS, BUXTON

Required for May, 1973, TEACHER/INSTRUCTOR to take responsibility for the canoeing department at the above centre. Applicants should hold, or be working towards, the B.C.U. Senior Instructor's Certificate and should be prepared to take an active interest in mountain activities, rock climbing and caving.

The post will be resident with accommodation for a single man or a married man without children.

Burnham Scale 1 plus an Extraneous Duties Allowance of £375 p.a.

Application forms and further details may be obtained by sending s.a.e. to H. K. Fowler, Director of Education, County Offices, Matlock, to whom completed forms should be returned by 8th January, 1973.

About January 1976

DERBYSHIRE
EDUCATION COMMITTEE
WHITE HALL CENTRE FOR OPEN
COUNTRY PURSUITS
INSTRUCTOR

Applications are invited for this residential teaching post which will become vacant at the beginning of the Summer Term 1976. Applicants must be genuinely interested in young people and have considerable experience of caving and mountaineering. Experience of canoeing and M.L.C. work would be an advantage. Single bed-sitter available. Salary, Burnham Scale I with additional duties allowance £690 per annum from which a deduction will be made for accommodation.

Further details from the undersigned to whom completed application form should be returned by February 10, 1976.

C. W. Phillips, Director of Education, County Offices, Matlock, Derbyshire.

Guardian, 9 January 1990, p. 30.

OUTDOOR PURSUITS

Female Teacher of Outdoor Education HW/32/18

To work with girls and mixed groups.

White Hall Centre for Open Country Pursuits, Long Hill, Buxton, Derbyshire SK17 6SX.

Salary: Main Scale plus extraneous duties allowances and sleeping-in payments.

Required for April, 1990, or earlier if possible. Applicants should be qualified teachers with enthusiasm, commitment, experience and qualifications in outdoor pursuits and residential work with young people and adults.

Experience of leading groups in wild environments is essential together with leadership expertise in some of the following: sailing, canoeing, rock climbing, orienteering, caving and problem-solving.

Accommodation is available for a single person, a clean driving licence is essential.

Application form and further details may be obtained from the Principal, White Hall Centre for Open Country Pursuits, Long Hill, Buxton, Derbyshire SK17 6SX.

Guardian, 7 April 1992, p. A23.

OUTDOOR EDUCATION TEACHER

Main Professional Grade and Extraneous duty allowance plus sleeping in payments (under review).

Location: White Hall Centre for Open Country Pursuits. Applicants should be qualified teachers with experience and qualifications in outdoor pursuits and residential work with young people and adults.

Application form and job description available from the Staffing Office, Education Department, County Offices, Matlock, Derbyshire. Tel: Matlock 580000, ext 6428. Closing date: April 24, 1992.

JOB SHARE — Applications will be considered from those who wish to share a job with another person.

The Council's policy is that all people receive equal treatment regardless of their sex, marital status, sexual orientation, race, creed, colour, ethnic or national origin, or disability.

DDERBYSHIRE County Council

We're proud of Derbyshire.

Notes

1   'Outdoor Education', *The Times*, 14 Jan 1908, p. 7.

2   'Classified Ad 10: The Children's Model Farm School', *Manchester Guardian*, 18 Aug 1917, p. 1.

3   'Outdoor Education', *Yorkshire Post and Leeds Mercury*, 25 Feb 1953, p. 4.

4   Marjorie McDaniel, 'Outdoor Education in Winter', *Teachers College Journal*, 32, no. 5 (1 Mar 1961), p. 128.

5   Ken C Ogilvie, *Roots and Wings: A History of Outdoor Education and Outdoor Learning in the UK* (Lyme Regis, UK: Russell House Publishing, 2013), pp. 355, 360–361.

6   Ibid., p. 362.

7   Ibid., p. 362.

8   Christine Doyle, 'Joining Camp America', *The Observer*, 29 Mar 1970, p. 28.

9   Ken C Ogilvie, *Roots and Wings: A History of Outdoor Education and Outdoor Learning in the UK* (Lyme Regis, UK: Russell House Publishing, 2013), pp. 422–423.

10 T M Parker and K I Meldrum, *Outdoor Education* (London: J M Dent and Sons, 1973), p. 26.

11 W Burdon, 'Outdoor Education [Review]', *Geography*, 59, no. 2 (Apr 1974), p. 182.

12 Ken C Ogilvie, *Roots and Wings: A History of Outdoor Education and Outdoor Learning in the UK* (Lyme Regis, UK: Russell House Publishing, 2013), p. 421.

13 Lyn Noble, 'Fortieth Anniversary: Forty Years of Adventure at White Hall', *Head Teachers' Review*, (Autumn 1991), pp. 14–16 (p. 16).

14   Department of Education and Science, *Safety in Outdoor Pursuits*, DES safety series; no. 1 (London: HMSO, 1972).

15   Department of Education and Science, *Safety in Outdoor Education* (London: HMSO, 1989).

16   Ken C Ogilvie, *Roots and Wings: A History of Outdoor Education and Outdoor Learning in the UK* (Lyme Regis, UK: Russell House Publishing, 2013), pp. 682–691.

17   Ibid., p. 701.

18   Michael Kent, *The Oxford Dictionary of Sports Science and Medicine*, 3rd edn (Oxford: Oxford University Press, 2006).

19   *A Dictionary of Education*, ed. by Susan Wallace (Oxford: Oxford University Press, 2009).

Part Three:
Routine Adventure, 1970–92

15. LN, DD, and Fantastic Freedom, 1970–83

When Lyn Noble arrived at White Hall in 1970, the centre had developed steadily for twenty years and was entering a stable and very successful period – the whole of the 1970s – that could be characterised as routine adventure. Few of the staff there, however, will have been aware of the brief but concrete purpose statements made in 1949–50, which we looked at in Chapter 7. Most of these statements were now buried deeply in physical newspaper archives. In 1970, whereas the writings of Baden-Powell (and those of his sister and wife) still underpinned the Boy Scout and Girl Guide movements, and the theories of Kurt Hahn were still available to be revered or reinterpreted by Outward Bound, no such institutional mission statements or personal educational theories had been formally acknowledged and adopted by the county-council administrators or previous bosses of White Hall.

Even so, Lyn Noble's account of the years 1970–8, contributed by him to A B Afford's history, included a concise summary of his aims, and by implication the centre's.[1] This summary was in tune with White Hall's traditional operations and it endorsed the established blend of recreation, social and personal development, and countryside awareness. It was not some official statement that he had been able to pick off a shelf in the office. It had by necessity come out of his head, and the result was accurate. Luckily for everyone, in the 1970s the aims were part of the spirit of the place and were axiomatic and enshrined, as obvious to most people as if they had been carved in capital letters on a block of granite in the front porch.

Noble also pointed out that the motivation of youngsters who attended introductory schools' courses varied greatly. He repeated the message that Longland, Mosedale, Afford, Langmuir and Drasdo had all broadcast: that introductory schools' courses needed to be enjoyable.[2]

Despite the absence of any Seven Laws of White Hall, the 1970s at the house on the hill went remarkably well. Tradition and favourable staff chemistry and the centre's long name and sheer luck and intense commitment and a continuing (but vulnerable) optimism combined productively to provide an energetic decade. Dave Draper, who was the deputy principal in the 1970s, reminiscing from the more highly regulated and intellectualised world of 2014, wrote: 'I'm sure in the modern day approach of Elf n Safety and rules for all, no-one will really ever fully appreciate the fantastic freedom that we had [in the 1970s] in the way in which we tailored what we did to suit the abilities and expectations of those in our charge – but in many ways that is exactly what the activities that we were involved in were about – freedom and escape.'[3]

A Draper specialism was the improvising of aerial ropeways, a frequent location being the first pitch of P8 (Jackpot). Here, some local knowledge and a bit of cunning enabled the quick and efficient descent (and later the ascent) of a group of ten novice cavers, by an unconventional technique that probably does not appear in caving-instructor manuals. A more outrageous location, only used once, was the Miller's Dale viaduct, where a titanic zoom from the heights to a distant tree blurred the boundary between perceived risk and real risk. The Bohemian liberty to play these games was indeed memorable.

Here, I need to interrupt this pleasant thought for a moment to expand and clarify the comparison of the different periods. In actuality, regarding the managing of risk when instructing outdoor pursuits, the 1950s were less regulated than the 1960s, the 1960s less than the 1970s, the 70s less than the 80s, and so on through the century and into the 21st. In the 1970s at White Hall, the principal, the deputy principal and the instructors jointly regulated themselves and were proud of their competence to do so; they were not subject to formulaic risk management prescribed and imposed and approved by an external body set up and empowered by central government.

The one phrase 'freedom and escape', picked from an email, seems to me to fit the 1970s perfectly, but it is not the whole story. On its own, it would oversimplify the picture. A quite detailed perspective on the 1970s, more sober and more measured, exists in Lyn Noble's writing. Describing the White Hall of his first decade as principal, and writing when the time was fresh in his memory, Noble saw 'a period of restraint and scrutiny. Gone were the days of growth and development in material terms and the catch phrase became "maintenance of existing facilities"'. Describing the wider picture – outdoor education in general – he wrote of 'scarcely veiled threats of closure that hung over many centres'.[4] (This may have been more true of the end of the 1970s than of the start.)

Another aspect of the 1970s that Noble mentioned was the growing self-analysis engaged in by outdoor educators, an inward-looking search for motives and a questioning of effectiveness. Increasingly, academics and managers were seeking 'convincing reasons for continuing to operate what many felt were marginal establishments in times of economic difficulty'.[5] Bear in mind that by 1973 Britain had replaced Turkey as the 'sick man of Europe'.[6] In 1975, price inflation in Britain reached about 25 per cent and the country could not pay its debts. In 1976 the Labour government went to the International Monetary Fund for a bale-out loan of $3.9 billion (£2.3 billion).[7] There was a need for frugality; the television in the White Hall staffroom was black and white, not colour, and it would remain so throughout the 1980s.

Noble continued:

Against this background of change White Hall continued to offer its range of courses and at a time when 'outdoor pursuits' and 'outdoor activities' became very unfashionable (it all had to be 'outdoor education') the original title – 'Centre for Open Country Pursuits' – took upon itself a jubilant ring of happy inspiration.[8]

Schools and outdoor centres and youth clubs sometimes need to reappraise themselves and then, when necessary, may decide to adjust what they do and the way that they do it, to suit new social conditions and to remain relevant. These institutional changes tend to occur in cycles rather than continuously at a steady rate. The 1950s and 60s at White Hall had seen continual programme development, rapid acquisition of managerial experience and of staff members' teaching and technical skills, frequent building alterations and compelling equipment improvements; and all these achievements had started from zero. In the 1970s the pace of change slowed. Programmes did change, but less frequently. The stock of outdoor equipment did grow in size and did advance in design, but more slowly and less urgently. Most courses were full; many could probably have been filled twice over. The annual total of student overnights gradually rose. For the teaching staff, routine became both a friend and a foe, concomitantly. The most routine thing of all was the consistent success of the standard schools' courses, a testament to the value of routine. Paradoxically, this same routine could potentially lead to monotony and tediousness; later in this chapter we will discuss a condition that Bill March called instructoritis.

Four x 10, Three Minibuses, and Course Reports

Throughout the whole period of Part Three, the basic schools' courses consisted of forty pupils, usually from several schools, accompanied by three or four of their teachers. On most courses there was a roughly equal mix of boys and girls.

Course 991, a full course of the early 1970s. A total of forty pupils, working in four activity groups, was routine for most schools' courses from about 1969 until the mid-1990s.

In the early 1970s the centre transport consisted of two navy-blue minibuses and an elephant of a bus that held two groups but which was less than ideal for Derbyshire's narrow lanes. In about 1976 a third minibus replaced the ponderous old vehicle. Soon after this, someone at county hall decided that orange would be a safer colour than navy-blue. One of the defining characteristics of White Hall for the rest of the 1970s, the whole of the 1980s, and the early 1990s became its transport: three orange Ford Transits.

Let me say here, in case you don't spot it, that another repetition is on the way. Some things need saying more than once, and expanding upon. A durable and largely unquestioned feature of this long period, valued by many schools, was the writing of course reports on each pupil on every schools' course. Containing a paragraph or two on each pupil, these reports were thoughtful and wide-ranging, as much character sketches as records of daring. In some ways a White Hall report on a pupil was the antithesis of a traditional secondary-school subject report of that era.

Earlier chapters of this book told that the whole White Hall machine flourished, for several decades, without any precise written mission statement. Similarly, its report-writing functioned without any written guidelines. One unwritten principle did exist, however: the reports tried to pick out positive aspects of a pupil's character. There was an assumption that the schools already knew about the less captivating sides of some of their inmates. Also, the erring on the bright side was a precautionary policy that recognised that a White Hall report was merely the subjective opinion of one person.

The practice of report-writing hugely influenced the basic characteristics of White Hall's schools' courses of the 1970s. Report-writing was not some sort of backwoods tokenism, a sop to personal and social development; it ensured that a focus on personal and social development was a permanent feature of these courses. One cannot stress this enough. Each week, each group instructor needed to get to know ten young people well enough to be able to offer some helpful and preferably positive observation on each of them. Putting pen to paper at the end of each course required mental effort and sometimes considerable soul-searching. Often the observations were surprisingly penetrating. Many school principals replied to White Hall, acknowledging the depth and insight of the reports. A frequent comment was that the White Hall course had revealed more about a pupil than the school had discovered in three or four years. The reports enriched the links between White Hall and the schools.

Analysing the operations of an LEA residential outdoor education centre of this period, in the context of basic schools' courses, requires an assessment of the emphasis put on the acquisition of skill compared to the emphasis put on the nurturing of general personal and social attributes. At a superficial level, there may be a grain of truth in the anecdotal 1980s picture of a divided British outdoor education movement, polarised between narrow-minded activity-oriented traditionalists, working in outdoor centres, and more progressive trail-breaking theoreticians, working in colleges of education and universities. If we take this crude generalisation a hesitant step further – to expose its weaknesses – the teaching staff at White Hall in the 1970s and 80s fitted the first of the two stereotypes, yet their report-writing contributed to a strongly holistic approach that was broad minded, not narrow minded, and which balanced and regulated the focus on the outdoor pursuits. It is true that, in the 1970s, the group instructors starred the reports of pupils they thought might particularly suit and enjoy a follow-up course. Yet the reports themselves were not narrow. White Hall's report-writing set it apart from some other LEA centres.

(Another aspect of the gulf between theory and practice will appear in Chapter 21, in a discussion about the 1980s publication, the *Journal of Adventure Education*.)

In the mid-1980s, course departure afternoons became taken up with staff meetings, leaving insufficient time for report-writing. Instructors often wrote their reports at home or on the first morning of the following course. The time commitment of instructors was huge without this burden. Leaving report-writing until the morning of the next course was unsatisfactory as it ate into scarce maintenance, development, preparation and staff-meeting time. This issue was one of a number of management matters that arose in the late-1980s.

Having mentioned the first mornings of courses, I need here to diverge briefly from the subject of reports. An essential part of successfully providing years of routine adventure was the hundreds of Monday mornings of routine maintenance and development. These were busy times, countless hours spent on necessary tasks you won't find mentioned much in histories of outdoor education. Typically, before 11am, instructors occupied themselves maintaining the ropes course, attending to the needs of the lead-acid caving batteries, fashioning skegs out of fibreglass, adding nice tight deck-lines to kayaks, covering newly arrived maps, labelling climbing ropes, mending wetsuits (an aromatic job), stocktaking equipment stores, preparing equipment orders, enhancing the collections of colour slides, preparing evening sessions, planning specialist courses, writing syllabuses, and, if there was any time left, writing reports. Always, after 11am, there was the pre-course staff meeting and the filling-in of the duties board.

One other happening in connection with reports is worth a mention. Until the 1990s, each group instructor wrote ten reports by hand. The principal checked them, and then his secretary typed them and posted them to the schools, where they ended up in the Records of Achievement. In about 1987, Dave Edwards recognised the potential usefulness of the Amstrad word-processor, thus becoming the first White Hall instructor to enter the electronic age. Pete McDonald followed his lead in 1990, buying an Elonex PC, a so-called IBM clone. The November 1990 course reports reproduced in Appendix 3 were written on this Elonex PC and printed at home on a dot-matrix printer, the printout being passed on to Joan Howard, the White Hall secretary. The first ripples of the digital revolution had reached the house on the hill. But the internet had not yet arrived, so the postman's job would be safe for a while longer.

Near the end of the Lyn Noble era, there was some talk of replacing the group-instructors' reports with self-analysis sheets, completed by the course members themselves.

The wobbly beam, November 1980.

Part of the makeshift ropes course, January 1981.

On the ropes course, January 1981.

The homemade zip-line (aka aerial ropeway or flying fox), May 1976.

Staffing, 1970–83

None of the four wardens or principals and none of the permanent instructors of the period 1950–70 had stayed at White Hall for more than seven years. One difference between the White Hall of Part Two of this book and that of Part Three was that from 1970 onwards, principals and some of the permanent instructors tended to stay longer – ten, fifteen, or twenty years – rather than following their careers in new directions.

Between 1970 and 1977, the White Hall teaching staff comprised a principal, a deputy principal and four instructors. In late 1970 they were Lyn Noble, Dave Draper, Rick Scott, Alan Alldred, Janet Richards (later Davies) and Dick Wilkinson.

Lyn Noble was a gifted rock climber. In the years that I knew him he almost never overstretched himself, always climbing impressively well, in control and with talent to spare. He was also an able alpinist and an old friend of Doug Scott, whom he had met while they were both at Loughborough College of Education. In July 1961 Noble and Scott and a few others had climbed together in the Bregaglia in southern Switzerland, a holiday made memorable by a retreat down the Ago di Sciora after Noble, who seldom fell off any climb, uncharacteristically fell more than a hundred feet and sustained a fractured femur.[9] In the late 1960s he was one of a small group of climbers who developed some new cliffs in Pembrokeshire.

Before his move to White Hall, Noble had been the chief instructor at Ghyll Head, Manchester city council's outdoor centre on the edge of Lake Windermere. While there he had tried to start a Lakeland organisation for centre instructors to enable them to network. A few meetings had taken place, but the need for the local group would end when the NAOE came into being.[10]

Ken Ogilvie, the warden of Ghyll Head, had 'changed the orientation of the centre so that courses were group – rather than teacher – led', giving Ghyll Head an unusual or even unique approach.[11] However, the transition at White Hall from Meldrum's principalship to Noble's seems to have been seamless, with Noble largely continuing the established White Hall approaches rather than making any radical changes.

Dave Draper, the deputy principal, was a mountaineer and caver from Leicester. He was an old mate of the guidebook publisher and distributer Ken Vickers. Before coming to White Hall, he had been one of three male instructors at Rhowniar Girls Outward Bound School, near Aberdovey. He had then temped at several centres in north Wales, which was followed by an appointment as a permanent instructor at Aberglaslyn Hall in 1967.[12] While in Wales, Draper had become closely involved with the mountaineering first-aid courses run by Dr Ieuan Jones.

He was a more experienced and more committed caver than most White Hall instructors before him. After his arrival at White Hall, he became heavily involved in the Derbyshire Cave Rescue Organisation (DCRO). An inventive extrovert with a propensity for occasional bouts of harmless madness, Draper was the perfect foil to the more cautious and reserved Noble. Nobody who saw Draper the showman would ever forget him, spicing his teaching with spontaneous theatrical performances unrivalled for getting a message across to inattentive teenagers. For a decade or so, the Noble–Draper combination would work well, the restrained and responsible and correct boss and the outgoing and uninhibited deputy, sustaining a vigorous and confident and occasionally creative centre culture.

Dave Draper, 1970s.

By 1970, national discussions about forming some sort of national association for people involved in outdoor education had continued sporadically for about four years. In June 1970, Lyn Noble edited the first broadsheet of the proposed body, called *Sort Out*, and he contributed an article, 'Another Course, Another Hill'. Dave Draper also contributed an article, 'First Signs of Exposure'. The NAOE came into being on 4 October 1970, with a list of officers that read like a who's who of the world of outdoor centres, including Lyn Noble as honorary treasurer.[13]

Janet Richards left White Hall in August 1971, being replaced by Barbara Hulley. Alan Alldred left in 1972 and was replaced by Trev Morris, a climber and caver. Rick Scott moved on at Christmas 1972 to work at I M Marsh College of Physical Education with Ron James. Gwyn Edwards, whose specialism was canoeing, replaced him. Richards, Hulley, Scott and Edwards had all found a way into outdoor instructing by taking the well-known one-year Post Graduate Certificate in Education (PGCE) course established by Barbara Spark (later Roscoe) at the University College of North Wales in September 1965. The aim of this course was to 'select and train graduates to become more effective teachers of outdoor activities for the secondary school age group'.[14]

In 1976, Trev Morris and Dick Wilkinson left, followed shortly afterwards by Barbara Hulley. Dave Edwards, a man with a head full of karst geomorphology and with an irrepressible enthusiam for hands-and-knees crawling, arrived in May 1976. Pete McDonald arrived at the same time, emotionally scarred from teaching maths in Rotherham. Lynda Welham arrived soon after.

1977 saw the arrival of Phil Booth, raising the number of teaching staff to seven. It would remain at seven, with very occasional changes, until McDonald's departure in 1992.

Regarding the best way to run a residential outdoor pursuits centre, it is possible to identify far-reaching advantages and equally important disadvantages in having teaching staff who remain in the same roles for many years. Stability worked quite well at White Hall in the period 1976–1983; it may not have served the centre so well in 1984–92.

On the basic schools' courses, three or four of their teachers usually accompanied the forty pupils. Lyn Noble supported this practice:

> Encouraging the participation of teachers had a secondary effect which fell into line with one of Kim Meldrum's stated objectives. By creating personal links with teachers involved or at least interested in outdoor work the Centre was in a better position to help train these people to carry out their own activities at school.[15]

Although the visiting teachers were sometimes PE teachers, many taught other subjects. Often one or two were hillwalkers or climbers or cavers or dinghy sailors whose presence helped reduce the staff-pupil ratios. Voluntary instructors continued to play a vital part at weekends. Paid temporary instructors were occasionally brought in during the absence of permanent staff.

From my memory, among the many people who worked at White Hall in the 1970s or 80s either as VIs or as paid temporary instructors were Alan ('Soppy') Allsop, Terry Ashman, Nigel Atkins, Dave Baines, ('Big') John Boden, Phil Burke, Bruce Combes, Jeff Connor, George Cooper, Ralph Cooper, Joan Cooper, Geoff Creake, Stew Dale, Bill Dark, John Davies, Pete Denver, Mike ('Chunky Giblet') Gilbert, Bob Gillott, Bill Hartle, Dave Hassall, Perry Hawkins, Darran Hawkins, Adam Haynes, Al Hindle, Jill Hindle, Chris Jackson, Gary Kwant, Bill Lounds, Des Marshall, Roger ('Scog') Martin, Dave McDowell, Keith McDowell, Neil McKechnie, Steve Murphy, Ian McNeill, Steve Meyers, John de Montjoy, Dave Pownall, Paul Ramsden, Wendy Scott, Nigel Shepherd, Fred Smith, Andy ('Spanner') Spenser, Dave Waters, Phil Watkins, Keith ('Worm') Worsencroft and the totally unforgettable Buster, whose real name I've forgotten.

The ancillary staff in the 1970s and 1980s comprised a secretary, a housekeeper, two cooks, a storeman, two cleaners and (for part of this period) a caretaker-boilerman. Over the two decades, many people occupied these roles, some for a short time, other for more than ten years. Rather than attempting to draw up a complete record of all the comings and goings, I will give a rough summary, using late 1974 as a starting point.

The secretary was Mary Leahy; the next secretary, later in the 1970s, was Joan Howard, who stayed for many years. The housekeeper in 1974 was Ros Stroud, who was followed in about 1978 by Dorothy Yuille, before Sara Lingard took on the job, bringing invaluable stability. The cook in late 1974 was a youthful Bob Higginbotham. Joe Cook was the chain-smoking storeman; he was followed briefly by Neil McKechnie, and then John Dennis arrived, to start his many years of service in charge of the thousands of items of clothing, footwear and equipment that underpinned the daily life of a busy outdoor centre. The caretaker-boilerman in 1974 was the long-serving Bert Heathcote.

I am acutely aware of this book's minimal and sketchy coverage of the contributions of non-teaching staff. I hope, though, that some recognition is preferable to none at all. In November 1974 Bob Higginbotham was at the start of over forty years of work at White Hall and of unflagging commitment to its cause, firstly as cook and later as house manager. Similarly, in 1976 Sara Lingard started a thirty-eight-year stint as cook and then housekeeper. In those days, the aroma of the dining room was redolent of roast beef and Yorkshire pudding. Popular desserts included jam roly-poly, Bakewell tart and rice pudding. Food alergies were almost unheard of. As well as producing innumerable breakfasts and dinners suitable for outdoor appetites, Bob and Sara also steered the White Hall catering through the evolution of mass sandwich-making, from the time of pyramids of sandwiches delivered to the table-tennis room to the time of make-your-own lunch. Among the splendid packed-lunch components of the 1970s were generously proportioned sugar-coated doughnuts and oversized slabs of flapjack sturdy enough to survive, without any packaging, whatever mistreatment came their way. Bob and Sara also revolutionised the organising of camp food, supercharging this regular and quite complicated routine.

Lyn Noble's arrival roughly coincided with another Derbyshire managerial change: in August 1970, Jack Longland retired. One of Jack's colleagues later recalled:

> I worked at Derbyshire County Education Office for the whole of Jack's reign as director of education. He was a great boss to work for, easily approachable and always joined in the office social activities, including playing in the office cricket team – always with the ubiquitous pipe in his mouth. One memorable occasion springs to mind. I was arranging the Christmas party and suggested to Jack that it would be appropriate if, as is the tradition in the services, for the officers to wait on the other ranks at dinner. He immediately issued a 'three-line whip' to all the assistant directors, who duly turned out in full evening dress for the occasion.
>
> … The education authority was extremely fortunate in being able to bring Jack to Derbyshire. I am sure that one of the factors persuading him was the attraction of the Peak District, which enabled him to pursue his climbing activities.[16]

As we shall see later, in retirement Longland remained heavily involved in voluntary roles, particularly as chairman of the MLTB, for another ten years.

Qualifications, Ever Evolving

Another difference between the periods of Part Two and Part Three concerned instructing qualifications. Before 1970, instructing and coaching qualifications in climbing, caving and canoeing either did not exist or were newly established and not yet well known. The first mountain leader course had taken place in 1964. The BCU senior-instructor qualification was created in 1966 as a minimum qualification for leading groups of canoeists. The first MIC course happened in October 1968. A qualification called the Cave Leadership Certificate was launched in 1970. In 1972, the RYA and the National School Sailing Association jointly produced a scheme of qualifications. For each sport, a hierarchical group of qualifications evolved. During the 1970s, these newish qualifications became well-established parts of the world of outdoor centres. In December 1972, for example, an advertisement for a vacancy at White Hall said: 'Applicants should hold, or be working towards, the B.C.U. Senior Instructor's Certificate and should be prepared to take an active interest in mountain activities, rock climbing and caving.'[17]

Some LEAs began to expect every leader or instructor of school pupils to hold an appropriate qualification for the activity being undertaken, such as the MLC for hillwalking in summer conditions. Further up this particular hierarchy, centre staff members who ran MLC courses usually held the MIC.

In 1966, as described in Chapter 13, Kim Meldrum had questioned the need for the burgeoning bureaucracy of adventurous outdoor pursuits. Qualifications were a part of that bureaucracy. Many professional instructors viewed them with a pragmatic and necessary ambivalence. On the one hand, in a multi-activity centre like White Hall, an instructor did not just need one high-level qualification, such as the MIC; you needed also to obtain and sometimes revalidate basic or intermediate qualifications in several other sports. There was never an end to the paper chase, with its attendant registration fees and annual subscriptions. Occasionally a requirement to hold a qualification could seem to be excessive in a particular circumstance. On the other hand, by running training and assessment courses, LEA centres – along with the national centres – had become the main deliverers of qualifications like the MLC. You did not bite the hand that fed you.

Gradually, a total reliance on the national qualifications, run by the national governing bodies (NGBs), was relaxed. In Derbyshire this process began in 1975 when a group of teachers, advisers, lecturers in further education and Lyn Noble met to produce guidelines on the minimum standards required of leaders of rock climbing parties. The only national qualifications for instructing climbing were the BMC Mountain Guide award and the MIC, which were both more advanced than was necessary for all instructing. The meeting led to the production of a small booklet containing suggestions on the teaching of rock climbing and on the skills demanded of leaders. White Hall staff began assessing potential leaders for either single-pitch climbing or multi-pitch climbing.[18] These local assessments were fairly informal. Candidates were required to have considerable prior experience.

Similar meetings in 1976 contemplated extending the written Derbyshire guidelines to cover 'how to do everything from lighting a primus stove to laddering a vertical shaft'. Instead, however, the county adopted a policy that 'leaders of activities must either hold appropriate national qualifications or have equivalent experience and be vetted by White Hall staff'.[19] In 1977 the White Hall office began a register of approved leaders of hillwalking, caving, climbing and canoeing parties. A similar register, listing sailing instructors, was started at Lea Green (near Matlock), which in the 1970s was a county centre for sporting excellence. No local qualification was available for the person in overall charge of a sailing session; he or she was required to hold the RYA Senior Instructor certificate.

In 1977 the widening role of White Hall resulted in the addition of a seventh member of staff. In the years that followed, Noble and his teaching staff gradually developed a range of local qualifications, approved by Derbyshire education committee, for teachers and youth leaders who wished to operate locally at a basic level below that of the national qualifications. If a teacher just wanted to take pupils on moorland walks in Derbyshire, he or she could apply for approval as a local hillwalking leader. The practical assessment usually took the form of night navigation on Kinder Scout or Bleaklow.

Like many wardens and principals of this period, as well as running a centre and presiding over the sort of developments that I have just described, Noble remained involved in a variety of local and national committee work, such as chairing the BMC's Peak District guidebook committee executive, which he did from 1979 to 1984.[20]

Dave Edwards coordinated the development of a Derbyshire local cave leader qualification that could be partly tailored to people's needs by specifying approval for leading trips into named caves. Gwyn Edwards and Phil Booth built up a local canoeing leader qualification for running basic canoeing sessions on flat water. White Hall's single-pitch climbing qualification developed over ten years to become a mature and relevant scheme accompanied by a clear syllabus. Applications for this respected qualification arrived quite frequently. Sometimes teachers or youth leaders from other counties applied for the Derbyshire single-pitch climbing qualification, their own counties having no valid equivalent.

In parallel with its training and assessment slots for the Derbyshire local registrations, White Hall continued to run training and assessment courses for national qualifications: the MLC, the BCU Senior Instructor certificate, and a range of RYA awards from the Elementary Day Boat certificate to the Instructor certificate.

Expeditioning and Other Professional Development, 1970–83

Bill March, a leading ice-climber of the 1970s, was for a while the deputy director of Glenmore Lodge, the Scottish Sports Council's centre in the Cairngorms. He later became, for just eighteen months, the director of Plas y Brenin. March was a talented instructor with an extrovert and sometimes abrasive streak. Jeff Connor caught the essence of him: '"Big Bill" was a very large, very strong and outgoing six-footer with a huge toothy grin and a formidable appetite for climbing, drinking and occasionally fighting. People either loved or hated March.'[21] He had little sympathy for unnecessary bureaucracy and he held some strong views on risk.[22]

One of March's suppositions, which received widespread attention throughout British outdoor centres, was that instructors of outdoor pursuits were prone to what he called 'instructoritis'. The matter deserves some consideration here, in Part Three of this book, because instructoritis was a penalty imposed on professionals for tirelessly and successfully providing – week after week, month after month – routine adventure.

March said that the job of being a full-time instructor, outside in all weathers, all the year round, often working at a novice level and heeding numerous safety rules and regulations, tended to lead to stagnation, a loss of enthusiasm for the job, and a lack of experimentation. The situation could also blunt your desire to remain involved in the sport in your free time and at a higher level. In arguing that this was the case, and labelling the condition as a disease, March was implying that instructors should recognise the tendency and should guard against it. You could avoid instructoritis, he said, by taking preventive measures:

The treadmill of repetitive courses with the same content should be avoided and an attempt should be made to programme as great a variety of work as possible … The exchange of instructors between different [centres] should be given active and financial encouragement.[23]

As well as recommending these programming initiatives, March suggested that instructors should continue their personal climbing or kayaking, etc. By maintaining the interest that attracted you to the sport in the first place, the argument went, you would refresh your enthusiasm for the routine daily job.

There are different ways to refresh one's enthusiasm. In the early 1970s, the climber Pete Livesey worked for a while at Humphrey Head outdoor centre on the southern side of the Lakes. Looking back at Livesey's life from 2014, John Barraclough illustrated one way to mitigate the effects of spending a lot of time instructing: 'Around 1973 I bumped into [Livesey] at Wallowbarrow Crag. In his lunch break from guiding his students, I saw him strung out in the overhangs on *The Plumb*. When he got down, I congratulated him on such an impressive solo ascent. "Climbing with beginners all the time brings your standard down. You've got to do what it takes to maintain it," he told me.'[24]

Whatever the validity of these arguments about instructoritis, Derbyshire county council tended to look favourably upon requests for special leave, especially if the purpose of the leave had the word 'expedition' tagged onto it. When the leave – typically a couple of months – was a mixture of annual leave and unpaid leave, these arrangements did not cost the county any extra expense.

Following the examples of Kim Meldrum and Joe Brown, several of the White Hall instructors of the 1970s took part in trips to the greater ranges: the Himalayas, the Hindu Kush and the Andes.

In September 1971 Dave Draper joined the ex-White Hall instructor John Cheesmond on an Anglo-Welsh expedition to attempt to climb Patrisi Himal (21,742 feet) in Nepal.[25] This was Draper's second trip to Asian mountains, as he had taken part in an expedition to the Munjan area of the Hindu Kush in northeastern Afghanistan in 1966, during which a couple of virgin 20,000-foot summits were reached.[26]

Also in 1971, Rick Scott spent six weeks bagging peaks in brilliant sunshine in the Bashgal valley area of the central Hindu Kush. Afghanistan was a safer place then than it is now and was closer to Europe than was Nepal. 'A shorter journey, shorter approach march and nothing to pay for your peak. It [was] good-value, cut-price mountaineering.'[27] Thirty peaks were climbed, nineteen of which were, as far as was known, previously unclimbed.[28] Among the other members of this expedition were John Davies (the future husband of the White Hall instructor Janet Richards) and Ali Kellas (a London civil engineer and a future White Hall deputy principal).

In the same year, Janet Richards, immediately after leaving White Hall, joined four other women on an expedition to the Cordillera Carabaya in southeastern Peru. All five members of this trip were mountaineering instructors: Kate Dilworth, Barbara Spark, Molly Porter, Carol McNeill and Richards herself.[29]

Three years later, in 1974, the White Hall instructor Barbara Hulley joined Janet Davies (née Richards), Kate Dilworth and Carol McNeill on an expedition to the Cholakhola Glacier area of the Everest range. A report in the *Sheffield Evening Telegraph* included a photograph of the women standing beside their Ford Transit van in the White Hall courtyard, before setting off to drive overland to Kathmandu. The article was headed: 'All-girl Team Set to Conquer Himalayas'.[30] Janet Davies has recently pointed out to me that the loathsome wording was not of their choosing. 'No "conquering" was planned, just some climbing.' (Some journalists still today reach automatically for the word 'conquer', which has raised the ire of Jim Perrin who says: 'Any mountain-themed book or article with "conquest" in the title deserves to be studiously ignored – not even post-modern irony can justify this uncomprehending nonsense.')[31]

In summer 1975 Rick Scott, three years after leaving White Hall, and another well-known instructor Dave Bland died in an avalanche while approaching the Gervasutti Pillar of Mont Blanc du Tacul.[32]

In 1977 the White Hall instructor Gwyn Edwards joined two Bewerley Park Centre instructors, Sam Cook and John Anderson, and a Derbyshire teacher Keith McDowell on a pioneering sea kayak exploration of northwest Spitsbergen.[33]

I wouldn't go so far as to say that instructoritis was unknown at White Hall in the 1970s, but the chance of contracting it was low.

In the 1950s and 60s, occasional days had been allocated for the permanent instructors to improve their skills in activities other than their specialisms. This was known as staff training. In 1952 the caver John Plowes introduced Peter Mosedale, Donald Blair, John Hird and Cyril Machin to caving, 'a whole new activity'.[34] Skiing featured in the staff training undertaken during Eric Langmuir's time. Joe Brown wrote that 'the opportunities for doing new things at White Hall were tremendous'; taking advantage of those opportunities, he had taken up canoeing.[35] Also in the 1960s, instructors took part in mountain-rescue exercises, especially stretcher lowering.

In the 1970s, these sorts of occasions during work time became almost nonexistent. To an extent, some new and young instructors were arriving with a wider range of skills than their forebears, hence lessoning a part of the need for staff training. Another cause for the end of staff training was a gradual increase in the use of the centre, measured in annual overnights, throughout the 1970s, which virtually extinguished the time slots previously available for staff development. This would become one of a number or internal issues of the 1980s.

Sheffield Evening Telegraph, 15 August 1974.

(From left) Janet Davies, Barbara Hulley, Kate Dilworth and Carol McNeil in the White Hall courtyard, before setting off overland to Kathmandu, on an expedition to the Cholakhola Glacier area of the Everest range. August 1974.

Warding off instructoritis. Adam Haynes, training in the tent loft, November 1982.

Running Costs of White Hall Centre in 1983

In 1983 White Hall cost about £217,000 to run. This money came from several sources:

Source of funds for White Hall	Amount in £
County rates and the Treasury	
Budget, excluding salaries	51,000
Salaries – teaching staff	87,000
Salaries – clerical staff	12,000
Salaries – domestic staff	29,000
Student fees	38,000
Total	£ 217,000

Based on a diagram from *A Comparison of Two Outdoor Adventure Centres*, 1983.

The cost to the community (ie the net expenditure) was £179,000. The fees for Derbyshire school pupils were about £2.70 per day.

Notes

1   A B Afford, *The Story of White Hall Open Country Pursuits Centre; vol. 2* (Buxton, Derbyshire, UK: A B Afford, 1978), pp. 30–31.

2   Ibid., p. 31.

3   David Draper, Email to P McDonald, subject 'Voices', 1 July 2014 [Email].

4   A B Afford, *The Story of White Hall Open Country Pursuits Centre; vol. 2* (Buxton, Derbyshire, UK: A B Afford, 1978), p. 29.

5   Ibid., p. 29.

6   *The Oxford Illustrated History of Britain*, ed. by Kenneth O Morgan (Oxford: Oxford University Press, 1986), p. 578.

7   The National Archives, 'Sterling Devalued and the IMF Loan' (no date) <http://www.nationalarchives.gov.uk/cabinetpapers/themes/sterling-devalued-imf-loan.htm> [accessed 18 Jan 2016].

8   A B Afford, *The Story of White Hall Open Country Pursuits Centre; vol. 2* (Buxton, Derbyshire, UK: A B Afford, 1978), p. 29.

9   Doug Scott, *Up and About: The Hard Road to Everest* (Sheffield: Vertebrate Publishing, 2015), p. 102.

10   Ken C Ogilvie, *Roots and Wings: A History of Outdoor Education and Outdoor Learning in the UK* (Lyme Regis, UK: Russell House Publishing, 2013), p. 357.

11   Lynn Cook, 'Outdoor Education: Its Origins and Institutionalisation in Schools with Particular Reference to the West Riding of Yorkshire Since 1945' (PhD thesis, University of Leeds, 2000), p. 222.

12   David Draper, Email to P McDonald, subject 'Fading Memory', 1 Apr 2016 [Email].

13   Ken C Ogilvie, *Roots and Wings: A History of Outdoor Education and Outdoor Learning in the UK* (Lyme Regis, UK: Russell House Publishing, 2013), pp. 361–362.

14   Ibid., p. 424.

15   A B Afford, *The Story of White Hall Open Country Pursuits Centre; vol. 2* (Buxton, Derbyshire, UK: A B Afford, 1978), p. 33.

16   Roy King, 'The Centres That Jack Built Are His Great Legacy', *Derby Evening Telegraph*, 8 Dec 2008, p. 24.

17   'Classified Ad 13', *Guardian*, 12 Dec 1972, p. 18.

18   A B Afford, *The Story of White Hall Open Country Pursuits Centre; vol. 2* (Buxton, Derbyshire, UK: A B Afford, 1978), p. 34.

19   Ibid., p. 34.

20   *The First Fifty Years of the British Mountaineering Council*, ed. by Geoff Milburn, Derek Walker and Ken Wilson (Manchester: British Mountaineering Council, 1997), p. 121.

21   Jeff Connor, *Creagh Dhu Climber: The Life and Times of John Cunningham* (no place given: Ernest Press, 1999), pp. 178–179.

22   John Cleare, 'William J March 1941–1990', *Alpine Journal*, 96 (1991–92), pp. 304–306.

23   Bill March, 'Instructoritis', *Climber and Rambler*, 14 (June 1975), pp. 294, 296.

24   John Sheard, Mark Radtke and others, *Fast and Free: Pete Livesey, Stories of a Rock Climbing Legend* (Lancaster, Lancashire: 2QT, 2014), p. 46.

25   David N Draper, 'Asia, Nepal, P 19,580, Patrisi Himal', *American Alpine Journal*, 18, no. 1 (1972), p. 188.

26   E J Hammond, 'Expedition Reports: Munjan Expedition (1966)', *Geographical Journal*, 134, no. 4 (Dec 1968), p. 617. Also David Draper, Email to P McDonald, subject 'Fading Memory', 1 Apr 2016 [Email].

27   R Scott, 'British Central Hindu Kush Expedition, 1971', *Alpine Journal*, 77 (1972), pp. 170–171.

28   [Anon.], 'Hindu Kush Men Home', *Climber and Rambler*, 10 (1971), p. 387.

29   Kate Dilworth, 'Cordillera Carabaya Expedition 1971', *Alpine Journal*, 77 (1972), pp. 211–214.

30   Pat Roberts, 'All-girl Team Set to Conquer Himalayas', *Sheffield Evening Telegraph*, 15 Aug 1974.

31   Jim Perrin, *Shipton and Tilman: The Great Decade of Himalayan Exploration* (London: Hutchinson, 2013), p. 78.

32   [Anon.]*Climber and Rambler*, 14 (1975), p. 518.

33   John Anderson, *British Sea Kayak Exploration of North West Spitsbergen, 1977* (UK: John Anderson, 1977).

34   A B Afford, *The Story of White Hall Open Country Pursuits Centre; vol. 2* (Buxton, Derbyshire, UK: A B Afford, 1978), p. 7.

35   Joe Brown, *The Hard Years* (1967; repr. London: Penguin Books, 1975), p. 227.

16. The Hill and Water Sports, 1970–92

By 1970, several activities had become core elements of most White Hall schools' introductory courses (subject to the season and the weather). These long-established activities were rock climbing, caving, map-reading, hillwalking, camping and canoeing. Throughout the period 1970–92, they remained at the heart of things, founding members of the programmes for basic schools' courses. (Except for caving, which was suspended in about 1989, after the discovery of concerning levels of radon gas in some Derbyshire caves.) The coverage of these core activities in this chapter will focus on any changes that took place over the twenty-three years.

In 1970 the centre's expanding stock of equipment was stored in separate parts of the stone outbuilding somewhat misleading known as the Cottage. Here were the general store (holding camping units, walking boots, anoraks and overtrousers), a caving store, a climbing store and a canoeing store. Wetsuits were stored in a room in the main building.

Two other outdoor pursuits – pony trekking and cycling – had remained on the periphery of White Hall's menu. Special arrangements to include them had occasionally been made. In the case of pony trekking, participants had paid a surcharge. Neither activity had become a regular feature on the programmes.

The practice of hiring ponies for pony trekking died out completely in the early 1970s. Cycling, in contrast, arrived at White Hall as a major new initiative in 1991. So cycling will gain a mention near the end of this chapter.

The period 1970–92 saw one other important addition to the range of activities offered on schools' courses. This was dinghy sailing. Chapter 3 sketched the historical background of dinghy sailing up to 1949. The section on sailing in this chapter will add a little more background and will then cover White Hall's sailing from its start in the early 1970s, after the building of Errwood Reservoir, to its end in about 1991.

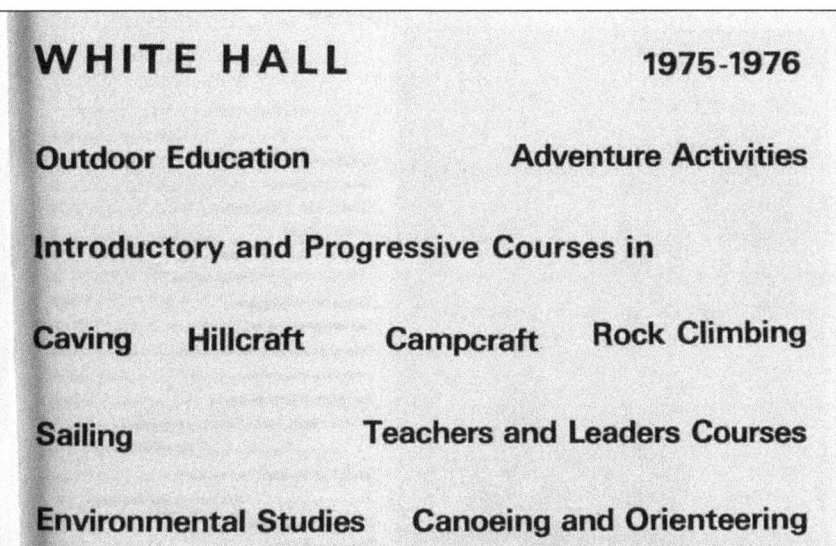

D3272\2, courtesy of Derbyshire Record Office

Page (i) from Programme No. 39, September 1975 – September 1976. This utilitarian page epitomises the White Hall brand of the 1970s. The activities were at the centre of things, but the inclusion of 'Outdoor Education' and 'Environmental Studies' on this page acknowledged the wider aspects of White Hall's purpose.

Climbing, 1970–92

In the 130 years since the start of rock climbing as a sport, the equipment used to protect climbers from death or injury has evolved from rudimentary to scientifically sophisticated. The period 1970–92 brought a surge in that progression, producing a number of far-reaching innovations. In a parallel process, the climbing community has adapted and diversified the sport's unwritten rules – its so-called ethics – to cater for new situations. These changes to the ethics have sometimes been controversial, especially when tending to liberalise one's conduct on the rock, such as tolerating the daubing of crags with chalk. In examining the changes that took place, this section will look mainly at how they affected novice climbing on White Hall courses.

By 1970, the hawser-laid three-strand nylon ropes in the White Hall climbing store had been replaced by kernmantel ropes. Pupils on climbing sessions wore their walking boots and were issued with nylon webbing waistbelts.

Whether the pupils wore climbing helmets in 1970 is uncertain. Photographs from the 1950s and early 1960s show helmet-less pupils and instructors. Joe Brown's helmet manufacturing in the mid-1960s may have helped to promote the necessity for pupils to wear helmets when climbing. For a few years, there was a transitional phase, which is evident in one of the few written safety rules of the early 1970s: a sheet of instructions on a noticeboard in the staffroom included a statement that said something like: 'Helmets should be worn when climbing on limestone'. By 1973 the wearing of helmets by pupils on climbing sessions was routine irrespective of what sort of rock was being climbed.

Among other essential items in the climbing store in 1970 were long leather gauntlets for use when giving a waist belay. Friction belay devices had not yet been invented.

P McD

Pamela Edwards instructing at Windgather Rocks in about 1973. Helmets have become expected in instructed climbing. The footwear is walking boots. Pam is using a waist belay and is wearing long gauntlets. The climbers are using waistbelts.

In 1970, recent additions to the gear in the climbing store included artificial chockstones made of aluminium, in various sizes and shapes, such as hexagonal and tapered wedges. These had become available from climbing shops in the late 1960s. Other state-of-the-art gear was nylon webbing tape for use for main belays and running belays. Also, by this time, the strength of karabiners had improved greatly, as a result of better alloys and design.

By 1975, the equipment in the climbing store included Chouinard chockstones in the form of Stoppers and Hexcentrics, in a wide range of sizes and better designed than anything that had been available before.

Jumping ahead ten years, by 1985 two further important innovations had filtered down to the instructional situation from mainstream climbing, and a third idea had been copied from Plas-y-Brenin. Friction belay devices called Sticht plates, an invention patented in 1970, had arrived at White Hall at some point in the 1970s. In the late 1970s, Dave Edwards had built the White Hall weight-drop machine, based on one at Plas-y-Brenin. Luckily for the novices who practised holding leader falls on this mechanical brute, they now had the belay plates, which were far superior to the waist belay. Sit-harnesses, invented by Don Whillans in 1970, had replaced White Hall's waistbelts in the early 1980s.

The improved gear at White Hall trickled down from developments that were not just national but global. In the case of mountaineering equipment, Paul Nunn summed up the overall effects:

> In 1970 ice axes tilted downwards, ice screws improved, but boots remained leather, heavy and primitive, gaiters were poor and shell clothing defective. Subsequently massive improvements continued – ice axes and hammers, crampons, outer and under clothing, boot manufacture, ice pitons, harnesses, rucksacks, gaiters, karabiners, tents, stoves, down and other warm wear, and in rock equipment also. Overwhelmingly, equipment became lighter, allowing survival in conditions unthinkable a decade earlier.[1]

By 1985 the use of chalk by climbers in Britain, which in the mid-1970s had been controversial, had become accepted.[2] This innovation did not directly affect instructional climbing with beginners, but it contributed to a general rise in climbing standards.

Another influence that had this effect was the increasing availability and popularity of indoor climbing walls. The oldest UK indoor

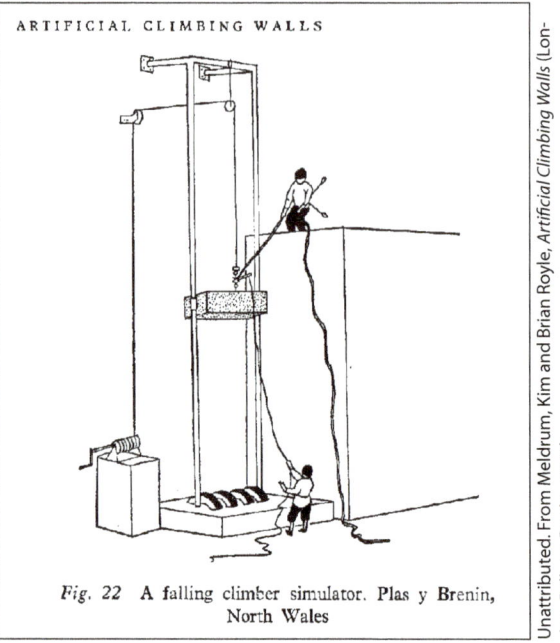

Fig. 22 A falling climber simulator. Plas y Brenin,
North Wales

Unattributed. From Meldrum, Kim and Brian Royle, *Artificial Climbing Walls* (London: Pelham Books, 1970).

Plas y Brenin weight drop machine, 1960s?

P McD

Weight-drop machine, White Hall Centre,
September 1981. Built by the White Hall
instructor Dave Edwards, based on the Plas
y Brenin prototype.

climbing wall had been built in 1960.[3] Buxton's Fairfield Centre, a recreation facility built in 1969, had a climbing wall of a primitive design but usable. White Hall in 1985 was still waiting for this vital indoor addition. In this respect it had fallen behind some other LEA outdoor centres.

Bob Higginbotham on the east wall of the Chapel Traverse, June 1975.

The mid-1980s also saw the arrival in Britain of its first bolt-protected sports climbs, legitimising the controversial offshoot of traditional climbing.[4] By using steel expansion bolts for running belays, leaders could fall off vertical or overhanging rock with impunity, a revolution. The old saying, 'The leader must not fall', did not apply to this new version of rock climbing. Generations of climbers had learnt from Edward Whymper that 'courage and strength are nought without prudence, and that a momentary negligence may destroy the happiness of a lifetime'. Now, in sports climbing, prudence and negligence were hardly parts of the equation any more. (They would remain vital factors in traditional climbing and alpinism). Climbers themselves, barely five years after the mountain-training dispute (which will be covered in Chapter 19), were changing the sport fundamentally to a degree infinitely greater than the old and damned MLTB had ever done.

In 1985 the White Hall climbing store still lacked climbing shoes such as EBs, the French footgear that had been popular for twenty years, or Boreal Firés, the sticky-rubber shoes that had appeared in Spain in about 1982; most course members still climbed in the centre-issue bendy walking boots.[5] On the other hand, by the late 1980s, a few fifteen-year-olds were turning up for climbing weekends already possessing £70 rock shoes and with their agility and strength boosted by many teenage hours spent on indoor climbing walls.

Several staff members now owned Friends, the spring-loaded camming devices for fixing in cracks to make belays. The inventing of Friends had been a technical advance comparable to the advent of nylon rope. Friends had been on sale by mail order or in climbing shops since February 1978, but were expensive and in 1987 had yet to arrive in the White Hall climbing store.[6]

In 1988 Rory Gregory masterminded and drove along the construction of an indoor climbing-wall in the old chapel. The work, with help from all the other instructors, took eighteen months. They finished the wall in time to coincide with the alarming loss of caving, abruptly stopped because of a worry about radon. (Disturbingly high levels of radon had been recorded in some Derbyshire caves, and further testing was under way.) The climbing-wall was the most important addition to the indoor resources since Derbyshire opened White Hall.

In November 1989, Simon Nadin, at the age of twenty-four, became the world champion of competition climbing. He had started climbing after taking part in courses at White Hall about ten years earlier.

And so we reach 1992, the end of the period under consideration. The equipment and some of the ethics of rock climbing had undergone numerous changes since 1970, changes whose total impact on the sport was considerable. Most British climbers had come to accept, enthusiastically or lamentably, the use of bolt belays – permanent anchors fixed to the rock – on some limestone cliffs. Two distinct branches of rock climbing had evolved: traditional climbing and sport climbing. But none of these changes looked likely to erode the place of climbing as one of White Hall's core activities.

On the contrary, climbing's place in education would in some ways become more secure. In December 1991, the Foundry, the first of a new generation of climbing walls, had opened in Sheffield. It had made a huge impact, amounting to 90,000 user-visits during its first year, including many youngsters. Other new walls had begun to appear. Mark Vallance, the Foundry's owner, described one of the effects of this development:

> The advent of walls changed my view of teaching young children to climb. I used to think climbing was an activity best confined to consenting adults, because of the inherent danger. It wasn't something to be encouraged. With the levels of safety and control possible in climbing gyms, it's become possible for even very young children to climb in safety and have a whale of a time.[7]

Few observers of the 1991 climbing scene, however, would have predicted that, by 2013, the BMC magazine *Summit* would be providing articles such as 'How to Climb Outside'. Even fewer would have imagined that, by 2015, an eleven-year-old boy, Josh Ibbertson, would be climbing well enough outside to tick his first 8a+, and that he would subsequently comment: 'I'm definitely interested in getting into trad when I get a bit older.'[8]

Caving, 1970–92

The year 1967 had brought two caving fatalities. On Wednesday 16 May 1973, a third White Hall caving death occurred. As in the Carlswark accident of 1967, the cause was drowning. This second drowning happened during a schools' introductory course. According to newspaper reports, ten pupils from Heanor Gate County Secondary School were on a trip down Wood Mine, an ancient copper mine at Alderley Edge, Cheshire. They were accompanied by their teacher, Roger Moakes, and a White Hall instructor, Gwyn Edwards. The boys were divided into two groups of five, one under the supervision of Edwards, the other under Moakes. A boy in Edwards's group, Paul Shaw of Kilburn, aged fourteen, fell into an underground pool while wearing a heavy battery, boots and bulky protective clothing. Although Edwards dived into the pool to try to save Paul, he was unable to find him, searching in what must have been total darkness.

The cave rescue service was called out. After a five-hour search, a diver, Phil Burke, found the boy's body caught in a narrow constriction about twelve feet underwater.[9]

Several people involved in the rescue expressed the opinion that Wood Mine was very safe. Organised and licensed groups had been visiting it for three years. It was technically straightforward with easily negotiated passages and a few simple scrambles. Two days after the accident, a newspaper reported that White Hall Centre was preparing a report on it for Derbyshire county council education officials.[10]

In July, *Descent* magazine reported this accident briefly and in a factual way.[11] In September, a preliminary report appeared in the newsletter of the Derbyshire Caving Association:

Alderl[e]y Edge Mine
Early in May a party of ten schoolboys from a Kilburn school, accompanied by one instructor from Whitehall Outdoor Pursuits Centre and one schoolteacher, went down Alderl[e]y Edge Mines. During the visit one boy apparently fell or walked into deep water in a flooded part of the mine. The instructor was unable to find him and after some confusion (either on the part of the police or owing to an incorrect callout, it is not sure which at present) the cave rescue was eventually called out to search for the missing boy and found him drowned. The inquest which is due to be held will, of course, find out what really happened, but at present no detailed report is available.

To forestall the question which is already being asked by some people – no member of the staff of Whitehall is either a member of B.A.C.I. [British Association of Caving Instructors] or holds or has shown any interest in the Cave Leadership Certificate. J. E. Potts.[12]

There may have been an understandable reason behind the mildly critical implication of the last paragraph. The caving world was split on the merits of the Cave Leadership Certificate, which had been launched in 1970 by the Cave Leader Training Board, a subcommittee of the British Association of Caving Instructors. Jenny Potts obviously supported the cave-leadership scheme (if we interpret the paragraph as a complaint). Some other cavers did not. In June 1970, Ben Lyon had written that 'instructed caving has been a favourite target of abuse from caving organisations for a long time'.[13]

It seems to me unlikely that any of the permanent staff at White Hall will have opposed the existence of the Cave Leadership Certificate. Several staff members were involved in the Derbyshire Cave Rescue Organisation (DCRO). The White Hall ethos encouraged high standards of instructing in all outdoor pursuits.

Research for this book has not located the report that White Hall was said to be preparing on this accident. Neither have any details from the inquest been found.

Six year earlier, in May 1967, after the two fatal caving accidents, the board of inquiry had recommended that novice caving trips should have one instructor to every three pupils. Eventually, in the mid-1970s, the staff-pupil ratio for caving trips on schools' courses became, in practice, 3:10, the three usually being two White Hall instructors and one visiting teacher.

Only recently, in the last year, have I learnt the details of the Bar Pot near-fatal accident of 1957 and of the three caving deaths of 1967 and 1973. Institutions and their staff members have to move on from such tragedies. The passage of time tends to blur the facts. But our memories of the lost boys, and the knowledge of the circumstances of their deaths, should never be allowed to fade completely.

Roger Moakes, the teacher involved (blamelessly) in the 1973 Alderley Edge accident, continued to bring Heanor Gate groups to White Hall for many years, introducing hundreds of young people to the outdoors.

*

A novice caving trip into Carlswark Cavern in 1992 was in many ways much the same as a novice trip into Carlswark in 1970, except that by 1992 the earthy Gin Entrance had been severely eroded by the passage of thousands of beginners. Before the start of this period, miners' cap-lamps and Oldham lead-acid batteries, capable of giving twelve hours' light, had already replaced the antiquated acetylene cap-lamps for most White Hall novice caving. The caving store had gained an industrial charging rack with capacity for charging about twelve batteries. From then on, throughout this period, lighting changed only slightly, the heavy Oldham batteries being replaced by FX battery packs. (Whereas, if we were to look at the whole period of this book, the lighting would progress from candles and the smoky yellow flames of 1950s acetylene lamps, through several intermediate technologies, to the piercing blue beams of 2010s LED bulbs.) The footwear issued to participants – wellington boots – did not change. On many beginners' trips, the pupils wore old clothes and a boiler-suit. In the early 1970s, the boiler-suits were standard cotton industrial wear. Later in the 70s, tough nylon boiler-suits, designed for caving, replaced the cotton ones.

For wet trips, such as Jackpot (P8), wetsuits were available, initially made out of unlined neoprene. Instructors spent much time on Monday mornings repairing the seams of dozens of wetsuits. The coming of wetsuits made out of lined neoprene, in the late 1970s, was a welcome improvement.

The Carlswark example given above, in which improved boiler-suits were the main change between 1970 and 1992, applies to White Hall's novice caving. The example does not mean that the sport of caving changed little during this period. In fact, vertical caving methods changed fundamentally in the 1970s with the widespread adoption of single-rope techniques (SRT), which had first been used by French cavers in 1934.[14] Single-rope techniques replaced laddering techniques. By the mid-1970s, the White Hall caving store contained minimal-stretch abrasion-resistant ropes designed for single-rope techniques. Ladders remained in use for novice caving that included short vertical sections.

Specialist caving courses at White Hall made much use of the weight-drop machine, constructed by Dave Edwards in the late 1970s. Using this machine, course members practised lifelining. Some items of caving equipment, such as the c-links of wire ladders, were limited in strength. To demonstrate this to members of cave leader courses, Dave entertained them by testing equipment to destruction. Very few of the caving centres in Britain at this time, LEA or otherwise, were equipped with the weight-drop machines required for this sort of training.

In the 1980s, a job-creation team converted the courtyard stables into a caving store and a room with large sinks for cleaning caving equipment.

Clothing for caving improved again in the 1980s, with the advent of the combination of polyester one-piece undersuits and very tough PVC oversuits. But old clothes and nylon boiler-suits remained the most common arrangement for pupils on White Hall's introductory caving trips.

In about 1989, White Hall temporarily suspended its caving after the discovery of disquieting levels of radon gas in some Derbyshire caves.

Exit from the pool, back into the first chamber, Gautries Hole. Introductory schools' course, March 1979.

After a trip down Gautries Hole. Introductory schools' course, March 1979.

Teamwork, coping with the heavy battery before a trip into Gautries Hole. Introductory schools' course, June 1981.

Teamwork, pulling off the welling-tons after a trip through Carlswark Cavern. Introduc-tory schools' course, February 1981.

Cleaning up after a trip down Gautries Hole, March 1979.

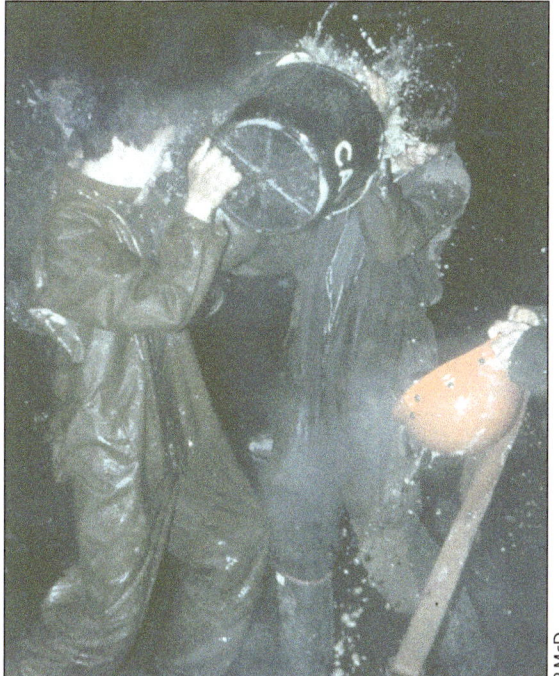

Cleaning up after a caving trip, February 1981.

Map-reading and Orienteering

There are a few aspects of map-reading and orienteering that previous chapters have touched on but which I will list together here as a reminder of the historical background.

As early as 1889, the *Boy's Own Paper* was telling its readers about Ordnance Survey maps and was encouraging every boy to have at least an inch-to-the-mile sheet of the area where he lived.[15]

In 1908, in his book *Scouting for Boys*, Baden-Powell mentioned map-reading as a necessary skill for walking and cycling expeditions. However, he did not allocate this subject as much space and attention as he gave to his yarns on tracking (men or animals) or on pioneering or on 'chivalry and brave deeds'.[16] The sections on map-reading were enlarged in later editions.

In early 1941 Gordonstoun school was in Wales, having been evacuated from Scotland in June 1940. Dr B Zimmermann, a Gordonstoun teacher, introduced the Gordonstoun pupils to orienteering, then known as Norwegian compass games:

Open Country Games (Compass Games)

These were introduced in the middle of the term as part of regular school work. Two mornings a week up to the break (11-20) were used for these games; their object, restricted, due to the season, was to teach the boys how to handle a compass, how to read a map, and how to make simple sketches in connection with estimating distances, training in description and exploitation of the open country.

The various exercises were not practised in separate groups, but in the form of simple types of competitive games. As the countryside offers large opportunities for these games, the training developed satisfactorily, and with the better summer weather still better progress is to be hoped for.

B. Z.[17]

Map-reading formed an important part of White Hall first schools' course in February–March 1951. It quickly became a core activity for all schools' courses. Peter Mosedale added a competitive element by developing wide games that relied heavily on map-reading, such as Bandits.

In 1955 John Disley, well known as an Olympic steeplechaser, became chief instructor at Plas y Brenin. He soon introduced to Britain the Scandinavian sport of orienteering, which involved running and navigation across wild countryside. The two key skills involved were route choice and map-reading. The first UK orienteering event took place later that year in the forest near Plas y Brenin.[18]

In the early 1960s, Joe Brown walked purposefully (and perhaps surreptitiously) around the Goyt Valley with a hammer and chisel, creating the carved-number circuit, a cleverly designed whole-day circular map-reading walk that started and finished at White Hall.

In June 1967 various orienteering associations met and formed the British Orienteering Federation.

In 1972 the Ordnance Survey published *The Dark Peak*, a sheet in the 1:25,000 Outdoor Leisure Map series. Each of the maps in this series, printed on large sheets of paper, covered an area previously requiring a handful of standard 1:25,000 sheets.

By the mid-1970s, specially drawn coloured orienteering maps began to appear in Britain, replacing the primitive black-and-white photo-copied maps. In 1976, the World Orienteering Championships took place at Aviemore.

In 1983 a coloured 1:5,000 plan of the White Hall grounds and the immediate surrounds became available. Extracts from this plan, about twelve centimetres square, were ideal – conveniently small – for the orienteering on the schools' courses. Gwyn Edwards perfected a method of encasing them in a thin coating of fibreglass, making a rigid sheet, transparent on one side. These convenient and sturdy orienteering maps were used four times on most courses, in all weathers and all the year round, and they lasted almost indefinitely.

The centre had enough Ordnance Survey 1:25,000 and 1:50,000 maps to equip four groups of ten pupils operating simultaneously any-where in the Peak District. As well, adequate stocks of maps for Wales, the Lake District and Scotland were held. Transparent self-adhesive film, such as Transpaseal and Coverlon, became available in the 1970s, extending the life of a paper map up to ten or twenty times over. White Hall teaching staff spent many a Monday morning expertly rolling out metre-wide film across metre-wide flat paper maps. In the late 1970s the Ordnance Survey experimented with waterproof plastic maps, sending several prototypes to White Hall for testing. Although these samples survived abuse and prolonged wetness remarkably well, the Ordnance Survey did not take the idea beyond the experimental stage.

In the 1970s and 80s, a consistent feature of most White Hall schools' courses, summer and winter, for year after year, was a progression of three sessions that each included some map-reading: firstly, a half-day introduction to map-reading, close to the centre, using a large-scale plan based on part of an Ordnance Survey 1: 10,560 map; then a day walk requiring map-reading or a two-day expedition requiring map-reading, using 1:63,360 (later, 1:50,000) or 1:25,000 maps; and then an end-of-course orienteering competition for all forty pupils, often a popular way of bringing a course to a close.

The grounds of Errwood Hall were the most frequent destination for the end-of-course orienteering event. At 9am one instructor left early to walk around the course, placing the stakes that marked the checkpoints. An hour later, three minibuses disgorged forty lively teenagers at the Errwood Hall carpark. A busy master-of-ceremonies issued a map and a checkpoint card to each pair of competitors and recorded their departure times. When the carpark was empty – about twenty minutes after the arrival of the minibuses – there was time for that staff member to put down the clipboard and to pour a cup of coffee and perhaps to begin writing ten reports. Whatever the meteorological embellishments of the morning, these events were reliable and popular parts of the course programmes and they required only one or two White Hall instructors. The Errwood Hall area was an ideal site, close to White Hall. In the 1980s, partly in a search for some variety for staff, alternative orienteering sites came into occasional use, such as Tegg's Nose Country Park (near Macclesfield), Lyme Park (near Disley) and Cromford Moor.

As well as being a core element on all White Hall schools' courses, map-reading was a core activity for many other outdoor centres in Britain. At a meeting of the AWMC in November 1979, Ken Oldham reported that a survey of forty-five outdoor centres had shown that 93 per cent of them provided hillwalking or orienteering as one of their activities, which was a greater proportion than any other pursuit. Eighty-seven per cent of the centres included water activities in their mix of pursuits, 75 per cent of them included mountaineering activities and climbing, 67 per cent included some field studies, and 60 per cent provided caving or mine exploration on their programmes.[19]

In 1982, Penguin Books published *The Penguin Book of Orienteering* by Roger Smith. In a section titled 'Orienteering as a School Activity', Smith argued that orienteering was an excellent school activity, combining elements of geography, navigation, mathematics, competition and self-reliance. Orienteering provided both physical and mental activity, the latter being easily incorporated into classroom work. Unfortunately, though, 'schools orienteering in the UK [had] struggled to establish itself and still [had] to rely largely on the efforts of enthusiastic orienteers who [happened] to be teachers'. Because of cutbacks in spending on education, Smith said, the situation seemed unlikely to change.[20]

Competitors on an end-of-course orienteering competition at Errwood Hall. Introductory schools' course, October 1981. The map is an extract encased in fibreglass by Gwyn Edwards.

An orienteering marker, as used for White Hall's orienteering events at Errwood Hall. October 1981.

Hillwalking and Camping, 1970–1992

Most schools' courses between May and October included a two-day 'expedition', which consisted of a reasonably long walk, with or without packs, and an overnight camp. Listing the purpose of these outings reads like a weary pedagogic cliché, but there's no avoiding it. The walks often required some prior route-planning and they included some practice in navigation and some development of the skill of walking on rough terrain. The young explorers also had to meet the physical challenge of walking a long way. From their perspective, this aspect may often have occupied most of their attention. They may not have been consciously aware of the elements of environmental education or the social aspects. Typically the social facets include cooperating with others, considering others and contributing towards the group spirit.

The Derbyshire terrain often allowed groups of teenagers to operate alone, monitored closely but without the continuous presence of staff.

Another regular and dependable part of White Hall's schools' courses, instead of or in addition to the overnight expedition, was a whole-day walk, either on the moorland of Kinder Scout or through Derbyshire dales, or locally, around the Goyt Valley.

The back road (the Roman road), looking up to Combs Moss from White Hall, February 1979.

The back road (the Roman road), looking south towards Buxton, February 1979.

By the early 1970s, the White Hall store was well equipped to kit out pupils with effective sleeping bags, rucksacks, tents, stoves, waterproof jackets and overtrousers, and other essential gear. The centre was benefitting from twenty years' development of the equipment storage and issue system; its twenty camp units, five to a group and stored in custom-built shelving, made the issuing and returning of equipment simplicity itself. Also, as four of the White Hall staff tended to each use the same five camp units each course, there was an added incentive to take a personal interest in the care and maintenance of the equipment.

As for all the other activities, the equipment available for camping went through long phases of stability, interrupted by occasional technological advances. At the start of the 1970s, all the tentage was cotton. The most common type in use at White Hall was the Blacks Good Companion, a well-established design, first developed in about 1935, which used a single central pole or a single 'A' pole. These tents were popular but were poorly suited to upland sites exposed to any wind. By the mid-1970s, they had been replaced by Vango tents, still of cotton but with a sewn-in groundsheet, two 'A' poles and a ridge pole. The Vango tents remained reliable workhorses for a decade, almost infinitely repairable and resistant to all the perils of centre use except mildew. Cotton tents rotted rapidly if they were packed away slightly damp. A notable breakthrough, both against this fungus and against stormy weather, took place in the 1980s, with the arrival of nylon dome tents.

Throughout the 1970s and early 80s, the camp units included paraffin pressure stoves, similar to the stoves relied on by Captain Scott and other polar explorers. In the mid-1980s, these were replaced by Trangia non-pressure methylated-spirits stoves.

At Wetton Mill campsite in the Manifold Valley, May 1976. Vango tents like this one were the workhorse tents of the 1970s and early 1980s.

Bogged down, Kinder Scout, October 1980.

Swimming at Threes Shires Head, schools' course, June 1978.

A group on Kinder Scout one winter in the 1970s, during an introductory schools' course. They are wearing Helly-Hansen waterproofs, heavy PVC-on-cotton jackets from Norway, designed for the fishing industry.

Two members of a White Hall group at the top of Kinder Downfall. Introductory schools' course, January 1979.

Members of a White Hall group at the top of Kinder Downfall. Introductory schools' course, January 1979.

Following the Kinder River across the plateau. Schools' course, January 1979.

Canoeing, 1970–92

Canoeing, like climbing and caving, was a core activity at White Hall, always an essential feature on the programmes of schools' courses, except when the water in the reservoirs and canals froze. The last detailed mention of canoeing occurred back in Chapter 10; it finished with the arrival at White Hall of two-seater fibreglass kayaks in about 1959. We need to catch up. In 1962, even Percy Blandford, who had spent at least fifteen years designing and building fabric-covered wooden canoes, conceded that 'glass fibre has much to commend it. The result is very strong and needs no maintenance'. However, he also said: 'It is heavier than other methods and there are building difficulties which make it unsuitable for most amateurs.'[21] In actuality, canoe moulds were proliferating and the age of the wood-and-canvas canoe was ending, except among nostalgic revivalists.

Something else that Blandford wrote in 1962 was: 'Single-seater or two-seater? Most enthusiasts favour single-seaters. You are independent. You are your own skipper.'[22] There is another side to this argument, connected with the value of teamwork. However, at some point in the 1960s, White Hall's fleet of fibreglass canoes changed from two-seaters to single-seaters. Wally Blake remembers that when he arrived in January 1966, the production of fibreglass single-seaters by Dick Wilkinson was in full swing.

No statistical information exists on how much canoeing activity was taking place in Derbyshire schools and youth clubs in the late 1960s. However, a 1968 survey of canoeing activity in schools and youth clubs in industrial Lancashire produced some figures, which were probably conservative. Fifty-seven schools of various kinds were offering the chance to canoe (or to build a canoe), either in curriculum time or in school clubs; 1,939 children were involved. In further education and youth work, 2,271 individuals were involved. The staff involved totalled 215.[23]

Then came the 1970s and a major development located in Nottinghamshire but close to Derby. A section of the Trent Valley lies to the southeast of Derby and Nottingham. In 1970 the Nottinghamshire county planning department published *Trent Valley Study*, which, among other things, examined the increasing use of the River Trent by rowers, anglers, canoeists, dinghy sailors and water-skiers. On canoeing, the study said: 'Six years ago there were only two canoe clubs in the whole of Derbyshire, Leicestershire, Lincolnshire and Nottinghamshire, whereas now there are eighteen.'[24] Partly in response to this study, by

March 1971 the work was well under way to transform 270 acres of barren floodlands and worked-out gravel pits at Holme Pierrepont into gently rolling parkland and a 2,000-metre outdoor still-water rowing and canoeing course.[25] The Holme Pierrepoint National Water Sports Centre came into use in 1972 and was officially opened by the prime minister, Edward Heath, on 27 July 1973.[26]

A significant change for the sport of canoeing in Derbyshire happened in late 1972 when the Midland Canoe Club moved its headquarters from Trent Lock to a site in Darley Abbey, formerly the home of the Derwent Sailing Club.[27] This move from the River Trent to the River Derwent may have shifted the focus of some members from sprint racing to slalom.

Canoeing developments at White Hall reflected the freedom that suitably qualified and experienced instructors enjoyed in deciding on venues, subject to the availability of transport and to legal access considerations. Combs Reservoir and the Peak Forest Canal remained frequent destinations for flat-water canoeing. These were supplemented occasionally by driving further to either the Caldon Canal in the Churnet Valley or to Flash Dam on Matlock Moor. On all these flat-water sites, most beginner sessions included canoe games as well as basic paddling skills. Gwyn Edwards, skilled in working with fibreglass, fabricated skegs for the whole fleet of canoes, tailoring each skeg to fit a particular hull shape. Having a skeg on the canoe made it far easier for a novice to paddle in a straight line.

On the Peak Forest Canal at Whaley Bridge, introductory schools' course, October 1973. The single-seat fibreglass kayaks have replaced the earlier two-seat kayaks. The pupils wear wetsuit tops over their jerseys.

P McD

Victory Quarry, Doveholes, summer 1982. A swimming test, sometimes held before kayaking or sailing. Dennis Richardson (in shorts) and a teacher look on.

In the early 1980s, after thirty years of fibreglass kayaks, polyethylene – a tough plastic that is unaffected by water and many chemicals – revolutionised kayak construction again. Manufacturers developed a way to build the shell in one piece by loading plastic pellets into a heated rotational mould. Kayaks could now be mass produced using recycled plastics; supplies of polyethylene became available from recycled plastic beverage bottles. The resulting boats were affordable and particularly suited to recreational kayaking. White Hall gradually replaced its older fibreglass kayaks with new plastic ones.

In the late 1980s, White Hall gained canoeing access to Victory Quarry lake near Dove Holes.

The centre also bought open Canadian double-seat canoes and obtained permission to use them on Errwood Reservoir, which had previously been used only for sailing. The addition of open Canadian canoes anticipated a national trend that would gather pace in the 1990s. They were more stable than kayaks and could take two or three people.

One of White Hall's main venues for river canoeing, accessible as a day trip, was the slalom course on the River Derwent at Matlock. Canoeists benefitted from legal access here to about one kilometre of river, the slalom section usually being a gentle grade 2 with a few eddies to play in. Another main moving-water venue was further down the Derwent at Darley Abbey. At certain river levels, this site was ideal for novices under instruction.

Much of the rest of the River Derwent presented canoeists with legal-access headaches. The four-kilometre stretch from Darley Dale to Matlock, for example, was a gentle grade 1, potentially a suitable trip for novices but fraught with uncertainties about legal access.

The Milford to Darley Abbey section was similarly problematic. Little has changed since then. A canoe website in 2015 offered the following advice on this section of about eleven kilometres: 'At lower levels, it is a good tourist paddle, ideal for opens [open canoes] and novices, but spoilt by fishermen, farmers and other busybodies who contest the access … We usually start in the dark, first thing in the morning to clear the most contentious bit first.'[28]

Another local venue for river canoeing was the River Goyt. White Hall groups occasionally paddled a section near Marple that included the Manchester Canoe Club slalom site. Another possibility on the Goyt combined a section of the river with a section of the canal, making a circular trip that included the magnificent Marple aqueduct, completed in 1800.

In the 1950s and 60s, White Hall's away canoeing courses mainly involved river kayaking, such as on the River Wye on the Welsh border or on rivers in Scotland. In 1969 and 1970, the course was on the River Spey.[29] Later in the 1970s, influenced by Gwyn Edwards, the focus for away canoeing courses switched from rivers to the sea, Anglesey being a frequent destination, particularly the exquisite sheltered inlets and coves of Trearddur Bay and Rhoscolyn.

Midlands canoeists gained an important new facility on 13 September 1986 when Princess Anne opened the 700-metre canoe slalom course at Holme Pierrepont National Water Sports Centre.[30] In October 1986 it was reported that up to a hundred paddlers a day were using the course.[31]

General Adventure (GA), Rock-hopping and Gorge Walking

In the 1950s and 60s, activities like rock-hopping and gorge walking had happened as planned or opportunist parts of days programmed as hillwalking. Occasionally these and other adventurous activities had taken place during overnight expeditions.

In March 1963 Richard Beeching had produced what had become known as the Beeching Report, in which he had proposed to close five thousand miles of railway track and 2,636 stations. Among the railway lines that subsequently closed was the line through Chee Dale and

Miller's Dale (part of the Midland Railway line from Manchester to Derby). It closed in 1968. It became part of the Monsal Trail.

Thanks to Mr Beeching, in the early 1970s a half-day activity called general adventure (GA) began to appear on White Hall's programmes for basic schools' courses, as an end in itself. General adventure usually took place at a disused railway viaduct upstream of Miller's Dale. White Hall paid rent to British Railways for the use of this viaduct.[32] In the 1970s the session included an abseil, a giant Tarzan swing across the river, and the building of a makeshift rope bridge. Two instructors were required.

P McD

Abseiling off the disused railway viaduct in Millers Dale. Introductory schools' course, November 1974.

The GA equipment, used four times a week, was kept conveniently available in the climbing store. The device used for the Miller's Dale abseil throughout the 1970s and 80s was a figure of eight. The ropes were protected from abrasion on the lip by a piece of thick carpet. At first, the pupils abseiled on normal climbing ropes, the sit harnesses were improvised, and the safety rope was held with a waist belay and using gloves.

From the late 1970s onwards, they abseiled on a non-stretch abrasion-resistant caving rope. Proper sit harnesses arrived in the early 1980s. The safety rope was now held with a mechanical friction brake, often an Italian hitch.

For a while in the 1980s, because of access limitations on one side of the river, a caving-ladder climb superseded the swing.

Minor dramas were an accepted part of GA. Now and again, an abseiler with long hair would get their hair caught in the figure of eight; the result of this was usually more awkwardness than anything more serious. The abseil was often deliberately positioned exactly above the middle of the river (except when the river was in spate). The abseiler stopped descending when they were just above the water and was then pulled sideways onto the river bank; occasionally they would end up wading or floating in the middle of the river.

The main perceived danger – the danger in the minds of the pupils – of the Miller's Dale GA session was the possibility of something going wrong during the abseil. Some of the main real dangers involved the spectators: the seven or eight kids milling around at the top of the abseil, waiting for their turn, and leaning over the parapet or throwing stones while the instructor's attention was on the abseiler. The safety briefing at the start of these sessions had to ram home some absolute noes.

Other activities with an adventurous element included rock-hopping down the River Goyt and clambering down Padley Gorge (which later became a nature reserve).

A Goyting session. Introductory schools' course, April 1975.

A Goyting session, April 1975. On the left is George Lowe of Everest 1953, who was visiting White Hall in his capacity as an Her Majesty's Inspector (HMI).

Skiing

Skiing at White Hall in the 1970s and 80s was an opportunist activity. When it snowed heavily, which could be anytime between December and April, groups dropped the scheduled activities and headed for the snow. But staff could seldom write 'Skiing' on the programme until the day before, or even the morning of, the event. Even so, White Hall was equipped to put twenty students out on skis. In the 1970s the skis were wooden ones with cable bindings. These were replaced in the 1980s with compact skis equipped with step-in bindings.

The unpredictable aspect of skiing in Derbyshire did not mean that money spent on skiing equipment was wasted. It was well spent. On the few occasions each winter when the snow fell heavily, it would have been incredibly frustrating not to have any skiing equipment. These occasional days of skiing broke up the winter for the instructors and benefitted staff morale. Over an extended time-span, many students were introduced to skiing, and the outlay per year, if calculated, would probably have been considerably less than what was spent on some other activities.

Walking to the skiing field below the Combs road. Schools' course, January 1977.

First time on skiis, on the field below the Combs road, January 1977. In the fawn jacket is Dave Draper. On the right are Gwyn Edwards (in blue) and visiting teachers Roger Moakes and Jack Inman.

Rope tow on the slopes below the Combs road.
Schools' course, January 1982.

P McD

Polybagging on the field below the Combs road, January 1977.

Dinghy Sailing, a Latecomer

We saw in Chapter 4 that, as far as school pupils were concerned, for the first half of the 20th century, dinghy sailing in the UK was largely a sport for the lucky few. Even for adults with some spare money, before 1950 only two sailing clubs operated in Derbyshire, if you counted the River Trent as part of Derbyshire: Burton SC and Trent Valley SC both sailed on the Trent, parts of which marked the county border.

Before we examine dinghy sailing at White Hall in the Lyn Noble years, we need to catch up with national developments of the 1950s and 60s. Nationally, opportunities for young people to try sailing began to increase in the 1950s, with the advent of courses run by the CCPR and the Scottish Council of Physical Recreation. In the 1953 season, 'close on one thousand men and women [were] introduced to a sport which [would] provide them with an absorbing leisure-time activity for the rest of their lives. They came from all parts of Britain, and from all walks of life: students, nurses, school teachers, typists, housewives, shop assistants, youth leaders, doctors, farmers, miners'.[33]

The dinghy-sailing scene in Derbyshire came alive, slowly at first, after the second world war, when attitudes to sailing on reservoirs began to change. Looking back at the national situation, Gordon Fairley wrote: 'Many of those who sail on reservoirs in these enlightened days [1983] perhaps do not realise what a debt of gratitude they owe to the far-sightedness of Council members of the Y.R.A. [Yacht Racing Association] away back in 1949.'[34] The first lengthy YRA council discussion about access to reservoirs took place in January 1950. Since the early 1930s, most reservoir managers had insisted that sailing on reservoirs was not practicable, for health reasons. The early discussions in the 1950s were confined to canal feeder systems.

Just two miles north of White Hall is Combs Reservoir, created in 1797 to feed the Peak Forest Canal. It is just over a kilometre long and 400 metres wide at the dam. The surrounding hills rise gently to create a picturesque setting. Recreational access to a canal-feeder reservoir was a less sensitive issue than recreational access to a drinking-water reservoir. In January 1950, Combs Sailing Club was founded. It was the only sailing club within a forty-mile radius and was the second sailing club to be formed in Derbyshire.[35]

The object of the club was 'to encourage and practise the arts of sailing, racing, rowing and paddling of small craft'. The use of any form of power was totally excluded; this even applied to the safety boat until 1970.

The club's constitution limited membership: 'Only gentlemen resident within a radius of three miles from the Hanging Gate Inn, Cockyard, Chapel-en-le-Frith shall normally be eligible for Membership with the exception that a proportion of the Membership, not exceeding one third, may be outside the area.' Women were specifically excluded: 'Ladies shall not be eligible for full membership but may take part in Club activities as guests, or as permitted by the Bye-Laws'. Recalling these male-only days, one of the founder members said: 'We pioneers were devoted to our calling and had not yet thought about socialising with wives and children.'[36]

We should pause here and remind ourselves that the original Combs Sailing Club constitution was written in 1950, the same year as White Hall Centre opened. There could hardly be a better or more local example of the social norms of those times.

The club's constitution and social atmosphere changed gradually over decades. In 1956, the policy on female membership became: 'Ladies shall be eligible for election as Sailing Members but not as Ordinary Members'. Even after this change, a restriction on women becoming full members stayed until the end of 1965. Further constitutional and attitudinal changes followed, and by the mid-1980s the club could justifiably call itself a family sailing club.[37]

White Hall groups did not sail in the 1950s, despite Combs Reservoir being only two miles away. But technological change was happening that would make sailing practicable and affordable. Plywood, developed for building aircraft during the war, was adapted for build-ing dinghies. By the late 1950s, schools were building boats as part of woodwork lessons. In 1958 a correspondent to *The Times* wrote:

> It is probably the 'build-it-yourself' movement which, more than anything else, has been responsible for the spread of yachting in recent years … The widespread prefabrication of parts and their sale in kit form have made the home-builder's task still easier …
>
> Undoubtedly, the boom has been most pronounced in the sphere of sailing dinghies … Instead of being the sport of a few rich men, as it was before the war, yachting to-day is well within reach of ordinary people.[38]

In 1947, the Yacht Racing Association had 373 affiliated clubs and only 336 individual members. In 1952 it changed its name to Royal Yachting Association.[39] At the end of 1957 the RYA had 909 clubs and 5,177 individual members.[40]

In Derbyshire, the Derwent Sailing Club was formed in 1959 to use the River Derwent at Darley Abbey. (This club later became the Swarkestone Sailing Club.)

Philip Davies.

Cynthia Rollaston and Christopher Davies of the Derwent Sailing Club sailing a Merlin Rocket 620 on the River Derwent at Darley Abbey, near Derby, in about 1962.

During the 1950s, filtration methods had improved, raising the possibility of sailing on drinking water. Some opposition to this idea had to be overcome. 'Many fears were expressed that sailors would pollute the waters whereas dead sheep and seagulls seemed not to be too great a health hazard.'[41] In Derbyshire, Ogston Sailing Club started in 1960; apparently Ogston Reservoir, near Alfreton, was the first drinking-water reservoir in the country to be used for sailing.[42]

By the early 1960s, dinghy sailing had become fashionable and affordable. The 1960s saw a boom in dinghy racing in Britain.

In January 1963 a new boat, the Mirror Dinghy, was exhibited at the International Boat Show in London. A complete kit for home building cost £63 11s. 0d. The kits cleverly used glass tape to fasten the seams. In the first ten weeks after the Boat Show, customers ordered over 300 kits and enquiries arrived from all over the world.[43]

*

A need for some sort of national sailing organisation for schools arose, leading to the first formal meeting of the National School Sailing Association on 11 February 1961.[44] The NSSA aimed to promote and help school sailing, canoeing and allied activities. In December 1965, Derbyshire education committee agreed to appoint a full-time sailing master so that pupils from thirty schools could be taught sailing on Ogston Reservoir.[45]

In March 1964, Stockport Corporation awarded a contract for the construction of a second dam across the Goyt Valley. The Duchess of Kent opened Errwood Reservoir on 14 June 1968.[46] In September 1968 the *Guardian* reported that the Peak Park Planning Board was negotiating with three water authorities for their reservoirs in the national park to be used for recreation.[47] Water authorities were beginning to accept their social responsibilities. Stockport and District Water Board decided to allow sailing on Errwood Reservoir. Errwood Sailing Club was founded in November that year.

There were public concerns, shared by planners, that the presence of dinghies on Errwood Reservoir would increase the traffic on the narrow road up the Goyt Valley. On 5 February 1970, the Peak Park Planning Board and the Countryside Commission announced that, as an experiment, a four-mile stretch of road through the most scenic part of the valley would be closed to all but authorised motorists at weekends and on public holidays from July to September. The scheme was reported to be 'Britain's first attempt to protect an area of natural beauty from strangulation by sightseers' cars'.[48]

Glossop Sailing Club was formed in 1970 after prolonged negotiations between the water authority, the Peak Park Planning Board and the dinghy sailors, dating back at least four years.[49] At first the club was based at Bottoms Reservoir. In about 1980 Glossop Sailing Club moved further up Longdendale to Torside Reservoir, which provided a sailing area of 170 acres.

Staunton Harold Sailing Club, which sails on Staunton Harold Reservoir, was formed in 1974. Which brings us up to date and ready to cover the place of sailing at White Hall from the early 1970s to 1991.

*

In about 1970 the county council's schools' sailing unit, based at Ogston, set up an outpost at Errwood Sailing Club, consisting of about five GP14 dinghies, a fibreglass dory safety boat, a petrol locker and a set of bulky life jackets that met British Standard 3595. Also about this time, Helly-Hansen PVC-on-cotton jackets and overtrousers became available, imported from Norway. In the early 1970s, using the facilities at Errwood on weekdays only, and the improved clothing when necessary, White Hall Centre added dinghy sailing to its menu. For about six months each year, sailing became a regular and important part of basic schools' courses. On nine-day basic schools' courses, each pupil had half a day's introduction to sailing; those who then chose sailing as their first choice had a full day of sailing during which most crews progressed to sailing alone, without an instructor in the boat.

One of the Derbyshire county council GP14s on Errwood Reservoir, June 1981. Dennis Richardson on the tiller.

P McD

Capsize drill on Errwood Reservoir. Sailing follow-up course, 1978.

To run a sailing session on Errwood Reservoir an instructor needed to hold the RYA senior instructor qualification. For a while, only Lyn Noble, Dave Draper and Dennis Richardson were qualified. This limited the flexibility of the staffing on most courses that included sailing. This problem was eventually resolved by the other instructors all gaining the necessary qualification.

White Hall ran one specialist sailing course each summer, offered as a follow-up opportunity open to pupils who had enjoyed the sailing on basic schools' courses. Among the other users of the Derbyshire county-council boats were schools in Buxton and Chapel-en-le-Frith. On occasions, for certain courses, the Errwood outpost borrowed a trailer-load of Optimist dinghies from Ogston.

In the 1980s, young dinghy sailors from Derbyshire achieved some notable successes in the annual National School Sailing Association (NSSA) regatta. These included the 420 Class Bowl (best 420 crew) in 1984 and the Felixstowe Salver (best under-fourteen crew) in 1985 and 1986.

One day in about 1986, a precocious young dinghy sailor from Whatstandwell, the ten-year-old Ellen MacArthur, joined in a club race on Ogston Reservoir and crossed the line in front of all the club members.[50]

In April 1991, the *Guardian* reported that Derbyshire county council had cut £16.6 million (5 per cent) from its education budget to avoid rate-capping. Among many changes was the ending of tuition in sailing at Ogston Reservoir and Errwood Reservoir.[51]

Carsington Sailing Club, probably Derbyshire's youngest dinghy sailing club, was formed in 1992.

Despite the spending cuts severely reducing the opportunities to take up sailing, dinghy sailors from schools in Derbyshire continued to perform well at the annual NSSA regatta. The awards included the 420 Class Bowl in 1994 and 1996; the Ellis Trophy (fast-handicap class winner) in 1999 and 2001; the Laser Radial Trophy in 2004; the Plymouth Salver (best under-twelve crew) in 1999 and 2002; and the Mount Haes Trophy (the most prestigious prize at the national regatta) in 2004.[52]

Just after 10pm on 7 February 2005, Ellen MacArthur crossed an imaginary line in the sea off Brittany to become the fastest person ever to sail solo around the world. The *Daily Telegraph* said: 'MacArthur embarked on this journey as a yachtswoman and return[ed] as a symbol of human aspiration.'[53]

P McD

Sailing on Errwood Reservoir, September 1979.

Notes

1   Paul Nunn, *At the Sharp End* (London: Unwin Hyman, 1988), p. 121.
2   Phil Kelly, Graham Hoey and Giles Barker, *Peak Rock: The History, The Routes, The Climbers* (Sheffield: Vertebrate Publishing, 2013), p. 174.

3   Kim Meldrum and Brian Royle, *Artificial Climbing Walls* (London: Pelham Books, 1970), p. 66.

4   Simon Thompson, *Unjustifiable Risk? The Story of British Climbing* (Milnthorpe, UK: Cicerone, 2010), p. 294.

5   Mark Vallance, *Wild Country: The Man Who Made Friends* (Sheffield: Vertebrate Publishing, 2016), pp. 142–143.

6   Ibid., pp. 117–118.

7   Ibid., pp. 187–188.

8   Sarah Stirling, '11-year-old Josh Ibbertson Talks Getting Strong and Ticking his First 8a+', British Mountaineering Council (25 Nov 2015) <https://www.thebmc.co.uk/interview-josh-ibbertson> [accessed 8 Nov 2016].

9   'Boy, 14, Drowns in Mine Lagoon', *Guardian*, 17 May 1973, p. 24. Also 'Boy of 14 Dies in Mine on School Outing', *The Times*, 17 May 1973, p. 1.

10 'Report on Boy's Death in Mine', *Guardian*, 18 May 1973, p. 9.

11 'Alderley Edge Fatality', *Descent: The Magazine for Cavers and Potholers*, July 1973, p. 6.

12 J E Potts, 'Alderl[e]y Edge Mine', *Derbyshire Caving Association Newsletter*, 24 Sept 1973, p. 5.

13 Quoted in Ken C Ogilvie, *Roots and Wings: A History of Outdoor Education and Outdoor Learning in the UK* (Lyme Regis, UK: Russell House Publishing, 2013), p. 349.

14 Ralph Crane and Lisa Fletcher, *Cave: Nature and Culture*, Earth (London: Reaktion Books, 2015), p. 78.

15 G A Hutchison, ed., 'Ordnance Maps, and How They Are Made', in *The Boy's Own Annual: 1889–1890* (London: Boy's Own Paper Office, 1890), vol. 12, pp. 203–204.

16 Robert S S Baden-Powell, *Scouting for Boys: A Handbook for Instruction in Good Citizenship*, Reprint of six-part (1908) edn (Oxford: Oxford University Press, 2005), p. 155.

17 B Zimmermann, 'Open Country Games (Compass Games)', *Gordonstoun Record: Christmas 1939 – Easter 1941*, no. 5 (1941), p. 22.

18 Ken C Ogilvie, *Roots and Wings: A History of Outdoor Education and Outdoor Learning in the UK* (Lyme Regis, UK: Russell House Publishing, 2013), p. 296.

19 Ibid., p. 415.

20 Roger Smith, *The Penguin Book of Orienteering* (Harmondsworth: Penguin Books, 1982), pp. 163, 173–174.

21 Percy W Blandford, *Canoes and Canoeing* (London: Lutterworth Press, 1962), p. 19.

22 Ibid., p. 15.

23 Ken C Ogilvie, *Roots and Wings: A History of Outdoor Education and Outdoor Learning in the UK* (Lyme Regis, UK: Russell House Publishing, 2013), p. 327.

24 Nottinghamshire County Planning Department, *Trent Valley Study* (West Bridgford: Nottinghamshire County Planning Dept, 1970), p. 56.

25 Christopher Dodd, 'A Water Playground for Britain', *Guardian*, 12 Mar 1971, p. 20.

26 Jim Railton, 'Rowing', *The Times*, 24 July 1973, p. 11.

27   Midland Canoe Club, 'History of the Midland Canoe Club' (2015) <http://
     www.derbycanoeclub.co.uk/> [accessed 24 Mar 2015].

28   Jimmy of Midland Canoe Club, 'Guide to the River Derwent: Milford to Darley
     Abbey' (23 Jan 2011) <http://www.ukriversguidebook.co.uk/rivers/england/
     midlands/river-derwent-milford-to-darley-abbey> [accessed 25 Mar 2015].

29   Janet Davies, Email to P McDonald, subject 'Re: TSoWH', 3 Dec 2016 [Email].

30   'Court Circular', *The Times*, 13 Aug 1986, p. 14.

31   Anne Warden, 'Nottingham Course a Great Success', *The Times*, 2 Dec 1986, p.
     37.

32   A B Afford, *The Story of White Hall Open Country Pursuits Centre; vol. 2* (Buxton,
     Derbyshire, UK: A B Afford, 1978), p. 31.

33   G A McPartlin, 'Sailing Holidays', *Physical Recreation*, 5, no. 4 (Oct–Dec 1953),
     pp. 15–18 (p.15).

34   Gordon Fairley, *Minute by Minute: The Story of the Royal Yachting Association
     (1875–1982)* (Woking, UK: Royal Yachting Association, 1983), pp. 118–119.

35   J E A 'Sandy' Broadbent, *The History of the Combs Sailing Club 1950–2000*
     (Chapel-en-le-Frith: Combs Sailing Club, 2000), pp. 4, 11.

36   Ibid., pp. 12–14, 47.

37   Ibid., pp. 47–48.

38   'Boom in Sailing Small Craft', *The Times*, 11 Jan 1958, p. 7.

39   Gordon Fairley, *Minute by Minute: The Story of the Royal Yachting Association
     (1875–1982)* (Woking, UK: Royal Yachting Association, 1983), p. 115.

40   'Boom in Sailing Small Craft', *The Times*, 11 Jan 1958, p. 7.

41   Gordon Fairley, *Minute by Minute: The Story of the Royal Yachting Association
     (1875–1982)* (Woking, UK: Royal Yachting Association, 1983), p. 119.

42   'The History of Ogston Sailing Club', Ogston Sailing Club (no date) <http://
     www.ogstonsc.co.uk/history.htm> [accessed 25 Apr 2015].

43   'Rush to Push Out the Boat', *Daily Mirror*, 16 Mar 1963, p. 11.

44   'The NSSA Archives', National School Sailing Association (Feb 2015) <https://
     sites.google.com/site/nssasailing/> [accessed 18 Mar 2015].

45   'Lessons Ahoy?', *Guardian*, 23 Dec 1965, p. 12.

46   'News in Brief', *The Times*, 23 May 1968, p. 12.

47   George Hawthorne, 'Planners See Leisure Pleasure in Peak District Reservoirs',
     Guardian, 14 Sept 1968, p. 4.

48   Dennis Johnson, 'Saving Goyt Valley from Traffic', *Guardian*, 6 Feb 1970, p. 22.

49   George Hawthorne, 'Manchester May Open Reservoirs for Recreation',
     Guardian, 9 Feb 1966, p. 18.

50   Ellen MacArthur, *Taking On the World* (London: Michael Joseph, 2002), pp.
     21–22.

51   'Making a Meal of Dinners', *Guardian*, 16 Apr 1991, p. 21.

52   'Trophies', National School Sailing Association (Feb 2015) <https://sites.google.
     com/site/nssasailing/trophies> [accessed 18 Mar 2015].

53   Sue Mott, 'The Greatest Ever? Surely There Can Be No Doubt', *Daily Telegraph*,
     9 Feb 2005.

17. A Year's Courses, 1975–6

Research into White Hall's history has so far found surprisingly few centre documents from the period 1950–92, the era before the electronic revolution. Some White Hall material may be waiting to be discovered among fifty boxes of education-committee papers at the Derbyshire Record Office. In the meantime, the few physical documents that have been unearthed include a copy of Programme No. 39, listing the courses that were available from September 1975 to September 1976.[1] This programme is a useful record of a typical year in the 1970s. As well as listing course numbers and dates, it provided advice on clothing and equipment and on the booking procedure. It also described each type of course, providing about sixteen descriptions in total. This chapter is a straightforward record of the courses available in 1975–6, based mainly on Programme No. 39.

White Hall Centre Programme for 1975–6

In the Number-of-Days column in the table below, a two-day course meant a course providing two nights' accommodation. A four-day course meant four nights' accommodation, and so on. A typical winter schools' course, listed in the table as four days, went from 2pm on the Monday to 3pm on the Friday, ie five days, not four. The figures in the Number-of-Days column, if misinterpreted, can make a course appear to be a day shorter than it actually was.

Course	Date	No. of Days	Description
1093	Sept 5 – 7, 1975	2	Specialist Activity Weekend
1094	Sept 8 – 16	8	Schools O.C.P.
1094a	Sept 8 – 12	4	Bunkhouse
1095	Sept 19 – 21	2	Specialist Activity Weekend
1096	Sept 26 – 28	2	Specialist Activity Weekend

Course	Date	No. of Days	Description
1097	Sept 29 – Oct 7	8	Schools O.C.P.
1097a	Sept 29 – Oct 3	4	Bunkhouse
1098	Oct 10 – 12	2	Teachers Weekend
-	Oct 22 – 24	3	Maintenance Break
1099	Oct 25 – Nov 1	7	M.L.C. Assess. and Train.
1100	Nov 3 – 9	6	Schools O.C.P.
1100a	Nov 3 – 7	4	Bunkhouse
1101	Nov 14 – 16	2	Youth Service Weekend
1102	Nov 17 – 21	4	Schools O.C.P.
1102a	Nov 17 – 21	4	Bunkhouse
1103	Nov 24 – 28	4	Schools O.C.P.
1103a	Nov 24 – 28	4	Bunkhouse
1104	Dec 1 –5	4	Schools O.C.P.
1104a	Dec 1 –5	4	Bunkhouse
1105	Dec 8 –12	4	Schools O.C.P.
1105a	Dec 8 –12	4	Bunkhouse
1106	Dec 15 – 19	4	Schools O.C.P.
1106a	Dec 15 – 19	4	Bunkhouse
1107	Jan 5 – 9, 1976	4	Schools O.C.P.
1107a	Jan 5 – 9	4	Bunkhouse
1108	Jan 12 – 16	4	Schools O.C.P.
1108a	Jan 12 – 16	4	Bunkhouse
1109	Jan 19 – 23	4	Schools O.C.P.
1109a	Jan 19 – 23	4	Bunkhouse
1110	Jan 26 – 30	4	Schools O.C.P.
1110a	Jan 26 – 30	4	Bunkhouse
1111	Jan 30 – Feb 1	2	Youth Service Weekend
1112	Feb 7 – 14	7	M.L.C. Assess. and Train.
1113	Feb 16 – 20	4	Schools O.C.P.
1114	Feb 23 – 27	4	Schools O.C.P.
1114a	Mar 1 – 5	4	Bunkhouse
-		3	Maintenance Break
1115	Mar 8 – 12	4	Schools O.C.P.
1116	Mar 15 – 19	4	Schools O.C.P.
1117	Mar 21 – 28	7	M.L.C. Assess. and Train.

Course	Date	No. of Days	Description
1118	Apr 2 – 8	6	D. of E. Training
1118a	Apr 5 – 9	4	Bunkhouse
1119	Apr 9 – 11	2	Voluntary Instructors Weekend
1120	Apr 16 – 18	2	Family Weekend
1121	Apr 19 – 27	8	Schools O.C.P.
1121a	Apr 19 – 23	4	Bunkhouse
1122	Apr 30 – May 2	2	Specialist Activity Weekend
1123	May 3 – 11	8	Schools O.C.P.
1123a	May 3 – 7	4	Bunkhouse
1124	May 14 – 16	2	Specialist Activity Weekend
1125	May 22 – 29	7	M.L.C. Train. or Sailing Course
1126	June 4 – 6	2	Youth Service Weekend
1127	June 7 – 11	4	Special Schools
1128	June 14 – 22	8	Schools O.C.P.
1129	June 28 – July 6	8	Schools Supplementary
1130	July 12 – 20	8	Schools O.C.P.
1131	July 26 – Aug 3	8	Specialist
1132	Aug 9 – 17	8	Schools Supplementary
1133	Aug 23 – 31	8	Specialist

Introductory Courses

Schools' Open Country Pursuits (OCP) Courses

Before describing the courses that appeared on the 1975–6 programme, I need to mention a development that occurred at the start of the 1970s and which, I think it's fair to say, improved some of the basic schools' courses. This development took the form of a link between Derbyshire and Lincolnshire. Lyn Noble explained:

> During times of economic difficulty there is an understandable anxiety amongst administrators to maximise the use of any establishment or facility. In 1970 White Hall came under close scrutiny which resulted in a demand for an immediate increase in 'student days' (i.e. numbers of students in residence at any one time multiplied by the number of resident days in a year). Within weeks an agreement was made with Lindsey Education Committee, later to be absorbed into Lincolnshire Education Committee, which

made available 1200 student days a year to Lindsey schools. At the same time recruitment within Derbyshire was stepped up and we were soon turning down late applicants for courses. By 1971 [the] demand for places was such that in order to accommodate new schools as well as the Lindsey groups it became necessary to limit schools to twenty places per year.[2]

The Schools' OCP courses varied in length, being either four, six or eight days long. In the twelve months of the 1975–6 programme, there were twenty of these introductory courses, fourteen of them taking place between November and March. The programme described the schools' courses as follows:

These courses may be taken as an introduction to the outdoors or as an integral part of a school outdoor education programme.

At the introductory level students are encouraged to discover and develop the potential of the countryside and the potential of themselves at every level from the quietly appreciative to the stren-uously physical. A taste of a number of the following activities is offered, depending on the weather and the time of year: campcraft, caving, climbing, canoeing, hill walking, orienteering, sailing and incidental environmental studies and general adventure.

Wherever possible groups are encouraged to integrate their White Hall courses into Outdoor Education schemes that may be in operation at school. Realistic preparation and follow up work can greatly increase the value and enjoyment of a relatively short residential course. The Principal and Staff of White Hall will be happy to visit schools and offer advice about linking school based topics with outdoor activities at the centre.

For many school groups one of the most valuable aspects of these courses is the opportunity to experience community living and develop a sense of communal responsibility.

On most introductory schools' courses in the 1970s and 80s, the forty places were allocated to two blocks of twenty pupils from two schools. A note in the 1975–6 programme added the advice or request that at least one visiting teacher should accompany each group of twenty.

Writing about these courses in 1978, Lyn Noble mentioned a change that had occurred in the 1970s, the development of some half-day ses-sions. He explained the reasons for this move:

Anyone who has climbed, walked or canoed on the continent will appreciate that for a large part of the time in Britain we carry out our activities in conditions which would send those from sunnier climes straight back to bed. Also it doesn't take much observation to realise that only in the best possible conditions do British outdoor sportsmen (particularly climbers, cavers and canoeists) spend many more than three or four hours per day actually pursuing their sport. It therefore seemed reasonable to work on the assumption that those undertaking activities for the first time would be satisfied with a half-day session. The theory proved true and courses now offer a quick fire range of half-day activities, morning and afternoon, which serve to rouse enthusiasm as well as create new insights.[3]

The half-days worked very well, except for Peak Plumbago, which Chapter 18 will deal with.

The longer schools' courses included Sundays. In the early 1970s, arrangements were occasionally made, on request, for course members to attend church services on Sunday mornings. By the end of the 1980s, such requests were very seldom made. God was facing some stiff competition.

*

Most evenings on schools' courses included a talk or film or slide show, held in the briefing room and lasting about three-quarters of an hour. The indispensable audio-visual aids of the 1970s and 80s were – as well as chalk and a blackboard – an overhead projector, a 16mm film projector and a Kodak Carousel slide projector.

The film cupboard in the briefing room held a dozen or so films, about four of which were used quite frequently. *Hazard*, a 1959 film made for the British Iron and Steel Federation, carried a safety message about the need for helmets. It featured Joe Brown and Don Roscoe climbing in the Dolomites. *White Hall*, shot in Eric Langmuir's time at White Hall, provided a general idea of what a schools' course entailed. *Cold Can Kill*, a 1972 documentary, explained the causes of hypothermia, with examples on land and sea. *Summer Holiday* was about a bold voyage across the North Sea in a Wayfarer dinghy.

The evening session on the first evening of a schools' course was invariably 'The Week Ahead'. On the longer schools courses, the evening before the expedition always included an expedition briefing. On the final evening of a schools' course, an illustrated talk titled 'Where to Now?' explained the opportunities available to individuals to return to White Hall on a supplementary course or on a specialist courses.

Other evening sessions were less regular and more opportunist. Sometimes on fine evenings, instead of an indoor session, the duty instructor, with the help of the four visiting teachers, organised a night walk of some sort (in the dark), most commonly from White Hall down to the northern end of Fernilee Reservoir. Long summer evening occasionally saw the front lawn in use for impassioned and vigorous welly-throwing.

A more cerebral occupation on some of the 1970s schools' courses was diary-writing. Some schools issued exercise books to their pupils and required each person to write a daily diary. This practice dated from White Hall's earliest days, when 'the Day's Log book of activities, which each child [was] required to record, [was] regarded as a valuable medium of education.'

Somewhere, one or two of these diaries may be awaiting discovery. But in the 1970s the requirement to record their adventures in writing was one White Hall challenge that many young visitors were happy to opt out of. The centre tended to become littered with near-empty exercise books. Pupil power won, and the practice of keeping a diary, as a compulsory part of the course, was dropped. On diary-writing, some other outdoor centres may have achieved greater success than White Hall. Hundreds of Outward Bound course members kept daily logbooks. Many have since retained them. Bob Newton, for example, attended a course at Ullswater OBMS in 1963 and he recently posted an excerpt from his logbook:

Thursday 11th April 1963
6.30am Almost flew out of bed this morning, last one out of bed gets 30 seconds extra in the cold shower (Poor old Smith!).
8.00am Breakfast.
8.45am Inspection – although we desperately needed 10/10, we were only able to get 9 – well there's always tomorrow!
9.15am Rock climbing – left the school in a very happy mood, singing all the way to Gowbarrow. The climbing was very enjoy-able and although I was not afraid, I experienced a sinking feeling when I thought my left foot was slipping.[4]

During the 1980s, White Hall's 16mm film projector and films began to gather dust, as the use of film began a long worldwide decline, being replaced by video cameras, video cassettes and, at first, video players connected to televisions. (High-resolution digital projectors would not appear until about 2006.) Recent efforts to locate the early 1960s film *White Hall* have been unsuccessful.

Finally, if we stay for a moment on the subject of technological progress, in the White Hall front porch in the 1970s and 80s was a payphone available to course members. But the year 1983 saw the appearance, somewhere in the world, of the Motorola DynaTAC 8000x, the first commercially available handheld mobile phone. According to the United Nations, this new technology would spread faster than any other technology in history. By the early 1990s, some pupils on schools' courses would be arriving at White Hall and alighting from the bus while speaking into a cell phone, 'Just got there, Mum. It's miles from anywhere. We're in the cloud ... Yes. It's a spooky looking house ... like summat outa *Dracula*.' By 1996 the Duke of Edinburgh's Award scheme would be providing written guidance on the use of mobile phones by young people on unaccompanied self-reliant journeys.[5] Smartphones with GPS (Global Positioning System) capability were still some years away.

The house on the hill, miles from anywhere, in the cloud, a spooky looking place.

		Group A DE	Group B GE	Group C PM	Group D BH
Mon	am				
	pm	2.30pm Course arrives, welcome, dormitory allocation 3.00pm Group allocation, tour of centre 7.30pm The Week Ahead			
Tue	am	Caving	Orienteering	Camp prep	Sailing
	pm	Orienteering	Caving	Sailing	Camp prep
		7.30pm Film: Cold Can Kill			
Wed	am	Sailing	Camp prep	Climbing	Canoeing
	pm	Camp prep	Sailing	Canoeing	Climbing
		7.30pm Expedition briefing			
Thurs	am				
	pm				
		———— E x p e d i t i o n s ————			
Fri	am				
	pm				
		7.30pm Disco			
Sat	am	Climbing	Canoeing	Caving	Orienteering
	pm	Canoeing	Climbing	Orienteering	Caving
		7.30pm Illustrated talk: Where to Now?			
Sun	am	9.15am Orienteering competition 12noon Equipment return			
	pm	1.00pm Lunch 2.00pm Final course meeting 2.15pm Final group meetings 2.30pm Course departs			

A typical course programme for a seven-day course in the 1970s and 80s. (Called a six-day course in the annual programme of courses.) The inclusion of the evening lecture 'Where to Now?' on the last night of each course was consistent with one of White Hall's purposes, the promotion of outdoor recreation.

P McD

It rained and rained and rained. Trev Morris and his group after bivouacking in one of the Danebower quarries. Introductory schools' course, October 1973.

Special School Courses (4 days)

The 1975–6 programme lists only one of these courses. In later years there may have been two. The usual forty places were reduced to thirty to improve the staff-pupil ratio. On these courses, some activities that normally needed only one White Hall instructor, such as rock-hopping down the River Goyt, required two instructors. The course description in the programme said:

> The content of these courses is best arranged in consultation with the Principal. Emphasis may be placed on community living, outdoor pursuits, environmental studies or simple field studies. It is essential that groups are accompanied by their own teachers and that early contact is made with White Hall in order that the course may be planned to the best advantage.

Youth Service Weekends

Youth Service Weekend courses were founding members of White Hall's range of provision. The weekends offered a choice of activities including hill walking, climbing, canoeing, caving, orienteering and general adventure. The 1975–6 programme listed three of these weekends. Forty places were available on each.

Some of these adventure weekends were, by common consensus, very successful, albeit sometimes requiring an initial adjustment of one's expectations. Youth clubs are different from schools, and youth leaders are different from teachers; the atmosphere on a youth service weekend was often very different from that of a schools' course.

The minimum age on these weekends was fourteen. There was no upper age limit, which meant that occasionally a few course members were legally old enough to buy alcoholic drinks, making Friday evenings a test of the duty instructor's tact and diplomacy and sometimes making the whole weekend a test of everyone's tolerance until Sunday evening and the private thought, Thank goodness we've got rid of that lot.

Family Adventure Weekend

This weekend was open to family groups only, consisting of at least one parent and one child. The minimum age for children was eight. The course was 'an opportunity for parents and children to share in an introductory weekend which [offered] a choice of walking, climbing, canoeing, caving and general adventure'. Social activities took place on the Saturday evening.

Follow-up Courses

Providing follow-up courses as a natural progression from the schools'
introductory courses was seen in the 1960s and 70s not as an optional
choice for the centre but as an obvious obligation. Lyn Noble spelt this
out in 1978. This happened to be at the height of the mountain-training
dispute, hence his careful use of the words 'risk' and 'safety':

> Clearly it would be very wrong to 'switch on' an individual if we
> were unable to provide the follow up tuition necessary to direct
> his [*sic*] new found enthusiasm. For this reason White Hall has
> continued to offer specialist courses in hillcraft, caving, canoeing
> and rock climbing. The aim in each case is to provide the student
> with the basic skills necessary to pursue his own development in
> reasonable safety. I use the word 'reasonable' deliberately for there
> is no way that risk activities may be rendered entirely safe. Indeed
> most practitioners, educationally based or otherwise, whilst sanely
> valuing life and limb, would deplore any attempt to emasculate
> their sports.[6]

Supplementary Course (8 days)

The supplementary courses were open to pupils who had previously
attended a schools' course. The course members on a supplementary
course had usually been invited back because of their enthusiasm and
ability on the earlier schools' introductory course. The minimum age
was fourteen. Individuals usually booked their own places on these
courses, but small block bookings were possible. The activities included
hillcraft, rock climbing, canoeing, caving and sometimes dinghy sailing. These courses culminated in a drive to a base camp in the Lake
District or north Wales, from which three days of walking, canoeing
and climbing took place.

Specialist Activity Weekends

These weekends were designed for students who wished to extend
their experience and improve their skills in one particular activity. The
available activities were canoeing, caving, climbing and hillcraft. The
courses took place at two levels: proficiency (minimum age fifteen) and
leader (minimum age eighteen). The leader courses included training
and assessment for the Derbyshire single- or multi-pitch climbing
approval; training and assessment for the BCU inland proficiency, sea
proficiency, and senior-instructor qualifications; and training in hillcraft
as a supplement to MLC training courses.

Mountaineering Course (8 days)

This annual course was for the enthusiastic hillwalker and camper. It included the crossing of remote mountainous terrain, usually in Scotland and very strenuous. The 1975–6 programme described the mountaineering course as 'suitable for enthusiasts, trainee mountain leaders or Duke of Edinburgh's Award gold expedition training'. The minimum age was sixteen.

Rock Climbing (8 days)

This annual course usually took place on the igneous crags of the Lake District or north Wales, a contrast to the sedimentary rocks of the Peak District. In some years the organising staff member opted to drive the extra distance to Cornwall, hoping to be rewarded with sunbaked lichenous granite and views down to a shimmering seascape, dotted with seagulls, shags and cormorants. The 1975–6 programme described the course as 'a specialist course for the budding rock enthusiast'. Students who reached the necessary standard of proficiency were encouraged to lead climbs. The minimum age was sixteen.

Canoeing Course (8 days)

This annual course was a mobile course for the paddler with an established interest. The accommodation was under canvas. The programme provided eight days of still-water, river and sea canoeing, and, if you were lucky, some lolling around in the sun. The minimum age was sixteen.

Caving Course (8 days)

This annual course usually took place in Yorkshire. Applicants needed previous experience of caving and were told to be prepared for a strenuous week. The minimum age was sixteen.

Supplementary course campsite, Maentwrog, north Wales, July 1975. Each course member did three activities: climbing, hillwalking and kayaking.

Making packed lunches at the supplementary-course campsite, Maentwrog, north Wales, July 1975.

Some members of Pete McDonald's group, supplementary course, Duddon Valley, Lake District, August 1979. Supplementary courses had thirty course members, working in three groups of ten.

On the way down after a wet day on Gearr Aonach, Glencoe. Scottish hillwalking course, 1980.

Starting along the Aonach Eagach, Glencoe. Scottish hillwalking course, 1980.

Partway up The Saddle. In the distance are the Five Sisters of Kintail. Reading the map is Pete Denver. Scottish hillwalking course, 1980.

Longland's Continuation to Red Wall, Lliwedd, north Wales, August 1973.

Practising climbing a caving ladder, specialist caving course, August 1976.

Practising lifelining, specialist caving course, August 1976.

Other Courses for Young People

Duke of Edinburgh's Award Expedition Training (6 days)

This annual course concentrated on expedition training at bronze, silver and gold levels. It also included rock climbing, caving and canoeing. These courses also met the requirements needed to count as the residential experience part of the Duke of Edinburgh's Award.

Environmental Studies (4 days)

Groups wishing to study aspects of the local White Hall environment or of the Peak District countryside could book a four-day Schools' OCP course and arrange a special programme in consultation with the principal. Also, the bunkhouse was available for self-programming groups that required accommodation only.

Very few schools requested the first option. Some White Hall staff members had university degrees relevant to various fields of outdoor investigating, but no coordinated methodical development of well-planned environmental sessions took place. Chapter 18 discusses this issue.

Bunkhouse

The bunkhouse had originally been developed as a part of AB Afford's mobile scheme. AB left White Hall in the mid-1960s. It is not clear exactly when the mobile scheme ended; a decision to end it seems to have been made in about 1969.[7] The bunkhouse subsequently became available for small self-programming groups from all over the country. They operated independently, catering for themselves and not using the main building much except possibly for the showers. The 'Bunkhouse' listings in the 1975–6 programme were merely indications of the availability of the bunkhouse.

The bunkhouse also became useful to accommodate an increasing number of university or college of education students on teaching practice. 'These students [were] invariably specialists in some relevant aspects of outdoor pursuits and in exchange for the opportunity to observe a centre in action and practise their skills they contribute[d] in no small measure to the running of the centre.'[8]

Courses for Adults

Voluntary Instructor Training Weekend

This annual course had the longest pedigree of all the White Hall courses, the opening weekend in 1950 having been for the training of volunteer instructors. Voluntary instructor training weekends were open to all VIs and potential VIs aged over eighteen. These weekends dealt in depth with the techniques of caving, climbing, canoeing and hillcraft, laying emphasis on teaching methods and group safety. Each course member kept to his or her own specialist activity. Most sessions were largely practical, but some discussion took place on emergency procedures and on the educational aims of the centre.

Teachers' Weekend Courses
One of these was held each year, with forty places available to teachers, to teachers in training and to youth leaders. The 1975–6 programme summarised this course as 'an introduction to Outdoor Education in Derbyshire'. The course included an explanation of the qualifications required by teachers and youth leaders running outdoor schemes in schools or clubs in Derbyshire. It also included a discussion about the opportunities available at White Hall and at other Derbyshire centres.

Mountain Leadership Courses (7 days)
The 1975–6 programme listed four of these seven-day slots. Four MLC training courses and three MLC assessment courses took place in these four weeks. The courses were open to anyone; fees for out-county applicants were higher than for Derbyshire residents. White Hall's MLC courses often spent a few days in the Peak District followed by an expedition in north Wales or the Lake District.

For the MLC assessment courses, whenever possible, Lyn Noble arranged small groups of 'real' novices for the candidates to take on expedition, this being a more genuine leader situation than having the assessees lead the assessors. This was a welcome development that happened more frequently in the 1980s than in the 1970s.

In 1980 the name Mountain Leadership Certificate was changed to Mountain Leader. Chapter 19 will examine the story behind this semantic nicety.

Sailing Course (7 days)
This seven-day course was designed for people wishing to gain RYA proficiency awards. The 1975–6 programme gives a minimum age of eighteen. In later years this minimum age was reduced, and this annual sailing course became more like a follow-up course for school pupils.

Alpine Course
In 1976 White Hall ran its first alpine mountaineering course in the French Alps. Planned and organised by Lyn Noble, its success exceeded all expectations. His brief description, written in 1978, understated

both his own achievement in running the course and the remarkable efforts of ten alpine beginners: 'The ethos was the same as for all our specialist courses: we set out to provide, for those without mountaineering club or personal contacts, tuition in the basics of Alpinism which would enable students to organise their own mountaineering trips in the future. The course was blessed with perfect weather and six major peaks were climbed in twelve days.'[9]

Two more alpine courses followed in the late 1970s.

MLC training course, Rhinog Fawr, north Wales, May 1979.

MLC training course, Helvelyn, Lake District, October 1977.

P McD

Roger Moakes and two other course members (Rob and Chris) arrive at the summit of the Montagne des Agneaux during the 1978 alpine course.

P McD

Roger Moakes, a course member, on an ascent of the Roche Faurio during the 1978 alpine course.

Notes

1   Derbyshire Record Office, Programme of courses for White Hall Centre for Open Country Pursuits, Buxton. Date: 1975–1976, D3272/2.

2   A B Afford, *The Story of White Hall Open Country Pursuits Centre; vol. 2* (Buxton, Derbyshire, UK: A B Afford, 1978), pp. 32–33.

3   Ibid., p. 32.

4   Bob Newton, 'Write Your Story', The Outward Bound Trust (2016) <https://www.outwardbound.org.uk/test-area/your-stories/bob-newton/> [accessed 3 Jan 2017].

5   Wally Keay, 'The Use of Mobile Phones by Young People on Unaccompanied, Self-reliant Journeys', *Journal of Adventure Education and Outdoor Leadership,* 12, no. 4 (Winter 1995–6), p. 33.

6   A B Afford, *The Story of White Hall Open Country Pursuits Centre; vol. 2* (Buxton, Derbyshire, UK: A B Afford, 1978), p. 32.

7   Ibid., p. 31.

8   Ibid., p. 35.

9   Ibid., p. 32.

18. The Rocks and Vegetation and So Forth

We saw in Chapter 2 that in March 1891 an editorial in the *Manchester Guardian* welcomed the fact that young people on bicycles – 'persons who [were] by no means well-to-do' – were escaping from the towns into the pure air of the countryside; they were rediscovering that place. This process continued into and through the 20th century, and it spread beyond cyclists to walkers, campers, cavers, climbers and canoeists, helped by the train, the bus and the motor car. So it was hardly a new idea when Jack Longland, addressing Ilkeston Rotary Club in October 1950, included as one of the purposes of his planned centre the aim of helping young people to understand the countryside and to appreciate its beauty. About four months later, Ken Oldham, a rural-studies teacher, took about fifty-three photographs during White Hall's first schools' course. Some of the subjects and captions show that learning about the countryside was, for Oldham, an important aspect of the week; among the captions are 'Field mouse at Combs', 'Parts of a sheep', 'Rock strata exposed – Shooters' Clough', 'Dying forest – Shooters' Clough', 'Limestone at Winnats', and 'Entrance to a cave at Winnats'.

It is clear from Oldham's writing that he also attached importance to the social aspects of the course and to the physical challenge that the activities, done for their own sake, provided. Oldham's course diary disappeared, so we do not know whether he allocated any half-days or days specifically to a field-studies topic. But this seems unlikely. It is more likely that the biological or geological or agricultural points of interest were spontaneous moments, seized when the opportunities arose. If they were, then he set the pattern for the next forty years: activity-anchored days containing a fluctuating mixture of physical, environmental and social ingredients. (I warned you, in Chapter 7, that I would be repeating this point.)

Over the 1950s, the White Hall staff built up the start of a small library that contained geographical, geological, botanical and historical books as well as mountaineering books and climbing guides. Also the briefing room acquired several glass cases displaying a variety of rocks and crystals. There is a photograph of the Duke of Edinburgh being shown these geological displays in 1958.

Outdoor Schoolwork – Someone Else's Business?

Five years later, as mentioned in Chapter 11, the 1963 HMI report on White Hall said little about environmental studies. It merely mentioned, cautiously, the possibility of more systematically observing 'the rocks and vegetation and so forth'. The inspectors did not go so far as suggesting that the basic schools' courses include a half-day or a day heavily weighted towards outdoor studies. No move in this direction would occur at White Hall until the late 1970s. Even then, the outdoor-studies half-day would be experimental and short-lived.

Another nine years went by before Harold Drasdo, in 1972, observed that 'discussion of the use of wild country for educational purposes usually contrives to divide activity into two groups. First we have Field Studies or Environmental Education … Second, we have Outdoor Pursuits or Adventure Activities'. He then discussed the short history of deliberate attempts to combine the two approaches on the same half-day or day, such as collecting samples of stream water, for later examination, while doing a challenging hill walk. He left it to the reader to decide on the pros and cons of combining both approaches simultaneously.[1]

Nationally, some differences of opinion existed on whether a schools' basic course at a residential outdoor-pursuits centre should include a day or two unequivocally devoted to field studies (later called environmental studies). As discussed in Chapter 14, some people interpreted the new label 'outdoor education' as being an umbrella term that covered both outdoor pursuits and field studies. In April 1974 a reviewer of the Parker–Meldrum book *Outdoor Education* complained about its allocating much space to outdoor pursuits and little to field studies. Tensions existed between on the one side the ideas of some members of the field-studies community, the older of the two movements, and on the other side the ideas of the qualified teachers who were working in residential outdoor-pursuits centres, the younger movement. These two broad areas had grown from different beginnings and were based on different priorities and values.

Some people may have felt that a dedicated environmental session should be an automatic component of every schools' course at places like White Hall. Others may have argued that some environmental content was already included in the school curriculum but that few schools were equipped and staffed to provide the outdoor adventure that young people craved. Putting this argument another way, its supporters might have claimed that explicit outdoor schoolwork was someone else's business.

These polarised arguments missed an important point. I will spell it out, for the third or fourth time in this book: the idea of an outdoor-pursuits centre, such as White Hall, staffed by Philistines and concentrating solely on providing outdoor adventure and nothing else, was hardly fair to the climbers, canoeists, sailors and cavers who worked in this sort of a centre. Even if the word 'environmental' did not appear on White Hall's standard schools' programmes, the word 'environment' had entered everyday English. Passing on environmental knowledge was part of daily work, but often in a spontaneous opportunist way rather than in a planned way. (Incidentally, the term 'climate change' had hardly been heard of.)

Nationally, it is probably true to say that, as the 1970s passed, most people gave the term 'outdoor education' a wide interpretation but not an ultra-wide one. Outdoor education and environmental education remained separate but related movements and would eventually be allocated their separate slots in the curriculum for schools in England and Wales. Chapter 21 will touch upon this matter.

Peak Plumbago

For a while in the late 1970s – maybe six months or so – the programmes for schools' courses included an experimental half-day called Peak Plumbago. These sessions centred on a surface visit to Magpie Mine, a lead mine near Sheldon with a long history and plenty of potential for a reliable couple of hours of outdoor learning. However, as far as I can remember, the White Hall instructors had not joined in any preparatory research, and no consultation with subject specialists had taken place. There may have been a duplicated sheet of information or questions; other than that, little groundwork had preceded the introduction of the new activity. Group instructors were left to their own devices to develop a session that would grab the attention of ten teenagers. These half-days met mixed success: limited interest or uninterest from some pupils and a correspondingly lukewarm enthusiasm from White Hall staff. Secondary pupils fully engaged in the excitement of an outdoor-pursuits course will not tolerate an environmental session that is inexpert and half-hearted.

The overall approach was underdone. The resulting sessions were a token gesture. Peak Plumbago had quietly appeared on the programme and was just as quietly dropped. Unlike several later issues that arose in the 1980s, the question of whether to include this half-day never grew into an understorey of disagreement.

We had barely scratched the surface of the potential. Had some thorough preparation taken place jointly between White Hall staff and an appropriate adviser, the result could have been less perfunctory and more professional.

Robert Morris / Alamy ANYAYP

Magpie Mine, a disused lead mine near Sheldon in the Peak District National Park.

*

In 1983 I spent an exchange year in Victoria, Australia, working at two residential outdoor education centres, Rubicon School Camp and Bogong School Camp. Rubicon School Camp's teaching staff had developed a two-day environmental session based at Royston House, an old house up in the ranges. Some of Rubicon's schools' outdoor activities courses included this overnight field-studies element. During these visits, the pupils trapped, recorded and set free small mammals. They also examined artificial hollow-tree nesting sites and they spotlighted possums at night.

The trappings, artificial hollows, and spotlightings were often very productive, making these visits to the bush intensely interesting for staff and pupils alike. It was evident that there was some ignorance among urban Australian youngsters about their wildlife, so the educational value of these sessions was considerable.

As regards ideas for White Hall, one important aspect was the thoroughness of the planning and preparation that had gone into developing these sessions successfully. Another was the bringing-in of outside experts to assist the camp staff with the development work. After several years of help from outside experts, by 1983 the Rubicon staff possessed a high level of expertise in this area and were almost ready to operate without any further aid.

Like Rubicon, Bogong School Camp had a well-developed environmental element in its schools' courses. On Bogong's ten-day summer courses, the environmental proportion amounted to three half-day sessions: an introductory lecture and a short walk to set the mammal traps; the next morning, an examination of the mammal traps; later in the course, learning stations.

Using its acres of indoor space, Bogong had developed a three-hour classroom circuit, during which the pupils visited twelve learning stations. Groups of twenty-four pupils were divided into twelve pairs, and each pair spent about ten minutes at each station. The twelve stations were: 1. Mammals; 2. Insects; 3. Reptiles; 4. Dangerous species; 5. Geology; 6. Birds; 7. 3-D map of Bogong with aerial photograph and flat map; 8. Fish; 9. 3-D map of Kiewa hydro power scheme; 10. Kiewa Valley history, since settlement; 11. Land use in Kiewa Valley; 12. History of Kiewa Valley.

The learning stations were attractive and informative. They must have taken hundreds of hours to build. The Bogong staff had used every tool in the teachers' audio-visual armoury to make the stations come alive: stuffed mammals, stuffed birds, dioramas, coloured spot lighting, huge creepy crawlies, preserved snakes, microscopes, rock samples to touch, 3-D models, live fish, tape recordings, slide projectors, photographs and posters.

Seeing the professionalism of the Rubicon School Camp and Bogong School Camp environmental sessions opened my eyes to what might be possible at White Hall Centre. But not until the turmoil of the 1990s would White Hall, in collaboration with visiting teachers, begin to link some of the content of its courses more deliberately to the school curriculum.

*

Magpie Mine is an ancient monument, scheduled in January 1974. Now, in January 2016, the National Heritage List for England (NHLE), available on the website of Historic England, lists all of England's so-called designated assets. A search of this list reveals, not surprisingly, that Derbyshire has no protected wreck sites. Happily for the pacifists among us, neither does it have any registered battlefields. But Derbyshire does possess 494 scheduled archaeological sites and 5596 listed buildings (or structures). If you have climbed on Birchen Edge, you might have used one of these buildings as a convenient spike belay: Nelson's Monument is a Grade II listed building, 'a tapering obelisk-like shaft of gritstone … about ten feet tall … inscribed OCT 21 1805'.

Regarding things botanical or geological or biological, Derbyshire in January 2016 has ninety-eight sites of special scientific interest (SSSI). Many of them are in the White Peak. At least thirteen of these designated sites are within about ten kilometres of Buxton. They are Combs Reservoir, Duchy Quarry, Poole's Cavern and Grin Low Wood, Monk's Dale, Topley Pike and Deep Dale, Fox Hole Cave, Colshaw Pastures, Moss Carr, Calton Hill, Waterswallows Quarry, Leek Moors, Chrome and Parkhouse Hills, and a large part of the Goyt Valley watershed.[2]

Many of these places of historical interest or environmental importance were worthy of young people's attention but, viewed from the White Hall perspective and in the context of a five-day course for secondary pupils, they had to compete with the attractions of the Peak District's world-renowned climbing, some of Britain's finest caves, and Derbyshire's wild moorland walks and perfect limestone rambles, as well as the excitement of canoeing and sailing. Rightly or wrongly, in the 1970s and 80s the provision of days or half-days dedicated to historical or environmental subjects remained, for want of a better description, someone else's business.

Part 4 of this book will indicate whether this clear demarcation, at White Hall, continued into the 1990s. Throughout the 1980s a series of environmental disasters put green issues on the political agenda in many countries. Environmental education in UK schools was slow to respond to these new concerns, but in 1988 the European Year of the Environment raised public awareness of the state of the planet.[3] The status of environmental education began to rise, a process that continues today.

Arbor Low stone circle, a Neolithic henge monument set on high limestone moorland about 20 km (12.5 miles) southeast of White Hall. Arbor Low is the most important prehistoric site in the east Midlands.

The magnificent Marple aqueduct, completed in 1880. It carries the Peak Forest Canal over the River Goyt. White Hall canoeing groups occasionally combined sections of the river and the canal to complete a circuit.

Arkwright Society

The mill yard at Sir Richard Arkwright's Cromford Mills, a UNESCO World Heritage Site.

Derbyshire Libraries and www.picturethepast.org.uk'

Bolsover Colliery, near Chesterfield, in about 1930. Many of the schoolpupils and youth-club members who visited White Hall came from the industrial areas of Derbyshire. Bolsover Colliery closed in 1993.

Robert Morris / Alamy D1FD5N.

Millstones near Stanage Edge. A reminder of the stone industry. The National Stone Centre is at Wirksworth.

Notes

1   Harold Drasdo, *Education and the Mountain Centres*, 2nd edn (1972, 1973; repr. Penrith: Association for Outdoor Learning, 1998), pp. 6–7.

2   'Designated Sites View', Natural England (no date) <https://designatedsites. naturalengland.org.uk/SiteSearch.aspx> [accessed 30 Jan 2016].

3   Ken C Ogilvie, *Roots and Wings: A History of Outdoor Education and Outdoor Learning in the UK* (Lyme Regis, UK: Russell House Publishing, 2013), pp. 493–495.

19. Mountain Training Dispute, 1970–80

The mountain training row of the 1970s was a national power struggle. It shook up the lives of the BMC and the MLTB, with reverberations reaching the Association of Wardens of Mountain Centres (AWMC), the Sports Council and grassroots climbers. Yet the row hardly caused a ripple in the daily routine of a White Hall Centre instructor on schools' courses. Even the MLC training and assessment courses carried on much the same as usual – energetically and enjoyably – during the dispute.

If that were the complete picture, the dispute would not warrant much space in this book. However, Jack Longland stood his ground at the fiery centre of the controversy, and this book is partly the story of Longland. Also, Lyn Noble, as a member of the AWMC, was closer to the affair than were the other White Hall staff. The mountain training dispute, therefore, although clearly national in character and importance, is also of enough local interest to deserve this chapter to itself.

Origins of the Mountain Leadership Certificate, 1951–69

To understand what went wrong in the 1970s, we need to glance back at the convoluted origins of the MLC. In the early 1950s, the CCPR convened meetings to discuss the growing number of mountain accidents involving led school parties. Many members of mountain rescue teams welcomed this initiative and saw a need for intervention; what form this might take was unclear. In contrast, the general response from mountaineering representatives – those not involved in mountain rescue or outdoor instructing – emphasised the importance of traditional freedoms. Amateur club climbers on the whole opposed intervention; some even opposed the publication of guidelines and many were strongly against certification.[1]

The sports of hillwalking and climbing had no written rules. When climbers went into the mountains, they left most rules and regulations behind them. They entered a place of freedom, subject to some consensual precepts that ranged from the inviolable (eg, the almost universal rejection of the practice of chipping holds in the rock) to the debatable (eg, the mid-1970s controversy over the use of chalk). Most hillwalkers and climbers wanted things to stay that way. The BMC saw itself, and was viewed by the mountaineering fraternity, as a representative organisation, not a governing body that would make and impose irksome rules. Putting this another way: climbers were not inclined to be governed by anyone.

Furthermore, the BMC was nothing like the force it is today. It had no paid staff. The honorary secretary, as one retiring president remarked, 'was in fact the BMC'.[2] The council was not, and could not be, a training organisation. In October 1956 a special correspondent to *The Times* made this clear:

> … the British Mountaineering Council is in no sense a training body, regarding the introduction of beginners to mountaineering as essentially a task for the clubs and similar organizations. So it is constantly at work matching requests for help and information with the facilities provided by the many member clubs that are willing to accept and teach beginners, and by such organizations as the Central Council of Physical Recreation, the Youth Hostels Association, the Outward Bound movement, the Ramblers' Association, and the Mountaineering Association.[3]

The issue hibernated for a few years and then quietly re-emerged at a meeting of the CCPR outdoor activities advisory group in 1961. By the end of 1961, John Jackson, the warden of Plas y Brenin, had drawn up a draft programme for a three-week training course for leaders of hill walks. Evidence in correspondence suggests that the support of the Ministry of Education for the scheme was conditional upon the scheme awarding a certificate of competence.[4]

Subsequent developments over a couple of years were delicate and entangled. Suffice to say that the first meeting of the AWMC took place at White Hall Centre from 28 February to 1 March 1963. This small exclusive body would considerably influence the development of mountain training and would play an important part in the training dispute.[5] Six months later, on 25 September 1963, a meeting of the CCPR outdoor activities advisory committee, under Jack Longland's chairmanship, agreed that some sort of hillwalking leader certificate was needed. At the time, Longland, as well as chairing the CCPR outdoor group, was also the president of the BMC. This dual role would later be seen as having complicated the issue of who said and did what in these early days of the MLC. According to Ken Wilson, this agreement to develop a certificate amounted to a major policy decision, taken without warning and late at night at just one meeting:

> Was Jack Longland launching a completely personal initiative, or was he responding to some urgent Government 'encouragement'? The fact that each of the interested bodies had their supposed views expressed by 'individuals' rather than mandated 'representatives' is an unconventional way of formulating policy, to say the least …
>
> Whether Jack Longland deliberately kept discussion to a minimum or was merely displaying his efficient committee skills is difficult to say. He may well have felt that speed was necessary to counter the reactionary attitudes of the traditional clubs that he had fought all his life. In this he was probably mistaken as the BMC was already fully aware of its responsibilities. In hindsight it is clear that it would have been better for the BMC to have had a fuller debate on such a major policy development.[6]

The crucial meeting, however, had taken place. The die was cast. Certificates were on the horizon.

In November 1963 the CCPR set up a working party 'to consider the desirability and practicability of establishing some sort of certificate of competence in the leadership of mountain activities'. The working party subsequently added an extra idea by recommending that there should be a training body called a Joint Board, comprising representatives of the BMC, the CCPR, and the CCPR outdoor activities advisory committee, and also including a Department of Education observer.[7]

In June 1964, at the third meeting of the AWMC, John Jackson presented his proposals for a certificate of competence, which had been evolving for about three years. The meeting examined these proposals and suggested further improvements. By then, the association, and some wardens in particular, as well as Jack Longland, had heavily invested their own ideas and desires in the developments under way.

The first proper working meeting of the Mountain Leadership Training Board took place on 15 September 1964 at the London office of the CCPR, where the board would continue to meet until February 1975.

Present were three CCPR representatives (John Jackson, J B Bradley and Jack Longland); two BMC reps (J H Della Porta and A Oakes); a Scout Association rep; a Duke of Edinburgh's Award rep (Sir John Hunt); and an Outward Bound Trust/AWMC rep (Tom Price). Also, an inspector of schools attended as an observer, to keep the Department of Education and Science informed on developments. Longland was unanimously elected chairman, a position he would hold until 1980. Writing in 1986, Tom Price said: 'Looking back one realises that [Longland] was really the prime mover in getting the scheme started.'[8]

The meeting agreed that the name of the board's qualification for leading hill walks in summer conditions would be the Mountain Leadership Certificate. The first MLC training course took place at Plas y Brenin in December 1964.

To sum up on the origins of the MLTB, Geoffrey Young, helped by Longland, had played a major role in the creation of the BMC in 1944. Both men were keen on mountain training. A concern for safety spurred the final determined institutional push in 1961–4 to create the MLTB, a push that came from the CCPR outdoor activities advisory committee (of which Longland was chair) and the AWMC. The BMC (of which Longland was president in 1962–5) was on the edge of these proceedings, a hesitant onlooker, wary of safety initiatives but swept up in the current.

(Still today, 2017, different versions of this story vie for acceptance. In January 2014 the BMC website posted an article by Ed Douglas on the origins of mountain training. Discussing the creation in 1964 of the Mountain Leader [*sic*] Training Board, he wrote: 'It was inevitably the BMC, together with the CCPR …, which took the lead in establishing the new training organisation.'[9] This sweeping statement differs from my interpretation of the happenings. At best it is superficial and misleading, if it is not wholly fallacious.

Also in 2014, reminiscing in *A Passion for Mountains*, Ron James recalled having been involved in the 1960s 'in several big rescues for young people under so-called "instruction"'. He explained the result of these experiences: 'Johnnie Lees and I pressed the BMC to do something about this and the Mountain Leadership Certificate was initiated.'[10] This broad statement positions the BMC as having been a prime mover behind the setting up of the MLTB and the introduction of the MLC. Again, as I see things, the attributing is incorrect, even if James and Lees, with dozens of other folk, did for very good reasons contribute to the genesis of the MLTB.

Perhaps the only thing inevitable about the complex events preceding the forming of the MLTB was that the full intricacies would take a long time to surface and that a consensus on them would take a long time to be reached.)

The MLC became the main responsibility of – and emotionally owned by – the MLTB, a near-autonomous body that the BMC influenced to an extent but did not control. In 1965 the Scottish Mountain Leadership Training Board came into existence and created the Scottish winter MLC, a far more demanding qualification. Then a wider qualification, the Mountaineering Instructor Certificate (MIC), was developed, and the first MIC course was held at Plas y Brenin on 9–16 October 1968.[11] The Northern Ireland MLTB was formed in 1969. (A separate Welsh MLTB would not appear until June 1980.)

By 1970 the BMC had run its admirable British Mountain Guides scheme for twenty-three years, providing registration for a small number of professional climbers, but the BMC had otherwise been a minor presence in mountain training. The three mountain leadership training boards, viewed collectively, were running the MLC, the Scottish winter MLC and the MIC schemes. This stable duality had about two more years ahead of it free from interference, before being violently assailed by a reawakened BMC, inspired by the arrival of Dennis Gray as its national officer and suddenly anxious to assume monopoly control of all mountain training.

Widening Gulf, 1970–5

In his 1970 autobiography *Rope Boy*, written two years before he became the first professional officer of the BMC, the mountaineer Dennis Gray conceded reluctantly that there was a need for professional instructors of mountaineering, but he also said: 'The very word "certificate" is abhorrent to me in this connection'.[12]

The essence of Gray's alarm lay in the fundamental changes that, he said, were happening in rock climbing and mountaineering:

> British climbing is at present being re-shaped by pressure groups completely outside the traditional basis of individuals and clubs. Many of the old-established clubs don't seem to realise this; their members do not appear to grasp the size of the numbers now taking part or wishing to participate. They have lost contact with the latest newcomers to the sport who are taking their lead more and more from the climbing photographers and journalists, training

and quasi-educational organisations, suppliers of equipment and the mass media in general. The coming flood of new climbers will accentuate this trend and if to-day's climbers ... do not act, climbing will soon become just another commercialised spectator sport with the same sort of ethic as football or horse-racing ... far away from the idealistic concept of mountaineering as a physical and aesthetic recreation for individuals.[13]

In February 1971, Jack Longland, now six months into his retirement, chaired the National Mountain Safety Conference, which was attended by nearly 400 delegates. Dave Draper was one of the speakers, giving a talk on the accident black spots of Langdale and Snowdon.

About nine months later, on Saturday 20 November 1971, a well-equipped party of six school pupils, an eighteen-year-old student teacher and one adult leader were benighted in blizzard conditions on the Cairngorm plateau. It was impossible to make snow holes. They sat all night in their sleeping bags and polythene bivouac sacks. Sunday dawned but the appalling weather – normal Cairngorm conditions – kept them pinned down. They spent a second night out in the open. Five of the pupils and the student teacher died. One of the pupils and the leader, twenty-one year old Cathy Davidson, survived.[14]

On the Saturday, another group from the same school, led by one of their teachers, Ben Beattie, had been an hour ahead of Davidson's group and had reached the relative safety of the Curran Bothy, a shelter.

Beattie was well qualified, being one of a then small number of holders of the MIC. Davidson had climbed in the Alps and had been exempted from taking the MLC. (In the early days of the MLC, the MLTB granted exemption to many applicants, as a way to fast-track patently experienced people to meet the shortage of qualified leaders.) She did not have the Scottish winter MLC. She had planned to obtain the MIC.[15]

This Cairngorm tragedy immediately sparked off a nationwide debate about and scrutiny of mountaineering in education. A six-day fatal-accident inquiry took place. The jury returned a verdict that found no-one guilty of gross negligence. It made seven recommendations. But this public inquiry merely intensified the debate that had already erupted.

Locally, within Scotland, some undercurrents alleged that excessively ambitious expectations had arisen at the school.[16] Expert witnesses at the inquiry had disagreed on whether the Cairngorm plateau in winter was a suitable place for a school group. Nationally and very publicly, many grassroots climbers thought not. Many were also concerned that the tragedy might lead to new rules, not drawn up by mountaineers and advisory in form, but concocted by bureaucratic authorities and mandatory. Some people questioned the worth of the MLC and MIC. Stripped down to its essentials, a sentiment common among hill-hardened club mountaineers was that teachers with scant real experience and holding qualifications of doubtful worth were giving mountaineering a bad name. To make matters worse, this was all happening totally out of the clubs' control.

Nobody has bettered Tom Price's explanation of why this dispute arose:

> Before long the sporting and educational interests came into conflict as far as mountaineering was concerned. [No equivalent feuds happened over canoeing or sailing.] Education was earnest and respectable; climbing was wild, iconoclastic and irreverent. Education was for the good of society; climbing was for the delectation and aggrandisement of the individual. Education demanded safety; climbers wanted to be free to kill themselves in their own way. No one was more strongly aware of this dichotomy than Ken Wilson, the owner and editor of *Mountain* magazine. To him climbing was a bit like bull fighting, a question of skill, courage and style in the face of danger. It was not sport so much as drama. Educational programmes demanded the elimination of risk and this, according to Ken Wilson, impoverished climbing and indeed sowed the seeds of its destruction.[17]

In January 1972, Dennis Gray, now thirty-six, took up the post of national officer for the BMC. Gray became the council's first full-time paid employee. By then the mountain leader training scheme, run by the MLTB, was one of the biggest training schemes in British sport.[18] The name of the much sought basic hillwalking qualification, Mountain Leadership Certificate, had become well established. The scheme wasn't perfect – far from it – yet the people responsible for creating it had every reason to be proud of it. The stage was set for an intense debate on the appropriateness of the word 'certificate' and for a prolonged and damaging power struggle for the control of the whole training scheme.

A part of the controversy was semantic. Some high-profile mountaineers and many rank-and-file club members, often self-taught and sometimes having learnt from their harmless mistakes or dangerous blunders, contended that the continued use of the word 'certificate' would irreversibly damage the whole character of mountaineering.[19]

A more concrete and undeniable problem was that the prior experience of applicants for MLC training courses was ill-defined, if defined at all. The approaches of different providers of MLC training courses differed widely. Some centres stated clearly what hillwalking experience a person should have before attending a training course. At the opposite extreme, for some centres, bums-on-seats was an absolute priority, often resulting in the members of a training course possessing a huge range of experience. For some professional instructors, who were running several MLC training courses each year, the need to cope with groups ranging from total novices to seasoned hillwalkers was a far more obvious problem than the alleged undesirable connotations of the word 'certificate'.

Another part of the row involved a principle, a belief that the national representative body of a sport, and not some other organisation, should control the general character of that sport's state-subsidised training scheme.

Another aspect of the situation was the presence, among the frontline troops of both sides, of complex and strong-willed people, confident in the rightness of their cause. Their tenacious personalities turbocharged the debate.

Dennis Gray, after being an underfed teenage pillion-rider of the Bradford Lads, anti-club and anarchic, had moved on to join the all-conquering muscularity of the Rock and Ice, undeniably a club, albeit without some of the trappings of clubship; and he had then reconstructed himself again to become a servant of the mountaineering clubs of Britain and a tradition-loving admirer of the literature of the old-established club journals.[20] A *Climber and Rambler* article described him as an initiator and driving force, 'unlikely to be a mere figurehead or passive servant of the [BMC] Committee'.[21] According to Ken Ogilvie, some people in outdoor education circles referred to him as 'Gauleiter Gray'.[22] Tom Price, looking back from 2000, saw Gray as 'the man who really ran the BMC ... by nature a radical, never afraid of stirring things up. His hero in politics was Tony Benn, whom he always referred to as Wedgie'.[23]

Jack Longland, now sixty-six and a Sir for his services to education, was thirty years older than Gray. He had been involved in the slow build-up of mountain training for at least twenty-nine years, since writing a tribute to Colin Kirkus in 1943 (quoted in Chapter 1). This period of his life had been one long campaign to fill a training vacuum, a gap in provision that some amateur climbers were happy to tolerate for doctrinaire reasons. In January 1972 he was sixteen months into retirement, yet still captaining the MLTB ship and with plenty of time on his hands to steer it through any storms.

In March 1972, at the third annual conference of the NAOE, Longland spoke in favour of training for leaders of adventurous outdoor pursuits. The Cairngorm tragedy had subjected outdoor education to a greater public scrutiny than any other occurrence since White Hall had opened. He repeated a message he had been disseminating for years: 'We are trying to give as many children as possible the chance of outdoor activities which would never have come their way before … We are very much under trial and in the public eye.'[24] In April 1972 the *Guardian* reported that outdoor pursuits organised at home and abroad for Edinburgh schoolchildren were to be cut by 30 per cent immediately, in the interests of safety.[25]

To distinguish between the two sides of the dispute, some written accounts use the terms 'educational mountaineers' and 'sporting mountaineers'. I will occasionally resort to these labels, but reluctantly because the distinction is questionable. Many professional outdoor instructors, most of whom accepted the need for a mountain leader qualification, remained active climbers in their spare time; some eminent climbers who supported the BMC's criticism of the use of mountains by teachers had themselves been involved at some point in outdoor education or in instructing adult novices.

In March 1973 the BMC held a national safety conference in Leeds. The organisers deliberately chose speakers both from professional outdoor educators and from the BMC side, representing the thousands of club members who climbed in their spare time. Far from clarifying and diffusing the issues surrounding certificates and regulations, the proceedings inflamed them. After one volatile exchange at question time, one of the four hundred delegates offered 'to meet the editor of *Mountain* outside!'[26]

This incident illustrates a general feature of the events of this chapter. At its managerial and representational levels, outdoor education was male dominated. Similarly, mountaineering clubs and their national representative body, the BMC, were male dominated. Hence the event described above, in which a need for logical discussion seems to have been subordinate to a more primitive male impulse. Although none of the subsequent confrontations led to a solution by duelling, 'some of these meetings left one absolutely smashed and churned up'.[27]

Tom Price was one of the speakers at the Leeds conference. In an address titled 'Bridging the Gap', he asked himself, 'Is the teaching mountaineer really any different from the sporting mountaineer?'

> ... my first cautious reply was: 'He doesn't have to be' ... Nevertheless, all too often one can see a difference, and when one does it is basically a difference in attitude. I can well recall the time when I myself became a teaching mountaineer, after many years of private climbing and fell-walking and club membership. It was when I became Warden of a Mountain Centre. My friends were very generous about it, they made allowances, they conceded that everyone has to earn a living somehow, and that no one could be blamed for wanting to go and live in Eskdale; but few of them really approved of what I was doing, and one or two said as much. I felt they had the same kind of reservations that the contemporaries of the Abraham brothers must have had when the brothers went into the postcard business. I was no longer quite pure.[28]

You wonder how common this outcast feeling was, in outdoor instructors. Numerous 'sporting mountaineers' spent periods as 'teaching mountaineers'. Most of these dual-role characters were unknown outside their own local circles. If they did feel impure or torn in two directions, they may have shared the dichotomy with some better-known sporting-and-teaching mountaineers, all of them accomplished risk-takers, including Joe Brown, Don Roscoe, Ray Greenall, Slim Sorrell, Harold Drasdo, John Cunningham, Bob Pettigrew and Peter Boardman.

In July 1973, *Climber and Rambler* sounded the alarm: ' ... there are signs of an ugly schism developing in the sport. The schism is between those who see the old happy spirit of climbing being eroded in a mass of safety regulations, and those who want to put safety first, above all else. There is no denying that the increasing concern with safety has largely been brought about by the involvement of educational bodies in climbing'.[29] There were few signs on the horizon, however, of any sedatives. Both publicly and privately, the arguments and language would become increasingly inflammatory and partisan.

Later that year, the BMC formed a Future Policy Committee. In January 1974, this committee produced a draft report that Walter

Unsworth described as 'dynamite with a short fuse'.[30] The report was unsympathetic to the aims of the educational mountaineers. It contained outspoken and elitist statements such as 'it is not the function of the BMC to encourage people to take up mountaineering'. Using the hills for educational purposes, according to the draft report, would be 'prejudicial to the interests of mountaineers'.[31] The reader was left with the feeling that the BMC didn't believe in organised training. Paradoxically, the implication of the report was clear: the BMC intended to take over the training function of the MLTB. According to Walt Unsworth, 'Sir Jack Longland, known for the way he can express his views forcibly in impeccable English, is said to have expressed himself *very* forcibly in language worthy of the Bard.'[32]

Two months later the first BMC national conference was held in Buxton. Colin Mortlock, the author of a recent book on adventure education, attempted to explain the education viewpoint but was drowned out by heckling. 'Even Sir Jack Longland chairing the sessions, became something of an Aunt Sally, receiving a cool and noisy reception which made him visibly uncomfortable.'[33]

Following this conference, Ken Wilson, the influential founder and editor of *Mountain*, publicly joined the fray on the BMC side by writing an abrasive and uncompromising editorial headed 'The Educational Threat':

> The mountaineering world must seriously examine the price that might have to be paid for this extension of regulation and certification into a sport that has previously enjoyed complete freedom
> ...
>   These climber/educators, many of them honourable and experienced mountaineers, have become the fifth columnists of responsible society in our midst. Our sport is, always had been, and should always remain essentially irresponsible ...
>   The real climbing world must therefore seriously consider its attitude towards this educational tumour that is gnawing away at its vitals ...[34]

A practical example of the essential irresponsibility of the real climbing world concerned helmets. Most climbers wanted to retain the choice of whether to wear a helmet. In 1975 Tom Proctor famously decided to put a helmet on, a rare event for him, for his first ascent of Great

Arête on Millstone Edge.[35] In contrast, by the early 1970s, the wearing of helmets had become expected in instructed climbing.

As well as being the creative brain behind *Mountain*, an internationally respected magazine that had set new standards of style and quality, Wilson was also a co-author and the designer of *The Black Cliff: The History of Rock Climbing on Clogwyn du'r Arddu* (1971). In the combination of Gray and Wilson, Longland now faced the determined and organised opposition of two combative characters from a younger generation of climbers. In the eyes of some grassroots climbers, Longland was just a name from climbing's history. Gray, they could see, was still an active climber and the author of a recent and well-received autobiography. Wilson was a colourful character, entertainingly opinionated and disputative, a passionate lobbyist on numerous mountaineering issues, and a plain and forthright speaker whom Tom Price always thought of as 'the Che Guevara of the climbing world'.[36]

In the same month, the BMC set up a committee chaired by Lord Hunt to look at mountain training matters and specifically at what role the BMC should have in training.

Ogilvie summarises the situation that had been reached:

> Emerging from the plethora of opinion was the picture of a failure to make the vital distinctions between, on the one hand, the informal groups of friends in a party of 'sporting' mountaineers, and on the other, formally led 'educational' groups which were bound by, and unable to discount their legal responsibilities 'to take care' lest they be sued for negligence.[37]

The English, Scottish and Northern Ireland MLTBs held their sixth annual joint meeting on 19 October 1974. Longland re-emphasised that, in his view, the three boards were independent of the BMC and could determine their own constitutions and membership.

In March 1975 the *Guardian* published a lengthy article by Ken Wilson arguing that new safety measures, such as certification, were killing climbing and that the educational establishment was to blame, 'a Wooden Horse' in the mountaineers' midst. 'This insidious invasion by the educationalists is threatening the very foundations of British mountaineering, sapping the vitality of its new recruits, and bringing with it a host of unnecessary controls.'[38]

Was the situation as black and white as Wilson was portraying? Were all educators baddies, from some sort of ascendant safety-ocracy? Only four weeks earlier, the same newspaper had published a letter from Lyn Noble, undeniably someone deep within the outdoor-education establishment and inclined to conformity. Far from advocating new safety procedures, the letter, headed 'Don't Put Walkers in a Cocoon', opposed a bureaucratic Snowdonia National Park safety plan.[39] Furthermore, in alerting the public to the swelling safety bureaucracy, Noble's well-constructed letter was consistent with Kim Meldrum's satirical article of 1966, 'White Hell Pursuing Centre', which had given advance warning of an approaching epidemic of risk averseness.

The *Hunt Report on Mountain Training* was released in July 1975. It was balanced and nonpartisan. It did not come anywhere close to suggesting the end of mountain training, despite newspaper headings such as the *Guardian*'s 'Scrap Mountain Leadership Certificates, Says Hunt'.[40] However, it did contain some controversial findings and it did not forestall what Dennis Gray, long afterwards, described as 'the greatest confrontation in the history of British climbing'.[41] Tom Price, looking back at the Hunt report from 1986, pinpointed a couple of the impasse points:

> The Hunt Report, which while generally supportive of the MLTB, made two recommendations which caused tremors high on the Richter Scale. One was that the issuing of certificates should be discontinued. The other was that the name of the Scheme should be changed to something less high-powered, such as Hillcraft Leaders Course.[42]

Another sticking point, perhaps the most problematic of all, was the report's statement: 'The British Mountaineering Council cannot properly evade responsibility for training in the mountain areas. It seems to us anomalous that there should be two bodies operating at national level in the same field, pursuing policies which may become, and are already considered by some to be, at variance with one another.'[43]

Price summarised the resulting standoff:

> The MLTB rejected these recommendations. The BMC was disposed to insist upon them. Dennis Gray, an irresistible force, came into direct collision with Sir Jack Longland, an immovable object. Fire and fury was brought to the issue by Ken Wilson … Thus arose the Great Schism between the MLTB and the BMC which lasted from 1976 until 1980.[44]

Wilson, incidentally, when he wasn't busy with fire and fury, had been busy compiling and designing *Hard Rock: Great British Rock-climbs*, which was published in 1975 to universal acclaim, further raising his standing in the British climbing world.

The fourth annual joint conference of the English, Scottish and Northern Island MLTBs took place on 14–16 November 1975. The atmosphere was highly charged. A clear consensus opposed the proposals of the Hunt report.

Turmoil, 1976–80

In November 1976 the BMC published its future-policy report, which strongly endorsed the proposals of the Hunt report. The onus was now on the BMC to effect change; the MLTB was content with the status quo.

In December 1976, during his valedictory address to the Alpine Club, Longland directly confronted the heart of the Wilson–Gray reasoning, the claim that educationists would eliminate risk and that this would eventually destroy the sport of climbing. 'It is current cant that climbing is "a risk sport", and that but for this, it would lose its savour. I prefer the doctrine that mountaineering is a hard-won *craft*, without which the climber would find himself too often in wholly unjustifiable danger. Moreover, the *cult* of danger is a sign of neurosis and not of a healthy man or a healthy society.'[45]

Over the six months following the Hunt report, several meetings of various committees failed to produce agreement on compromise proposals.[46]

At one of these meetings, Lyn Noble, representing the AWMC, warned that the MLTB and the BMC were on a collision course. He said that both parties had made errors but that in his opinion the BMC Management Committee did not sufficiently understand several compromises proposed by the MLTB. The wardens, he said, had made a positive and constructive contribution.[47]

The wardens' willingness to be constructive, however, had limits. On several occasions the AWMC had expressed its belief that the MLTB should be autonomous. Meanwhile, back at White Hall, the MLC courses were carrying on as normal, largely unaffected by the increasingly vitriolic national deadlock.

On 14 July 1977, during an MLTB meeting at the BMC offices in Manchester, the dispute leapt up several levels of intensity in a few minutes. There are two main published accounts of the whole training dispute. The first is a detailed chapter in Ogilvie's *Roots and Wings*. The second account consists of fragments of a chapter contributed by Gray to *The First Fifty Years of the British Mountaineering Council*. Unfortunately, Gray does not go into details about the rancorous and alarming meeting held on 14 July. The next three paragraphs rely mainly on Ogilvie's description of that day.

Early in the meeting, one of the BMC representatives announced that the council was preparing a constitution for its own Mountain Training Board. (In John Hunt's words, written shortly afterwards, the BMC 'took the unilateral step of setting up a training board of its own, which purported to supplant the MLTB'.[48]) After some acrimonious discussions, Dave Parsons, representing the BMC, produced and read from a prepared list of criticisms of the MLTB. He was flanked by the BMC general secretary[49], Dennis Gray, and the BMC president, Bob Pettigrew. (Twenty-six years earlier, in happier times, Pettigrew and Longland had joined in the postwar optimism and vigour of White Hall's opening weekend, the birth of LEA residential outdoor education.) Ogilvie describes the confrontation:

> The list itemised all the nitty gritty faults in the working of the MLTB allegedly due to Longland's incompetence – a censorious and disparaging diatribe that amounted to character assassination. A BMC vote for no confidence in the Chairman was defeated with 4 for and 9 against … Observing Longland throughout all this unrelenting and very adversarial engagement, I was shocked to see the effect upon him of this onslaught – face drawn and hands shaking, struggling to maintain his composure.[50]

Ogilvie then intervened, proposing that the MLTB meeting should stop and reconvene elsewhere. The MLTB members walked out of the BMC offices.

Four days later, under the heading 'Mountaineers in High-level Row', the *Guardian* reported that

> an argument of increasing ill-will is reverberating through the British mountaineering world and shows no signs of dying … Sir Jack at the weekend described the [British Mountaineering] Council's behaviour towards the Board as constituting a 'vendetta'

and said that if it was not called off, the Board would seek another home for the servicing and administration of its work.[51]

The MLTB subsequently resolved to meet in future somewhere less hostile. The newspapers thrived on the episode, with headlines like 'Mountaineering Men Refuse to Let Go' and 'The Board That Just Won't Climb Down'.[52] In the eyes of some journalists, the BMC had sacked Longland.

Headlines from July to October 1977, at the height of the mountain-training dispute.

Writing in his autobiography, when describing the aftermath of the BMC's unilateral decision to set up a training board of its own, Hunt remained analytic and nonjudgmental:

The ensuing crisis threatened to engulf not only those who train and teach, but the whole body of people who climb as a leisure pastime. Even more serious was the harm which this schism could do to the interests of the young people whose enthusiasm for adventure needs to be wisely and competently guided by adults.[53]

More privately, Hunt was less guarded. In a letter to the MLTB, after the 14 July break-up, he said that the way that the BMC was pursuing its policies disturbed him. After the break-up, Hunt resigned from the BMC.

The money for running the MLTB came from a Sports Council quarterly grant, but indirectly, through the BMC. However, Longland had close links with the Sports Council, having been its vice-chairman in 1966–74. Also, the vice-chairman of the Sports Council in 1977 was John Disley, who had strong links with outdoor education. What happened next is that Longland played his ace. On 10 October 1977 the Sports Council, probably at Longland's suggestion, withheld from the BMC the MLTB's part of the quarterly grant. In a flash, the BMC lost £3,390 of its £6,700 quarterly grant, more than half the total. The BMC responded by appealing to all its members to write to their MPs, which hundreds did.[54] Walt Unsworth, the editor of *Climber and Rambler*, sent a telegram signed by the editors of three climbing magazines to Denis Howell, the minister for sport, protesting about the Sports Council's action. But because of the Sports Council's independent Royal Charter, Howell could not intervene.[55]

There were now two boards claiming the money. The Sports Council felt that, until this was resolved, it could not pay the grant to anyone. Journalists continued to make hay, with headlines like 'Parting of Ways' and 'Pique Among the Peaks'.[56] According to Mark Vallance, the Sports Council would have been acting unconstitutionally had it transferred the withheld £3,390 to the MLTB, 'a self-appointed group that had no legal status'.[57]

Reports in national newspapers tended to present the mountain training dispute as being a majestic two-sided power struggle: the MLTB versus the BMC; Longland versus Gray; educational mountaineers versus sporting mountaineers. Articles in the two main climbing magazines, *Mountain* and *Climber and Rambler*, repackaged the same story to suit the readership: baddies versus goodies.

Underneath these simplifications, the realities were more complicated. Other institutions and other people had been involved for many years. The main battalion behind the MLTB was the AWMC, comprising in 1977 about sixty-five individuals with full membership.[58] Also backing the MLTB, in reserve and kept informed, lay the whole giant education machine, seen by the BMC side as a potential marauding invader. The main forces backing the BMC in 1977 were 208 mountaineering clubs, whose members were a large proportion of Britain's climbing populace. The BMC also had 1,753 individual members, a number that was growing rapidly, heading for over 10,000 by 1994.[59]

If there was one point in Jack Longland's life when his consummate public-relations skills were less effective than normal, it was now. Forty-two years earlier, in March 1935, Longland had been a bright young innovator in the internal politics of the Alpine Club, determined to confront the old buffers of the Mount Everest Committee and to effect change. Now, he was occupying the opposite role. In the battle for the hearts and minds of grassroots climbers in the late 1970s, Longland was ineffectual and was outmanoeuvred by Dennis Gray and Ken Wilson, two younger men whom we might now recognise as pioneer spin doctors and the equals to Longland in well-meant obduracy. In 1976, *Climber and Rambler* became the official organ of the BMC, a successful arrangement that would last until 1985.[60] Looking back from 1997, Gray wrote: 'Although Jack and his Board [the MLTB] may have had the ear of the establishment, the BMC began to win the media battle being characterised as a poor downtrodden national voluntary sports body ill-used by heartless bureaucrats in a David [BMC] and Goliath [Sports Council] struggle.'[61] Ken Ogilvie, one of the alleged heartless bureaucrats, recalled the public-relations contest differently: 'One aspect that rankled at the time was that the mountaineering press was so effectively controlled by the "sporting" mountaineers, that the viewpoint of the "educational" mountaineers was rarely given a chance properly to express itself publicly, answer all the accusations or correct mistaken impressions.' According to Ogilvie, throughout the long dispute, from 1972 to 1980, only two statements from Longland and one from the AWMC were given space in the climbing press.[62]

Despite losing its Crawford Street administrative facilities, the MLTB continued to operate, meeting elsewhere, such as at the Sports Council's regional offices in Manchester. Meanwhile, the BMC unilaterally pronounced the MLTB to have been abolished and replaced by the new Mountain Training Board. A furious AWMC wrote to the minister of sport and recreation, putting the other side of the story.[63]

Divided Loyalties

One of the complications of the prolonged row had been the presence of prominent personalities who had connections with both sides. Longland himself, for example, had been the president of the BMC from 1962 to 1965, and in 1973 had been made an honorary member.

A few of the people involved in the dispute, either closely or on the periphery, managed successfully to wear two hats. The events forced others to pick one of their hats and discard the other.

Regarding Bob Pettigrew's role, he was the BMC president in the later phase of the dispute, 1976–9. He had also been an educational adviser. He nevertheless identified totally with the BMC's cause and was resolute throughout the whole period in maintaining the Council's position as set out by the Hunt Report. Gray later wrote that 'it is to him more than any other single person that the Council owes a successful outcome to the Training Dispute.'[64] Ogilvie added a different slant: 'Pettigrew was one who might have been expected to sympathise with the education lobby but did not – with his divided loyalties the mountaineering values side prevailed.'[65]

Another man caught up in the events of 14 July 1977 had been Mark Vallance, an old schoolmate and climbing partner of Jack Longland's son Nick and a friend of the Longland family. Vallance was one of three BMC nominees on the MLTB, the others being Dennis Gray and Pete Livesey. When the no-confidence motion was put to the vote, rather than abstaining, Vallance voted in favour of the motion. Although the vote of no confidence failed, Vallance's support for the motion soured his relationship with Jack Longland for several years.[66]

Livesey was another person with a foot in both camps. Most well known as a transformational top rock climber of the early and mid-1970s, by 1977, as a lecturer in outdoor education at Bingley College of Education, Livesey was also a renowned and charismatic outdoor educator.[67] (Remaining true to his principles, in about 1980 Livesey decided to quit climbing, turning his back on a game he had dominated for six of seven years. He was pessimistic about climbing's future, seeing – perhaps wrongly – bolt protection as potentially jeopardising adventure in the interests of safe leisure for all.[68])

Tom Price, an ex-warden of Eskdale OBMS who was vice-chairman of the Hunt committee, remained close enough to the sporting mountaineers to later become the BMC president (1982–5).

Perhaps the person rooted most firmly in both camps was John Hunt. He had directed the Duke of Edinburgh's Award scheme for ten years and had been the BMC president from 1965 to 1968. Ever since running a toughening-up course for soldiers in Snowdonia in 1942, Hunt had believed in the value to young people of expedition work. But the expedition parts of the Duke of Edinburgh's Award scheme had quite frequently run into difficulties and had been criticised by mountain-rescue teams and by experienced hillwalkers. Hunt, therefore, was fully aware of the perspectives of both sides of the dispute. He emerged from his demanding Hunt-committee involvement with his reputation for impartiality intact or even enhanced. However, he had not been under quite the same personal strain as Longland: the BMC was not planning to take over the Duke of Edinburgh's Award scheme. (But some negativity among outside observers of the expeditioning part of the award scheme would persist. Simon Thompson, writing in 2010, was pessimistic about expeditioning that appeared to lack enjoyment: 'Participants in the scheme – normally wet and bedraggled youths – and their anxious adult overseers are a common sight in the British countryside to this day.'[69])

Arbitration

On 28 October 1977, Peter Lloyd, the president of the Alpine Club, offered to arbitrate an agreement, provided that the warring parties called a truce. In February 1978 the MLTB and the BMC agreed to put the matter to arbitration, although not in the strictest meaning of 'arbitrate', which would have implied a binding commitment to accept the panel's decisions. The highly formal arbitration hearing took place at the Inns of Court on 30–31 May 1979. The findings of the tribunal of 'four wise men' became known five months later, in November.

The main thrust of the tribunal's report favoured the BMC: 'We think that the case for the BMC to assume a positive role in training for mountaineering is almost unanswerable and we find ourselves at this point in full agreement with the findings of the Hunt Committee.'[70]

A secondary recommendation, subject to the above, went some way towards the MLTB's stance on independence. It also responded to the BMC's claim that the MLTB had been operating without a constitution: 'The MLTB which, whatever the constitutional position may have been, has enjoyed de facto autonomy since its formation, should remain autonomous within a constitutional framework.'[71]

The report recommended getting rid of certificates. Instead of awarding a certificate to a successful candidate, the directors of assessment courses would complete a report page in the person's logbook. In other words, one piece of paper (the certificate) would be replaced by another piece of paper (a page in a logbook). The tribunal also suggested name changes for the qualification and for the board itself.

An important and penetrating tribunal comment on the attitude of the BMC said:

The BMC is concerned with the interests of club mountaineers and does not by any means represent all those who visit the hills in Britain. In particular it does not understand the large and still growing phenomenon of outdoor education, particularly in a mountain environment. The objectives of this education are much wider than the sport of mountaineering, and are properly to be described under several headings such as aesthetic, ethical, scientific, social, physical and spiritual. The value of mountains in education is to help in social and personal development, to provide adventurous outdoor activities, to develop cognitive skills, and to encourage a responsible attitude to the natural environment. The BMC, in common with the club members whom it represents, is ambivalent towards the use of the mountains for such broader educational purposes.[72]

A note needs adding here, in sympathy with the BMC's position in the 1970s. The confusion of climbers about the objectives of outdoor education was understandable, as outdoor educators were still arguing among themselves about these objectives. This will become apparent when we reach the White Hall Centre of the late 1980s.

MOUNTAIN LEADERSHIP TRAINING BOARD

This is to certify that

MALCOLM PAUL CREASEY

has completed the training required by the Board and has been awarded the

MOUNTAIN LEADERSHIP CERTIFICATE

Date 19.3.75.　　　　Jack Longland. Chairman

Fred A. Smith Secretary

Details of courses attended are entered on the back of this certificate

A Mountain Leadership Certificate (summer), issued in 1975. In December 1979, after more than four years of controversy, the BMC and the MLTB agreed to replace the certificate with a report page in the candidate's logbook.

Section 4

MOUNTAIN LEADER TRAINING SCHEME

(Summer Conditions)

ASSESSMENT REPORT

Mr/M̶r̶s̶/M̶x̶ Ian Duncan McNeill

of 50, Stafford St.,Long Eaton, Notts. attended

an Assessment Course at White Hall Centre

from 17th October to 24th October 1987

The Director of Assessment was satified that the candidate fulfilled the requirements of the syllabus and demonstrated the technical competence to lead walking parties in the mountain areas of the United Kingdom in summer conditions.

N.B. THE CANDIDATE HAS NOT BEEN ASSESSED IN THE SKILLS OF MOVEMENT ON SNOW AND ICE OR IN ROCK-CLIMBING.

COMMENTS: Ian McNeill has performed with a high degree of skill and competence in all aspects of the syllabus. Personal skills were assessed in appalling weather conditions over three days in Snowdonia and leadership was tested on a two day expedition over the Dark Peak with a group of novices.

Signed ⟍⟋ 𝓓 ᴸᴺᵒᴸᴸ   Date 26th October '87

Director of Assessment

Centre White Hall Centre, Long Hill, Buxton, Derbys.

IMPORTANT: THIS REPORT SHOULD ALWAYS BE READ IN CONJUNCTION WITH THE LOG BOOK WITH SPECIAL REFERENCE TO THE POST-ASSESSMENT PAGES (PP 31 ONWARDS) BEFORE A FINAL DECISION IS TAKEN AS TO THE CANDIDATE'S SUITABLITY TO LEAD WALKING PARTIES IN THE U.K. MOUNTAINS AND MOORLANDS.

The assessment report page from the logbook of a candidate for the Mountain Leader qualification.

In December 1979 the BMC management committee and the MLTB both decided to accept the arbitrators' report. But there were many details still to be decided. One sentence in the report touched upon a philosophical contradiction facing outdoor educators that was already widely acknowledged to exist but which was becoming more acute: 'There is a pressing need to explore the paradox which seems to exist between the desire to provide adventure training on the one hand, and the attempt to eliminate all risk on the other.'[73] We met this contradiction in Chapter 7, when it led us to ask the questions, in the context of 1950: was climbing a suitable sport for young people to take up? Would their parents understand it?

On the morning of 26 February 1980, the old MLTB met for the last time. Jack Longland gave a valedictory address. He had served on the board for nearly thirty years. It was the end of an era. In the opinion of Ken Ogilvie, no other person had put their mark on the early development of outdoor education in as many ways as Longland.[74] Between 1964 and 1980 some twenty thousand people had attended an introductory MLC course and about five thousand had qualified.

On the afternoon of the same day, the new MLTB held its inaugural meeting. The board invented a new word, 'mountainwalking', and agreed a new title for itself, the Mountainwalking Leader Training Board, but kept the initials MLTB. Out went the MLC; in came the Mountain Leader qualification or award.

In April the MLTB adopted a constitution. Things were looking up.

John Disley, as vice-chairman of the Sports Council from 1974 to 1982, was well informed on the mountain training dispute. In 1993, looking back at this period in Longland's life, Disley wrote:

> Jack fought on for his principles even when in his 70s. His refusal to allow Ken Wilson to impose BMC politically-correct modes – the young should climb or fall without benefit of organised training – on the work of the Mountain Leadership Board and of Plas y Brenin was steadfast. Jack as Chairman and Ken as BMC representative on many committees of this era made for very difficult meetings, but Jack stuck it out until more moderate and reasonable voices prevailed at the BMC. In my opinion, his unflinching response to attacks which were often extremely personal in nature stopped the BMC being completely rejected by the fair minded climbers of the day. I followed him as Chair-

man at the ML Board and PYB, and would not have taken on the jobs if Jack had not previously won the day.[75]

In 1966, Kim Meldrum, writing from deep within outdoor education, had noticed the start of what he called – tongue in cheek – a qualifications rat race.[76] In 1970 a critical Dennis Gray, when writing *Rope Boy*, had only very reluctantly accepted that Britain needed any sort of mountain leader qualification. They were both swimming against a strong current. By the time Gray retired from his job as the BMC general secretary in 1989, the demand for Eric Langmuir's *Mountain Leadership* (1969) had required several reprints and a second edition (renamed *Mountaincraft and Leadership*). Iain Peter, the MLTB secretary, was energetically seeking European Equivalence for the ML award. A number of lower-level qualifications were about to sprout. Leader, instructor and coach qualifications were an established part of British outdoor education.

Writing in 2014, John Porter remarked that anyone brought up after the debate would find it difficult to see what the fuss had been about. The mountain leader qualifications for summer and winter were now generally accepted as a good thing.[77] The education system, whether climbers approved of it or not, had become acutely risk averse, and certification had penetrated every corner of outdoor education, but the fears that the regulations of education would affect 'the freedom of the hills' cherished by the grassroots climber had not translated into reality. Most ML courses (and previously most MLC courses) were very enjoyable, both for students and staff. 'The spirit that pervaded them was the same spirit that brings climbers and fell-walkers together in enjoyment and companionship.'[78]

The mountain training dispute had contained a rich vein of irony. While the mass of grassroots climbers had fended off a perceived threat from a safety-mongering educational bureaucracy, many of them, at the same time, had begun to shift their own activities fundamentally towards a safer form of the sport, a seismic shock that was far greater than any changes that a secessionist MLTB could have effected and which, moreover, an older but still passionate Ken Wilson relentlessly opposed.

The mountain training dispute was not, of course, the first controversy in mountaineering. In a 1930 article titled 'Some Mountaineering Controversies', Theo Chorley of the Fell and Rock Climbing Club discussed guideless alpinism, a vexed matter of the 19th century.

In a clever introduction that appears at first to be discursive but is not, he describes a chance observation that he made one day in a hotel in Grasmere. He had overheard a fellow-guest spouting on about the 'silly fools who clamber about the crags'. Inwardly Chorley lamented the average person's lack of understanding of mountaineering, an ignorance that at its worst sometimes led to contempt. But he kept silent. The incident set him thinking about controversies in general:

> Restraining myself with difficulty from making some cutting remark … I continued to watch these products of cultivated England with a jaundiced eye. Their talk turned to golf. I gathered that there was a question of the highest moment agitating the country, or at any rate the responsible part of it, and this had to do with whether the golf ball should be large and light or small and heavy …
>
> The humour of the situation dawned upon me at last. I really ought to have appreciated that these controversies are part and parcel of every sport, indeed of every human activity.[79]

The next chapter will briefly touch upon controversial times in another human activity, that of running an outdoor pursuits centre.

Notes

1   Ken C Ogilvie, *Roots and Wings: A History of Outdoor Education and Outdoor Learning in the UK* (Lyme Regis, UK: Russell House Publishing, 2013), p. 335.

2   *The First Fifty Years of the British Mountaineering Council*, ed. by Geoff Milburn, Derek Walker and Ken Wilson (Manchester: British Mountaineering Council, 1997), p. 8.

3   'Climbers in Council', *The Times*, 15 Oct 1956, p. 11.

4   Ken C Ogilvie, *Roots and Wings: A History of Outdoor Education and Outdoor Learning in the UK* (Lyme Regis, UK: Russell House Publishing, 2013), pp. 335–336.

5   Tom Price, 'What Led to the Leaders', *High Magazine*, no. 46 (Sept 1986), pp. 38–42 (p. 38).

6   *The First Fifty Years of the British Mountaineering Council*, ed. by Geoff Milburn, Derek Walker and Ken Wilson (Manchester: British Mountaineering Council, 1997), pp. 36–37.

7   Ken C Ogilvie, *Roots and Wings: A History of Outdoor Education and Outdoor Learning in the UK* (Lyme Regis, UK: Russell House Publishing, 2013), p. 336.

8   Tom Price, 'What Led to the Leaders', *High Magazine*, no. 46 (Sept 1986), pp. 38–42 (p. 38).

9   Ed Douglas, 'Mountain Training: 50 Years of Showing the Way', British Mountaineering Council (7 Jan 2014) <https://www.thebmc.co.uk/mountain-training-50-years-of-showing-the-way> [accessed 23 July 2015].

10 Ron James, 'A Guide's Life – More Ups than Downs!', in *A Passion for Mountains*, ed. by Hannah Burrows-Smith (London: Robert Hale, 2014), pp. 82–87 (p. 86).

11 Ken C Ogilvie, *Roots and Wings: A History of Outdoor Education and Outdoor Learning in the UK* (Lyme Regis, UK: Russell House Publishing, 2013), pp. 337, 339.

12 Dennis Gray, *Rope Boy* (London: Victor Gollancz: 1970), p. 312.

13 Ibid., p. 310.

14 Jeff Connor, *Creagh Dhu Climber: The Life and Times of John Cunningham* (no place given: Ernest Press, 1999), pp. 198–202.

15 Ken Wilson, 'The Cairngorm Tragedy: A Mountain Report', in *The Games Climbers Play*, ed. by Ken Wilson (London: Bâton Wicks, 1996), pp. 618–636.

16 Jeff Connor, *Creagh Dhu Climber: The Life and Times of John Cunningham* (no place given: Ernest Press, 1999), pp. 203–204.

17 Tom Price, *Travail So Gladly Spent* (Ty Croes, Wales: Ernest Press, 2000), p. 183.

18 *The First Fifty Years of the British Mountaineering Council*, ed. by Geoff Milburn, Derek Walker and Ken Wilson (Manchester: British Mountaineering Council, 1997), pp. 44–45.

19 Ibid., p. 48. Also Dennis Gray, *Rope Boy* (London: Victor Gollancz: 1970), p. 312.

20 Dennis Gray, *Rope Boy* (London: Victor Gollancz: 1970), pp. 313–314.

21 Talkaround [W Unsworth], 'The New National Officer', *Climber and Rambler*, 11 (Feb 1972), p. 45.

22 Ken C Ogilvie, *Roots and Wings: A History of Outdoor Education and Outdoor Learning in the UK* (Lyme Regis, UK: Russell House Publishing, 2013), p. 440.

23 Tom Price, *Travail So Gladly Spent* (Ty Croes, Wales: Ernest Press, 2000), p. 210.

24 [Anon.], 'Mountain Safety "on Trial"', *Climber and Rambler*, 11 (July 1972), p. 182.

25 'Cut in School Trips', *Guardian*, 25 Apr 1972, p. 7.

26 *The First Fifty Years of the British Mountaineering Council*, ed. by Geoff Milburn, Derek Walker and Ken Wilson (Manchester: British Mountaineering Council, 1997), pp. 49–50.

27 Ken C Ogilvie, *Roots and Wings: A History of Outdoor Education and Outdoor Learning in the UK* (Lyme Regis, UK: Russell House Publishing, 2013), p.456.

28 Tom Price, 'Bridging the Gap', in *The Games Climbers Play*, ed. by Ken Wilson (London: Bâton Wicks, 1996), pp. 637–642.

29 Talkaround [W Unsworth], 'The Safety Factor', *Climber and Rambler*, 12 (July 1973), p. 307.

30 Walt Unsworth, 'Dynamite – With a Short Fuse', *Climber and Rambler*, 13 (Mar 1974), p. 85.

31 Quoted in ibid.

32 Ibid.

33   Ken C Ogilvie, *Roots and Wings: A History of Outdoor Education and Outdoor Learning in the UK* (Lyme Regis, UK: Russell House Publishing, 2013), p. 445.

34   Ken Wilson, 'The Educational Threat', *Mountain*, no. 33 (Mar 1974), p. 8.

35   Phil Kelly, Graham Hoey and Giles Barker, *Peak Rock: The History, The Routes, The Climbers* (Sheffield: Vertebrate Publishing, 2013), p. 174.

36   Tom Price, *Travail So Gladly Spent* (Ty Croes, Wales: Ernest Press, 2000), p. 212.

37   Ken C Ogilvie, *Roots and Wings: A History of Outdoor Education and Outdoor Learning in the UK* (Lyme Regis, UK: Russell House Publishing, 2013), p. 446.

38   Ken Wilson, 'Advice and Ascent', *Guardian*, 8 Mar 1975, p. 11.

39   D L Noble, 'Don't Put Walkers in a Cocoon', *Guardian*, 12 Feb 1975, p. 14.

40   Peter Hildrew, 'Scrap Mountain Leadership Certificate, Says Hunt', *Guardian*, 15 Sept 1975, p. 6.

41   *The First Fifty Years of the British Mountaineering Council*, ed. by Geoff Milburn, Derek Walker and Ken Wilson (Manchester: British Mountaineering Council, 1997), p. 47.

42   Tom Price, 'What Led to the Leaders', *High Magazine*, no. 46 (Sept 1986), pp. 38–42 (p. 39).

43   Training Committee, *Hunt Report on Mountain Training, July 1975* (Manchester: British Mountaineering Council, 1975), para. 43.

44   Tom Price, 'What Led to the Leaders', *High Magazine*, no. 46 (Sept 1986), pp. 38–42 (p. 39).

45   Jack Longland, 'Valedictory Address: Jack Longland', *Alpine Journal*, 82 (1977), pp. 3–12 (p. 6).

46   Ken C Ogilvie, *Roots and Wings: A History of Outdoor Education and Outdoor Learning in the UK* (Lyme Regis, UK: Russell House Publishing, 2013), pp. 452-454.

47   Ibid., p. 454.

48   John Hunt, *Life Is Meeting* (London: Hodder & Stoughton, 1978), p. 143.

49   Ogilvie (p. 455 of *Roots and Wings*) wrongly describes Gray as the BMC national officer. In 1974 Gray had moved from the national officer role to the general secretary role.

50   Ken C Ogilvie, *Roots and Wings: A History of Outdoor Education and Outdoor Learning in the UK* (Lyme Regis, UK: Russell House Publishing, 2013), p. 455.

51   'Mountaineers in High-level Row', *Guardian*, 18 July 1977, p. 4.

52   'Mountaineering Men Refuse to Let Go', *Guardian*, 20 Sept 1977, p. 3. Also 'The Board That Just Won't Climb Down', *Guardian*, 23 Sept 1977, p. 4.

53   John Hunt, *Life Is Meeting* (London: Hodder & Stoughton, 1978), p. 143.

54   *The First Fifty Years of the British Mountaineering Council*, ed. by Geoff Milburn, Derek Walker and Ken Wilson (Manchester: British Mountaineering Council, 1997), p. 60.

55   'Pique among the Peaks', *Guardian*, 15 Oct 1977, p. 1.

56   'Parting of Ways', *Guardian*, 7 Oct 1977, p. 2. Also 'Pique among the Peaks', *Guardian*, 15 Oct 1977, p. 1.

57   Mark Vallance, *Wild Country: The Man Who Made Friends* (Sheffield: Vertebrate Publishing, 2016), p. 32.

58   Ken C Ogilvie, *Roots and Wings: A History of Outdoor Education and Outdoor Learning in the UK* (Lyme Regis, UK: Russell House Publishing, 2013), p. 416.

59   *The First Fifty Years of the British Mountaineering Council,* ed. by Geoff Milburn, Derek Walker and Ken Wilson (Manchester: British Mountaineering Council, 1997), p. 98.

60   Ibid., pp. 32, 70.

61   Ibid., p. 60.

62   Ken C Ogilvie, *Roots and Wings: A History of Outdoor Education and Outdoor Learning in the UK* (Lyme Regis, UK: Russell House Publishing, 2013), p. 441.

63   Ibid., p. 456.

64   *The First Fifty Years of the British Mountaineering Council,* ed. by Geoff Milburn, Derek Walker and Ken Wilson (Manchester: British Mountaineering Council, 1997), p. 63.

65   Ken C Ogilvie, *Roots and Wings: A History of Outdoor Education and Outdoor Learning in the UK* (Lyme Regis, UK: Russell House Publishing, 2013), p. 442.

66   Mark Vallance, *Wild Country: The Man Who Made Friends* (Sheffield: Vertebrate Publishing, 2016), pp. 31–32, 201.

67   John Sheard, Mark Radtke and others, *Fast and Free: Pete Livesey, Stories of a Rock Climbing Legend* (Lancaster, Lancashire: 2QT, 2014), pp. 33, 156–161, 317.

68   Ibid., pp. 271–273.

69   Simon Thompson, *Unjustifiable Risk? The Story of British Climbing* (Milnthorpe, UK: Cicerone, 2010), p. 127.

70   J H Emlyn Jones, *Report of the Tribunal on Mountain Training* (London: Alpine Club, 1979), p. 17.

71   Ibid., p. 18.

72   Ibid., p. 15.

73   Ibid., p. 22.

74   Ken C Ogilvie, *Roots and Wings: A History of Outdoor Education and Outdoor Learning in the UK* (Lyme Regis, UK: Russell House Publishing, 2013), p. 462.

75   Jim Perrin, 'Sir John Laurence ('Jack') Longland: 1905–1993', *Climbers' Club Journal: 1993,* 21, no. 3 (new series) (1994), pp. 79–83 (pp. 82–83).

76   K I Meldrum, 'White Hell Pursuing Centre', *Climbers' Club Journal: 1966,* 15, no. 1 (new series) (1966), pp. 61–67 (p. 61).

77   John Porter, *One Day as a Tiger: Alex MacIntyre and the Birth of Light and Fast Alpinism* (Sheffield: Vertebrate, 2014), pp. 125–126.

78   Tom Price, 'What Led to the Leaders', *High Magazine,* no. 46 (Sept 1986), pp. 38–42 (p. 41).

79   R S T Chorley, 'Some Mountaineering Controversies', *Fell and Rock Journal,* 8, no. 3 (1930), pp. 293–303 (p. 293).

20. Never a Dull Moment, 1983–92

The 1970s at White Hall, under Lyn Noble and Dave Draper, had been stable and confident times, great years. I might not have emphasised this enough. The years 1983–92 were less contented. Decidedly bumpy. Both of these contrasting periods were covered in my book *Climbing Lessons* (1997), an autobiographical account of working in outdoor education. I wrote the book in 1993–7, when the memories were still fresh and, in some cases, raw. This may have been a mistake. Samuel Goldwyn, the film producer, once said: 'I don't think anyone should write their autobiography until after they're dead.' Another sceptic, the British historian Philip Guedalla, suggested that 'autobiography is an unrivalled vehicle for telling the truth about other people', to which the writer Hugh Leonard added that it is also a felicitous vehicle 'for telling lies about oneself'.

If I used the latter vehicle, then I have transgressed, but it is now too late for me to confess to and thereby enlighten my ex-colleague of sixteen years, Dave Edwards, who told me he was amazed how honest the book was. Perhaps that honesty was premature and was itself some sort of contravention. Maybe I should have delayed the writing until now, twenty-five years later, allowing memories to fade and providing the time for what had once seemed to be important issues to shrink to minor blips of local history, which they are now. Yet I did not delay. And the book was not just honest; it was brutally so, too frank for some people to stomach.

Climbing Lessons was an autobiography, a genre that describes events and people through one person's eyes. *The Story of White Hall Centre* is a history, a genre that attempts to amalgamate many people's perspectives.

Autobiography and history are poles apart. This chapter of the history, if it were comprehensive, would need to examine a time of some generalised disaffection among the teaching staff, accompanied by occasional fractiousness and compounded by internal division. Some of the people involved will have memories different from mine. Truth is many-sided. Accounts of disunity and discontent are sometimes best written by outsiders, detached in time and distance from the events and the visceral beliefs. A historical account of the eight years 1984–92 should reflect the diverse perspectives of an assortment of staff members. My views are already in writing, albeit in the different genre and in a more informal register. Other opinions remain in people's heads. I am wary of the risk of accidentally ascribing sentiments to my ex-colleagues which they did not hold. With these considerations in mind, in February 2015 I started looking for another author, rather than me, for this chapter. This search has been unsuccessful, a result that has blocked the progress of the writing. To get past this impasse, I decided to summarise the period ruthlessly, leaving just enough content to provide some continuity. This condensing will allow uncomfortable truths and forgotten discord to remain undisturbed behind a superficial blandness.

For the rest of this chapter I will refer to myself in the third person. This will help to keep the book a history rather than another autobiography, but it will not necessarily eliminate any personal slant that I may have on the events.

Disruption, 1983

In January 1983, several staffing situations affected the make-up of the team of five group instructors. Gwyn Edwards was away from White Hall, halfway through two years of secondment; Dennis Richardson, after a road accident in France, lay seriously injured in a French hospital; and Pete McDonald had recently arrived in Australia, starting an exchange year organised by the League for the Exchange of Commonwealth Teachers. Back at White Hall, Rory Gregory continued a long stint of standing in for Gwyn, on a fixed-term contract; a temporary instructor was doing Dennis's job; and Pete Dingle, McDonald's exchange partner, was feeling his way into such mysteries as the group-instructor system and hand-jamming at Ramshaw Rocks. The other four staff members were Lyn Noble, Dave Draper, Dave Edwards and Phil Booth. The period was one without a female permanent instructor, a situation that would last for about nine years.

Pete McDonald and Pete Dingle, the Australian, had met briefly in London while travelling from and to Britain. As the months of 1983 passed, they exchanged occasional letters, partly because they had swapped houses but also to discuss aspects of the exchange. In a letter in July, halfway through the exchange year, Dingle told McDonald that he felt that the UK led Victoria in many aspects of outdoor education.

This was hardly surprising. In the UK, state-subsidised residential out-door education had been going for thirty years longer than in Victoria. Dingle also said he thought that the main exception was management, and that White Hall could learn something from Rubicon on that. He added that he was mystified by the deputy's role at White Hall. With the benefit of hindsight, these comments now look like telling signs of issues on the horizon.

Internal Reappraisal, 1984–90

By the time McDonald returned to White Hall, in January 1984, the deputy principal Dave Draper was tidying up loose ends and packing his bags ready for a move north to become an estate manager at a holiday park in the Lake District. An era was ending. White Hall was to miss Draper's charismatic influence. Dennis Richardson, who had suffered a serious leg injury a year earlier, had not recovered enough mobility to return to his job at White Hall, but he had regained enough movement to be able to undertake an instructing role at the Derbyshire schools' sailing unit at Ogston Reservoir.

To meet a requirement of the League for the Exchange of Commonwealth Teachers, McDonald produced a professional study, 'A Comparison of Two Outdoor Adventure Centres'.[1] Partly in response to this study, several important managerial improvements occurred in the mid-1980s. The governors approved the allocation of sixteen development days a year for teaching staff. Responsibilities were put into writing, specific to each member of staff. The centre rules, such as the policy on smoking, were put on paper.

Following these considerable changes, the full teaching staff met several times to consider the most fundamental area of all, the centre's purpose. This resulted in the adoption, internally at least, of written aims that were general and wide-ranging. Couching the aims in broad and accommodating language was perhaps the wisest approach to this task, but it meant that different members of staff could read the aims with emphasis on different aspects. No copies of these 1984 aims and objectives documents have survived, as far as I know.

This internal attempt to clarify the centre's purpose was a micro-cosm of a national debate that years of expanding and diversifying had intensified. You can detect a hint of the existence of that debate in some comments made to me recently by John Cheesmond after he had read a draft of this book:

I was interested to read of Jack Longland's philosophy for open country pursuits of encouraging children to have enjoyable experiences. I was delighted to be reminded of that as, after all my years in the field of OE and hearing of many aims and approaches, even up to the present, I have a strong sense that what makes the best outdoor experiences so powerful and memorable is that they are truly 'joyful' for participants. The only downside of this for me was that when I moved on from Whitehall [in November 1969], I found that other employers were not satisfied with such a rationale. While I did meet Jack Longland very briefly, I'm sad to say that I didn't spend time with him. He does sound to have been a truly inspiring figure.[2]

The new deputy principal, Ali Kellas, arrived sometime in 1984 and competently filled the gap left by Dave Draper's departure, bringing a combination of experience, technical skills and administrative proficiency. Another development, almost unprecedented for White Hall, took place at about the same time as Kellas's arrival. The five instructors – Gwyn Edwards, Dave Edwards, Booth, Gregory and McDonald – met one evening and decided to ask the education authority to review their conditions of service. They subsequently put the request through the normal channels. The negotiations would take three years, against the background of a protracted national teachers' dispute.

Early in 1985, ill health forced Gwyn Edwards onto three months of sick leave.

In 1986, as part of a review of outdoor education in the county, Lyn Noble produced an outline 'Derbyshire Approach to Outdoor Education'. Other developments of the mid-1980s included a complete revision of the county's climbing-leader syllabuses and improvements to the ropes course. In January 1987, Hilary Sharp joined the staff to fill the vacancy left by Gwyn Edwards's prolonged absence. Gwyn died of cancer in March 1987.

Coincident with these happenings at White Hall, Noble continued his involvement in national developments. In November 1986 he became chairman of the AWOEC. In November 1987, at the association's annual general meeting and conference, he spoke on the theme 'The Wider View of Outdoor Education'.

Also in November, Noble, concerned about deteriorating relationships within the centre, brought in a management consultant, Derrick Rowland. A series of three meetings took place over a year. All staff,

Instructors' Hours of Work, White Hall Centre, Early 1980s

White Hall instructor, typical workload on a 5-day course

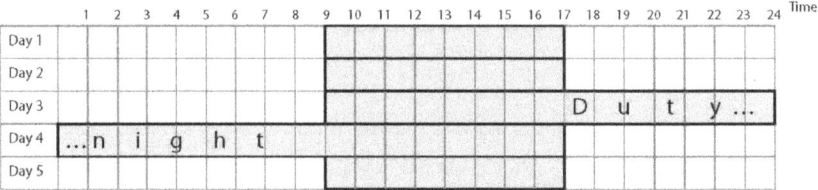

Total hours worked in five days = 56

White Hall instructor, typical workload on a 7-day course

Total hours worked in seven days = 88

White Hall instructor, worst-case workload,
weekend followed by a 9-day course (discontinued)

Total hours worked in eleven days = 136

including non-teaching staff, joined in these meetings. Rowland worked tactfully and hopefully, but the atmosphere among the teaching staff remained strained.

McDonald later maintained that, despite the drawing-up of written White Hall aims, one of the causes of the tense relationships was that several staff members were interpreting the aims differently and were prioritising different aspects. Opinions may differ on the extent to which this was the case.[3] McDonald said that this internal issue was never adequately ventilated at the time.

In December 1988, following Lyn Noble's outline suggestions of 1986, the county council produced 'Outdoor Education in Derbyshire – a Consultation Document'. (Work on a final version of this would still be under way in mid-1992.)

Even with the local disruptions and divisions of the 1980s, indeed amid them, White Hall instructors continued to practise their sports privately at a high level. In March 1983, Rory Gregory took part in an attempt on the East Ridge of Tawche in the Nepal Himalayas. In autumn 1986 and again in summer 1988, Ali Kellas took part in attempts to climb the North East Ridge of Mount Everest. In September 1989 Phil Booth and two companions made the first official ascent of Hagshu (6330 metres) in Kishtwar, Kashmir, a fine looking peak that had defied many attempts.[4]

Ali Kellas left White Hall in December 1989 to become principal of Derwent Hill, near Keswick. His replacement, Doug Jones, came in May 1990. Jones was a graduate of John Brailsford's outdoor education degree at Coleg Normal, part of the University College of North Wales. He had worked in a number of posts, mostly in North Wales, combining full time instructing with several related activities. These included a spell in an RNLI lifeboat crew, team leader of one of the UK's busiest mountain rescue teams and running his friend Dr Ieuan Jones's mountain first aid scheme for several years. For the seven years immediately before his arrival at White Hall, Jones had been deputy principal of Marle Hall, Warwickshire county council's outdoor centre in Llandudno Junction on the north Wales coast. As with the staff at White Hall in the same era, Jones had also enjoyed secondment to other centres and expedition leave to the greater ranges.

Jones arrived at a time when he was involved in an initiative that would usefully meet a growing need among British mountaineering instructors. In 1975, the British Mountain Guides had formed the British Mountain Guides Association (BMGA) after an amicable break from the BMC. They applied to join the International Federation of Mountain Guides Associations. Although their first and second applications were declined, in 1977 a third application was accepted, giving the British Mountain Guides parity with their international counterparts. Alongside the international acceptance of their qualifications, the BMGA opened up opportunities for tailored insurance and retail discounts. In 1989, Simon Powell, who had worked at Plas y Brenin and for Outward Bound at both Rhowniar and Loch Eil, conceived the idea of forming a similar association for MIC holders. He approached Jones and they co-founded the Association of Mountaineering Instructors (AMI) with the aim of providing a unified voice for qualified instructors and the expectation that this would lead to similar opportunities to those that the qualified guides enjoyed. The inaugural meeting of the AMI took place at Plas y Brenin on 31 March 1990, a month before Jones's move to Derbyshire. Powell became the first chairman and Jones the first secretary. Jones also subsequently became AMI's second chair. Now, in 2017, the AMI is recognised as one of the foremost professional bodies in the field, providing MIC and MIA holders with a united voice.

In February 1990, Hilary Sharp moved to Vallorcine in France, where she set up her own trekking business. She also wrote several walking and climbing guides to the European Alps. Gill Berrow, an international K1 canoeist, came down from Scotland to replace her.

In 2016 Simon Beames interviewed White Hall's first six female permanent instructors. They were Meriel Blake (formerly Evans), 1965–9; Janet Davies (formerly Richards), 1969–71; Barbara Hall (formerly Hulley), 1971–5; Lynda Welham, 1976–7; Hilary Sharp, 1987–90; and Gill Berrow, 1990–3. A preliminary finding was that the first four interviewed did not perceive that they had been treated differently due to their gender by their manager, colleagues or course members.

Cycling's Time Arrives, 1990–2

In June 1890, with the coming of summer, as mentioned in Chapter 4, the pupils of Abbotsholme school undertook cycling expeditions to explore the Derbyshire and Staffordshire countryside in their vicinity. But it took a hundred years and radon gas to bring recreational cycling to White Hall. In January 1990, national newspapers reported that the cancer risk of exposure to radon gas was three times higher than had previously been thought.[5] At about the same time, a Manchester scientist discovered disquieting levels of radon in some Derbyshire caves.

White Hall subsequently suspended its caving, awaiting the results of further scientific surveys.

In March 1990, Pete McDonald proposed the development of cycling as a core activity that could, at least partly, fill the gaps left by the loss of caving.[6] This proposal met the approval of all staff. By March 1991, the courtyard garage held about sixteen new mountain bikes and a flat-bed trailer fitted with Automaxi upright bike carriers. Adjoining the garage, the old boiler room was now a bike workshop. The first bike rides took place in about April. The role of leading groups of young cyclists was a skill that all the teaching staff had to acquire from a beginning of minimal experience. In September 1991, guidance notes on the leading of cyclists were distributed to the teaching staff.[7] Everything possible to develop cycling as a reliable and affordable activity had been done. Time would determine the long-term success or otherwise of this experiment.

Having fun on the new bikes was interrupted once or twice in October and November 1991 when officers of the county council inspected the management and operation of White Hall. A report made available to the governors in February 1992 suggested that the centre should re-examine its aims.

A sad postscript is necessary here. In September 1992, an article in the *New Scientist* reported that radon readings in summer for Giant's Hole, Derbyshire finest cave, were the highest ever recorded for a natural limestone cave anywhere in the world.[8] The article mentioned that Dave Edwards, who had become the chairman of a National Caving Association working party on radon, had cut his time underground from 200 hours a year to about twenty-six hours in the past year.

School groups did subsequently begin to visit Derbyshire caves again, but only selected caves, with very low levels of radon.

About twelve years later, Dave Edwards developed small-cell lung cancer. He died on 27 January 2005. He had never smoked cigarettes. An amiable guy, a pleasure to work with. He was in his element in Lancaster Hole, roaming casually yet expertly along the labyrinthine high-level route, basking in the perfection of the Minarets passage, skirting carefully around two old friends, Scylla and Charybdis, and forging ahead up the Manchester Bypass.

D Edwards

In the courtyard at the start of a bike ride, 1991–2. Standing behind the group is Dave Edwards.

D Edwards

Heading north on the back road during a schools' course, 1991–2. White Hall is behind the trees.

Biking, during a schools' course,1991–2.

Crossing the River Goyt near Taxal, on a schools'
course, 1991–2.

On a forestry road to the west of Fernilee Reservoir, during a
schools' course, 1991–2.

The bike trailer, 1991–2.

Bike stand, bike workshop, 1991–2.

Notes

1   Derbyshire Record Office, A Comparison of Two Outdoor Adventure Centres:
     Pete McDonald, 1983, D7786/BOX/1/Bundle 1.

2   John Cheesmond, Email to P McDonald, subject 'Impact of the Outdoors', 9
     June 2016 [Email].

3   Pete McDonald, *Climbing Lessons: Inside Outdoor Education* (Kaikohe, NZ: Pete
     McDonald, 1997), pp. 293–317.

4   Phil Booth and Max Holliday, 'Kishtwar Dialogue', *Climber and Hill Walker,* May
     1990, pp. 24–26. (Two Polish climbers had reached the summit two weeks earlier
     but since they did not have a permit, their ascent remained undisclosed.)

5   Nigel Williams, 'Number of Homes at Risk from Radon Gas Triples', *Guardian,*
     20 Jan 1990, p. 2.

6   Derbyshire Record Office, Development of Cycling as an Activity at White
     Hall: Pete McDonald, March 1990, D7786/BOX/1/Bundle 3.

7   Derbyshire Record Office, Cycling: Notes for Staff: Pete McDonald, September
     1991, D7786/BOX/1/Bundle 3.

8   William Brown, 'Cavers Risk Cancer from Underground Radon', *New Scientist,*
     135, no. 1838 (12 Sept 1992), p. 4.

21. Other National Developments, 1970–92

Earlier chapters of Part Three have already covered several national developments of the Lyn Noble principalship, such as the proliferation of qualifications, organisations and regulations, the steady improvement in outdoor-pursuits equipment and the mountain training dispute of the 1970s. A number of other national happenings, ranging from isolated miscellaneous events to far-reaching reform of primary and secondary education, warrant at least a mention and sometimes a page or two. They occurred over twenty-three years. This chapter covers the whole of that period chronologically.

In February 1970, the British Schools Canoeing Association was formed, 'to encourage, promote and help canoeing in schools'. In the 1960s, canoeing in schools and youth groups had grown considerably, and this growth looked set to continue.[1]

On 4 October 1970, the NAOE was formally established. The object of the association was 'to bring into closer communication and co-operation those involved in a wide range of educational activities in the outdoors'.[2] By the end of its first year, the association had 300 members.

In 1972 the Department of Education and Science published *Safety in Outdoor Pursuits*, offering detailed guidance on good practice. Also in 1972, Harold Drasdo was moved to write: 'In all the mountain regions of Britain the adventure industry is in full swing.'[3] (Note that some people dislike this use of the word 'industry'; they prefer 'sector' or 'field'.)

In 1973 the Council for Environmental Education published the second edition of the *Directory of Centres for Outdoor Studies in England and Wales*. It contained 298 centres, 132 of which had described themselves as providing mostly outdoor pursuits.[4]

*

In the three years 1972–5, three former White Hall staff members produced writing on outdoor pursuits or outdoor education. The first was *Education and the Mountain Centres* (1972), a lengthy essay by Harold

Drasdo. The second was *Outdoor Education* (1973), a book by Terry Parker and Kim Meldrum. The third was *Hill and Watersports in British Education* (1975), the unpublished manuscript by Peter Mosedale.

In the 1960s, residential outdoor pursuits centres had become so universally in vogue that many an LEA had rushed out to buy a rural building without pausing to think in any depth about its purpose. Although White Hall's operational approach served as an example to imitate or adapt or reject, no matching prototype purpose document was available to copy. Drasdo's *Education and the Mountain Centres* set people's minds thinking, Hang on a moment! What is the aim of these places? He examined, critically, some of the philosophical issues behind the *raisons d'être* of residential centres for outdoor pursuits. Only a few writers had ventured this way before, although the matter had been discussed casually at conferences.

The first print-run of 1,000 copies, self-published, sold out within six months. A second print-run of 2,000 copies was sold by the mid-1970s. A reprint was published in 1998.

Parker and Meldrum's *Outdoor Education* outlined – with all the authority, merited or not, of a commercially published hardback – the historical development of outdoor education nationally and it gathered evidence to detail the current practices of the time. Parts of this book now form a historical record, a snapshot of the early 1970s, supported by some rudimentary statistics and some basic graphs.

Meldrum and Parker said that the UK's residential outdoor pursuits centres were generally regarded as serving four aims:

1. Character training.
2. An introduction to lasting leisure-time pursuits.
3. An experience in community living.
4. Countryside appreciation.

Discussing the first aim, they gave short shrift to the idea of changing a pupil's personality by exposing him or her to hardships and to the anxiety of a hostile and unfamiliar environment. If this was what was meant by 'character training', it had no place in the aims of LEA outdoor centres.[5] These comments accurately reflected a feeling that, by the 1970s, was widespread within outdoor education. According to Ken Ogilvie, by 1977 character building (or character training) was seen as an outmoded idea that had been by-passed and was out of tune with the post-imperial times and pop youth culture. However, part of what went on at residential outdoor pursuits centres could legitimately be called social and personal development.[6]

Perhaps a view representative of many teachers in LEA outdoor centres was that of Mike McEvoy, headmaster of Bewerley Park Centre from 1965 to 1975. McEvoy valued some aspects of Outward Bound training but rejected Outward Bound's character-building aims because he felt that change could not be imposed on young people but had to come from within.[7]

Meldrum and Parker also questioned the second and third aims. Some elementary cost-benefit analysis raised doubts about these two aims. Some of the book's reasoning on this, however, may have been debatable; the statement that 'most mountaineers cease their activities during their mid twenties' may have been correct in the 1950s; I doubt whether it was accurate in 1973, when their book was published.[8]

The fourth aim, an introduction to the appreciation of the country-side, the authors felt, could be the *raison d'être* of many centres.

On a different subject – the professional qualifications of instructors – the situation was noticeably changing. In the mid-1960s, Joe Brown and Gordon Mansell had each very competently shouldered the full responsibilities of a White Hall staff member despite not being quali-fied teachers. Nationally by 1973, the appointing of non-teachers to jobs at LEA outdoor centres was becoming less common:

> In the outdoor pursuits centres there was a tendency some time ago to appoint experts well versed in the technical skills who may or may not have been good instructors or teachers. There is now a trend to appoint teachers who also have the necessary expertise. Most staff are expected to help in a wide range of activities.[9]

Meldrum and Parker supported this trend towards appointing qualified teachers. They also offered an analysis of the roles of an instructor at an outdoor centre and of the skills required to fulfil those roles. This was an early attempt to pinpoint what makes a good instructor. (At this place in their book, the authors deliberately changed from the word 'instructor' to 'teacher'.) In their opinion, the expertise required of centre teachers was expanding and would continue to do so. It was inevitable, they thought, that outdoor centres would increasingly be staffed by university- and college-trained specialist teachers:

> Specialist instructors will have to live up to their specialist role, and the combination of three years' teacher training in outdoor education, and the accumulation of experience, is an inevitable requirement of all specialists, particularly those in the educational field [ie, in LEA outdoor centres].[10]

Moving on to the third mid-1970s publication, we return to Peter Mosedale. In describing the 1950s, Chapter 8 drew heavily on *Hill and Watersports in British Education*. We did not, however, reach even halfway through the Mosedale manuscript. For some readers, the second half may be the meaty, controversial half, albeit discovered forty years too late.

One clue to the contents of the second half is the manuscript's title. It is fairly specific. Although I have no explicit evidence to prove it, the title is also, I believe, very deliberate, like the name of the centre he once ran: White Hall Centre *for Open Country Pursuits*. An author only has a few words to play with when deciding on a title. Most authors of nonfiction are careful to make the title match the book's main subject or message. Mosedale chose to use the title 'hill and water sports in British education' rather than the obvious title that would have been more in keeping with the emerging fashion, 'outdoor education in Britain'. We know that he knew of Parker and Meldrum's book *Outdoor Education* (1973); it is possible, and again I am speculating, that he deliberately chose a less ambiguous title for his own book.

The title he decided on is a shorthand way of saying: the subject of this manuscript is the place of hillwalking, climbing, camping, orienteering, skiing, caving, kayaking and sailing in British education. We should not be surprised that the manuscript's library record at the University of Canberra in 2014 listed the manuscript's subject as 'Physical education and training – Great Britain'. The library record did not mention outdoor education.

Despite the emphasis of its title, however, the manuscript does range widely over the overlapping territories of outdoor recreation, outdoor education and physical education. The term 'outdoor education' appears in the manuscript nine times (excluding in titles). Large parts of the manuscript would fit comfortably into a book about outdoor education. But the term 'outdoor recreation' appears thirty-four times, and that was Mosedale's main focus and passion.

In promoting the importance of outdoor recreation, Mosedale was in tune with one main strand of Jack Longland's views of twenty-five years earlier, discussed in Chapter 7. Longland had talked about making the most of the opportunities offered by our wilder national playgrounds.

In practice, making the most of these opportunities was complicated, as the resources were limited. The opportunities needed to be rationed out. Mosedale examines the practical difficulties, financial constraints, social issues, moral dilemmas and philosophical considerations involved in promoting and managing outdoor recreation in Britain. He asks, and attempts to answer, some of the hard questions of 1975. He questions nearly everything. Can we justify the inclusion of a selected group of outdoor pursuits in the provision of education made from public funds? Are we to rationalise this development by staying on the grounds that appear to be firmest of all, those of physical education (whatever that may mean at present)? (*Déjà vu!*) Is the state getting value for money from the outdoor centres that it funds? Has the odd week at a residential training centre any value? How old should young people be before we introduce them to sports like climbing and kayaking? Should we be catering for the young person who is already interested in mountaineering or other outdoor pursuit, in the same way as we cater for those who are interested in swimming or dancing or throwing the discus? Can we regard the training of adults as a legitimate part of provision for life-long recreation and leisure?

Mosedale concluded that 'outdoor recreational activities when taught under the guidance of those who accept a broad and liberal concept of education can properly claim to contribute to formal education'.[11]

Throughout this manuscript, behind the historian Mosedale and the centre-warden Mosedale and behind the philosophising Mosedale and the analytic Mosedale, there is a person with a consistent, straightforward and unshakeable belief in the benefits of outdoor recreation. On the penultimate page, this belief comes across strongly in plain English:

It becomes difficult for some experts to appreciate the value of simple exposure to hills and forests, rivers and the sea, and to understand how imprisoned are so many children and young people in the streets of the great conurbations, and how unaware they can remain as to the nature even of their own country.

The perpetual problem is how to interest the ordinary young man and woman in outdoor activities of a general kind. It is a truism to say that those who need the help of centres and specialists least are those who find their way to them most easily. Naturally a restricted island such as Britain could not possibly hope that most of its young people would take up sailing or mountain activities. A whole range of interests associated with open country has to be catered for. Even to get a larger proportion of young people interested in their own country, even to see thousands more walking the magnificent country and coastal footpath systems would be advantageous.[12]

Now, in 2017, after the worldwide recession and, in Britain, the closing of many state-funded centres, some of Mosedale's questions of 1975 will have been replaced by much newer ones. But one or two of Mosedale's questions were prophetic: 'Several questions arise for the future. Is it possible to have existing publicly-financed centres return to the original concept? Would it be best in extending provision to put money into much simpler ventures staffed more cheaply, and less expensive in capital and recurrent costs: a cross between the early youth hostels in mountain districts and the first centre opened in Derbyshire in 1959 when only the warden and assistant warden were full-time employees?'[13] (The 'first centre' he was referring to was a Peak Park Planning Board hostel for walkers and climbers opened in Longdendale in 1959.[14])

*

Returning now to the national developments of the Lyn Noble era, we have reached the period 1975–92.

On 8 October 1975, Joe Tasker and Dick Renshaw reached the summit of Dunagiri, having climbed the southeast ridge of this 7,066-metre peak in alpine style.[15] Their ascent was a notable British contribution to the long evolution of light and unsupported Himalayan mountaineering, fulfilling Jack Longland's prediction of 1933[16] and echoing the style of mountain travelling and exploring demonstrated in 1934 and 1935 by Eric Shipton and Bill Tilman.

Meanwhile, back in Britain in the same month, at Dartington Hall in Devon, a conference took place to examine the expanding scale and scope of outdoor education. Perhaps influenced by the recent Drasdo and Parker–Meldrum writings, the delegates attempted to identify and categorise the goals of outdoor education. By the mid-1970s, harder times and diversification were making it necessary to defend, justify and promote outdoor education as a viable option.[17]

In the middle of the freezing winter of 1978–9, infamously coined the Winter of Discontent, more than 2,000 strikes erupted across Britain as workers rejected the Labour government's attempts to curtail wage increases. Some disruption occurred in the transport of pupils from their homes to outdoor centres.

White Hall's thirtieth birthday was on 29 December 1980. Ken Ogilvie has summarised where outdoor education had reached nationally: 'by 1980 ... the movement for Outdoor Education had blossomed, diversified and rapidly matured into a self-organising, albeit miscellaneous collection of confident partisan groups enthusiastically loyal to their own particular philosophies and choices.'[18] In the midst of the confident optimism, however, a prescriptive curriculum was on the horizon for schools in England and Wales, as also were government policy changes that would reduce funding for LEA residential outdoor centres.

*

September 1980 saw the publication of the first issue of the *Journal of Adventure Education*. In 1981 it became the official journal of the NAOE. Over the following decade, this periodical would evolve to wander nomadically across the land between parish newsletter and peer-reviewed journal, never really settling in one place; many of its articles sat somewhere between these two extremes. It would have three other titles (variants of the first) before finally, in 1997, becoming the magazine *Horizons*. Ken Ogilvie writes that this magazine's 'value to the industry was inestimable in being the main channel for disseminating all manner of grass-roots information and local news pertinent to OE ...'[19]

Ogilvie's appraisal of the merits of the *Journal of Adventure Education* may accurately reflect that publication's national position, but admiration for the journal in the 1980s was less than universal. One could argue about the extent to which this particular ferment of ideas ever won the attention of the outdoor-centre workforce. Far from viewing this multidimensional magazine as pertinent, some professional instructors considered it to be unappetising and unrepresentative, only very occasionally relevant. What proportion of White Hall instructors – deep in the grassroots – read this magazine in the 1980s is debatable. To get their attention, the *Journal of Adventure Education* had to compete with *Mountain* magazine, *Climber and Rambler*, *Canoeist* and *Descent*. White Hall instructors also had to keep abreast of the publications of the BMC, the BCU, the RYA and the National Caving Association. Most White Hall instructors were members of a teachers' union, but few joined the NAOE. They tended to spend much of their spare time climbing or caving or canoeing, trying to maintain a reasonable level of skill in their main interests. Increasingly, many instructors also had family responsibilities.

*

In 1982 the Association of Wardens of Mountain Centres renamed itself the Association of Wardens of Outdoor Education Centres, reflecting the diversifying situations of its members.

The Conservative party, led by Margaret Thatcher, easily won the 1983 general election. Her government set about privatising and deregulating, a process that included introducing market mechanisms into health and education.

The UK coalminers' strike of 1984–5 was one of the biggest and most bitter industrial disputes in British history. It has been called 'more a civil war than an industrial dispute'. In some of the pit villages of eastern Derbyshire, minibuses carrying working miners were regularly stoned by pickets and striking miners. The strike tore families apart. The minibuses, mainly Ford Transits, were fitted with steel mesh grilles to protect the windscreens, wire mesh screens to protect the radiators, and Perspex covers on the headlamps. The glass in the side windows was replaced with shatterproof Perspex. Underside fire extinguishers were installed to protect against petrol bombs. Children in the villages witnessed the minibuses daily running the gauntlet, like armoured personnel carriers; their dads or brothers were either in the vehicles or on the pavement, lobbing stones. This became apparent to the White Hall teaching staff when they noticed that some pupils from the coalmining areas of Derbyshire expressed a reluctance to travel in the centre's Ford Transit minibuses.

Peter Arkell

Miners or their supporters attacking the police vans carrying strike breakers. 1984, Rossington, Yorkshire. Similar scenes took place in southeast Derbyshire.

The strike ended in March 1985 following a National Union of Mineworkers vote to return to work. The union's defeat was a political triumph for Margaret Thatcher and the Conservative Party. In the years that followed, many mines would close for ever.

County councils in England and Wales were an upper tier of local government. They provided major local services such as education, social services and transport. In 1984 Margaret Thatcher's Conservative government had introduced legislation that would give it powers to limit the spending of local councils. The limiting was known as rate-capping. The powers to rate-cap first came into effect in the financial year 1985–6. Central government determined the rate-capping criteria each year; if the government thought a local council's budget to be excessive with regard to general economic conditions, the government could set a maximum budget.[20]

Over the following three decades, the willingness of Margaret Thatcher and of her successors to rate-cap, limit and control local democracy in England would be one of several causes of a widespread fall in the number of LEA residential outdoor education centres.

*

In 1987, legislation to outlaw corporal punishment in state schools came into effect, but corporal punishment remained legal in independent schools. Not until 1999 would caning be banned in all schools.

Also in 1987, Marion Shoard's erudite and penetrating book *This Land is Our Land* appeared, exposing a rural ownership regime still based on feudal principles.

Regarding excessive and inflexible safety regulations, an important and original piece of writing appeared in 1988. This was *Outdoor Education Safety and Good Practice – Guidelines for Guidelines*. Published by the Duke of Edinburgh's Award, it was an unusually successful result of collaborative writing by representatives of about five organisations. The climber Pete Livesey called it 'a revolutionary, and against the grain, guide to the construction of operating regulations in outdoor pursuits in educational or instructional settings.'[21]

*

The government's assault on the local authorities intensified after Margaret Thatcher was returned to power as prime minister for the third time, in June 1987. 'The power of the local education authorities had to be destroyed – or, at least, undermined – because LEAs were a focus of opposition to the Conservative Government and could impede the process of transforming secondary education.'[22] The Education

Reform Act 1988 set into motion the most radical reorganisation of education since the Butler act of 1944. The July 1988 act included, for schools in England and Wales, a prescriptive curriculum that was mainly concerned with measurable skills and with learning fashioned towards attainment targets and graded tests. The act designated three or four core subjects (English, maths and science, plus Welsh in Welsh-speaking schools) and seven foundation subjects (history, geography, a foreign language, technology, music, art and physical education). The act did not contain the words 'outdoor education'. In a letter to the education secretary Kenneth Baker, the NAOE included the statement: 'We fear ... that Outdoor Education may become pushed to one side and starved of resources by the introduction of a National Curriculum, particularly one which is based mainly upon academic achievement.'[23]

According to Ken Ogilvie, letters of this sort were 'received' or 'noted' but then quietly filed away.

Most countries have some form of national curriculum, but the levels of detail vary. In comparison to many countries' schemes, the National Curriculum for England and Wales that arose from the Education Reform Act 1988 was relatively rigid. To some observers, schooling appeared dependent on a recipe handed down by the government rather than being the exercise of professional expertise by teachers.

A further reform called the Local Management of Schools granted schools the option of directly controlling their own budgets. Those schools that chose this option would also be able to decide how the money was spent. A county council would retain only 10 per cent of this money as a central fund to maintain linked services such as school meals and outdoor centres. The figure of 10 per cent was scheduled to shrink to 7 per cent in about 1994. The money available to keep LEA outdoor centres running would decrease.

Following the Education Reform Act 1988, the Curriculum Council set up national working parties to thrash out the practical details for each subject on the curriculum. The outdoor-education community – scattered across the UK, diverse and disjointed – now needed to involve itself in a long struggle to retain outdoor education in the curriculum. If you have read the whole of this book, your mind might now be going back to Chapter 10, to the year 1955, and to 'Seeking Respectability'.

In 1989 various outdoor education and environmental education organisations threw themselves into this process, stressing the cross-curricular or holistic contributions that their movements could make if officially recognised by the curriculum. In April 1989, the heads of outdoor education centres, meeting at White Hall, discussed the low prominence of outdoor education in the draft curriculum papers and they agreed to produce a paper explaining and promoting outdoor education's links with other subjects in the curriculum.[24]

Nationally, some competition between environmental education and outdoor education had bubbled on for years, perhaps occasionally flaring up among Men of Affairs (there weren't many women involved) but hardly registering at a grassroots level. Compared to English departments and mathematics departments, outdoor studies and outdoor pursuits were low-status departments in most schools, always vulnerable to funding cutbacks, always defending their spots on the edge of the educational stage. In this struggle for recognition, they ought to have been allies, and they sometimes were, but sometimes they competed against each other.

An example of this staking-out of territory (some of it overlapping) and of the competing for position at the tough end of the curriculum hierarchy, and of the gradual development of policy, can be seen if we compare the first, second and third editions of the *Directory of Centres for Outdoor Studies in England and Wales*, published by the Council for Environmental Education. The first (1970) and second (1973) editions attempted to scoop up every outdoor centre that existed (in England and Wales), ranging from places that offered solely outdoor pursuits to places wholly concerned with environmental education. White Hall appeared in the 1970 directory. It came into a category labelled 'Field studies [are] subsidiary'.[25] The third (1981) edition dropped all the centres that offered only outdoor pursuits, including White Hall. It carried a note: 'Those centres which are exclusively concerned with outdoor recreational pursuits have not been included. Details of these centres may be obtained from the Sports Council ...'[26]

It is interesting to reflect that in the early 1900s at Bootham School – a place that was mentioned in Chapter 4 – field studies (the Natural History Society) and outdoor pursuits (the summer camps) coexisted happily, as they still do in many schools today.

October 1989 saw the timely arrival of *In Search of Adventure: A Study of Opportunities for Adventure and Challenge for Young People*, edited by John Hunt. A review in *The Times* judged it to be 'probably the most thorough analysis yet undertaken of the adventure provision that has become woven into the fabric of education ...'[27]

On 22 January 1990, a delegation led by Lord Hunt briefed the minister for education, Angela Rumbold, about the effects the Education Reform Act 1988 was having or was expected to have on outdoor education.[28] The delegation raised six areas of concern:

1. Because outdoor education was not mentioned in the national curriculum, it would have a low priority in curriculum planning. Residential experiences would be less likely to take place within school hours. Teachers needing outdoor qualifications would be at the end of the queue for in-service training money.

2. Under the Local Management of Schools, money previously allocated to outdoor education could be used for other purposes. The priorities and opinions of school principals would become all important. LEA centres were likely to disappear or become commercial.

3. A tight control of staffing levels under Local Management of Schools had made it more difficult for teachers to involve themselves actively in outdoor education. The general level of teacher competence in adventurous outdoor pursuits was likely to decline.

4. Charging for out-of-school activities – often involving asking parents for 'voluntary contributions' – was hindering outdoor education. Children in poorer areas would be less likely to participate.

5. LEA residential outdoor centres were a unique provision, unparalleled in other countries, but they had no formal recognition as schools. This lack of official status increased their vulnerability to the other changes already listed.

6. In addition, unconnected with the Education Reform Act, some recent accidents involving school parties had heightened public concern about safety on school trips. Teachers were becoming increasingly wary of the responsibility involved in providing adventurous outdoor pursuits.

The outlook for outdoor education looked grim. Without any specific recognition in the curriculum documents, outdoor education would not be a subject and would therefore be irrelevant as it would not meet the stipulated criteria.

School-based management was not just a British initiative; it was part of an international trend. The implementing of local management of schools began in April 1990. For LEA-owned outdoor education centres, which were considered by many teachers to have spearheaded a major advance in educational philosophy and practice, 'survival in a cut-throat business world became the name of the game'.[29]

One indication of the likely influence of market forces was already visible in the branding literature coming from some outdoor centres, especially from privately owned ones. In 1964 Jack Longland had warned the delegates at the second conference of mountain centres against making excessive claims for the benefits of short courses at residential outdoor centres. Also in the 1960s, Tom Price, when he was warden of Eskdale Outward Bound MS, had been embarrassed by the extravagant claims made by the Trust's public relations person. That was a long time ago. By 1990, grandiose claims for the benefits of short residential outdoor education courses had begun to appear in glossy centre information brochures, more eye-catching than anything previously available and accompanied by declarations of academic verification. But Longland was now eighty-five and Price was about seventy-one, and no comparable younger figure possessed the authority and charisma to question the rhetoric influentially. Besides, most of outdoor education's movers and shakers were fully occupied themselves in talking up the value of outdoor education, not pointing out its limitations or that some of its main benefits were immeasurable.

In a 1990 document on the whole curriculum, the National Curriculum Council recognised, to the relief of outdoor educators, the cross-curricular value of outdoor education:

> Outdoor Education can make a significant contribution as a focus of cross-curricular work. Many youngsters leave home for the first time when going to an outdoor centre and the experience of living in a community with others, sharing objectives and testing themselves in new environments can be rewarding. There is value in sampling activities which may become the basis of life-long outdoor pursuits: in addition, outdoor education provides an ideal opportunity for fieldwork in geography, science, physical education, environmental education and for education for citizenship.[30]

There was one niche in which outdoor education could claim to have subject status rather than merely cross-curricular value. This was, of course, physical education. The connection between OE and PE remained obvious and indisputable, despite the lifelong efforts of some outdoor educators to downplay this connection or even deny that it existed, sometimes in a way that let slip a subliminal message to their PE-friendly peers, Pity you! We know best.

On 19 February 1991, the government published the interim report of its working group for the curriculum in physical education. The report recommended that children should participate in six components of physical education, two of which were 'swimming and water-based sports' and 'outdoor education and adventure activities'. On the same day, Kenneth Clarke, the education secretary, voiced his disquiet on many of the recommendations. In particular he questioned whether money and time would be available for the teaching of swimming and dance and outdoor education.[31]

Later the same year, among the hundreds of pages of curriculum material, just a few words dangled a gossamer lifeline to outdoor educators, in a paragraph in the final report of the working group:

> Outdoor education can make its unique contribution through: sharing experience with others, perhaps in a challenging environment; exploring personal beliefs, attitudes and values whilst living and learning with one's peers; working in small groups in a collective enterprise such as a science or arts based outdoor study or a challenging journey; and using the gifts of each individual toward the development of the group as a whole.[32]

Some of us at White Hall in the early 1990s were only vaguely aware of the spreading plight of LEA centres nationally. I, for one, had hardly noticed the arrival of the Education Reform Act 1988. I had been wrapped up in a local world since the mid-1980s. Developing the cycling had engrossed me creatively. But if I had been a *Guardian* reader, an article in April 1991 might have alarmed me. The newspaper reported that Derbyshire had cut £16.6 million (5 per cent) from its education budget to avoid rate-capping. Schools that had their own swimming pools would receive no money to run them. The peripatetic music service would be scrapped, meaning forty-five jobs lost. Cuts would also be made in sixty other areas. Four hundred teaching jobs and seventy administrative jobs would be lost. Tuition in sailing for pupils at Ogston Reservoir and at Errwood Reservoir would end.[33] White Hall was facing at least funding cuts, if nothing worse.

Doug Jones remembers the abrupt beginning of the end of the schools' sailing unit at Ogston: 'I can't recall the exact date but sailing was stopped very unexpectedly and even the three staff working there did not know about it. They were given days to mothball the boats and kit and lock the doors behind them. They were then to be made redundant but were actually redeployed.'

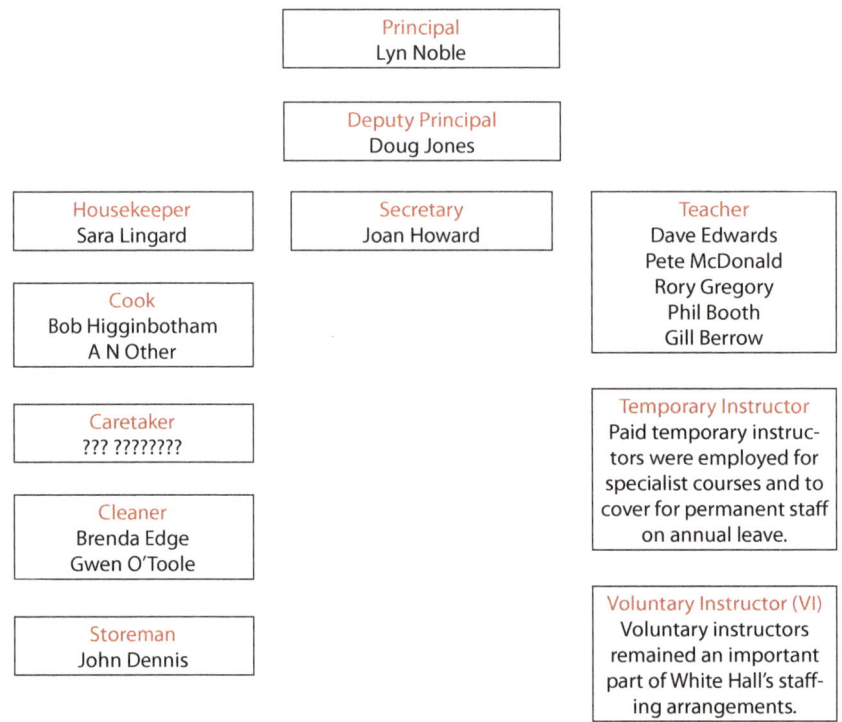

White Hall's staffing structure in February 1992, before the centre entered a long period of frequent change. All positions, except temporary instructors and voluntary instructors, were full-time and permanent.

In February 1992, I left, heading for New Zealand. Max Holliday, a well-qualified and experienced instructor and teacher, replaced me, initially on a temporary basis. In March, Lyn Noble retired after twenty-two years in charge of White Hall, an enigmatic period: viewed close up, a time of two sharply contrasting halves; viewed from a distance, and blurred by the magnitude of subsequent events, a time of adequate funding and relative stability. Our departures cleared the decks for new blood to invigorate the centre. But the new principal and his or her staff would be facing not just unprecedented funding cutbacks and fundamental changes in operations, but also the possibility of closure. Ten years later, in 2002, writing about the role and status of LEAs in 1945–2000, Clyde Chitty summarised the changing circumstances as having been times of 'post-war pride and *fin de siècle* uncertainty'.

From the mid-1940s until the mid-1970s, most of Britain's political establishment had shared a tacit governing philosophy which had embraced a broad commitment to the idea of a national system of education, locally administered. 'It was believed that the tripartite partnership established between central government, local government and the individual schools and colleges involved a network of checks and balances which would ensure the effective distribution of power throughout the system.'[34] Part Two and Part Three of this book have been about outdoor education in this period of consensus and postwar pride, the earliest decades of which involved bold and usually productive advances into uncharted terrain.

The tripartite partnership had begun to break down in the late 1970s when economic dislocation and a national identity crisis had ushered in a new era of accountability and sanctions. The trust and confidence that central government had once placed in the competence of LEAs had gradually collapsed.[35] By the early 1990s, LEA education in general and outdoor education in particular were firmly in the grip of the *fin-de-siècle* state of suspense.

Part 4 will trace the turbulence through the 1990s and into the 21st century. It will try to determine whether the wretched uncertainty has lingered into the most recent years.

Endnotes

1   Ken C Ogilvie, *Roots and Wings: A History of Outdoor Education and Outdoor Learning in the UK* (Lyme Regis, UK: Russell House Publishing, 2013), pp. 305–306.

2   Quoted in ibid., p. 361.

3   Harold Drasdo, *Education and the Mountain Centres*, 2nd edn (1972, 1973; repr. Penrith: Association for Outdoor Learning, 1998), p. 6.

4   Ken C Ogilvie, *Roots and Wings: A History of Outdoor Education and Outdoor Learning in the UK* (Lyme Regis, UK: Russell House Publishing, 2013), pp. 383–384.

5   T M Parker and K I Meldrum, *Outdoor Education* (London: J M Dent and Sons, 1973), pp. 87–90.

6   Ken C Ogilvie, *Roots and Wings: A History of Outdoor Education and Outdoor Learning in the UK* (Lyme Regis, UK: Russell House Publishing, 2013), p. 433.

7   Lynn Cook, 'Outdoor Education: Its Origins and Institutionalisation in Schools with Particular Reference to the West Riding of Yorkshire Since 1945' (PhD thesis, University of Leeds, 2000), pp. 186–187.

8   T M Parker and K I Meldrum, *Outdoor Education* (London: J M Dent and Sons, 1973), p. 89.

9   Ibid., p. 90.

10   Ibid., p. 115.

11   Derbyshire Record Office, Monograph: Hill and Water Sports in British Education: Peter Mosedale, 1975, D7786/BOX/1/Bundle 5.

12   Ibid., p. 68.

13   Ibid., p. 30.

14   'New Youth Hostel in Longdendale', *Manchester Guardian*, 12 Feb 1958, p. 5.

15   John Porter, *One Day as a Tiger: Alex MacIntyre and the Birth of Light and Fast Alpinism* (Sheffield: Vertebrate, 2014), pp. 22–23.

16   J L Longland, 'Everest, 1933', *Fell and Rock Journal*, 9, no. 3 (1933), pp. 327–343 (p. 342).

17   Ken C Ogilvie, *Roots and Wings: A History of Outdoor Education and Outdoor Learning in the UK* (Lyme Regis, UK: Russell House Publishing, 2013), p. 468.

18   Ibid., p. 489.

19   Ibid., p. 539.

20   Carl Emmerson, John Hall and Michael Ridge, *The Impact of Expenditure Limits on Local Government Spending: Evidence from the United Kingdom*, Working Paper Series; no. 98/5 (London: The Institute for Fiscal Studies, 1998), pp. 1–3.

21   Quoted in Ken C Ogilvie, *Roots and Wings: A History of Outdoor Education and Outdoor Learning in the UK* (Lyme Regis, UK: Russell House Publishing, 2013), p. 533.

22   Clyde Chitty, 'The Role and Status of LEAs: Post-war Pride and Fin de Siècle Uncertainty', *Oxford Review of Education*, 28, no. 2 & 3 (2002), pp. 261–273 (p. 266).

23   Quoted in Ken C Ogilvie, *Roots and Wings: A History of Outdoor Education and Outdoor Learning in the UK* (Lyme Regis, UK: Russell House Publishing, 2013), p. 508.

24   Ibid., pp. 514–515.

25   Council for Environmental Education, *Directory of Centres for Outdoor Studies in England and Wales* (London: Council for Environmental Education, 1970), pp. ii, 4.

26   Council for Environmental Education and Carolyn Cocke, *Directory of Centres for Outdoor Studies in England and Wales*, 3rd edn (Reading: Council for Environmental Education, 1981), p. 1.

27   David Tytler and Ronald Faux, 'Are the Young Game for a Lesson?', *The Times*, 13 Nov 1989, p. 35.

28   Ken C Ogilvie, *Roots and Wings: A History of Outdoor Education and Outdoor Learning in the UK* (Lyme Regis, UK: Russell House Publishing, 2013), pp. 518–520.

29   Ibid., pp. 509–511.

30   Department of Education and Science, *Curriculum Guidance 3: The Whole Curriculum* (London: HMSO, 1990). Quoted in David Hopkins and Roger Putnam, *Personal Growth through Adventure* (London: David Fulton Publishers, 1993), p. 194.

31   John Goodbody, 'Clarke Sends Advisers back to Think Tank', *The Times*, 20 Feb 1991, p. 38.

32   Department of Education and Science and Welsh Office, *Physical Education for Ages 5 to 16: Final Report of the National Curriculum Physical Education Working Group* (London: HMSO, 1991). Quoted in David Hopkins and Roger Putnam, *Personal Growth through Adventure* (London: David Fulton Publishers, 1993), p. 67.

33   'Making a Meal of Dinners', *Guardian,* 16 Apr 1991, p. 21.

34   Clyde Chitty, 'The Role and Status of LEAs: Post-war Pride and Fin de Siècle Uncertainty', *Oxford Review of Education,* 28, no. 2 & 3 (2002), pp. 261–273 (p. 261).

35   Ibid. (p. 261).

Part Four:
Change, 1992–2017

22. Doug Jones and Chronic Uncertainty, 1992–2004

We start Part Four in March 1992. Doug Jones is the acting White Hall principal. He is living in, as all the previous principals had done. He would not be appointed principal until the post of Director of Derbyshire Outdoors was established. Outdoor education in the UK is entering a very long period of destructive uncertainty and enforced change. The funding of many LEA residential outdoor education centres has become vulnerable to cuts caused by two national policy reforms. The first is the government's general policy of limiting the spending of local councils, if necessary by rate-capping their budgets; this policy is part of an overall strategy to reduce public spending as a share of national GDP. The second influence is the 1988 Education Reform Act, which has fundamentally changed the relationship between the Department of Education and Science (DES) and local education authorities in England and Wales.[1] The act has reduced local authorities' discretion to set policy. It has defined a new role for local education authorities. It has given new responsibilities to schools and colleges. In effect, the act has challenged each local authority's role both from above (the DES) and from below (the schools and parents). Two particular consequences of the act look set to affect outdoor education in England and Wales: the local management of schools and the national curriculum. The act has also reformed the education system in Scotland, but at a slower pace.

For Doug Jones, the step up, working in a job that is dear to his heart, should be a career high point for all the right reasons; instead he finds himself grappling with the first severe cuts in spending, the start of a long fight to keep the centre open.

In 1992, all over the country, LEA outdoor centres are beginning to wrestle, somewhat shell-shocked, with a period that Ken Ogilvie would later call 'the numbing nineties'. I will adapt a couple of his sentences: at the start of the 1990s, the curriculum reforms (entailing for outdoor education philosophical shifts or adjustments) and the financial difficulties brought on by the Education Reform Act 1988 and by local management of schools mean that for many LEA centres it is a survival time of 'adapt or die'.[2] After decades of beneficial development and of relative constancy, the LEA centres are facing a period of turmoil, confusion and anxiety in a climate that is anything but benign.[3]

Locally in 1992, some aspects of Derbyshire are now very different from their state in the Derbyshire of White Hall's birth. In 1950, eastern and southern Derbyshire had over fifty collieries, employing 60,000 people. In Derbyshire in 1992, only three British Coal collieries remain – Bolsover, Markham and Shirebrook. They would all close in 1993.[4] On the other hand, in 1992 the headquarters of Rolls-Royce are still in Derby. Rolls-Royce, with over a hundred years of history behind it, has recently emerged from state ownership. The firm is still making jet engines, some of the most complex machines on the planet, and is in the early stages of becoming an industrial star and a wealth creator.

Derbyshire education committee has already experienced a squeeze on expenditure. It had been forced to cut £16.6 million from its education budget for 1991–2. Despite this, nobody at White Hall in March 1992 is expecting the teaching-staff redundancies that are soon to occur. These will be the first of several unavoidable changes, beyond the control of Derbyshire county council.

Before we continue, let's pause for a moment to sketch the centre that we are leaving behind. To do this, I will turn the clock back a few weeks, from March back to February. In late February 1992, White Hall had seven permanent full-time teaching staff: Lyn Noble (who had announced his coming retirement), Doug Jones, Dave Edwards, Pete McDonald (who was about to emigrate), Phil Booth, Rory Gregory and Gill Berrow. All seven were qualified teachers, vaguely familiar with although not necessarily users of the word 'pedagogy'. (If this word is new to you, 'pedagogy' is to 'teaching' what 'speleology' is to 'caving': the scientific aspect, but not the art, of the activity.)

Schools' courses were almost exclusively for secondary schools (just one or two primary school courses had been piloted in 1991). The schools' courses had changed only slightly in twenty years and were fully booked. Group instructors wrote course reports. The instructor-pupil ratio for activities like climbing and general adventure was often 2:10. The equipment stores were well stocked. Caving had been suspended because of concerns about radon gas; in an effort to compensate for the loss of this core activity, the centre had a new mountain-biking unit.

Transport took the form of three Ford Transit minibuses, an arrangement dating back to about 1976. The centre had a governing body,
which I think had been set up in the 1980s. The term 'risk management'
had not arrived at White Hall. The office had acquired a second-hand
IBM computer but only one or two people knew how to use it. The
internet hadn't arrived.

Still imagining ourselves at White Hall in late February 1992, for
forty-two years the minimum age for course members on White Hall
schools' courses had been thirteen. On supplementary courses and specialist courses it had been fourteen and fifteen respectively. Just a few
rare exceptions to the minimum age had occurred. The annual family
weekend, listed in the 1975–6 programme, had taken children of eight
years old or older. An occasional primary-school group had begun to
appear in the late 1980s. But nobody in February 1992 was anticipating
the sudden and urgent imposed change that in the mid-1990s would
greatly reduce the minimum age limit for White Hall courses, sweeping
away the tradition of working mainly with the secondary age group.
This change would amount to an emergency reversal of the previous
secondary-only policy. It would be White Hall's adaptive response to a
fall-off in bookings from the secondary schools, connected to the local
management of schools policy and the national curriculum.

Another national change that would affect White Hall would result
from several high-profile accidents at other British outdoor centres.
Generations of White Hall instructors had prided themselves on their
professionalism, but in February 1992 the Lyme Bay tragedy had not
yet occurred, and nobody at White Hall was predicting that the government would bring in the compulsory licensing of many outdoor
pursuits centres, or that this change would hasten the arrival of formal
risk management.

Finally, nobody knew that, after adjusting to these extensive changes,
White Hall and other surviving outdoor centres would need to weather
the global financial crisis of 2007–8 and the subsequent global recession of 2008–12.

Part Four examines White Hall's determined but uncertain advance
through the traumatic 1990s and into the first seventeen years of the
21st century. One of the main thematic aspects of this book has been
the division of the happenings into local developments (at White Hall)
and national developments (in England and Wales and sometimes also
in Scotland). In Chapters 8, 10, 11 and 13 of Part Two, the national
developments were separated from the local ones and were relegated

to the end of each chapter. In Part Three, the national developments were allocated whole chapters, 19 and 21. The three chapters of Part Four will approach the task differently, to suit a very different era. Throughout the period 1992–2017, the national developments, coming from London, were to the fore, setting the local agendas; the LEA centres could only try steadfastly to stay afloat, before being swamped by the backwash of another indiscriminate ideological wave coming from Westminster. So Chapters 22, 23 and 24 will leave the local and national strands entwined and will switch back and forth between the two. The chronology and the themes will compromise with each other, taking turns to be in charge.

One other thing. Except for a few brief mentions, Part Four will not attempt to cover the growth and accomplishments (or difficulties) of Britain's hundreds of privately owned or trust-subsidised residential outdoor education centres. The intention, in examining the national happenings, will be to discover their effect on the LEA residential outdoor centres and in particular on White Hall Centre.

April 1992 – the Inevitable Bombshell

One day in April 1992, the *Guardian* reported that Derbyshire county council's education committee had agreed on £6.27 million of cuts, which were necessary for the county to avoid rate-capping. County officers had advised the councillors that staff reductions were inevitable and that 'there could be redundancies at outdoor pursuits centres and in the youth service'.[5] The council's narrow boat and sailing dinghies were to be sold. (Initially the dinghies were mothballed. They would be sold later, in 1993 or 1994.)

In looking more closely at how the national happenings of the early 1990s affected White Hall Centre, we are fortunate in having an MA dissertation scrutinising this precise subject. In 1992 Phil Booth took a year's unpaid leave to examine the potential impact of a proposed reduction in net expenditure of £50,000 during the financial year 1992–3. The introduction to his dissertation laid out the guts of a critical situation that confronted White Hall in April 1992. The fees for places on the schools' courses had traditionally remained very low in comparison with the fees charged by some other LEA outdoor centres. In March 1992, for example, a place on a five-day schools' course cost £13. 'The declared policy of Derbyshire county council had been to enable "participation by all"'. White Hall's income had remained low; the county councillors had expressed few concerns about this. In 1991–2, the gross expenditure had been about £382,000 and the gross income had been about £42,000, a subsidy of £340,000.[6]

> Over the years DCC [had] been happy to let things continue, so long as Whitehall [sic] seemed to be 'doing a good job'. [I will use the more common spelling 'White Hall' in any further quotes from the dissertation.] Elected members appeared satisfied in the knowledge that the centre was 'getting kids out into the country-side' … There were no major crises.[7]

All this was about to change, and in a way that justifies the oxymoron in the subheading of this section. On 23 April 1992 the education com-mittee decided to require White Hall to generate an additional income of £50,000 in the financial year 1992–3 by increasing the course fees. Ie, the committee required the centre to more than double its income from £42,000 to £92,000. Although some commentators had viewed this change as inevitable, the size and urgency of the stipulation came 'as something of a bombshell for which White Hall was totally unpre-pared in terms of a planned practical response'.

Booth summed up the implications of the education committee's requirement:

> White Hall [in April 1992] is certainly at one of the most criti-cal points in its history. Its future is in the balance. If it can 'save' £50,000 by March 1993 it may have a future. Even then, that future is uncertain since DCC will almost certainly be facing another round of expenditure cuts.[8]

After several crisis budget meetings between the White Hall teaching staff and county council representatives, a final proposal emerged that required the centre to save £24,000 in costs while also raising income by £40,697. This modified proposal was approved by a members' execu-tive group of the Community Education Consultative Committee on 22 May 1992.

The aims of Booth's research were:
- to build a picture of the management of White Hall prior to April 1992;
- to examine the immediate impact of the cuts upon the centre;
- to consider the longer term implications of those cuts; and

- to apply an action-research approach to the problem of the cuts in order to make a positive contribution to the process of change at White Hall.[9]

Specific objectives arising from these aims included examining the purpose of White Hall, examining the managerial decision-making, and examining the marketing of the centre.

At the outset of his research, Booth identified several themes that would obviously become relevant parts of the wider enquiries. One was the management of change, an area that had received little attention in the past but which would now be critical for the survival of the centre. Closely related to this theme was the possibility or likelihood of resistance to change. The White Hall teaching staff were committed idealists, immensely experienced, impressively qualified, thoughtful and articulate, but they were hardly business-minded; they were more familiar with vigorous exercise than with vigorous marketing. Another theme identified at the start was the clarity of White Hall's objectives. For example, did a mission statement exist? For whom did the centre exist?[10]

A short chapter explained the study's methodology. A key feature of Booth's approach had consisted of semi-structured in-depth interviews with sixteen people involved directly or indirectly with White Hall. These interviews, mostly about an hour long, had taken place between 17 June and 23 July 1992. Among the interviewees were county councillor Geoff Lennox, chair of White Hall's governors, and county councillor Martin Doughty, the leader of Derbyshire county council. Booth also interviewed Ken Chapman, assistant chief education officer.

A large chapter – half of the dissertation (pages 37–92) – then listed the study's findings. Section One of these findings described the historical factors that, if not overcome or reduced in influence, could hinder the process of change. These factors included the lack of a formal well-defined purpose statement for the centre (despite the 1980s efforts to produce one); the absence of a clear rationale stating where White Hall fitted into a county-wide scheme for providing residential outdoor experiences; the lack of financial planning at a strategic level (spending had tended to be random and spontaneous, responding to necessity, rather than planned); the neglect of marketing (which had come about partly because most courses were oversubscribed); the lack of criteria for deciding the balance between different sorts of courses; and the difficulty of evaluating the centre's overall performance.[11]

Regarding the centre's governing body, Booth said that

its main role has been to provide political 'clout', to get things done at County Offices, and to lobby for White Hall particularly in securing funds for improvements and developments. It has had a passive role regarding the overall purpose of the centre, exerting little influence over general policy. One governor felt uncertain as to how much power the governing body actually had in terms of determining the centre's purpose.[12]

Not all historical factors were potential handicaps. Many were strengths, to be appreciated and preserved. In Chapter 8 of this book, during a mention of gender bias, I stressed that mixed groups had become, in the 1950s, the most common arrangement for White Hall's schools' courses. So it was interesting to read in this authoritative dissertation, in a section on equal opportunities, that several of the people Booth interviewed in 1992 saw White Hall as 'one of the finest examples of real equality of opportunity in action'. In the words of one interviewee, White Hall was 'where I first learnt what equal opportunities really meant in practice'. Some interviewees mentioned the lack of distinction made between boys and girls by White Hall staff in terms of expectations and responsibilities given.[13] In 1991, slightly more girls than boys had attended courses at White Hall.

Section Two of the findings discussed the immediate impacts of the cuts, as observed by Booth in 1992. One immediate impact was improved cooperation between the managers of White Hall and Lea Green, a second residential centre run by Derbyshire county council. This cooperation led to the modified final budget proposal mentioned earlier. Booth viewed the cooperation between the two managements as an improvement in financial planning and in decision-making.

An immediate effect of the retrenchment part of the changes involved staffing. On 7 April 1992 the county had advertised for a permanent full-time replacement for Pete McDonald. But before this vacancy could be filled, the job was changed from full-time to 0.5 of a teaching post. Booth reported that this reduction in staffing had unsettled some of the centre's permanent teaching staff. The impact on staff morale had been heightened by the temporariness of the centre managers' appointments: having an acting principal and an acting deputy principal exacerbated the misgivings of some staff about the future. Doug Jones was doing Lyn Noble's job and Dave Edwards was doing Jones's job, but the county did not advertise for a permanent full-time replacement for Edwards. In just two months, the teaching staff had changed from a principal, a deputy and 5 teachers to an acting principal, an acting deputy and 3.5 teachers. The 0.5 post to replace Pete McDonald was filled by Max Holliday, a very experienced instructor.

A third instant consequence had to do with income generation, in several ways. After May 1992, the course fees for school pupils for a five-day course rose from £13 to £44, a 340 per cent increase. This initially resulted in some reduction in demand, but the new fees still represented excellent value for money. There was a consensus among the interviewees that in the longer term the increased fees would not produce a permanent fall-off in the demand for places. However, most of the people interviewed 'felt that youngsters from a low income background, especially one of unemployment, would not be able to afford the new fees'.[14]

Other immediate changes connected with bringing in more money included efforts to increase the number of pupils attending on day visits, especially from primary schools. Also, the county council allowed the centre managers slightly more freedom in raising income from commercial operations, such as running management-development courses and hiring the accommodation to a business with no connection to Derbyshire schools or to the youth service. Regarding management development, using income from such courses to subsidise less profitable courses was an established strategy of some private outdoor centres. At Brathay Hall the practice was known as 'surplus with a purpose'; in 1992 this approach was already helping Brathay to recover from a financial crisis that had hit the centre in 1988–91.[15]

In summing up the immediate impacts of the cuts, Booth said that since the completion of his interviewing, certain working practices had been suspended to enable more flexible programming and the development of new ideas. After an initial down in the mood of the staffroom, morale seemed to have improved, with a noticeable determination to ensure the success of the measures taken to meet financial imperatives. There was a feeling that the future existence of the centre would depend, in part, upon the success of these measures.

Section Three of Booth's findings examined the longer-term implications of the 1992 funding cuts. The long-term ramifications for the centre's finances were profound. Martin Doughty, the leader of Derbyshire county council, had described the county's financial situation for 1993–4 as 'likely to be dire'. Further reductions in White Hall's subsidy looked not only likely but inescapable. Basic changes in the way that the county council operated were on the horizon. The knock-on effects could possibly

> see White Hall operating under a system of cost centre management. As a local cost centre White Hall would manage itself, and be responsible for planning, budgeting and income generation. The framework for this would be a 'service level agreement' with the County Council whereby White Hall would provide a certain service on the basis of agreed costs which would be underwritten by the authority.[16]

For cost centre management to work at White Hall, several areas would need considering. The centre managers would require expertise in financial management; the existing managers had received no formal training in this. A coherent business plan, looking ahead several years, would be essential. The county would need to decide to what extent White Hall would become market driven, selling its services in what would be a very competitive marketplace.

The funding cuts of 1992 also raised far-reaching questions about White Hall's purpose. Different perspectives existed on the *raison d'être* of the centre. The uncertainty surrounding the future role of White Hall even extended to the process of how this role should be determined:

> Should DCC inform the centre what its role should be? How far should the centre governors take responsibility for deciding the future direction of the centre? What part should the Principal and staff of the centre take in this process?[17]

Booth allocated ten pages to a discussion of these questions and of other longer-term aspects of the centre's purpose. A common concern queried whether the traditional purposes of White Hall, described with some justification by Booth in 1992 as ambiguous (but now exhaustively recorded in this book), might become lost as a result of the pressure of financial imperatives. Bearing in mind that Booth raised this concern in 1992, we should now, in 2017, be able to gain some idea of which aspects of the traditional purposes have survived. Chapter 24 will attempt to answer this question.

Another concern connected with income generation was the possibility that a bums-on-seats priority might develop that would emphasise the throughput of numbers rather than the quality of the learning.

On the other hand, there was also an argument that a slightly diluted experience for a larger number of visitors might be more equitable than a very intense experience for a smaller number.[18]

There was a strong feeling that youngsters from low-income backgrounds would not be able to afford the new fees and that this would become a long-term problem, not just a momentary blip in the centre's user profile, quickly and easily reversed.[19]

Furthermore, White Hall's sudden budget cuts of April 1992 had resulted in much uncertainty about the centre's future role in the training of adult outdoor leaders. Traditionally, Derbyshire county council had heavily subsidised White Hall's INSET courses for Derbyshire teachers and youth leaders. Under the local management of schools policy, the money for training was being devolved directly to the schools. Already, in 1992, the fees increases for White Hall's accreditation courses had resulted in teachers facing very big increases in the personal expenses involved in attending these courses. It was impossible to foresee what importance, if any, the schools would give to training their teachers in outdoor leadership skills. Of critical importance, Booth said, was 'the need to go out and talk to schools in order to identify their training and other needs and to attempt to offer solutions to these needs in as flexible a way as possible'.[20]

Finally, still on the likely longer-term repercussions of the budget cuts, Booth's research had revealed crucial implications for marketing and staffing. He had also found that most interviewees felt that the national curriculum would have a major impact on the centre.[21]

Chapter Five of the dissertation discussed some political and philosophical aspects of White Hall's predicament, such as the power relationship between central and local government. Here, if it's your sort of stuff, you will find some ideas on the pros and cons of second-order change, ie on the pros and cons of profound transformation in basic assumptions and underlying values.

Chapter Six completed the dissertation by providing conclusions and recommendations. The conclusions extracted and summarised the study's main findings, such as the need for White Hall's purpose to be more clearly defined (a move suggested by Pete McDonald in 1983[22] and acted upon internally in 1984). There was hope that the context in which White Hall would operate might be clarified by the publication by the county council of the second version of 'A Derbyshire Approach to Outdoor Education', which in November 1992 was in draft form. On 6 November 1992 the White Hall teaching staff produced another draft aims-and-objectives statement for the centre (the detailed 1984 aims-and-objectives documents having been lost or filed and forgotten). The new statement on the centre's aim said:

> The aim of White Hall is to provide opportunities for all areas of the community to broaden and enhance the quality of their educational experience through active involvement out of doors.[23]

White Hall had waited a long time for this slender but very elastic statement. It was wide enough to accommodate many different needs. But a mission statement means nothing if a centre no longer exists. In 1992, all mission statements in the LEA sector were about to become subordinate to the need to survive and particularly to the demands of financial imperatives and of the national curriculum.

Included among the dissertation's recommendations was a list of practical suggestions. Present and future managers and other staff of White Hall may be curious to know which of these suggestions have subsequently been acted upon; unfortunately, space considerations prevent my reproducing the list here.

White Hall Centre had reached a precarious and pivotal point in its history. The whole of Booth's penetrating dissertation was frank and compelling and urgent. The year 1992 in the life of the centre was not a suitable time for understatement or inflexibility or procrastination. Booth wrote: 'With further cuts [in local authority spending] likely in 1993/94, it is inconceivable that White Hall can continue to rely upon the same level of subsidy as it has enjoyed in the past.'[24]

LEA Funding Cuts and Other Changes, 1992–4

In June 1992 the long-awaited National Curriculum Council's scheme for PE was published. It included Outdoor Adventure Activities (OAAs) as compulsory elements for pupils up to the age of eleven (Key Stages 1–2). The OAAs would be optional after Key Stage 2.[25] The irony was luminous. Outdoor education was finally gaining a mention on the statutory list of what schools should teach, while, concurrently, government policies were ruthlessly demolishing the machine that delivered outdoor education.

White Hall's managers tolerated the irony, stoically, and responded quickly to this curriculum development, deciding in about July to offer more courses for younger pupils.[26] Twenty-five years later, recalling the national curriculum issue, Phil Booth said that there was considerable talk about linking courses to the new National Curriculum through Outdoor and Adventurous Activities. Much of the talk was openly critical because it was felt, by many of us, that the notion represented a dumbing down of the essence of outdoor education, which was all about an approach aimed at developing the whole person in a different way to the traditional school-based approach. Reducing it to a mere add-on to PE … was seen as derisory. In my time (until 1998) I don't think that linking courses to the National Curriculum was ever considered seriously at White Hall in a way that might have had major expression in the content of courses.

Other influences became more significant, particularly adjustment to an increasing number of younger, ie primary-age youngsters, attending courses. This did in part reflect an impact of the National Curriculum in that White Hall could provide in a neat package a means whereby schools could meet one required aspect of the PE curriculum, that being Outdoor Adventure Activities. (Incidentally I recall Dance was an alternative here. The idea that Dance and Outdoor Education could somehow be seen as having equivalent value reinforced the view expressed above that the proposed role of Outdoor Education in the new National Curriculum was seen by many as derisory)

I do recall that early on there was considerable opposition from some staff to primary-age youngsters attending courses. Similarly there was much opposition to the idea that youngsters with special needs might be capable of participating in outdoor activities, both aspects of which were to become standard in the 2000s.[27]

On seeing the OAAs included in the official curriculum, some outdoor educators may have breathed sighs of relief. But any momentary euphoria triggered by this recognition did not last long. In July 1992, a government white paper, *Choice and Diversity: A New Framework for Schools*, proposed an increase in the delegation of funding to schools, thus leaving less money in each LEA's central fund.[28] At the 1992 Conservative Party conference, the prime minister, John Major, said: 'We want to see large numbers of our schools opt out of local authority control and go for grant-maintained status.'[29] The government applied the same destabilising ideology to LEA-run support services. 'There was this immoveable belief in Government circles that local enterprise in free competition would fill any gap arising in LEA provision and that Centres and the Advisory Service could easily be transferred to the commercial sector.'[30]

Amid the gloom, in September 1992 a micro-ray of hope lit up one corner of the scene when, as expected, Outdoor Adventure Activities (OAAs) became compulsory components for pupils up to the age of eleven.

In November, at the annual general meeting of the Association of Heads of Outdoor Education Centres (AHOEC), a list of sixteen centres under threat of closure was drawn up. Some other outdoor centres had faced closure but had found ways to continue, such as by becoming charitable trusts or by transforming themselves into privately owned enterprises. Few LEA residential outdoor centres could any longer consider their futures to be safe. However, regarding the overall effects of the Education Reform Act on outdoor education, 1992 was still early days. The rest of the 1990s would need to unfold before the full effects of the act on LEA centres and on outdoor education in LEA-maintained schools would become apparent.

Outdoor education in many independent schools would continue vigorously – as it had done for a century, since the summer bicycling expeditions at Abbotsholme in the 1890s and the Bootham School summer camps that started in 1903 – perhaps subject to future new safety legislation but untouched by government funding cutbacks imposed on LEAs. The message to any young teacher aspiring to be involved in outdoor education was: find a job in an independent school.

On 30 March 1993 the *Guardian* published a national analysis in tabular form of where the funding cuts were taking place. The physical size of the table, spreading across the whole width of the newspaper page, served to emphasise the widespread national impact of the severe reductions. Of the 116 local authorities surveyed, seventy-four gave figures showing cuts in real terms in education spending. Derbyshire county council was just one out of the seventy-four. In the financial year 1993–4, Derbyshire county council's spending on education would be £12.5 million less than it had been in 1992–3. The county's spending on social services would fall by £11 million.[31]

Writing in the *Guardian*'s weekly education supplement on the same day, Iain McMorrin, a former chair of the AHOEC, spoke for many of the seventy-four LEAs: 'after more than half a century of development, the whole infra-structure of Outdoor Education and Field Studies is in danger of collapse'.[32] An area of education that the UK had successfully pioneered was looking likely to vanish.

The Arrival of Freelance Instructors

March 1993 also saw the appearance of a young and energetic Clare Reading at White Hall, the first of a new, post-bombshell generation of White Hall instructors. Her arrival into what is sometimes called the outdoor industry coincided with the rise of the Great British fixed-term (and often part-time) job. The late 1980s had witnessed an increase, throughout a range of British labour markets, in the use of short-term contract staff. The trades and professions affected ranged from council carpenters to university lecturers. The growing prevalence of fixed-term contracts had led to the term the 'gig economy': workers do a gig here, a gig there. The change was very apparent in education's outdoor sector, many of whose centres were trying to save money. Along with the increase in the use of short-term contracts, there was an increase in the number of self-employed instructors, some of whom operated their own businesses while also working occasionally at residential outdoor centres. Reading remembers the prospect confronting her when she began the freelancing: 'As I emerged [from a postgraduate certificate in education year] the scene had changed, centres had closed and there were more qualified outdoor activity teachers chasing the few jobs remaining in a reduced market.'[33]

The outdoor sector had always hosted a scattering of freelance instructors, seeking paid temporary work. A number of them had worked at White Hall. But most of the instructing at White Hall had always been done by the permanent staff and unpaid voluntary instructors. The employing of Clare Reading, initially as a paid temporary freelancer, marked the start of a wholesale shift – locally at White Hall and also nationally – towards the use of self-employed freelance instructors.

The Arrival of Personal Computers and the Internet

Along with freelance instructors came personal computers. Joan Howard, White Hall's long-serving secretary and office stalwart, retired shortly after Lyn Noble. The position was redesignated to that of administrative assistant. Judith Nicoll was appointed in October 1993, arriving just in time to pilot the office into and through the world of personal computers, word processing, spreadsheets, fax machines, laser printers, scanners, the internet, Wi-Fi, emailing and mobile phones. On 15 November 1994, for example, the *Daily Telegraph* became the first

UK national newspaper to be available online. The web was about to revolutionise the way in which people obtained and consumed information. Also, changes at County Hall in Matlock in the mid-1990s led to the need for White Hall to undertake more of its own administration. Nicoll was the right person at the right time. 'Judith became a real mainstay as the centre took on more of the work from Matlock. She is IT savvy and with the help of Lyndsay Jones and Sue Hallsworth she assembled database records of freelance instructors, client schools and course participants. When Sara was ill, which sadly was on several occasions, Judith was an even greater asset to the centre than normal, coping with some of Sara's work as well as her own.'[34]

Judith Nicoll's efficiency and her dedication to her job – anchored on her belief in the value of the courses that White Hall was providing – would help greatly to sustain the survival of the centre over the following two decades. (At some point in this period, her role would be renamed from administrative assistant to business services officer.)

A significant loss at this time, about 1993 or 1994, was the sale of the Derbyshire schools' fleet of sailing dinghies, which had sat mothballed for a year or two since the closure of the schools' sailing unit at Ogston. Doug Jones found himself in the role of liquidator:

> I was asked to organise the disposal of the sailing assets and was given keys to the storage facility. This was an old school gym in Clay Cross. When I got there there had been a break-in and anything easy to move and worth something had been stolen. This included video recorders and TVs as well as outboard motors. I organised a sale of the boats and was told to sell them for whatever I could. I put an advert in a sailing magazine and word around the county. The wetsuits, life jackets etc came to White Hall and were put into the canoe store.[35]

*

Jack Longland died on 29 November 1993 aged eighty-eight. *The Times* reported that 'his last years, as he had to sit by and watch his educational work being undone by successively tougher Conservative secretaries of state, were sad and frustrating ones.'[36] Jim Perrin quoted Longland's own words: 'I watch with appalled disgust what Mrs Thatcher's successive administrations have visited upon the community of Britain – in the education service, for example, the substitution of a reasonably non-pompous altruism by unashamedly vulgar self-interest.'[37] John Hunt summed up Longland's contribution to education:

> Jack was numbered among a small group of brilliant young men who emerged from the old universities with double firsts in the mid-twenties; they included John Wolfenden and John Redcliffe-Maud, who played leading parts in extending the perspectives and scope of formal education beyond the classroom and into outdoor experience beyond the confines of school playing fields. Those ideas had their genesis in the private sector of education; Abbotsholme and Gordonstoun both preached the equal and complementary values of academic or technical learning on the one hand, and outdoor activities additional to, or instead of, competitive organised sport on the other. This was a concept of education by no means generally accepted in the years immediately after the War ... The establishment of the first local authority Outdoor Activities Centre in Britain, at White Hall, is a monument to the inspirational lead which Jack Longland gave to a more holistic concept of education.[38]

In 2015 the entry for 'Longland, Sir John Laurence (Sir Jack)' in the online version of *Who Was Who* showed the width of Longland's contribution to education and sport: it listed eighteen national commissions, committees and advisory bodies that he had served on.

Derbyshire Outdoors

The review of White Hall staffing, mentioned earlier, had been delayed throughout 1993 because a relevant wider review was already taking place. This was a feasibility study into the provision of outdoor education in Derbyshire. Judith Cook, the head of Lea Green Centre, conducted this county-wide study in 1993–4. From this study, a proposal emerged for Derbyshire to close some self-catering and field-studies facilities and to create one body to oversee and manage White Hall, Lea Green, some urban studies centres and the remaining self-catering accommodation. This new body, which later came to be called Derbyshire Outdoors, would be headed by a 'cost centre principal' appointed from among the existing staff.[39]

The county subsequently advertised, internally, the post of cost centre principal. Between the acceptance of the study's proposal by county councillors and the interviews for the new post there was a notable change of senior positions within the county's education department.

Doug Jones was appointed to the role of cost centre principal. He remembers:

> Had the head of Lea Green been appointed the story of the next ten years may have been very different. On a personal note I was very moved by the level of support from staff during the run up to the interviews. When I got back to White Hall, after being given the news at County Hall that I had been appointed, the staff had been out to buy bubbly and cream cakes and even John Dennis emerged from the stores to celebrate. It is very easy to look back on all the difficult decisions and changes imposed from outside and not remember that overall most staff recognised the changes that were coming and all worked together to respond to them.[40]

Almost immediately the county council made large cuts to the outdoor education budget and informed Jones that he would not be replaced at White Hall but would continue to be the principal of White Hall *and also* the director of what became Derbyshire Outdoors. The next four years were to be ones of survival with budget cuts every year and the need to increase prices and reduce expenditure.

One effect of the cuts at White Hall was an increasing reliance on paid temporary freelance instructors. Jones recalls: 'White Hall was now expected to increase the number of courses whilst at the same time working with a reduction of 30 per cent in its teaching staff. This was only possible by the use of freelance staff. Of course the use of freelance staff increased the administration and management time immensely but as they were not permanent staff they did not appear on the overall staff quota of the county.'[41]

Lyme Bay and Statutory Regulation, 1993–6

Balancing the books was only one component of the challenges facing many UK outdoor educators in the early 1990s. On 22 March 1993, a canoeing tragedy took place that was predictable and preventable and correspondingly shocking, and which would become a defining event comparable to the Cairngorm tragedy of 1973.

On 21 March, twenty-two pupils and two teachers from Southway Comprehensive School, Plymouth, arrived at St Albans Centre in Lyme Regis, which was part of the company Active Learning and Leisure Limited. On the following morning, eight of the pupils and one of their teachers, Norman Pointer, chose to go canoeing. All nine were novices.

The canoeing instructors for the trip, Tony Mann and Karen Gardner, held only the BCU one star award, which was not even a qualification for instructing on a local pond, let alone on the sea in March. The ill-conceived and poorly executed trip – later described in *The Times* as 'an appalling catalogue of errors' – began at the Town Beach at Lyme Regis harbour just before 10am.[42] The eleven canoeists left the beach, intending to paddle two or three miles along the coast to Charmouth and to return to Lyme Regis by lunchtime. The novices were wearing life jackets, the instructors buoyancy aids.

The instructors had not checked the weather forecast before setting off.[43] The novices' canoes did not have spray decks to keep the water out.[44] The centre did not provide any distress flares, nor did the group of eight schoolchildren and a teacher have any other emergency equipment. The only emergency equipment carried by Karen Gardner was a whistle.[45] No support boat was provided for the trip.

The party ran into difficulties immediately. One of the pupils capsized. Tony Mann helped him back into the canoe. Then Norman Pointer capsized, and Mann went to his aid. While Mann was helping Pointer, an offshore wind blew Karen Gardner and the eight pupils out to sea. By 12.30pm, Gardner and the eight pupils were all swimming.

A series of critical delays meant that the first rescue helicopter was not scrambled until 3.56pm. Similarly, the Lyme Regis inshore lifeboat was not launched until 4.20pm. Over the next two and a half hours, all eleven canoeists were picked up, but one pupil had died in the water and three others succumbed to hypothermia in hospital. The pupils who died were Dean Sayer, seventeen years old, and Simon Dunne, Claire Langley and Rachel Walker, all sixteen.[46]

A few days after the deaths, David Jamieson, the Labour MP for Plymouth Devonport, put forward an all-party motion in the Commons proposing a national register to regulate outdoor activity centres.[47] Partly as an attempt to forestall the imposition of a mandatory scheme, several voluntary codes of practice and systems of centre accreditation had already been evolving under the control of various organisations. The campaigners for a statutory scheme welcomed these voluntary initiatives but considered that they did not go far enough.[48] Most coverage in the national press supported these campaigners. Much public opinion favoured statutory supervision of all providers.

On 30 July, two months after the tragedy, a Devonshire county council inquiry report said that 'the immediate cause of the tragedy was … the lamentable failure of the St Alban's Centre to organise and supervise the canoeing activity, to employ suitable staff and to have prepared and operated sensible and predetermined procedures when difficulties arose.'[49]

The report also backed up Jamieson's idea, calling for the national register of adventure activity centres. Jamieson welcomed this support. He said: 'Hundreds of thousands of children are at risk this summer – and I don't think that is any exaggeration.'[50] The pros and cons of his proposal, however, immediately became the subject of complicated argument. The matter became highly controversial. Informed opinion was divided on whether new laws were required to regulate outdoor education in schools and other educational establishments. People disagreed on the need for the mandatory licensing scheme, on the form of the proposed regulator, and on to whom the regulations should apply. The Conservative government was joyfully deregulating a range of areas and was not inclined to create new rules that might stymie private enterprises. In particular, having expressed confidence in the ability of private providers to replace the LEA outdoor centres, the Tories were reluctant to increase the compliance costs of those providers.

Writing in December 1994 in the *Independent*, Celia Dodd gave a parent's perspective:

> This week my son came home from school begging me to let him go on a residential trip next summer. Like many parents, I was apprehensive at the prospect. It has always been hard to send your children away, but the tragedy at the St Albans Centre in Lyme Bay in March 1993 has made many parents question whether such trips are worth the risk.
>
> Accidents happen, but the deaths of those four teenagers should have been avoided. Parents are bound to ask: how many centres are inappropriately staffed? And has anything been done to bring them into line?[51]

A court verdict on the same day may have partly answered Dodd's last question. Since the Lyme Bay deaths, Active Learning and Leisure Limited, the company that ran St Albans Centre, had changed its name to OLL Limited. At Winchester Crown Court, Peter Kite, the managing director of OLL Limited, was found guilty of manslaughter and was jailed for three years. In addition, his company became the first in Britain to be found guilty of manslaughter, a decision that swept away 400 years of legal history.[52] The company was fined £60,000.

By the 1990s, many national-governing-body (NGB) instructing awards, such as BCU Senior Instructor, RYA Senior Instructor, and Mountain Leader, had been evolving for two or three decades or more. These awards' rough edges, if they had once possessed any, had been smoothed off. Much was known about the craft and art of instructing adventurous activities. A person's holding an NGB qualification for instructing or leading at a certain level indicated that he or she could operate competently at that level with the ease of long practice. Qualifications did not guarantee safety, but they went a long way towards achieving it. The manifest negligence evident in the Lyme Bay case – an apparent denial of the need for instructors to be appropriately qualified – was rare.

In the 1950s, knowledge of the dangers of and prevention of hypothermia, which was usually called exposure or exhaustion-exposure, had been sadly lacking. By the 1970s, however, all professionals and most amateurs were alert to the insidiousness and seriousness of hypothermia. From 1972 onwards, for about ten years, the 1972 documentary film *Cold Can Kill* was shown to every member of nearly every White Hall schools' course. But the disastrous Lyme Bay trip had gone ahead, in March, as if immersion hypothermia did not exist.

According to a court report in *The Times*, nine months before the disaster two experienced St Albans Centre instructors had quit their jobs after just five weeks because of their concerns about safety. 'They sent a letter to Kite telling him to take a "careful look" at safety, otherwise he might find himself explaining "why someone's son or daughter will not be coming home".'

Referring to this letter, the judge, Mr Justice Ognall, said Kite had been given notice in 'chilling, clear terms' of the risks he was running. But Kite had completely failed to heed the warning.[53]

The judge called for an immediate and thorough appraisal of the running of activity centres. He said the potential for injury or death was too obvious for safety procedures to be left 'to the inadequate vagaries of self-regulation'.[54] He was essentially demanding government action. This was a rare and stark example of a judicial pronouncement that would lead to legislative intervention.[55]

*

Undeterred by or perhaps bolstered by the furious debate, David Jamieson pressed ahead in parliament with a private member's bill, the Activity Centres (Young Persons' Safety) Bill. This piece of enabling legislation had its first reading on 14 December 1994.[56]

The second reading of Jamieson's bill occupied three and a half hours on 27 January 1995. In his speech introducing the bill, Jamieson mentioned the great changes that were taking place in outdoor education nationally:

> I wish to examine briefly the present position of activity centres and the framework in which they operate. There has been a rapid growth in those wishing to participate in such activities. Local education authority centres have declined in number as more funds have been delegated to individual schools and less has been held back by authorities. Squeezes on budgets have meant that many local education authority centres have closed and commercial centres have filled the gap.[57]

Later in the debate, Mark Wolfson, the Conservative MP for Sevenoaks and an ex-warden of Brathay Hall in Cumbria, voiced an extract from Outdoor Education 101, speaking about the two aspects that were competing for attention: safety and adventure:

> Safety must be balanced against the importance of adventure and, therefore, as others have said in the debate, of some risk. There is a real possibility that safety could become so dominant a theme that the thrill, excitement and challenge of the activities could be squeezed out. Safety standards must be high, exacting and sensible, but an acceptable risk is and should remain part of the activity … The Bill is a necessary sledgehammer to crack a nut, the nut being those very few cowboy centres. They must go. Therefore, the Bill is justified. They must either go or their standards must be dramatically raised.[58]

The bill enjoyed cross-party support. The atmosphere in the House was polite. The speakers were almost sycophantic in their praise for David Jamieson. Nobody dared to disturb the bonhomie by condemning the closures that indiscriminate government policies had wreaked – and were still wreaking – on the LEA centres, most of which had excellent safety records stretching back decades.

The bill received Royal Assent on 28 June 1995, becoming law and bringing in a statutory licensing scheme for a defined range of activities when provided commercially for minors (people under eighteen years old). Many providers fell outside the remit of the act. The act did not apply to schools providing activities for their own pupils or to voluntary bodies that were providing activities to their own members. The act attracted criticism from some individuals in the education sector. The winter 1995–6 issue of the *Journal of Adventure Education and Outdoor Leadership* carried a full-page editorial by Chris Loynes titled 'Why I think the licensing scheme should be scrapped'.[59] Replying frankly to this on the letters page of a subsequent issue, John Driscoll, who had been involved in developing the statutory scheme, was more optimistic:

> Although I have the greatest respect for Chris Loynes' experience in adventure education, I cannot let the pessimistic diatribe against the licensing scheme which formed recent editorials in both the Winter and Spring issues go unanswered. His comments are based on assumptions he has made before the Licensing Authority has even had the chance to formulate its operating procedures, let alone begin to look ahead.[60]

The safety debate centred on whether regulation would be best achieved by voluntary self-supervision or by statutory mandate. Loynes's suggestion, although based on some valid concerns, fell on indifferent ears, or maybe it never reached London. On 26 March 1996, in line with the intention of the Activity Centres (Young Persons' Safety) Act, Lord Henley, the education and employment minister, announced a new adventure activities licensing scheme, whose purpose was to improve safety for children and young people by introducing a regular improved inspection programme beginning on 16 April 1996.[61] In April, the Adventure Activities Licensing Authority (AALA) was set up to implement the scheme, under the guidance of the Health and Safety Executive (HSE). The voluntary-versus-statutory debate, however, was set to rumble on for years.

The attitude of the White Hall staff to the coming of compulsory licensing seems to have been acceptant, with some reservations. Clare Reading recalls:

> I remember two feelings: firstly, that we were happy and confident in our own safety standards, so we would expect to be given a licence and carry on as normal. Secondly, that although we were glad that the 'cowboys' would be identified and [that] the cheap competition they posed would be found out, we were all concerned about the Scout Association not falling within the remit

of the AALA. We all knew of or saw instances of underqualified volunteers continuing to take scouts outdoors.[62]

The first AALA inspection of White Hall Centre took place on 14 January 1997. Kevin Danforth was the inspector. White Hall's first licence, effective from 3 April 1997, specified the activities kayaking (April to October), open canoeing (April to October), paddle surfing (April to October), improvised rafting, sailing (summer), rock climbing, ice climbing, abseiling, gorge scrambling, hill walking and mountaineering, mountain biking, caving and overnight camping (April to October). The licence also acknowledged that other activities might be offered that did not come within the scope of the Adventure Activities Licensing Regulations 1996.

Clare Reading recalls that 'there was grumbling that we had to pay £400 for the licence, when actually we were doing things to the same standard as before', but that this complaint was partly allayed by being granted a licence for two years, while some other centres only received a one-year licence. The new paperwork was also a concern: 'I think we had to do written risk assessments for AALA. We grumbled a bit because we realised that we'd still be doing real-time ones as well.'[63]

Also in January 1997, Marcus Bailie (the head of the AALA inspection services) floated the idea of a voluntary approval scheme for the many operators whose outdoor activities fell outside the statutory scheme, but the cost of implementing such a scheme looked likely to be a stumbling block.[64]

By September 1997 the AALA had issued 875 licences.[65] Legislators had originally envisaged a total of 3,000. The figure 3,000 had been mentioned six times in the second reading of the Activity Centres (Young Persons' Safety) Bill.

I have dwelt at some length on the Lyme Bay tragedy because White Hall Centre, as were hundreds of other outdoor centres, was affected by the resulting Activity Centres (Young Persons' Safety) Act. In the overall scheme of things, the act was just another tightening of the regulatory screw, part of a national and local process that had continued, incrementally, since White Hall's first serious accident involving a pupil (in Bar Pot in 1957). Kim Meldrum had written about the 'slough of certifications' in 1966. But whereas any previous tightenings of procedures had comprised small changes over a long period, the introduction of compulsory licensing was a seismic change in the regulating of outdoor activities. Compulsory inspection is a very severe form of regulation. Only five industries were licensed in this way in the UK. They were the asbestos stripping, the explosives, the nuclear, the offshore oil, and the adventure activity industries.[66]

Doug Jones describes one particular trend that happened in many outdoor centres during this period and which was probably connected, to some extent, to the arrival of statutory regulation:

> Licensing hugely affected people's perception of adventure activities and the risks they apparently offered. At White Hall there was much rear-guard action trying to maintain the adventure in what we did and trying not to just offer activities that may have had perceived risk but whose adventure was minimal or artificial. Throughout the outdoor sector, the advent of on-site activities – purpose-built ropes courses, climbing walls, abseil towers, cycling tracks and artificial caving systems – became the norm. Even White Hall, close to all the attractions of the Peak District, was not immune to this.[67]

By the 1990s, an increasing number of people from all walks of life had begun to ask the questions: where is this regulatory process leading us to? Are we, in attempting to shield our young people from all real risk, denying them a vital part of life: a sense of adventure? Some of the advocates of statutory regulation had conceded that the new layer of legislation could exacerbate the dichotomy between risk aversion and the need for adventure. In July 1993 Simon Jenkin and Philip Jenkinson, the two chief officers from Devonshire county council who had led the internal inquiry into the Lyme Bay deaths, said: 'We do not wish to see a reduction in the number and type of outdoor activities undertaken by young people, and we recognise that there will always be a degree of risk when young people undertake such activities. However, we believe ... a national system of registration is inevitable and, indeed, desirable.'[68]

Risk aversion – or the culture of overprotection – having grown in prominence over many decades, was a constant aspect of society in the 1990s.

Looking back from 2017 at the coming of compulsory licensing, Doug Jones wrote:

> Like many LEA centre heads in the mid-1990s, I felt the licensing scheme was a sledgehammer being used to crack a walnut. It was severely limited in scope, both in the activities and the

people it covered. The saving grace was that it was not run by HSE inspectors with little understanding of how our industry operated, but by inspectors appointed from our field who had the respect of their peers. It brought a new understanding of where the real risks are (many serious accidents involve water) and how they are best managed. I don't think we at White Hall had to change anything we did, but we had to produce a vast amount of paperwork. Gradually over the coming years it became obvious, and the AALA were willing to state, that paperwork did not save lives; experienced, competent, well-led staff did.

By about 2005 the outdoor field felt confident enough in itself to begin to question licensing and to fight back against having a scheme which looked only at safety. We had always felt that safety was only part of the overall equation with quality and learning equally important. This led to the various Quality Mark schemes and Adventuremark which operated to the same standard as AALA but covered all activities and all ages.

White Hall's early inspections were always a collegiate affair with the inspector learning as much from us as we did from him. Very few recommendations were ever made and even those were adapted to work as we wished them to with the blessing of the chief inspector.[69]

Concurrently with the deepening of society's culture of fear, a steady supply of adult mountaineers, canoeists and sailors had of course been heading boldly in the opposite direction. On 13 May 1995, while David Jamieson's bill was on its parliamentary journey, Alison Hargreaves, an ex-pupil of Belper High School, Derbyshire, climbed Everest unsupported and without bottled oxygen, the first woman to do so. Three months later she would make the fifth British ascent of K2 but would die in a savage storm on the descent.

In 1997 the book *The Culture of Fear*, written by Frank Furedi, a sociologist at the University of Kent, gave a fresh impetus to the growing questioning of people's exaggerated perception of the risks present in normal life. A few journalists took up the challenge of warning their readers of the consequences of making safety such an ingrained moral imperative that children would never learn how to assess risk accurately and would be denied any outdoor excitement or adventure. Writing in the *Guardian* in July 1997, Decca Aitkenhead titled her article 'School's out – but the kids are locked up'. She said that in a consumer society which fetishises safety, we are deluded into believing risk *can* be eliminated. We must just try harder, and spend more, and then our children will be safe … in fact, all we end up with is a grotesque blame culture, where we cannot come to terms with the fact that, sometimes, bad things just happen.[70]

Inherently linked to the blame culture was another behavioural phenomenon, not previously mentioned in this book, the compensation game. With the help of no-win no-fee lawyers, an increasing number of people were pursuing border-line or doubtful lawsuits, in which the cards were stacked against innocent defendants. Clare Reading provides a local perspective on this aspect of the 1990s:

> The daytime television got overtaken by adverts from lawyers wanting to take on any case where they might act for someone who has had an accident and hence gain an opportunity to sue someone else. At first County just paid out, being afraid of the legal costs of contesting. We had an example at White Hall where there was a small injury to a pupil properly briefed who slipped from about one foot high on the ropes course. I think it was so obviously a scam for compensation that DCC fought it, and won.
>
>   I had a boy break his arm on Bleaklow. We got him to A&E and his parents were full of thanks for our looking after him, etc. Two weeks later we got a letter of intention to sue for negligence … The loss adjuster visited the site with Doug and declared it to be appropriate. The teaching assistant wrote a verbatim recollection of my briefing, and the claim was halted. The law stated that the child itself has until twelve months after their eighteenth birthday to claim on their own behalf – so the incident hung on the record for another eight years or so.[71]

Risk aversion and alarmism would remain issues in the 2000s, frequently receiving attention in newspapers as well as in books and academic papers. Chapter 23 will touch upon this subject again.

Watch Your Language, 1994–6

Writing in October 2004, Peter Higgins said that the outdoor sector had 'been very poorly informed by research findings'. In the thirty to forty years of higher education involvement (roughly 1960–1995) there had been less than a dozen PhD theses written on the subject area and no major grants awarded.[72] Despite the remorseless uncertainty of the 1990s, however, and sometimes because of it, from about the mid-1990s onwards outdoor education's body of written knowledge had accumulated faster than in earlier times. Perhaps adversity was driving people to the libraries. Higgins continued:

> The research situation in the UK has been changing over the past five to 10 years, and paradoxically at the same time as formal out-of-classroom experiences opportunities have been in decline academic interest has been increasing. It is clearly impossible to summarise the results from this research in a few lines, however, the weight of evidence from MSc and PhD theses, projects supported by small research grants and Government commissioned studies do generally show benefits in out-of-classroom experiences. Perhaps more importantly this evidence points to a latent and undeveloped potential in relation to both curricular studies and lifelong learning.[73]

The situation in the 1990s meant that academic justification for the existence of outdoor education became, for many but not for all practitioners, more necessary than before. But outdoor education's workforce had not always welcomed the influence of academia. There were valid reasons for some people holding reservations about this influence.

Chapter 21 mentioned the beginning in September 1980 of a new magazine called the *Journal of Adventure Education*. Over the course of the 1980s and early 90s, a growing proportion of this magazine[74] (and of its renamed successors, including *Horizons* magazine) consisted of academic articles containing psychological and sociological terms. Outdoor education was not unique in this respect. The infiltration of jargon into the literature of outdoor education reflected the growing use by many other educationists of obscure and technical words, terms that were acceptable when used in moderation and in their proper place, but which 'when put into long, rolling, polysyllabic cadences … induce[d] in the reader listlessness, ennui and ultimately, nausea'.[75] In 1994 Stephen Pimenoff suggested that

> jargon probably has a more deleterious effect on the relationship between theory and practice in education than in any other profession. Scientific papers are written for scientists, medical ones for

doctors; but education theory is not written for teachers, who have little patience with any of it. This is the cause of the tremendous gulf that exists between teachers and educationists.[76]

Pimenoff wondered if the reason for the prolixity had 'something to do with the comparative newness of "Education". The subject had to fight for recognition as an academic discipline, and [was] still not universally accepted. Perhaps educationists [felt] that having their own language [would] bolster their claims to respectability.'[77] If this comment was tenable about educationists in general, it applied even more strongly to writers on outdoor education, who were involved in a subject on the fringe of the curriculum.

Here is an example of a remote tribal dialect, taken from an article connected with abseiling, which appeared in the autumn 1995 *Journal of Adventure Education and Outdoor Leadership*:

> Fifteen Sports Studies students (age 20 ±1.52 years) completed a simple 80 foot abseil. The CSAI-2 reported significant differences ($p<0.01$) in their somatic anxiety scores and an associated reduction in self-confidence, immediately prior to their commitment to the abseil. The data supported a weak inverse relationship ($rho=0.32$ $p=0.24$) between total sensation seeking scores measured using Zuckerman's SS-V inventory and somatic anxiety immediately prior to the abseil.[78]

This conversation would have been perfectly at home in an isolated valley of a neighbouring smaller mountain range. It may have produced iridescent excitement around the fireplaces in that valley. But not everyone was greatly taken with this new way of talking. In spring 1996 an anonymous letter to the journal's editor complained of 'looking at the Journal and finding it all a little academic':

> My colleagues and I haven't yet found on[e] article in this issue that grabs our interest other than to try and analyse the titles. What do they mean? ... Would it, could it, be possible to have one article that is of an inspiring nature ... rather than a ... dry nightmare of long words and boring ideas.[79]

As I have now strayed from the main 1990s story, I might as well complete the digression by taking this topic forwards courageously to today. In 2017, the excessive use of jargon in education remains a cause of poor communications and of a subsequent divide between theory and practice. Ten minutes spent on Google brings up dozens of UK websites dedicated to education jargon-busting.

Redundancies and Closures, National and Local, 1995–8

Moving on now from the polysyllabic cadences, and returning to the fate of Britain's LEA outdoor centres, whatever year we examine from the 1990s, we find closures and redundancies. In the mid-1990s, while the government was considering its response to the Lyme Bay tragedy, the effects of government policies were savaging many LEA centres and their instructors. In April 1995, a television programme reported that thirty outdoor centres had closed over the previous six years and that fifty more were under threat. Neither had the local authority advisers been spared. The number of local authority advisers in outdoor education, able to expertly help schools and teachers, had fallen dramatically. One estimate said the total number of advisers in outdoor education had dropped from fifty in the mid-1980s to five in the mid-1990s.[80] Between 1989 and 1997, Pat Keighley, the outdoor-education adviser for Northumberland, had the unenviable responsibility for closing six residential centres and making their staff redundant, and then he himself was made redundant, a casualty of the only constancy left in the outdoor sector: retrenchment.[81]

Sooner or later the ripples of change were bound to lap White Hall Centre. Some of the timing has been difficult to pin down. The first ripples appear to have arrived in about 1994, when the demand from secondary schools for basic courses began to fall. Bob Higginbotham recalls the time and the onset of adaptation:

> While we carried on, taking lower numbers, we started doing day courses for a couple of local primary/junior schools. Then when the secondary numbers really plummeted, we did our first residentials for primary/juniors. The numbers remained at a pretty constant 40 for quite a while.[82]

Clare Reading remembers that by the mid-1990s, the 340 per cent price rise for schools' five-day courses, imposed in 1992, had contributed towards secondary schools bringing fewer pupils. Doug Jones adds that 'the move from secondary to primary schools was a factor common to much of outdoor education after 1990. It was not only White Hall that was affected by this trend. The change came about for many reasons … Also we were caught up in the increasing worldliness of young people [of the secondary age group] who saw a trip to Derbyshire as less exciting than one to Europe or even further afield.'[83] Reading concurs: 'At one point, secondary schools had a choice of ski trip, cruise (!), Spanish trip (based at a sports complex with one cultural day-trip and not much chance to practise Spanish) or White Hall. I think the foreign trips sounded more exotic but involved two days on a coach. White Hall was the cheapest, so it suffered and was undervalued in two ways.'[84]

At White Hall, typically only about twenty-seven places were being filled out of the forty that had initially been available. In an attempt to fill the empty places, Dave Edwards, who was acting deputy principal, approached the primary schools that had been attending day courses and he persuaded them to try residentials. This development seems to have been a key moment in White Hall's adapting to the new circumstances. The price of the courses did not deter the primary-school parents, who were not usually aware of the previously extremely low fees.[85]

Doug Jones adds that 'increasing the number of schools coming to White Hall inevitably meant running more courses for primary pupils as this was where the demand was. Looking back one can see that this change was happening on a national scale but it would be some years before it became obvious that this was the case.'[86]

*

In February 1995, Jones, observing the parliamentary progress of David Jamieson's bill from an increasingly cash-strapped White Hall office, was well aware that forty-three years of public trust, built up in Derbyshire, was in danger of being eroded and nullified by the failures of one substandard and recalcitrant outdoor centre, located nearly 200 miles away, whose actions had been bereft of both professionalism and common sense. White Hall and hundreds of other well-run outdoor centres would be caught up in the shrapnel from Lyme Bay, but White Hall's reputation was second to none, which made the Jamieson proposals a potential distraction, not to be entirely ignored, but to be kept in perspective. The financial consequences of the local management of schools reform was a far heavier burden on Jones's mind than any curriculum issues or the possibility of having to apply for inspection to stay open. This is clear from a letter he wrote, as a representative of the AHOEC, to the chair of the NAOE on 14 February:

The current budget crisis in education is having a major effect on many outdoor centres and it would be pointless to detail every threat as it would simply be a list of every centre in the country. Some centres are under immediate threat of closure and a worrying trend is the speed with which this happens …

Those centres which are not facing closure are facing a major cut in their subsidies. Cuts of up to 50% are common and the impact that this has on staffing and course costs passed on to students is obvious.

We hope that the current emphasis being placed on quality will ensure the continuing existence of local authority outdoor education provision. The AHOEC feels this is a card we must continually play as it is undoubtedly one of our greatest strengths.[87]

A year later, on 27 March 1996, the *Manchester Evening News* reported that Derbyshire education committee had been forced to chop £12.4 million from its education budget for 1996–7. The article included the blunt news: 'Derbyshire Outdoors, which runs adventure courses for youngsters from Buxton's White Hall pursuits centre, will be told to save £150,000.' Councillor Dave Wilcox, the chairman of the education committee, had said: 'Huge cash cuts of this order will clearly affect scores of adults and youngsters right across the county. But every element of the education service, even services for children with special needs, [has] faced cut-backs. It's time this perpetual erosion of our services was halted.'[88]

Despite the dispiriting background, a 1996–7 White Hall programme of adventure activity courses open to individuals was as ambitious as any annual programme of the past. It listed forty-two courses. The enterprising and partly innovative range included seven different levels of rock climbing course, five levels of hillwalking and mountaineering course, one level of skiing course, three levels of caving course, six levels of canoeing course, two levels of mountain biking course, three types of general activities course for the younger adventurer (minimum age eight), and one type of family weekend. A five-day Peak District Classic Climbs course with an instructor-pupil ratio of 1:3 cost £220 for an adult and £115 for a Derbyshire resident in full-time education. A two-day Moving into Vertical Caving course cost £90 for an adult and £40 for a Derbyshire resident in full-time education.[89]

In about September 1998, in a major and sudden retrenchment, Dave Edwards and Phil Booth were made redundant. When the two of them walked out of White Hall for the last time, out of the door went about forty-three years of institutional knowledge and a considerable state investment in excellence. Wasteful and often precipitate departures of this sort were taking place all over Britain. The way in which the county officers handled these two redundancies in summer 1998, and the haste involved, is not something that Booth and Doug Jones are likely to forget. I will draw on three accounts, starting with a summary from Jones, written in the third person:

> By 1998 further reduction in costs were not possible without losing staff and DCC asked for two teaching staff from Derbyshire Outdoors to take voluntary redundancy. Originally this was to be one from Lea Green and one from White Hall. Two WH staff requested voluntary redundancy (no LG staff requested it) and this was opposed by DJ. DJ was overruled by DCC and Phil Booth and Dave Edwards both left. The feeling in DCC was that WH and LG could share staff and that staff from LG could cover for loss of staff at WH. This ignored completely the fact that the Centres worked in very different fields with differently qualified staff. While it was possible for WH staff to occasionally help out at Lea Green, the reverse was not the case.[90]

Booth adds more details:

> I'm sure there will also be differing perspectives and recollections on our redundancies. I recall there had been an offer for voluntary redundancy (I think for non-teaching as well as teaching staff) on the table in mid-1998 which didn't appear very attractive. However, it became clear that two redundancies from the teaching staff were going to become necessary and that they would be compulsory if a voluntary agreement could not be reached.
>
> We went into a staff meeting on a Monday morning (I think early September) to be presented with an offer which we were told had to be decided upon by the following afternoon. We had the evening to discuss with family etc our choice.
>
> I was given informal advice by my union rep that, for a number of reasons, I was likely to be one of the two compulsory redundancies if I didn't go for the offer. I was pretty indignant about the whole process but, after brief discussion with my wife and two teenage sons, decided to accept the offer. We were all amazed that

Dave also went for the offer since as acting deputy he was under no threat. However, he was appalled at the process and at the way county staff had conducted themselves and he decided to go.

We were presented with the offer on Monday morning and had our leaving interview at County Offices on Wednesday afternoon. We were offered no redundancy advice and were told we could not use any of the county's support services since we were no longer employees.

In view of what I did professionally post White Hall I was happy to have departed at that juncture. Dave and I worked closely together in the following years until his sad death. I went on to teach in a special school as well as running a range of my own training courses before becoming head of Dukes Barn [an outdoor activity centre in Beeley, near Bakewell]. I never heard Dave express regret at leaving White Hall, only disgust at the manner of our departure.

I know my wife and Dave's wife had different perspectives [from ours]. They were both much more aware of the financial downside of leaving secure and relatively well paid jobs for what was potentially a much more stressful and insecure financial future.[91]

Several accounts from onlookers tell a similar story. Clare Reading:

It was very sudden. Everyone knew something drastic might happen … Phil or Dave got their letter on Saturday … It said they had to decide on Monday. The wife of one of them was away for the weekend. On Monday there was a fearful panic. Somebody's figures had been worked out wrongly. Everyone was appalled that county could get something so crucial wrong. They got an extension to Tues or Wed for the revised figures and discussions with partners to be considered. I think it was probably the Wednesday when both Phil and Dave arrived and announced that they were both taking redundancy, as they didn't want to work for such an incompetent authority. Everyone was properly shocked … [Phil and Dave] were so upset at the callous deadline that they just wanted out.[92]

The relationships between White Hall teaching staff and the county councillors and officers had been predominantly harmonious and productive for long periods of White Hall's history. But there had also been some regretful episodes. The handling of the 1998 redundancies was one of these atypical incidents.

Looking back at these redundancies from 2017, it is now possible to see a silver lining for Booth and Edwards: they left just in time to miss the first of three occasions, spread over the years, when the future of White Hall seemed particularly at risk. Memory is a fickle thing, and people I've talked to about those years disagree on whether an explicit proposal to close White Hall was ever made. However, several discussions on reducing White Hall's subsidy to zero definitely took place, and understandably some staff interpreted these discussions as being tantamount to closure proposals. After Booth and Edwards left, some of the remaining staff would still be wary of the possibility of closure twelve years later, in about 2010–12.

One of those survivors was Clare Reading. She recalls the 1998 'closure' plan. There was a real risk that White Hall Centre would cease to exist. She took part in what is sometimes referred to as the first petition against closure: 'Darran and I went down to Matlock to plead our case … It was pretty hostile, especially a councillor whose child had recently been to PGL [a privately owned activity provider] or similar: "You haven't even got quad bikes?" … We tried to sell the developmental and educational values of the centre and of the residential experience. DH and I went because it was after PB and DE had left.'[93]

Doug Jones adds that 'many of the battles to save the centre went on behind closed doors and the staff knew nothing about them. Sometimes there were threats that came to very little or nothing, at other times it felt like a real triumph that we had survived. I remember after Rory became my deputy that he commented one day that he had never fully appreciated before what fights went on in the background.'[94]

Also in this period, some White Hall support staff took voluntary redundancy, and hours were lost from the cleaning and caretaking provision. It was not just teaching staff who bore the brunt of the cuts. Across the county at Lea Green, in a further round of redundancies, two Lea Green staff lost their jobs.

Linking Course Content to the School Curriculum

We saw in Chapter 1 that in the early 1940s some Hertfordshire teachers involved in the County Badge scheme were linking outdoor pursuits and field studies to a range of normal curricular subjects. But most other counties put the badge scheme on hold. As a result of this shelving, two issues that a booming badge scheme might have highlighted were left dormant: the first was the relationship between outdoor pursuits and field studies; the second was the links between both of these sectors and the school curriculum.

Chapters 7, 11, 18 and 21 touched again very briefly on these matters. Nearly sixty years after the Hertfordshire badge scheme, however, the connections between outdoor pursuits and environmental education remained a matter for discussion, if no longer a bone of contention. As also did the connections between the content of adventurous residential outdoor courses and the school curriculum. In 1999, in a book section titled 'Changing Roles for Outdoor Education Centres', Geoff Cooper argued that outdoor centres should become more a part of mainstream education by developing links across the curriculum:

> Arguably, outdoor centres have suffered by the division into field studies and outdoor pursuits. Field study centres have been regarded as more academic and their work linked more closely to the schools curricula. Leaders in these centres are usually referred to as teachers or tutors which reinforces this role. Outdoor pursuits centres have had more problems in justifying their existence partly because the activities they offer are frequently perceived to be associated with leisure and recreation rather than education. This problem can be exacerbated when their 'leaders' are often called instructors rather than teachers, which implies that they are imparting technical skills rather than educating young people.[95]

In reality, said Cooper, the two approaches had much in common and each had a great deal to offer to the other. As regards improving the links with the school curriculum, Chapter 23 will observe how sheer necessity – a will to survive – would drive many centres, including White Hall, in this direction.

A section in Chapter 21 looked at how the job titles of the White Hall teaching staff had changed over the decades. This renaming had not yet ended. Clare Reading, who started working half-time at White Hall in 1993 and who still works there, was called a teacher until 1997. Then, after she was put on Joint Negotiating Committee (JNC) conditions, her job title changed to chief instructor (a job-share with Max Holliday). More recently, her job title became team leader, a label used throughout Derbyshire for employees on her pay scale, in numerous disparate departments.[96]

The change from teachers' pay and conditions to JNC pay and conditions, in about 1996–7, was part of Derbyshire county council's cost cutting. In combination with the European Working Time Directive, which had been introduced in 1993, this cost cutting resulted in several fundamental alterations to the way that White Hall operated as a residential centre. Before this change, whoever was the overnight duty instructor slept in, as had been the routine for decades. In recognition of this work, teaching staff had received an extraneous duties allowance. Under the JNC pay and conditions, the instructors' annual holidays shortened and the extraneous duties allowance ended. From then onwards, except for some summer holiday courses when there were no accompanying adults, White Hall teaching staff ceased to sleep in. The duty instructor worked until about 10pm and then went home; he or she received time off in lieu of the evening hours worked. The overnight supervision after 10pm and the breakfast supervision was done by paid centre assistants, a new role.[97]

The county council appointed four centre assistants to organise evening activities, sleep in, supervise breakfast, run the equipment stores, help with maintenance and assist with activity groups. The involvement on activities was both for the assistants' professional development and to support the increasing presence in standard school groups of children with special needs. 'You would be shocked', Clare Reading told me, 'at the number of children we meet who are labelled ADHD, autistic, "on the spectrum" and as having behaviour difficulties.'[98]

Until 1996, Doug Jones and his family lived in the deputy's house, sometimes called the Cottage, fronting onto the courtyard. He had never moved across the courtyard to the principal's house, a detached newer house built in 1983, the Cottage 'giving more privacy, in as much as it was possible to have privacy when a busy centre was in full swing around your home'.[99] In 1996, as a result of the changes to teaching staff pay and conditions of service, together with the employing of overnight assistants, the requirement for the principal to live in ceased. Jones and his family moved down to live in Buxton, Jones becoming the first White Hall principal to live out.

Access to Land

Chapters 2 and 8 mentioned the legal access issues connected, in the 1950s and earlier, with Combs Moss, Combs Edge, Castle Naze, Windgather Rocks and the Roaches. Since then, the Peak District National Park Authority had purchased the land containing Windgather Rocks (in 1961) and the Roaches Estate (in 1980), thus giving climbers and walkers legal access to these places. Combs Moss and much of Combs Edge remained private land, where in the 1990s some confrontation between walkers and landowners continued to occur. Clare Reading recalls the access situation on this oblong of moorland above White Hall, literally White Hall's backyard, in the late 1990s:

> One of the Combs Moss landowners had fences put up all around his land, so that he had control of the access points. He made no attempt to work with us when the CROW Act was imminent and inevitable. He could have asked us to only use the edges and not to invade the heathery bits, but instead he provoked Doug or Rory whenever possible, ringing up and ranting, blaming White Hall if he had seen anyone on the Moss – and most of the time the trespassers weren't White Hall people. We didn't use the walk along Combs Edge much … We didn't like to expose groups to the rudeness of the gamekeeper.[100]

I am reminded of a verse from 'The Manchester Rambler', written in 1932:

> The day was just ending and I was descending
> Down Grinesbrook just by Upper Tor
> When a voice cried 'Hey you' in the way keepers do
> He'd the worst face that ever I saw
> The things that he said were unpleasant
> In the teeth of his fury I said
> 'Sooner than part from the mountains
> I think I would rather be dead'

April 2000 brought the Countryside and Rights of Way Act 2000 (the CROW Act), a substantial reform of the laws governing walking access to land in England and Wales, after nearly a century of debate and various levels of conflict. The National Parks and Access to the Countryside Act 1949 had assumed that planning authorities in England and Wales would negotiate with private landowners to establish access land, typically comprising open moorland rather than enclosed fields. In these agreed areas of uncultivated land, whose boundaries would be shown on the topographic maps, the public would have the 'right to roam'. Nearly forty years later, only about 100,000 acres or just 0.3

per cent of the total area of England and Wales was covered by access arrangements.[101] Several planning authorities had not made any access agreements whatsoever. Reasoned discussion had largely not fulfilled the vision of the 1949 act (or of the two acts that had replaced it).

The CROW Act set in motion the mandatory creation of areas of open countryside known as 'access land'. The act led to a statutory right of pedestrian access to about 1.6 million hectares of access land in England and Wales. The act included limitations on the new right, to ensure that landowners would not suffer significant losses or costs.

In the lead-up to the CROW Act, Clare Reading attended a public meeting in the Palace Hotel in Buxton, where the draft access maps were revealed, showing the proposed areas of access land.

> There were loads of farmers and landowners, one walker, one person from World Challenge, and me … There was a lot of shouting and interrupting in the middle of one presentation as the farmers couldn't restrain themselves. Some wanted to scrap the CROW bill, although it was way too late for that. They were allowed to object to the boundaries and in lots of cases they got their way. The public were not given any chance to come back on those adjustments. The outcome was that several landowners clawed back a bit of land between the road and the open land, making the open land difficult to access.[102]

Rory Gregory expands on Reading's account:

> I pushed to begin using the local area including Combs Moss as much as possible as soon as the CROW Act came into force. For a while everything was fine despite a few skirmishes with the local gamekeeper. However, the landowners of Combs Moss, a shooting consortium with offices in London, wrote to the powers that be at DCC stating that we could not use the Moss for our activities as we were doing it for financial gain! This was not permissible under the act.
>
> Despite me getting enthusiastic support for our cause for permitted educational use from the Peak Park authority and from local rangers and the BMC, the leaders at DCC told us to back off until the matter was resolved – it never was. Sometime later English Nature were involved and they surprisingly asked us not

to use the Moss on environmental grounds due to its delicate and extra-special nature.[103]

Access difficulties on Combs Moss had occurred sporadically ever since White Hall's opening. The latest information that I have received, in November 2017, indicates that access to this fantastic bit of moorland has recently improved. White Hall groups now use the moor for night hikes, for a stream walk, and for a walk back from Castle Naze.

The CROW Act was not perfect. Some access black spots remained, such as the access to Mouldridge Mine near Pikehall, where a locked gate increased the hazard of crossing a straight section of road carrying high-speed traffic. Putting this law change into a historical context, however, and remembering some of the stories of exciting encounters in the 1950s and 60s, there is no doubt that this act diminished the opportunities for people to take part in the ancient sport of trespassing.

Campaign for Adventure

On 29 November 2000, a national conference took place to discuss risk and adventure in society.[104] Titled 'A Question of Balance' and including an address by the Duke of Edinburgh, this important conference was attended by about 350 people from all corners of outdoor education. Prince Philip concluded by proposing a 'Campaign for Adventure', a movement 'to help combat the risk averse society and compensation culture which had arisen from the excessively negative reporting of accidents to school parties and [from] the growing "culture of fear".'[105]

The conference organisers released a well-crafted list of aims and objectives, worth reading in its entirety but from which I will limit myself to just one example of the objectives: '2.1.4 To reinforce the key principle that the great majority of people are well intentioned, reliable and trustworthy; and to recognise that those who make misjudgements should not necessarily be blamed.'[106] Putting this another way, society should not overreact to rare and uncharacteristic oversights or mis-calculations, otherwise society would make risk-taking and adventure impossible. It was a question of balance.

This initiative was a welcome development after the gloom of the 1990s. The news media covered the conference reasonably well. If you compare the stance and tone of 1990s press articles on safety and risk with the general drift of articles published in the 2000s, the reporting of this conference can be seen as an early stage in a correction to the balance of such articles. To illustrate this noticeable shift, I will quote from a mixture of press reports and formal sources from the period 2001–9.

On 5 March 2001, some former White Hall course members attended a reunion lunch at the centre to celebrate its fiftieth year and the lifelong influence of the outdoors.[107] By apt coincidence, about a week later the *Observer* and the *Guardian* both carried sizeable reviews of Frank Furedi's controversial new book *Paranoid Parenting*, in which he said that it was cruel to keep children indoors and that obsessive fears about children's safety were a bigger threat than bullies or paedophiles.[108]

I need to pause here to add that the enlightenment was neither universal nor immediate. The obstacles to a better informed and more sophisticated public understanding of safety and risk were considerable. The formal launch of the Campaign for Adventure took place in June 2001. As if on cue, in July, after a series of accidents, Nigel de Gruchy of the National Association of Schoolmasters, Union of Women Teachers (NASUWT) advised teachers not to do school trips. This was not the first time a teachers' union had advised its members against taking part in out-of-school activities, nor would it be the last. Speaking to *The Times*, De Gruchy said:

> We have been advising teachers not to go on trips for years now. They are fraught with risk. Before the facts are known, people are pointing the finger of blame. Accidents happen all the time on family holidays but there's no one to sue so you don't hear about it. It is sad that we have to give this advice and children will miss out as a result.[109]

De Gruchy's advice was not completely without justification. Even so, Rory Gregory, a member of the NASUWT, who was still settling into survival mode in the White Hall office, may well have been thinking, With friends like that, who needs enemies?

About eighteen months after the Question of Balance conference, writing in a Young Explorers' Trust publication, Tony Land acknowledged some hints of progress but also was aware of the difficulties facing outdoor educators: 'There are encouraging signs that the pendulum may be swinging back a little … But it is unlikely to be an easy victory as the entrenched vested interests of the bureaucrats, insurance companies, media and lawyers have all the effective guns, while government departments and quangos are much more concerned with PE and sport than with outdoor adventure as we know it.'[110]

In its effort to encourage that swing of the pendulum, the Campaign for Adventure would run energetically for four more years (and its website would still be accessible and informative in 2017). To try to detect the changing balance, and the difficulties facing the promoters of adventure, we will glance through a few more extracts from press reports and other sources.

On 4 August 2002, the *Sunday Express* carried a two-page spread with a banner headline, 'The Death of the School Trip?' The article quoted Chris Keates, deputy general secretary of the NASUWT, who had said:

> Teachers take on a tremendous responsibility whenever they take children off the school premises, finding themselves subject to all sorts of litigation. We recognise that children can get a lot out of school trips but it isn't worth the risk for teachers any more.[111]

David Hart, the general secretary of the National Association of Head-teachers, had given the newspaper a different perspective:

> I don't want to see the vast majority of schools imposed upon because of the incompetence of a very small minority ... School trips are absolutely critical for many children who would never otherwise have the opportunity to experience things like adventure holidays.[112]

Just three months earlier, however, an adventure break for a group of fifteen children from Fleetwood High School, Lancashire, had gone tragically wrong when a ten-year-old boy, Max Palmer – the son of an education support worker at the school – had drowned while swimming in a rain-swollen stream. On 23 September 2003 the *Daily Mail* reported that Paul Ellis, the geography teacher in charge of the party, had pleaded guilty to manslaughter. He had ignored a warning that heavy rain had turned the rocky Glenridding Beck into a dangerous torrent. The water temperature had been just 8°C. He was jailed for twelve months.

This tragedy shared one or two similarities with the Lyme Bay tragedy, such as the ignoring of warnings. According to a *Guardian* article that followed an HSE report:

Ellis lied to his school about his leadership qualifications. He failed to make the most basic inquiries to discover whether the children in his care could swim. He took his group to the hills in conditions that were completely unsuitable for the planned activity. The children had no protective clothing: no wetsuits, windproofs or buoyancy aids. Ellis had no rescue equipment and it seems that, even if he had taken a rope, he would not have known how to use it.

Detective chief inspector Bill Whitehead of Cumbria Police said the court case was a landmark one but he had sympathy for Ellis: 'We were not dealing with a career criminal here but a schoolteacher who had made a severe error.'[113]

While the national debate on safety and risk enjoyed considerable prominence, other national issues continued to tick over. On 27 January 2004, *The Times* found room for a letter from Bob Pettigrew, questioning the millions of pounds that the Labour government had allocated for Britain's bid to host the Olympics, while, in contrast, the local and national programmes of outdoor recreation would 'be progressively starved of even the limited funding they currently enjoy[ed]'. Writing from his home in Derbyshire, Pettigrew reached into the past to resurrect one of Longland's most basic and persistent arguments:

> When will this Government finally realise that it will achieve its so-called fitness targets only by promoting and encouraging further active participation by the public at large in the open country pursuits at which large numbers of Britons of all ages currently excel?[114]

Change Had Become the Norm

By the end of the 1990s at White Hall, frequent change had become an ever-present feature of the centre's operations. Doug Jones has summarised the effects of the changes:

> Looking back, the 1990s were a series of crises not of our making that we were responding to without seeing the whole picture. 20/20 hindsight is a wonderful thing but I'm not sure we could have done very much different. There was a real risk that White Hall would cease to exist completely.

We should also note that although in the 1990s there were major changes in the role and make up of White Hall the centre managed to respond to these and still maintain a level of adventure and quality that resulted in schools wanting to book as far as two or three years in advance. By the end of the 1990s White Hall had more operational and support staff than at the start of the decade. These staff were on very different pay and working conditions from those of their predecessors, but the centre was still providing courses to the young people of Derbyshire, at a time when many LEA centres were closing. New courses had been introduced, including weeks for young carers and Rotary Young Leaders Award courses. Thousands of young people continued to enjoy the activities that White Hall offered. Indeed as the decade progressed the number of young visitors increased.

It was great to see the centre responding to the imposed changes and coming out at the other end stronger and busier than ever. Seeing staff respond to the challenges and/or move on to their own challenges was one of the great joys of managing White Hall.[115]

There's no avoiding the cliché: during his time at White Hall, Jones had come through the best of times and the worst of times. One of his last initiatives was his pushing through of an application for a Big Lottery Fund grant to extend the dining room and to rebuild the climbing wall. The actual work on these improvements took place after his departure.

Throughout his tenure, Jones, like the three principals immediately preceding him, was involved in national developments in the outdoor sector as well as in local ones at White Hall. He was a member of the working party that formulated what eventually became adventure activity licensing. He served on the MLTB (later Mountain Leader Training England), becoming chairman in 1999, following in the footsteps of Jack Longland. In 2003–6 he chaired Mountain Leader Training United Kingdom. From 1999 to 2010 he was a director of the Mountain Training Trust, which ran the National Mountain Centre, Plas y Brenin, in that period.

After twelve years of coping with cutbacks ad nauseam, a time unlike anything that any other White Hall warden or principal had faced, Doug Jones left White Hall in September 2004 to become Bedfordshire's county officer for outdoor education and adventure activities. He later set up an adventure-activity consultancy, providing a range of services including inspecting on behalf of several industry quality standards and appearing as an expert witness on court cases involving mountaineering or abseiling. Derbyshire remained his home.

Rory Gregory became White Hall's seventh warden or principal and, as Jones had done latterly, would live out.

Notes

1   P John, '4 The Education Reform Act', Policy Studies Institute, University of Westminster (1990) <http://www.psi.org.uk/publications/archivepdfs/Recent/CENLOC4.pdf> [accessed 5 Mar 2017], p. 30.

2   Ken C Ogilvie, *Roots and Wings: A History of Outdoor Education and Outdoor Learning in the UK* (Lyme Regis, UK: Russell House Publishing, 2013), p. 588.

3   Ibid., p. 586.

4   Derbyshire County Council, 'Derby and Derbyshire Minerals Local Plan Apr 2000, as altered Nov 2002' (Nov 2002) <https://www.derbyshire.gov.uk/images/DD%20MLP%20Part%202_tcm44-189490.pdf> [accessed 17 Jan 2016].

5   David Ward, 'County's £6m Cut Likely to Cost Jobs', *Guardian*, 24 Apr 1992, p. 5.

6   Philip David Booth, 'The Impact of Financial Cuts upon an Outdoor Centre … during the Financial Year 1992/93' (MA dissertation, University of Sheffield, Jan 1993), p. 4.

7   Ibid., p. 41.

8   Ibid., p. 6.

9   Ibid., p. 12.

10 Ibid., pp. 13–18.

11 Ibid., pp. 37–58.

12 Ibid., p. 43.

13 Ibid., p. 45.

14 Ibid., p. 62.

15 Maurice Dybeck, *A Broad River: Brathay Hall Trust, 60th Anniversary Edition* (Ambleside, Cumbria: Brathay Hall Trust, 2005), pp. 142–149, 190.

16 Philip David Booth, 'The Impact of Financial Cuts upon an Outdoor Centre … during the Financial Year 1992/93' (MA dissertation, University of Sheffield, Jan 1993), p. 67.

17 Ibid., p. 73.

18 Ibid., p. 76.

19 Ibid., pp. 77–79.

20 Ibid., pp. 79–81.

21 Ibid., pp. 82–93.

22 Derbyshire Record Office, A Comparison of Two Outdoor Adventure Centres: Pete McDonald, 1983, D7786/BOX/1/Bundle 1., p. 74.

23   Philip David Booth, 'The Impact of Financial Cuts upon an Outdoor Centre ...
      during the Financial Year 1992/93' (MA dissertation, University of Sheffield, Jan
      1993), p. 106.

24   Ibid., p. 115.

25   National Curriculum Council, *Physical Education in the National Curriculum*
      (York: National Curriculum Council, 1992).

26   Philip David Booth, 'The Impact of Financial Cuts upon an Outdoor Centre ...
      during the Financial Year 1992/93' (MA dissertation, University of Sheffield, Jan
      1993), p. 30.

27   Philip Booth, Email to P McDonald, subject 'Re: 1992-2000', 7 June 2017
      [Email].

28   Department of Education and Science and Welsh Office, *Choice and Diversity: A
      New Framework for Schools*, Cm. 2021 (London: HMSO, July 1992).

29   Clyde Chitty, 'The Role and Status of LEAs: Post-war Pride and Fin de Siècle
      Uncertainty', *Oxford Review of Education*, 28, no. 2 & 3 (2002), pp. 261–273 (p.
      270).

30   Ken C Ogilvie, *Roots and Wings: A History of Outdoor Education and Outdoor
      Learning in the UK* (Lyme Regis, UK: Russell House Publishing, 2013), p. 590.

31   Frances Rickford, 'Council Spending Survey', *Guardian*, 30 Mar 1993, pp. 6–7.

32   Quoted in Ken C Ogilvie, *Roots and Wings: A History of Outdoor Education and
      Outdoor Learning in the UK* (Lyme Regis, UK: Russell House Publishing, 2013),
      p. 626.

33   Clare Reading, to P McDonald (1), 14 June 2017 [Letter].

34   Doug Jones, Email to P McDonald, subject 'Office manager', 20 July 2017
      [Email].

35   Doug Jones, Email to P McDonald, subject 'Chapter 22', 18 Aug 2017 [Email].

36   'Sir Jack Longland', *The Times*, 2 Dec 1993, p. 23.

37   Jim Perrin, 'Sir John Laurence ('Jack') Longland: 1905–1993', *Climbers' Club
      Journal: 1993*, 21, no. 3 (new series) (1994), pp. 79–83 (p. 82).

38   John Hunt, 'Sir Jack Longland 1905–1993', *Alpine Journal*, 99 (1994), pp.
      336–341.

39   Doug Jones, Email to P McDonald, subject 'Notes for your book', 15 Aug 2017
      [Email].

40   Ibid.

41   Ibid.

42   John Young, 'Parents Demand Facts on Canoeing Disaster', *The Times*, 24
      Mar 1993, p. 3. Also Kathryn Knight, 'Catalogue of Mistakes That Led to
      Drownings', *The Times*, 9 Dec 1994, p. 3.

43   Kathryn Knight, 'Catalogue of Mistakes That Led to Drownings', *The Times*, 9
      Dec 1994, p. 3.

44   Maurice Chittenden, 'Errors and Delays That Turned Canoe Adventure into
      Tragedy', *Sunday Times*, 28 Mar 1993, p. 2.

45   Lin Jenkins, 'Activity Centre Head Who Ignored Risks Jailed for Three Years',
      The Times, 9 Dec 1994, p. 3.

46   Maurice Chittenden, 'Errors and Delays That Turned Canoe Adventure into
      Tragedy', *Sunday Times*, 28 Mar 1993, p. 2.

47   Ibid.

48   Jan Bradford, 'From Lyme Bay to Licensing', Adventure Activities Licensing
     Authority (Apr 2000) <http://www.aals.org.uk/lymebay01.html> [accessed 11
     Oct 2014].

49   Quoted in ibid.

50   Anne Benson, 'Canoe Tragedy Inquiry Calls for Regulation of Outdoor Centres',
     Guardian, 30 July 1993, p. 3.

51   Celia Dodd, 'Education – Are Outdoor Trips Worth the Risk?', *Independent*, 8
     Dec 1994, p. 27.

52   Lin Jenkins and Frances Gibb, 'Canoe Centre Chief and Company Are Found
     Guilty', *The Times*, 9 Dec 1994, p. 1.

53   Lin Jenkins, 'Activity Centre Head Who Ignored Risks Jailed for Three Years',
     The Times, 9 Dec 1994, p. 3.

54   Quoted in Jan Bradford, 'From Lyme Bay to Licensing', Adventure Activities
     Licensing Authority (Apr 2000) <http://www.aals.org.uk/lymebay01.html>
     [accessed 11 Oct 2014].

55   Julian Fulbrook, *Outdoor Activities, Negligence and the Law*, First paperback edn
     (London: Routledge, 2016), p. 28.

56   Kathryn Knight, 'Watchdogs Call for Statutory Scheme', *The Times*, 9 Dec 1994,
     p. 3.

57   United Kingdom Parliament, 'Hansard Online: Orders of the Day: Activity
     Centres (Young Persons' Safety) Bill Order for Second Reading: columns
     590–633' (27 Jan 1995) <https://www.publications.parliament.uk/pa/cm199495/
     cmhansrd/1995-01-27/Debate-1.html> [accessed 13 Feb 2017].

58   Ibid.

59   Chris Loynes, 'Why I Think the Licensing Scheme Should Be Scrapped', *Journal
     of Adventure Education and Outdoor Leadership*, 12, no. 4 (Winter 1995–6), p. 2.

60   John Driscoll, 'Letter to the Editior', *Journal of Adventure Education and Outdoor
     Leadership*, 13, no. 2 (Summer 1996), p. 13.

61   [Editorial], 'Lord Henley Announces New Outdoor Activity Safety Measures',
     Journal of Adventure Education and Outdoor Leadership, 13, no. 1 (Spring 1996), p.
     38.

62   Clare Reading, to P McDonald (1), 14 June 2017 [Letter].

63   Ibid.

64   Pete Allison and John Telford, 'Turbulent Times: Outdoor Education in Great
     Britain 1993–2003', *Australian Journal of Outdoor Education*, 9, no. 2 (2005), pp.
     21–30 (p. 22).

65   Jan Bradford, 'From Lyme Bay to Licensing', Adventure Activities Licensing
     Authority (Apr 2000) <http://www.aals.org.uk/lymebay01.html> [accessed 11
     Oct 2014].

66   Julian Fulbrook, *Outdoor Activities, Negligence and the Law*, First paperback edn
     (London: Routledge, 2016), p. 17.

67   Doug Jones, Email to P McDonald, subject 'Notes for your book', 15 Aug 2017
     [Email].

68   'Report into Canoe Deaths Calls for Regulation: National Register for Activity
     Centres Urged', The Independent Online (1993) <http://www.independent.

co.uk/news/uk/report-into-canoe-deaths-calls-for-regulation-national-register-for-activity-centres-urged-disaster-1487975.html> [accessed 13 Feb 2017].

69   Doug Jones, Email to P McDonald, subject 'Nuggets from a …', 10 Oct 2017 [Email].

70   Decca Aitkenhead, 'School's Out – But the Kids Are Locked Up', *Guardian*, 25 July 1997, p. 17.

71   Clare Reading, to P McDonald (2), 1 July 2017 [Letter].

72   House of Commons Education and Skills Committee, *Education Outside the Classroom: Second Report of Session 2004–05* (London: The Stationery Office, 10 Feb 2005), p. Ev 112.

73   Ibid., p. Ev 112.

74   Not to be confused with the peer reviewed international *Journal of Adventure Education and Outdoor Learning*, which started in 1997.

75   Stephen Pimenoff, 'In Plain English, Your Jargon Makes Me Sick …', Independent (6 May 1994) <http://www.independent.co.uk/voices/in-plain-english-your-jargon-makes-me-sick-why-are-educational-theorists-torturing-the-language-stephen-pimenoff-is-astounded-1434084.html> [accessed 16 May 2014].

76   Ibid.

77   Ibid.

78   Peter Bunyan and Maggie Boniface, 'The Interaction of Sensation Seeking and Anxiety in Abseiling', *Journal of Adventure Education and Outdoor Leadership*, 12, no. 3 (Autumn 1995), pp. 25–27 (p. 25).

79   [Anon.], 'Letter to the Editor', *Journal of Adventure Education and Outdoor Leadership*, 13, no. 1 (Spring 1996), p. 38.

80   Ken C Ogilvie, *Roots and Wings: A History of Outdoor Education and Outdoor Learning in the UK* (Lyme Regis, UK: Russell House Publishing, 2013), pp. 637–638.

81   Ibid., (p. 627).

82   Bob Higginbotham, Email to P McDonald, subject '40', 14 Nov 2015 [Email].

83   Doug Jones, Email to P McDonald, subject 'History project', 30 Mar 2017 [Email].

84   Clare Reading, to P McDonald (2), 1 July 2017 [Letter].

85   Clare Reading, to P McDonald (1), 14 June 2017 [Letter].

86   Doug Jones, Email to P McDonald, subject 'Notes for your book', 15 Aug 2017 [Email].

87   Private correspondence quoted in Ken C Ogilvie, *Roots and Wings: A History of Outdoor Education and Outdoor Learning in the UK* (Lyme Regis, UK: Russell House Publishing, 2013), p. 634.

88   'Hard-up County Chops Cash for Community', *Manchester Evening News*, 27 Mar 1996.

89   Derby Local Studies and Family History Library, White Hall Centre: Adventure Activity Courses 1996/97, LA796.

90   Doug Jones, Email to P McDonald, subject 'Notes for your book', 15 Aug 2017 [Email].

91   Philip Booth, Email to P McDonald, subject 'Re: 1992-2000', 7 June 2017 [Email].

92   Clare Reading, to P McDonald (1), 14 June 2017 [Letter].

93   Clare Reading, to P McDonald (2), 1 July 2017 [Letter].

94   Doug Jones, Email to P McDonald, subject 'History project', 30 Mar 2017 [Email].

95   Geoff Cooper, 'Changing Roles for Outdoor Education Centres', in *Outdoor Education and Experiential Learning in the UK*, ed. by P Higgins and B Humberstone (Luneburg: Verlag Erlebnispadagogik, 1999), pp. 43–49 (pp. 43–44).

96   Clare Reading, to P McDonald (1), 14 June 2017 [Letter].

97   Clare Reading, to P McDonald (2), 1 July 2017 [Letter].

98   Clare Reading, Email to P McDonald, subject 'Draft Chapter 22', 19 Sept 2017 [Email].

99   Doug Jones, Email to P McDonald, subject 'Notes for your book', 15 Aug 2017 [Email].

100   Clare Reading, to P McDonald (2), 1 July 2017 [Letter].

101   Quoted in Deborah Pearlman and J J Pearlman, 'Is the Right To Roam Attainable? An Aspiration or a Pragmatic Way Forward?', in *Rights of Way: Policy, Culture and Management*, ed. by Charles Watkins, Rural Studies Series (London: Pinter, 1996), pp. 49–68 (p. 55).

102   Clare Reading, to P McDonald (2), 1 July 2017 [Letter].

103   Rory Gregory, Email to P McDonald, subject 'Chronological blunder', 19 Aug 2017 [Email].

104   Ian F Lewis, *'A Question of Balance': Risk and Adventure in Society: Wednesday 29th November, 2000, Royal Geographical Society, London: verbatim report* (Penrith, Cumbria: Institute for Outdoor Learning, 2001).

105   Ken C Ogilvie, *Roots and Wings: A History of Outdoor Education and Outdoor Learning in the UK* (Lyme Regis, UK: Russell House Publishing, 2013), p. 703.

106   Ian Lewis, 'Campaign for Adventure: Aims and Objectives' (27 Feb 2014) <http://www.campaignforadventure.org/aims-and-objectives.html> [accessed 23 Feb 2017].

107   'Reunion to Mark Activity Centre's Half-century', *Derby Evening Telegraph*, 26 Feb 2001.

108   Maureen Freely and Martin Bright, 'Don't Be Paranoid, Parents Told', *Observer*, 11 Mar 2001, p. 13. Also Joanna Moorhead, 'Scared Silly', *Guardian*, 14 Mar 2001, p. A10.

109   Vanora Bennett, 'How Long Can the School Trip Survive?', *The Times*, 7 July 2001, p. 3(S).

110   Young Explorers' Trust, *Safe and Responsible Expeditions*, Rev. edn (London: Expedition Advisory Centre of the Royal Geographical Society, March 2002).

111   Julia Hartley-Brewer, 'The Death of the School Trip?', *Sunday Express*, 4 Aug 2002, pp. 10–11.

112   Ibid.

113 Jaya Narain, 'Teacher Jailed over Death of Pupil', Daily Mail (23 Sept 2003) <http://www.dailymail.co.uk/news/article-197221/Teacher-jailed-death-pupil. html> [accessed 18 Nov 2015].

114 Robert Pettigrew, 'Britain's Olympic Bid', *The Times*, 27 Jan 2004, p. 19.

115 Doug Jones, Email to P McDonald, subject 'Notes for your book', 15 Aug 2017 [Email].

23. Rory Gregory and Transition, 2004–12

In July 2004 Doug Jones went on annual leave that ran up to the end of his employment in September. So Rory Gregory became the acting head of centre in July 2004, twenty-two years after starting as a temporary instructor and six years after becoming deputy principal.

Gregory was a BEd graduate of the University of Sheffield. While at university he had started climbing and mountaineering. Before arriving at White Hall, he had worked at Parsons House Farm, dealing with kids from Knowsley, a very deprived area of Liverpool. Parsons House Farm, near Fox House Inn, ran under the strong and authoritative leadership of Paul Reaney. At the old farm, Reaney and his staff got through to tearaways and the occasional young thug with plain, old-fashioned adventure: much climbing, canoeing and expeditioning. Gregory's manner with young people was fair, direct and effective. All they had to do to gain his respect was make an honest effort.

In the 1980s Gregory completed the long training required to become a British Mountain Guide. The only other holder of that qualification on the permanent staff of White Hall had been Bob Downes in 1956–7. Over the 1960s and 70s, the role of certified mountain guide had gradually become more wide-ranging and the training and assessments had become more exacting. When in 1977 the Association of British Mountain Guides was accepted into the International Federation of Mountain Guide Associations (IFMGA), the certified British guides became IFMGA guides, internationally qualified to lead parties in the world's most challenging mountain environments. Becoming an IFMGA Guide requires high levels of competence in four disciplines – rock climbing, ice climbing, mountaineering and ski mountaineering – and takes many years and exceptional skills and commitment to achieve. Gregory was also an experienced caver and a holder of the Caving Instructor Certificate (CIC), valuable attributes for a head of White Hall, in view of the importance of caving in Derbyshire. Very few people in Britain were both IFMGA Guides and CIC holders.

The themes in this chapter play second fiddle to the chronology. The result does not lend itself to the use of subheadings, so I will dispense with them, except to mark the years. However, be prepared for the persistent competing sounds of risk aversion and adventure promotion, against the steady background beat of cuts in funding, interrupted occasionally by other tunes.

2004

For England and Wales, the body that inspected and regulated schools was the Office for Standards in Education (Ofsted). On 24 September 2004, the Ofsted report *Outdoor Education: Aspects of Good Practice* was published. In launching the report, David Bell, the chief inspector of schools, followed the emerging trend away from the culture of fear, stating that 'the benefits of outdoor education are far too important to forfeit, and by far outweigh the risks of an accident occurring. If teachers follow recognised safety procedures and guidance they have nothing to fear from the law.'[1]

The report listed ten main findings, the first of which was: 'Outdoor education gives depth to the curriculum and makes an important contribution to students' physical, personal and social education. However, not all students in schools benefit from such opportunities.'[2] The backhanded twist of this compliment drew some comment from outdoor educators. Did all the secondary pupils who played rugby or soccer benefit from those opportunities? At a local level, how tiny was the proportion of children who went home from White Hall, at the end of their course, regretting taking part?

Four days later, Alexandra Blair, the education correspondent for *The Times*, discussed Ofsted's report. He said that the Professional Association of Teachers (PAT) had welcomed the report and its support for school trips. However, Jim O'Neill, a former PAT chairman, had been sceptical about David Bell's assurances to teachers over litigation. O'Neill had said: 'No matter how much preparation is done accidents will, of their very nature, occur and the teacher involved then has to carry the guilt and worry of uncertainty and possible litigation.'[3]

Writing in 2005, Pete Allison and John Telford pointed out several inconsistencies between some of the suggestions in the Ofsted report and the basic position of the Campaign for Adventure.[4]

The Ofsted report took its place on the library shelves among decades of other reports, guidelines and codes of practice. Since the 1960s, the burgeoning and diversifying outdoor sector – or, more precisely, its administrators and office-holders, with input from their members or associates – had produced a steady stream of best-practice guides and safety guides. So numerous were the examples of this genre, which ranged from flimsy utilitarian booklets to eye-catching glossy brochures, that in 1988 the AHOEC and others had thought it a jolly good idea to draw up and publish a forty-page mother of all guides, *Outdoor Education Safety and Good Practice: Guidelines for Guidelines.*[5]

We have nearly reached the end of 2004. Looking back at the period 1993–2003, which they called turbulent times, Allison and Telford said that outdoor education in Great Britain had changed radically in these ten years. They suggested, tentatively, that the changes looked set to continue. Many of these changes, they thought, were for the better and would help to develop the field:

> The precise way in which the field grows and develops and the way the wide variety of practices merge or fragment remains to be seen, it seems safe to speculate that growth is and will continue to occur. It is, we believe, fair to say that in the past 10 years outdoor education has undergone many transitions but … British outdoor education is strengthening in many areas and receiving funding and support from sources outside mainstream education such as social services and community education. Hopefully, in coming years, a balance of safety issues and educational issues can be reached in order to address the current imbalance and over emphasis on safety.[6]

Allison and Telford were commenting on the broad national situation and were viewing it from Edinburgh. Down in Derbyshire, White Hall Centre was still in the early stages or mid-stages of transition. Nobody knew whether White Hall would survive to play a part in the rejuvenated sector. Work went ahead, however, on boring a hole for a new water supply for the centre. On 18 May 2004, the Environment Agency granted Derbyshire county council a licence to extract water from this borehole.

2005–7

In 2005, when the English Outdoor Council (EOC) published its twenty-five-page guide *High Quality Outdoor Education*, written by members of the Outdoor Education Advisers' Panel, the council was both meeting a perceived need and following a familiar pathway.[7] The guide was well written and well informed. However, there was something sadly ironic in the arrival of a smart document offering advice on good practice, and decorated with confident logos, at a time when many LEA centres, arguably all being models of best practice, were closing, becoming casualties of vicious cuts in funding.

White Hall Centre had been spared that fate, so far. It was still busily adapting to the changing circumstances. The number of pupils on each course, having dropped in the mid-1990s, had crept back up to forty and had then climbed to fifty. Recalling this period, Bob Higginbotham said: 'No-one is sure when the numbers rose [from 40 to 50+], but the extension to the dining room (the conservatory) was built with lottery money in about 2005 in response to the higher numbers. I remember that meal times were a pretty cramped affair before the extension.'[8] In the financial year 2004–5, the Big Lottery Fund granted Derbyshire county council £165,454 for a climbing wall and dining room extension at White Hall.[9]

According to a BBC news report, the total amount of money available for these improvements later rose to £260,000, after an outreach facility was added to the package. Work on the dining room extension began in August 2006, a year later than Bob's estimate in the last paragraph. (Meanwhile, unconnected with the Lottery money, some major maintenance to the centre buildings took place, the main building being totally reroofed in September 2006.)

The Lottery grant also paid for a half-time post to administer and promote the outreach service. Deb Cook, an enthusiastic and active canoeist, volunteered to take on this role, resurrecting a service last seen at White Hall in the form of Arthur Afford's mobile unit of 1963–9. The outreach facility was completed in March 2007.[10] It comprised an outreach store full of kit, six outreach canoes and an outreach trailer.

Lottery money, then, was something to cheer about in Derbyshire, and so was an event that took place on 7 February 2005, when Ellen MacArthur, who had grown up in Whatstandwell near Matlock and had learnt to sail with her family, sailed across the finishing line near the French coast at Ushant to break the world record for the fastest solo nonstop circumnavigation of the globe.

Just three days later, parliament's Education and Skills Committee published a report on education outside the classroom. Although the report said much that was positive about the potential of outdoor education, the report's main message was that there had been 'a general decline in opportunities for education outside the classroom'. The committee said that the 'evidence paints a picture of extremely patchy provision. Individual good practice in many schools and local authority areas is set against a more negative national situation. It is clear to the Committee that outdoor education is a sector suffering from considerable unexploited potential.'[11]

Perhaps the most important aspect of the committee's look at education outside the classroom was not the committee's findings, although these were significant; of equal or even greater value was the written evidence submitted by various groups or individuals and reproduced at the end of the report.

An impeccably informed submission from Peter Higgins of the Outdoor and Environmental Education Section of the University of Edinburgh provided an authoritative summary of the chequered history of the UK's 'outdoor learning sector' since 1949 and a succinct executive overview of the nature and potential of outdoor learning, as observed in October 2004. The section was committed to a broad vision of learning outdoors as the corollary to learning indoors. Higgins continued: 'In this context the outdoors offers a multitude of sensory, aesthetic, intellectual, physical, intellectual, personal, social and spiritual opportunities which can be approached in an interdisciplinary way which is very difficult to achieve in the classroom.'[12]

To illustrate the range and scope of outdoor education, Higgins's section had developed the three circles Venn diagram reproduced on the next page. This interpretation saw the outdoor educator 'as someone who facilitates learning in each, or all three, of the circles according to the needs of the individuals they teach and the requirements of the curriculum'. Normally I distrust diagrams that attempt to explain human behaviour, but this particular one represents the sector effectively and has been widely adopted:

The White Hall aims statements that were quoted in Chapter 7, mainly from 1949–50, included all three main aspects. Bob Pettigrew's 1954–5 thesis recognised the same three areas, although with a clear emphasis on the acquisition of outdoor pursuits skills.[13] A B Afford's 1978 history of White Hall listed the same three purposes in a passage contributed by Lyn Noble.[14] A skeletal version of the three purposes, based partly on the general approach at White Hall, appeared in my 1997 book *Climbing Lessons*.[15] However, regarding the requirements of the school curriculum, none of these written descriptions of the aims of White Hall Centre ventured any more than peripherally into linking these aims with official detailed school curriculums. Making that

The range and scope of outdoor education.

explicit connection precisely was not a high priority in 1949 or 1954–5 or 1978. The need for the connection might have become slightly more apparent by 1997. By the mid-2000s, though, establishing and nurturing and publicising that link to schoolwork was a key strategy for survival and a part of a new orthodoxy.

I hasten to emphasise that this picture of there having been only weak links between what pupils did at White Hall and what they did at school is a generalisation to which there were some exceptions. In Chapter 8, Peter Mosedale recounted that 'much work was done on the geography and ecology of the local district'. The 1952 course involving a group from Longdendale School, accompanied by Ken Oldham, was a residential extension of classroom work. Someone in the 1950s installed several glass display cases in the briefing room, containing rock and crystal samples.

In spring 2004, *Environmental Education* had contained a paper by Geoff Cooper discussing the changing roles of outdoor education centres. Cooper was the head of Wigan LEA's two outdoor education centres in the Lake District. For at least fourteen years, he had advocated the strengthening of the links between outdoor education, environmental education and the school curriculum. In the 2004 paper, he maintained his consistent message.[16]

It would be wrong of me to imply that Jack Longland had down-played the links between what went on at White Hall and what went on in schools. This book has emphasised that he viewed the hill and water sports as a worthwhile extension of the standard physical education provided in schools. In his detailed submission to the Education and Skills Committee, covering many aspects of outdoor education, Higgins had included a message that had been dear to Jack Longland's heart:

> In light of the fact that outdoor activities can be viewed as sport-ing activities in their own right, and indeed ones at which the UK has traditionally excelled (mountaineering, sailing, canoeing etc) the lack of emphasis in the curriculum seems puzzling. All the more so considering the well-recognised long-term health benefits of such activities which are often pursued well after individuals have forsaken the team-sports which characterise school-based physical education. Perhaps this is the nub of the issue, it is much easier to organise a class into two teams to play a ball-game than to provide outdoor activities which often require specialist equip-ment, transport and particular teaching skills.[17]

Strike while the iron is hot, goes the old saying. Twelve days after the publication of the report of the Education and Skills Committee, Lem-bit Öpik, the MP for Montgomeryshire, took up the cause, speaking in a House of Commons adjournment debate on the 'outdoor pursuits industry'. Perhaps galvanised by the magnitude of Ellen MacArthur's achievement, and unusually well informed on outdoor education, Öpik offered an eloquent analysis of the debate about safety and risk. Space considerations allow me to quote merely a fragment of his speech:

> Have you ever been in love, Mr. Deputy Speaker? If so, it is probable that you have experienced all the emotions associated with uncertainty, excitement, attraction and fear of the unknown, because love is a risk and a commitment to emotions, which may backfire in your face. That risk is at the heart of some of the great-est literary, political and cultural achievements of the human race. It is an example of what I am here to discuss: the politics of risk, and why I believe that an obsessive approach to health and safety, coupled with an increasingly litigious culture is contributing to the problems that face our society.[18]

Öpik suggested that society should seek to manage risks instead of trying to remove them. He said that 'by treating risk as a kind of social asbestos, to be eliminated at all costs, we forget that an element of risk is a good component of all our lives – and outdoor activities are a perfect example of positive risk.'

Winding up this adjournment debate, Jane Kennedy, the minister for work, said that the government and the Health and Safety Commission were working to discover and uncover the middle ground:

> The debate has highlighted the significance of risk as an issue of public interest, but unfortunately that discussion is often polarised. At one extreme, there are those who appear to take an excessively risk-averse approach and who want a risk-free society. I regard them as bonkers, because it happily rhymes with conkers, which they want to ban. At the other extreme, there are those who dismiss health and safety out of hand as being an unnecessary infringement of their freedom of action – one might categorise them as critics of the so-called nanny state.[19]

As we have seen in the last few pages, within the space of five months Ofsted, the English Outdoor Council, parliament's Education and Skills Committee and Lembit Öpik had all raised issues connected with the dangers of allowing a government or its policies to overprotect individuals or to interfere unduly with personal choice. The three groups and Öpik were well aware of both the nanny state and the cowboy operators, the two extremes. I wouldn't describe the positions of any of the four as being polarised. All four were seeking a balance.

Meanwhile, the news media maintained their fondness for stories with titles like 'Bring Back Adventure' or 'School Trips on the Way Out' (although the statistical evidence for the latter prediction was weak).

In the *Guardian* on 15 March 2005, Phil Revell, an educational journalist and former teacher, examined the repercussions of the Glenridding Beck drowning. An HSE report on the tragedy, like the Manchester Crown Court, had found the teacher, Paul Ellis, fairly and squarely to blame for the tragedy. Revell said that the finding had reignited the controversy surrounding outdoor education:

> On the one side are the columnists and leader writers who point to a decline in adventurous activities and bewail the 'cottonwool

culture' that denies children the opportunity to experience the challenges of nature.

In the opposite camp are safety campaigners and the second largest teaching union, the National Association of Schoolmasters, Union of Women Teachers ... The NASUWT argues that teachers are at risk if they lead a school trip.

Also in 2005, an all-party parliamentary group for Adventure and Recreation in Society was set up. The Campaign for Adventure had been instrumental in the lead-up to this development.[20]

This year also saw the release of Julian Fulbrook's *Outdoor Activities, Negligence and the Law*. In this particularly timely book, published while debate was raging around the 'compensation culture', Fulbrook examined the legal responsibilities of the organisers of school and youth expeditions and adventurous outdoor activities. Referring to the period 1995–2005 he wrote: 'In recent years ... there has developed what amounts to an almost irrational terror, particularly in staff rooms, on what the law seeks to do.'

Fulbrook questioned the common assumption that the compensation culture and blame culture were so overwhelming that no youth worker or teacher could sensibly involve themselves in outdoor pursuits with children or teenagers. Drawing on many examples from his wide-ranging research, he emphasised the very low risk for those involved in organised outdoor activities and the advantages to be gained from participation. Referring to the NASUWT policy of advising its members not to go on school trips, he said: 'Unfortunately such an attitude imperils the off-site learning of millions of young people, who lose out on an array of experiences which could do much to enhance their education and develop their maturity.'[21]

*

Chapter 22 included a mention of the Countryside and Rights of Way Act 2000, which created new rights of walking access to uncultivated land in England and Wales. Having achieved the right to roam (in defined areas), the access reformers shifted their attention onto the right to float. Ie, they began to scrutinise the legal and political complexities of gaining canoeing access to the rivers of these two countries. Locally, Derbyshire possessed a prime example of the access situation affecting numerous rivers in England and Wales. Chapters 3 and 16 touched upon canoeists' lack of legal access to much of the River Derwent, especially upstream of Darley Dale. In the 1950s and 1960s, White Hall groups had regularly paddled on this river, but I have found no details of exactly where. What is clear is that by the early 1970s, and possibly earlier than this, some landowners along the river opposed canoeing access, and it had become impossible for organised educational groups to use any sections of the river between Ladybower Reservoir and Darley Dale without making special private arrangements.

In England and Wales, of the 41,000 miles of waterways that were more than three yards wide, only 1,400 miles were open to canoeists. In 2006, the BCU became involved in a campaign for the 'right to float'. Advocates for improved canoeing access to rivers and to other waterways argued that 'most countries in the world have an automatic right for canoes, and other unpowered craft, to use rivers'.[22]

The Times reported that one hundred MPs led by John Grogan, the Labour member for Selby, had backed the right to float in a Commons early day motion. But government ministers were resisting any change in the laws controlling who does what on rivers. Jim Knight, the rural affairs minister, wanted the rivers to be opened up by voluntary agreement between canoeists and riparian landowners.[23] The canoeists were split on the merits of this idea; this internal rift put the country's four million anglers, many of whom opposed canoeing access, into the advantageous position of divide and rule.

No resolution of this access problem looked likely in the short or medium term. Neither would the issue evaporate.

*

On 26 November 2006 the Department for Education and Skills (DfES) published *Learning Outside the Classroom Manifesto*, after much consultation with the English Outdoor Council and other bodies. Whereas a political party usually addresses its manifesto to the general public, the DfES addressed its outdoor-learning manifesto to all young people. The manifesto promised to provide them 'with a wide range of experiences outside the classroom'. These ventures, whether into the school grounds or into local woodlands or onto far-off hills or lakes or rivers, were to be 'of agreed high quality'.[24]

As well as publishing the manifesto, the DfES put into action a scheme for any person or organisation to sign up to publicly endorse the manifesto. All the signatories were to pledge to take actions to promote and improve education outside the classroom.[25]

Speaking at the launch of the manifesto, Alan Johnson, the education secretary, said that 'learning outside the classroom should be at the heart of every school's curriculum and ethos'.[26]

If lavish graphic design indicates an underlying high quality of thought, this manifesto should have met its purposes admirably. Unfortunately, though, the launch coincided with the news of many potential closures of or threats of cuts in funding to outdoor centres. This was highly embarrassing for the DfES. The splendid photographs and resolute optimism of the manifesto can only have worsened that discomfort.

On 1 April 2007, the Adventure Activities Licensing Service (AALS) came into existence, operated by TQS Ltd under contract to the AALA. The role of the AALS was to deliver the licensing regime on a day-to-day basis.[27]

Also early in 2007, about eleven years after the setting-up of the AALA, a paper in the *Journal of Experiential Education* examined the impact of the licensing of adventure activities in Great Britain. The study focused on sea kayaking, the activity involved in the Lyme Bay tragedy. In the mid-1990s, during the national debate on the pros and cons of licensing, while the general public and the news media had supported the proposed statutory regulation of outdoor centres, many people working in the outdoor sector had condemned the idea.

The research behind the paper sought to discover whether this negative perception of licensing had persisted into the first ten years of the AALA. The study found that this had not happened; on the contrary, at the eighteen centres studied, the respondents and interviewees viewed the AALA as an advance.[28] Outdoor providers had learnt to live with the licensing regulations. This finding backed up a conclusion that Julian Fulbrook had reached in April 2005, when he had written that 'outside its narrow legislative focus, the AALA … has had an immensely powerful influence on safety generally in the outdoors in Britain'.[29] But whether the benefits were worth the considerable cost and effort involved was less clear. The continued existence of the AALA and the AALS could not be predicted with certainty, as we will see later in this chapter.

The year 2007 also saw the publication of Bob Barton's *Safety, Risk and Adventure in Outdoor Activities*, a down-to-earth and balanced examination of its subject, informed by Barton's practical experience as an instructor and mountain guide and humanely restrained in its occasional recourse to indigestible theory. His book included some basic statistics that suggested that risk averseness had become excessive. Here is Barton seeking the balance that we talked about earlier in this chapter:

We all deplore serious accidents in adventure activities or in any
out of school learning. Such events, mercifully rare, justifiably raise
great public concern and highlight the need for teachers, instructors and providers continually to aspire to the highest standards
of risk management, but a public obsession with safety and blame
and an ever greater aversion to any kind of risk threatens the
availability of adventure in any meaningful form. The waste of
young lives through lack of purpose and lack of self-esteem barely
registers on the scale of public concern, yet many see this as the
direct corollary of a diminution in the availability of opportunities
for self-discovery, self-expression and self-belief. I do not pretend
that outdoor experiences are the only remedy here, simply that
they are too valuable, of too great a proven effect, to be rejected
or neglected.[30]

Barton says that several uncertain variables make it difficult to compare
overall safety in outdoor education with that in everyday life. However,
'by making a number of assumptions, it is possible to make an analysis
which indicates that the average risk of death for young people during
a day of adventure activities is roughly the same as that for an average
day in the rest of their lives, in and out of school.'[31]

*

The White Hall ropes course, in the trees to the north of the centre,
did not escape the relentless advance of safety regulations. The course
had evolved haphazardly in the 1980s, largely by the efforts of Dave
Edwards on Monday mornings, assisted by other instructors. At first,
Edwards built the bridge elements using discarded climbing and caving
ropes. Later he rebuilt some of the bridges using thick ropes purchased
for the purpose. Rory Gregory constructed a robust wooden assault wall.

Some outdoor centres in the 1980s paid specialist contractors to
design and build sophisticated ropes courses. Compared to these elabo-
rate and expensive jungle gyms, the White Hall ropes course was limited and obviously home-made. Yet, as an on-site activity, it was useful
for filling in an empty hour or even as a programmed activity. On-site
facilities can be very helpful and worthwhile, especially if financial constraints limit the available transport; on the other hand, such transport
constraints can become a problem if the grounds become overcrowded,
with too much of the programme happening as short on-site sessions.

In about 1993 Edwards bought a load of pea gravel to spread on the
ground under the elements that pupils fell or jumped off. But more

radical changes became necessary to satisfy ever-tightening societal and legal expectations. 'The ropes course elements were lowered and lowered until there was no challenge left – that was in the mid-1990s. In 1997 we got someone to rebuild the whole lot with the same materials (it had been a hotchpotch), and we put a thick layer of bark chips under everything. This is still added to each year as it compacts quickly.'[32]

The ropes course having been totally rebuilt to pose much less risk to pupils than crossing the A5004 at White Hall's front entrance, the managers were then obliged to consider the safety of instructors, in response to the Work at Height Regulations 2005 (WAHR). An official brief guide to these regulations states that 'work at height means work in any place where, if there were no precautions in place, a person could fall a distance liable to cause personal injury.' The guide advises readers: 'Take a sensible approach when considering precautions for work at height. There may be some low-risk situations where common sense tells you no particular precautions are necessary and the law recognises this.'[33]

These new regulations raised questions about the carrying-out of ropes-course maintenance. The days of an instructor grabbing half an hour on a Monday morning to replace a worn section of rope or to tighten a bridge or to check the zip-wire take-off were over. Chapter 24 will briefly return to this maintenance matter to discover what sort of 'sensible approach' evolved.

*

Since the completion of White Hall's new indoor climbing wall in March 2007, the demand to use it had been very high. A new junior climbing club held on Friday nights had soon become oversubscribed. The wall had three main sections: a top-roping zone six metres high, a bouldering section five metres high, and ten metres of traversing.

On 21 October 2007, with the start of the global financial crisis visible across the Atlantic, White Hall opened the climbing wall to members of the public on Sunday evenings from 6pm to 10pm. This session would cost £4. Places would be filled on a first come first served basis. Before this opening, the nearest indoor climbing walls in the White Hall area were at Longnor and Marple.[34]

Also about this time, Deb Cook, running the outreach service and recognised by everyone as 'a person who got things done', was mixing business with pleasure, negotiating outreach contracts with schools, setting up a thriving Buxton-based canoe club called Peak Paddlers, and paddling for the British women's rafting team. Her outreach work paid for a hired minibus, which became available for mainstream centre use for part of the time, a godsend at a time when the overnight numbers were creeping up from forty to fifty and then sixty.[35]

Cook left White Hall in December 2007, moving to Wales. Her leaving was a real loss to the centre. Pat Bell, who had started working at White Hall as a freelance instructor in about 2002, took over the running of the outreach unit. At some point the outreach store and equipment became part of the general centre resources. The outreach service continued to operate.

In September 2008 Fiona Thomson began working at White Hall as a centre assistant. She would become a senior instructor in about 2011 and then centre manager in 2015, a role that she would share with Pat Bell.

2008–12

Only twice has this book needed to widen its range of vision to include global developments. The Great Depression, with its soup kitchens and its influence on Jack Longland, appeared in Chapter 1. The second world war, and its popularising of climbing, appeared in Chapter 6. We now need to add a third world-wide happening: the global financial crisis of 2007–8. This began in the housing market in the United States in 2007 and it reached its UK climax in late 2008.

On Monday 6 October 2008, one of several meltdown Mondays, the Financial Times Stock Exchange 100 Index spiralled down 7.85 per cent, one of the bigger one-day falls ever. Four days later, on Black Friday, the same index dropped 8.9 per cent, the third-biggest one-day fall in its history.[36] Stock markets around the world recorded similar falls to those in London. *MoneyWeek* said: 'We really are facing a massive global slowdown, and even if our governments could do anything about it (which is debatable), they are in fact all running around like headless chickens panicking.'[37]

A global recession would follow the financial crisis, lasting for different periods in different countries. In the UK, this recession would linger from 2008 to 2012. In 2009–10, the hole in public finances would reach 9.9 per cent of GDP, £152 billion, the biggest shortfall since the Second World War. The Labour government under Tony Blair and then, from May 2010, the Conservative government under David Cameron would both implement severe austerity measures. This would not be a good time for trying to persuade any government to restore the funding of LEA residential outdoor education centres.

*

One obvious way for LEA outdoor centres to heighten their relevance and importance, and thereby to help to secure their futures, was to strengthen their links to the school curriculum. This could happen in several ways. A centre and a school could collaborate to add an explicit link between a short residential course at the centre and the school's physical education (PE) curriculum. Similarly, parts of a residential course might connect to a school's social and personal development programme and goals. Or the connection could involve integrating some practical work on a short residential course with school-based theoretical studies in subjects such as history, geography, science and art.

In June 2009, the *Derby Evening Telegraph* reported on a history project undertaken by students at Anthony Gell School, Wirksworth and involving at one stage several caving instructors from White Hall Centre. The subject of the project was the history of lead-mining in the Peak District, old lead mines being a prominent part of Derbyshire's industrial landscape, above ground as well as below. The work included filming underground, a task enabled by White Hall instructors accompanying the Anthony Gell students down disused mines. The students also interviewed staff at Matlock Bath Mining Museum. The project culminated in the production and publication of a DVD, *Our Hidden Heritage: The History of Lead Mining in the Peak District*.[38] Tracy Critchlow, the Derbyshire county council cabinet member for young people, said: 'This is an impressive project which has created an excellent teaching aid for use in the county's schools.'[39] A £17,000 grant from the Young Roots Programme of the Heritage Lottery Fund paid for the project.

In 2004, Peter Higgins had pointed out that there was rarely a consistent approach, across a county or over the long term, to link short-term residential experiences with curricular work. The linking, when it did happen, was often the result of enthusiastic teachers rather than consistent approaches.[40] The Ofsted report *Outdoor Education: Aspects of Good Practice* of September 2004 had singled out the integrating of centre and school work as an area for improvement nationally.[41] One way to achieve greater consistency was to improve the links between schools and outdoor centres.

The links between White Hall Centre and Anthony Gell school, and between White Hall and dozens of other Derbyshire schools, had always been strong, stretching back not just decades but generations. But there was no harm in making them even stronger.

I would add one caveat to the welcome that many outdoor educators would extend to developments that link outdoor courses to the curriculum. In some words of Jack Longland that appeared at the start of this book: 'We have umpteen schools where people learn to work but now we have one where they can learn to play.'

Which brings us neatly back to the subject of excitement and adventure and having fun. In July 2009, *The Times* reported that canoeists in England and Wales were renewing their campaign for the 'right to float' on rivers. The broadcaster Griff Rhys-Jones and MPs from across the political spectrum were supporting the campaign. Tamsin Phipps, who headed the access campaign for Canoe England, said: 'The Environment Agency promised us these voluntary agreements, but it has not worked. Take the River Teme in Shropshire – we used to be able to paddle [it] 365 days a year; now we have got 10 days.'[42]

In summer 2009, sixteen years after the Lyme Bay deaths, the balance between having fun and avoiding danger remained a subject for debate. On 1 July 2009, the Countryside Recreation Network held a seminar in Birmingham under the banner 'Taking a Chance Outdoors – Is Fear of Risk Damaging Our Children?' Presenters provided strong evidence that an unreasonable fear of risk by people in many sectors of society was inhibiting the use of the outdoors by many children. It also became clear, though, that the culture of overprotection was only one factor of several that were causing a decline in the use of the natural environment.[43] Some young people preferred to stay indoors at home, going climbing in virtual reality while tucking into Kentucky Fried Chicken.

Technological progress continued, despite the global recession. In 2009, manufacturers sold 150 million GPS-enabled cell phones worldwide. The new technology looked certain to affect navigation on the hills and possibly the sport of orienteering, but to what extent was difficult to forecast. Regarding one long-standing core element of White Hall's schools' courses – map-reading – you might have half-expected the advent of GPS to have reduced the importance of learning to navigate with a map. However, a BBC news item in June 2011 suggested that frequent exposure to online maps from an early age was making children more familiar with map reading than in the past.[44]

For the time being at least, people would continue to use both paper and digital maps. For some people, nothing would ever replace a paper map. In 2009, Mike Parker, a self-confessed map addict, wrote about exploring a whole new world, 'as captured by the gods of the Ordnance Survey'. Parker could not understand anyone moving to a new area without buying a map first ... and 'without taking it out on a nightly basis, stroking its contours, gently murmuring the unfamiliar names, idly following with your finger footpaths and streams, back lanes and bridleways, feeling faintly, randomly intimidated by the angular blocks of planation forestry and sumps of squelchy moorland, excited by the wide beaches, towering peaks, nestled lakes and market towns, all spread beguilingly across the paper'.[45]

This chapter has lurched frequently between national developments and local happenings affecting White Hall Centre. As we near the end of the chapter, still guided by the chronology, there will be no abatement in the national-local mix.

In April 2010, a House of Commons select-committee report *Transforming Education Outside the Classroom* expressed concern that school trips would become the preserve of the pupils of private schools. The report said that 'all children should have opportunities to experience environments away from their local area, and to visit museums and galleries and other sites of interest, including the natural environment of the English countryside. We call on the Department [for Education] to ensure that families' ability to pay is not a deterrent to schools offering or pupils participating in school trips and visits. We commend to the Department the principle of subsidies for children from low-income families for school trips.'[46]

*

Since the Lyme Bay tragedy (1993) and the setting-up of the AALA (1996), some argument over the desirability of the statutory licensing of outdoor activity centres had continued. Some tourism bodies, for example, wanted licensing to be replaced by a code of practice. In October 2010, the government released *Common Sense, Common Safety*, a sixty-one-page report into health and safety regulations by Lord Young of Graffham. Young, a former Tory minister dubbed 'the enterprise czar', proposed changes that would remove needless bureaucracy. *The Times* reported that 'school trips and "good Samaritan" acts of kindness are to be freed from stifling red tape and fear of the compensation culture under reforms outlined in a Cabinet-backed report'.[47] The report recommended that the AALA be abolished and that a code of practice should replace the statutory licensing scheme.

The HSE later announced that it was working towards implementing Lord Young's recommendations, but that the licensing would remain in place until late 2012.[48] In actuality it would remain in place much longer than this. There were some reasonable arguments for retention as well as for abolition. There were also political aspects, as shown by a heading in the *Plymouth Herald*, 'Mum's anger at plan to scrap law brought in after four Plymouth children died'.[49] Newspaper stories massively oversimplified the details of the issue. An article in the *Journal of the Law Society of Scotland* discussed some of the complexities.[50]

*

Near the end of *Roots and Wings*, Ken Ogilvie made the point that wise historians confine themselves to the past. He said that forays into the future are best restricted to questions rather than reckless predictions. He posed some of the questions that he thought needed asking in 2010, 'a time of uniquely immense change':

> Has OL [outdoor learning] burned itself out? Outlived its useful-ness? … Has the world passed OL by and moved on? Is OL no longer relevant to the conditions now prevailing in 2010 which are very changed from those of the 1950s–60s? Is OL a great experiment in learning that is fizzling out because it was seen by the gate keepers of power as a minor player, a fringe luxury to be deleted from the list of priorities when the money became tight?[51]

In 2010 there were pessimistic and optimistic answers to these ques-tions. Overcoming his reluctance to look into the future, Ogilvie briefly explored some of these predictions. We've endured plenty of gloom in recent chapters, so I will confine myself to the views of the optimists. Outdoor education/outdoor learning in 2010, said Ogilvie, had a his-tory of which it could be proud so far, but it was out of sync with what was around it.

> Some optimists think its time may now have come. There is still a need for youngsters to be fit and re-connected to the outdoor natural environment, to be independent, confident, enterprising, aware of self, others and the environment more than ever. There is still a need for OE/OL to be strong enough to carry out its commitments against enduring, innate opposition.[52]

I will raise the same questions again near the end of this book, when we reach 2017.

In December 2010, a paper in the *British Educational Research Journal* explored the extent to which the provision of opportunities to engage in out-of-school learning activities was unevenly distributed, spatially and institutionally. The paper highlighted the uneven, precarious and uncertain nature of such activities. It also demonstrated that important regional and structural variations in the support and provision of opportunities for these activities by local authorities appeared to have an important role in determining the provision of activities at the level of the schools.[53]

Meanwhile, in Derbyshire, despite the future of outdoor education appearing to be more precarious than ever, if that was possible, the county council went ahead with a complete rewiring of White Hall, the work being done between November 2010 and February 2011. Concurrently, the cuts in funding continued. On 5 March 2011, the *Derby Telegraph* reported that

> outdoor activities paid for by Derbyshire County Council are to be reviewed in a bid to save cash. The authority has revealed that support for the Duke of Edinburgh Award, the Lea Green Development and Conference Centre and [the] Chesterfield-based Adventure Activity Team could be cut. Whitehall [*sic*] Activity Centre and self-catering residential centres at Cromford Wharfshed and Grinlow Cottage are also under review.[54]

Nationally, between 1956 and 2009, four million people had taken part in the Duke of Edinburgh's Award (the DofE), which had usually included an expedition.[55] The scheme had reviewed and updated itself in 2008. In 2009 the old system of keeping track of progress through paper record books had been replaced by the introduction of an online system, eDofE. Participants use this system to track their progress, while leaders use it to oversee this progress. According to the charity's website, 'in 2009 ground breaking independent research from the University of Northampton … provided conclusive evidence about the DofE's positive impact on young people'.[56]

The DofE had been running in many Derbyshire schools for decades. White Hall's annual programme had included one or two DofE expedition training courses for as long as anyone could remember. Clare Reading notes:

> I think it's significant that DofE renewed itself in 2008. They realised that private schools were all offering the award, but that the less academic children in normal schools who could have gained so much from it were not getting the chance. They also realised

that standards had become variable – some children were given
a route to walk, for example, while others were expected to plan
the expeditions themselves.[57]

Among the DofE changes that took place nationally was the introduction of a requirement for potential participants to attend a half-day
introductory course, a requirement for supervisors to attend a supervisor's course, and one for assessors to do an assessor's course. The latter
did not go down well with some long-serving volunteers who felt that
they were not trusted and who were also asked to pay for the courses.

In Derbyshire, despite the *Derby Telegraph* report of possible cuts to
the county's funding of the DofE, participation in the award remained
strong. Clair Reading again:

> With firstly the Walking Group Leader award being introduced
> and then the Lowland Leader, and in spite of strict supervision
> limits (numbers of groups to one trained or qualified supervisor),
> the DofE did grow and it reached the target students. Derbyshire
> set up a group for any students who for whatever reason could not
> do the DofE at their school, or for those who needed to catch up
> with the expedition element.
>
> I think it was Rory who devised a policy on the adult-student
> ratio for Derbyshire. We revived the local hillwalking accreditation
> so that teachers who were experienced walkers but who lacked
> walking leader qualifications could continue the DofE work while
> the scheme was expanding. This internal assessment mostly took
> place with me – one day on Combs Moss for those supervising
> the Silver and Bronze levels.[58]

Three months after the *Derby Telegraph* story, in a three-minute report
on the BBC television news, Andrew Bomford said that the BBC
had contacted all the remaining LEA outdoor centres in England
and Wales. Almost all of them had had their entire funding cut. They
expected the cost of their courses to double, and that this change would
deny the children of poorer families the opportunity to attend residential courses. A third of these council-run centres felt their futures to be
uncertain. Twelve were expecting to close.[59]

A few days later, writing in a Liberal Democrat newsletter, John
Russell tried to rally the troops:

Outdoor education is a challenging service to provide. It is a soft underbelly that is too easily cut. Scrutiny reports all too often recommend centre closures as the challenge of restructuring, increasing occupancy and finding funding to repair buildings appears impossible.

The challenges can be overcome. Another way is possible and this is an appeal to all our ministers and MPs to rise up to the challenge and to fight in response to this crisis that the BBC has so starkly revealed and to make a commitment to preserving the wonder and unique transformational educational experiences that outdoor education provides.[60]

Russell then suggested that local authorities should establish trusts to preserve their residential outdoor centres. He gave an example in which two local councils had transferred the physical assets of a centre building to a trust to manage, on condition that an affordable outdoor education service was maintained. The trust was free to seek funding and to raise much needed investment for refurbishing the 'dilapidated infrastructure'. However, he also conceded that 'these services must be subsidised to some degree to survive'.[61]

Discussions on Self-sufficiency

During Rory Gregory's eight years of heading the centre, he was involved twice behind the scenes in exploratory discussions on the scope for White Hall to move further towards complete self-sufficiency, such as by increasing its income and by money-saving initiatives. These White Hall issues were part of a bigger picture of all Derbyshire county council departments undertaking the same process. As far as Gregory knows, no written records of his informal conversations were kept. The first discussion was with the assistant director of the county council's Children and Young Adults Department:

Donald Rae tasked me early on with investigating the possibility of WH moving towards zero funding over an unspecified period of time. I produced a short report which I have been unable to locate. Basically I told him that existing with no subsidy would not be possible to do while maintaining high standards of outdoor education with highly experienced, qualified members of teaching staff and working with 1:10 teaching ratios that the activity governing bodies specified at the time.

Then came a move towards Single Status, during which everyone's job and role within DCC was compared and evaluated.
People were then placed in groups allocated to a specific pay scale.
(We had lost teachers' pay and conditions a while before.) Not
surprisingly, most people's salaries were reduced. This reduced
the WH staff budget which took the heat off of us for a while.

A similar conversation happened later with Ian Price, the head of Derbyshire Outdoors and Lea Green Learning and Development Centre:

It was several years later that Ian Price asked me to look into how
we could make WH operate without DCC funding. He asked
me to examine things like charitable trusts, etc. Again, nothing
was written down.

Over a period of about six months Darran and I looked at this.
Through the AHOEC I spoke to various heads who were already
operating without local authority funding or were preparing to do
so. Eventually I made a presentation to Ian Price in which I made
it clear that the only way that zero funding could work would be
to completely change the way that WH operated. Ie, operate with
large groups of students on low-grade activities, on site, and run
by junior staff members with help from visiting teachers. In short
I told him that in the long term this would probably put off our
existing customers because formulaic on-site activities were not
what they wanted to come to WH for. Also WH was too small;
centres with over a hundred beds were the only ones that could
raise sufficient funds to cover their operating costs and make this
model work. The matter was dropped …

At WH we increased numbers at the centre but continued with
proper traditional outdoor educational activities run by outdoor
professionals and enthusiasts, mostly off-site in wild adventurous
surroundings.[62]

These accounts by Gregory are characteristically frank. In the meetings,
he had expressed his ideas forthrightly. Robust argument of this sort
happens in all professional situations. Gregory was worried, understandably, that further reductions in the subsidy would lower the quality
of the provision. He was also still grappling with a question aired by
Phil Booth in 1993: would a slightly diluted experience for a larger

number of visitors be more equitable than a very intense experience for a smaller number?

Regarding Gregory's point about the minimum size for a residential outdoor centre, developments at White Hall over the following six or seven years would call into question the notion that residential centres needed at least a hundred beds to survive unsubsidised. There is efficiency in numbers, but the viability threshold might be less than a hundred.

As regards Gregory's concerns about the quality of the future courses, Darran Hawkins has argued that, despite an ever diminishing subsidy, the addition of an on-site mountain-bike trail, opened in May 2013 after Gregory's departure, increased the opportunities for adventure education, hence reinforcing the quality of the school's courses.[63] Chapter 24 will include a look at where the subsidy has got to. It will also mention the centre's diversifying and its developing a more commercial way of operating, aspects that Gregory's reviews had not considered.

One day in June 2011, White Hall held a celebratory day packed with outdoor activities to mark its sixtieth year. Among those present were pupils from Earl Sterndale Primary School, who had recently completed a six-week bike-ability course at White Hall, organised through the High Peak Schools Sport Partnership. Also present were county councillor Robin Baldry, the chair of White Hall's advisory committee, and county councillor Barrie Taylor, another member of the committee.[64]

White Hall Centre had survived, thanks to local pride and some splendid obstinacy. Three generations of Derbyshire people loved the place. Whole families – grandparents, parents and today's children – shared indelible memories of their visits. The centre had received immense support from county councillors (of all colours) and officers, despite the economic constraints that LEAs were under. In an age of sustainability and global warming and obese kids and the culture of fear, and in a county a large part of which was a national park, its future ought to have been secure. Whether that was the case remained to be seen. Rory Gregory retired in July 2012, after thirty years at White Hall. Darran Hawkins took on the leadership, facing the challenge of moving the centre forwards from survival to stabilisation and rejuvenation.

The dining room before its conservatory extension.

View from the front lawn, January 2010. The conservatory was completed in 2006.

Combs Reservoir, June 2009

White Hall Centre

Combs Reservoir, December 2007.

White Hall Centre

Scrambling, Higgor Tor, August 2007.

Scrambling, Higgor Tor, August 2007.

White Hall Centre

Scrambling, Higgor Tor, October 2008.

White Hall Centre

Scrambling, Roaches, November 2009.

Windgather Rocks, November 2007.

Yarncliff Quarry, October 2008.

On the new indoor climbing wall, August 2007.

Belaying, August 2007.

White Hall Centre

Devonshire Mine, Matlock Bath, August 2007.

White Hall Centre

Navigating underground, Devonshire Mine, August 2007.

White Hall Centre

Ropes course, White Hall, November 2007.

White Hall Centre

Ropes course, White Hall, May 2012.

Ropes course, White Hall, November 2007.

Ropes course, White Hall, March 2007.

White Hall Centre

Stream scrambling, Beeley Brook, March 2009.

White Hall Centre

Swamp walking, White Hall grounds, March 2012.

The top of the hill, January 2009.

White Hall Centre

Night hike, August 2007.

White Hall Centre

Notes

1   Alexandra Blair, 'Pupils Miss Out on School Trips Because of Legal Fears', *The Times,* 28 Sept 2004, p. 9.

2   'Outdoor Education: Aspects of Good Practice', Office for Standards in Education (24 Sept 2004) <http://dera.ioe.ac.uk/id/eprint/4914> [accessed 25 Feb 2017], p. 2.

3   Alexandra Blair, 'Pupils Miss Out on School Trips Because of Legal Fears', *The Times,* 28 Sept 2004, p. 9.

4   Pete Allison and John Telford, 'Turbulent Times: Outdoor Education in Great Britain 1993–2003', *Australian Journal of Outdoor Education,* 9, no. 2 (2005), pp. 21–30 (p. 23).

5   Association of Heads of Outdoor Education Centres and others, *Outdoor Education Safety and Good Practice: Guidelines for Guidelines* (London: Duke of Edinburgh's Award, 1988).

6   Pete Allison and John Telford, 'Turbulent Times: Outdoor Education in Great Britain 1993–2003', *Australian Journal of Outdoor Education,* 9, no. 2 (2005), pp. 21–30 (pp. 27–28).

7   Outdoor Education Advisers' Panel, *High Quality Outdoor Education: A Guide to Recognising and Achieving High Quality Outdoor Education in Schools, Youth Services, Clubs and Centres* (No place: English Outdoor Council, 2005).

8   Bob Higginbotham, Email to P McDonald, subject '40', 14 Nov 2015 [Email].

9   Big Lottery Fund, 'New Opportunities Fund Details of Grants Made for the Financial Year Ended 31 March 2005' (2005) <https://www.biglotteryfund.org.uk/-/media/.../pub_grants_list_nof05.pdf> [accessed 14 Apr 2016], p. 10.

10   BBC, 'Funding Boost for Outdoor Centre' (2 May 2007) <news.bbc.co.uk/2/hi/uk_news/england/derbyshire/6614281.stm> [accessed 14 Apr 2016].

11   House of Commons Education and Skills Committee, *Education Outside the Classroom: Second Report of Session 2004–05* (London: The Stationery Office, 10 Feb 2005), pp. 9–10.

12   Ibid., p. Ev 111.

13   Robert G Pettigrew, 'A Short History of Some Outdoor Activities and Their Application in the Current Work of a Typical Centre – White Hall' (Supp. Cert. in PE thesis, Loughborough Training College, 1954–5), p. 72.

14   A B Afford, *The Story of White Hall Open Country Pursuits Centre; vol. 2* (Buxton, Derbyshire, UK: A B Afford, 1978), pp. 30–31.

15   Pete McDonald, *Climbing Lessons: Inside Outdoor Education* (Kaikohe, NZ: Pete McDonald, 1997), pp. 293–296.

16   Geoff Cooper, 'Changing Roles of Outdoor Education Centres', *Environmental Education,* 75 (Spring 2004) (pp. 30–35).

17   House of Commons Education and Skills Committee, *Education Outside the Classroom: Second Report of Session 2004–05* (London: The Stationery Office, 10 Feb 2005), p. Ev 114.

18   United Kingdom Parliament, 'Hansard Online: 22 Feb 2005: Outdoor Pursuits Industry' (22 Feb 2005) <https://www.publications.parliament.uk/pa/cm200405/cmhansrd/vo050222/halltext/50222h05.htm> [accessed 26 Feb 2017].

19   Ibid.

20 Ken C Ogilvie, *Roots and Wings: A History of Outdoor Education and Outdoor Learning in the UK* (Lyme Regis, UK: Russell House Publishing, 2013), p. 718.

21 Julian Fulbrook, *Outdoor Activities, Negligence and the Law*, First paperback edn (London: Routledge, 2016), p. vi.

22 Valerie Elliott, 'Let's Go up Every Creek with a Paddle', *The Times*, 2 May 2006, p. 23.

23 Ibid.

24 Department for Education and Skills, *Learning Outside the Classroom: Manifesto* (Nottingham: DfES, 2006), pp. 8, 12.

25 Ibid., pp. 6–7.

26 Anushka Asthana, 'Teachers Told: Bring Back Adventure', *Observer*, 26 Nov 2006.

27 Health and Safety Executive, 'The Adventure Activities Licensing Service' (no date) <http://www.hse.gov.uk/aala/aals.htm> [accessed 12 Feb 2017].

28 Rowland Woollven, Pete Allison and Peter Higgins, 'Perception and Reception: The Introduction of Licensing of Adventure Activities in Great Britain', *Journal of Experiential Education,* 30, no. 1 (2007), pp. 1–20 (p. 1).

29 Julian Fulbrook, *Outdoor Activities, Negligence and the Law*, First paperback edn (London: Routledge, 2016), p. vii.

30 Bob Barton, *Safety, Risk and Adventure in Outdoor Activities* (London: Paul Chapman Publishing, 2007), p. 3.

31 Ibid., p. 9.

32 Clare Reading, to P McDonald (2), 1 July 2017 [Letter].

33 Health and Safety Executive, 'Working at Height: A Brief Guide', HSE (Jan 2014) <http://www.hse.gov.uk/pubns/indg401.pdf> [accessed 10 July 2017].

34 'All-year Round Climbing', *Buxton Advertiser,* 18 October 2007.

35 Clare Reading, to P McDonald (2), 1 July 2017 [Letter].

36 Sarah Arnott, 'Credit Crisis Rocks the World', *The Independent* (11 Oct 2008) <http://www.independent.co.uk/news/business/analysis-and-features/credit-crisis-rocks-the-world-957956.html> [accessed 18 Oct 2008].

37 John Stepek, 'The Darkest Day for Global Markets – So Far', *MoneyWeek* (6 Oct 2008) <http://www.moneyweek.com/investments/stock-markets/the-darkest-day-for-global-markets-so-far-69190.aspx> [accessed 11 Oct 2008].

38 Derbyshire County Council Education Committee and Anthony Gell School, 'Our Hidden Heritage: The History of Lead Mining in the Peak District', Matlock, Coracle Films (2008) [DVD].

39 'Mining Heritage Brought to Life in Pupils' Documentary', *Derby Evening Telegraph,* 22 June 2009, p. 10.

40 'Memorandum submitted by Dr Peter Higgins …', House of Commons: Select Committee on Education and Skills (31 Jan 2005) <http://www.publications.parliament.uk/pa/cm200405/cmselect/cmeduski/120/120we06.htm> [accessed 18 Nov 2015].

41 'Outdoor Education: Aspects of Good Practice', Office for Standards in Education (24 Sept 2004) <http://dera.ioe.ac.uk/id/eprint/4914> [accessed 25 Feb 2017], p. 14.

42   Valerie Elliott, 'Canoeists up the Creek as Barbed Wire Blocks Access to
      Waterways', *The Times*, 11 July 2009, p. 23.

43   *Taking a Chance Outdoors – Is Fear of Risk Damaging Our Children?*, ed. by Kim
      Haigh and Magali Fleurot (Sheffield: Countryside Recreation Network, 2009),
      p. 7.

44   Tim Muffett, 'Ordnance Survey Marks 220 Years of Mapping' (21 June 2011)
      <http://www.bbc.com/news/uk-13853690> [accessed 4 Apr 2017].

45   Mike Parker, *Map Addict: A Tale of Obsession, Fudge and the Ordnance Survey*
      (London: Collins, 2009), p. 1.

46   House of Commons Children Schools and Families Committee, *Transforming
      Education Outside the Classroom: Sixth Report of Session 2009–10* (London: The
      Stationery Office, 1 Apr 2010), p. 3.

47   Frances Gibb and Alex Ralph, '"Common Sense" Curb on Safety Promises
      Freedom for Schools', *The Times*, 16 Oct 2010, p. 38.

48   Health and Safety Executive, 'Recommendation to Abolish the Adventure
      Activities Licensing Authority' (Mar 2011) <http://www.hse.gov.uk/aala/
      recommendation-to-abolish-aala.htm> [accessed 22 Jun 2017].

49   'Mum's Anger at Plan to Scrap Law Brought in after Four Plymouth Children
      Died', *Plymouth Herald*, 12 Oct 2011.

50   David McArdle, 'Future of Adventure Activities Licensing', The Journal of
      the Law Society of Scotland (17 Oct 2011) <http://www.journalonline.co.uk/
      Magazine/56-10/1010300.aspx> [accessed 22 June 2017].

51   Ken C Ogilvie, *Roots and Wings: A History of Outdoor Education and Outdoor
      Learning in the UK* (Lyme Regis, UK: Russell House Publishing, 2013), p. 738.

52   Ibid., p. 739.

53   Chris Taylor, Sally Power and Gareth Rees, 'Out-of-School Learning: The
      Uneven Distribution of School Provision and Local Authority Support', *British
      Educational Research Journal*, 36, no. 6 (Dec 2010), pp. 1017–1036 (p. 1017).

54   'Funding Cuts Feared for Outdoor Activities after Authority Starts Review',
      Derby Telegraph (5 Mar 2011) <http://www.derbytelegraph.co.uk/Funding-
      cuts-feared-outdoor-activities-authority-starts-review/story-11604453-detail/
      story.html> [accessed 8 Feb 2016].

55   Nick Veevers and Pete Allison, *Kurt Hahn: Inspirational, Visionary, Outdoor and
      Experiential Educator* (Rotterdam: Sense Publishers, 2011), p. xxi.

56   Duke of Edinburgh's Award, 'Our History' (June 2011) <http://www.dofe.info/
      go/history/> [accessed 8 July 2017].

57   Clare Reading, to P McDonald (2), 1 July 2017 [Letter].

58   Ibid.

59   Andrew Bomford, 'Cuts May Deny Poorer Children Outdoor School Trips',
      BBC (9 June 2011) <http://www.bbc.com/news/uk-13715804> [accessed 14
      Apr 2016].

60   John Russell, 'Opinion: The Death of Affordable Outdoor Education?', Liberal
      Democrat Voice (13 June 2011) <http://www.libdemvoice.org/opinion-the-
      death-of-affordable-outdoor-education-24432.html> [accessed 14 Apr 2016].

61   Ibid.

62   Rory Gregory, Email to P McDonald, subject 'Chronological blunder', 19 Aug
      2017 [Email].

63   Darran Hawkins, Email to P McDonald, subject 'Mid-November', 1 Sept 2017 [Email].

64   'Thanks a Million from UK's Kids', Buxton Advertiser Online (19 June 2011) <http://www.buxtonadvertiser.co.uk/news/local/thanks-a-million-from-uk-s-kids-1-3493014> [accessed 26 Mar 2014].

24. Darran Hawkins and a Gritty Optimism, 2012–

Darran Hawkins is the first White Hall principal to be a local, Derbyshire born and bred. He grew up in Belper, a former textile mill town eleven kilometres north of Derby. He attended Belper High School, which in the 1970s and 1980s was a progressive secondary school. There was no school uniform. The head teacher, Michael Tucker, had asked the teachers to prompt the pupils to address them by their first names. Climbing, caving and canoeing were treated as part of the school curriculum.[1] The River Derwent runs through Belper. The town is only thirteen kilometres (eight miles) away from the climbing at Cromford's Black Rocks. There is some caving near Matlock. The school had a strong outdoor pursuits department, which benefitted from the presence of a succession of able and committed teachers, including Pete Clark, Roger Smith, Hilary Collins and Alan Thomson. Hawkins had been one of many pupils influenced by the enthusiasm of these teachers. The well-known mountaineers Nigel Vardy and Alison Hargreaves came through the same course. Hawkins's main sport, as for the seven preceding White Hall wardens or principals, is rock climbing.

The White Hall Centre that Hawkins took charge of in August 2012 was now minimally subsidised, in transition to break even, a goal supported by the county council. The dominant theme of the story of the council's support for White Hall, over a period of seventy years, had been one of nonpartisan enthusiasm and commitment. This backing had continued through the 1990s and 2000s, despite the financial constraints imposed on the county. There had been a few hiccups on the way – the loudest being the regrettable 1998 redundancies episode – but these had been atypical, unrepresentative of the county's long-standing proud ownership of White Hall and of the county's determination to keep White Hall operating. This chapter looks at the last five years of that determination, up to the present day, which means that it is more of a commentary on relatively recent events than a history of the past. Furthermore, the scope for the present staff to frankly express their views to me is limited by contractual restraints. So I write this chapter from a less than fully informed position. To insiders it may reflect what I do not know as much as it reflects what I have found out.

White Hall in 2012 was now operating in a competitive market with various other outdoor centres – local authority and commercial – seeking the custom of similar client groups. The priorities for White Hall were clear: to balance the books, while maintaining standards and keeping course fees as low as possible; to provide day and residential courses to suit the requirements of the schools; to provide an outreach service to schools; to provide accreditation courses for adults in hillwalking, climbing, canoeing and caving; to maintain adequately the equipment; and to develop new income-generating business, such as charging for advisory services, renting out the building on a self-catering basis during the quieter periods when it would otherwise be empty, and running bespoke courses for commercial clients.

White Hall's outreach service remained available, coordinated by Pat Bell. Outreach offered a flexible approach that provided high-quality outdoor education in the local area of a school or further afield. White Hall instructors visited Netherthorpe School in Chesterfield, to provide training and assessment in the outdoor pursuits elements of GCSE physical education. They visited primary schools in northeast Derbyshire to provide bikeability training and assessment. They also responded to requests from some secondary schools for Duke of Edinburgh's Award expedition training and assessment.

The umbrella managerial arrangement Derbyshire Outdoors remained in place, now overseeing White Hall, Lea Green Learning and Development Centre, Meadow Lodge (accessible accommodation at Lea Green) and the Adventur Mobile Activities Team (a mobile unit based in Chesterfield). The head of Derbyshire Outdoors was now Ian Price, who was also the head of Lea Green.

*

In 2012, the *Guardian* ran a roundtable on learning outside the classroom, sponsored by Zurich Municipal (an insurer of schools) and conducted under the Chatham House rule, which states that comments are not attributed to speakers. This rule is said to encourage open debate. An article in late 2012 discussed the roundtable group's findings. I will extract the main ones, to provide a rough idea of the national trends in outdoor education at that time (in England and Wales), a background that could limit the speed and scope of any rejuvenation at White Hall.

During the group's discussions on barriers to outdoor learning, the members had barely mentioned health and safety regulations. The group had even noticed a recent reduction in form-filling and red tape. However, many schools were still reluctant to offer opportunities for learning outside the classroom, particularly for the riskier kinds of activity. The group believed that learning outside the classroom had reduced as a result of funding cuts, inadequate teacher training, parental reluctance and an increased policy emphasis on passing exams and meeting targets. 'In particular, the increasing policy shift in emphasis away from creative subjects such as art and music and towards subjects such as maths, English and science, was felt by some participants to hinder attempts to take children on trips outside the classroom.' Yet, the group thought, 'children experience numerous benefits from learning outside the classroom, such as the opportunity to take risks, learn new physical skills, improve self-confidence and develop better relationships with teachers.'[2]

Meanwhile, in many independent schools there were few if any barriers to outdoor learning. Outdoor education remained a permanent part of the philosophy at Gordonstoun and an enticement to prospective borders (or their parents), a selling point for an education that would cost £29,000 a year.[3]

In the last chapter and in this one, you may have noticed that in some contexts the terms 'outdoor learning' and 'learning outside the classroom' have begun to replace the older term 'outdoor education'. Whether these three terms would become perfect synonyms was difficult to judge. The book *Learning Outside the Classroom: Theory and Guidelines for Practice*, published in 2012, concerned itself entirely with outdoor learning close to schools and the pupils' homes, rather than at faraway residential outdoor centres.[4] The local sites envisaged in this book included built-up areas as well as natural places.

One of the threads that will run through this chapter will be a growing public recognition, nationally, of the health benefits of physical activity. A related thread will be a mounting concern about the number of children whose young bodies were seldom called upon to run or swim or dance or cycle or even walk. In this connection, it was perhaps a sign of this recognition and concern that in 2012 Sport England granted White Hall Centre £20,000 towards the building of an off-road mountain-bike track of about one kilometre in the grounds of the centre. Staff thought that this track would assist the development of cycling within the programme and would also complement the already successful cycle ability training programmes being run at the centre.[5]

A further £20,000 was found by restructuring the spending on equipment for one financial year and by using income generated by outreach services. The mountain-bike trail was built in spring 2013 by Architrial at a cost of £40,000. Groups began using it in May 2013.[6]

The year 2014 at White Hall saw the end of an era on the domestic side. In November, Sara Dawson retired after thirty-eight years as a much loved cook and housekeeper. She had spent most of her working life at White Hall, only a mile and a quarter from Combs, the village where she had grown up. For about eighteen years she had battled through recurring bouts of cancer. She died on 5 February 2016. Her funeral took place at St John the Baptist in Chelmorton. A huge turnout that filled the church included many faces connected with White Hall.

In the same year, Bob Higginbotham completed his fortieth year as cook and then catering supervisor. When he had started, in 1974, two cooks and one housekeeper took care of all the catering for courses of forty pupils and four visiting teachers. Serious food allergies and special diets and religious requirements such as halal meat (permissible meat) were almost unheard of at White Hall. There was just the occasional vegetarian or diabetic pupil or teacher. Much of the written organisation behind the catering – the ordering, the menus, the recipes, the portion sizes, etc – took the form of handwriting on paper.

By 2014, the kitchens were catering for up to seventy-two pupils and about seven accompanying adults. Individual requirements, such as gluten-free and nut-free diets, had become more common than in the past. No cook could afford to ignore the workings of the immune system and anaphylactic shock. The resulting culinary complications had gradually encroached upon the simplicity of the 1970s and 80s. Menus were more complex. Much of the office side of the catering was now done electronically. Bob had witnessed and taken part in a revolution in professional catering.

Petitions, 2012–14

In January 2012 several education organisations had launched a national petition calling on the government to protect outdoor education centres from imminent closure. The organisations included the AHOEC, the EOC, the IOL, the Field Studies Council and the National Association of Field Studies Officers. According to the petition statement, a third of the surviving local authority centres were threatened and closures could deny millions of children the opportunity for potentially life-changing experiences. The petition called for the government to create a fixed-term transition fund and to provide business training that would enable LEA centres to survive long enough to become self-sufficient. It was thought that many of the threatened centres would then be able to remain open. If they were forced to close immediately, many would never reopen. [7]

Steve Tilling, the director of communications at the Field Studies Council, had said that the potential loss of these opportunities for children had come at a time when health, physical activity and contact with nature were all declining. The loss would impact the most, he said, on children from poorer and more disadvantaged groups who had few or no other opportunities to share an overnight experience away from home and to visit places they would not otherwise see. [8]

The deadline for signing this petition was 23 January 2013, by which time it carried 6,432 signatures. It was submitted to the 2010–15 Conservative–Liberal Democrat coalition government. [9]

A curious sub-plot of this petition story was the delayed support for the petition from the BMC, which allocated a webpage to it six months later, titled 'Campaign to Save Outdoor Education Centres'. Better late than never. We saw in Chapter 19 that the BMC and the AWMC (Association of Wardens of Mountain Centres) had been on opposing sides of the prolonged mountain training dispute of the 1970s. In March 1974 Ken Wilson had written that 'climber/educators … have become the fifth columnists of responsible society in our midst … The real climbing world must therefore seriously consider its attitude towards this educational tumour that is gnawing away at its vitals'. [10] This bitter row had ended in December 1979, but the arbitrated truce had not suddenly transformed the BMC into a natural ally and defender of the LEA outdoor sector. On the contrary, twenty years of funding cuts had slipped by before the BMC had woken up to the fact that the closing of dozens of outdoor centres was a matter that the national governing body of hillwalking, rockclimbing and mountaineering ought to concern itself about.

While the generalised national petition was collecting signatures, the supporters of many outdoor centres under the threat of closure were organising local petitions, each opposing the proposed closure of a particular centre or small group of centres. In March 2014, for example, Birmingham city council confirmed that its outdoor learning services for schools would end at eight sites. The council said the closures would save £133,000 in 2014–15, and that the sale of the sites would raise about £2.8 million. More than 600 people signed a petition against the council's plans.

Similar stories were unfolding all over the UK.[11] There seemed to be no light at the end of this tunnel. Yet in June 2014, the National Institute of Economic and Social Research released figures to show that in spring 2014 the UK's economy had passed its pre-recession peak after six years in the doldrums.[12] The recession was over.

Playing Outside, 2012–15

If we judge from press reports, 2012–15 was notable for a marked increase in public concern about a significant drop in the time that children were spending playing outside. Sometime in 2012 or earlier, the television adventurer and Chief Scout, Bear Grylls, had added his voice to this discussion. He had reportedly said that health and safety regulations prevented children from getting the most out of life. In response to this claim, in 2012 the Institution of Occupational Safety and Health (IOSH) had written to him, making clear that its stance was that people should be 'risk aware, not risk averse'.[13]

In April 2013, some statistics emerged in a study by JCB Kids to mark the launch of its Fresh Air Campaign. Modern children were playing outdoors just half as much as their parents had done when they were young. About 54 per cent of the 2,000 parents interviewed worried that their child did not spend enough time playing outdoors. Cath Prisk, a director of Play England, a charity that promoted outdoor play for children, said: 'It's a sad reality that many kids don't get outside to play every day any more. And because they don't go out, they don't know their own communities as well as their parents did, they don't have as many friends in the area and they don't have the same fun that many of their parents did.'[14]

Some of the statistics that emerged were dramatic. In 1971, 86 per cent of primary school children were allowed to travel home from school alone. By 1990, this had dropped to 35 per cent. In 2010 the proportion allowed was only 25 per cent.[15]

To help tackle the problem, Play England was encouraging parents 'to reclaim the streets' for their kids, by thinking about how they themselves had played in the street as children, and about what could be possible where they live. In a few areas in Hackney, Bristol and Oxford, residents were being allowed to regularly close their streets to traffic so that children could play outside.

In the early 1950s, Jack Longland had viewed White Hall as a place where children would learn to play. Sixty years later, this purpose remained, along with other aspects, at the core of White Hall's interpretation of outdoor education. But courses at White Hall Centre involved playing in the countryside, not playing in town streets. What connection has playing in the countryside got to playing in the street or playground? Both of these forms of play can be casualties of risk aversion, such as – on the street – the desire to avoid stranger danger. And both forms of play are essential for 'the development of children who are healthy and active, take a robust approach to risk and relish being outdoors'.[16] According to research undertaken by Nike for its Designed to Move campaign, there was a possibility that the ten-year-olds of 2014 would be the first generation in recent history to have a shorter life expectancy than their parents.[17] In this connection, White Hall's change to running courses for primary schools, although basically a response to falling demand from secondary schools, fitted perfectly into the contemporary thinking: targeting children before the age of ten was the key to breaking the cycle of physical inactivity, because that was when preferences and motivation were hard-wired and when life-long physical activity patterns were instilled.[18]

In May 2014, following the example of Bear Grylls (whose UK merchandising arm, incidentally, made £3.3 million profit that year[19]), another television celebrity adventurer Ben Fogle joined in the conversation. I have not checked his figures:

A recent survey reported that children in the UK were spending an average of half an hour a week outdoors. Half an hour? That's less than a prisoner would expect. It's enough to make me want to weep. As a father I fear for my own children, chained to their classroom rather than exploring the great outdoors.

Learning and education should be as much about the natural world in which we live as they are about books. I realise our education system is stretched, but it seems that sport, outdoor activities, school outings and field trips have been sacrificed to meet government targets in the classroom.

As a child, it was the great outdoors that helped me overcome my own lack of self-esteem and confidence. The great outdoors

has bettered me as a person. It has made me who I am, and it's
something I am desperate to instil in my own children.[20]

In April 2015, the IOSH backed up Grylls's argument that children
should take more risks and spend more time outdoors.[21]

Earlier in this chapter I mentioned the increasing use of the terms
'outdoor learning' and 'learning outside the classroom'. On 21 April
2015 Lea Green Learning and Development Centre hosted the Derbyshire Learning Outside the Classroom Conference. Nine workshops
took place, ranging from Woodland Tots and Outdoor Natural Music
Making to Pond and River Studies and Outdoor Education to Aid
Learning. Providers' stands in the Lea Green sports hall represented
thirty-three organisations that included residential centres, environmental bodies and heritage sites.[22] On a fine spring day, over 130 people came 'together to share best practice, [to] explore new ideas and
opportunities and [to] show that learning outside the classroom [was]
not just "outdoors" but encompasse[d] a wealth of "beyond four walls"
experiences available to our young people'.[23]

Women Instructors at White Hall

Throughout much of White Hall's existence until the major changes
that began in 1992, the permanent teaching staff had been all male.
Even in the six periods when the staff did include a permanent female
instructor, she was the sole woman. Commenting on this in January 1993, Phil Booth had said that attempts to achieve a balanced
staff (50/50 male and female) were regarded as desirable but had not
succeeded.

> At best [there had been] one female in a teaching staff of seven in
> recent years. One view was [that] this arose because traditionally
> female staff with good experience and qualifications [had] not
> been available. The nature of the work (anti-social hours, over-
> nights, weekend working) has also tended to discourage women
> staff, especially those with children.[24]

In 2016 Simon Beames interviewed White Hall's first six female permanent instructors. They were Meriel Blake (formerly Evans), 1965–9;
Janet Davies (formerly Richards), 1969–71; Barbara Hall (formerly
Hulley), 1971–5; Lynda Welham, 1976–7; Hilary Sharp, 1987–90;
and Gill Berrow, 1990–3. Perhaps the strongest finding was that all
six women did not perceive that they had been treated differently due

to their gender by their manager, colleagues or course members. This would seem to contradict much of the gender-based outdoor education literature, which highlights a long history of sexism. This finding suggests that the organisational culture at White Hall and the attitudes and actions of the six female instructors were somewhat extraordinary.

Outdoor Recreation, the Economy, and Health, 2014–17

As we near the end of Part Four of White Hall's story, having left behind the global recession, you might be expecting the influence on outdoor education of national developments to quieten, leaving White Hall Centre and other outdoor centres – publicly owned or privately owned – to flourish or to wither in the market economy. Or to soldier on, doing great work in spite of government policies. Instead, another national development took place that would significantly affect these policies. While the lead-up to and the implementing of the Scottish independence referendum (held on 18 September 2014) transfixed Britain and while subsequently the suspense before and the implementing of the Brexit referendum (held on 23 June 2015) transfixed Europe, a national organisation called the Sport and Recreation Alliance concentrated on things that really mattered, precipitating a well-informed and determined campaign in support of outdoor recreation.

The Sport and Recreation Alliance (SRA) is an umbrella body for sport and recreation, representing over 300 governing and representative bodies. In June 2014 it published a report, *Reconomics: The Economic Impact of Outdoor Recreation in the UK: The Evidence*. This report established the value of the UK outdoor economy, collating a wide and disparate literature and bringing the results together into one comprehensive eighty-eight page document.

The authors of the report acknowledged that defining outdoor recreation is complex and problematic. The concept can mean all things to all people. One earlier researcher had interpreted 'outdoor recreation' to mean anything from 'rock-climbing, equestrian sports or adventure racing … to more leisurely activities such as bird watching, dragon boat racing, or a walk along a marked path.' The concept covers an extremely broad range of leisure pursuits including camping, hunting and fishing.[25] For the purpose of their research, the authors took outdoor recreation to mean physical activities that take place in the natural environment.

As well as making the full report available, the SRA provided a summary document, condensing the results and presenting them partly in pictorial form. Compressing the findings into four main points, the last page of this summary said that outdoor recreation (in 2014):

- was the UK's favourite pastime – three in four adults in England regularly got active outdoors;
- drove the visitor economy – people spending their day enjoying outdoor recreation had spent £21 billion in 2012–13;
- created jobs and skills – walking tourism alone supported up to 245,500 full-time equivalent jobs; and
- promoted a healthy nation – outdoor recreation could make a significant contribution to tackling the £10 billion cost of physical inactivity.[26]

On the last point, the report said that the health benefits of an active lifestyle were well documented; they were so important that experts had referred to physical activity as a 'wonder drug'. 'We know that outdoor recreation is good for the mind, body and soul. As such it has a very significant role to play in the challenge to get the nation more active and more healthy.'[27]

Many outdoor instructors and teachers of outdoor education will have welcomed this report. But its real importance for the outdoor education sector lay not when viewed in isolation but when viewed in partnership with subsequent related developments.

We saw in Chapter 23 that in 2010 a government report had recommended the abolition of the AALA, as part of a general policy of cutting the red tape that was hampering businesses. In March 2015 the same government, the Conservative–Liberal Democrats coalition, reversed this proposal. The AALA would be retained, ministers having decided that 'there remains a place for AALA because it is important that parents and other carers of children can have confidence that activity providers are following good safety practices. Therefore AALA will be retained, albeit that in the longer term its scope and future delivery mechanisms may change.'[28]

On 28 October 2015, the House of Commons debated outdoor recreation. David Rutley, the MP for Macclesfield and a lover of the Peak District, opened the debate and soon got to the nub of things, putting the case for outdoor recreation very clearly:

Although many would be reluctant to put on a pair of football or rugby boots, some 20 million people [who were not currently active] said that they would like to participate in outdoor recreation of some kind when they contributed to Sport England's commissioned research 'Getting Active Outdoors'. Some will need a nudge and others will need to be empowered or enabled to achieve their aspiration, but it will be worth it, because if we can inspire people and get more people off the sofa and active in one or more kinds of outdoor recreation, we can harvest considerable economic benefits in terms of health spending saved and productive value added.[29]

He closed his introduction by asking for a broad interpretation of the word 'sport':

> Let me conclude by saying that … we now need a fundamental shift in social attitudes to being active so that it is more usual to take part and be physically active than to not participate. We need to interpret sport in the widest sense of outdoor active participation and recreation. It will help to improve physical and mental health and wellbeing, and productivity gains, and, as *Reconomics* shows, will add a huge amount to our rural economies.[30]

As you plough through the remarkably similar speeches in the Hansard record of this important and good-natured debate, the more incomprehensible becomes the memory of the previous two decades, a tale of protracted government indifference to the plight of the LEA outdoor education centres.

There was widespread agreement that a cross-departmental approach would be needed to promote outdoor recreation, involving the Department for Culture, Media and Sport, the Department of Health, and the Department for Education. Several speakers mentioned the role of schools in promoting outdoor recreation. John Mann, the MP for Bassetlaw, said: 'There should be a proper debate across Government about all year 6 pupils, who are in their final year of primary school, having a residential week in the great outdoors.'[31] This idea alone, if implemented, would probably secure the future of many outdoor education centres, including White Hall.

On the day after the parliamentary debate, the BMC website reported on it enthusiastically. This influential website received three million hits a year. The post pointed out that the debate had seen repeated calls for the outdoors to be made central to the government's physical activity strategy.[32]

That strategy arrived about a month later in an eighty-four page document titled *Sporting Future: A New Strategy for an Active Nation*. Very significantly, the new policy broadened the traditional meaning of 'sport' to include outdoor recreation: 'The UK is fortunate to have some of the best countryside and outdoor space in the world, where people can take part in a wide variety of activities, many of which have not necessarily been supported as much as other more traditional sports. This needs to change if we are to provide a variety of different opportunities to engage in sport and physical activity that meets the demand from the customer, rather than telling them what type of activity we think they should be doing.'[33]

We saw in Chapter 13 that by the early 1960s some colleges of physical education were starting to broaden their syllabuses to include sports like canoeing and rockclimbing. However, for some 'traditional' PE lecturers, who were most at home in the gym or on the tennis court, getting to grips with the aesthetics of the hill and water sports, and accepting these sports as worthy curriculum members, had been problematic, taking the lecturers out of their comfort zone. Now, over fifty years later – déjà vu! – outdoor recreation and its aesthetics were at last receiving some recognition in the government's strategy for sport:

> The insight in *Getting Active Outdoors* [a recent study into the supply of and demand for outdoor activities in England] showed that 'being outdoors' itself is important rather than the sport or activity; it is the environment which is enticing. We are very encouraged by the report's findings and want to see the outdoor activities sector thrive and grow as an important alternative way that people can engage in sport and physical activity.[34]

Sporting Future was widely welcomed. It spelt out one of the changes that needed to take place in implementing the new strategy: 'In order to deliver the most for this sector, Sport England will need to work with organisations it has not traditionally worked with on outdoor recreation.'[35]

Little by little by little by little, outdoor recreation, including its aesthetic aspects, was beginning to receive the informed attention that it deserved. The next change was a noticeable shift in Sport England's approach, observable in *Towards an Active Nation*, released by Sport England in May 2016. In *Towards an Active Nation*, Sport England stated an intention to spend more money on tackling inactivity. It also committed itself to invest more in children and young people from the age of five to build positive attitudes to sport and activity as the foundations of an active life.[36]

Sport England wanted to make life easier for the millions of people who were trying to be active but who found that the physical, social and emotional cues and incentives to act were just not strong or relevant enough to their lives. In this connection, Sport England thought that some activities had a 'particularly strong potential to move the market' because they had wide appeal and were relatively easy for people to fit into their busy lives. These activities included walking, cycling, and outdoor activities.[37]

Outdoor recreation was now being seen as an important component of government plans to improve people's fitness and health and to hence eliminate avoidable costs to the national health service. A main snag in the recent history – the last twenty-five years – of LEA outdoor activity centres had been the inability of successive governments (and of some educationists) to appreciate the long-term value to the nation of outdoor recreation, and by extension of outdoor education. Westminster policies strongly supporting the growth of outdoor recreation were a welcome change after decades of funding cuts and risk aversion.

What had these national developments got to do with White Hall Centre? Promoting the hill and water sports had been at the heart of White Hall's *raison d'être* since 7 June 1949, when a county council subcommittee had anticipated the possible use of the premises 'in connexion with open-country pursuits'. Chapter 17 included a typical course programme from the 1970s, showing an illustrated talk 'Where to Now' on the last evening of the course. This matched one of White Hall's purposes, the promotion of outdoor recreation. In only one aspect of its approach to this task might White Hall have underachieved or been slow to join the fashion: occupying glittering exhibitors' stands at industry gatherings, networking with other delegates and potential clients, and running an extravagant website, frequently revamped.

My mention of the centre's *raison d'être* in the last paragraph reminds me that in Chapter 23 I promised to look into which aspects of White Hall's traditional purposes have survived into 2017. I shall do so now, but only in the broadest terms. In 2017, schools continued to be White Hall's main clients, seeking the three-circles residential educational courses that the centre had been providing since 1950. Other users, such as the youth service, were smaller in number. But every paying user helped to keep the centre afloat.

In the late 1970s and the 1980s, many outdoor centres had become involved in providing the residential part of the government's Youth Opportunities Programme (YOP) and its successor the Youth Training Scheme (YTS). These two post-school schemes had aimed to develop young people's life skills and social skills to improve the employability of the nation's workforce. However, White Hall had played little part in these enterprises as its schools' courses were in heavy demand and were always fully booked, even with minimal promotion.

In more recent times – since 1992 but I cannot be more specific than that – White Hall has involved itself successfully in several local initiatives focused on the social and personal development of young people. One of these enterprises was called Derbyshire Educational Leisure Time Activities (DELTA). The DELTA courses, Darran Hawkins wrote in 2017,

> were and still are immensely important ... for the opportunity WH can give to some of the most disadvantaged young people of Derbyshire. This was ... and still is valuable work ... This is why we're here, to help young people get the best opportunities and chances in life and if we can contribute through a residential holiday with outdoor activities then we're of value. Feedback and evaluations from social workers, young people and parents/carers showed that we did and [shows that we] still do make an important contribution.[38]

Clare Reading remembers the DELTA courses evolving after initial minor difficulties. Her frank description glimpses some of the sort of tensions that can lie beneath the surface of residential outdoor education:

> Rising costs for young people on our summer courses led to a reduction in the number of more specialist low staff-student ratio courses. This happened around the time that DELTA funding came in. After some initial teething problems, we got better and better at placing a young person on the right course to meet their needs. These solutions ranged from taster days and one-night camps to full five-day residentials.
>
> Instructors worked in pairs with small groups, so we chose whole days out using venues farther afield, and there was extra money too for visiting climbing walls and going ten-pin bowl-

ing on the last night. There were always challenges, but it was rewarding too.[39]

Previously in Part Four, few discrepancies have appeared between the accounts of different staff members. But differing perceptions can occur between the members of the teaching staff of an outdoor centre, just as they can between the members of the teaching staff of a school. The Hawkins and Reading views on DELTA courses come from slightly different perspectives, each being no less professional than the other.

In about 2015, Fiona Thomson was promoted from senior instructor to centre manager, a role she would share with Pat Bell.

In 2016 Derbyshire Sport published its strategy *Towards an Active Derbyshire: 2016–2021*, a local response to Sport England's *Towards an Active Nation*. This local interpretation lacked the term 'outdoor recreation' and almost completely lacked the word 'recreation'.[40] The Derbyshire strategy had not caught up with the national policy statements. However, a careful search of the Derbyshire document found a quote from *Getting Active Outdoors*: 'Early exposure to outdoor activities can make a lasting impression. People who are introduced to outdoors activities as children and adolescents are more likely to grow up to choose an active outdoors lifestyle.' As well as this recognition of the value of outdoor activities, quoted from a national document, the authors added a local ambition:

> We will engage a wide range of providers and influencers, building a culture of activity outdoors, engaging people in the fantastic countryside, landscapes and urban parks that Derbyshire, the Peak District National Park and the National Forest are known and celebrated for.[41]

Derbyshire Sport is a voluntary partnership that exists to enable many organisations to work together to promote sport and recreation in the county.

On 16 September 2016 David Rutley took a group of about thirteen MPs for a walk on the Carneddau, being the annual walk of the all-party parliamentary group for mountaineering. The fact that this had become an annual event was evidence of a rising parliamentary interest in outdoor recreation. After the walk Rutley said: 'It's vital to help get more people off the sofa and become more active outdoors.

The health and well-being benefits are clear, and this will also create a real boost to rural tourism.'[42]

Sometime in 2016 Darran Hawkins became Assistant Head of Service, overseeing White Hall. Part of this role involved establishing the county's School Visits Service, which advises schools on matters connected with learning-outside-the-classroom. Hawkins's full job title became Assistant Head of Service and Outdoor Education Advisor.

In an initiative to maximise the centre's income, during quiet periods the building was rented out to private groups on a self-catering basis; this practice had been evolving for several years.

In February 2017, shortly before I finished work on the manuscript for this book, the SRA published *Reconomics Plus*, updating and expanding the well-received *Reconomics* (2014) to reflect the significant recent changes in government strategies, especially the broadening of 'sport' to include a wide range of outdoor recreations.

Course Fees, Staffing and Capacity in 2017

While we are on the subject of money, and nearing the end of this book, how much were young people now paying for their White Hall residential courses? The full price list differentiated between Derbyshire young people, City of Derby young people, out-county individuals, and people on bespoke courses for commercial firms. Arguably the fee of interest to most potential users was the fee that a Derbyshire school pupil paid. For a five-day (four nights) course in October 2016, a school pupil paid the high-season fee of £236.60.[43] This fee covered full board, all tuition at a standard staff-pupil ratio of 1:10, all equipment, and the use of the centre's minibuses. The five-day courses lasted from 12 noon on the Monday to 2pm on the Friday. For a similar course in March 2017, the school pupil paid the low-season fee of £212.00. The following table is an extract from the full price list:

High season (1 September – 31 October 2016)

COURSE	Derbyshire Young People	Derby City	All other groups and Individuals	Commercial and Management
5 Day	236.60	271.20	319.00	410.20
3 Day	118.30	135.60	159.50	205.10
Fri - Sun	111.65	128.95	152.85	198.45
Saturday - Sunday	88.30	110.40	133.60	178.10

Course No. 3169	Group A	Group B	Group C	Group D	Group E	Group F
Group Tutors						
Group Rooms	Coffee Lounge	Dining Room	Lounge	Briefing Room	Conservatory	Kinder Annexe

Monday 9th		
am	12 noon Arrive, Course Introduction, Packed **Lunch**, **Settle** into Dormitories, **Equipment** Issue	
pm	Grounds Activities and Introduction to Maps	
Evening	Night Hike	Evening session staff:............ Overnight Duty:............

Tuesday 10th		Group A	Group B	Group C	Group D	Group E	Group F
	am	Adventure Day	Adventure Day	Canoe	C Wall/Ropes/Zipwire	Scramble	Mountain Bike
	pm			C Wall/Ropes/Zipwire	Canoe	Mountain Bike	Scramble
	Evening	Shelter Building				Staff on duty:............	

Wednesday 11th		Group A	Group B	Group C	Group D	Group E	Group F
	am	Scramble	Mountain Bike	Adventure Day	Adventure Day	Canoe	C Wall/Ropes/Zipwire
	pm	Mountain Bike	Scramble			C Wall/Ropes/Zipwire	Canoe
	Evening	Secret Agents				Staff on duty:............	

Thursday 12th		Group A	Group B	Group C	Group D	Group E	Group F
	am	Canoe	C Wall/Ropes/Zipwire	Scramble	Mountain Bike	Adventure Day	Adventure Day
	pm	C Wall/Ropes/Zipwire	Canoe	Mountain Bike	Scramble		
	Evening	Mini Olympics				Staff on duty:............	

Friday 13th		
am	Team Challenges including Orienteering Competition, Equipment Return, Course Summary	
pm	2.00 pm Pack and Clear Dormitories, Depart	

A programme for a residential five-day (four nights) primary school course in September 2013.

By moving the office out to the vacant principal's house, extra dormitory space had been created in the main building, which could now accommodate seventy-two students. Each school was allocated one free teacher place per activity group. For example, if a school brought twenty children, there would be two activity groups and therefore two free places for the accompanying teachers or other adults.

White Hall's transport in 2017 consisted of three minibuses, as it had done for over forty years.

Although courses for school groups remained White Hall's main provision, the annual programme still found room for some courses for individuals. Some of these courses targeted young people, while others were open to people of any age. People could book these courses individually or in groups of friends or in family groups.

Five-day (four nights) 'adventure activity breaks in the Peak District' were available for 9–13 year olds and for 14–17 year olds. These weeks ran from 10am on the first day to 4pm on the last day. The activities on offer included climbing, canoeing, kayaking, mountain-biking, ropes courses, zip-wires, orienteering, hill adventures and rock scrambles. The price for a Derbyshire resident in 2016, with an 'early bird discount', was £276. The full price (if not booked early) for a Derbyshire resident was £345.[44]

Similar but shorter three-day (two nights) adventure activity breaks were also available, for the same age groups.

Not all courses were residential. Multi-activity days, running from 10am to 4pm and introducing a range of activities, were open to people of all ages and abilities, at £21 per person in 2016. Activity taster days were similar, for £24.20 per person in 2016.

In response to the need to increase the centre's income, the briefing room and the boardroom were now available for hire as meeting rooms when not in use by White Hall's course members. To hire one of these rooms cost £15 per hour. On the few occasions each year when White Hall was empty, with no courses being run, the whole centre was available for hire. The cost of hiring the whole centre, for accommodation only, was £24 per person per night (with a minimum total charge of £720 per night).[45]

In the financial year 2016–17, the county council subsidy met 18 per cent of White Hall's total running costs. This subsidy covered a much lower proportion of the running costs than in earlier years, as shown starkly by the following table:

Year	1982–3[i]	1991–2[ii]	2016–17
Subsidy	179,000	340,000	Unobtained
Student fees	38,000	42,000	Unobtained
Total running costs	217,000	382,000	Unobtained
Subsidy as a % of total running costs	82%	89%	18%[iii]

[i] Derbyshire Record Office, A Comparison of Two Outdoor Adventure Centres: Pete McDonald, 1983, D7786/BOX/1/Bundle 1, p. 78.

[ii] Booth, Philip David, 'The Impact of Financial Cuts upon an Outdoor Centre … during the Financial Year 1992/93' (MA dissertation, University of Sheffield, Jan 1993), p. 4.

[iii] Nicoll, Judith, Note to P McDonald, 17 Nov 2017 [Note].

The county council expected White Hall's income and costs to break even, with zero subsidy, by 2019. No less notable than the magnitude of the cut in the subsidy had been the remarkable collective resilience of those many people who, over two decades, had worked to help White Hall to adjust to the new reality. The untiring efforts of everyone connected with White Hall throughout the period of Part Four had achieved a transformation in the centre's financing.

The total number of staff employed at White Hall in 2017, either full-time or part-time, was three or four times as many as at the end of Part Three. Also, the range of roles they occupied had deepened, as shown by the diagram on the next page:

```
┌─────────────────────────────┐
│ Assistant Head of Service &  │
│  Outdoor Education Advisor   │
│        Darran Hawkins        │
│           FTE: 1             │
└─────────────────────────────┘

┌─────────────────────────────┐
│       Centre Manager         │
│          Pat Bell            │
│        Fiona Thomson         │
│           FTE: 2             │
└─────────────────────────────┘
```

Business Services Officer		Team Leader
Judith Nicoll		Clare Reading
FTE: 1		FTE: 0.5

Catering Supervisor	Business Services Assistant	Programme Leader
Robert Higginbotham	Vacant	Dave Barker (0.5)
FTE: 1	FTE: 1	Rory Guy (0.5)
		Jennifer Harding (0.75)

Cook	Business Services Assistant	Andrew Waring (0.5)
Paula Camenzuli	Diane Cox	Leon Zablocki (0.5)
Ann Copstick	Margaret Jackson	FTE: 2.75
FTE: 1.7	FTE: 0.7	

Catering Assistant		Permanent Instructor
Janet Davenport		Tom Wild
Bethany Baily		Mark Cudahy
FTE: 0.4		Kathryn Breen
		FTE: 3

Caretaker		Apprentice Instructor
Paul Bailey		Samuel Hooper
FTE: 1		FTE: 1

		Relief Instructor
		About 27 freelance
		instructors are listed as
		relief instructors

Cleaner		Relief Night Care As-
Michelle Lownds		sistant
Diana Brassington		Matthew Gould
Kay Doxey		Paul May
Karen Eley		Lauren Fielding
FTE: 2		Anna Welsh
		Andrew Westley
		Nicola Parkin
		Simon Ramwell

White Hall's staffing structure in November 2017. Adapted from a fuller version drawn up by Judith Nicoll. The abbreviation 'FTE' stands for 'full-time equivalent'.

Staff photographs on a centre noticeboard, November 2017. The thirty-nine people include part-time staff and freelance instructors.

Stream-beds That Flash in the Sunlight

In 1950, when White Hall opened, the UK had about 900 National Coal Board collieries employing a total of 697,000 men, who that year produced 216 million tons of coal.[46] Sixty-five years later, on Friday 18 December 2015, miners worked the last shift at Kellingley Colliery in North Yorkshire, ending centuries of deep coalmining in Britain. This is one example of the national changes that have taken place during the life of White Hall Centre.

The hill and water sports have changed also. In 1950, the British Mountaineering Council had no paid staff. By 1974, it had a number of paid staff, but during the mountain training dispute a BMC future policy committee had produced a draft report containing statements like 'it is not the function of the BMC to encourage people to take up mountaineering'. Using the hills for educational purposes, the report had said, would be 'prejudicial to the interests of mountaineers'.

Now the BMC is a sizeable organisation with about twenty-five employees. Climbing has become an established part of the entertainment, recreation and tourism industries, driven by commerce such as selling insurance, equipment and guiding services.[47] The BMC has also expanded its services to and its influence upon walkers. In 2017, among nine BMC core policies was one on young people that said:

> The BMC is committed to supporting and encouraging young people who are interested in climbing, hill walking and mountaineering. The BMC's role is to act in an advisory capacity and to facilitate youth activities such as indoor competitions and appropriate outdoor activities. The BMC encourages the provision of outdoor youth training by competent agencies.[48]

Canoeing in 1950 was still a minority sport. White Hall groups regularly canoed on stretches of the River Derwent. (My enquiries to discover exactly where have only revealed a missing fraction of history.) Sometimes the White Hall canoeists camped beside this river. Since then, canoeing has grown steadily. In April 2014 the BCU underwent a rebranding. The British Canoe Union, Canoe England and Great Britain Canoeing joined forces to become British Canoeing. Publicity connected with this change said that 1.6 million British people paddled a canoe once or twice a year; 100,000 paddled ten times a year or more; and 36,000 paddlers were affiliated to the BCU (at the time of the name change).[49] And these large numbers were likely to grow. To ensure the long-term success and growth of the sport, British Canoeing intended to increase its focus on attracting new people into canoeing.

This book started, in Chapter 1, with Jack Longland marching across the plains of Tibet in 1933 in a mile-long column, as a member of a large expedition to Everest. Now, if you are an affluent mountaineer and in a hurry, you can arrive at Everest base camp by helicopter. At base camp, you might phone home to deal with some business matter, before setting off up the mountain, taking advantage of a good and reliable weather forecast, a beaten track in the snow, and the fixed ropes and fixed ladders that have become the semi-permanent infrastructure of Everest tourism. With a bit of luck you could be on your way home a week later.

In Chapter 11, I mentioned Chris Bonington and Ian Clough climbing the north face of the Eiger in 1962, a notable achievement accomplished competently in three days. In November 2015, the Swiss climber Ueli Steck climbed the north face of the Eiger at least four times in two weeks. On one of these ascents, he 'reclaimed the speed record … climbing the ca. 5,500-foot face in 2 hours 22 minutes 50 seconds'.[50]

At a grass-roots level, 'cheap flights and a move away from risk-taking has meant that overcrowding on the UK crags has shifted to crags in France, Spain and Thailand, leaving many British mountain crags to gather moss.'[51]

Against this background of enormous change over sixty-seven years, it would be surprising if White Hall Centre had not also undergone innovation and modification. This book has recorded a steady stream of incremental alterations and adjustments occurring over the whole period. It has also described, in the last three chapters, the fundamental changes forced upon the centre by a financial crisis.

Shortly after I started writing this book, Darran Hawkins said to me, in an email: 'The place hasn't changed much, new dining room conservatory, new bigger climbing wall in the chapel and a few more bunk beds to increase from the 40 of your day to 70 now.' The remark was a casual one with a limited context, not part of a discussion on all aspects of the centre.

I knew of course that a hell of a lot had changed, nationally and locally. Transformation and innovation had affected White Hall's financing, management, staffing, communicating, marketing and programming. Here is one more example: from the 1950s to the 1980s, pupils often wrote thank-you letters to White Hall; now some of them post video clips on YouTube or they post comments on school blogs. But in another sense, Hawkins was right. The setting of the manor house, on a windswept broad spur, has not changed. The views from the house in all directions have hardly altered. If you don't believe me, take a walk to retrace the steps of the many 1950s visitors to White Hall whose buses dropped them off in Buxton, the highest market town in England. Put some boots on, if it's winter, and head up Manchester Road (A5004), passing the Devonshire Dome on your right and, after ten minutes, leaving the town behind and below you. Stay on the busy main road for another kilometre, hugging the safety of the verge, well out of reach of Tarmac trucks. After passing Cold Springs Farm, take the right fork to follow the Roman Road steadily uphill. Initially thinly tarmacked and hemmed in by dry-stone walls, this narrow lane soon deteriorates markedly into an exquisitely ordinary ancient byway. It has all the characteristics you would expect of such a route: a battered gate, remnants of tarmac, muddy ruts, water-filled potholes (often frozen in winter), loose pebbles and sizeable rocks, an occasional unkempt

sheep that doesn't look capable of reaching the meatworks or perhaps
a gaudily dressed mountain-biker too breathless to say hello and – as
you gain height, meandering slightly – increasingly expansive view in
all directions. On the left are boggy fields where grass competes with
rush and tussock. On the right, the hummocky moorland rises steeply to
Combs Moss. Here and there, ugly scatterings of old bricks attempt to
fill washed-out sections of the track. The tattered track levels out before
reaching a high point, and then the narrow strip of tarmac reappears
and the road drops gently to White Hall.

Old Road has not changed much in living memory. There is nothing
new on it, unless you are a geocacher, in which case you might be playing
a new version of Bandits, searching for a small Tupperware container
hidden by the side of the stony track and containing a yo-yo and a toy
aeroplane. The unmaintained lane is now a part of the Midshires Way,
a 362-kilometre footpath (and in places a bridleway) through middle
England.

To fully appreciate that nothing has altered, and provided that you
are feeling energetic and are suitably clad, when you reach the back of
White Hall but before you reach the narrow side gate you could ignore
the persistent light rain and head across the sedgy hillside roughly
eastwards along the footpath below Combs Edge, and then you could
continue around the thirty kilometres of Joe's carved-number scheme
that circles the Goyt Valley. This should convince you that this glorious
part of Derbyshire has little changed.

Land use in Britain's countryside can change. Agriculture changes.
Cattle may replace sheep. Farm buildings may grow bigger. The techniques of forestry change, and forests wax and wane. New reservoirs
appear. Old ones can vanish. Wind turbines and motorways may appear,
controversially. But, compared to townscapes, rural landscapes change
only slowly, especially in the national parks, and often remain unaltered
over several lifetimes.

In his eloquent and inspiring book *The Wild Places*, the travel writer
Robert MacFarlane described his search for any genuinely wild places
left in Britain. The search saw him climbing, walking and swimming
by day and spending his nights sleeping on cliff-tops and in ancient
meadows and wildwoods. Conventional wisdom tells us that Britain
has no true wilderness, but MacFarlane discovered fifteen locations
that, he suggested convincingly, deserved to be called wild places. On
moorland, he wrote:

… despite the human influences in their making, the moors of Britain and Ireland have become wild places for numberless people, who leave behind the confines of their cities to enter another realm: of mazes made by troughs and hags, of wheatears flicking between stones, and of mica sand that causes stream-beds to flash in the sunlight with a silver fire.[52]

MacFarlane's celebrated book has become a modern classic. Time will tell whether he has singlehandedly and permanently broadened the meaning of the adjective 'wild'. For MacFarlane, a wild place was 'somewhere remote, where starlight fell clearly, where the wind could blow upon [you] from its thirty-six directions, and where the evidence of human presence was minimal or absent.'[53] I am happy to follow his lead and to label Combs Moor, for example, as a wild place. The broken and ramshackle rocks of Combs Edge and the treeless spongy moor itself, with its eroding peat beds and its emerald-green cushions of bog-moss, are only about a hundred metres lower in height above sea level than Kinder Scout and Bleaklow, Derbyshire's wildest moors. White Hall, sitting on its broad spur, is only ten minutes' walk below Combs Edge. Most Derbyshire children live in areas that are manifestly unwild: the county's towns and suburbs. White Hall is perfectly sited for introducing these children to one of Derbyshire's trackless expanses. This was the case in 1950, and it remains so today.

We humans are forever adapting our lives to suit changing circumstances. Whenever we do so, particularly during tumultuous times, some of our organisations and some of our ideas, such as our educational priorities, do not survive. The underground mining of coal in the UK ended either because people no longer used coal or because they could buy it more cheaply from other countries. Should we now treat climbing and canoeing and sailing as activities that we have moved on from and can discard, like coalmining and haystack building and bus conducting? Do children need these traditional adventurous outdoor pursuits any more? Or are privately-run ropes courses like Go Ape ('31 sites across the UK … and counting!'), and long zip wires (£30 a go, given as birthday presents), seen as the same thing, but better? Will educators discard the child-development aspects (costly) and only keep the big-thrill, no-skill funfair amusements?

If we judge from Key Stages 1 and 2 (for children aged five to eleven) of the national curriculum for PE, outdoor activities are not about to follow coal into the history books. How well the activities will be provided in the future, however, is difficult to anticipate. In 2006 the *Learning Outside the Classroom Manifesto* had promised young people that ventures in the school grounds would be 'of agreed high quality', Clare Reading, commenting in 2017, was less than impressed by the quality of some of the provision that had been added since the manifesto: 'Many primary schools now have a bit of bouldering wall in their playground, to "tick that box", but it has to be so unchallenging as to not need supervision, so of-agreed-high-quality it generally is not.'[54]

Orienteering is perhaps a more successful activity in school grounds than bouldering walls are. Many schools now, in 2017, have some orienteering exercises that are easily set up in their grounds. British Orienteering is working to improve the quality and extent of these orienteering activities through training for teachers.

On a similar matter – that of the facilities in the White Hall grounds – Chapter 23 mentioned the White Hall ropes course and the repercussions of the Work at Height Regulations 2005. Employers, managers and employees were to 'take a sensible approach when considering precautions for work at height'. Before 2005, maintaining the ropes course had been an odd job for an instructor on a Monday morning; now it was a business. Clare Reading brings us up to date on the ropes-course maintenance: 'Although some checking and maintenance is done in house, White Hall also pays someone to make decisions about what needs doing, when to replace cables, etc. He does the biggest time-consuming jobs too. I think he builds courses, so is following best practice in that world.'[55] You could argue whether this change resulted from a sensible approach or from the need to meet regulations that nobody really believed in. Darran Hawkins pointed out to me that the White Hall managers were not risk averse; they were 'risk aware, and aware of the present view of risk in Britain'.[56]

This chapter has allocated much space to the subject of outdoor recreation, merely one aspect of outdoor education, because outdoor recreation in 2012–17 was receiving some positive and hopeful attention nationally. Government policies in health and education were placing increased emphasis on the value of activities like hillwalking and cycling, over a lifetime. A possibility existed that outdoor recreation could become a salutary catalyst that would help to haul the surviving outdoor centres out of irritating uncertainty and into more stable times. Meanwhile, the other main aspects of outdoor education – environmental appreciation and social and personal development – remained as fundamentally important as the hill and water sports. In articles about outdoor pursuits written in the 1950s, the word 'environment' had scarcely appeared; by 2017, the state of the environment had become the most important story of the age, encompassing rights and responsibilities, pollution, overconsumption, climate change and loss of biodiversity. The world had never needed environmental education as much as it needed it in 2017. In connection with all three of these aspects of outdoor education, developing stronger links to the school curriculum continued to be a priority in the outdoor centres' tussles to survive.

An example of the increasing emphasis on linking residential outdoor education to the school curriculum occurred in July 2017 on a blog of the School of Sport and Exercise Science of the University of Lincoln. A group of undergraduates had attended a course on 'Teaching Key Stage 2 Outdoor Education', based at Hagg Farm Outdoor Education Centre, on the Snake Road above Bamford. The blog said that 'Hagg Farm Centre provides primary and secondary schools in Nottingham with outdoor learning experiences which meet the requirements of the National Curriculum for Physical Education'.[57] Two months later, Nottinghamshire county council advertised a vacancy at Hagg Farm for a 'tutor of outdoor and environmental education'. The successful applicant would 'be part of a small team offering curriculum linked outdoor activities to young people from schools'.[58]

The White Hall management team was similarly occupied. 'We get schools to choose the emphasis of their course, eg cooperation, listening skills, independence, … and these priorities are worded in school-target-speak so that the residential course is clearly linked to the school's objectives.'[59]

Making an explicit connection between the residential course and the school curriculum had become a normal part of the marketing of many centres.

In Chapter 23 I suggested that White Hall's traditional approach to adventurous outdoor pursuits, comprising three main areas of learning and little changed between 1950 and 1992, had been perfectly in line with the Edinburgh three-circles model of outdoor education. However, writing in 1992, Phil Booth had pondered whether all the aspects of the traditional purposes of White Hall would survive the imminent changes enforced by financial imperatives. Now, twenty-five years later, there seems to be good reason to be confident that White Hall's schools' courses in 2017, despite the centre's transformation, are still achieving a balanced spread of opportunities across the three broad circles. Putting this another way, the White Hall brand is alive and well.

Darran Hawkins emphasises that the two goals of preserving the quality of the courses while also chasing budgetary targets are both being achieved:

> Improving the quality of courses has been and still is essential. Perhaps more so than in past times, understanding our customer relationships with teachers, students, parents and other stakeholders has been fundamental in reaching our joint goal of maintaining quality and meeting financial targets.
>
> This process has included increasing the opportunity for adventurous activities, especially for primary pupils with the building of the mountain bike track. This development coincided with the increasing use of Combs Moss's Grande Couloir gully as a local scramble and the use similarly of Lightwood Stream (which runs southeast from the plateau) to enable adventure with a minimum of transport. Some of these changes required an adjustment in mindset. Instructors can get comfortable with the known; because we've always driven to the Roaches for scrambling doesn't mean we have to for every scrambling session.
>
> Regarding the economies of scale – the idea that a residential centre needed at least a hundred beds to function unsubsidised – what hadn't been considered [by Rory Gregory's investigations a few years earlier] was a different way of working and operating. Commercial pressures required commercial answers and a recognition of the new knowledge and skills that were required. Yes: marketing, financial, IT and management skills, which will probably have a few of the old guard foaming at the mouth. Terminology has changed; we now have commercialisation and customers. However, these are the drivers that have enabled White Hall and Derbyshire Outdoors to succeed.
>
> A commercial attitude also encourages a different way of utilising and maximising our assets, leading to diversification into rentals, self-catering and even wedding receptions. Diversification has allowed us to continue delivering high-quality adventure education and a product that is greatly valued by the schools that use us, as our bookings into 2022 demonstrate.[60]

Evaluations completed by visiting staff in 2016–17 endorse Hawkins's remarks about the continuing high quality of the schools' courses. One teacher wrote: 'The best residential I have ever had the pleasure of taking part in. Thank you to all the staff who have made us feel so welcome and have worked so hard to make our experience amazing. I cannot wait to bring other groups of children back here. The children have gained in confidence, independence and respect.' Another contented visitor wrote: 'I wish I knew how White Hall staff can almost immediately understand the needs of individual children.'[61]

Chapters 13, 18 and 21 touched upon the occasionally awkward relationship between the environmental studies sector and the outdoor education sector. The two sectors had sometimes been allies, and sometimes competitors. From time to time, people had staked out what they thought was their territory. So it was fascinating to notice, in 2016, that the National Association of Field Studies Officers had become a part of the IOL, an establishment whose roots lay firmly in adventure education. According to Rosie Napier, writing on the Allnatt Outdoors blog, all the delegates at a field studies conference in January 2016 had agreed that being part of the IOL would 'bridge the gap between field studies and activity providers and [would give] the potential for the disciplines to be combined', which would provide teachers with better opportunities to become informed on best practice and on curriculum changes.[62]

The last few years, 2014–17, have brought a sanguine relief from the gloom of the rest of Part Four. This book can now end on an upward trajectory. The post-recession national developments that I have described give cause, collectively, for some optimism in the outdoor education sector. However, it is too early to know whether that optimism will translate into healthier finances for residential outdoor centres and practical progress.

Where to now, for White Hall Centre? The prospect of calmer waters? Further transition? And rejuvenation? Such changes are real possibilities. They could take place under the present county-council ownership. Alternatively, they could happen under community-interest ownership or private ownership. None of these three forms of ownership is a panacea for balancing the books. People hold different opinions on the extent to which outdoor centres operating under the rigours of free enterprise will meet educational needs, especially those of children from impoverished families. Some of these centres may face significant problems retaining staff. Some centres operated by community trusts may have to get by with minimal investment income.

In the 1950s, during a time of memorable postwar austerity, when neither green issues nor our need for exercise were high on the national agenda, Jack Longland and Peter Mosedale had forged ahead establishing White Hall. In doing so, they had departed from some of the convictions and priorities of Kurt Hahn and Robert Baden-Powell. Longland and Mosedale had carved out their own distinctive approach to residential outdoor pursuits, one that recognised the importance of the countryside and of landscape, and which appreciated the potential lifetime health benefits of the hill and water sports.

In 2015, post-recession austerity policies were still in place and the national debt was a concern. Yet, Britons on overnight trips in Britain involving outdoor recreation spent £11.8 billion. The estimated retail value of the outdoor specialist market in 2015 was £1.2 billion.[63] On Thursday 16 March 2017, Toyota Manufacturing UK announced that it would be spending £240 million in upgrading its car plant at Burnaston, near Derby. The small Derbyshire town of Shirebrook, whose colliery had closed in 1993, was now the home of a vast warehouse complex (SportsDirect.com) and of hundreds of migrant workers from eastern Europe; you would probably not have described Shirebrook as thriving, bearing in mind SportsDirect's controversial employment practices, but the town was getting by.[64] So, as in the 1950s, in 2017 there was still some money around, albeit spread quite thinly in some segments of the population. White Hall Centre was a newcomer in the process of gathering some of this money in exchange for rendering educational services. It had shown resilience and flexibility in surviving the cutbacks of 1992–2012. Yes, it was still feeling its way, getting to grips with commercial reality, but it was achieving remarkable success in this task. Even during the difficult times described throughout Part Four, thousands of young people had benefitted greatly from their visits to the house on the hill. Despite the constraints placed on LEAs by central government, the councillors and officers of Derbyshire county council had resolutely supported White Hall Centre. During an unprecedented and seemingly endless period of cutbacks, the centre had been reroofed and fully rewired. A borehole had been drilled for water. The dining room had been extended. An on-site mountain biking circuit had been created and a new climbing wall had been built. Laudatory evaluations had been received. In 2014 a much needed new website had come into operation. The link with schools in Lincolnshire, a popular arrangement in the 1970s and early 1980s, had recently been successfully revived. In September 2017, there were no spare weeks for the next eighteen months. Booking were being taken for 2022. There was every prospect that the services of another amateur historian would be required later in the century.

Windgather Rocks, November 2016. The belayers are working as teams of three.

Combs Reservoir, August 2012.

Finding a balance, Combs Reservoir, August 2012.

Water sport, Combs Reservoir, August 2012.

Winter sports, January 2015.

White Hall Centre

White Hall Centre

The mountain-bike trail, during its construction, February 2013. The trail
was completed in May 2013.

The High Peak Trail, August 2017.

White Hall Centre

One of the disused railway tunnels of the Monsal Way, June 2014.

White Hall Centre

Chee Dale, June 2014.

The Chee Dale stepping stones, June 2014.

White Hall Centre

Night hike, October 2016.

White Hall Centre

Problem solving, May 2015.

White Hall Centre

Stream scrambling, Errwood, October 2013.

White Hall Centre

Stream scrambling, Errwood, October 2013.

Errwood, October 2013.

A helping hand, Errwood, February 2016.

White Hall Centre

Carlswark Cavern, January 2015.

White Hall Centre

Giant's Hole, May 2015.

Subterranean explorer, Higgor Tor, July 2015.

Exiting the underworld, Higgor Tor, February 2016.

White Hall Centre

Zip wire, White Hall, September 2016.

White Hall Centre

Ropes course, White Hall, October 2016.

Notes

1   David Rose and Ed Douglas, *Regions of the Heart: The Triumph and Tragedy of Alison Hargreaves* (Washington, DC: National Geographic Society, 2000), pp. 14–15.

2   Kim Thomas, 'Outdoor Learning is in a Class of Its Own', *Guardian,* 4 Dec 2012.

3   Diana Hinds, 'A World Away from the Frantic Pursuit of Grades', *The Times,* 25 Mar 2011, p. 5 (S2).

4   Simon Beames, Peter Higgins and Robbie Nicol, *Learning Outside the Classroom: Theory and Guidelines for Practice* (London: Routledge, 2012).

5   Ian Price, *The Building of a Mountain Bike Trail at White Hall Centre – Inclusion in the Capital Programme – (Young People)*, Unpublished report (Matlock, Derbyshire: Derbyshire County Council, 16 Apr 2013).

6   Bob Higginbotham, Email to P McDonald, subject 'White Hall History Project', 16 May 2013 [Email].

7   'Petition: Save Our Outdoor Education Centres', UK Government and Parliament (23 Jan 2013) <https://petition.parliament.uk/archived/petitions/26661> [accessed 15 Mar 2017].

8   Tony Ryan, 'Campaign to Save Outdoor Education Centres' (26 July 2013) <https://www.thebmc.co.uk/campaign-to-save-outdoor-education-centres> [accessed 3 May 2014].

9   'Petition: Save Our Outdoor Education Centres', UK Government and Parliament (23 Jan 2013) <https://petition.parliament.uk/archived/petitions/26661> [accessed 15 Mar 2017].

10   Ken Wilson, 'The Educational Threat', *Mountain,* no. 33 (Mar 1974), p. 8.

11   'Outdoor Learning Cuts Approved by Birmingham Council', BBC (18 Mar 2014) <http://www.bbc.com/news/uk-england-26630526> [accessed 15 Apr 2016].

12   Matt West, 'UK Finally Lifts out of Depression' (10 June 2014) <http://www.thisismoney.co.uk/money/news/article-2653837/Official-figures-industrial-output-rises-fastest-rate-three-years-April-economic-recovery-continues-widen.html> [accessed 16 Mar 2017].

13   [Anon.], 'Bear Grylls' Outdoor Claims Backed', *The Safety & Health Practitioner,* 33, no. 4 (Apr 2015), p. 24.

14   Katy Winter, 'Children today would rather read …', MailOnline (11 Apr 2013) <http://www.dailymail.co.uk/femail/article-2307431/Children-today-read-chores-HOMEWORK-play-outside.html> [accessed 15 Apr 2016].

15   Grace Hammond, 'Put the Risks in Perspective and Let Children Play Outside', *Yorkshire Post,* 23 Apr 2013.

16   'Healthy Children: White Paper', Playforce (Aug 2014) <http://www.academiesshowbirmingham.co.uk/wp-content/uploads/2014/08/Playforce-Healthy-Children-White-Paper.pdf> [accessed 14 Mar 2017], p. 2.

17   'Designed to Move: A Physical Activity Action Agenda', Nike Inc (2013) <http://www.designedtomove.org/resources/designed-to-move-report> [accessed 14 Mar 2017].

18 'Healthy Children: White Paper', Playforce (Aug 2014) <http://www.academiesshowbirmingham.co.uk/wp-content/uploads/2014/08/Playforce-Healthy-Children-White-Paper.pdf> [accessed 14 Mar 2017], p. 8.

19 Sam Creighton, 'From SAS to VIP', Daily Mail (8 Sept 2015) <http://www.dailymail.co.uk/news/article-3225748/From-SAS-VIP-Bear-Grylls-s-profits-run-wild-survival-expert-makes-3-3million-year-business-empire.html> [accessed 22 Mar 2017].

20 Ben Fogle, 'Ben Fogle's Country Travels: Why Don't Children Play Outside?', Telegraph (18 May 2014) <http://www.telegraph.co.uk/sport/10836804/Ben-Fogles-country-travels-why-dont-children-play-outside.html> [accessed 15 Apr 2016].

21 [Anon.], 'Bear Grylls' Outdoor Claims Backed', *The Safety & Health Practitioner*, 33, no. 4 (Apr 2015), p. 24.

22 Derbyshire County Council, 'Derbyshire Learning Outside The Classroom Conference: 21 April 2015 – Lea Green Development Centre' (2015) <http://www.derbyshire.gov.uk/images/Derbyshire%20LOTC%20Conference%202015%20Delegate%20Pack_tcm44-264294.pdf> [accessed 13 Sept 2017].

23 Derbyshire County Council, 'Derbyshire Learning Outside the Classroom Conference 2015 [Review]' (2015) <http://www.derbyshire.gov.uk/images/Derbyshire%20LOTC%20Conference%202015%20Review_tcm44-264295.pdf> [accessed 13 Sept 2017].

24 Philip David Booth, 'The Impact of Financial Cuts upon an Outdoor Centre … during the Financial Year 1992/93' (MA dissertation, University of Sheffield, Jan 1993), p. 47.

25 Verity Comley and Chris Mackintosh, *Reconomics: The Economic Impact of Outdoor Recreation in the UK: The Evidence* (London: Sport and Recreation Alliance; Liverpool John Moores University, June 2014), p. 8.

26 Simon Butler, Verity Comley and Chris Mackintosh, *Reconomics: The Economic Impact of Outdoor Recreation* (London: Sport and Recreation Alliance; Liverpool John Moores University, June 2014), p. 22.

27 Ibid., p. 19.

28 Department for Work and Pensions, 'A Final Progress Report on Implementation of Health and Safety Reforms', DWP (25 Mar 2015) <http://www.hse.gov.uk/aboutus/meetings/hseboard/2015/250315/pmarb1525b.pdf> [accessed 26 June 2017], p. 12.

29 United Kingdom Parliament, 'Hansard Online: 28 Oct 2015: Outdoor Recreation' (28 Oct 2015) <https://hansard.parliament.uk/Commons/2015-10-28/debates/15102834000003/OutdoorRecreation> [accessed 17 Mar 2017].

30 Ibid.

31 Ibid.

32 Carey Davies, 'MPs Agree: "The potential for outdoor recreation is massive"', British Mountaineering Council (29 Oct 2015) <https://www.thebmc.co.uk/mps-agree-the-potential-for-outdoor-recreation-is-massive> [accessed 15 Apr 2016].

33 Cabinet Office, *Sporting Future: A New Strategy for an Active Nation* (London: H M Government, Dec 2015), pp. 23–24.

34   Ibid., p. 24.

35   Ibid., p. 25.

36   Sport England, *Towards an Active Nation: Strategy 2016–2021* (London: Sport England, May 2016), pp. 6, 45.

37   Ibid., p. 24.

38   Darran Hawkins, Email to P McDonald, subject 'Mid-November', 1 Sept 2017 [Email].

39   Clare Reading, to P McDonald (2), 1 July 2017 [Letter].

40   Derbyshire Sport, 'Towards an Active Derbyshire: 2016–2021', Derbyshire Sport (2016) <http://www.derbyshiresport.co.uk/uploads/towards-an-active-derbyshire-strategy.pdf> [accessed 18 Mar 2017].

41   Ibid., p. 48.

42   David Rutley, 'MPs Spend Day In Hills To Become Outdoor Champions' (5 Oct 2016) <https://www.davidrutley.org.uk/news/mps-spend-day-hills-become-outdoor-champions> [accessed 3 July 2017].

43   White Hall Outdoor Education Centre, 'Bookings and Information: Prices' (Apr 2016) <http://whitehall.derbyshire-outdoors.org/bookings-info/prices/> [accessed 27 Aug 2017].

44   White Hall Outdoor Education Centre, 'Outdoor Adventures: Challenge, Learn, Achieve', Derbyshire County Council (2015) <http://whitehall.derbyshire-outdoors.org/wp-content/uploads/2015/04/White-Hall-Activities-Leaflet-2015.pdf> [accessed 27 Aug 2017].

45   White Hall Outdoor Education Centre, 'Room and Centre Hire', Derbyshire County Council (no date) <https://www.derbyshire.gov.uk/education/outdoor_learning/white_hall/hire/default.asp> [accessed 28 Aug 2017].

46   B R Mitchell, *British Historical Statistics* (Cambridge: Cambridge University Press, 1988), pp. 250, 254.

47   John Porter, *One Day as a Tiger: Alex MacIntyre and the Birth of Light and Fast Alpinism* (Sheffield: Vertebrate, 2014), p. 189.

48   British Mountaineering Council, 'BMC Core Policies' (no date) <https://www.thebmc.co.uk/bmc-core-policies?s=5> [accessed 12 June 2017].

49   'A New Look for Canoeing', Go Canoeing! (Apr 2014) <
http://www.gocanoeing.org.uk/go/index.cfm/news/news/a-new-look-for-canoeing/> [accessed 2 Jun 2017].

50   Dougald MacDonald, 'Ueli Steck Takes Back Eiger Speed Record', Climbing (19 Nov 2015) <http://www.climbing.com/news/ueli-steck-takes-back-eiger-speed-record/> [accessed 2 Apr 2016].

51   John Porter, *One Day as a Tiger: Alex MacIntyre and the Birth of Light and Fast Alpinism* (Sheffield: Vertebrate, 2014), pp. 164–165.

52   Robert Macfarlane, *The Wild Places* (London: Granta Books, 2007), p. 80.

53   Ibid., p. 8.

54   Clare Reading, to P McDonald (2), 1 July 2017 [Letter].

55   Ibid.

56   Darran Hawkins, Email to P McDonald, subject 'Mid-November', 1 Sept 2017 [Email].

57   School of Sport and Exercise Science, 'Teaching Key Stage 2 Outdoor Education: Student Residential Trip', University of Lincoln (21 July 2017) <https://sportex.blogs.lincoln.ac.uk/2017/07/21/teaching-key-stage-2-outdoor-education-student-residential-trip/> [accessed 14 Sept 2017].

58   Nottinghamshire County Council, 'Tutor of Outdoor and Environmental Education' (13 Sept 2017) <https://www.indeed.co.uk/Farm-Education-jobs> [accessed 14 Sept 2017].

59   Clare Reading, Email to P McDonald, subject 'Book project update', 29 Oct 2017 [Email].

60   Darran Hawkins, Note to P McDonald, 17 Nov 2017 [Note].

61   Fiona Thomson, Email to P McDonald, subject 'WH Book', 29 Nov 2017 [Email].

62   Rosie Napier, 'Field Studies Professional Development Event in London', Allnatt Outdoors (14 Jan 2016) <http://allnatt.co.uk/field-studies-professional-development-event-in-london/> [accessed 4 Apr 2017].

63   Quoted in Sport and Recreation Alliance, *Reconomics Plus: The Economic, Health and Social Value of Outdoor Recreation* (London: Sport and Recreation Alliance; Manchester Metropolitan University, Feb 2017), pp. 11, 14.

64   John Humphreys, 'How Sports Direct and Migrant Labour Changed Shirebrook', BBC Radio 4 (20 May 2017) <http://www.bbc.com/news/election-2017-39973990> [accessed 22 May 2017].

Appendix 1. Charlie Wilson and Keswick Youth Centre

In Chapter 8, I wrote that Peter Mosedale's position, as the first warden of White Hall Centre for Open Country Pursuits, was a lonely and vulnerable one. One other LEA residential outdoor pursuits centre may have existed, albeit virtually unannounced. This was in Keswick. Documents and newspapers from that time call it either Keswick Youth Centre or Cumberland County Youth Centre. (Later it became known as Denton House or Denton House Outdoor Centre.) The story of Keswick Youth Centre starts with a man by the name of Charles R Wilson.

Charlie Wilson was a well-known Lake District climber of the 1930s. He knew and climbed with and may have been influenced by Mabel Barker, an early enthusiast for outdoor learning who set up a small residential school at Caldbeck in Cumberland in 1927.[1] The book *Cumbrian Rock* (1988) contains some of Wilson's 'comprehensive set of hundreds of climbing photographs' from the 1930s. He took part in the first ascent of May Day Climb (1938) and of Overhanging Bastion (1939).

On 1 January 1939, Wilson, Jim Birkett and Len Muscroft formed themselves into the Cumberland and Westmorland Guides. The standard daily charge for a route such as Central Buttress was £1.50 with a maximum of three in the party.[2]

Before the second world war, the building that later became Keswick Youth Centre was a casual ward, which provided food and overnight accommodation to 'casuals', ie tramps and itinerants.[3] The onset of war led to the closure of many casual wards in the northwestern counties. By July 1943 the Keswick casual ward had been converted into a children's home.[4]

Charlie Wilson spent the war years in the Royal Air Force and then returned to Cumberland and restarted his guiding. In September 1947, he was one of the first five people recognised as climbing guides by the BMC.[5]

According to Ken Ogilvie, in the late 1940s, Wilson 'started the Carlisle Mountaineering Club'.[6] An early mention of the club occurred in a newspaper article on 1 March 1948. The story described a climbing accident involving Harold Stephenson (25), a member of Carlisle

Mountaineering Club. Also mentioned was 'the leader of the party, Mr C Wilson'.[7]

At some point, the Cumberland education committee decided that the casual-ward building would become Keswick Youth Centre, a residential facility. On 1 February 1948, a married couple, designated 'warden' and 'steward', took up their appointments there. They were Mr and Mrs T McCambridge of Workington.[8] (Jack and Maysie. One meaning of 'steward' was a person who manages the eating arrangements at a club or hotel.) Also that month the director of education for Cumberland reported that the Ministry of Education and the Ministry of Health had approved the appropriation of the premises for educational purposes. On 16 April 1948 the Cumberland education committee approved a scale of charges for this residential facility.[9] It is likely that the building opened as a day and residential youth centre about this time. The charges were:

Breakfast	1s 6d
Lunch	1s 6d
Tea	1s
Supper	6d
Bed	1s for members of youth organisations recognised by the county youth subcommittee
Bed	1s 6d for others

You cannot tell from this list of charges whether the education committee expected Keswick Youth Centre to be used by school groups as well as by youth organisations. Superficially, if we judge by the list and the centre's name, this Keswick facility of 1948 looks no different from hundreds of other youth centres in Britain's towns and cities. In November 1939, a key government circular (1486), 'The Service of Youth', had been issued. In the following ten years, LEA-run youth centres had seen prolific growth. One enquiry, published in 1949, estimated that 70 out of 113 local authorities contacted had between them opened about 900 youth centres.[10]

There are many accounts of general-purpose youth centres organising occasional outdoor-pursuits days or weekends in the late 1940s and even during the war. However, Charlie Wilson's involvement suggests that Keswick Youth Centre may have focused mainly on outdoor pursuits from its very beginning. According to Ken Ogilvie, the centre, which he calls Denton House, was 'the first LEA centre to provide courses in outdoor activities in the modern mode'.[11]

Whether you consider the Keswick centre of 1948 to have been an LEA outdoor centre depends partly on what characteristics you think distinguished a residential outdoor pursuits centre from a general-purpose residential youth centre. A desirable though not essential part of setting up an LEA outdoor centre in the 1940s and 1950s was a public statement of the intent to do so, either spoken or written. Derbyshire education committee stated such an intent during a meeting on 28 June1949, announcing its plan to establish 'a training centre for open country pursuits, including walking, camping, and climbing'.[12] Again, on 26 May 1950, an advertisement for the post of Warden described the new facility as 'White Hall, Buxton: Open Country Pursuits Centre'.[13] In June, Longland had to front up and answer the *Spectator*'s editor's criticism of Derbyshire's plans. Again, in December, he answered a harsh critic in the letter columns of the *Derby Evening Telegraph*.

In researching the early years of Keswick Youth Centre, I have looked in particular for an explicit council minute or newspaper report announcing the purpose of the centre to be the provision of outdoor pursuits such as fell-walking, climbing and canoeing.

In July 1948, Brigham Boys' School, Keswick, applied for permission to use the Keswick youth centre. A sub-committee approved this for physical training classes from 1.45pm to 3.30pm on Monday and Thursday each week from September to Easter, subject to the centre not being required for youth activities.[14]

On 21 January 1949, the director of education submitted a report on the work of the Keswick Youth Centre. Searches of the county council's records have not yet unearthed this report.

On 1 September 1949 a new director of education for Cumberland, Gordon S Bessey, took up his appointment.[15]

Jack Longland visited the Keswick Youth Centre sometime in 1949, perhaps to look at the set-up and to adopt some of the ideas for White Hall. He signed the visitors' book.[16]

Much of the initiative behind the setting-up of Keswick Youth Centre seems to have come from Charlie Wilson, supported by consecutive directors of education. At some point in the late 1940s or early 1950s, Wilson became the assistant county youth officer for Cumberland. (He later became one of the outdoor-activities advisers for Cumberland education authority.) Wilson's connections with the Carlisle Mountaineering Club gave him ready access to a potential pool of voluntary instructors for courses in outdoor pursuits.[17] Some of these courses were based at Keswick Youth Centre.

An account of one of these courses described a climbing weekend run by Wilson at Keswick Youth Centre on 11–12 March 1950.[18] 'Twenty-two Lancashire and Cumberland youths attended the first [of a] series of three week-end schools in rock climbing, organised by Cumberland Education Committee in conjunction with the Central Council for Physical Training and Recreation ... They had lectures on equipment and the theory of rock climbing and mountain rescue work by leaders of the Carlisle Mountaineering Club'. Among the instructors were S F Marshall, the deputy director of education for Cumberland, and J R Clarke, a county youth organiser. The all-in fee for the weekend was fifteen shillings.[19]

According to Derek Stansfield, Keswick Youth Centre courses that took place on weekdays in the 1950s, before the appointment of a teacher head of centre, were self-programming.[20]

In June 1952, the Keswick Youth Centre ran its first full week's mountaincraft course, after running just weekend courses in 1951.[21] Twenty-five 'young people' (whatever that means) attended.

Among the courses that Charlie Wilson ran in 1953 were fell-walking weekends for soldiers and Durham University students. On the first of these weekends, held on 24–25 October, there were twenty places, for which forty Service men and women had applied.[22]

Charlie's son Bill Wilson, who lives in Canada, remembers the youth centre of the late 1950s: 'All I know is I had great times with Mr and Mrs Jack McCambridge who were the custodians at the time. Visited there lots of times with Dad who was the Youth Organiser for Cumberland at the time, taking school kids from the centre on fell walking, rock climbing and canoeing. I think he would take Royal Marines from there on week-end climbing courses too ... There was great atmosphere at the centre, with people from all over meeting there.'[23]

Keswick Youth Centre was later renamed Denton House, probably in the 1960s. In February–March 1963, Charlie Wilson, representing Denton House, attended the first meeting of the AWMC.[24] The earliest occurrence I know of the name Denton House being used in a Cumberland county council document, to refer to the youth centre, is in a report by Gordon Bessey recorded in the county youth subcommittee minutes of 8 December 1966.[25] This report, on activities among young people, included mentions of a Duke of Edinburgh's Award conference, canoe-rolling sessions for teachers and youth leaders, a canoe-building course, and skiing classes at the nylon ski slope in Carlisle. The director reported that 'Mr. Wilson has also been concerned with arrangements for the use of Dun Fell as a ski-ing area and has taken a film on ski-ing techniques. There is no other film of this nature available in the country and the film should prove valuable for training.'[26]

During some reorganising of local government in 1974, Carlisle education authority and Cumberland education authority were amalgamated to form Cumbria education authority. Denton House outdoor centre became one of three residential outdoor centres run by Cumbria county council. The other two were Fellside and Hawse End. Derek Stansfield, who was appointed Head of Centre at Fellside in September 1973, says that Denton House 'was the brainchild of Gordon Bessey … and Charlie Wilson'.[27]

Charlie Wilson, with the help of members of Carlisle Mountaineering Club, contributed greatly to the development of outdoor pursuits in Cumberland schools and youth organisations. Ken Ogilvie has described Wilson's work as nationally significant: 'As a Youth Service Officer for Cumberland after World War II, he was one of the foremost pioneers in the country developing outdoor pursuits within an education authority.'[28]

Further research may reveal whether Cumberland education committee clearly decided, either at the very beginning or later, that Keswick Youth Centre would be a residential outdoor pursuits centre. The information that has emerged, so far, suggests that it was initially similar to many other youth centres around Britain and that it evolved by stealth into an outdoor centre. Denton House is now a private residential outdoor pursuits centre.

Notes

1   Ken C Ogilvie, *Roots and Wings: A History of Outdoor Education and Outdoor Learning in the UK* (Lyme Regis, UK: Russell House Publishing, 2013), pp. 221–223.

2   Trevor Jones and Geoff Milburn, *Cumbrian Rock: 100 Years of Climbing in the Lake District* (Glossop, UK: Pic Publications, 1988), pp. 4, 106–109, 111.

3   Helen Cunningham, *Report on Search: HRC/EP/16479, 27 Oct 2014*, Unpublished report (Carlisle: Cumbria Archive Service, 2014).

4   'Round the North-west', *Lancashire Daily Post*, 14 July 1943, p. 4.

5   *The First Fifty Years of the British Mountaineering Council*, ed. by Geoff Milburn, Derek Walker and Ken Wilson (Manchester: British Mountaineering Council, 1997), p. 224.

6   Ken C Ogilvie, *Roots and Wings: A History of Outdoor Education and Outdoor Learning in the UK* (Lyme Regis, UK: Russell House Publishing, 2013), p. 285.

7   'Hull Man Injured on Lakeland Climb', *Daily Mail,* 1 Mar 1948, p. 1.

8   Helen Cunningham, *Report on Search: HRC/EP/16479, 27 Oct 2014,* Unpublished report (Carlisle: Cumbria Archive Service, 2014).

9   Ibid.

10   Bernard Davies, *From Voluntaryism to Welfare State: A History of the Youth Service in England: 1939–1979,* History of the Youth Service in England, 2 vols (Leicester: Youth Work Press, 1999), vol. 1, pp. 18, 26.

11   Ken C Ogilvie, *Roots and Wings: A History of Outdoor Education and Outdoor Learning in the UK* (Lyme Regis, UK: Russell House Publishing, 2013), p. 284.

12   'Encouraging a Life in the Open Air', *Derby Evening Telegraph,* 29 June 1949, p. 7.

13   'Public Notices', *The Times,* 26 May 1950, p. 1.

14   Helen Cunningham, *Report on Search: HRC/EP/16479, 27 Oct 2014,* Unpublished report (Carlisle: Cumbria Archive Service, 2014).

15   'New Somerset Officer', *Western Daily Press,* 24 Oct 1949, p. 1.

16   Derek Stansfield, Email to P McDonald, subject 'Early history of Denton House Outdoor Centre', 14 Sept 2014 [Email].

17   Ken C Ogilvie, *Roots and Wings: A History of Outdoor Education and Outdoor Learning in the UK* (Lyme Regis, UK: Russell House Publishing, 2013), p. 285.

18   Frederick P Knowlson, 'Climbing in Lakeland', *Yorkshire Post,* 13 Mar 1950, p. 1.

19   Ibid. Also 'School for Young Rock Climbers', *Manchester Guardian,* 13 March 1950, p. 4.

20   Derek Stansfield, Email to P McDonald, subject 'Early history of Denton House Outdoor Centre', 14 Sept 2014 [Email].

21   'Sunrise on Scafell', *Northern Daily Mail,* 3 June 1952, p. 4.

22   'Soldiers Who Like Walking', *Yorkshire Post and Leeds Mercury,* 6 Nov 1953, p. 4.

23   William Wilson, Email to P McDonald, subject 'Keswick Youth Centre', 1 Jan 2015 [Email].

24   Ken C Ogilvie, *Roots and Wings: A History of Outdoor Education and Outdoor Learning in the UK* (Lyme Regis, UK: Russell House Publishing, 2013), p. 352.

25   Carlisle Archive Centre (Cumbria County Council), Cumberland CC, Minutes of Council & Committees, County Youth Sub-committee, 8 Dec 1966, pp. 583–584.

26   Ibid.

27   Derek Stansfield, Email to P McDonald, subject 'Early history of Denton House Outdoor Centre', 14 Sept 2014 [Email].

28   Ken C Ogilvie, *Roots and Wings: A History of Outdoor Education and Outdoor Learning in the UK* (Lyme Regis, UK: Russell House Publishing, 2013), pp. 222–223.

Appendix 2. Founding Purpose

Purpose Statements and Mentions from before White Hall Opened

Statement or Mention	Source	Notes
'The primary purpose of Whitehall will be to provide a place where short training courses for leaders and members of youth organisations can be organised both by the [youth service] sub-Committee and by voluntary bodies.'	Derbyshire Local Studies Library, Derbyshire Record Office (Matlock, UK), Derbyshire Education Committee: Youth Service in Derbyshire 1944–1945, Section 4 – Whitehall, Buxton, Ref 369.4.	Youth Service report.
(Jack Longland was appointed Director of Education for Derbyshire on 17 November 1948.)		
On 7 June 1949 at a meeting of the Further Education Sub-Committee 'it was resolved to take no further action with regard to the negotiations for the sale of Whitehall ... pending the submission of a report by the Director of Education regarding the possible use of the premises in connexion with open-country pursuits'.	Derbyshire Record Office, Education minute books, D919 C/1/17/29, 7 June 1949, no. 7459.	DCC education committee minutes.
'Derbyshire Education Committee decided yesterday to authorise the Director of Education ... to inspect suitable properties with a view to establishing a training centre for open country pursuits, including walking, camping, and climbing'.	'Encouraging a Life in the Open Air', *Derby Evening Telegraph*, 29 June 1949, p. 7.	Newspaper report.
'[Mr Longland] says: "We mean to show climbing can be a cheap and safe sport for all. At present, there are too many unnecessary accidents." ... There will be courses in climbing, camping, and rambling, by qualified teachers.'	'School for Climbers: £3,000 Project for Buxton', *Nottingham Evening Post*, 23 Aug 1949, p. 5.	Newspaper, direct quote of Longland's words.
'Derbyshire Education Committee is going ahead with plans to provide a training centre for open country pursuits, including walking, camping and climbing ... Mr J. L. Longland instigated the scheme, and one of its main objects will be to show that climbing can be a cheap and safe sport.'	'Training Centre', *Derby Evening Telegraph*, 26 Aug 1949, p. 3.	Newspaper report.

Statement or Mention	Source	Notes
'Whitehall, a building off Long Hill owned by the Derbyshire Education Authority, may be converted into the first centre for open country pursuits, at a cost of over £2,000. Training would be given all the year round in rambling, camping, hiking, rock climbing, mountain walking, and the proper use of the countryside.'	'"Whitehall" May Be First Country Pursuits Centre', *Buxton Advertiser*, 27 Aug 1949, p. 3.	Newspaper report.
'Mr. J. L. Longland, Director of Education, Derbyshire, said that in physical training in schools we had concentrated too much on sports which were later enjoyed by only a few. The focus should be on a wider and more relevant renewal of physical activities after schooldays than we had yet conceived.'	'Work – A Pleasure or a Hardship? Plain Speaking at Southport Conference', *Manchester Guardian*, 6 Jan 1950, p. 2.	Newspaper, indirect quote of what Longland said.
'As most accidents are simply through lack of experience the Derbyshire Education Committee are providing a training centre at Whitehall ... where youngsters with the keen-ness to want to climb really well can receive the help and advice of experienced men [*sic*], thereby being in less of a danger to themselves and a worry to others.'	'Mr. Longland Gives Hints on Climbing', *Derby Evening Telegraph*, 3 Feb 1950, p. 4.	Newspaper, indirect quote of what Longland said.
'Applications are invited for the post of WARDEN. The centre will be used for short residential courses for young people in rambling, mountain-walking, rock-climbing and camping.'	'Public Notices', *The Times*, 26 May 1950, p. 1.	Advertisement placed by County Hall.
'White Hall ... is to be opened ... in September as a training centre where townsfolk will learn how to take care of themselves in the country and how to take care of the country in which they enjoy themselves ... [The location is] ideal for a centre for training in "open country pursuits". The authority considers these an essential part of education, as they develop initiative and self-reliance, qualities not easily inculcated in classroom or on playing-field. On different levels, each [course] will teach the technique of camping and hill walking, the importance of proper equipment, map and compass work, and, for those who with, rock climbing. They will lay an equal stress on the countryside itself, local history, geology, natural history, and the duty of proper conduct in a National Park area.'	'The Townsman in the Country', *Manchester Guardian*, 5 June 1950, p. 4.	Newspaper report.

Statement or Mention	Source	Notes
'Derbyshire may soon have an Outward Bound School to teach young people how to understand the countryside, Mr. Jack Longland … told Ilkeston Rotary Club yesterday … Mr. Longland said that, in order to provide a proper place for the youngsters to develop their own potentialities and to give them a legitimate outlet for adventure, courage and endurance, the Derbyshire Education Committee were hoping shortly to open a training centre at Whitehall, Buxton, which would be known as an Outward Bound School. The aims of the schools [sic], said Mr. Longland, are to get together a group of young girls and boys, preferably between the ages of 16 and 20, in as natural surroundings as possible and teach them to understand the countryside and appreciate its beauty.'	'Countryside Teaching Plan: Outward Bound School in Peak', *Derby Evening Telegraph*, 24 Oct 1950, p. 7.	Newspaper, indirect quote of what Longland said.
Reproduced later in this appendix.	'Why provide mountain training centres?', in private papers of Jack Longland, sent to *Out of Doors*, 13 Dec 1950.	1,900-word article by Longland on the purpose of White Hall.
'Large sums are spent annually on the gymnasia and playing fields required for physical exercises and national games and, whether or not it be true that Waterloo was won on such playing fields, nobody disputes the worthwhileness of this expenditure. We ought not to overlook the fact that our wilder national playgrounds, like the High Peak, with their less artificial rules-of-the-game, offer disciplines of adventure and self-reliance which are of high educational value and which the young are, of themselves, seeking on an unprecedented scale. White Hall is a modest and experimental attempt to make the most of these opportunities.'	'Needs of County's "Tragic Children"', *Derby Evening Telegraph*, 27 Dec 1950, p. 2.	Letter written by Longland.

Statement or Mention	Source	Notes
'[White Hall] is intended for young people, of both sexes, between the ages of 15 and about 25, who are interested in open country pursuits. It is for those – Youth Hostellers, Ramblers, Scouts and Guides, Cyclists and others – who have already "discovered" the hills and have done a good deal of walking and, perhaps, some camping or rock-climbing. It is also – and equally – for the complete beginner who wants to try some of these things.'	White Hall Open Country Pursuits Centre: Programme, January – May 1951.	The annual programme was probably written by Longland or Mosedale.
'It is a pioneer venture intended … for the young people of Derbyshire … who already, perhaps, have "discovered" the hills and have done a good deal of walking and maybe some camping and rock-climbing. It is open also to the complete beginner who wants to try some of these pursuits … to anyone, in fact, who is young and looks for happiness and interest in the sort of countryside in which White Hall stands … The programme for each course will not be planned, cut and dried, in advance. It will depend on many things – the interests and abilities of the members on each course, the season and the weather. The basis will be fell-walking or rambling and there will be opportunities to learn and practise some of the skills and techniques of hillcraft on which, to an important extent, the enjoyment of wild country depends – walking, path-finding, outdoor cooking, rock-climbing, and the study of country life and work.'	'Country Pursuits Centre', *Derby Evening Telegraph*, 27 Dec 1950, p. 4. Adapted from the White Hall programme of courses for January to May 1951.	Newspaper report.
'Mr. Jack Longland … said last night: "This centre represents an advance in the physical and general education of normal children and young people. Our wilder national playgrounds, like the High Peak, offer disciplines of adventure and self-reliance, which are of high educational value."'	'Boy of 14 to Train Tough Climbers', *Sheffield Daily Telegraph*, 28 Dec 1950, p. 3.	Newspaper, direct quote of Longland's words.

Jack Longland's 1950 *Out of Doors* Article

This article was sent to *Out of Doors* magazine on 13 December 1950. A look through the issues for 1951–1953 did not find it. It may never have been published. It is the longest and most deliberate piece of writing by Longland on the purpose of White Hall Centre. It is reproduced here by kind permission of Nick Longland.

Why provide mountain training centres?
Jack Longland.
Submitted to *Out of Doors* magazine on 13 December 1950
Three large houses have been taken over since the war as schools or centres for a type of training which makes full and very use of the background of mountains against which these houses are set. Glenmore Lodge, run by the Central Council of Physical Recreation, lies at the gateway to the biggest mountain group in Great Britain, the Cairngorms. The Outward Bound Trust, pioneers of the Sea School Aberdovey, have taken the Lord Rea's fine house in Eskdale, with its lovely surrounding estate, and those who go there have the unmatched Lakeland hills as their training ground. And now, in January 1951, Derbyshire Education Authority are opening White Hall, built 1400 feet above sea level in the Peak District National Park. These new ventures are not identical in their conception of the opportunities which the mountains give, nor in the type of training courses which they offer, and this is as it should be, since Britain's mountains are richly diverse in character, and there are many ways in which they can bring strengths and health to those who learn to use them well. Nevertheless these mountain centres are all attempting to meet a common need, and their rapid development reflects the urgency of the need.

What is this need, and why should we think that mountain training centres are the right way of meeting it? To find the answers we must start with the truism that few Englishmen are citydwellers at heart and most have their roots in the countryside. Traditionally holidays are taken in the country or by the sea but apart from these holidays, which for most are family affairs, there has in the last 30 years or so been a literally unprecedented flow of young people at weekends and for longer periods into wilder country, the mountains, hills, the moorlands and the remote parts of the coastline. There are many causes for this enormous expansion in the numbers of walkers, cyclists, campers and climbers. On the negative side there are the drabness of many of our big towns, particularly in the industrial North, and the monotony and unadventurousness of the jobs which fill the working day. But these negative inducements might drive young holidaymakers no further than to football matches and dogs tracks, Butlin's camps or coach tours, and more positive explanations of the movement into open country must be sought. One reason, frequently forgotten, is the interest in country matters awakened by the richer education now given in schools. Allied to this is the growing realization, fostered by modern physical education teaching, that team games, whether played or watched, do not afford sufficient outlet for adventure, nor offer a real test of what a boy or girl can do on their own, or in a small group, when facing genuine difficulties which are not man-made, nor adopted as an artificial code of rules for the better playing of a game. A further economic reason is that better wages and holidays with pay bring longer expeditions and the purchase of the simple equipment required within the reach of young wage earners.

The result is that throughout the year, and not only at summer weekends, by-roads and moorland tracks and lonely dales are thronged with cyclists: that mountains and moors, until recently tenanted only by sheep and grouse, are vivid with the bright and often unsuitable costumes of hikers: that the railways and motor coaches run special Sunday excursions into remote places unvisited 20 years ago and that rock-climbing, until recently the sport of a few eccentric and well-to-do people, is now so popular that parties have to queue up at the foot of favourite climbs.

If all this has happened, and the numbers are increasing each year, why bother about schools and training centres for open country pursuits? There are a number of good and urgent reasons.

First, this large influx mainly of young town-dwellers creates a sharp problem of relations with countryfolk and their property and occupations. It is not easy for the town-bred youngster to realize that a moorland farm in someone else's factory premises, and that to leave the gate open for stock to stray may be just as stupid piece of industrial sabotage as putting sand into a turbine. Bad manners, careless habits with hedges and stone walls and growing crops, and occasional acts of wilful destructiveness are all bedevilling relations between townspeople and countryfolk and the mutual hostility is growing dangerously. There is specially important in solving this problem now that the National Parks Bill has become law, and the big experiment begins of testing whether the public at large are fit to be trusted to use and enjoy the areas of wild beauty which will be dedicated to their enjoyment. We shall not solve this problem by putting up notices thickly sprinkled with large DON'T's nor by direct moral instruction to school children and others. Most youngsters have an innate capacity for disregarding direct moral instruction, and in general it is not an unhealthy sign. What is needed is the demonstration by positive means that walker, cyclist or climber can only get full enjoyment out of his country expeditions if he is inspired to get to know more and more about the countryside, its people and their jobs, its birds and plants, weather and geology. From this deeper understanding good manners, considerateness and eventually friendship with countryfolk will come as byproducts.

The second problem is that of safety. Mountain walking in general and rock-climbing in particular offer outlets unmatched by other sports for adventure, and exploration, and the self-reliance the comes from learning the various techniques needed for safe passage over the mountains in all seasons and weathers. But the experience of the last few years proves that far too many young people are venturing among mountains and into wilder country without any of the necessary knowledge which would guarantee their safety. There is a melancholy record of accidents, deaths from exposure, falls while rock climbing and so on, nearly all of which could be prevented if the right training was readily accessible for boys and girls who needed it. Played by the rules, mountain walking and rock-climbing are safe enough. If the rules are not known or disregarded then the courage often shown by these youngsters is no safeguard in itself. It should be added that these far too frequent accidents nearly always involve large numbers of local people, shepherds, policemen, quarry workers and other climbers in lengthy and sometimes hazardous rescue operations, and thus, in turn, relations between countryfolk on the week-ending walkers are worsened.

What has been done up to now to provides training for those who need it? Climbing, rambling, cycling clubs and associations nearly all do splendid work in accepting beginners as members, and their experienced members devote time and knowledge to teaching them what to do and what not to do during their visits into open country. The Mountaineering Association is doing a specially valuable job in finding and training many who are outside the membership of the established clubs. The Youth Hostels Association has shown great resource in providing hostels among the mountains and moors so that youngsters are not barred from their chosen ground by reasons of cost and inaccessibility. But there are multitudes more that these agencies do not yet reach, and the number increases each year of boys and girls venturing into the mountains without the knowledge and training, clothing and equipment and maps and compasses which are needed to turn hazardous, disappointing and often inconsiderate excursions into full and safe enjoyment of what wild country can give to its pilgrims. There is room then for a great expansion of opportunities for this kind of training and education. The new mountain training centres are not competing for members of the established clubs. Their function is complimentary, and it is their task to try and reach those who can be reached in no other way. If some at least of their students graduate later as welcome well-trained members of good cycling, climbing and walking clubs, they will be all the better pleased with this evidence that they are doing their job properly. If new clubs spring into existence to meet the continuing needs of those to whom the mountain centres have given their initial training, there is more cause still for believing that that special function is a very necessary one. Even the most inverately solitary climber or walker now realizes that the mountains are the playground of all wish to visit them. He may at times go further afield, to mountain groups like those which lie in lovely loneliness between loch Broom and Cape Wrath, but in his normal excursions it is surely of great importance to him that he should meet only young explorers who are not lost, who do not need rescuing, who are not spoiling the countryside by the inconsiderate behaviour or the sandwich papers and tins which they stuff into the summit cairns. And the ordinary walker, who is less in love of solitude, and gladly welcome the parties who have learnt to share his hobby, provided down genuinely "of the brotherhood" and that they realize with him that the right relationship between men and mountain springs from the knowledge that mountains are large and men are very small, and that the lover of mountains is learning from them all the time.

And what fun the leaders and helpers at the mountain training centres are going to have! What is better than the opportunity of teaching crafts that you love, and which you are proud to have spent so long learning yourself – and to do all this in those delectable places which you would sooner have visited than anywhere else in the wide world! We shall have too, the advantage of catching our students young, before they got themselves into danger, and been frightened away from the mountains, before they have learnt the bad habits which are often not unlearnt. No-one who loves the hills and the mountains, and who does not want to hug his passion to himself, could fail to be impressed if he has visited one of the mountain centres, and watched these groups of boys and girls, mostly late teens and coming from school and some from city jobs far from mountains, all learning seriously and happily the crafts that are the passport to the best regions of this island.

It may be added finally that the right kind of training in open country pursuits is just as important a part of the education of healthy boys and girls as anything else they learn in and out of school. Without making an exaggerated claims about value of walking and climbing in building character, it can safely be said that these pastimes can help to produce self-reliant people who trust and are trusted by their companions in difficulties and dangers and who then develop the ability to think and act independently difficult circumstances in a way which is not without value to themselves and to the nation in both peace and war.

Purpose Statements or Mentions from after White Hall Opened

Statement or Mention	Source	Type of Source
' … at the inauguration [30–31 December 1950] the Director of Education, Jack Longland, supported by the Warden of the Centre, Peter Mosedale, stated their aims. These included the provision of basic training in hillcraft in all weathers and in the allied sports of climbing, caving, camping, canoeing, and ski-ing wherever conditions are suitable; to set before those coming to the Centre a vision of greatness in Nature and in Man, to inspire them with it and to persuade them to approach it in humility. This involves the training of self-reliance, the discipline of living together, the opportunity for the boy and girl to use their abundant physical and nervous energies in activities which can do nothing but good. It involves an uplifting of the spirit and a challenge to the whole personality. It provides natural penalties, sharper than a referee's whistle, for inefficiency, slackness and selfishness. All these advantages can be gained without overtaxing strength, providing the work is continuously adjusted to the age and condition of the student and to the weather.'	Machin, Cyril B, 'The Educational Value of Open Country Pursuits', *Journal of the Midland Association of Mountaineers*, 3, no. 1 (1956), pp. 16–18.	Jack Longland's opening-weekend speech (1950), as reported by Cyril Machin in 1956.
'The first parties set out to-day from White Hall, Derbyshire Education Committee's new open country pursuits centre, for snow rambles and instruction in rock climbing and skiing … [The courses] are elastic enough to suit prevailing conditions, and to meet the abilities and interests of the students … Beginners, as well as experienced students, have to be catered for in planning hill walks, pathfinding, rambling, camping, climbing and ski-ing and the other diversity of interests which are grouped under the title of "open country pursuits".'	'The Alpine Touch to Open Centre', *Derby Evening Telegraph*, Saturday 30 Dec 1950, p. 7.	Newspaper report.
'[The centre] is intended for young people of both sexes who are interested in open country pursuits. It is for those who have already discovered the hills. It is also – and equally – for the complete beginner. On the hills, as at sea, the beginner has much to learn. White Hall is a place where young people may learn and practice [sic] the skills of hill-craft which will equip them to go into mountain country with enterprise and confidence. It is a place where they may discover the joy, the challenge, the invigoration and the special comradeship which the hills offer. And it is a place where the beginner will meet experienced mountaineers and fell-walkers, not only as instructors but as friends.'	From early 1950s annual programme, quoted in Peter R Mosedale, *Hill and Water Sports in British Education*, Manuscript, unpublished (Canberra: 1975), p. 22.	The annual programme was probably written by Longland or Mosedale.

Statement or Mention	Source	Type of Source
'It is "a place where young people of a specially adventurous spirit may practice the techniques of hill-walking, of camping and cooking, of where and where not to ski, of rock-climbing – in short a place where young people may learn to enjoy the hills without unnecessary danger or discomfort".'	'Learning Hillcraft in Comfort', *Manchester Guardian*, 2 January 1951, p. 3.	Newspaper report, quoting from unknown source.
Same wording as above.	'"Enjoy the Hills" – Derbyshire Centre', *Education*, 26 Jan 1951, p. 157.	Newspaper report, quoting from unknown source.
'What we have to persuade the young walker or climber is that he [*sic*] has much to learn, and that he will live a much more full and interesting life as well as a safer one if he does take the trouble to learn. These are the lessons which are being successfully taught at the courses of ... and at our own Derbyshire training centre on the moors above Buxton.'	Longland, J L, 'Mountain Risks and Remedies', *Observer*, 13 Apr 1952, p. 4.	Article written by Longland.
'The centre provides short residential courses for young people in hill walking, climbing, camping, caving, ski-ing and canoeing. Applications are invited from experienced enthusiasts ... for the post of WARDEN.'	'Derbyshire Education Committee: White Hall Centre for Open Country Pursuits, Buxton: Warden and Housekeeper [vacancy]', *The Times*, 12 Aug 1955, p. 1.	Advertisement placed by County Hall.
'Here [at White Hall] school children, students, teenagers, and teachers receive their first lessons in climbing, caving, canoeing and fell walking, and acquire a love for and knowledge of the countryside ... [White Hall] is by no means run for profit (the low fees demanded of pupils barely cover maintenance costs), but to give Derbyshire's rising generation a love of healthy outdoor sports and the self-reliance and discipline so essential in life.'	Haddington, Peter, 'Gateway to Adventure at the White Hall Centre for Open Country Pursuits, near Buxton', *Derbyshire Countryside*, 23, no. 5 (Sept 1958), pp. 30–33.	Magazine article.

Statement or Mention	Source	Type of Source
'Our students learn to walk, to read a map, to steer a compass course in cloud or darkness, to camp and cook in the open, and to acquire the basic skills of some open-air sports. Our youngsters ... get cheerfully wet and muddy exploring the limestone caves, develop from tumbling novices to quite accomplished skiers on the nursery slopes of the Combs Valley, learn to use their own canoes and explore the countryside on horseback. They emerge, after only a week's course, not only with a wealth of valuable new experience, but also more alive, more self-reliant, and with the humility that comes from pitting yourself against natural obstacles much larger than the ordinary human scale.'	'Getting a Firm Foothold in Open-country Skills', *Guardian*, 6 Mar 1961, p. 19.	Reproduced from an official description of the centre.
In 1950 the Derbyshire Education Committee opened [White Hall] as a school where young people could learn the skills of living and moving with safety in hilly country, and in doing so learn to master themselves and their environment ... There are two main kinds of course. Week-end courses cater for those whose work only allows them freedom at such times, and provide both elementary and advanced training, at the choice of the student, in fell-walking, map-reading, rock climbing, caving, canoeing in summer, and skiing when there is snow ... School courses are of four days or longer, and provide a more comprehensive scheme of training, including emphasis on self-reliance, comradeship and living in a community. More specialised courses are indicated on the programme.'	Derby Local Studies and Family History Library, White Hall Centre for Open Country Pursuits: programme no. 31 September 1967 - September 1968, LA369.4.	Similar or identical wording appeared in earlier annual programmes and in the 1963 inspectors' report.

Appendix 3. Sample Course Reports

Reports were an important part of White Hall's basic schools' courses in the 1970s and 1980s. My enquiries to schools have not yet obtained any examples, but one old course report turned up in my filing cabinet. This report was for a particularly responsive and engaged group of ten young people. It is reproduced below with names obscured.

1897   26–30th Nov 1990

The following 5 pupils from ▓▓▓▓▓ joined 5 from ▓▓▓▓▓ to work as a group of 10 on the activities this week. A friendly, mature and cheerful atmosphere developed immediately. This continued to be the main characteristic of the week, and, coupled with some very good weather for the time of year, and the hard working efforts of the visiting staff, the course must go down as one of the most successful of the year. I feel that the group response this week was so uniformly positive, supportive, tolerant, and friendly that the emphasis of the report writing should be on this aspect and that joint congratulations would make more sense than trying to pick out individuals, but some short individual reports follow. Suffice it to say that, with young people like this around, your faith in human nature gets a mighty boost. Many of them were on the quiet side and it's a paradox that with a group of very mature, slightly reserved people like this you have less to write about in the individual reports than after a problematical course, but it's a problem which I wish we had more often!

▓▓▓▓▓ was a quiet girl, not inclined to show her feelings much, but quite confident and at ease socially, reliable and attentive. On the long walk over Kinder Scout on the Tuesday she kept up with a fast pace with determination and no complaints, though obviously having to push herself quite hard to do so. On a number of subsequent occasions she again showed the same persistent, stoic effort.

▓▓▓▓▓ was quite a fit, agile person who showed a fair amount of natural ability and confidence on all the activities and enjoyed a corresponding amount of success. For instance, she was one of the best 2 or 3 rock climbers in the group, including the lads. Again, on quite an ambitiously long canoeing trip she ended up with the fittest lads at the front, a result of strength, stamina and effort. ▓▓▓▓▓ was a polite, reliable and mature person who made a sensible and friendly contribution to the cheerful group atmosphere this week.

▓▓▓▓▓ was a friendly, cheerful type, at ease socially and with a good sense of humour and a ready smile, and the ability to see the funny side of things. Her approach to the more intimidating challenges was usually fairly cautious but she had a go at everything in the end. She made her own easy going, relaxed contribution to the cheerful group atmosphere.

▓▓▓▓▓ was yet another quiet, reliable type who never needed any special attention but just got on with things sensibly and quite successfully. On the canoeing session I was glad of his help as an assistant leader (he has canoed quite a bit before); he would enjoy a canoeing follow-up weekend to work more on skills now. ▓▓▓▓▓ was an undemonstrative sort, not inclined to show his feelings much, but he seemed to enjoy the whole week and made his own very quiet contribution to the positive group atmosphere.

▓▓▓▓ was a very reserved chap, I had to make a little note on
Tuesday evening to remind myself the next day to work out who the
▓▓▓▓ was on my group list, but at the same time he seemed quite
at home socially, at ease within the mature and sensible group
atmosphere, willing to have a go at all the activities on offer
when his turn came up, and at all times a polite and reliable
person.

(Introduction - similar to that for ▓▓▓▓▓).

▓▓▓▓ was great company, a talkative, delightfully cheerful sort,
even when struggling at the back of the group up the side of
Derbyshire's biggest hill. She was also that surprisingly rare one
out of a hundred pupils who spontaneously and openly expresses
appreciation of the situation and the scenery in wild places. I
suspect that she's probably equally intuitive and observant in more
mundane situations. ▓▓▓▓ had a go at nearly every activity, despite
obvious nerves and doubts on the more intimidating ones. Her
friendly and lively personality was an important influence on the
success of the group.

▓▓▓▓▓ was a real character, a popular and sometimes hilarious
member of the group who tended to say what she thought, whether it
be something about hating walking, the worst day of her life, or
whatever, but who at the same time never stopped smiling and joined
in the thick of it - literally so in the case of the mud of the
night line activity. Also, despite often protesting difficulty or
whatever, from a technical point of view ▓▓▓▓ really did quite
reasonably, in particular on the climbing when she climbed neatly
and in good balance. ▓▓▓▓ supplied that very necessary
extrovert influence to a group of predominantly reserved
characters.

▓▓▓▓ was a quietly able lad who enjoyed a good deal of quiet
success this week, modestly and politely. He was fit, agile and
strong for his build, and did well on each activity, especially
rock climbing. Neither was it a surprise to see him (with ▓▓▓▓
and ▓▓▓▓) get 2nd place in the end of course orienteering
competition.

▓▓▓▓ was an open, friendly lad with a good sense of humour, even
when the laughs were at his own expense. This open and tolerant
side of his nature was an important influence on the friendly group
atmosphere and, though we laughed at his expense at times, we also
appreciated his company and in this sense he was a popular member
of the group. ▓▓▓▓ was the uncomplicated, keen, volunteering
sort, happy for instance to carry some of the emergency equipment
on Kinder. He took every opportunity to try each new activity, and
wasn't afraid to go first on occasions.

▓▓▓▓ was a strong and reasonably confident lad who joined in the
whole course enthusiastically and energetically. From a technical
point of view he did quite well at every activity but seemed to
particularly enjoy the challenge of climbing. It was no surprise
to see him (with ▓▓▓▓ and ▓▓▓▓) achieve 2nd place in the end of
course orienteering competition. ▓▓▓▓ was a cheerful, amiable
person with a ready smile and a sort of tolerant and generous side
to his nature.

Appendix 4. Recent Evaluations

At the end of each White Hall schools' course, the visiting staff write client evaluations. The following quotes are taken from the evaluations received in the twelve months before November 2017:

- The quality of the staff and their work enables children to develop life skills and grow as individuals.
- Amazing staff … encouraged and supported the children with understanding and support. The positive experience will stay with the children and staff throughout their lives.
- The course aims were fully achieved, beyond expectations. Some children were expected to struggle with self- reliance, but the place is structured so well that they have coped well with being out of their familiar situations.
- I have found the experience at White Hall a fantastic, fun and friendly few days. The children have loved it. It is lovely to see them supporting each other and overcoming difficulty when out on activities.
- Stunning organisation, delivery of activities and relationships with kids.
- The best residential I have ever had the pleasure of taking part in. Thank you to all the staff who have made us feel so welcome and have worked so hard to make our experience amazing. I cannot wait to bring other groups of children back here. The children have gained in confidence, independence and respect.
- Thanks again to everyone at White Hall for another fab experience. The kids have all had a 'ball'! they have worked together as a team and all achieved personal goals.
- As always White Hall Centre has provided our children with the opportunity to achieve new goals, develop their independence and boost their confidence. They also make new friendships which they see through to secondary school.
- I wish I knew how White Hall staff can almost immediately understand the needs of individual children.
- I have used many outdoor centres over the years – and this is by far my favourite! All of the activities are well managed with a good balance of fun and challenge. I would definitely recommend it.
- The relationship with the centre staff was superb – they worked out the individual children's needs (and we had many special needs and

behavioural problems) and got the very best from them. This is why we come to White Hall.

- The centre staff without exception were incredible and couldn't have been more helpful, they bent over backwards to accommodate all our needs. Your kindness and attention to detail was fantastic.
- I have found the experience at White Hall a fantastic, fun and friendly few days. The children have loved it. It is lovely to see them supporting each other and overcoming difficulty when out on activities.

Abbreviations

AALA	Adventure Activities Licensing Authority.
AALS	Adventure Activities Licensing Service.
AMI	Association of Mountaineering Instructors.
AWMC	Association of Wardens of Mountain Centres. Later renamed Association of Wardens of Outdoor Education Centres (AWOEC). Then renamed again to Association of Heads of Outdoor Education Centres (AHOEC).
BCU	British Canoe Union. Later became British Canoeing.
BMC	British Mountaineering Council.
BMGA	British Mountain Guides Association.
BOP	*Boy's Own Paper.*
CCPR	Central Council of Physical Recreation. Later renamed the Sport and Recreation Alliance (SRA).
CIC	Caving Instructor Certificate.
CROW	Countryside and Rights of Way.
DCC	Derbyshire County Council.
DELTA	Derbyshire Educational Leisure Time Activities.
DofE	Duke of Edinburgh's Award.
EOC	English Outdoor Council.
GA	General Adventure.
HMI	Her Majesty's Inspectorate.
HSE	Health and Safety Executive.
IFMGA	International Federation of Mountain Guide Associations. In French, the *Union Internationale des Associations des Guides de Montagne* (UIAGM).
INSET	in-service training.
IOL	Institute for Outdoor Learning.
IOSH	Institution of Occupational Safety and Health.
JNC	Joint Negotiating Committee.
LEA	Local Education Authority.
MIA	Mountaineering Instructor Award
MIC	Mountaineering Instructor Certificate
MLC	Mountain Leadership Certificate. Later renamed Mountain Leader Award (ML).

MLTB	Mountain Leadership Training Board. Later renamed Mountain Leader Training England (MLTE). Then renamed again to Mountain Training England (MTE).
NAOE	National Association for Outdoor Education. Later became the Institute for Outdoor Learning (IOL).
OAA	Outdoor Adventure Activity.
OBMS	Outward Bound Mountain School.
OBSS	Outward Bound Sea School.
Ofsted	Office for Standards in Education.
RYA	Royal Yachting Association.
SRA	Sport and Recreation Alliance.
VI	Voluntary Instructor
WAHR	Work at Height Regulations.

Acknowledgments

Casting my mind back to the origins of this book, I am indebted to Bob Higginbotham who in August 2012 had the idea of collecting people's memories of White Hall, an enterprise that grew into an archive and then, at Dennis Gray's suggestion and with the encouragement of Darran Hawkins, into the book.

The research behind the writing has been like most detective work: incremental routine punctuated by some special moments of progress. One happening stands out. In September 2014 two men called in at White Hall to say hello. Bob Pettigrew (eighty-something) and George Sutton (a sprightly ninety-one) had attended White Hall's opening weekend in 1950, as voluntary instructors. Their surprise visit sixty-four years later was an early example of the enthusiasm with which many people would greet the archive and book idea. It also evidenced the deep impression that White Hall had left on some of its visitors, a characteristic I would encounter frequently during my subsequent research.

Many people contributed information relevant both to the White Hall Centre archive and to the research for the book. I owe thanks to the skills and help of the staff of the Derbyshire Record Office, who catalogued the material in the White Hall collection and who dealt with the reprographics orders of a researcher 11,800 miles away. Also, archival material from other sources forms many parts of the story, thanks to the existence of local history societies and regional and national museums, libraries and archives. Mary Wilde of the British Cave Research Association and Bill Whitehouse of the Derbyshire Cave Rescue Organisation retrieved and sent me caving papers from the 1950s and 1960s.

My brother Mike, with the help of Peter Higgins, tracked down some long forgotten magazine articles in the library of the University of Edinburgh. Ron Brightmore interrupted two holidays in the UK to undertake some research, which led to the discovery of the 1951 Spring-bank School photographs. Ron, Nick Longland, Mark Lambert, Wally Blake and Janet Davies read and improved the manuscript, without necessarily agreeing with everything in it. Mark alerted me to the existence of Jack Longland's unpublished 1950 *Out of Doors* article. Lynn Cook retrieved and sent me several of Ken Oldham's private papers from her own archived material. Bob Pettigrew lent me his 1954–5 Loughborough Training College thesis on outdoor activities. Stew Dale, Keith Bridgens, Des Marshall and Bob Higginbotham scoured their local knowledge to identify the scenes shown in several photographs from the 1950s and earlier. Brian Sharp described a White Hall course he attended as a thirteen-year-old in 1957. Maureen Drasdo wrote to me about the late 1950s. Meriel Blake, Wally Blake, Alan Alldred and John Cheesmond reached fifty years into the past to fill in some evocative details of the 1960s. Janet Davies helped me with the late 1960s and the early 1970s. Dave Draper helped me to recall the Bohemian liberty of the mid-1970s. Bob Higginbotham rolled out names from the 1970s and 80s, set in pastry. Doug Jones and Phil Booth remembered the turbulent 1990s. Pete Denver examined some 1990s material at the Derbyshire Records Office. Rory Gregory wrote about the period 2004–12. My gathering of information for Part Four met an obliging team response, with input from Judith Nicoll, Clare Reading, Fiona Thomson, Darran Hawkins, Jenny Harding, Pat Bell and Lyndsay Jones.

In 2016 my research sprouted an offshoot, a study into the experiences of White Hall's first six full-time female instructors. I thank Karen Stockham for her involvement in the early stages of this idea and Simon Beames for taking on the study.

The interloan staff of Dunedin Public Libraries proved that there is still a role for physical books and human posties, while the custodians of Otago University Library retrieved from storage numerous bound copies of *The Boy's Own*. During the initial stages of my research, I deliberately delayed reading Ken Ogilvie's book *Roots and Wings*, a bulging chronicle of a sector once possessing, according to Geoff Cooper, 'the most extensive system of outdoor education centres in the world'. I wanted to reach my own conclusions on the main divisions of the period. Eventually I did open *Roots and Wings*, and it became a frequent source.

My thanks also go to the many people who have permitted me to quote from their emails. For other help I am grateful to:

Lina Arthur, Oxford University Mountaineering Club Library; Pauline Asker, Derby Coroner's Office; Louise Avery, Gordonstoun Archive; Dave Baines; Ann Barton, Dunedin Public Libraries; Gill Berrow; Elaine Broughton, Derby Local Studies Library; Martyn Carr, Fell and Rock Climbing Club; Pete Clark; Sue Clayton, Buxton Library; Debs

Cousin, Outward Bound Trust; Jacqueline Cox, University of Cambridge Archives; Malcolm Creasey, Mountain Training; Helen Cunningham, Cumbria Archive Service; Pat Dallman, Sheffield Archives and Local Studies; Philip Davies, Swarkestone Sailing Club; Barry Dent, New Mills Local History Society; Deborah Elliott, Burton Library; Stuart Fisher, *Canoeist* magazine; Keith Foster, The Magic Attic; John Frankland, Skipton Library; Tina Gardner, British Mountaineering Council; Linda Geddes, Dunedin Public Libraries; Christine Gladwin, Sidcot School Archive; Frank Grant; Dennis Green, Cave and Crag Club; Barbara Hall; Andy Hemsted, Cave and Crag Club; John Heyes, Glossop Sailing Club; Mike Higgins, Derbyshire Caving Association; Pete Higgins, University of Edinburgh; Mark Higginson, Picture the Past; Anne Horn, University of Sheffield Library; Ian Housley-Tatton, Abbotsholme Archive; Chris Howes, *Descent* magazine; Glyn Hughes, Alpine Club Archives; Alan Jeffreys, Grampian Speleological Group; Ben Jones, Buxton Museum and Art Gallery; Hazel Jones, Pinnacle Club; Charles Knighton, Clifton College Archives; Richard Knisely-Marpole; Paul Knowles, Manchester Metropolitan University; Moira Langmuir; Philip Leach, Media Archive for Central England; Jenny Liddle, National Trust Images; Donald Macdonald, Clapham Old Xaverians; David Medcalf, Climbers' Club Archives; Alex Messenger, British Mountaineering Council; Roy Morgan, Cave and Crag Club; Nigel Mosedale; Bill Myers, North West Evening Mail; Simon Nadin; John Needham; Martin Nelson, Burton Sailing Club; Michael Nichols, Clapham Old Xaverians; Eddie O'Brien, Clapham Old Xaverians; Jenny Orwin, Bootham School Archive; Suzanne Pearson; Emily Pitts, womenclimb.co.uk; Bob Pyett, Combs Sailing Club; Glyn Rawson, Ogston Sailing Club; Mel Reid; Eliza Richardson, Media Archive for Central England; Katy de las Rivière, Sedbergh School Archive and Heritage Centre; Shaun Roberts, Glenmore Lodge; Kate Ross; Frank Salt; Doug Scott; Ben Seal, British Canoeing; Derek Sederman, Old Abbotsholmians; Hilary Sharp; Chris Sherwin, Fell and Rock Climbing Club; Naomi Shewan, University of Warwick Library; Otto Smart, Manchester Grammar School Archives; Derek Stansfield; Paul Stevens, Repton School; Paul Stillman, Mendip Cave Registry and Archive; Andy Syme, Yorkshire Ramblers' Club; Mike Tinnion, Carlisle Mountaineering Club; Bill Truscott, Midland Association of Mountaineers; Blair Turnbull, Robertson Library; Ros Westward, Buxton Museum and Art Gallery; Anne-Maree Wigley, Dunedin Public Libraries; Joy Wheeler, Royal Geographical Society; Maxine Willett, Mountain Heritage Trust; William Wilson; Colin Wood, University of Worcester; Keith Worsencroft; Mike Worsencroft.

Index

Lightning Source UK Ltd.
Milton Keynes UK
UKHW02n1314170118

316320UK00002B/6/P